D1519275

The Works of John Dryden

General Editor

H. T. SWEDENBERG, JR.

Associate General Editor

EARL MINER

Textual Editor

VINTON A. DEARING

VOLUME NINE

EDITOR

John Loftis

TEXTUAL EDITOR

Vinton A. Dearing

VOLUME IX

The Works
of John Dryden

Plays

THE INDIAN EMPEROUR
SECRET LOVE
SIR MARTIN MAR-ALL

University of California Press
Berkeley, Los Angeles, London

UNIVERSITY OF CALIFORNIA PRESS
Berkeley and Los Angeles, California

UNIVERSITY OF CALIFORNIA PRESS, LTD.
London, England

*The copy texts of this edition have been drawn in the
main from the Dryden Collection of the
William Andrews Clark Memorial Library*

© *1966 by The Regents of the University of California*
Second Printing, 1974
ISBN: 0-520-00360-8
Printed in the United States of America
Library of Congress Catalog Card Number: 55-7149
Designed by Ward Ritchie

Acknowledgments

The editors gratefully acknowledge their debt to the community of scholarship for aid rendered in the preparation of this volume:

To the staffs of the University of California, Los Angeles, Library, the Stanford University Library, the William Andrews Clark Memorial Library, the Folger Shakespeare Library, and the Henry E. Huntington Library for expert and expeditious service accorded with unfailing courtesy.

To the Research Committee of the University of California, Los Angeles, for annual grants-in-aid.

To Mrs. Carol Pearson, Mrs. Nancy Shea, and Mr. Robert Chamberlain for research assistance and to Miss Jeanette Dearborn and Mrs. Dorothy Modafferi for stenographic assistance.

To Mrs. Geneva Phillips for meticulous care in the preparation of the manuscript. To Mrs. Grace H. Stimson of the University of California Press for her expert attention to the book as it proceeded through the press. To Dr. James G. McManaway for a detailed bibliographical account of the unique copy of Sir Martin Mar-all and of the other copies of the first edition of the play in the Folger Shakespeare Library. To Professors Emmett L. Avery and Arthur H. Scouten for information regarding details of Restoration stage history. To the Master and Fellows of Magdalene College, Cambridge, for permission to reprint the list of errata found in a copy of The Duke of Lerma (1668), now in the Pepys Library.

To Chancellor Franklin D. Murphy and Vice-Chancellor Foster H. Sherwood of the University of California, Los Angeles, for their encouragement of the General Editor and for their generous support of this edition of Dryden.

H. T. S., Jr.

June 1965

Contents

THE INDIAN EMPEROUR

OR

THE CONQUEST OF MEXICO

BY THE SPANIARDS

THE
Indian Emperour,

OR,

THE CONQUEST OF

MEXICO

BY THE

SPANIARDS.

Being the Sequel of the *Indian Queen*.

By JOHN DRYDEN Esq;

*Dum relego scripsisse pudet, quia plurima cerno
Me quoque, qui feci, judice, digna lini.* Ovid.

LONDON,
Printed by *J. M.* for *H. Herringman* at the Sign of the *Blew Anchor*
in the Lower walk of the *New Exchange.* 1667.

TITLE PAGE OF THE FIRST EDITION (MACDONALD 69A)

A Defence of an Essay of Dramatique Poesie, being an Answer to the Preface of *The Great Favourite, or the Duke of* Lerma.

THE former Edition of the *Indian Emperour* being full of faults which had escaped the Printer, I have been willing to over-look this second with more care: and though I could not allow my self so much time as was necessary, yet by that little I have done, the Press is freed from some gross errours which it had to answer for before. As for the more material faults of writing, which are properly mine, though I see many of them, I want leisure to amend them. 'Tis enough for those who make one Poem the business of their lives, to leave that correct: yet, ex-
10 cepting *Virgil*, I never met with any which was so in any Language.

But while I was thus employ'd about this Impression, there came to my hands a new printed Play, called, *The Great Favourite, or the Duke of* Lerma, the Author of which, a noble and most ingenious Person, has done me the favour to make some Observations and Animadversions upon my *Dramatique Essay*. I must confess he might have better consulted his Reputation, than by matching himself with so weak an Adversary. But if his Honour be diminished in the choice of his Antagonist, it is sufficiently
20 recompens'd in the election of his Cause: which being the weaker, in all appearance, as combating the received Opinions of the best Ancient and Modern Authors, will add to his glory, if he overcome; and to the opinion of his generosity, if he be vanquished, since he ingages at so great odds; and so, like a Cavalier, undertakes the protection of the weaker party. I have only to fear on my own behalf, that so good a cause as mine may not suffer by my ill management, or weak defence; yet I cannot in Honour but take the Glove when 'tis offer'd me: though I am only a Champion by succession; and no more able to defend the

---

14 Lerma, the] Lerma. The Q2, D. [These and other sigla are identified in the textual notes, where also fluctuations in the texts cited are explained.]
24 and so,] and, so Q2, D.

right of *Aristotle* and *Horace,* than an Infant *Dimock* to maintain the Title of a King.

For my own concernment in the Controversie, it is so small,
that I can easily be contented to be driven from a few Notions
of Dramatique Poesie; especially by one, who has the reputation of understanding all things: and I might justly make that
excuse for my yielding to him, which the Philosopher made to
the Emperour; why should I offer to contend with him who is
Master of more than twenty Legions of Arts and Sciences? But
10 I am forc'd to fight, and therefore it will be no shame to be
overcome.

Yet I am so much his Servant as not to meddle with any thing
which does not concern me in his Preface: therefore I leave the
good sense and other excellencies of the first twenty lines, to be
consider'd by the Critiques. As for the Play of the Duke of
Lerma, having so much alter'd and beautifi'd it, as he has done,
it can justly belong to none but him. Indeed they must be extream ignorant as well as envious, who would rob him of that
Honour; for you see him putting in his claim to it, even in the
20 first two lines.

> *Repulse upon repulse like waves thrown back,*
> *That slide to hang upon obdurate rocks.*

After this let detraction do its worst; for if this be not his, it
deserves to be. For my part I declare for distributive Justice, and
from this and what follows he certainly deserves *those advantages,*
which he acknowledges to have received from the opinion of
sober men.

In the next place I must beg leave to observe his great Address
in courting the Reader to his party. For intending to assault all
30 Poets, both Ancient and Modern, he discovers not his whole
design at once, but seems only to aim at me, and attacques me on
my weakest side, my defence of Verse.

To begin with me, he gives me the Compellation of *The*
Author of a Dramatique Essay; which is a little Discourse in
Dialogue, for the most part borrowed from the observations of
others: therefore, that I may not be wanting to him in civility, I

return his Complement by calling him *The Author of the Duke
of* Lerma.

But (that I may pass over his salute) he takes notice of my
great pains to prove Rhyme as natural in a serious Play, and
more effectual than blanck Verse. Thus indeed I did state the
question; but he tells me, *I pursue that which I call Natural in a
wrong application: for 'tis not the question whether Rhyme or
not Rhyme be best or most natural for a serious subject, but
what is nearest the nature of that it represents.*

10   If I have formerly mistaken the Question, I must confess my
ignorance so far, as to say I continue still in my mistake: But he
ought to have prov'd that I mistook it; for 'tis yet but *gratis
dictum;* I still shall think I have gain'd my point, if I can prove
that Rhyme is best or most natural for a serious subject. As for
the question as he states it, whether Rhyme be nearest the nature
of what it represents, I wonder he should think me so ridiculous
as to dispute whether Prose or Verse be nearest to ordinary Conversation?

It still remains for him to prove his inference; that, since
20 Verse is granted to be more remote than Prose from ordinary
Conversation, therefore no serious Plays ought to be writ in
Verse: and when he clearly makes that good, I will acknowledge
his Victory as absolute as he can desire it.

The question now is which of us two has mistaken it, and if it
appear I have not, the world will suspect what Gentleman that
was, *who was allowed to speak twice in Parliament, because he
had not yet spoken to the Question;* and perhaps conclude it to
be the same, who, as 'tis reported, maintain'd a contradiction *in
terminis,* in the face of three hundred persons.

30   But to return to Verse, whether it be natural or not in Plays,
is a Problem which is not demonstrable of either side: 'tis enough
for me that he acknowledges he had rather read good Verse than
Prose: for if all the Enemies of Verse will confess as much, I shall
not need to prove that it is natural. I am satisfied if it cause delight: for delight is the chief, if not the only end of Poesie; instruction can be admitted but in the second place, for Poesie only

---

25-26 what Gentleman that was] *what Gentleman that was* Q2, D.

instructs as it delights. 'Tis true that to imitate well is a Poets
work; but to affect the Soul, and excite the Passions, and above
all to move admiration (which is the delight of serious Plays) a
bare imitation will not serve. The converse therefore which a
Poet is to imitate, must be heighten'd with all the Arts and
Ornaments of Poesie; and must be such, as, strictly consider'd,
could never be supposed spoken by any without premeditation.

As for what he urges, that *a Play will still be supposed to be a
composition of several Persons speaking* ex tempore; *and that*
10 *good Verses are the hardest things which can be imagin'd to be
so spoken:* I must crave leave to dissent from his opinion, as to
the former part of it: for, if I am not deceiv'd, a Play is suppos'd
to be the work of the Poet, imitating, or representing the conversation of several persons: and this I think to be as clear, as he
thinks the contrary.

But I will be bolder, and do not doubt to make it good, though
a Paradox, that one great reason why Prose is not to be us'd in
serious Plays, is because it is too near the nature of converse:
there may be too great a likeness; as the most skilful Painters
20 affirm, that there may be too near a resemblance in a Picture: to
take every lineament and feature is not to make an excellent
piece, but to take so much only as will make a beautiful Resemblance of the whole; and, with an ingenious flattery of Nature,
to heighten the beauties of some parts, and hide the deformities
of the rest. For so says *Horace,*

> *Vt pictura Poesis erit, &c.*————
> *Hæc amat obscurum, vult hæc sub luce videri,*
> *Judicis argutum quæ non formidat acumen.*
> ————*Et quæ*
> 30 *Desperat, tractata nitescere posse, relinquit.*

In *Bartholomew-Fair,* or the Lowest kind of Comedy, that
degree of heightning is used, which is proper to set off that
Subject: 'tis true the Author was not there to go out of Prose, as
he does in his higher Arguments of Comedy, *The Fox* and
Alchymist; yet he does so raise his matter in that Prose, as to

34 and] D; *and* Q2.

render it delightful; which he could never have performed, had he only said or done those very things that are daily spoken or practised in the Fair: for then the Fair it self would be as full of pleasure to an ingenious person as the Play; which we manifestly see it is not. But he hath made an excellent Lazar of it; the Copy is of price, though the Original be vile. You see in *Catiline* and *Sejanus*, where the Argument is great, he sometimes ascends to Verse, which shews he thought it not unnatural in serious Plays: and had his Genius been as proper for Rhyme,
10 as it was for Humour; or had the Age in which he liv'd, attain'd to as much knowledge in Verse, as ours, 'tis probable he would have adorn'd those Subjects with that kind of Writing.

Thus Prose, though the rightful Prince, yet is by common consent depos'd, as too weak for the government of serious Plays; and he failing, there now start up two Competitors; one the nearer in blood, which is blanck Verse; the other more fit for the ends of government, which is Rhyme. Blanck Verse is, indeed, the nearer Prose, but he is blemish'd with the weakness of his Predecessor. Rhyme (for I will deal clearly) has somewhat
20 of the Usurper in him, but he is brave, and generous, and his Dominion pleasing. For this reason of delight, the Ancients (whom I will still believe as wise as those who so confidently correct them) wrote all their Tragedies in Verse, though they knew it most remote from Conversation.

But I perceive I am falling into the danger of another rebuke from my Opponent: for when I plead that the Ancients used Verse, I prove not that they would have admitted Rhyme, had it then been written: all I can say is only this, That it seems to have succeeded Verse by the general consent of Poets in all Modern
30 Languages: for almost all their serious Plays are written in it: which, though it be no demonstration that therefore they ought to be so, yet, at least the practice first, and then the continuation of it, shews that it attain'd the end, which was to please; and if that cannot be compass'd here, I will be the first who shall lay it down. For I confess my chief endeavours are to delight the Age in which I live. If the humour of this, be for low Comedy, small Accidents, and Raillery, I will force my Genius to obey it, though

with more reputation I could write in Verse. I know I am not so
fitted by Nature to write Comedy: I want that gayety of humour
which is required to it. My Conversation is slow and dull, my
humour Saturnine and reserv'd: In short, I am none of those who
endeavour to break Jests in Company, or make reparties, so that
those who decry my Comedies do me no injury, except it be in
point of profit: reputation in them is the last thing to which I
shall pretend. I beg pardon for entertaining the Reader with so
ill a Subject; but before I quit that Argument, which was the
10 cause of this digression, I cannot but take notice how I am corrected for my quotation of *Seneca,* in my Defence of Plays in
Verse. My words are these. *Our Language is Noble, Full, and Significant, and I know not why he who is Master of it, may not
cloath ordinary things in it as decently as the* Latine, *if he use the
same diligence in his* choice of Words. *One would think* Unlock
a door *was a thing as vulgar as could be spoken; yet* Seneca *could
make it sound high and lofty in his* Latine.

Reserate Clusos Regii postes Laris.

But he says of me, that *being fill'd with the Precedents of the
20 Ancients who writ their Plays in Verse, I commend the thing,
declaring our Language to be Full, Noble, and Significant, and
charging all defects upon the* ill *placing of words, which I prove
by quoting* Seneca *loftily expressing such an ordinary thing as*
shutting a door.

Here he manifestly mistakes; for I spoke not of the placing,
but of the choice of words: for which I quoted that Aphorism of
Julius Cæsar, Delectus verborum est origo Eloquentiæ: but
delectus verborum is no more *Latine* for the placing of words,
than *Reserate* is *Latine* for shut the door, as he interprets it,
30 which I ignorantly construed unlock or open it.

He supposes I was highly affected with the sound of those
words; and I suppose I may more justly imagine it of him: for if

---

5 reparties, so] reparties. So Q2, D.
12–18 *Our . . . Laris.] romans and italics reversed from Q2, D, except for*
"Latine" (*bis*).
19 that] *That* Q2, D.   28, 29 *Latine*] D; Latine Q2.

he had not been extreamly satisfied with the sound, he would
have minded the sense a little better.

But these are now to be no faults; for ten days after his Book
is publish'd, and that his mistakes are grown so famous, that they
are come back to him, he sends his *Errata* to be printed, and
annexed to his Play: and desires that instead of *shutting* you
would read *opening;* which it seems, was the Printers fault. I
wonder at his modesty, that he did not rather say it was *Seneca's*
or mine, and that in some Authors *Reserare* was to *shut* as well
10 as to *open,* as the word *Barach,* say the Learned, is both to *bless*
and *curse.*

Well, since it was the Printer, he was a naughty man to commit
the same mistake twice in six lines: I warrant you *delectus
verborum* for placing of words was his mistake too, though the
Author forgot to tell him of it: if it were my Book I assure you it
should. For those Rascals ought to be the Proxies of every
Gentleman Author, and to be chastis'd for him, when he is not
pleas'd to own an Errour. Yet since he has given the *Errata,* I
wish he would have inlarged them only a few sheets more, and
20 then he would have spar'd me the labour of an Answer: for this
cursed Printer is so given to mistakes, that there is scarce a
sentence in the Preface, without some false Grammar, or hard
sence in it: which will all be charg'd upon the Poet, because he is
so good natur'd as to lay but three Errours to the Printers
account, and to take the rest upon himself, who is better able
to support them. But he needs not apprehend that I should
strictly examine those little faults, except I am call'd upon to do
it: I shall return therefore to that quotation of *Seneca,* and
answer not to what he writes, but to what he means. I never
30 intended it as an Argument, but only as an illustration of what I
had said before concerning the election of words; and all he can
charge me with is only this, that if *Seneca* could make an ordinary
thing sound well in *Latine* by the choice of words, the same with
the like care might be perform'd in *English:* if it cannot, I have
committed an Errour on the right hand, by commending too
much the copiousness and well sounding of our Language, which

33 *Latine*] D; Latine Q2.   34 *English*] D; English Q2.

I hope my Country men will pardon me. At least the words which follow in my Dramatique Essay will plead somewhat in my behalf; for I say there, that this Objection happens but seldom in a Play, and then too either the meanness of the expression may be avoided, or shut out from the Verse by breaking it in the midst.

But I have said too much in the defence of Verse; for after all 'tis a very indifferent thing to me, whether it obtain or not. I am content hereafter to be ordered by his rule, that is, to write it sometimes because it pleases me, and so much the rather, because
10 he has declared that it pleases him. But he has taken his last farewel of the Muses, and he has done it civilly, by honouring them with the name of *his long acquaintances,* which is a Complement they have scarce deserved from him. For my own part I bear a share in the publick loss, and how emulous soever I may be of his fame and reputation, I cannot but give this testimony of his Style, that it is extream poetical, even in Oratory; his Thoughts elevated, sometimes above common apprehension; his Notions politick and grave, and tending to the instruction of Princes, and reformation of States; that they are abundantly
20 interlac'd with variety of Fancies, Tropes, and Figures, which the Criticks have enviously branded with the name of obscurity and false Grammar.

Well *he is now fetter'd in business of more unpleasant nature:* the Muses have lost him, but the Commonwealth gains by it; The corruption of a Poet is the Generation of a Statesman.

He will not venture again into the civil Wars of Censure, ubi————*nullos habitura triumphos:* if he had not told us he had left the Muses, we might have half suspected it by that word, *ubi,* which does not any way belong to them in that place; the
30 rest of the Verse is indeed *Lucans,* but that *ubi* I will answer for it, is his own. Yet he has another reason for this disgust of Poesie; for he says immediately after, that *the manner of Plays which are now in most esteem, is beyond his power to perform:* to perform the manner of a thing I confess is new English to me. *However, he condemns not the satisfaction of others, but rather their unnecessary understanding, who, like* Sancho Panca's *Doctor, pre-*

23   Well] *Well* Q2, D.

scribe too strictly to our appetites; for, says he, *in the difference of* Tragedy *and* Comedy, *and of* Farce *it self, there can be no deter-mination but by the taste, nor in the manner of their composure.*

We shall see him now as great a Critick as he was a Poet, and the reason why he excell'd so much in Poetry will be evident, for it will appear to have proceeded from the exactness of his judg-ment. *In the difference of* Tragedy, Comedy *and* Farce *it self, there can be no determination but by the taste.* I will not quarrel with the obscurity of his Phrase, though I justly might; but beg his pardon if I do not rightly understand him: if he means that there is no essential difference betwixt *Comedy, Tragedy,* and *Farce,* but what is only made by the peoples taste, which distin-guishes one of them from the other, that is so manifest an Errour that I need not lose time to contradict it. Were there neither Judge, Taste, nor Opinion in the world, yet they would differ in their natures; for the action, character, and language of *Tragedy,* would still be great and high; that of *Comedy* lower and more familiar; Admiration would be the Delight of one, and Satyr of the other.

I have but briefly touch'd upon these things, because, whatever his words are, I can scarce imagine, that he *who is always con-cern'd for the true honour of reason, and would have no spurious issue father'd upon her,* should mean any thing so absurd as to affirm, that *there is no difference betwixt* Comedy *and* Tragedy *but what is made by the taste only:* Unless he would have us understand the Comedies of my Lord *L.* where the first Act should be Pottages, the second Fricassés, *&c.* and the Fifth a *Chère Entière* of Women.

I rather guess he means, that betwixt one *Comedy* or *Tragedy* and another, there is no other difference but what is made by the liking or disliking of the Audience. This is indeed a less errour than the former, but yet it is a great one. The liking or disliking of the people gives the Play the denomination of good or bad, but does not really make, or constitute it such. To please the

1 says he] D; *says he* Q2.   21 he] *he* Q2, D.
24 that] *that* Q2, D.   27 Fricassés] Fricasses Q2, D.
28 *Chère Entière*] *Chere Entiere* Q2, D.   31 errour] D; errrour Q2.

people ought to be the Poets aim, because Plays are made for
their delight; but it does not follow that they are always pleas'd
with good Plays, or that the Plays which please them are always
good. The humour of the people is now for *Comedy,* therefore in
hope to please them, I write *Comedies* rather than serious Plays:
and so far their taste prescribes to me: but it does not follow from
that reason, that *Comedy* is to be prefer'd before *Tragedy* in its
own nature: for that which is so in its own nature cannot be
otherwise; as a man cannot but be a rational creature: but the
10 opinion of the people may alter, and in another Age, or perhaps
in this, serious Plays may be set up above Comedies.

  This I think a sufficient Answer; if it be not, he has provided
me of an Excuse; it seems in his wisdom, he foresaw my weakness,
and has found out this expedient for me, that *it is not necessary
for Poets to study strict reason, since they are so used to a greater
latitude than is allowed by that severe inquisition; that they must
infringe their own jurisdiction to profess themselves oblig'd to
argue well.*

  I am obliged to him for discovering to me this back door; but I
20 am not yet resolv'd on my retreat: For I am of opinion that they
cannot be good Poets who are not accustomed to argue well. False
Reasonings and colours of Speech, are the certain marks of one
who does not understand the Stage: For Moral Truth is the
Mistress of the Poet as much as of the Philosopher: Poesie must
resemble Natural Truth, but it must *be* Ethical. Indeed the
Poet dresses Truth, and adorns Nature, but does not alter them:

  Ficta voluptatis causâ sint proxima veris.

Therefore that is not the best Poesie which resembles notions of
things that are not, to things that are: though the fancy may be
30 great and the words flowing, yet the Soul is but half satisfied
when there is not Truth in the foundation. This is that which
makes *Virgil* be preferred before the rest of Poets: In variety of
fancy and sweetness of expression, you see *Ovid* far above him:
for *Virgil* rejected many of those things which *Ovid* wrote. *A
great Wits great Work is to refuse,* as my worthy Friend Sir *John*

14 that] *That* Q2, D.

Berkenhead has ingeniously express'd it: you rarely meet with
any thing in *Virgil* but Truth, which therefore leaves the
strongest impression of pleasure in the Soul. This I thought my
self oblig'd to say in behalf of Poesie: and to declare, though it be
against my self, that when Poets do not argue well, the defect is
in the Work-men, not in the Art.

And now I come to the boldest part of his Discourse, wherein
he attacques not me, but all the Ancients and Moderns; and
undermines, as he thinks, the very foundations on which Drama-
10 tique Poesie is built. I could wish he would have declin'd that
envy which must of necessity follow such an undertaking, and
contended himself with triumphing over me in my opinions of
Verse, which I will never hereafter dispute with him; but he must
pardon me if I have that Veneration for *Aristotle, Horace, Ben.
Johnson,* and *Corneille,* that I dare not serve him in such a Cause,
and against such Heroes, but rather fight under their protection,
as *Homer* reports of little *Teucer,* who shot the *Trojans* from
under the large Buckler of *Ajax Telamon.*

Στῆ δ' ἄρ' ὑπ' Αἴαντος σάκεϊ Τελαμωνιάδαο &c.

20   *He stood beneath his Brothers ample shield;*
          And, cover'd there, shot death through all the field.

The words of my noble Adversary are these:
*But if we examine the general Rules laid down for Plays by
strict reason, we shall find the errours equally gross; for the great
foundation which is laid to build upon, is nothing as it is
generally stated, as will appear upon the examination of the
Particulars.*

These Particulars in due time shall be examin'd: in the mean
while let us consider what this great foundation is, which he says
30 is nothing, as it is generally stated. I never heard of any other
foundation of Dramatique Poesie than the imitation of Nature;
neither was there ever pretended any other by the Ancients or

Moderns, or me, who endeavour to follow them in that Rule.
This I have plainly said in my definition of a Play; that it is *a just
and lively image of humane Nature, &c.* Thus the Foundation, as
it is generally stated, will stand sure, if this definition of a Play
be true; if it be not, he ought to have made his exception against
it, by proving that a Play is not an imitation of Nature, but somewhat else which he is pleas'd to think it.

But 'tis very plain, that he has mistaken the foundation for that
which is built upon it, though not immediately: for the direct
10 and immediate consequence is this; if Nature be to be imitated,
then there is a Rule for imitating Nature rightly, otherwise there
may be an end, and no means conducing to it. Hither-to I have
proceeded by demonstration; but as our Divines, when they
have prov'd a Deity, because there is order, and have infer'd that
this Deity ought to be worshipped, differ afterwards in the
manner of the Worship; so having laid down, that Nature is to
be imitated, and that Proposition proving the next, that then
there are means which conduce to the imitating of Nature, I
dare proceed no farther positively: but have only laid down
20 some opinions of the Ancients and Moderns, and of my own, as
means which they used, and which I thought probable for the
attaining of that end. Those means are the same which my
Antagonist calls the Foundations, how properly the world may
judge; and to prove that this is his meaning, he clears it immediately to you, by enumerating those Rules or Propositions against
which he makes his particular exceptions; as namely, those of
time and place, in these words: *First we are told the plot should
not be so ridiculously contrived, as to crowd two several Countries into one Stage; secondly, to cramp the Accidents of many
30 years or days into the representation of two hours and an half;
and lastly, a Conclusion drawn, that the only remaining Dispute
is, concerning time, whether it should be contained in* 12 *or*
24 *hours; and the place to be limited to that spot of ground where
the Play is supposed to begin: and this is called nearest Nature;
for that is concluded most natural, which is most probable, and
nearest to that which it presents.*

2–3 *a just* . . . [*italics*] . . . *&c.*] a just . . . [romans] . . . &c. Q2, D.

Thus he has only made a small mistake of the means conducing to the end, for the end it self, and of the superstructure for the foundation: but he proceeds. *To shew therefore upon what ill grounds they dictate Laws for Dramatique Poesie, &c.* He is here pleased to charge me with being Magisterial, as he has done in many other places of his Preface. Therefore in vindication of my self, I must crave leave to say, that my whole Discourse was Sceptical, according to that way of reasoning which was used by *Socrates, Plato,* and all the Academiques of old, which *Tully*
10 and the best of the Ancients followed, and which is imitated by the modest Inquisitions of the Royal Society. That it is so, not only the name will shew, which is *an Essay,* but the frame and Composition of the Work. You see it is a Dialogue sustain'd by persons of several opinions, all of them left doubtful, to be determined by the Readers in general; and more particularly defer'd to the accurate Judgment of my Lord *Buckhurst,* to whom I made a Dedication of my Book. These are my words in my Epistle, speaking of the persons whom I introduc'd in my Dialogue: *'Tis true they differ'd in their opinions, as 'tis probable*
20 *they would; neither do I take upon me to reconcile, but to relate them, leaving your Lordship to decide it in favour of that part which you shall judge most reasonable.* And after that in my Advertisement to the Reader I said this; *The drift of the ensuing Discourse is chiefly to vindicate the Honour of our* English *Writers from the Censure of those who unjustly prefer the* French *before them. This I intimate, lest any should think me so exceeding vain, as to teach others an Art which they understand much better than my self.* But this is more than necessary to clear my modesty in that point: & I am very confident that
30 there is scarce any man who has lost so much time, as to read that trifle, but will be my Compurgator as to that arrogance whereof I am accus'd. The truth is, if I had been naturally guilty of so much vanity as to dictate my opinions; yet I do not find that the

19 Dialogue:] ~ . Q2, D.
19–22 *'Tis true* . . . [italics] . . . *reasonable*] 'Tis true . . . [romans] . . . reasonable Q2, D.
23–28 *The drift* . . . *my self*] romans and italics reversed from Q2, D, except for "English" *and* "French".

Character of a positive or self-conceited person is of such advantage to any in this Age, that I should labour to be publickly admitted of that Order.

But I am not now to defend my own Cause, when that of all the Ancients and Moderns is in question: for this Gentleman who accuses me of arrogance, has taken a course not to be taxed with the other extream of modesty. Those propositions which are laid down in my Discourse as helps to the better imitation of Nature, are not mine (as I have said) nor were ever pretended so to be, but derived from the Authority of *Aristotle* and *Horace,* and from the Rules and Examples of *Ben. Johnson* and *Corneille.* These are the men with whom properly he contends, and against whom *he will endeavour to make it evident, that there is no such thing as what they All pretend.*

His Argument against the Unities of place and time, is this; that *'tis as impossible for one Stage to present two Rooms or Houses truly, as two Countries or Kingdoms, & as impossible that five hours or twenty four hours should be two hours, as that a thousand hours or years should be less than what they are, or the greatest part of time to be comprehended in the less: for all of them being impossible, they are none of them nearest the Truth or Nature of what they present; for impossibilities are all equal, and admit of no degree.*

This Argument is so scattered into parts, that it can scarce be united into a Syllogism; yet, in obedience to him, *I will abbreviate* and comprehend as much of it as I can in few words, that my Answer to it may be more perspicuous. I conceive his meaning to be what follows as to the unity of place: (if I mistake, I beg his pardon, professing it is not out of any design to play the *Argumentative Poet.*) If one Stage cannot properly present two Rooms or Houses, much less two Countries or Kingdoms, then there can be no Unity of place: but one Stage cannot properly perform this; therefore there can be no Unity of place.

I plainly deny his minor Proposition; the force of which, if I mistake not, depends on this; that the Stage being one place, cannot be two. This indeed is as great a Secret, as that we are all

13 whom] *whom* Q2, D.   16 that] *That* Q2, D.

mortal; but to requite it with another, I must crave leave to tell him, that though the Stage cannot be two places, yet it may properly represent them, successively, or at several times. His Argument is indeed no more than a meer fallacy, which will evidently appear when we distinguish place, as it relates to Plays, into real and imaginary. The real place is that Theater, or piece of ground on which the Play is acted. The imaginary, that House, Town, or Country where the action of the *Drama* is supposed to be; or more plainly, where the Scene of the Play is laid. Let us
10 now apply this to that Herculean Argument, which *if strictly and duely weighed, is to make it evident, that there is no such thing as what they all pretend.* 'Tis impossible, he says, for one Stage to present two Rooms or Houses: I answer, 'tis neither impossible, nor improper, for one real place to represent two or more imaginary places, so it be done successively, which in other words is no more than this; That the imagination of the Audience, aided by the words of the Poet, and painted Scenes, may suppose the Stage to be sometimes one place, sometimes another, now a Garden, or Wood, and immediately a Camp: which I appeal to
20 every mans imagination, if it be not true. Neither the Ancients nor Moderns, as much Fools as he is pleased to think them, ever asserted that they could make one place two; but they might hope by the good leave of this Author, that the change of a Scene might lead the imagination to suppose the place alter'd: So that he cannot fasten those absurdities upon this Scene of a Play, or imaginary place of Action, that it is one place and yet two. And this being so clearly proved, that 'tis past any shew of a reasonable denial, it will not be hard to destroy that other part of his Argument which depends upon it, namely, that 'tis as impossible for
30 a Stage to represent two Rooms or Houses, as two Countries or Kingdoms: for his reason is already overthrown, which was, because both were alike impossible. This is manifestly otherwise; for 'tis proved, that a Stage may properly represent two Rooms or Houses; for the imagination being Judge of what is represented, will in reason be less chocqu'd with the appearance of two rooms in the same house, or two houses in the same City, than

10 which] *which* Q2, D.

with two distant Cities in the same Country, or two remote
Countries in the same Universe. Imagination in a man, or reasonable Creature, is supposed to participate of reason, and when that
governs, as it does in the belief of fiction, reason is not destroyed,
but misled, or blinded: that can prescribe to the reason, during
the time of the representation, somewhat like a weak belief of
what it sees and hears; and reason suffers it self to be so hood-
wink'd, that it may better enjoy the pleasures of the fiction: but
it is never so wholly made a captive, as to be drawn head-long
10 into a perswasion of those things which are most remote from
probability: 'tis in that case a free-born Subject, not a Slave, it
will contribute willingly its assent, as far as it sees convenient,
but will not be forc'd. Now there is a greater vicinity in Nature,
betwixt two Rooms than betwixt two Houses, betwixt two
Houses than betwixt two Cities, and so of the rest: reason therefore can sooner be led by imagination to step from one room into
another, than to walk to two distant houses, and yet rather to go
thither, than to flye like a Witch through the Air, and be hurried
from one Region to another. Fancy and Reason go hand in hand,
20 the first cannot leave the last behind; and though Fancy, when
it sees the wide Gulph, would venture over, as the nimbler; yet it
is with-held by Reason, which will refuse to take the leap, when
the distance over it appears too large. If *Ben. Johnson* himself
will remove the Scene from *Rome* into *Tuscany* in the same Act,
and from thence return to *Rome,* in the Scene which immediately follows; reason will consider there is no proportionable
allowance of time to perform the journey, and therefore will
chuse to stay at home. So then the less change of place there is,
the less time is taken up in transporting the persons of the
30 *Drama,* with Analogy to reason; and in that Analogy, or resemblance of Fiction to Truth, consists the excellency of the
Play.

    For what else concerns the Unity of place, I have already given
my opinion of it in my *Essay,* that there is a latitude to be allowed
to it, as several places in the same Town or City, or places adjacent to each other in the same Country; which may all be comprehended under the larger denomination of one place; yet with

this restriction, that the nearer and fewer those imaginary places are, the greater resemblance they will have to Truth: and Reason which cannot make them one, will be more easily led to suppose them so.

What has been said of the Unity of place, may easily be applyed to that of time: I grant it to be impossible, that the greater part of time should be comprehended in the less, that twenty four hours should be crowded into three: but there is no necessity of that Supposition. For as *Place,* so *Time* relating to a Play, is either imaginary or real: The real is comprehended in those three hours, more or less, in the space of which the Play is represented: The imaginary is that which is supposed to be taken up in the Representation, as twenty four hours more or less. Now no man ever could suppose that twenty four real hours could be included in the space of three: but where is the absurdity of affirming that the feigned business of twenty four imagin'd hours, may not more naturally be represented in the compass of three real hours, than the like feigned business of twenty four years in the same proportion of real time? For the proportions are always real, and much nearer, by his permission, of twenty four to three, than of four thousand to it.

I am almost fearful of illustrating any thing by similitude, lest he should confute it for an Argument; yet I think the comparison of a Glass will discover very aptly the fallacy of his Argument, both concerning time and place. The strength of his Reason depends on this, That the less cannot comprehend the greater. I have already answered, that we need not suppose it does; I say not that the less can comprehend the greater, but only that it may represent it: As in a Glass or Mirrour of half a yard Diameter, a whole room and many persons in it may be seen at once: not that it can comprehend that room or those persons, but that it represents them to the sight.

But the Author of the Duke of *Lerma* is to be excus'd for his declaring against the Unity of time: for if I be not much mistaken, he is an interested person; the time of that Play taking up so many years as the favour of the Duke of *Lerma* continued; nay, the second and third Act including all the time of his Prosperity, which was a great part of the Reign of *Philip* the Third: for in the beginning of the second Act he was not yet a Favourite, and before the end of the third, was in disgrace. I say not this with the least design of limiting the Stage too servilely to 24 hours, however he be pleased to tax me with dogmatizing in that point. In my Dialogue, as I before hinted, several persons maintained their several opinions: one of them, indeed, who supported the Cause of the *French* Poesie, said how strict they were in that Particular: but he who answered in behalf of our Nation,

10 was willing to give more latitude to the Rule; and cites the words of *Corneille* himself, complaining against the severity of it, and observing what Beauties it banish'd from the Stage, *pag.* 44. of my *Essay*. In few words my own opinion is this, (and I willingly submit it to my Adversary, when he will please impartially to consider it,) that the imaginary time of every Play ought to be contrived into as narrow a compass, as the nature of the Plot, the quality of the Persons, and variety of Accidents will allow. In Comedy I would not exceed 24 or 30 hours: for the Plot, Accidents, and Persons of Comedy are small, and may be naturally

20 turn'd in a little compass: But in Tragedy the Design is weighty, and the Persons great, therefore there will naturally be required a greater space of time in which to move them. And this, though *Ben. Johnson* has not told us, yet 'tis manifestly his opinion: for you see that to his Comedies he allows generally but 24 hours; to his two Tragedies, *Sejanus* and *Catiline,* a much larger time: though he draws both of them into as narrow a compass as he can: For he shews you only the latter end of *Sejanus* his Favour, and the Conspiracy of *Catiline* already ripe, and just breaking out into action.

30 But as it is an errour on the one side, to make too great a disproportion betwixt the imaginary time of the Play, and the real time of its representation; so on the other side, 'tis an oversight to compress the accidents of a Play into a narrower compass than that in which they could naturally be produc'd. Of this last errour the *French* are seldom guilty, because the thinness of

---

8, 35 *French*] D; French Q2.

their Plots prevents them from it: but few *Englishmen*, except
Ben. Johnson, have ever made a Plot with variety of design in it,
included in 24 hours which was altogether natural. For this
reason, I prefer the *Silent Woman* before all other Plays, I think
justly, as I do its Author in Judgment, above all other Poets.
Yet of the two, I think that errour the most pardonable, which in
too straight a compass crowds together many accidents, since it
produces more variety, and consequently more pleasure to the
Audience: and because the nearness of proportion betwixt the
imaginary and real time, does speciously cover the compression
of the Accidents.

Thus I have endeavoured to answer the meaning of his Argument; for as he drew it, I humbly conceive that it was none: as
will appear by his Proposition, and the proof of it. His Proposition was this.

*If strictly and duely weighed, 'tis as impossible for one Stage to
present two Rooms or Houses, as two Countries or Kingdoms,
&c.* And his Proof this: *For all being impossible, they are none of
them nearest the Truth or Nature of what they present.*

Here you see, instead of a Proof or Reason, there is only a
Petitio principii: for in plain words, his sense is this; Two
things are as impossible as one another, because they are both
equally impossible: but he takes those two things to be granted
as impossible, which he ought to have prov'd such before he had
proceeded to prove them equally impossible: he should have
made out first that it was impossible for one Stage to represent
two Houses, & then have gone forward to prove that it was as
equally impossible for a Stage to present two Houses, as two
Countries.

After all this, the very absurdity to which he would reduce
me, is none at all: for he only drives at this, That if his Argument
be true, I must then acknowledge that there are degrees in
impossibilities, which I easily grant him without dispute: and if
I mistake not, *Aristotle* and the *School* are of my opinion. For
there are some things which are absolutely impossible, and others

---

1 *Englishmen*] D; English men Q2.

which are only so *ex parte;* as 'tis absolutely impossible for a thing *to be,* and *not be* at the same time; but for a Stone to move naturally upward, is only impossible *ex parte materiæ;* but it is not impossible for the first Mover, to alter the Nature of it.

His last Assault, like that of a *Frenchman,* is most feeble: for whereas I have observed, that none have been violent against Verse, but such only as have not attempted it, or have succeeded ill in their attempt, he will needs, according to his usual custom, improve my Observation to an Argument, that he might have the glory to confute it. But I lay my Observation at his feet, as I do my Pen, which I have often employ'd willingly in his deserved commendations, and now most unwillingly against his Judgment. For his person and parts, I honour them as much as any man living, and have had so many particular Obligations to him, that I should be very ungrateful, if I did not acknowledge them to the World. But I gave not the first occasion of this difference in opinions. In my Epistle Dedicatory, before my *Rival Ladies,* I had said somewhat in behalf of Verse, which he was pleased to answer in his Preface to his Plays: that occasioned my Reply in my Essay, and that Reply begot this rejoynder of his in his Preface to the Duke of *Lerma.* But as I was the last who took up Arms, I will be the first to lay them down. For what I have here written, I submit it wholly to him; and if I do not hereafter answer what may be objected against this Paper, I hope the World will not impute it to any other reason, than only the due respect which I have for so noble an Opponent.

5 *Frenchman*] D; French man Q2.

To the most Excellent and most Illustrious Princess ANNE,
Dutchess of Monmouth, *and Countess of* Bucclugh,
Wife to the most Illustrious and High-born Prince James
Duke of Monmouth.

May it please your Grace,

THE favour which Heroick Plays have lately found upon
our Theaters has been wholly deriv'd to them, from the
countenance and approbation they have receiv'd at
Court, the most eminent persons for Wit and Honour in the
Royal Circle having so far own'd them, that they have judg'd no
way so fit as Verse to entertain a Noble Audience, or to express a
noble passion. And amongst the rest which have been written in
this kind, they have been so indulgent to this Poem, as to allow it
10 no inconsiderable place. Since, therefore, to the Court I owe its
fortune on the Stage, so, being now more publickly expos'd in
Print, I humbly recommend it to your Graces Protection, who by
all knowing persons are esteem'd a Principal Ornament of the
Court. But though the rank which you hold in the Royal Family,
might direct the Eyes of a Poet to you, yet your beauty and goodness only could detain and fix them: High Objects may attract
the sight; but it looks up with pain on Craggy Rocks and Barren
Mountains, and continues not intent on any object, which is
wanting in shades and greens to entertain it. Beauty, in Courts,
20 is so necessary to the young, that those who are without it, seem
to be there to no other purpose then to wait on the triumphs of
the fair; to attend their motions in obscurity, as the Moon and
Stars do the Sun by day, or at best to be the refuge of those
hearts which others have despis'd; and, by the unworthiness of
both, to give and take a miserable comfort. But as needful as
beauty is, Virtue, and Honour are yet more: the reign of it

Caption: and Countess of Bucclugh, *Wife to the most Illustrious and High-born*
Prince James *Duke of* Monmouth.] Q2–12, F, D; Countess of *Bucclugh*, &c. Q1.
5 Court, the] ∼ . *The* Q1–12, F, D.
15–16 goodness only could] Q3–5; *goodness* Q1–2, Q6–12, F, D.
16 Objects may] Q3–5; *Objects, 'tis true,* Q1–2, Q6–12, F, D.
21 there to] Q2–12, F, D; *there* Q1.   21 on] Q2–12, F, D; *upon* Q1.

without their support is unsafe and short like that of Tyrants.
Every Sun which looks on Beauty wasts it; and, when once it is
decaying, the repairs of Art are of as short continuance, as the
after Spring, when the Sun is going farther from us. This,
Madam, is its ordinary Fate; but yours which is accompanied
by Virtue, is not subject to that common destiny. Your Grace
has not only a long time of Youth in which to flourish, but you
have likewise found the way by an untainted preservation of
your Honour, to make that perishable good more lasting. And if
10 Beauty like Wines could be preserv'd, by being mix'd and
embodied with others of their own nature, then your Graces
would be immortal, since no part of *Europe* can afford a parallel
to your Noble Lord, in masculine Beauty, and in goodliness of
shape. To receive the blessings and prayers of mankind, you
need only to be seen together; we are ready to conclude that
you are a pair of Angels sent below to make Virtue amiable in
your persons, or to sit to Poets when they would pleasantly
instruct the Age, by drawing goodness in the most perfect
and alluring shape of Nature. But though Beauty be the Theme,
20 on which Poets love to dwell, I must be forc'd to quit it as a
private praise, since you have deserv'd those which are more
publick. For Goodness and Humanity, which shine in you, are
Virtues which concern Mankind, and by a certain kind of
interest all people agree in their commendation, because the
profit of them may extend to many. 'Tis so much your inclination to do good that you stay not to be ask'd; which is an approach so nigh the Deity, that Humane Nature is not capable
of a nearer. 'Tis my Happiness that I can testifie this Virtue by
my own experience; since I have so great an aversion from
30 solliciting Court Favours, that I am ready to look on those as
very bold, who dare grow rich there without desert. But I beg

4 from us.] Q3–5; *off.* Q1–2, Q6–12, F, D.
4–5 This, Madam] *This,* Madam Q1–12, F, D.
7 in which to flourish] Q2–12, F, D; *to flourish in* Q1.
11 nature] Q3–5; *natures* Q1–2, Q6–12, F, D.
15 only to] Q2–12, F, D; *only* Q1.   25 many] Q2–12, F, D; *mauy* Q1.
28 Virtue] Q3–5; *Virtue of your Graces* Q1–2, Q6–12, F, D.

your Graces pardon for assuming this Virtue of Modesty to my self, which the sequel of this discourse will no way justifie. For in this address I have already quitted the character of a modest Man, by presenting you this Poem as an acknowledgment, which stands in need of your protection; and which ought no more to be esteem'd a Present, then it is accounted bounty in the Poor, when they bestow a Child on some wealthy Friend, who can give it better Education. Offsprings of this Nature are like to be so numerous with me, that I must be forc'd to send some of
10 them abroad; only this is like to be more fortunate then his Brothers, because I have landed him on a Hospitable shore. Under your Patronage *Montezuma* hopes he is more safe than in his Native *Indies:* and therefore comes to throw himself at your Graces feet; paying that homage to your Beauty, which he refus'd to the violence of his Conquerours. He begs only that when he shall relate his sufferings, you will consider he is an *Indian* Prince, and not expect any other Eloquence from his simplicity, then that, with which his griefs have furnished him. His story is, perhaps the greatest, which was ever represented in
20 a Poem of this nature; (the action of it including the Discovery and Conquest of a New World.) In it I have neither wholly follow'd the truth of the History, nor altogether left it: but have taken all the liberty of a Poet, to adde, alter, or diminish, as I thought might best conduce to the beautifying of my work; it being not the business of a Poet to represent Historical truth, but probability. But I am not to make the justification of this Poem, which I wholly leave to your Graces mercy. 'Tis an irregular piece if compar'd with many of *Corneilles,* and, if I may make a judgement of it, written with more Flame then Art;

7–8 can give it better Education] Q3–5; *will better breed it up* Q1–2, Q6–12, F, D.
13 Native *Indies*] Q3–5, Q8–12, F, D; *Native Indies* Q1–2, Q6–7.
16 he is] Q3–5; *him as* Q1–2, Q6–12, F, D.
17 *Indian* Prince] Indian Prince Q1–12, F, D.
18 that, with which . . . him] Q3–5; *what . . . him withal* Q1–2, Q6–12, F, D.
24 work; it] Q4–5, Q9–12, F, D (It Q4–5); ~ . *It* Q1–3, Q6–8.
25 Historical truth] Q2–12, F, D; *truth* Q1.

in which it represents the mind and intentions of the Author, who is with much more Zeal and Integrity, then Design and Artifice,

MADAM,

October *the 12*th.

Your Graces most Obedient

1667.

And most Obliged Servant,

JOHN DRYDEN.

Connexion of the *Indian Emperour,* to the *Indian Queen.*

THE Conclusion of the *Indian Queen,* (part of which Poem
was writ by me) left little matter for another Story to
be built on it, there remaining but two of the considerable Characters alive, (*viz.*) *Montezuma,* and *Orazia;* thereupon
the Author of this, thought it necessary to produce new persons
from those two; and considering that the late *Indian* Queen,
before she lov'd *Montezuma,* liv'd in clandestine Marriage with
her General *Traxalla;* he has rais'd from them a Son and two
Daughters, supposed to be left young Orphans at their Death:
10 On the other side, he has given to *Montezuma* and *Orazia,* two
Sons and a Daughter; all now supposed to be grown up to
Mens and Womens Estate; and their Mother *Orazia* (for whom
there was no further use in the story) lately dead.

So that you are to imagine about Twenty years elapsed since
the Coronation of *Montezuma;* who, in the Truth of the
History, was a great and glorious Prince; in whose time happened
the Discovery and Invasion of *Mexico* by the *Spaniards;* under
the conduct of *Hernando Cortez,* who, joyning with the
Taxallan-Indians, the inveterate Enemies of *Montezuma,* wholly
20 Subverted that flourishing Empire; the Conquest of which, is
the Subject of this *Dramatique* Poem.

I have neither wholly followed the story nor varied from it;
and, as near as I could, have traced the Native simplicity and ignorance of the *Indians,* in relation to *Europæan* Customes: The
Shipping, Armour, Horses, Swords, and Guns of the *Spaniards,*
being as new to them as their Habits and their Language were to
the Christians.

---

3 on it] Q3–5; on Q1–2, Q6–12, F, D.
6 those two; and considering that] Q3–5; the old ones; and considering Q1–2,
Q6–12, F, D.
6 Queen] *Queen* Q1–12, F, D.
8 he has rais'd from them] Q3–5; from those two, he has rais'd Q1–2, Q6–12,
F, D.
16 in] Q3–5; and in Q1–2, Q6–12, F, D.   26 Habits] Q2–12, F, D; ~ , Q1.
26–27 Language were to the Christians] Q2–12, F, D; Language Q1.

The difference of their Religion from ours, I have taken from the Story it self; and that which you find of it in the first and fifth Acts, touching the sufferings and constancy of *Montezuma* in his Opinions, I have only illustrated, not alter'd from those who have written of it.

The Names of the Persons Represented.

Indians Men,
- *Montezuma,* Emperour of *Mexico.*
- *Odmar,* his Eldest Son.
- *Guyomar,* his Younger Son.
- *Orbellan,* Son to the late *Indian* Queen by *Traxalla.*
- High Priest of the Sun.

Women,
- *Cydaria, Montezuma's* Daughter.
- *Almeria* ⎫ Sisters; and Daughters to the late
- *Alibech* ⎭ *Indian* Queen.

Spaniards,
- *Cortez,* the *Spanish* General.
- *Vasquez* ⎫ Commanders under him.
- *Pizarro* ⎭

The Scene *MEXICO* and two Leagues about it.

Indians Men,] Indians Men, Q1–12, F, D; *omitted from M2.*
Queen] M2; *Queen* Q1–12, F, D.
High Priest of the Sun] M2; *High Priest* of the *Sun* Q1–6, D; *High Priest of the Sun* Q7–12, F.
Daughters] Q6–12, F, D, M2; Daughter Q1–5.
Queen] M2; *Queen* Q1–12, F, D.
Spaniards] Spaniards Q1–12, F, D; *omitted from M2.*

PROLOGUE.

ALMIGHTY *Critiques! whom our* Indians *here*
Worship, just as they do the Devil, for fear;
In reverence to your pow'r I come this day
To give you timely warning of our Play.
The Scenes are old, the Habits are the same
We wore last year, before the Spaniards *came.*
Our Prologue, th' old-cast too————
For to observe the new it should at least
Be spoke, by some ingenious Bird or Beast.
10 *Now if you stay, the blood that shall be shed*
From this poor Play, be all upon your head.
We neither promise you one Dance, or Show,
Then Plot and Language they are wanting too:
But you, kind Wits, will those light faults excuse:
Those are the common frailties of the Muse;
Which who observes, he buyes his place too dear:
For 'tis your business to be couz'ned here.
These wretched spies of wit must then confess
They take more pains to please themselves the less.
20 *Grant us such Judges,* Phœbus, *we request,*
As still mistake themselves into a jest;
Such easie Judges, that our Poet may
Himself admire the fortune of his Play;
And arrogantly, as his fellows do,
Think he writes well, because he pleases you.
This he conceives not hard to bring about
If all of you would join to help him out.
Would each man take but what he understands,
And leave the rest upon the Poets hands.

2 *fear;*] D; ∼ . Q1–12, F.   5 *same*] Q6–12, F, D; ∼ , Q1–5.
16 *observes,*] Q5, D; ∼∧ Q1–4, Q6–12, F.
20 Phœbus,] Q6–12, F, D; ∼∧ Q1–5.   23 *Play;*] Q6–12, F, D; ∼ . Q1–5.

THE INDIAN EMPEROUR.

ACT I. SCENE I.

The Scene a pleasant Indian *Country.*

Enter Cortez, Vasquez, Pizarro, *with* Spaniards *and* Indians *of their party.*

Cort. On what new happy Climate are we thrown,
So long kept secret, and so lately known;
As if our old world modestly withdrew,
And here, in private, had brought forth a new!
Vasq. Corn, Wine, and Oyl are wanting to this ground,
In which our Countries fruitfully abound:
As if this Infant world, yet un-array'd,
Naked and bare, in Natures Lap were laid.
No useful Arts have yet found footing here;
10 But all untaught and salvage does appear.
Cort. Wild and untaught are Terms which we alone
Invent, for fashions differing from our own:
For all their Customs are by Nature wrought,
But we, by Art, unteach what Nature taught.
Piz. In *Spain* our Springs, like Old Mens Children, be
Decay'd and wither'd from their Infancy:
No kindly showers fall on our barren earth,
To hatch the seasons in a timely birth.
Our Summer such a Russet Livery wears,
20 As in a Garment often dy'd appears.
Cort. Here nature spreads her fruitful sweetness round,
Breaths on the Air and broods upon the ground.

---

13   wrought] Q2–12, F, D, M1–2; taught Q1.

Here days and nights the only seasons be,
The Sun no Climat does so gladly see:
When forc'd from hence, to view our parts, he mourns:
Takes little journies, and makes quick returns.
    Vasq. Methinks we walk in dreams on fairy Land,
Where golden Ore lies mixt with common sand;
Each downfal of a flood the Mountains pour,
30 From their rich bowels rolls a silver shower.
    Cort. Heaven from all ages wisely did provide
This wealth, and for the bravest Nation hide,
Who with four hundred foot and forty horse,
Dare boldly go a New found World to force.
    Piz. Our men, though Valiant, we should find too few,
But *Indians* joyn the *Indians* to subdue,
Taxallan, shook by *Montezumas* powers,
Has, to resist his forces, call'd in ours.
    Vasq. Rashly to arm against so great a King
40 I hold not safe, nor is it just to bring
A War, without a fair defiance made.
    Piz. Declare we first our quarrel: then Invade.
    Cort. My self, my Kings Ambassadour, will go;
Speak, *Indian* Guide, how far to *Mexico?*
    Indi. Your eyes can scarce so far a prospect make,
As to discern the City on the Lake.
But that broad Caus-way will direct your way,
And you may reach the Town by noon of day.
    Cort. Command a party of our *Indians* out,
50 With a strict charge not to engage, but scout;
By noble ways we Conquest will prepare,
First offer peace, and that refus'd make war.   *Exeunt.*

---

23 seasons] Q2b–12, F, D, M1–2; season Q1–2a.
34 Dare] Q2–12, F, D, M1–2; We Q1.
38 Has,] Q5, Q8; ~∧ Q1–4, Q6–7, Q9–12, F, D, M1–2.
40 just] Q2b–12, F, D, M1–2; fit Q1–2a.
43 *Cort.* My self] Q2–12, F, D, M1–2; My self Q1.
44 Speak,] Q7–12, F, M1; ~∧ Q1–6, D, M2.

SCENE II.

A Temple, and the high Priest with other Priests.
To them an Indian.

Ind. Haste Holy Priest, it is the Kings command.
High Pr. When sets he forward?
Ind.————————————————He is near at hand.
High Pr. The Incense is upon the Altar plac'd,
The bloody Sacrifice already past.
Five hundred Captives saw the rising Sun,
Who lost their light ere half his race was run.
That which remains we here must celebrate;
Where far from noise, without the City gate,
The peaceful power that governs love repairs,
10 To feast upon soft vows and silent pray'rs.
We for his Royal presence only stay,
To end the rites of this so solemn day.   *Exit* Indian.

Enter Montezuma; *his eldest Son* Odmar; *his*
Daughter Cydaria; Almeria, Alibech, Orbellan, *and Train. They place themselves.*

High Pr. On your birth day, while we sing
            To our Gods and to our King,
            Her, among this beauteous quire,
            Whose perfections you admire,
            Her, who fairest does appear,
            Crown the Queen of all the year,

---

1 Priest,] Q2–12, F, D; ~∧ Q1, M1–2.   2 sets] Q2–12, F, D, M1–2; gets Q1.
12 rites] Q2–12, F, D, M1; rights Q1, M2.
12 day.] Q2–7, Q9–11, F, D, M1–2; ~ : Q1; ~∧ Q8, Q12.
12+ *s.d.* Cydaria;] Q8, D; ~ , Q1–7, Q9–12, F; ~ : M1; ~∧ M2.
13 *High Pr.*] Q2–12, F, D, M2; *Callib.* Q1, M1.
18 Crown the] Q3–5; Crown her Q1–2, Q6–12, F, D, M1–2.
18 year,] D; ~ . Q1–12, F, M2; ~∧ M1.

Of the year and of the day,

20   And at her feet your Garland lay.

Odm. My Father this way does his looks direct,

Heaven grant he give it not where I suspect.   [*Aside.*

> Montezuma *rises, goes about the Ladies, and at*
> *length stays at* Almeria *and bows.*

Mont. Since my *Orazia*'s death I have not seen

A beauty so deserving to be Queen

As fair *Almeria.*

Alm. ———Sure he will not know   [*To her Brother*

My birth I to that injur'd Princess owe,   *and Sister aside.*

To whom not only he his love deny'd,

But in her sufferings took unmanly pride.

Alib. Since *Montezuma* will his choice renew,

30   In dead *Orazia*'s room electing you,

'Twill please our Mothers Ghost that you succeed

To all the glories of her Rivals bed.   [*Aside to her.*

Alm. If news be carried to the shades below,

The *Indian* Queen will be more pleas'd, to know

That I his scorns on him, who scorn'd her, pay.   [*Aside.*

Orb. Would you could right her some more noble way. [*Aside.*

> *She turns to him who is kneeling*
> *all this while.*

Mont. Madam, this posture is for Heaven design'd, [*Kneeling.*

And what moves Heaven I hope may make you kind.

Alm. Heaven may be kind, the Gods uninjur'd live,

40 And crimes below cost little to forgive.

By thee, Inhumane, both my Parents dy'd;

One by thy sword, the other by thy pride.

Mont. My haughty mind no fate could ever bow,

---

22   suspect. [*Aside.*] suspect. Q1–12, F, D, M1–2.

27   To whom not only he his] Q3–5; Whom his hard heart not only Q1–2, Q6–
12, F, D, M1–2.

32   bed. [*Aside to her.*] bed. Q1–12, F, D, M1–2.

35   who] Q2–12, F, D, M2; that Q1, M1.

35   pay. [*Aside.*] pay. Q1–12, F, D, M1–2.

36   way. [*Aside.*] way. Q1–12, F, D, M1–2.

36+   s.d. kneeling] Q2–12, F, D, M2; *kneeliug* Q1; *omitted from* M1.

Yet I must stoop to one who scorns me now:
Is there no pity to my sufferings due?
    Alm. As much as what my mother found from you.
    Mont. Your mothers wrongs a recompence shall meet,
I lay my Scepter at her Daughters feet.
    Alm. He, who does now my least commands obey,
50 Would call me Queen, and take my pow'r away.
    Odm. Can he hear this, and not his Fetters break?
Is love so pow'rful, or his soul so weak?
I'le fright her from it.———   [*Aside.*
                  Madam, though you see
The King is kind, I hope your modesty
Will know, what distance to the Crown is due.
    Alm. Distance and modesty prescrib'd by you?
    Odm. Almeria dares not think such thoughts as these.
    Alm. She dares both think and act what thoughts she please.
'Tis much below me on his Throne to sit;
60 But when I do, you shall petition it.
    Odm. If, Sir, *Almeria* does your bed partake,
I mourn for my forgotten mothers sake.
    Mont. When Parents loves are order'd by a Son,
Let streams prescribe their fountains where to run.
    Odm. In all I urge I keep my duty still,
Not rule your reason, but instruct your will.
    Mont. Small use of reason in that Prince is shown,
Who follows others, and neglects his own.
                Almeria *to* Orbellan *and* Alibech, *who are*
                      this while whispering to her.
    Alm. No, he shall ever love, and always be
70 The subject of my scorn and cruelty.
    Orb. To prove the lasting torment of his life,
You must not be his Mistress, but his Wife.
Few know what care, an Husbands peace destroys,
His real griefs, and his dissembled joys.

---

44 who] Q2–12, F, D, M2; that Q1, M1.
53 it.——— [*Aside.* / Madam] it, Madam Q1–2, Q6–7, Q9, F, M2; it. Madam
Q3, Q8, Q10–12, D; it; Madam Q4–5; it? Madam M1.

Alm. What mark of pleasing vengeance could be shown,
If I to break his quiet lose my own?
    Orb. A brothers life upon your love relies,
Since I do homage to *Cydarias* eyes:
How can her Father to my hopes be kind
80 If, in your heart, he no example find?
    Alm. To save your life I'le suffer any thing;
Yet I'le not flatter this tempestuous King;
But work his stubborn soul a nobler way,
And, if he love, I'le force him to obey.
I take this Garland, not as given by you,   [*To* Montez.
But as my merit, and my beauties due.
As for the Crown that you, my slave, possess,
To share it with you would but make me less.

Enter Guyomar hastily.

    Odm. My brother *Guyomar!* methinks I spye
90 Hast in his steps, and wonder in his eye.
    Mont. I sent thee to the frontiers, quickly tell
The cause of thy return, are all things well?
    Guy. I went, in order, Sir, to your command,
To view the utmost limits of the land:
To that Sea shore where no more world is found,
But foaming billows breaking on the ground,
Where, for a while, my eyes no object met
But distant skies that in the Ocean set:
And low hung clouds that dipt themselves in rain
100 To shake their fleeces on the earth again.
At last, as far as I could cast my eyes
Upon the Sea, somewhat, methought, did rise
Like blewish mists, which still appearing more,
Took dreadful shapes, and mov'd towards the shore.

---

75   shown,] Q1b–10, F, D; ~ʌ Q1a, Q11–12, M2; ~ ? M1.
80   find?] Q2–12, F, D, M1; ~ . Q1, M2.
85   [*To*] Q3–5, Q8–12, F, D; ʌ*to* Q1–2; [*to* Q6–7, M2.
102   methought,] Q3–5; ~ʌ Q1–2, Q6–12, F, D, M1–2.

Mont. What forms did these new wonders represent?
Guy. More strange than what your wonder can invent.
The object I could first distinctly view
Was tall straight trees which on the waters flew,
Wings on their sides instead of leaves did grow,
110 Which gather'd all the breath the winds could blow.
And at their roots grew floating Palaces,
Whose out-bow'd bellies cut the yielding Seas.
      Mont. What Divine Monsters, O ye gods, are these
That float in air and flye upon the Seas!
Came they alive or dead upon the shore?
      Guy. Alas, they liv'd too sure, I heard them roar:
All turn'd their sides, and to each other spoke,
I saw their words break out in fire and smoke.
Sure 'tis their voice that Thunders from on high,
120 Or these the younger brothers of the Skie.
Deaf with the noyse I took my hasty flight,
No mortal courage can support the fright.
      High Pr. Old Prophecies foretel our fall at hand,
When bearded men in floating Castles Land,
I fear it is of dire portent.
      Mont. —————————Go see
What it fore-shows, and what the gods decree. *Exit High Pr.*
Mean time proceed we to what rites remain;
Odmar, of all this presence does contain,
Give her your wreath whom you esteem most fair.
130   *Odm.* Above the rest I judge one beauty rare,
And may that beauty prove as kind to me   *He gives* Alibech
As I am sure fair *Alibech* is she.   *the wreath.*
      Mont. You *Guyomar* must next perform your part.
      Guy. I want a Garland, but I'le give a heart:
My brothers pardon I must first implore,
Since I with him fair *Alibech* adore.
      Odm. That all should *Alibech* adore 'tis true,

---

113 are] Q3–5; were Q1–2, Q6–12, F, D, M1–2.
126 decree. *Exit High Pr.*] decree. Q1–12, F, D, M1–2.
127 remain;] Q3–5; ~ , Q1–2; ~ . Q6–12, F, D; ~∧ M1–2.

But some respect is to my birth-right due.
My claim to her by Eldership I prove.
140   *Guy.* Age is a plea in Empire, not in Love.
    Odm. I long have staid for this solemnity
To make my passion publick.
    Guy.————————So have I.
    Odm. But from her birth my soul has been her slave,
My heart receiv'd the wounds which first she gave:
I watcht the early glories of her Eyes,
As men for day break watch the eastern Skies.
    Guy. It seems my soul then mov'd the quicker pace,
Yours first set out, mine reach'd her in the race.
    Mont. Odmar, your choice I cannot disapprove;
150 Nor justly *Guyomar,* can blame your love.
To *Alibech* alone refer your suit,
And let her sentence finish your dispute.
    Alib. You think me Sir a Mistress quickly won,
So soon to finish what is scarce begun:
In this surprise I can no judgment make,
'Tis answering Riddles ere I'm well awake:
If you oblige me suddenly to chuse,
The choice is made, for I must both refuse.
For to my self I owe this due regard
160 Not to make love my gift, but my reward,
Time best will show whose services will last.
    Odm. Then judge my future service by my past.
What I shall be by what I was, you know:
That love took deepest root which first did grow.
    Guy. That love which first was set will first decay,
Mine of a fresher date will longer stay.
    Odm. Still you forget my birth.
    Guy.————————But you, I see,
Take care still to refresh my memory.

---

144 wounds which first] Q3–5; first wounds that Q1–2a, M1; first wounds which
Q2b, Q6–12, F, D, M2.
155 I can no] Q3–5; should I a Q1–2, Q6–12, F, D, M1–2.
158 refuse] Q2–12, F, D, M1–2; refufe Q1.
163 know:] Q2b–12, F, D, M1; ~ , Q1–2a; ~∧ M2.

Mont. My Sons, let your unseemly discord cease,
170 If not in friendship live at least in peace.
Orbellan, where you love bestow your wreath.
    Orb. My love I dare not, ev'n in whispers breath.
    Mont. A vertuous Love may venture any thing.
    Orb. Not to attempt the Daughter of my King.
    Mont. Whither is all my former fury gone?
Once more I have *Traxalla's* chains put on,
And by his Children am in triumph led,
Too well the living have reveng'd the dead!
    Alm. You think my brother born your enemy,
180 He's of *Traxalla's* blood, and so am I.
    Mont. In vain I strive,————
My Lyon-heart is with Loves toyls beset,
Strugling I fall still deeper in the net.
Cydaria your new lovers Garland take,
And use him kindly for your Fathers sake.
    Cyd. So strong an hatred does my nature sway,
That spight of duty I must disobey.
Besides you warn'd me still of loving two,
Can I love him already loving you?

Enter a Guard hastily.

190   *Mont.* You look amaz'd as if some sudden fear
Had seiz'd your hearts, is any danger near?
    1 *Guard.* Behind the covert where this Temple stands,
Thick as the shades, there issue swarming bands
Of ambush'd men, whom, by their arms and dress,
To be *Taxallan* Enemies I guess.

---

173   any thing.] Q2–12, F, D; ~ : Q1; ~∧ M1–2.
174   King.] Q2–12, F, D, M1; ~ ? Q1; ~∧ M2.
181   strive,————] ~,∧ Q1–12, F, D; ~ :———— M1; ~∧———— M2.
190   *Mont.* You] Q2–12, F, D, M2; *Mont.* How now———— / You Q1, M1.
195   *Taxallan*] Q10–12, D, M1; *Taxcallan* Q1–5; *Traxallan* Q6–9, F, M2.

Another Enters.

2 *Guard.* The Temple, Sir, is almost compast round.
Mont. Some speedy way for passage must be found.
Make to the City by the Postern Gate,
I'le either force my Victory, or Fate;
200 A glorious death in arms I'le rather prove,
Than stay to perish tamely by my Love.   *Exeunt omnes.*

An Alarm within. Enter Montez. Odm. Guy. Alib.
Orb. Cyd. Alm. *as pursued by* Taxallans.

Mont. No succour from the Town?
Odm.————————————————None, none is nigh.
Guy. We are inclos'd and must resolve to dye.
Mont. Fight for revenge now hope of life is past,
But one stroke more and that will be my last.

Enter Cortez, Vasquez, Pizarro, *to the* Taxallans, Cort. *stays them, just falling on.*

Cort. Contemn'd? my orders broke even in my sight! [*To his*
Did I not strictly charge you should not fight?   Indians.
Ind. Your choler, General, does unjustly rise,
To see your Friends pursue your Enemies;
210 The greatest and most cruel foes we have
Are these whom you would ignorantly save;
By ambush'd men, behind their Temple laid,
We have the King of *Mexico* betray'd.
Cort. Where, banish'd Vertue, wilt thou shew thy face

196   round.] Q2-4, Q6-12, F, D, M2; ∼ , Q1; ∼∧ Q5, M1.
201   Love. *Exeunt omnes.*] M1; Love. Q1-12, F, D; love (Exeunt M2.
201+   *s.d. within.*] Q2-4, Q6-12, F, D; ∼ , Q1, Q5, M1; ∼∧ M2.
201+   *s.d. by*] Q2-12, F, D; by Q1, M1-2.
207   *s.d.* Indians.] Q4-5, Q7-12, F, D; ∼∧ Q1-3, Q6; *s.d. omitted from M1-2.*
211   save;] Q3-5, M1; ∼ , Q1-2, Q6-12, F; ∼ . D; ∼∧ M2.
214   Where,] Q8-12, F, D, M1; ∼∧ Q1-7, M2.

If treachery infects thy *Indian* race!
Dismiss your rage, and lay your weapons by:
Know I protect them, and they shall not dye.
  Ind. O wond'rous mercy shown to foes distrest!
  Cort. Call them not so, when once with odds opprest,
220 Nor are they Foes my clemency defends,
Until they have refus'd the name of Friends:
Draw up our *Spaniards* by themselves, then Fire   *To* Vasq.
Our Guns on all who do not straight retire.
  Ind. O mercy, mercy, at thy feet we fall, Ind. *kneeling.*
Before thy roaring gods destroy us all;
See we retreat without the least reply, *The* Taxallans *retire.*
Keep thy gods silent, if they speak we dye.
  Mont. The fierce *Taxallans* lay their weapons down,
Some miracle in our relief is shown.
230 *Guy.* These bearded men, in shape and colour be
Like those I saw come floating on the Sea. [Mont. *kneels to* Cort.
  Mont. Patron of *Mexico* and god of Wars,
Son of the Sun, and brother of the Stars————
  Cort. Great Monarch, your devotion you misplace.
  Mont. Thy actions show thee born of Heavenly Race.
If then thou art that cruel god, whose eyes
Delight in Blood, and Humane Sacrifice,
Thy dreadful Altars I with Slaves will store,
And feed thy nostrils with hot reeking gore;
240 Or if that mild and gentle god thou be,
Who dost mankind below with pity see,
With breath of incense I will glad thy heart;
But if like us, of mortal seed thou art,
Presents of rarest Fowls, and Fruits I'le bring,
And in my Realms thou shalt be more then King.
  Cort. Monarch of Empires, and deserving more
Then the Sun sees upon your Western shore;

---

223 who] Q2–12, F, D, M2; that Q1, M1.
233 Stars————] M1; ~ . Q1–12, F, D, M2.
242 I] Q2–12, F, D, M2; we Q1, M1.
242 heart;] Q2–9, D; ~ , Q1, M1; ~ : Q10–12, F; ~ ∧ M2.
244 rarest] Q3–5; choicest Q1–2, Q6–12, F, D, M1–2.

Like you a man, and hither led by fame,
Not by constraint but by my choice I came;
50 Ambassadour of Peace, if Peace you chuse,
Or Herauld of a War if you refuse.
    Mont. Whence or from whom dost thou these offers bring?
    Cort. From *Charles* the Fifth, the Worlds most Potent King.
    Mont. Some petty Prince, and one of little fame,
For to this hour I never heard his name:
The two great Empires of the World I know,
That of *Peru,* and this of *Mexico;*
And since the earth none larger does afford,
This *Charles* is some poor Tributary Lord.
260   *Cort.* You speak of that small part of earth you know,
But betwixt us and you wide Oceans flow,
And watry desarts of so vast extent,
That passing hither, four Full Moons we spent.
    Mont. But say, what news, what offers dost thou bring
From so remote, and so unknown a King?
               While Vasq. *speaks,* Cort. *spies the Ladies*
               and goes to them, entertaining Cydaria
               with Courtship in dumb show.
    Vasq. Spain's mighty Monarch, to whom Heaven thinks fit
That all the Nations of the Earth submit,
In gracious clemency, does condescend
On these conditions to become your Friend,
270 First, that of him you shall your Scepter hold,
Next, you present him with your useless Gold:
Last, that you leave those Idols you adore,
And one true Deity with prayers implore.
    Mont. You speak your Prince a mighty Emperour,
But his demands have spoke him Proud, and Poor;
He proudly at my free-born Scepter flies,
Yet poorly begs a mettal I despise.
Gold thou may'st take, what-ever thou canst find,

265+ *s.d. them,*] Q2–12, F, D; ~∧ Q1; *s.d. omitted from* M1–2.
272 adore] Q3–5; implore Q1–2, Q6–12, F, D, M1–2.
273 prayers implore] Q3–5; him adore Q1–2, Q6–12, F, D, M1–2.

Save what for sacred uses is design'd:
280 But, by what right pretends your King to be
This Soveraign Lord of all the World, and me?
    Piz. The Soveraign Priest,———
Who represents on Earth the pow'r of Heaven,
Has this your Empire to our Monarch given.
    Mont. Ill does he represent the powers above,
Who nourishes debate not Preaches love;
Besides what greater folly can be shown?
He gives another what is not his own.
    Vasq. His pow'r must needs unquestion'd be below,
290 For he in Heaven an Empire can bestow.
    Mont. Empires in Heaven he with more ease may give,
And you perhaps would with less thanks receive;
But Heaven has need of no such Vice-roy here,
It self bestows the Crowns that Monarchs wear.
    Piz. You wrong his power as you mistake our end,
Who came thus far Religion to extend.
    Mont. He who Religion truely understands
Knows its extent must be in Men, not Lands.
    Odm. But who are those that truth must propagate
300 Within the confines of my Fathers state?
    Vasq. Religious Men, who hither must be sent
As awful guides of Heavenly Government;
To teach you Penance, Fasts, and Abstinence,
To punish Bodies for the Souls offence.
    Mont. Cheaply you sin, and punish crimes with ease,
Not as th' offended, but th' offenders please.
First injure Heaven, and when its wrath is due,
Your selves prescribe it how to punish you.
    Odm. What numbers of these Holy Men must come?
310   *Piz.* You shall not want, each Village shall have some;
Who, though the Royal Dignity they own,
Are equal to it, and depend on none.
    Guy. Depend on none! you treat them sure in state,
For 'tis their plenty does their pride create.

---

292 less] Q2–12, F, D, M1–2; least Q1.

Mont. Those ghostly Kings would parcel out my pow'r,
And all the fatness of my Land devour;
That Monarch sits not safely on his Throne,
Who suffers any pow'r, to shock his own.
They teach obedience to Imperial sway,
20 But think it sin if they themselves obey.
     Vasq. It seems then our Religion you accuse,
And peaceful homage to our King refuse.
     Mont. Your gods I slight not, but will keep my own,
My Crown is absolute, and holds of none;
I cannot in a base subjection live,
Nor suffer you to take, though I would give.
     Cort. Is this your answer Sir?
     Mont.————————————This as a Prince,
Bound to my Peoples and my Crowns defence,
I must return, but, as a man by you
30 Redeem'd from death, all gratitude is due.
     Cort. Honour requir'd that act, ev'n from a Foe,
But what I did were I again to do,
That reason which inclin'd my will before
Would urge it now, for Love has fir'd it more.
Is no way left that we may yet agree?
Must I have War, yet have no Enemy?
     Vasq. He has refus'd all terms of Peace to take.
     Mont. Since we must fight, hear Heav'n, what Prayers I make,
First, to preserve this Antient State and me,
40 But if your doom the fall of both decree,
Grant only he who has such Honour shown,
When I am dust, may fill my empty Throne.
     Cort. To make me happier than that wish can do,

318 suffers any pow'r, to shock] Q3–5; bears, within, a power that shocks Q1–2,
Q6–12, F, D, M1.
318 own.] Q3–12, F, D; ~ , Q1–2; ~∧ M1.
331 Honour requir'd that act, ev'n from a Foe,] Q3–5; It was an act my Honour
bound me to, Q1–2, Q6–12, F, D, M1–2.
333–334 That reason which inclin'd my will before / Would urge it now, for
Love has fir'd it] Q3–5; I could not do it on my Honours score, / For Love would
now oblige me to do Q1–2, Q6–12, F, D, M1–2.
338 Heav'n] Q3–5; Heavens Q1–2, Q6–12, F, D; Heav'ns M1; heaven M2.

Lies not in all your gods to grant but you;
Let this fair Princess but one minute stay,
A look from her will your obligements pay.
   Mont. to Cyd. Your duty in your quick return be shown.
Stay you, and wait my Daughter to the Town.   *To his Guards.*
           Exeunt Mont. Odm. Guy. Orbel. Alm. *and* Alib.
           Cyd. *is going, but turns and looks back upon*
           Cortez, *who is looking on her all this while.*
   Cyd. My Father's gone, and yet I cannot go,
350   Sure I have something lost or left behind!   *Aside.*
   Cort. Like Travellers who wander in the Snow,
    I on her beauty gaze till I am blind.   *Aside.*
   Cyd. Thick breath, quick pulse, and heaving of my heart,
    All signs of some unwonted change appear:
I find my self unwilling to depart,
    And yet I know not why I would be here.
Stranger you raise such storms within my breast,
    That when I go, if I must go again;
I'le tell my Father you have rob'd my rest,
360   And to him of your injuries complain.
   Cort. Unknown, I swear, those wrongs were which I wrought,
But my complaints will much more just appear,
Who from another world my freedom brought,
    And to your conquering Eyes have lost it here.
   Cyd. Where is that other world from whence you came?
   Cort. Beyond the Ocean, far from hence it lies.
   Cyd. Your other world, I fear, is then the same
    That souls must go to when the body dies.
But what's the cause that keeps you here with me,
370   That I may know what keeps me here with you?
   Cort. Mine is a love which must perpetual be,
If you can be so just as I am true.

347 *to Cyd.*] Q9–12, F; to Cyd. Q1–8, D; Going M2.
347 shown.] Q6–12, F, D; ~ , Q1–5; ~ₐ M2.
348+ *s.d. Exeunt . . . Alm. and Alib.*] in Q1–12, F, D, M1–2 follows l. 346.
348+ *s.d. looking*] Q2–12, F, D, M1; loooking Q1.
351 who] Q2–12, F, D, M2; that Q1, M1.
361 swear,] Q6–12, F, D; ~ₐ Q1–5, M1–2.
364 to] Q2–12, F, D, M2; by Q1, M1.
369 me,] M1; ~ ? Q1–12, F, D; ~ ! M2.

Enter Orbellan.

Orb. Your Father wonders much at your delay.
Cyd. So great a wonder for so small a stay!
Orb. He has commanded you with me to go.
Cyd. Has he not sent to bring the stranger too?
Orb. If he to morrow, dares in fight appear,
His high plac'd Love, perhaps may cost him dear.
Cort. That word was never spoke to *Spaniard* yet,
80 But forfeited his Life who gave him it;
Hast quickly with thy pledge of safety hence,
Thy guilt's protected by her innocence.
Cyd. Sure in some fatal hour my Love was born,
So soon o'rcast with absence in the morn!
Cort. Turn hence those pointed glories of your Eyes,
For if more charms within those Circles rise,
So weak my Vertue, they so strong appear,
I shall turn ravisher to keep you here.   *Exeunt omnes.*

ACT II. SCENE I.

SCENE, *The Magitians Cave.*

Enter Montezuma, *High Priest.*

Mont. Not that I fear the utmost Fate can do,
Come I th' event of doubtful War to know,
For Life and Death are things indifferent,
Each to be chose as either brings content;
My search does from a Nobler motive spring,

372+ *s.d.* Orbellan.] Q2–12, F, D, M1–2; Orb. Q1.
379 That] Q3–5; Dares———that Q1–2, Q6–12, F, D, M2; Dares!——— / that
M1.
380 who] Q2–12, F, D, M2; that Q1, M1.
386 within] Q3–5; beneath Q1–2, Q6–12, F, D, M1–2.
ACT II. SCENE I.] D; ACT II. Q1–12, F, M1; *omitted from M2.*
5 search does . . . motive] Q3–5; motive . . . cause does Q1–2, Q6–12, F, D,
M1–2.

Love rules my heart, and is your Monarchs King;
I more desire to know *Almeria*'s mind,
Then all that Heaven has for my state design'd.
   High Pr. By powerful Charms which nothing can withstand,
10 I'le force the Gods to tell what you demand.

Charm.

   Thou Moon, that aid'st us with thy Magick might,
And ye small Starrs, the scattered seeds of light,
Dart your pale beams into this gloomy place,
That the sad powers of the Infernal race
May read above what's hid from Humane Eyes,
And in your walks, see Empires fall and rise.
And ye Immortal Souls, who once were Men,
And now resolv'd to Elements agen,
Who wait for Mortal frames in depths below,
20 And did before what we are doom'd to do;
Once, twice, and thrice, I wave my Sacred wand,
Ascend, ascend, ascend at my command.

An Earthy Spirit rises.

   Spir. In vain, O mortal men your Prayers implore
The aid of powers below, which want it more:
A God more strong, who all the gods commands,
Drives us to exile from our Native Lands;
The Air swarms thick with wandring Deities,
Which drowsily like humming Beetles rise
From their lov'd Earth, where peacefully they slept,
30 And far from Heaven a long possession kept.
The frighted *Satyrs* that in Woods delight,

10+   *s.d. Charm.*] Q4–5, D; ~ , Q1–3, Q6–12, F; ~∧ M1–2.
12   ye] Q2–12, F, D, M2; yea Q1, M1.
17   who] Q2–12, F, D, M2; that Q1, M1.
19   Who] Q2–12, F, D, M2; That Q1, M1.
24   which] Q2–12, F, D, M2; that Q1, M1.
29   their . . . they] Q3–5; our . . . we Q1–2, Q6–12, F, D, M1–2.

Now into Plains with prick'd up Ears take flight;
And scudding thence, while they their horn-feet ply
About their Syres the little *Silvans* cry.
A Nation loving Gold must rule this place,
Our Temples Ruine, and our Rites Deface:
To them, O King, is thy lost Scepter given,
Now mourn thy fatal search, for since wise Heaven
More ill then good to Mortals does dispence,
40 It is not safe to have too quick a sense.   *Descends.*
     Mont. Mourn they who think repining can remove
The firm decrees of those who rule above;
The brave are safe within, who still dare dye,
When e're I fall I'le scorn my destiny.
Doom as they please my Empire not to stand,
I'le grasp my Scepter with my dying hand.
     High Pr. Those Earthy Spirits black and envious are,
I'le call up other gods of form more fair:
Who Visions dress in pleasing Colours still,
50 Set all the good to show, and hide the ill.
Kalib ascend, my fair-spoke servant rise,
And sooth my Heart with pleasing Prophecies.

          Kalib *ascends all in White in the shape*
               of a Woman and Sings.

     Kalib. I look'd and saw within the Book of Fate,
               Where many days did lower,
               When lo one happy hour
          Leapt up, and smil'd to save thy sinking State;
               A day shall come when in thy power
               Thy cruel Foes shall be;
               Then shall thy Land be free,
60   And thou in Peace shalt Raign:
          But take, O take that opportunity,
          Which once refus'd will never come again.   *Descends.*

---

42 who] Q2–12, F, D; that Q1, M1–2.
60 shalt] Q2–12, F, D, M3; shall Q1, M1–2.

Mont. I shall deserve my Fate if I refuse
That happy hour which Heaven allots to use;
But of my Crown thou too much care do'st take,
That which I value more, my Love's at stake.
        High Pr. Arise ye subtle Spirits that can spy
When Love is enter'd in a Females eye;
You that can read it in the midst of doubt,
70 And in the midst of frowns can find it out;
You that can search those many corner'd minds,
Where Womans crooked fancie turns, and winds;
You that can Love explore, and truth impart,
Where both lye deepest hid in Womans heart,
Arise.———

> *The Ghosts of* Traxalla *and* Acacis *arise,*
> *they stand still and point at* Montez.

High Pr. I did not for these Ghastly Visions send,
Their sudden coming does some ill portend.———
Begon,———begon.——— They will not dis-appear,
My Soul is seiz'd with an unusual fear.
80   *Mont.* Point on, point on, and see whom you can fright,
Shame and Confusion seize these shades of night;
Ye thin and empty forms am I your sport?   *They smile.*
If you were flesh———
You know you durst not use me in this sort.

> *The Ghost of the* Indian *Queen rises betwixt*
> *the Ghosts with a Dagger in her Breast.*

    Mont. Ha!
I feel my Hair grow stiff, my Eye-balls rowl,

---

66 Love's] Q2–12, F, D, M1–2; Lov's Q1.
67 spy] Q8, M1–2; ~ , Q1–7, Q9–12, F, D.
72 fancie] Q6–12, F, D, M1–2; ~ , Q1–5.
77 portend.———] ~ :∧ Q1–5, M2; ~ ,∧ Q6–12, F; ~ .∧ D; ~∧∧ M1.
78 begon.———They] M1 (they); begon,———they Q1–12, F, D, M2 (begon∧———Q7–12, F).
84+ *s.d. Queen*] Queen Q1–12, F, D, M1–2.
84+ *s.d. in*] Q2–12, F, D, M1–2; *into* Q1.

This is the only form could shake my Soul.
   Ghost. The hopes of thy succesless Love resign,
Know *Montezuma,* thou art only mine;
For those who here on Earth their passion show,
By death for Love, receive their right below.
Why doest thou then delay my longing Arms?
Have Cares, and Age, and Mortal life such Charms?
The Moon grows sickly at the sight of day,
And early Cocks have summon'd me away:
Yet I'le appoint a meeting place below,
For there fierce winds o're dusky Vallies blow,
Whose every puff bears empty shades away,
Which guidless in those dark Dominions stray.
Just at the entrance of the Fields below,
Thou shalt behold a tall black Poplar grow,
Safe in its hollow trunk I will attend,
And seize thy Spirit when thou doest descend.   *Descends.*
   Mont. I'le seize thee there, thou Messenger of Fate,
Would my short Life had yet a shorter date!
I'm weary of this flesh which holds us here,
And dastards manly Souls with hope and fear;
These heats and colds still in our breasts make War,
Agues and Feavers all our passions are.   *Exeunt.*

90

100

SCENE II.

Cydaria *and* Alibech, *Betwixt the two Armies.*

   Alib. Blessings will Crown your Name if you prevent
That Blood, which in this Battel will be spent;
Nor need you fear so just a sute to move,
Which both becomes your duty and your Love.
   Cyd. But think you he will come? their Camp is near,

90 who] Q2–12, F, D, M2; that Q1, M1.
93 Charms?] M1; ∼ ! Q1–12, F, D, M2.
s.d. Cydaria *and* Alibech,] Q2–12, F, D, M2; Cydaria, Alibeck Q1a; Cydaria,
Alibech Q1b; Cydaria. Alibech. M1.

And he already knows I wait him here.

    Alib. You are too young your power to understand,
Lovers take wing upon the least command;
Already he is here.————

Enter Cort. *and* Vasq. *to them.*

10   *Cort.* Methinks like two black storms on either hand,
Our *Spanish* Army and your *Indians* stand;
This only space betwixt the Clouds is clear,
Where you, like day, broke loose from both appear.

    Cyd. Those closing Skies might still continue bright,
But who can help it if you'l make it night?
The Gods have given you power of Life and Death,
Like them to save or ruine with a breath.

    Cort. That power they to your Father did dispose,
'Twas in his choice to make us Friends or Foes.

20   *Alib.* Injurious strength would rapine still excuse,
By off'ring terms the weaker must refuse;
And such as these your hard conditions are,
You threaten Peace, and you invite a War.

    Cort. If for my self to Conquer here I came,
You might perhaps my actions justly blame.
Now I am sent, and am not to dispute
My Princes orders, but to execute.

    Alib. He who his Prince so blindly does obey,
To keep his Faith his Vertue throws away.

30   *Cort.* Monarchs may err, but should each private breast
Judge their ill Acts, they would dispute their best.

    Cyd. Then all your care is for your Prince I see,
Your truth to him out-weighs your love to me;
You may so cruel to deny me prove,
But never after that, pretend to Love.

    Cort. Command my Life, and I will soon obey,
To save my Honour I my Blood will pay.

———

9 here.————] ~ .ᴧ Q1–12, F, D, M1–2.
17 ruine] Q2–12, F, D, M2; scatter Q1, M1.

Cyd. What is this Honour which does Love controul?
Cort. A raging fit of Vertue in the Soul;
40 A painful burden which great minds must bear,
Obtain'd with danger, and possest with fear.
Cyd. Lay down that burden if it painful grow,
You'l find, without it, Love will lighter go.
Cort. Honour once lost is never to be found.
Alib. Perhaps he looks to have both passions Crown'd:
First dye his Honour in a Purple Flood,
Then Court the Daughter in the Father's Blood.
Cort. The edge of War I'le from the Battel take,
And spare her Father's Subjects for her sake.
50   *Cyd.* I cannot Love you less when I'm refus'd,
But I can dye to be unkindly us'd;
Where shall a Maids distracted heart find rest,
If she can miss it in her Lovers breast?
Cort. I till to morrow will the fight delay,
Remember you have conquer'd me to day.
Alib. This grant destroys all you have urg'd before,
Honour could not give this, or can give more;
Our Women in the foremost ranks appear,
March to the Fight and meet your Mistress there,
60 Into the thickest Squadrons she must run,
Kill her, and see what Honour will be won.
Cyd. I must be in the Battel, but I'le go
With empty Quiver, and unbended Bow;
Not draw an Arrow in this fatal strife,
For fear its point should reach your Noble life.

Enter Pizarro.

Cort. No more, your kindness wounds me to the death,
Honour be gone, what art thou but a breath?

---

38   which] Q2–12, F, D, M2; that Q1, M1.
53   breast?] Q2–12, F, D, M1–2; ∼ ! Q1.
59   Fight] Q4–5, Q8, M2; ∼ , Q1–3, Q6–7, Q9–12, F, D, M1.
65+ *s.d. omitted from Q1, M1–2.*   67   breath?] Q2–12, F, D, M1–2; ∼ ! Q1.

I'le live, proud of my infamy and shame,
Grac'd with no Triumph but a Lovers name;
70 Men can but say Love did his reason blind,
And Love's the noblest frailty of the mind.
Draw off my Men, the War's already done.   *To* Piz.
     Piz. Your orders come too late, the Fight's begun,
The Enemy gives on with fury led,
And fierce *Orbellan* combats in their head.
     Cort. He justly fears a Peace with me would prove
Of ill concernment to his haughty Love;
Retire, fair Excellence, I go to meet
New Honour, but to lay it at your feet.
                         Exeunt Cort. Vasq. Piz.

Enter Odm. *and* Guy. *to* Alib. *and* Cyd.

80   *Odm.* Now, Madam, since a danger does appear
Worthy my Courage, though below my Fear,
Give leave to him who may in Battel dye,
Before his Death to ask his destiny.
     Guy. He cannot Dye whom you command to Live,
Before the Fight you can the Conquest give;
Speak where you'l place it.
     Alib. ————————————Briefly then to both,
One I in secret Love, the other Loath;
But where I hate, my hate I will not show,
And he I Love, my Love shall never know;
90 True worth shall gain me, that it may be sed,
Desert, not fancy, once a Woman led.
He who in fight his courage shall oppose
With most success against his Countries Foes,
From me shall all that recompence receive
That Valour Merits, or that Love can give:

71   mind.] Q2–12, F, D, M2; ~ , Q1, M1.
72   done. *To* Piz.] done. Q1–12, F, D, M1–2.
78   I] Q2–12, F, D, M2; I'le Q1, M1.
79+   *s.d.* Cyd.] Q2–12, F, D, M1; Cyd. Q1; *omitted from* M2.
86   it.] M1–2; ~ ? Q1–12, F, D.   92   who] Q2–12, F, D, M2; that Q1, M1.
95   That] Q2–12, F, D, M1–2; that Q1.

'Tis true my hopes and fears are all for one,
But hopes and fears are to my self alone,
Let him not shun the danger of the strife,
I but his Love, his Country claims his Life.

  0   *Odm.* All obstacles my Courage shall remove.
     Guy. Fall on, fall on.
     Odm. ——————For Liberty.
     Guy. —————————— For Love.

                   Exeunt, the Women following.

SCENE III.

SCENE Changes to the Indian *Country.*

Enter Mont. *attended by the* Indians.

     Mont. Charge, charge, their ground the faint *Taxallans* yield,
Bold in close Ambush, base in open Field:
The envious Devil did my Fortune wrong,
Thus Fought, thus Conquer'd I when I was young.   *Exit.*

Alarm, Enter Cort. *Bloudy.*

     Cort. Furies pursue these false *Taxallans* Flight,
Dare they be Friends to us and dare not Fight?
What Friends can Cowards be, what hopes appear
Of help from such, who where they hate show fear?

Enter Piz. Vasquez.

     Piz. The Field grows thin, and those that now remain,
 0 Appear but like the shadows of the Slain.

---

101   Liberty.] Q3–12, F, D; ∼ , Q1–2, M1; ∼ᴧ M2.
101+   s.d. Exeunt,] Q2–12, F. D; ∼ᴧ Q1, M1–2.
SCENE III. / SCENE] SCENE Q1–12, F, D, M1–2.
s.d. by the] Q2–12, F, D; by his Q1; omitted from M1–2.
8   who] Q2–12, F, D, M1; that Q1.   8   fear?] M1; ∼ ! Q1–12, F, D.

Vasq. The fierce old King is vanish'd from the place,
And in a cloud of dust pursues the Chase.
    Cort. Their eager Chase disorder'd does appear,
Command our Horse to charge them in the rear.   [*To* Vasq.
You to our old *Castillian* Foot retire,   [*To* Piz.
Who yet stand firm, and at their backs give Fire.

                                   Exeunt severally.

    Enter Odm. *and* Guy. *meeting each other in the Battel.*

    Odm. Where hast thou been since first the Fight began,
Thou less then Woman in the shape of Man?
    Guy. Where I have done what may thy Envy move,
20 Things worthy of my Birth, and of my Love.
    Odm. Two bold *Taxallans* with one Dart I slew,
And left it sticking ere my Sword I drew.
    Guy. I sought not Honour on so base a Train,
Such Cowards by our Women may be Slain;
I fell'd along a Man of Bearded face,
His Limbs all cover'd with a Shining case:
So wondrous hard, and so secure of wound,
It made my Sword, though edg'd with Flint, rebound.
    Odm. I kill'd a double Man, the one half lay
30 Upon the ground, the other ran away.   *Guns go off within.*

    Enter Mont. *out of breath, with him* Alib. *and an* Indian.

    Mont. All's lost———
Our Foes with Lightning and with Thunder Fight,
My Men in vain shun death by shameful Flight;
For deaths Invisible come wing'd with Fire,
They hear a dreadful noise and straight expire.

14   rear.] M1; ~ ; Q1–6, D; ~ : Q7–12, F; ~ᴧ M2.
14   *To* Vasq.] Q3–5; *To* Piz. Q1–2, Q6–12, F, D; *omitted from* M1–2.
15   *To* Piz.] Q3–5; *To* Vasq. Q1–2, Q6–12, F, D; *omitted from* M1–2.
16+ *s.d. other in the Battel*] Q2–12, F, D; *other* Q1; *omitted from* M1–2.
20   Love.] Q2–12, F, D, M1–2; ~ : Q1.   23 on] Q1b–12, F, D, M1–2; in Q1a.
34   deaths] Q2–6, D, M2; death's Q1, Q7–12, F, M1.

Take, gods, that Soul ye did in spight create,
And made it great to be unfortunate:
Ill Fate for me unjustly you provide,
Great Souls are Sparks of your own Heavenly Pride,
) That lust of power we from your god-heads have,
You'r bound to please those Appetites you gave.

>   *Enter* Vasq. *and* Piz. *with* Spaniards.

Vasq. Pizarro, I have hunted hard to day
Into our toyls the noblest of the prey;
Seize on the King, and him your Prisoner make,
While I in kind revenge, my taker take.
>   Piz. *with two goes to Attaque the King,* Vasq.
>   *with another to seize* Alib.
Guy. Their danger is alike, whom shall I free?
Odm. I'le follow Love.
Guy.————————I'le follow Piety.
>   Odm. *retreats from* Vasq. *with* Alib. *off the*
>   *Stage,* Guy. *Fights for his Father.*
Guy. Fly Sir, while I give back that life you gave,
Mine is well lost, if I your life can save.
>   Mont. *Fights off,* Guy. *making his*
>   *retreat, stays.*
> *Guy.* 'Tis more than Man can do to scape them all,
Stay, let me see where noblest I may fall.
>   He runs at Vasq., *is seized behind and taken.*
Vasq. Conduct him off,————
And give command he strictly guarded be.
Guy. In vain are guards, Death sets the Valiant free.
>   *Exit* Guy. *with Guards.*
Vasq. A Glorious day! and bravely was it Fought,

————
42   to day] Q6–12, F, D, M1–2; ~ , Q1–5.
45+   s.d. *King*] Q2–12, F, D; King Q1, M1–2.
47+   s.d. Alib.] Q2–12, F, D, M1; Alib∧ Q1; *Alibech*∧ M2.
51+   s.d. Vasq.] Q2–12, F, D; Vasq.∧ Q1; Pizarro M1; *vasq:*∧ M2.
52   off,————] ~ ,∧ Q1–12, F, D; ~ ;∧ M1; ~∧∧ M2.
54+   s.d. Guy.] Guy∧ Q1, M1; Guyomar Q2–12, F, D; *Gui:* M2.

Great fame our General in great dangers sought;
From his strong Arm I saw his Rival run,
And in a crowd, th' unequal Combat shun.

> *Enter* Cortez *leading* Cydaria, *who seems weeping,*
> *and begging of him.*

    Cort. Mans force is fruitless, and your gods would fail
60 To save the City, but your Tears prevail;
I'le of my Fortune no advantage make,
Those Terms they had once given, they still may take.
    Cyd. Heaven has of right all Victory design'd,
Where boundless power dwells in a will confin'd;
Your *Spanish* Honour does the World excel.
    Cort. Our greatest Honour is in loving well.
    Cyd. Strange ways you practice there to win a Heart,
Here Love is Nature, but with you 'tis Art.
    Cort. Love is with us, as Natural as here,
70 But fetter'd up with customs more severe;
In tedious Courtship we declare our pain,
And ere we kindness find, first meet disdain.
    Cyd. If Women Love they needless pains endure,
Their Pride and Folly but delay their Cure.
    Cort. What you mis-call their Folly, is their care,
They know how fickle common Lovers are:
Their Oaths and Vows are cautiously believ'd,
For few there are but have been once deceiv'd.
    Cyd. But if they are not trusted when they vow,
80 What other marks of passion can they show?
    Cort. With Feasts, and Musick, all that brings delight,
Men treat their Ears, their Pallats, and their Sight.
    Cyd. Your Gallants sure have little Eloquence,
Failing to move the Soul, they Court the Sence:
With Pomp, and Trains, and in a crowd they Woe,

58+ *s.d.* Cydaria] Q2–12, F, D, M1–2; Cidaria Q1.
58+ *s.d. weeping*] Q3–5; *crying* Q1–2, Q6–12, F, D, M1; *omitted from* M2.
84 Sence:] Q2–12, F, D; ∼ , Q1; ∼ . M1; ∼∧ M2.
85 Pomp] Q2–12, F, D; Pomps Q1, M1–2.

When true Felicity is but in two;
But can such Toys your Womens passion move?
This is but noise and tumult, 'tis not Love.
  Cort. I have no reason, Madam, to excuse
Those ways of Gallantry I did not use;
My Love was true and on a Nobler score.
  Cyd. Your Love! Alas! then have you Lov'd before?
  Cort. 'Tis true I Lov'd, but she is Dead, she's Dead,
And I should think with her all Beauty Fled,
Did not her fair resemblance live in you,
And by that Image, my first Flames renew.
  Cyd. Ah happy Beauty whosoe're thou art!
Though dead thou keep'st possession of his Heart;
Thou mak'st me jealous to the last degree,
And art my Rival in his Memory;
Within his Memory, ah, more then so,
Thou Liv'st and Triumph'st ore *Cydaria* too.
  Cort. What strange disquiet has uncalm'd your breast,
Inhumane fair, to rob the dead of rest!
Poor Heart! She slumbers in her silent Tomb,
Let her possess in Peace that narrow Room.
  Cyd. Poor-heart he pities and bewails her death!
Some god, much hated soul, restore thy breath
That I may kill thee; but some ease 'twill be,
I'le kill my self for but resembling thee.
  Cort. I dread your anger, your disquiet fear,
But blows from hands so soft who would not bear?
So kind a passion why should I remove?
Since jealousie but shows how well we Love.
Yet jealousie so strange I never knew,
Can she who Loves me not disquiet you?

_____

92 before?] Q3–5, M1; ~ ! Q1–2, Q6–12, F, D, M2.
94 Fled,] Q2–12, F, D, M1; ~ ; Q1; ~∧ M2.
105 Heart! She slumbers in . . . Tomb,] Q2–12, F, D, M2; Heart! / She slumbers deep, deep in . . . Tomb. Q1, M1.
107 death!] Q3–5, D; ~ , Q1–2, Q6–7, Q9–12, F; ~ . Q8; ~ : M1; ~∧ M2.
109 thee;] D; ~ , Q1–12, F, M1–2.
116 me not] Q2–12, F, D, M2; not me Q1, M1.

For in the Grave no Passions fill the Breast,
'Tis all we gain by Death to be at rest.
   Cyd. That she no longer Loves brings no relief,
120 Your Love to her still lives, and that's my grief.
   Cort. The object of desire once tane away,
'Tis then not Love, but pitty which we pay.
   Cyd. 'Tis such a pitty I should never have,
When I must lye forgotten in the Grave;
I meant to have oblig'd you when I dy'd,
That after me you should Love none beside,
But you are false already.
   Cort.————————If untrue,
By Heaven my falshood is to her, not you.
   Cyd. Observe sweet Heaven, how falsly he does Swear,
130 You said you Lov'd me for resembling her.
   Cort. That Love was in me by resemblance bred,
But shows you chear'd my sorrows for the Dead.
   Cyd. You still repeat the greatness of your grief.
   Cort. If that was great, how great was the relief?
   Cyd. The first Love still the strongest we account.
   Cort. That seems more strong which could the first surmount:
But if you still continue thus unkind,
Whom I Love best, you by my Death shall find.
   Cyd. If you should dye my death should yours pursue,
140 But yet I am not satisfied you'r true.
   Cort. Hear me, ye gods, and punish him you hear,
If ought within the World, I hold so dear.
   Cyd. You would deceive the gods and me; she's dead,
And is not in the World, whose Love I dread.
Name not the world, say nothing is so dear.
   Cort. Then nothing is, let that secure your fear.
   Cyd. 'Tis Time must wear it off, but I must go.
Can you your constancy in absence show?
   Cort. Mis-doubt my constancy and do not try,
150 But stay and keep me ever in your eye.
   Cyd. If as a Prisoner I were here, you might

Have then insisted on a Conqu'rours right,
And stay'd me here; but now my Love would be
Th' effect of force, and I would give it free.
   Cort. To doubt your Vertue or your Love were sin!
Call for the Captive Prince and bring him in.

         Enter Guyomar *bound and sad.*

You look, Sir, as your Fate you could not bear,   [*To* Guyomar.
Are *Spanish* Fetters then so hard to wear?
Fortune's unjust, she ruines oft the Brave,
o And him who should be Victor, makes the Slave.
   Guy. Son of the Sun, my Fetters cannot be
But Glorious for me, since put on by thee;
The ills of Love, not those of Fate I fear,
These I can brave, but those I cannot bear;
My Rival Brother, while I'm held in Chains,
In freedom reaps the fruit of all my Pains.
   Cort. Let it be never said, that he whose breast
Is fill'd with Love, should break a Lovers rest;
Haste, lose no time, your Sister sets you Free,
o And tell the King, my Generous Enemy,
I offer still those terms he had before,
Only ask leave his Daughter to adore.
   Guy. Brother (that Name my breast shall ever own, [*He em-*
The Name of Foe be but in Battels known;)   *braces him.*
For some few days all Hostile Acts forbear,
That if the King consents, it seem not fear;
His Heart is Noble, and great Souls must be
Most sought and Courted in Adversity.
Three days I hope the wisht success will tell.
   Cyd. Till that long time———
   Cort.———————————Till that long time, farewel.
                  Exeunt severally.

———————

155   sin!] Q6–12, F, D; ~ ; Q1–4; ~ : Q5; ~ₐ M1–2.
173   Brother (that] Q2–12, F, D, M2; Brother, that Q1; Brother; that M1.
174   known;)] Q2–12, F, D, M2; known;ₐ Q1, M1.
180   time———] Q6–12, F, D, M2; ~ .——— Q1–5; ~ . M1.

ACT III. SCENE I.

SCENE, *Chamber Royal.*

Enter Odmar *and* Alibech.

Odm. The gods, fair *Alibech,* had so decreed,
Nor could my Valour against fate succeed;
Yet though our Army brought not Conquest home,
I did not from the Fight inglorious come:
If as a Victor you the brave regard,
Succesless Courage then may hope reward,
And I returning safe, may justly boast   [*Enter* Guyomar
To win the prize which my dead Brother lost.   *behind him.*
    Guy. No, no, thy Brother lives, and lives to be
10 A Witness, both against himself and thee;
Though both in safety are return'd agen,
I blush to ask her Love for vanquisht Men.
    Odm. Brother, I'le not dispute but you are brave,
Yet I was free, and you it seems a Slave.
    Guy. *Odmar,* 'tis true, that I was Captive led
As publickly is known as that you fled;
But of two shames if she must one partake,
I think the choice will not be hard to make.
    Odm. Freedom and Bondage in her choice remain,
20 Dar'st thou expect she will put on thy Chain?
    Guy. No, no, fair *Alibech,* give him the Crown,

ACT III. SCENE I.] D; ACT III. Q1–12, F, M1–2.
1   gods, fair *Alibech,*] Q2–12, F, D; gods∧ fair *Alibech*∧ Q1, M2; Gods∧ fair *Alibech,* M1.
13   dispute] Q8, M2; ∼ , Q1–7, Q9–12, F, D, M1.
16   known] Q8, M2; ∼ , Q1–7, Q9–12, F, D, M1.
19   *Odm.* Freedom] Q2–12, F, D, M1–2; Freedom Q1.
19   remain] Q2–12, F, D, M2; remains Q1, M1.
20   Chain] Q2–12, F, D, M2; Chains Q1, M1.

My Brother is return'd with high **Renown**.
He thinks by Flight his Mistress must be won,
And claims the prize because he best did run.
    Alib. Your Chains were glorious, and your Flight was wise,
But neither have o'recome your Enemies:
My secret wishes would my choice decide,
But open Justice bends to neither side.
    Odm. Justice already does my right approve,
If him who Loves you most, you most should Love.
My Brother poorly from your aid withdrew,
But I my Father left to succour you.
    Guy. Her Country she did to her self prefer,
Him who Fought best, not who Defended her;
Since she her interest for the Nations wav'd,
Then I who sav'd the King, the Nation sav'd;
You aiding her, your Country did betray,
I aiding him, did her commands obey.
    Odm. Name it no more; in Love, there is a time
When dull Obedience is the greatest Crime;
She to her Countries use resign'd your Sword,
And you kind Lover, took her at her word;
You did your Duty to your Love prefer,
Seek your reward from Duty, not from her.
    Guy. In acting what my Duty did require,
'Twas hard for me to quit my own desire,
That Fought for her, which when I did subdue,
'Twas much the easier task I left for you.
    Alib. *Odmar* a more then common Love has shown,
And *Guyomar*'s was greater, or was none;
Which I should chuse some god direct my breast,
The certain good, or the uncertain best:
I cannot chuse, you both dispute in vain,
Time and your future Acts must make it plain;
First raise the Siege, and set your Country free,
I not the Judge, but the reward will be.

---

39   more;] Q8; ∼ , Q1–7, Q9–12, F, D; ∼ₐ M1–2.

To them, Enter Montezuma *talking with* Almeria
and Orbellan.

 Mont. Madam, I think with reason I extol
The Vertue of the *Spanish* General;
When all the gods our Ruine have fore-told,
60 Yet generously he does his Arms with-hold,
And offering Peace, the first conditions make.
 Alm. When Peace is offer'd 'tis too late to take;
For one poor loss to stoop to terms like those,
Were we o'recome what could they worse impose?
Go, go, with homage your proud Victors meet,
Go lie like Dogs, beneath your Masters Feet.
Go and beget them Slaves to dig their Mines,
And groan for Gold which now in Temples shines;
Your shameful story shall record of me,
70 The Men all crouch'd, and left a Woman free.
 Guy. Had I not Fought, or durst not Fight again,
I my suspected Counsel should refrain:
For I wish Peace, and any terms prefer
Before the last extermities of War.
We but exasperate those we cannot harm,
And Fighting gains us but to dye more warm:
If that be Cowardise, which dares not see
The insolent effects of Victory,
The rape of Matrons, and their Childrens cries,
80 Then I am fearful, let the Brave advise.
 Odm. Keen cutting Swords, and Engines killing far,
Have prosperously begun a doubtful War;
But now our Foes with less advantage Fight,
Their strength decreases with our *Indians* Fright.
 Mont. This Noble Vote does with my wish comply,
I am for War.
 Alm.———And so am I.
 Orb. ——————————And I.

56+ *s.d.* *To them, Enter*] Q2–12, F, D; *Enter* Q1, M1–2.
78 Victory,] Q2–3, Q6–12, F, D; ~ ; Q1, M1; ~ . Q4–5; ~∧ M2.

Mont. Then send to break the truce, and I'le take care
To chear the Souldiers, and for Fight prepare.
                              Exeunt Mont. Odm. Guy. Alib.
                              Almeria *stays* Orbellan.
Alm. to Orb. 'Tis now the hour which all to rest allow,
90 And Sleep sits heavy upon every brow;
In this dark silence softly leave the Town,   [Guyomar *returns*
And to the Generals Tent, 'tis quickly known,   *and hears them.*
Direct your steps: you may dispatch him strait,
Drown'd in his Sleep, and easie for his Fate:
Besides the truce will make the Guards more slack.
    Orb. Courage which leads me on, will bring me back:
But I more fear the baseness of the thing,
Remorse, you know, bears a perpetual sting.
    Alm. For mean remorse no room the Valiant finds,
100 Repentance is the Vertue of weak minds;
For want of judgement keeps them doubtful still,
They may repent of good who can of ill;
But daring Courage makes ill actions good,
'Tis foolish pity spares a Rivals Blood;
You shall about it streight.———   *Exeunt* Alm. Orb.
    Guy.————————————Would they betray
His sleeping Vertue, by so mean a way?
And yet this *Spaniard* is our Nations Foe,
I wish him dead———but cannot wish it so;
Either my Country never must be freed,
110 Or I consenting to so black a deed.
Would Chance had never led my steps this way,
Now if he dyes I Murther him, not they;
Something must be resolv'd e're 'tis too late,
He gave me freedom, I'le prevent his Fate.   *Exit* Guyomar.

88+ s.d. Alib. Almeria *stays* Orbellan.] Q2–12, F, D; Alib. Q1, M1; Manent
Alm: et Orbellan. M2.
89   *Alm. to Orb.*] Q2–12, F, D; *Alm.* Q1, M1–2.
92   known,] Q1b–12, F, D; ~∧ Q1a; ~) M1–2.
101   judgement] D, M1–2; ~ , Q1–12, F.   106   way?] M1–2; ~ ! Q1–12, F, D.
110   consenting] Q2–12, F, D, M1–2; confenting Q1.

SCENE II.

A Camp.

Enter Cortez *alone in a Night-gown.*

Cort. All things are hush'd, as Natures self lay dead,
The Mountains seem to nod their drowsie head;
The little Birds in dreams their Songs repeat,
And sleeping Flowers, beneath the night-dew sweat;
Ev'n Lust and Envy sleep, yet Love denies
Rest to my Soul, and slumber to my Eyes.
Three days I promis'd to attend my Doom,
And two long days and nights are yet to come.
'Tis sure the noyse of some Tumultuous Fight,   *Noyse within.*
10 They break the truce, and sally out by Night.

Enter Orbellan *flying in the dark, his Sword drawn.*

Orb. Betray'd! pursu'd! Oh whither shall I flye?
See, see, the just reward of Treachery;
I'm sure among the Tents, but know not where,
Even night wants darkness to secure my fear.
                    Comes near Cortez *who hears him.*
Cort. Stand, who goes there?
Orb.——————————Alas, what shall I say?   *Aside.*
A poor *Taxallan* that mistook his way,   *To him.*
And wanders in the terrours of the night.
Cort. Souldier thou seem'st afraid, whence comes thy fright?
Orb. The insolence of *Spaniards* caus'd my fear,
20 Who in the dark pursu'd me entring here.
Cort. Their Crimes shall meet immediate punishment,

---

8   come.] M₁; ∼ : Q₁–₁₂, F, D, M₂.   15   say?] M₂; ∼ ! Q₁–₁₂, F, D, M₁.
18   fright] Q₂–₁₂, F, D, M₁–₂; flight Q₁.
19   *Orb.* The] Q₁b–₁₂, F, D, M₁–₂; The Q₁a.

But stay thou safe within the Generals Tent.
  Orb. Still worse and worse.   *Aside.*
  Cort.————————Fear not but follow me,
Upon my Life I'le set thee safe and free.
                    Cortez *Leads him in, and returns.*

    To him Vasquez, Pizarro *and* Spaniards *with Torches.*

  Vasq. O Sir, thank Heaven and your brave *Indian* Friend
That you are safe, *Orbellan* did intend
This night to kill you sleeping in your Tent,
But *Guyomar* his trusty Slave has sent,
Who following close his silent steps by night
30 Till in our Camp they both approach'd the light,
Cryed seize the Traytor, seize the Murtherer:
The cruel Villain fled I know not where,
But far he is not, for he this way bent.
  Piz. Th' inraged Souldiers seek, from Tent to Tent,
With lighted Torches, and in Love to you,
With bloody Vows his hated life pursue.
  Vasq. This Messenger does since he came relate,
That the old King, after a long debate;
By his imperious Mistress blindly led,
40 Has given *Cydaria* to *Orbellan*'s Bed.
  Cort. Vasquez, the trusty Slave with you retain,
Retire a while, I'le call you back again.
                  Exeunt Vasquez, Pizarro.

        Cortez *at his Tent Door.*

  Cort. Indian come forth, your Enemies are gone,
And I who sav'd you from them, here alone;
You hide your Face, as you were still afraid,

---

23 worse. *Aside.*] worse. Q1–12, F, D, M1–2.
24 set] Q2–12, F, D, M1–2; let Q1.   25 Heaven] M1–2; ~ , Q1–12, F, D.
28 *Guyomar*] Q7–12, F, D, M2; ~ , Q1–6, M1.
31 Murtherer:] Q2–12, F, M2; ~ , Q1; ~ . D; ~∧ M1.

Dare you not look on him who gave you aid?

Enter Orbellan *holding his Face aside.*

Orb. Moon slip behind some Cloud, some Tempest rise
And blow out all the Stars that light the Skies,
To shrowd my shame.
Cort.————In vain you turn aside,
50 And hide your Face, your Name you cannot hide;
I know my Rival and his black design.
Orb. Forgive it as my passions fault, not mine.
Cort. In your excuse your Love does little say,
You might have taken a much nobler way.
Orb. 'Tis true my passion small defence can make,
Yet you must spare me for your Honours sake;
That was engag'd to set me safe and free.
Cort. 'Twas to a Stranger, not an Enemy:
Nor is it prudence to prolong thy breath,
60 When all my hopes depend upon thy death————
————Yet none shall tax me with base perjury,
Something I'le do, both for my self and thee;
With vow'd revenge my Souldiers search each Tent,
If thou art seen none can thy death prevent;
Follow my steps with silence and with haste.   [*They go out.*

SCENE III.

The Scene changes to the Indian
Countrey, they return.

Cort. Now you are safe, you have my out-guards past.
Orb. Then here I take my leave.

---

46 who] Q2–12, F, D, M2; that Q1, M1.
54 have taken a much nobler] Q3–5; how e're have took a fairer Q1–2, Q6–12, F, D, M1–2.
65 s.d. [*They go out.*] They go out, Q1–7, D, M1–2; [*Exeunt.* Q8–12, F.
SCENE III. / The] the Q1–7, D, M1–2; The Q8–12, F.

Cort.———————————*Orbellan,* no,
When you return you to *Cydaria* go,
I'le send a Message.
    Orb.————————Let it be exprest,
I am in haste.
    Cort.——I'le write it in your Breast.———   *Draws.*
    Orb. What means my Rival?
    Cort.————————————Either Fight or Dye,
I'le not strain Honour to a point too high;
I sav'd your Life, now keep it if you can,
Cydaria shall be for the bravest Man;
10 On equal terms you shall your Fortune try,
Take this and lay your flint-edg'd weapon by;   [*Gives him*
I'le arm you for my Glory, and pursue   *a Sword.*
No Palm, but what's to manly Vertue due.
Fame with my Conquest, shall my Courage tell,
This you shall gain by placing Love so well.
    Orb. Fighting with you ungrateful I appear.
    Cort. Under that shadow thou wouldst hide thy fear:
Thou wouldst possess thy Love at thy return,
And in her Arms my easie Vertue scorn.
20   *Orb.* Since we must Fight, no longer time delay,
The Moon shines clear, and makes a paler day.
    They Fight, Orbellan *is wounded in the Hand,*
        his Sword falls out of it.
    Cort. To Courage, even of Foes, there's pity due,
It was not I, but Fortune vanquish'd you;   [*Throws his*
Thank me with that, and so dispute the prize,   *Sword again.*
As if you Fought before *Cydarias* eyes.
    Orb. I would not poorly such a gift requite,
You gave me not this Sword to yield, but Fight;
But see where yours has forc'd its bloody way, [*He strives to hold*
My wounded Hand my Heart does ill obey.   *it, but cannot.*
30   *Cort.* Unlucky Honour that controul'st my will!
Why have I vanquish'd, since I must not Kill?

---

16 appear.] Q1b–12, F, D; ∼ : Q1a; ∼∧ M1–2.
20 time] Q3–5; let's Q1–2, Q6–12, F, D, M1–2.

Fate sees thy Life lodg'd in a brittle Glass,
And looks it through, but to it cannot pass.
     Orb. All I can do is frankly to confess,
I wish I could, but cannot love her less;
To swear I would resign her were but vain,
Love would recal that perjur'd breath again;
And in my wretched case 'twill be more just
Not to have promis'd, then deceive your trust.
40 Know, if I Live once more to see the Town,
In bright *Cydaria's* Arms my Love I'le crown.
     Cort. In spight of that I give thee Liberty,
And with thy person leave thy Honour free;
But to thy wishes move a speedy pace,
Or Death will soon o'retake thee in the Chace.
To Arms, to Arms, Fate shows my Love the way,
I'le force the City on thy Nuptial day.   *Exeunt severally.*

SCENE IV.

Mexico.

Enter *Montezuma, Odmar, Guyomar, Almeria.*

     Mont. It moves my wonder that in two days space,
This early Famine spreads so swift a pace.
     Odm. 'Tis, Sir, the general cry, nor seems it strange,
The face of plenty should so swiftly change;
This City never felt a Siege before,
But from the Lake receiv'd its daily store,
Which now shut up, and Millions crowded here,
Famine will soon in multitudes appear.
     Mont. The more the number still the greater shame.
10   *Alm.* What if some one should seek immortal Fame

----
41 I'le] Q2–12, F, D, M1–2; i'le Q1.
SCENE IV.] SCENE III. Q1–12, F, D, M2; Scene M1.

By ending of the Siege at one brave blow?
Mont. That were too happy!
Alm.————————Yet it may be so,
What if the *Spanish* General should be slain?
Guy. Just Heaven I hope does other-ways ordain.   [*Aside.*
Mont. If slain by Treason I should mourn his death.

Enter Orbellan *and whispers his Sister*

Odm. Orbellan seems in hast and out of breath.
Mont. Orbellan welcome, you are early hear,
A Bridegrooms hast does in your looks appear.
                              Almeria *Aside to her Brother.*
Alm. Betray'd! no, 'twas thy Cowardise, and Fear,
20 He had not 'scap'd with Life had I been there;
But since so ill you act a brave design,
Keep close your shame, Fate makes the next turn mine.

Enter Alibech, Cydaria.

Alib. O Sir, if ever pity touch'd your breast,
Let it be now to your own blood exprest:
In teares your beauteous Daughter drowns her sight,
Silent as dews that fall in dead of night.
Cyd. To your commands I strict obedience owe,
And my last Act of it I come to show;
I want the Heart to dye before your Eyes,
30 But Grief will finish that which Fear denies.
Alm. Your will should by your Fathers precept move.
Cyd. When he was young he taught me truth in Love.
Alm. He found more Love then he deserv'd, 'tis true,
And that it seems, is lucky too to you;

———————

12   Yet] Q3–5, Q7–12, F, D; yet Q1–2, Q6, M1–2.
14   ordain.] Q2–12, F, D, M1–2; ∼ , Q1.
15   should mourn] Q3–5; lament Q1–2, Q6–12, F, D, M1–2.
22   makes] Q3–12, F, D; make Q1–2, M1–2.

Your Fathers Folly took a head-strong course,
But I'le rule yours, and teach you Love by force.

Enter Messenger.

Mess. Arm, Arm, O King, the Enemy comes on,
A sharp assault already is begun;
Their Murdering Guns play fiercely on the Walls.
40   *Odm.* Now Rival, let us run where Honour calls.
    Guy. I have discharg'd what gratitude did owe,
And the brave *Spaniard* is again my Foe.
                        [*Exeunt* Odmar *and* Guyomar.
    Mont. Our walls are high, and multitudes defend:
Their vain attempt must in their ruine end;
The Nuptials with my presence shall be grac'd.
    Alib. At least but stay 'till the assault be past.
    Alm. Sister, in vain you urge him to delay,
The King has promis'd, and he shall obey.

Enter Second Messenger.

    Mess. 2. From several parts the Enemy's repel'd,
50 One only quarter, to th' assault does yield.

Enter Third Messenger.

    Mess. 3. Some Foes are enter'd, but they are so few
They only Death, not Victory pursue.
    Orb. Hark, hark they shout!———
From Vertues rules I do too meanly swerve:

36+ *s.d. Messenger*] D; Messenger Q1–12, F, M1–2.
37 *Mess.* Arm] Q3–5, D; Arm Q1–2, Q6–12, F, M1–2.
40 calls.] Q2–12, F, D, M1; ~ , Q1; ~∧ M2.
43 defend:] Q2–12, F, D, M2; ~∧ Q1; ~ ; M1.
48+ *s.d. Messenger*] D; Messenger Q1–12, F, M1–2.
49 *Mess.* 2. From] Q3–5, D; From Q1–2, Q6–12, F, M1–2.
50+ *s.d. Messenger*] D; Messenger Q1–12, F, M1–2.
51 *Mess.* 3. Some] Q3–5, D; Some Q1–2, Q6–12, F, M1–2.
53 shout!———] Q8–12, F; ~ !∧ Q1–7, D, M1–2.
54 do] Q3–12, F, D, M1–2; do, Q1–2.

I by my Courage will your Love deserve.   [*Exit.*
  Mont. Here in the heart of all the Town I'le stay:
And timely succour where it wants, convey.

     A Noise within. Enter Orbellan, Indians *driven in,* Cortez
       after them, and one or two Spaniards.

  Cort. He's found, he's found, degenerate Coward, stay:
Night sav'd thee once, thou shalt not scape by day.
                        [*Kills* Orbellan.
60   *Orb.* ———O I am Kill'd———   [*Dyes.*

          Enter Guyomar *and* Odmar.

  Guy. Yield Generous Stranger and preserve your life,   [*He is*
Why chuse you death in this unequal strife?   *beset.*
     Almeria *and* Alibech *seem to weep over* Orbellans *body.*
  Cort. What nobler Fate could any Lover meet?
I fall reveng'd, and at my Mistress feet.
       They fall on him and bear him down, Guyomar
          takes his Sword.
  Alib. He's past recovery; my Dear Brother's Slain:
Fates hand was in it, and my care is vain.
  Alm. In weak complaints you vainly wast your breath:
They are not Tears that can revenge his Death,
Dispatch the Villain strait.
    Cort. ————————The Villains Dead.
70   *Alm.* Give me a Sword and let me take his Head.
  Mont. Though, Madam, for your Brothers loss I grieve,
Yet let me beg,———

---

55 deserve. [*Exit.*] D, M1–2; deserve. Q1–12, F.
57+ *s.d.* Orbellan,] Q2–12, F, D, M1–2; Orbell. Q1.
59 once,] Q2–12, F, D; ~∧ Q1, M2; *different text in M1.*
60 *s.d.* [*Dyes.*] ∧Dyes. Q1, M1; ∧*Dyes.* Q2–12, F, D, M2.
62+ *s.d. seem to weep over*] Q3–5; *falls on* Q1; *fall on* Q2, Q6–12, F, D.
63 meet?] D; ~ , Q1–12, F, M2; ~∧ M1.
64 feet.] D, M1; ~ ? Q1–12, F; ~∧ M2.
66 hand] Q2–12, F, D, M1–2; head Q1.
69 Dead.] Q2–12, F, D, M1–2; ~ : Q1.

Alm.————————His Murderer may Live?
Cyd. 'Twas his Misfortune, and the Chance of War.
Cort. It was my purpose, and I kill'd him fair;
How could you so unjust and cruel prove
To call that Chance which was the act of Love?
    Cyd. I call'd it any thing to save your Life:
Would he were living still, and I his Wife;
That wish was once my greatest misery:
80 But 'tis a greater to behold you dye.
    Alm. Either command his Death upon the place,
Or never more behold *Almeria*'s face.
    Guy. You by his Valour, once from Death were freed:
Can you forget so Generous a deed?   [*To* Montezuma.
    Mont. How Gratitude and Love divide my breast!
Both ways alike my Soul is rob'd of rest.
But————let him Dye,————can I his Sentence give?
Ungrateful, must he Dye by whom I Live?
But can I then *Almeria*'s Tears deny?
90 Should any Live whom she commands to Dye?
    Guy. Approach who dares: he yielded on my word;
And as my Pris'ner, I restore his Sword;   [*Gives his Sword.*
His Life concerns the safety of the State,
And I'le preserve it for a calm debate.
    Mont. Dar'st thou Rebel, false and degenerate Boy?
That being which I gave, I thus destroy.
                    Offers to kill him, Odmar *steps between.*
    Odm. My Brothers blood I cannot see you spill,
Since he prevents you but from doing ill:
He is my Rival, but his Death would be
100 For him too glorious, and too base for me.
    Guy. Thou shalt not Conquer in this noble strife:

---

76   which was] Q2–12, F, D, M1–2; that was Q1.
79   once] Q3–12, F, D, M1–2; ~ , Q1–2.
88   Ungrateful,] Q2–4, Q6–12, F, D; ~∧ Q1, Q5, M1–2.
89   deny?] Q9–12, F; ~ ! Q1–8, D, M1; ~∧ M2.
95   Rebel,] Q6–12, F, D; ~∧ Q1–5, M2; ~ ! M1.
95   Boy?] Q2–12, F, D; ~ , Q1; ~∧ M1–2.

Alas, I meant not to defend my Life:
Strike, Sir, you never pierc'd a Breast more true:
'Tis the last Wound I e're can take for you.
You see I Live but to dispute your will;
Kill me, and then you may my Pris'ner Kill.
 Cort. You shall not, Gen'rous Youths, contend for me:
It is enough that I your Honour see,
But that your Duty may no blemish take,
10 I will my self your Father's Captive make:
When he dares strike I am prepar'd to fall: [*Gives his Sword*
The *Spaniards* will revenge their General.   *to* Montezuma.
 Cyd. Ah you too hastily your Life resign,
You more would Love it if you valued mine!
 Cort. Dispatch me quickly, I my Death forgive,
I shall grow tender else, and wish to Live;
Such an infectious Face her sorrow wears,
I can bear Death, but not *Cydaria's* Tears.
 Alm. Make haste, make haste, they merit Death all three:
20 They for Rebellion, and for Murder he.
See, see, my Brother's Ghost hangs hovering there,
O're his warm Blood, that steems into the Air,
Revenge, Revenge it cries.
 Mont.————————And it shall have;
But two days respite for his Life I crave:
If in that space you not more gentle prove,
I'le give a Fatal proof how well I Love.
'Till when, you *Guyomar,* your Pris'ner take;
Bestow him in the Castle on the Lake:
In that small time, I shall the Conquest gain
30 Of these few Sparks of Vertue which remain:
Then all who shall my head-long passion see,
Shall curse my Crimes, and yet shall pity me.   [*Exeunt omnes.*

---

127 when,] D, M1; ∼∧ Q1–12, F, M2.
130 which] Q2–12, F, D, M2; that Q1, M1.

ACT IV. SCENE I.

SCENE, *A Prison.*

Enter Almeria *and an* Indian, *they speak entring.*

Ind. A Dangerous proof of my respect I show.
Alm. Fear not, Prince *Guyomar* shall never know:
While he is absent let us not delay;
Remember 'tis the King thou doest obey.
    Ind. See where he sleeps.
                     [*Cortez appears Chain'd and laid asleep.*
Alm.————————Without, my coming wait:
And on thy Life secure the Prison Gate.———   [*Exit* Indian.
              [*She plucks out a Dagger and approaches him.*
Spaniard awake: thy Fatal hour is come:
Thou shalt not at such ease receive thy Doom.
Revenge is sure, though sometimes slowly pac'd,
10 Awake, awake, or sleeping sleep thy last.
    Cort. Who names Revenge?
    Alm.————————Look up and thou shalt see.
    Cort. I cannot fear so fair an Enemy.
    Alm. No aid is nigh, nor canst thou make defence:
Whence can thy Courage come?
    Cort.————————From Innocence.
    Alm. From Innocence? let that then take thy part,
Still are thy looks assur'd,———have at thy Heart:
                  [*Holds up the Dagger.*
I cannot kill thee; sure thou bear'st some Charm,   [*Goes back.*

———

ACT IV. SCENE I.] D; Act IV. Q1–12, F, M2; Act 4ᵗʰ 1ˢᵗ Sc: M1.
s.d. Indian,] Q2–12, F, D; ∼ₐ Q1, M1–2.
5 Without,] ∼ₐ Q1–12, F, D, M1–2.
6 Gate.——— [*Exit* Indian.] Q2–12, F, D, M2 (Gateₐ——— D); Gateₐ———
Q1, M1.
13 nigh] Q2–12, F, D, M2; near Q1, M1.
16+ *s.d. Holds*] Q2–12, F, D, M2; *Hold* Q1.

Or some Divinity holds back my Arm.
Why do I thus delay to make him Bleed,   [*Aside.*
20 Can I want Courage for so brave a Deed?
I've shook it off; my Soul is free from fear,   [*Comes again.*
And I can now strike any where,———but here:
His scorn of Death how strangely does it move!
A mind so haughty who could chuse but Love!   [*Goes off.*
Plead not a Charm, or any gods command,
Alas, it is thy heart that holds thy hand:
In spight of me I Love, and see too late
My Mothers Pride must find my Mothers Fate:
———Thy Country's Foe, thy Brother's Murtherer,
30 For shame, *Almeria,* such mad thoughts forbear:
It w'onnot be if I once more come on,   [*Coming on again.*
I shall mistake the Breast, and pierce my own.
                    [*Comes with her Dagger down.*
    Cort. Does your revenge maliciously forbear
To give me Death, till 'tis prepar'd by fear?
If you delay for that, forbear or strike,
Fore-seen and sudden death are both alike.
    Alm. To show my Love would but increase his Pride:
They have most power who most their passions hide.   [*Aside.*
Spaniard, I must confess I did expect
40 You could not meet your Death with such neglect;
I will defer it now, and give you time:
You may Repent, and I forget your Crime.
    Cort. Those who repent acknowledge they did ill:
I did not unprovok'd your Brother Kill.
    Alm. Petition me, perhaps I may forgive.
    Cort. Who begs his Life does not deserve to Live.
    Alm. But if 'tis given you'l not refuse to take?
    Cort. I can Live gladly for *Cydaria*'s sake.
    Alm. Does she so wholy then possess your mind?
50 What if you should another Lady find,

---

31 It] Q2–12, F, D, M1–2; I Q1 (*some copies of Q1 may have* It).
31 Coming] Q3–5, Q7–12, F, D; coming Q1–2, Q6.
47 refuse] Q2–12, F, D, M1–2; refufe Q1.

Equal to her in birth, and far above
In all that can attract, or keep your Love,
Would you so doat upon your first desire
As not to entertain a Nobler Fire?
    Cort. I think that person hardly will be found,
With Gracious form and equal Vertue Crown'd:
Yet if another could precedence claim,
My fixt desires could find no fairer Aim.
    Alm. Dull ignorance, he cannot yet conceive:
60 To speak more plain shame will not give me leave.   *[Aside.*
——Suppose one lov'd you, whom even Kings adore: *[To him.*
Who with your Life, your Freedom would restore,
And adde to that the Crown of *Mexico:*
Would you for her, *Cydaria*'s Love fore-go?
    Cort. Though she could offer all you can invent,
I could not of my Faith, once vow'd, repent.
    Alm. A burning blush has cover'd all my face:
Why am I forc'd to publish my disgrace?   *[Aside.*
What if I Love,———you know it cannot be, *[To him.*
70 And yet I blush to put the case 'twere me———
If I could Love you, with a flame so true
I could forget what hand my Brother slew?———
———Make out the rest,———I am disorder'd so
I know not farther what to say or do:
———But answer me to what you think I meant.
    Cort. Reason or Wit no answer can invent:
Of words confus'd who can the meaning find?
    Alm. Disordered words show a distemper'd mind.
    Cort. She has oblig'd me so, that could I chuse,
80 I would not answer what I must refuse.   *[Aside.*

---

61   you,] Q5; ~∧ Q1–4, Q6–12, F, D, M1–2.
61   *him.*] Q2–12, F, D; ~∧ Q1, M1.
66   vow'd,] Q2–6, D, M1; ~∧ Q1, Q7–12, F, M2.
68   disgrace? [*Aside.*] disgrace? Q1–12, F, D, M1–2.
69   Love,——— . . . be, [*To him.*] Love,∧ . . . be, Q1–12, F, D, M1–2.
70   me———] ~ . Q1–12, F, D, M1; ~∧ M2.

Alm. ———His mind is shook.   [*Aside*:
               ———Suppose I lov'd you, speak,
Would you for me *Cydaria*'s Fetters break?
Cort. Things meant in Jest, no serious answer need.
Alm. But put the case that it were so indeed.
Cort. If it were so, which but to think were Pride,
My constant Love would dangerously be try'd:
For since you could a Brothers death forgive,
He whom you save for you alone should live:
But I the most unhappy of mankind,
90 E're I knew yours, have all my Love resign'd:
'Tis my own loss I grieve, who have no more;
You go a begging to a Bankrupts door.
Yet could I change, as sure I never can,
How could you Love so Infamous a Man?
For Love once given from her, and plac'd in you,
Would leave no ground I ever could be true.
    Alm. You construed me aright,———I was in Jest:
And by that offer meant to sound your breast;
Which since I find so constant to your Love,
00 Will much my value of your worth improve.
Spaniard assure your self you shall not be
Oblig'd to quit *Cydaria* for me:
'Tis dangerous though, to treat me in this sort,
And to refuse my offers, though in sport.   *Exit* Almeria.
    Cort. In what a strange Condition am I left,   Cort. *solus.*
More then I wish I have, of all I wish bereft!
In wishing nothing we enjoy still most;
For even our wish is in possession lost:
Restless we wander to a new desire,
10 And burn our selves by blowing up the Fire:
We toss and turn about our Feaverish will,

---

81 shook. [*Aside.* / ———Suppose] shook; ———suppose Q1–12, F, D, M1–2
(shook∧——— M1; shook:∧ M2).
108 is] Q4–5, Q7–12, F, M1; ∼ , Q1–3, Q6, D.
110 up] Q2–12, F, D; of Q1, M1.

When all our ease must come by lying still:
For all the happiness Mankind can gain
Is not in pleasure, but in rest from pain.

> *Goes in and the Scene closes upon him.*

SCENE II.

Chamber Royal.

Enter Montezuma, Odmar, Guyomar, Alibech.

Mont. My Ears are deaf with this impatient crowd.
Odm. Their wants are now grown Mutinous and loud:
The General's taken, but the Siege remains;
And their last Food our dying Men sustains.
Guy. One means is only left, I to this hour
Have kept the Captive from *Almeria's* power:
And though by your command she often sent
To urge his doom, do still his death prevent.
Mont. That hope is past: him I have oft assayl'd,
10 But neither threats nor kindness have prevail'd;
Hiding our wants, I offerd to release
His Chains, and equally conclude a Peace:
He fiercely answer'd I had now no way
But to submit, and without terms obey:
I told him, he in Chains demanded more
Then he impos'd in Victory before:
He sullenly reply'd, he could not make
These offers now; Honour must give, not take.
Odm. Twice have I sallyed, and was twice beat back:
20 What desp'rate course remains for us to take?

---

s.d. Enter Montezuma, Odmar, Guyomar, Alibech.] M1–2 (*Enter omitted from M1;* Enter M2); Enter *Montezuma, Odmar, Guyomar, Alibech.* Q1–12, F, D.
1   crowd.] Q2–12, F, D; ∼ : Q1; ∼∧ M1–2.   5   hour] F, D, M1–2; ∼ , Q1–12.
20   take?] Q5, Q8, M2; ∼ ! Q1–4, Q6–7, Q9–12, F, D; ∼ . M1.

Mont. If either Death or Bondage I must chuse,
I'll keep my Freedom, though my life I lose.
    Guy. I'll not upbraid you that you once refus'd
Those means, you might have then with Honour us'd:
I'll lead your Men, perhaps bring Victory:
They know to Conquer best, who know to Dye.
                              [*Exeunt* Montezuma, Odmar.
    Alib. Ah me, what have I heard! stay, *Guyomar*,
What hope you from this Sally you prepare?
    Guy. A death, with Honour for my Countries good:
30 And to that use your self design'd my blood.
    Alib. You heard, and I well know the Towns distress,
Which Sword and Famine both at once oppress:
Famine so fierce, that what's deny'd Mans use,
Even deadly Plants, and Herbs of pois'nous juice
Wild hunger seeks; and to prolong our breath,
We greedily devour our certain death:
The Souldier in th' assault of Famine falls;
And Ghosts, not Men, are watching on the walls.
As Callow Birds———
40 Whose Mother's kill'd in seeking of the prey,
Cry in their Nest, and think her long away;
And at each leaf that stirs, each blast of wind,
Gape for the Food which they must never find:
So cry the people in their misery.
    Guy. And what relief can they expect from me?
    Alib. While *Montezuma* sleeps, call in the Foe:
The Captive General your design may know:
His Noble heart, to Honour ever true,
Knows how to spare as well as to subdue.
50   *Guy.* What I have heard I blush to hear: and grieve
Those words you spoke I must your words believe;
I to do this! I, whom you once thought brave,

---

27 stay,] Q9-12, F; ~ʌ Q1-8, D, M1-2.
30 And to that use] Q3-5; A death, to which Q1-2, Q6-12, F, D, M1-2.
33 use,] Q2-12, F, D; ~ʌ Q1; ~) M1.
38 Ghosts, not Men,] Q4-5, Q7-12, F, D, M1; Ghosts not Men Q1-3, Q6, M2.
40 the] Q2-12, F, D; their Q1, M1-2.

To sell my Countrey, and my King Enslave?
All I have done by one foul act deface,
And yield my right to you by turning base?
What more could *Odmar* wish that I should do
To lose your Love, then you perswade me to?
No, Madam, no, I never can commit
A deed so ill, nor can you suffer it:
60 'Tis but to try what Vertue you can find
Lodg'd in my Soul.
    Alib. —————I plainly speak my Mind;
Dear as my Life my Vertue I'll preserve:
But Vertue you too scrupulously serve:
I lov'd not more then now my Countries good,
When for it's service I employ'd your Blood:
But things are alter'd, I am still the same,
By different ways still moving to one fame;
And by dis-arming you, I now do more
To save the Town, then arming you before.
70   *Guy.* Things good or ill by circumstances be,
In you 'tis Vertue, what is Vice in me.
    Alib. That ill is pardon'd which does good procure.
    Guy. The good's uncertain, but the ill is sure.
    Alib. When Kings grow stubborn, slothful, or unwise,
Each private man for publick good should rise.
    Guy. Take heed, Fair Maid, how Monarchs you accuse:
Such reasons none but impious Rebels use:
Those who to Empire by dark paths aspire,
Still plead a call to what they most desire;
80 But Kings by free consent their Kingdoms take,
Strict as those Sacred Ties which Nuptials make;
And what e're faults in Princes time reveal,
None can be Judge where can be no Appeal.

---

56 should] Q2–12, F, D, M1; should Q1; shou'd M2.
61 ——I] ∧~ Q1–12, F, D, M1–2.
75 rise.] Q2–12, F, D, M2; rise; / As when the Head distempers does endure, / Each several part must join t'effect the cure. Q1; rise; / Virtue though
straight, doth of loose folds consist / which larger Soules can can [*sic*] widen as
they list. M1.

Alib. In all debates you plainly let me see
You love your Vertue best, but *Odmar* me:
Go, your mistaken Piety pursue:
I'll have from him what is deny'd by you;
With my Commands you shall no more be grac'd,
Remember, Sir, this trial was your last.
90   *Guy.* The gods inspire you with a better mind;
Make you more just, and make you then more kind:
But though from Vertues rules I cannot part,
Think I deny you with a Bleeding Heart:
'Tis hard with me what ever choice I make;
I must not merit you, or must forsake:
But in this streight, to Honour I'le be true,
And leave my Fortune to the gods and you.

Enter Messenger Privately.

Mess. Now is the time; be aiding to your Fate;
From the Watch-Tower, above the Western Gate,
100 I have discern'd the Foe securely lye,
Too proud to fear a beaten Enemy:
Their careless Chiefs to the cool Grottoes run,
The Bowers of Kings, to shade them from the Sun.
   Guy. Upon thy life disclose thy news to none;
I'le make the Conquest or the shame my own.
                              [*Exit* Guyomar *and Messenger.*

Enter Odmar.

Alib. I read some welcome message in his Eye,
Prince *Odmar* comes: I'le see if he'l deny.
Odmar I come to tell you pleasing News,
I beg'd a thing your Brother did refuse.

97+   s.d. *Enter*] Q2–12, F, D, M2; *Enter a* Q1, M1.
97+   s.d. *Messenger*] D; Messenger Q1–12, F, M1–2.
105+ s.d. *Messenger*] D; Messenger Q1–12, F, M2; *omitted from* M1.
109   beg'd] Q2–12, F, D, M1–2; beg Q1.

110   *Odm.* The News both pleases me and grieves me too;
    For nothing, sure, should be deny'd to you:
    But he was blest who might commanded be;
    You never meant that happiness to me.
        Alib. What he refus'd your kindness might bestow,
    But my Commands, perhaps, your burden grow.
        Odm. Could I but live till burdensome they prove,
    My Life would be immortal as my Love.
    Your wish, e're it receive a name I grant.
        Alib. 'Tis to relieve your dying Countries want;
120 All hope of succour from your Arms is past,
    To save us now you must our Ruine haste;
    Give up the Town, and to oblige him more,
    The Captive General's liberty restore.
        Odm. You speak to try my Love, can you forgive
    So soon, to let your Brother's Murderer live?
        Alib. Orbellan, though my Brother, did disgrace
    With treacherous Deeds, our Mighty Mothers Race;
    And to revenge his Blood, so justly spilt,
    What is it less then to partake his guilt?
130 Though my Proud Sister to revenge incline,
    I to my Country's good my own resign.
        Odm. To save our Lives our Freedom I betray———
    ———Yet since I promis'd it I will obey;
    I'le not my Shame nor your Commands dispute:
    You shall behold your Empire's absolute.   [*Exit* Odmar.
        Alib. I should have thank'd him for his speedy grant;
    And yet I know not how, fit words I want:
    Sure I am grown distracted in my mind,
    That joy this grant should bring I cannot find:
140 The one, denying, vex'd my Soul before;
    And this, obeying, has disturb'd me more:
    The one, with grief, and slowly did refuse,
    The other, in his grant, much haste did use:
    ———He us'd too much———and granting me so soon,

112   who] Q2–12, F, D, M2; that Q1, M1.
120   hope] hopes Q1–12, F, D, M1–2.

He has the merit of the gift undone:
Methought with wondrous ease, he swallow'd down
His forfeit Honour, to betray the Town:
My inward choice was *Guyomar* before,
But now his Vertue has confirm'd me more———
50 ———I rave, I rave, for *Odmar* will obey,
And then my promise must my choice betray.
Fantastick Honour, thou hast fram'd a toyl
Thy self, to make thy Love thy Vertues spoyl.   [*Exit* Alibech.

SCENE III.

*A pleasant Grotto discover'd: in it a Fountain spouting; round
about it* Vasquez, Pizarro, *and other* Spaniards *lying carelesly
un-arm'd, and by them many* Indian *Women, one of which
Sings the following Song.*

SONG.

Ah fading joy, how quickly art thou past?
          Yet we thy ruine haste:
As if the cares of Humane Life were few
          We seek out new:
And follow Fate which would too fast pursue.

See how on every bough the Birds express
          In their sweet notes their happiness.
They all enjoy, and nothing spare;
But on their Mother Nature lay their care:
10 *Why then should Man, the Lord of all below,*
          Such troubles chuse to know
As none of all his Subjects undergo?

---

5   which would] Q2–12, F, D, M4–5; *that does* Q1.
7   *In their*] Q1b–12, F, D, M4–5; *In the* Q1a.
10   *below,*] Q7–12, F, D; ~∧ Q1–6, M4–5.

Hark, hark, the Waters fall, fall, fall;
And with a Murmuring sound
Dash, dash, upon the ground,
        To gentle slumbers call.

After the Song two Spaniards *arise and Dance a Saraband with*
    Castanieta's: at the end of which, Guyomar *and his* Indians
    enter, and e're the Spaniards *can recover their Swords, seize*
    them.

Guy. Those whom you took without, in Triumph bring,
But see these streight conducted to the King.
    Piz. Vasquez, what now remains in these extreams?
20   *Vasq.* Only to wake us from our Golden Dreams.
    Piz. Since by our shameful conduct, we have lost
Freedom, Wealth, Honour, which we value most,
I wish they would our Lives a Period give:
They Live too long who Happiness out-live.

                            [Spaniards *are led out.*
    1 *Ind.* See, Sir, how quickly your success is spread:
The King comes Marching in the Armies head.

        Enter Montezuma; Alibech; Odmar, *Discontented.*

    Mont. Now all the gods reward and bless my Son: [*Embracing.*
Thou hast this day, thy Fathers Youth out-done.
    Alib. Just Heaven all Happiness upon him shower,
30 Till it confess it's will beyond it's power.
    Guy. The heavens are kind, the gods propitious be,
I only doubt a Mortal Deity:
I neither Fought for Conquest, nor for Fame,

---

13   *Hark, hark*] Q2–12, F, D, M4–5; *Hark, bark* Q1.
16+   *s.d. Saraband*] Saraband Q1–12, F, D, M1; *omitted from M2.*
16+   *s.d. Castanieta's*] Castanieta's Q1–12, F, D; *omitted from M1–2.*
16+   *s.d. Indians*] Q2–12, F, D, M2; Indian's Q1; *omitted from M1.*
17   without,] D; ~‿ Q1–12, F, M1–2.
26+   *s.d.* Montezuma; Alibech;] ~ , ~ , Q1–12, F, D; ~ , ~ . M1; *Mont:* ~ , M2.
29   all] Q2–12, F, D, M2; such Q1, M1.

Your Love alone can recompence my Flame.
  Alib. I gave my Love to the most brave in War;
But that the King must Judge.
  Mont.————————————'Tis *Guyomar.*
               [*Souldiers shout,* A Guyomar, *&c.*
  Mont. This day your Nuptials we will Celebrate;
But guard these haughty Captives till their Fate:
Odmar, this night to keep them be your care,
To morrow for their Sacrifice prepare.
  Alib. Blot not your Conquest with your Cruelty.
  Mont. Fate says we are not safe unless they Dye:
The Spirit that fore-told this happy day,
Bid me use Caution, and avoid delay:
Posterity be juster to my Fame;
  Nor call it Murder, when each private Man
In his defence may justly do the same:
  But private persons more then Monarchs can:
All weigh our Acts, and what e're seems unjust,
Impute not to Necessity, but Lust.
          [*Exeunt* Montezuma, Guyomar, *and* Alibech.
  Odm. Lost and undone! he had my Fathers voice,
And *Alibech* seem'd pleas'd with her new choice:
Alas, it was not new! too late I see
Since one she hated, that it must be me.————
————I feel a strange Temptation in my will
To do an action, great at once and ill:
Vertue ill treated, from my Soul is fled;
I by Revenge and Love am wholly led:
Yet Conscience would against my rage Rebel————
————Conscience, the foolish pride of doing well!
Sink Empire, Father Perish, Brother Fall,
Revenge does more then recompence you all.
————Conduct the Pris'ners in————

       Enter Vasquez, Pizarro.

36+   *s.d.* A *Guyomar*] *A* Guyomar Q1–4, Q6–12, F, D; Guyomar Q5; A Guyomar
M1; *a Guiomar* M2.

Spaniards, you see your own deplor'd Estate:
What dare you do to reconcile your Fate?
   Vasq. All that Despair, with Courage joyn'd can do.
   Odm. An easie way to Victory I'le show:
When all are Buried in their Sleep or Joy,
I'le give you Arms, Burn, Ravish, and Destroy;
70 For my own share one Beauty I design,
Engage your Honours that she shall be mine.
   Piz. I gladly Swear.
   Vasq.————————And I; but I request
That, in return, one who has touch'd my breast,
Whose name I know not, may be given to me.
   Odm. Spaniard 'tis just; she's yours who e're she be.
   Vasq. The night comes on: if Fortune bless the bold
I shall possess the Beauty.
   Piz.————————I the Gold.   *[Exeunt Omnes.*

SCENE IV.

A Prison.

Cortez *discovered, bound:* Almeria *talking with him.*

   Alm. I come not now your constancy to prove,
You may believe me when I say I Love.
   Cort. You have too well instructed me before,
In your intentions to believe you more.
   Alm. I'm justly plagu'd by this your unbelief,
And am my self the cause of my own grief:
But to beg Love, I cannot stoop so low;
It is enough that you my passion know:
'Tis in your choice; Love me, or Love me not,   *[Lays hold on*
10 I have not yet my Brother's Death forgot.   *the Dagger.*

—————
70 my own] Q3–12, F, D, M1–2; my one Q1–2.
77 ————I] ∧~ Q1–12, F, D, M1–2.
s.d. bound:] Q2–12, F, D, M2; *bound by one Foot,* Q1; bound by the feet M1.

Cort. You Menace me and Court me in a breath:
Your *Cupid* looks as dreadfully as Death.
    Alm. Your hopes, without, are vanish'd into smoak:
Your Captains taken, and your Armies broke.
    Cort. In vain you urge me with my miseries:
When Fortune falls, high Courages can rise.
Now should I change my Love, it would appear
Not the effect of gratitude, but fear.
    Alm. I'le to the King, and make it my Request,
Or my Command that you may be releast;
And make you Judge, when I have set you free,
Who best deserves your passion, I, or she.
    Cort. You tempt my Faith so generous a way,
As without guilt might constancy betray:
But I'm so far from meriting esteem,
That if I Judge, I must my self Condemn;
Yet having given my worthless heart before,
What I must ne're possess I will adore;
Take my devotion then this humbler way;
Devotion is the Love which Heaven we pay.   [*Kisses her hand.*

Enter Cydaria.

    Cyd. May I believe my Eyes! what do I see!
Is this her Hate to him, his Love to me!
'Tis in my Breast she sheaths her Dagger now.
False Man, is this the Faith? is this the Vow?   [*To him.*
    Cort. What words, dear Saint, are these I hear you use?
What Faith, what Vows are those which you accuse?
    Cyd. More cruel then the Tyger o're his spoyl;
And falser then the Weeping Crocodile:
Can you adde Vanity to Guilt, and take
A Pride to hear the Conquests which you make?
Go publish your Renown, let it be said

---

16 falls,] Q3–12, F, D, M1; ∼∧ Q1–2, M2.
28 ne're . . . I will] Q2–12, F, D, M2; not . . . I'le still Q1, M1.
36 those] Q2–12, F, D, M1–2; these Q1.

You have a Woman, and that Lov'd, betray'd.
   Cort. With what injustice is my Faith accus'd?
Life, Freedom, Empire, I at once refus'd;
And would again ten thousand times for you.
   Alm. She'l have too great content to find him true;
And therefore since his Love is not for me,
I'le help to make my Rivals misery.   [*Aside.*
Spaniard, I never thought you false before: [*To him.*
50 Can you at once two Mistresses adore?
Keep the poor Soul no longer in suspence,
Your change is such as does not need defence.
   Cort. Riddles like these I cannot understand!
   Alm. Why should you blush? she saw you kiss my hand.
   Cyd. Fear not, I will, while your first Love's deny'd,
Favour your shame, and turn my Eyes aside;
My feeble hopes in her deserts are lost:
I neither can such power nor beauty boast:
I have no tye upon you to be true
60 But that which loosned yours, my Love to you.
   Cort. Could you have heard my words!
   Cyd. ————————————————— Alas, what needs
To hear your words, when I beheld your deeds?
   Cort. What shall I say? the Fate of Love is such,
That still it sees too little or too much.
That act of mine which does your passion move
Was but a mark of my Respect, not Love.
   Alm. Vex not your self excuses to prepare:
For one you love not is not worth your care.
   Cort. Cruel *Almeria* take that life you gave;
70 Since you but worse destroy me, while you save.
   Cyd. No, let me dye, and I'le my claim resign;
For while I live, methinks you should be mine.
   Cort. The Bloodiest Vengeance which she could pursue,
Would be a triffle to my loss of you.
   Cyd. Your change was wise: for had she been deny'd,

63 say?] Q11–12; ~ ! Q1–10, F, D; ~ ∧ M1–2.
64 That] Q2–12, F, D, M2; As Q1, M1.

A swift Revenge had follow'd from her Pride:
You from my gentle Nature had no Fears,
All my Revenge is only in my Tears.
    Cort. Can you imagine I so mean could prove,
To save my Life by changing of my Love?
    Cyd. Since Death is that which Nat'rally we shun,
You did no more then I, perhaps, had done.
    Cort. Make me not doubt, Fair Soul, your constancy;
You would have dy'd for Love, and so would I.
    Alm. You may believe him; you have seen it prov'd.
    Cort. Can I not gain belief how I have Lov'd?
What can thy ends, malicious Beauty, be:
Can he who kill'd thy Brother live for thee?
                  [*A noyse of Clashing of Swords.*
                [Vasquez *within,* Indians *against him.*
    Vasq. Yield Slaves or dye; our Swords shall force our way.
                             [*Within.*
    Ind. We cannot, though o're-powr'd, our trust betray. [*Within.*
    Cort. 'Tis *Vasquez* voice, he brings me Liberty.
    Vasq. In spight of Fate I'le set my General Free: [*Within.*
Now Victory for us, the Town's our own.
    Alm. All hopes of safety and of love are gone:
As when some dreadful Thunder-clap is nigh,
The winged Fire shoots swiftly through the Skie,
Strikes and Consumes e're scarce it does appear,
And by the sudden ill, prevents the fear:
Such is my state in this amazing wo;
It leaves no pow'r to think, much less to do:
————But shall my Rival Live, shall she enjoy
That Love in Peace I labour'd to destroy?   [*Aside.*
    Cort. Her looks grow black as a Tempestuous wind;
Some raging Thoughts are rowling in her mind.
    Alm. Rival, I must your jealousie remove,

---

87 malicious Beauty,] Q2–12, F, D, M2; Inhumane Creature∧ Q1, M1.
89+ *s.d.,* 90 *Within*] Q9–12, F; *within* Q1–8, D; *omitted from M1–2.*
92 *Within*] Q9–12, F; *within* Q1–8, D, M2; *omitted from M1.*
105 jealousie] Q2–12, F, D, M2; jealous Thoughts Q1, M1.

You shall, hereafter, be at rest for Love.
    Cyd. Now you are kind.
    Alm. ————————He whom you Love is true:
But he shall never be possest by you.
                 [Draws her Dagger, and runs towards her.
    Cort. Hold, hold, ah Barbarous Woman! flye, oh flye!
110   *Cyd.* Ah pity, pity! is no succour nigh?
    Cort. Run, run behind me, there you may be sure,
While I have Life I will your Life secure.
                 [Cydaria gets behind him.
    Alm. On him or thee light Vengeance any where:
                 [She stabs and hurts him.
————What have I done? I see his blood appear!
    Cyd. It streams, it streams from every Vital part:
Was there no way but this to find his Heart?
    Alm. Ah! Cursed Woman, what was my design!
This Weapons point shall mix that blood with mine!
            *[Goes to stab her self, and being within his
                reach he snatches the Dagger.*
    Cort. Now neither Life nor Death are in your power.
120   *Alm.* Then sullenly I'le wait my Fatal hour.

      Enter Vasquez *and* Pizarro *with drawn Swords.*

    Vasq. He Lives, he Lives.
    Cort. ————————————Unfetter me with speed;
Vasquez, I see you troubled that I bleed:
But 'tis not deep, our Army I can head.
    Vasq. You to a certain Victory are led;
Your Men, all Arm'd, stand silently within:
I with your Freedom, did the work begin.
    Piz. What Friends we have, and how we came so strong,

---

110 pity! is . . . nigh?] Q9–12, F; pity, is . . . nigh! Q1–8, D; pitty! is . . . nigh! M2.
118 This Weapons point shall mix that blood with mine!] Q2–12, F, D, M2; At least this Weapon both our Blood shall joyn. Q1, M1.
124 *Vasq.*] Q1b–12, F, D, M1; *Vsq* . Q1a; V: M2.
125 Men,] Q8; ∼ʌ Q1–7, Q9–12, F, D, M1–2.

We'l softly tell you as we March along.

   Cort. In this safe place let me secure your fear: [*To* Cydaria.

No Clashing Swords, no Noyse can enter here.

Amidst our Arms as quiet you shall be

As Halcyons Brooding on a Winter Sea.

   Cyd. Leave me not here alone, and full of fright,

Amidst the Terrors of a Dreadful night:

You judge, alas, my Courage by your own,

I never durst in Darkness be alone:

I beg, I throw me humbly at your Feet.———

   Cort. You must not go where you may dangers meet.

Th' unruly Sword will no distinction make:

And Beauty will not there give Wounds but take.

   Alm. Then stay and take me with you; though to be

A Slave to wait upon your Victory.

My Heart unmov'd, can Noyse and Horrour bear:

Parting from you is all the Death I fear.

   Cort. Almeria, 'tis enough I leave you free:

You neither must stay here, nor go with me.

   Alm. Then take my Life; that will my rest restore:

'Tis all I ask for saving yours before.

   Cort. That were a Barbarous return of Love.

   Alm. Yet, leaving it, you more inhumane prove:

In both extreams I some relief should find:

Oh either hate me more, or be more kind.

   Cort. Life of my Soul do not my absence Mourn:

But chear your Heart in hopes of my return.   [*To* Cydaria.

Your Noble Father's Life shall be my care;

And both your Brothers I'm oblig'd to spare.

   Cyd. Fate makes you Deaf while I in vain implore,

My Heart forebodes I ne'r shall see you more:

I have but one request, when I am Dead

---

147 Life;] ∼ , Q1–12, F, D, M1; ∼∧ M2.
150 Yet, leaving it,] Q2–6, D; Yet leaving it Q1, M2; Yet Leaving it, Q7–12, F; Leaving mee Life M1.
154 your] Q2–12, F, D, M2; thy Q1, M1.
155 Your] Q2–12, F, D, M2; Thy Q1, M1.
156 your] Q2–12, F, D, M2; thy Q1, M1.

160 Let not my Rival to your Love succeed.
    Cort. Fate will be kinder then your Fears fore-tell;
Farewel my Dear.
    Cyd. ————A long and last farewel:
————So eager to imploy the cruel Sword;
Can you not one, not one last look afford?
    Cort. I melt to Womanish Tears, and if I stay,
I find my Love my Courage will betray;
Yon Tower will keep you safe, but be so kind
To your own Life that none may entrance find.
    Cyd. Then lead me there————   [*He leads her.*
170 For this one Minute of your Company,
I go methinks, with some content to Dye.
                    [*Exeunt* Cortez, Vasquez, Pizarro, Cydaria.
    Alm. Farewel, O too much Lov'd, since Lov'd in vain!   [*Sola.*
What Dismal Fortune does for me remain!
Night and Despair my Fatal Foot-steps guide;
That Chance may give the Death which he deny'd.   [*Exit.*

Cortez, Vasquez, Pizarro, *and* Spaniards, *return again.*

    Cort. All I hold dear, I trust to your defence;   [*To* Pizarro.
Guard her, and on your Life, remove not hence.
                    [*Exeunt* Cortez, *and* Vasquez.
    Piz. I'le venture that————
The gods are good; I'le leave her to their care,
180 Steal from my Post, and in the Plunder share.   [*Exit.*

---

164 afford?] M1–2; ~ ! Q1–12, F, D.
175+ *s.d.* Spaniards,] Q1b–12, F, D; ~ʌ Q1a, M1–2.
179 her to] Q1b–12, F, D, M1–2; to her Q1a.

ACT V. SCENE I.

The Chamber Royal, an Indian *Hamock discover'd in it.*

Enter Odmar *with Souldiers,* Guyomar, Alibech, *bound.*

Odm. Fate is more just then you to my desert,
And in this Act you blame, Heaven takes my part.
    Guy. Can there be Gods, and no Revenge provide?
    Odm. The gods are ever of the Conquering side:
She's now my Queen, the *Spaniards* have agreed
I to my Fathers Empire shall succeed.
    Alib. How much I Crowns contemn I let thee see,
Chusing the younger and refusing thee.
    Guy. Were she Ambitious, she'd disdain to own
The Pageant Pomp of such a Servile Throne:
A Throne which thou by Parricide do'st gain,
And by a base submission must retain.
    Alib. I Lov'd thee not before, but, *Odmar,* know
That now I hate thee and despise thee too.
    Odm. With too much Violence you Crimes pursue,
Which if I Acted 'twas for Love of you:
This, if it teach not Love, may teach you Fear:
I brought not Sin so far, to stop it here.
Death in a Lovers Mouth, would sound but ill:
But know, I either must enjoy, or Kill.
    Alib. Bestow, base Man, thy idle Threats elsewhere,
My Mothers Daughter knows not how to Fear.
Since, *Guyomar,* I must not be thy Bride,
Death shall enjoy what is to thee deny'd.
    Odm. Then take thy wish.——   [*Offers to stab.*

---

s.d. *Hamock*] Q5; Hamock Q1–4, Q6–12, F, D, M1; *omitted from M2.*
2   blame,] Q1b–12, F, D, M1; ~∧ Q1a, M2.
12   a] Q2–12, F, D, M2; most Q1, M1.
21   elsewhere,] Q2–12, F, D; elsewher∧ Q1a; elsewhere: Q1b; else where∧ M1–2.
25   wish.—— [*Offers to stab.*] M2; wish.—— Q1–12, F, D, M1.

Guy. Hold, *Odmar,* hold:——   [*Stops his hand.*
My right in *Alibech* I will resign;
Rather then see her Dye, I'le see her thine.
      Alib. In vain thou would'st resign, for I will be,
30 Even when thou leav'st me, Constant still to thee:
That shall not save my Life: wilt thou appear
Fearful for her who for her self wants Fear?
      Odm. Her Love to him shows me a surer way:
I by her Love, her Vertue must betray.   [*Aside.*
Since, *Alibech,* you are so true a Wife;   [*To her.*
'Tis in your power to save your Husbands Life:
The gods, by me, your Love and Vertue try:
For both will suffer if you let him Dye.
      Alib. I never can believe you will proceed
40 To such a Black and Execrable Deed.
      Odm. I only threatn'd you; but could not prove
So much a Fool to Murder what I Love:
But in his Death, I some advantage see:
Worse then it is I'm sure it cannot be.
If you consent, you with that gentle Breath
Preserve his Life: if not, behold his Death.
                    [*Holds his Sword to his breast.*
      Alib. What shall I do?
      Guy.——————What, are your thoughts at strife
About a ransom to preserve my Life?
Though to save yours I did my Interest give,
50 Think not when you were his I meant to Live.
      Alib. O let him be preserv'd by any way:
But name not the foul price which I must pay.   [*To* Odmar.
      Odm. You would and would not, I'le no longer stay.
                    [*Offers again to Kill him.*
      Alib. I yield, I yield, but yet e're I am ill,

---

26 hold:—— [*Stops his hand.*] M2; hold:—— Q1–12, F, D, M1.
34 betray.] ~ : Q1–12, F, D, M2; ~ .—— M1.
46 if not,] Q2–12, F, D, M1–2 (not∧ M2); I'le not Q1.
47 do?] M1; ~ ! Q1–12, F, D; ~∧ M2.
47 What, are] Q6–12, F, D; What are Q1–5, M1–2.
52 which] Q2–12, F, D; that Q1, M1–2.

An innocent desire I would fulfil:
With *Guyomar* I one Chast Kiss would leave,
The first and last he ever can receive.
    Odm. Have what you ask: that Minute you agree
To my desires, your Husband shall be free.
                             [*They unbind her, she goes to her Husband.*
60   *Guy.* No, *Alibech*, we never must embrace: [*He turns*
Your guilty kindness why do you mis-place?   *from her.*
'Tis meant to him, he is your private Choice:
I was made yours but by the publick Voice.
And now you leave me with a poor pretence,
That your ill Act is for my life's defence.
    Alib. Since there remains no other means to try,
Think I am false; I cannot see you dye.
    Guy. To give for me both Life and Honour too
Is more, perhaps, then I could give for you.
70 You have done much to cure my Jealousie,
But cannot perfect it unless both Dye:
For since both cannot Live, who stays behind
Must be thought fearful, or, what's worse, unkind.
    Alib. I never could propose that Death you chuse;
But am like you, too jealous to refuse.   [*Embracing him.*
Together dying, we together show
That both did pay that Faith which both did owe.
    Odm. It then remains I act my own design:
Have you your wills, but I will first have mine.
80 Assist me Souldiers.———   [*They go to bind her, she cries out.*

                Enter Vasquez, *two* Spaniards.

    Vasq. Hold, *Odmar*, hold! I come in happy time
To hinder my Misfortune, and your Crime.
    Odm. You ill return the kindness I have shown.

---

64   pretence] Q2–12, F, D, M1–2; prctence Q1.
73   be thought fearful, or, what's worse,] Q2–12, F, D, M2; think the other fearful, or Q1, M1.
77   Faith which] Q2–12, F, D, M2; Faith that Q1, M1.
81   hold! I] M1; ∼ , ∼ Q1–12, F, D; ∼∧∼ M2.

Vasq. Indian, I say desist.

Odm. —————————*Spaniard,* be gone.

Vasq. This Lady I did for my self design:

Dare you attempt her Honour who is mine?

    Odm. Your'e much mistaken; this is she whom I

Did with my Father's loss, and Countries buy:

She whom your promise did to me convey,

90 When all things else were made your common prey.

    Vasq. That promise made excepted one for me;

One whom I still reserv'd, and this is she.

    Odm. This is not she, you cannot be so base.

    Vasq. I Love too deeply to mistake the Face:

The Vanquish'd must receive the Victors Laws.

    Odm. If I am Vanquish'd I my self am Cause.

    Vasq. Then thank your self for what you undergo.

    Odm. Thus Lawless Might does Justice overthrow.

    Vasq. Traytors, like you, should never Justice name.

100   *Odm.* You owe your Triumphs to that Traytors shame.

But to your General I'le my right refer.

    Vasq. He never will protect a Ravisher:

His Generous Heart will soon decide our strife;

He to your Brother will restore his Wife.

It rests we two our claim in Combat try,

And that with this fair prize, the Victor flye.

    Odm. Make haste,———

I cannot suffer to be long perplext:

Conquest is my first wish, and Death my next.

                 [*They Fight, the* Spaniards *and* Indians *Fight.*

110 *Alib.* The gods the Wicked by themselves o'rethrow:

All Fight against us now and for us too! [*Unbinds her Husband.*

    [*The two* Spaniards *and three* Indians *kill each other,* Vasquez

       kills Odmar, Guyomar *runs to his Brothers Sword.*

    Vasq. Now you are mine; my greatest Foe is slain. [*To* Alibech.

    Guy. A greater still to Vanquish does remain.

    Vasq. Another yet!———

---

107 haste,———] M1; haste,∧ Q1–12, F, D, M2.
114 yet!———] M1; ∼ !∧ Q1–12, F, D, M2.

The Wounds I make but sow new Enemies:
Which from their Blood, like Earth-born-brethren rise.
 Guy. Spaniard take breath: some respit I'le afford,
My Cause is more advantage then your Sword.
 Vasq. Thou art so brave————could it with Honour be,
20 I'd seek thy Friendship, more then Victory.
 Guy. Friendship with him whose hand did *Odmar* kill!
Base as he was, he was my Brother still:
And since his Blood has wash'd away his guilt,
Nature asks thine for that which thou hast spilt.
   [*They Fight a little and breath,* Alibech *takes up a*
    Sword and comes on.
 Alib. My weakness may help something in the strife.
 Guy. Kill not my Honour to preserve my Life: [*Staying her.*
Rather then by thy aid I'le Conquest gain,
Without defence I poorly will be slain.
   [*She goes back, they Fight again,* Vasquez *falls.*
 Guy. Now, *Spaniard,* beg thy Life and thou shalt live.
30 *Vasq.* 'Twere vain to ask thee what thou canst not give:
My breath goes out, and I am now no more;
Yet her I Lov'd, in Death I will adore.   [*Dyes.*
 Guy. Come, *Alibech,* let us from hence remove:
This is a night of Horror, not of Love.
From every part I hear a dreadful noyse:
The Vanquish'd Crying, and the Victor's Joys.
I'le to my Father's aid and Countries flye;
And succour both, or in their Ruine Dye.   [*Exeunt.*

128+ *s.d. falls.*] Q1b–12, F, D, M1–2; ∼ʌ Q1a.
130 'Twere vain] Q2–12, F, D, M2; I scorn Q1, M1.

SCENE II.

A Prison.

Montezuma, Indian *High Priest bound,* Pizarro, Spaniards *with Swords drawn, a Christian Priest.*

Piz. Thou hast not yet discover'd all thy store.
Mont. I neither can nor will discover more:
The gods will Punish you, if they be Just;
The gods will Plague your Sacrilegious Lust.
    Chr. Priest. Mark how this impious Heathen justifies
His own false gods, and our true God denies:
How wickedly he has refus'd his wealth,
And hid his Gold, from Christian hands, by stealth:
Down with him, Kill him, merit Heaven thereby.
10   *Ind. High Pr.* Can Heaven be Author of such Cruelty?
    Piz. Since neither threats nor kindness will prevail,
We must by other means your minds assail;
Fasten the Engines; stretch 'um at their length,
And pull the streightned Cords with all your strength.
        [*They fasten them to the racks, and then pull them.*
    Mont. The gods, who made me once a King, shall know
I still am worthy to continue so:
Though now the subject of your Tyranny,
I'le Plague you worse then you can punish me.
Know I have Gold, which you shall never find,
20 No Pains, no Tortures shall unlock my Mind.
    Chr. Pr. Pull harder yet; he does not feel the rack.
    Mont. Pull till my Veins break, and my Sinews crack.
    Ind. High Pr. When will you end your Barb'rous Cruelty?
I beg not to escape, I beg to Dye.

---

s.d. Indian *High Priest*] Indian High Priest Q1–12, F, D, M2; Caliban M1.
s.d. Christian Priest] Christian Priest Q1–12, F, D; Jesuite M1; *omitted from M2.*
14+ *s.d. racks*] M1; *rack* Q1–12, F, D, M2.

Mont. Shame on thy Priest-hood that such pray'rs can bring:
Is it not brave to suffer with thy King?
When Monarchs suffer, gods themselves bear part;
Then well may'st thou, who but my Vassal art:
I charge thee dare not groan, nor shew one sign,
30 Thou at thy Torments doest the least repine.
　　Ind. High P. You took an Oath when you receiv'd your Crown,
The Heavens should pour their usual Blessings down;
The Sun should shine, the Earth it's fruits produce,
And nought be wanting to your Subjects use:
Yet we with Famine were opprest, and now
Must to the yoke of Cruel Masters bow.
　　Mont. If those above, who made the World, could be
Forgetful of it, why then blam'st thou me?
　　Chr. Pr. Those Pains, O Prince, thou sufferest now are light
40 Compar'd to those, which when thy Soul takes flight,
Immortal, endless, thou must then endure:
Which Death begins; and Time can never cure.
　　Mont. Thou art deceiv'd: for whensoe're I Dye,
The Sun my Father bears my Soul on high:
He lets me down a Beam, and mounted there,
He draws it back, and pulls me through the Air:
I in the Eastern parts, and rising Sky,
You in Heaven's downfal, and the West must lye.
　　Chr. Pr. Fond man, by Heathen Ignorance misled,
50 Thy Soul destroying when thy Body's Dead:
Change yet thy Faith, and buy Eternal rest.
　　Ind. High Pr. Dye in your own: for our Belief is best.
　　Mont. In seeking happiness you both agree,
But in the search, the paths so different be,
That all Religions with each other Fight,
While only one can lead us in the Right.
But till that one hath some more certain mark,
Poor humane kind must wander in the dark;
And suffer pains, eternally, below,

31　*High*] Q2–12, F, D, M1; ~ . Q1.
59　eternally,] Q8; ~∧ Q1–7, Q9–12, F, D, M1.

60 For that, which here, we cannot come to know.
    Chr. Pr. That which we worship, and which you believe,
    From Natures common hand we both receive:
    All under various names, Adore and Love
    One power Immense, which ever rules above.
    Vice to abhor, and Virtue to pursue,
    Is both believ'd and taught by us and you:
    But here our Worship takes another way.
        Mont. Where both agree 'tis there most safe to stay:
    For what's more vain then Publick Light to shun,
70 And set up Tapers while we see the Sun?
        Chr. Pr. Though Nature teaches whom we should Adore,
    By Heavenly Beams we still discover more.
        Mont. Or this must be enough, or to Mankind
    One equal way to Bliss is not design'd.
    For though some more may know, and some know less,
    Yet all must know enough for happiness.
        Chr. Pr. If in this middle way you still pretend
    To stay, your Journey never will have end.
        Mont. Howe're, 'tis better in the midst to stay,
80 Then wander farther in uncertain way.
        Chr. Pr. But we by Martyrdom our Faith avow.
        Mont. You do no more then I for ours do now.
    To prove Religion true———
    If either Wit or Suff'rings would suffice,
    All Faiths afford the Constant and the Wise:
    And yet ev'n they, by Education sway'd,
    In Age defend what Infancy obey'd.
        Chr. Pr. Since Age by erring Child-hood is misled,
    Refer your self to our Un-erring Head.
90   *Mont.* Man and not erre! what reason can you give?
        Chr. Pr. Renounce that carnal reason, and believe.
        Mont. The Light of Nature should I thus betray,
    'Twere to wink hard that I might see the day.
        Chr. Pr. Condemn not yet the way you do not know;

---

79 'tis] Q2–12, F, D; 'twas Q1.   81 *Chr.*] Q2–12, F, D; ~∧ Q1; Jes— M1.
88 *Pr.*] Q2–12, F, D; Pr.. Q1; *omitted from M1.*

I'le make your reason judge what way to go.
 Mont. 'Tis much too late for me new ways to take,
Who have but one short step of life to make.
 Piz. Increase their Pains, the Cords are yet too slack.
 Chr. Pr. I must by force, convert him on the Rack.
00 *Ind. High Pr.* I faint away, and find I can no more:
Give leave, O King, I may reveal thy store,
And free my self from pains I cannot bear.
 Mont. Think'st thou I lye on Beds of Roses here,
Or in a Wanton Bath stretch'd at my ease?
Dye, Slave, and with thee, dye such thoughts as these.
       [High Priest turns aside and dyes.

  Enter Cortez *attended by* Spaniards, *he speaks entring.*

 Cort. On pain of death kill none but those who fight;
I much repent me of this bloody night:
Slaughter grows murder when it goes too far,
And makes a Massacre what was a War:
10 Sheath all your weapons and in silence move,
'Tis sacred here to Beauty and to Love.
Ha————   *[Sees* Montezuma.
What dismal sight is this, which takes from me
All the delight that waits on Victory!
     [Runs to take him off the Rack.
Make haste: how now, Religion do you Frown?
Haste holy Avarice, and help him down.
Ah Father, Father, what do I endure *[Embracing* Montezuma.
To see these Wounds my pity cannot Cure!
 Mont. Am I so low that you should pity bring,
20 And give an Infants Comfort to a King?
Ask these if I have once unmanly groan'd;
Or ought have done deserving to be moan'd.

99 *Pr.*] Q2–12, F, D; *Pr..* Q1; *omitted from M1.*
105+ *s.d. High Priest*] M2; High Priest Q1–12, F, D; Caliban M1.
106 who] Q2–12, F, D, M2; that Q1.
113 What] Q6–12, F, D, M2; *Cort.* What Q1–5, M1.
117 Montezuma.] Q1b–12, F, D, M1; M Q1a.

Cort. Did I not charge thou should'st not stir from hence? [*To
But Martial Law shall punish thy offence.   Pizarro.
And you,———   [*To the Chr. Priest.*
Who sawcily, teach Monarchs to obey,
And the wide World in narrow Cloysters sway;
Set up by Kings as humble aids of power,
You that which bred you, Viper-like devour,
130 You Enemies of Crowns———
    Chr. Pr. ————————————Come, let's away,
We but provoke his fury by our stay.
    Cort. If this go free, farewel that discipline
Which did in Spanish Camps severely shine:
Accursed Gold, 'tis thou hast caus'd these crimes;
Thou turn'st our Steel against thy Parent Climes!
And into *Spain* wilt fatally be brought,
Since with the price of Blood thou here art bought.
                        [*Exeunt Priest and* Pizarro.
                [*Cortez kneels by* Montezuma *and weeps.*
    Cort. Can you forget those Crimes they did commit?
    Mont. I'le do what for my dignity is fit:
140 Rise, Sir, I'm satisfi'd the fault was theirs:
Trust me you make me weep to see your Tears:
Must I chear you?
    Cort. ————————Ah Heavens!
    Mont. ——————————————You're much to blame;
Your grief is cruel, for it shews my shame,
Does my lost Crown to my remembrance bring:
But weep not you, and I'le be still a King.
You have forgot that I your Death design'd,

125 you,———] Q8, M1; ~ ,∧ Q1–7, Q9–12, F, D.
130 Crowns———] ~ . Q1–12, F, D; ~ ! M1.
132 free,] Q1b–12, F, D; ~∧ Q1a, M2.
134 Gold,] Q1b–12, F, D; ~∧ Q1a, M2.
134 crimes;] Q1b–4, Q6–11, F, D; ~ : Q1a, Q12; ~ ! Q5; ~∧ M2.
135 Climes] Q1b–12, F, D; climes Q1a, M2.
136 brought,] Q1b–12, F, D; ~∧ Q1a, M2.
137+ s.d. *Priest*] D; Priest Q1–12, F; Jes M1; *omitted from M2.*
137+ s.d. *by*] Q1b–12, F, D; *to* Q1a.   139 is] Q2–12, F, D, M1–2; it Q1.
142 ———Ah] ∧~ Q1–12, F, D, M1–2.
145 weep not you,] Q2–4, Q7–12, F, D; weep not, you∧ Q1; weep you, Q5; weep
not∧ you∧ Q6, M1–2.

To satisfie the Proud *Almeria*'s mind:
You, who preserv'd my Life, I doom'd to Dye.
    Cort. Your Love did that, and not your Cruelty.

                    Enter a Spaniard.

50   *Span.* Prince *Guyomar* the Combat still maintains,
Our Men retreat, and he their ground regains:
But once incourag'd by our Generals sight,
We boldly should renew the doubtful Fight.
    Cort. Remove not hence, you shall not long attend: [*To* Mon-
I'le aid my Souldiers, yet preserve my Friend.   tezuma.
    Mont. Excellent Man!——   [*Exit* Cortez, &c.
But I, by living, poorly take the way
To injure Goodness, which I cannot pay.

                    Enter Almeria.

    Alm. Ruine and Death run Arm'd through every Street;
60 And yet that Fate I seek I cannot meet:
What guards Misfortunes are and Misery!
Death that strikes all, yet seems afraid of me.
    Mont. Almeria's here: oh turn away your Face!
Must you be witness too of my disgrace?
    Alm. I am not that *Almeria* whom you knew,
But want that pity I deny'd to you:
Your Conquerour, alas, has Vanquish'd me;
But he refuses his own Victory:
While all are Captives, in your Conquer'd State,
70 I find a wretched freedom in his hate.
    Mont. Could'st thou thy Love on one who scorn'd thee lose?
He saw not with my Eyes who could refuse:

154–155 *s.d.* Montezuma.] Q1b–6, D; Montezu Q1a; Montez. Q7–12, F; Mont.
M1–2.
156 Man!——] Q8; ~ !ʌ Q1–7, Q9–12, F, D, M1–2.
161 are and Misery!] Q2–12, F, D, M2; are! / Such is th' infectious strength of
Misery, Q1, M1.
171 who] Q2–12, F, D, M2; that Q1, M1.
172 who] Q1b–12, F, D, M2; that Q1a, M1.

Him who could prove so much unkind to thee,
I ne're will suffer to be kind to me.
    Alm. I am content in Death to share your Fate;
And dye for him I love with him I hate.
    Mont. What shall I do in this perplexing streight?
My tortur'd Limbs refuse to bear my weight: [*Endeavouring to*
I cannot go to Death to set me free: *walk and not*
180 Death must be kind, and come himself to me.   *being able.*
    Alm. I've thought upon't: I have Affairs below, [Alm. *musing.*
Which I must needs dispatch before I go.
Sir, I have found a place, where you may be,   [*To him.*
(Though not preserv'd) yet like a King dye free:
The General left your Daughter in the Tower,
We may a while resist the *Spaniards* power,
If *Guyomar* prevail,——
    Mont. ——Make haste and call;
She'l hear your Voice, and answer from the Wall.
    Alm. My voice she knows and fears, but use your own,
190 And to gain entrance, feign you are alone. [Almeria *steps behind.*
    Mont. Cydaria!
    Alm. ——Lowder.
    Mont. ——Daughter!
    Alm. ——Lowder yet.
    Mont. Thou canst not, sure, thy Father's voice forget.
        [*He knocks at the door, at last* Cydaria *looks
        over the Zoty.*
    Cyd. Since my Love went, I have been frighted so,
With Dismal Groans, and Noyses from below:
I durst not send my Eyes abroad, for fear
Of seeing dangers, which I yet but hear.
    Mont. Cydaria!——

173 Him who] Q2-12, F, D, M2; He that Q1a, M1; Him that Q1b.
177 streight?] M1; ~ ! Q1-12, F, D; ~∧ M2.
179 *walk and*] Q1b; *walk* Q1a, Q2-3, Q6; *walk,* Q4-5, Q7-12, F, D.
182 go.] M1; ~ : Q1-12, F, D; ~∧ M2.
187 Make haste] Q2-12, F, D, M2; Haste then, Q1, M1.
192+ *s.d. Zoty*] *Balcone* Q1a, Q2-12, F, D, M1-2; Zoty Q1b.
197 *Cydaria!*——] M1; ~ !∧ Q1-12, F, D, M2.

Cyd. Sure 'tis my Father calls.
Mont. ————————————Dear Child make haste;
All hope of succour, but from thee is past:
As when upon the sands the Traveller
Sees the high Sea come rolling from a far,
The Land grow short, he mends his weary pace,
While Death behind him covers all the place:
So I by swift mis-fortunes am pursu'd,
Which on each other, are like Waves renew'd.
Cyd. Are you alone?
Mont. ————————I am.
Cyd. ————————————I'le strait descend;
Heaven did you here for both our safeties send.
        [Cydaria *descends and opens the door,* Almeria
            rushes betwixt with Montezuma.
Cyd. Almeria here! then I am lost again.   [*Both thrust.*
Alm. Yield to my strength, you struggle but in vain:
Make haste and shut, our Enemies appear.

        Cortez *and* Spaniards *appear at the other end.*

Cyd. Then do you enter, and let me stay here.
        [*As she speaks,* Almeria *over-powers her,*
            thrusts her in, and shuts.
Cort. Sure I both heard her voice and saw her face,
She's like a Vision vanish'd from the place:
Too late I find my absence was too long;
My hopes grow sickly, and my fears grow strong.
        [*He knocks a little, then* Montezuma, Cydaria,
            Almeria *appear above.*
Alm. Look up, look up, and see if you can know

---

198   Sure] M2; ———— ∼ Q1–12, F, D, M1.
200   when upon the sands the] Q2–12, F, D, M2 (sand's M2); on the sand the
frighted Q1, M1 (Sands M1).
210+   *s.d.* Cortez] M1; [∼ Q1–12, F, D, M2.
211+   *s.d.* over-powers] Q2–12, F, D, M1–2; *oevr-powers* Q1.
212   *Cort.*] Q2–12, F, D, M2; *Cyd.* Oh Heavens! / *Cort.* Q1; Cyd— within Oh
heav'ns! / Cort— M1.
213   Vision] Q2–12, F, D, M1–2; ∼ , Q1.

Those whom, in vain, you think to find below.

 Cyd. Look up and see *Cydaria*'s lost estate.

 Mont. And cast one look on *Montezuma*'s Fate.

220 *Cort.* Speak not such dismal words as wound my Ear:

Nor name Death to me when *Cydaria*'s there.

Despair not, Sir, who knows but Conquering *Spain*

May part of what you lost restore again?

 Mont. No, *Spaniard,* know, he who to Empire born,

Lives to be less, deserves the Victors scorn:

Kings and their Crowns have but one Destiny:

Power is their Life, when that expires they dye.

 Cyd. What Dreadful Words are these!

 Mont. ————————————————Name Life no more;

'Tis now a Torture worse then all I bore:

230 I'le not be brib'd to suffer Life, but dye

In spight of your mistaken Clemency.

I was your Slave, and I was us'd like one;

The Shame continues when the Pain is gone:

But I'm a King while this is in my Hand,——— [*His Sword.*

He wants no Subjects who can Death Command:

You should have ty'd him up, t'have Conquer'd me,

But he's still mine, and thus he sets me free. [*Stabs himself.*

 Cyd. Oh my dear Father!

 Cort. ————————————Haste, break ope the door.

 Alm. When that is forc'd there yet remain two more.

    [*The Souldiers break open the first door, and go in.*

240 We shall have time enough to take our way,

'Ere any can our Fatal Journey stay.

 Mont. Already mine is past: O powers divine

Take my last thanks; no longer I repine:

I might have liv'd my own mishaps to Mourn,

While some would Pity me, but more would Scorn!

For Pity only on fresh Objects stays:

But with the tedious sight of Woes decays.

Still less and less my boyling Spirits flow;

And I grow stiff as cooling Mettals do:

---

218 estate] Q1b–12, F, D, M1–2; e stte Q1a.   239 *Omitted from* Q1.

Farewel *Almeria.*———   *[Dyes.*

    Cyd. ———————He's gone, he's gone,
And leaves poor me defenceless here alone.
    Alm. You shall not long be so: prepare to Dye,
That you may bear your Father Company.
    Cyd. Oh name not Death to me; you fright me so,
That with the Fear I shall prevent the blow:
I know your Mercy's more, then to destroy
A thing so young, so Innocent, as I.
    Cort. Whence can proceed thy cruel thirst of Blood?
Ah Barb'rous Woman! Woman! that's too good,
Too mild for thee: there's pity in that name,
But thou hast lost thy pity, with thy shame.
    Alm. Your cruel words have pierc'd me to the Heart;
But on my Rival, I'le revenge my smart.   *[Going to kill her.*
    Cort. Oh stay your hand! and to redeem my fault,
I'le speak the kindest words———
That Tongue e're utter'd, or that Heart e're thought.
Dear———Lovely———Sweet———
    Alm. ——————————This but offends me more,
You act your kindness on *Cydaria's* score.
    Cyd. For his dear sake let me my Life receive.
    Alm. Fool, for his sake alone you must not Live:
Revenge is now my Joy; he's not for me,
And I'le make sure he ne're shall be for thee.
    Cyd. But what's my Crime?
    Alm. ——————————'Tis Loving where I Love.
    Cyd. Your own example does my act approve.
    Alm. 'Tis such a Fault I never can forgive.
    Cyd. How can I mend, unless you let me live?
I yet am Tender, Young, and full of Fear,
And dare not Dye, but fain would tarry here.
    Cort. If Blood you seek, I will my own resign:

258 Blood?] Q8, F; ~ , Q1–7, Q9–12, D; ~∧ M1–2.
259 Barb'rous Woman!] Q8–12, F, M1; ~ ? Q1–7, D, M2.
263 smart. [*Going to kill her.*] M1; smart. Q1–12, F, D, M2.
267 ———This but offends] ∧This but offends Q2–12, F, D, M2; ∧These words offend Q1, M1.

280 O spare her Life, and in exchange, take mine.
   Alm. The Love you shew but hastes her Death the more.
   Cort. I'le run, and help to force the inner door.
                                  [Is going in haste.
   Alm. Stay, *Spaniard,* stay, depart not from my Eyes:
That moment that I lose your sight, she dyes.
To look on you I'le grant a short Reprieve.
   Cort. O make your gift more full, and let her Live:
I dare not go; and yet how dare I stay?
Her I would save, I murder either way.
   Cyd. Can you be so hard-hearted, to destroy
290 My ripening hopes, that are so near to joy?
I just approach to all I would possess:
Death only stands 'twixt me and happiness.
   Alm. Your Father, with his Life, has lost his Throne:
Your Countries Freedom and Renown are gone.
Honour requires your Death: you must obey.
   Cyd. Do you dye first; and shew me then the way.
   Alm. Should you not follow, my Revenge were lost.
   Cyd. Then rise again, and Fright me with your Ghost.
   Alm. I will not trust to that, since Death I chuse,
300 I'le not leave you that Life which I refuse:
If Death's a pain, it is not less to me;
And if 'tis nothing, 'tis no more to thee.
But hark! the noyse increases from behind,
They're near, and may prevent what I design'd:
Take there a Rival's gift.———   *[Stabs her.*
   Cort. Perdition seize thee for so Black a Deed.
   Alm. Blame not an Act which did from Love proceed:
I'le thus Revenge thee with this Fatal blow;   *[Stabs her self.*
Stand fair, and let my Heart-blood on thee flow.
                      [Cortez here goes in as to her.

287 stay?] Q9–12, F, M2; ∼ ! Q1–8, D; ∼ᴧ M1.
294 are] Q8; is Q1–7, Q9–12, F, D, M1–2.
301 pain, it is not] Q2–12, F, D, M2 (painᴧ M2); pain 'twill not be Q1, M1.
305 Take there] Q2, Q6–12, F, D, M1–2; Take, there's Q1; Take, there Q3–5.
307 which] Q2–12, F, D, M1–2; that Q1.
309 thee] Q2–12, F, D, M1–2; the Q1.
309+ s.d. [Cortez *here goes in as to her.*] M1; *omitted from* Q1–12, F, D, M2.

0   *Cyd.* Stay Life, and keep me in the chearful Light;
Death is too Black, and dwells in too much Night.
Thou leav'st me, Life, but Love supplies thy part,
And keeps me warm by lingring in my Heart:
Yet dying for him, I thy claim remove;
How dear it costs to Conquer in my Love!
Now strike: that thought, I hope, will arm my Breast.
     Alm. Ah, with what differing passions am I prest!
     Cyd. Death, when far off, did terrible appear;
But looks less dreadful as he comes more near.
0   *Alm.* O Rival, I have lost the power to kill;
Strength has forsook my Arm, and Rage my will:
I must surmount that Love which thou hast shown:
Dying for him is due to me alone.
Thy weakness shall not boast the Victory,
Now thou shalt live, and dead I'le Conquer thee.

Enter Souldiers above.

Souldiers assist me down.————
          [*Exeunt from above led by Souldiers, and enter*
               both led by Cortez.
     Cort. Is there no danger then?   [*To* Cydaria.
     Cyd. ————————————You need not fear
My Wound, I cannot dye when you are near.
     Cort. You for my sake, Life to *Cydaria* give: [*To* Almeria.
0 And I could dye for you, if you might Live.
     Alm. Enough, I dye content, now you are kind;
Kill'd in my Limbs, reviving in my Mind.
Come near, *Cydaria,* and forgive my Crime.
                    [Cydaria *starts back.*
You need not fear my rage a second time:

---

316   thought,] Q7–12, F, D, M1; ~∧ Q1–6, M2.
325+   s.d. *Enter Souldiers above.*] Enter Souldjers. M1; *omitted from* Q*1–12,* F,
D, M2.
326   down.————] ~ .∧ Q1–12, F, D, M1–2.
326+   s.d. *Exeunt*] Q3–5, Q7–12, F, D; Exeunt Q1–2, Q6, M1–2.
326+   s.d. *Souldiers*] M2; Souldiers Q1–12, F, D, M1.
332   Mind.] M1; ~ : Q1–12, F, D, M2.

I'le bathe your Wound in Tears for my Offence:
That Hand which made it makes this Recompence.
                    [*Ready to join their hands. Shoves her back.*
I would have joyn'd you, but my Heart's too high:
You will, too soon, possess him when I dye.
    Cort. She Faints, O softly set her down.
    Alm. ─────────────────────'Tis past!
340 In thy Lov'd Bosom let me breathe my last.
Here in this one short Moment that I Live,
I have what e're the longest Life could give.─────   [*Dyes.*
    Cort. Farewel, thou Generous Maid: ev'n Victory
Glad as it is, must lend some Tears to thee.
Many I dare not shed, lest you believe   [*To* Cydaria.
I Joy in you less then for her I Grieve.
    Cyd. But are you sure she's dead?─────
I must embrace you fast, before I know
Whether my Life be yet secure or no:
350 Some other hour I will to Tears allow;
But having you, can shew no sorrow now.

          Enter Guyomar *and* Alibech *bound, with Souldiers.*

    Cort. Prince *Guyomar* in bonds! O Friendship's shame!
It makes me blush to owne a Victors name.
                    [*Unbinds him, and* Cydaria, Alibech.
    Cyd. See, *Alibech, Almeria* lyes there:
But do not think 'twas I that Murder'd her.
                    [Alibech *kneels and Kisses her Dead Sister.*
    Cort. Live, and enjoy more then your Conquerour: [*To* Guy-
Take all my Love, and share in all my power.   omar.

───────

335 Wound] M1-2; Wounds Q1-12, F, D.
336+ s.d. *hands. Shoves her back.*] M1; *hands.* Q1-12, F, D, M2.
344 thee.] M1; ~ : Q1-10, F, D, M2; ~ ! Q11-12.
345 believe] Q2-12, F, D, M1-2; ~ ─── Q1.
347 dead?───] ~ ?ᴧ Q1-12, F, D, M1-2.
351+ s.d. *bound,*] Q2-9, D; ~ᴧ Q1, Q10-12, F, M1; ~ . M2.
353+ s.d. *him, and*] M1; *him,* Q1-12, F, D, M2.
355+ s.d. *Sister.*] Q2-12, F, D, M1; ~ᴧ Q1; *omitted from* M2.

Guy. Think me not proudly rude, if I forsake
Those Gifts I cannot with my Honour take:
I for my Country Fought, and would again,
Had I yet left a Country to maintain:
But since the Gods decreed it otherwise,
I never will on its dear Ruines rise.
  Alib. Of all your Goodness leaves to our dispose,
Our Liberty's the only gift we chuse:
Absence alone can make our Sorrows less;
And not to see what we can ne're redress.
  Guy. Northward, beyond the Mountains we will go,
Where Rocks lye cover'd with Eternal Snow;
Thin Herbage in the Plains, and Fruitless Fields,
The Sand no Gold, the Mine no Silver yields:
There Love and Freedom we'l in Peace enjoy;
No *Spaniards* will that Colony destroy.
We to our selves will all our wishes grant;
And nothing coveting, can nothing want.
  Cort. First your Great Father's Funeral Pomp provide:
That done, in Peace your Generous Exiles guide;
While I loud thanks pay to the powers above,
Thus doubly Blest, with Conquest, and with Love.   [*Exeunt.*

FINIS.

---

377   guide;] D; ~ . Q1–9, F, M1–2; ~ , Q10–12.

EPILOGUE
BY A
Mercury.

To all and singular in this full meeting,
    Ladies and Gallants, Phœbus sends me greeting,
    To all his Sons by what e're Title known,
Whether of Court, of Coffee-house, or Town;
From his most mighty Sons, whose confidence
Is plac'd in lofty sound, and humble sence,
Ev'n to his little Infants of the Time
Who Write new Songs, and trust in Tune and Rhyme.
Be't known that Phœbus (being daily griev'd
10   To see good Plays condemn'd, and bad receiv'd,)
Ordains your judgement upon every Cause,
Henceforth be limited by wholesome Laws.
He first thinks fit no Sonnettier advance
His censure, farther then the Song or Dance.
Your Wit Burlesque may one step higher climb,
And in his sphere may judge all Doggrel Rhyme:
All proves, and moves, and Loves, and Honours too:
All that appears high sence, and scarce is low.
As for the Coffee-wits he says not much,
20   Their proper bus'ness is to Damn the Dutch:
For the great Dons of Wit———
Phœbus gives them full priviledge alone
To Damn all others, and cry up their own.
Last, for the Ladies, 'tis Apollo's will,
They should have pow'r to save, but not to kill:
For Love and He long since have thought it fit,
Wit live by Beauty, Beauty raign by Wit.

---

2 greeting,] ∼ . Q1–12, F, D.   8 Who] Q2–12, F, D; That Q1.
21 Dons] Q9–12, F; Dons Q1–8, D.

SECRET LOVE

OR

THE MAIDEN QUEEN

SECRET-
LOVE,

OR THE
Maiden-Queen :

As it is Acted

By His Majesties Servants,

AT THE

THEATER-ROYAL.

Written by

JOHN DRYDEN Esq;

————————*Vitiis nemo sine nascitur* ; *optimus ille*
Qui minimis urgetur.　　　　　HORACE.

LONDON,

Printed for *Henry Herringman*, at the Sign of the *Anchor*,
on the Lower-walk of the New-*Exchange*, 1668.

TITLE PAGE OF THE FIRST EDITION (MACDONALD 70A)

PREFACE.

I T has been the ordinary practice of the *French* Poets, to dedi-
cate their Works of this nature to their King, especially when
they have had the least encouragement to it, by his approbation of them on the Stage. But I confess I want the confidence to
follow their example, though perhaps I have as specious pre-
tences to it for this Piece, as any they can boast of: it having been
own'd in so particular a manner by His Majesty, that he has
grac'd it with the Title of His Play, and thereby rescued it from
the severity (that I may not say malice) of its Enemies. But,
though a character so high and undeserv'd, has not rais'd in me
the presumption to offer such a trifle to his more serious view, yet
I will own the vanity to say, that after this glory which it has
receiv'd from a Soveraign Prince, I could not send it to seek protection from any Subject. Be this Poem then sacred to him without the tedious form of a Dedication, and without presuming to
interrupt those hours which he is daily giving to the peace and
settlement of his people.

For what else concerns this Play, I would tell the Reader that it
is regular, according to the strictest of Dramatick Laws, but that
it is a commendation which many of our Poets now despise, and
a beauty which our common Audiences do not easily discern.
Neither indeed do I value my self upon it, because with all that
symmetry of parts, it may want an air and spirit (which consists in
the writing) to set it off. 'Tis a question variously disputed,
whether an Author may be allowed as a competent judg of his
own works. As to the Fabrick and contrivance of them certainly
he may, for that is properly the employment of the judgment;
which, as a Master-builder he may determine, and that without
deception, whether the work be according to the exactness of the
model; still granting him to have a perfect Idea of that pattern
by which he works: and that he keeps himself always constant
to the discourse of his judgment, without admitting self-love,

---

1   *French*] D; French Q1–6, F.
28 he may] D; may Q1–6, F.

which is the false surveigher of his Fancy, to intermeddle in it.
These Qualifications granted (being such as all sound Poets are
presupposed to have within them) I think all Writers, of what
kind soever, may infallibly judg of the frame and contexture of
their Works. But for the ornament of Writing, which is greater,
more various and bizarre in Poesie then in any other kind, as
it is properly the Child of Fancy, so it can receive no measure, or
at least but a very imperfect one of its own excellencies or fail-
lures from the judgment. Self-love (which enters but rarely into
10 the offices of the judgment) here predominates. And Fancy (if I
may so speak) judging of it self, can be no more certain or demon-
strative of its own effects, then two crooked lines can be the adæ-
quate measure of each other. What I have said on this subject,
may, perhaps, give me some credit with my Readers, in my
opinion of this Play, which I have ever valued above the rest of
my Follies of this kind: yet not thereby in the least dissenting
from their judgment who have concluded the writing of this to
be much inferior to my *Indian Emperour*. But the Argument of
that was much more noble, not having the allay of Comedy to
20 depress it: yet if this be more perfect, either in its kind, or in the
general notion of a Play, 'tis as much as I desire to have granted
for the vindication of my Opinion, and, what as nearly touches
me, the sentence of a Royal Judg. Many have imagin'd the Character of *Philocles* to be faulty; some for not discovering the
Queens love, others for his joining in her restraint. But though
I am not of their number, who obstinately defend what they have
once said, I may with modesty take up those answers which have
been made for me by my Friends; namely, that *Philocles,* who was
but a Gentleman of ordinary birth, had no reason to guess so soon
30 at the Queens Passion, she being a person so much above him,
and by the suffrages of all her people, already destin'd to *Lysimantes:* Besides, that he was prepossessed, (as the Queen somewhere hints it to him) with another inclination which rendred
him less clearsighted in it, since no man, at the same time, can
distinctly view two different objects. And if this, with any shew of
reason, may be defended, I leave my Masters the Criticks to deter-

18   *Indian Emperour*] Q6, F, D; Indian Emperour Q1–5.

mine whether it be not much more conducing to the beauty of my Plot, that *Philocles* should be long kept ignorant of the Queens love, then that with one leap he should have entred into the knowledg of it, and thereby freed himself, to the disgust of the Audience, from that pleasing Labyrinth of errors which was prepar'd for him. As for that other objection of his joyning in the Queens imprisonment, it is indisputably that which every man, if he examines himself, would have done on the like occasion. If they answer that it takes from the height of his Character to do it; I would enquire of my over-wise Censors, who told them I intended him a perfect Character, or indeed what necessity was there he should be so, the variety of Images, being one great beauty of a Play? it was as much as I design'd, to show one great and absolute pattern of honour in my Poem, which I did in the Person of the Queen: All the defects of the other parts being set to show, the more to recommend that one character of Vertue to the Audience. But neither was the fault of *Philocles* so great, if the circumstances be consider'd, which, as moral Philosophy assures us, make the essential differences of good and bad; He himself best explaining his own intentions in his last Act, which was the restauration of his Queen; and even before that, in the honesty of his expressions when he was unavoidably led by the impulsion of his love to do it. That which with more reason was objected as an indecorum, is the management of the last Scene of the Play, where *Celadon* and *Florimell* are treating too lightly of their marriage in the presence of the Queen, who likewise seems to stand idle while the great action of the *Drama* is still depending. This I cannot otherwise defend, then by telling you I so design'd it on purpose to make my Play go off more smartly; that Scene, being in the opinion of the best judges, the most divertising of the whole Comedy. But though the Artifice succeeded, I am willing to acknowledg it as a fault, since it pleas'd His Majesty, the best Judg, to think it so. I have onely to add, that the Play is founded on a story in the *Cyrus*, which he calls the Queen of *Corinth;* in whose Character, as it has been affirm'd to me, he represents that of the famous *Christina*, Queen of *Sweden*. This is what I thought convenient to write by way of

Preface, to the *Maiden-Queen;* in the reading of which, I fear you will not meet with that satisfaction which you have had in seeing it on the Stage; the chief parts of it both serious and comick, being performed to that height of excellence, that nothing but a command which I could not handsomely disobey, could have given me the courage to have made it publick.

---

1   *Maiden-Queen*] Q6, F, D; Maiden-Queen Q1–5.

PROLOGUE.

I.

HE *who writ this, not without pains and thought*
From French *and* English *Theaters has brought*
Th' exactest Rules by which a Play is wrought:

II.

The Unities of Action, Place, and Time;
The Scenes unbroken; and a mingled chime
Of Johnsons *humour, with* Corneilles *rhyme.*

III.

But while dead colours he with care did lay,
He fears his Wit, or Plot he did not weigh,
Which are the living Beauties of a Play.

IV.

Plays are like Towns, which howe're fortifi'd
By Engineers, have still some weaker side
By the o'reseen Defendant unespy'd.

V.

And with that Art you make approaches now;
Such skilful fury in Assaults you show,
That every Poet without shame may bow.

VI.

Ours therefore humbly would attend your doom,
If Souldier-like, he may have termes to come
With flying colours, and with beat of Drum.

The Prologue goes out, and stayes while a Tune is play'd, after
which he returnes again.

---

3   *wrought:*] ∼ . Q1-6, F, D.

Second PROLOGUE.

I had forgot one half I do protest,
20   *And now am sent again to speak the rest.*
He bowes to every great and noble Wit,
But to the little Hectors of the Pit
Our Poet's sturdy, and will not submit.
He'll be before-hand with 'em, and not stay
To see each peevish Critick stab his Play:
Each Puny Censor, who his skill to boast,
Is cheaply witty on the Poets cost.
No Criticks verdict, should, of right, stand good,
They are excepted all as men of blood:
30   *And the same Law should shield him from their fury*
Which has excluded Butchers from a Jury.
You'd all be Wits————
But writing's tedious, and that way may fail;
The most compendious method is to rail:
Which you so like, you think your selves ill us'd
When in smart Prologues you are not abus'd.
A civil Prologue is approv'd by no man;
You hate it as you do a Civil woman:
Your Fancy's pall'd, and liberally you pay
40   *To have it quicken'd, e're you see a Play.*
Just as old Sinners worn from their delight,
Give money to be whip'd to appetite.
But what a Pox keep I so much ado
To save our Poet? he is one of you;
A Brother Judgment, and as I hear say,
A cursed Critick as e're damn'd a Play.
Good salvage Gentlemen your own kind spare,
He is, like you, a very Wolf, or Bear;
Yet think not he'll your ancient rights invade,
50   *Or stop the course of your free damning trade:*
For he, (he vows) at no friends Play can sit

But he must needs find fault to shew his Wit:
Then, for his sake, ne're stint your own delight;
Throw boldly, for he sets to all that write;
With such he ventures on an even lay,
For they bring ready money into Play.
Those who write not, and yet all Writers nick,
Are Bankrupt Gamesters, for they damn on Tick.

PROLOGUE

Spoken by Mrs. Boutell *to the* Maiden
Queen, *in mans Cloathes.*

WOMEN like us (passing for men) you'l cry,
Presume too much upon your Secresie.
There's not a fop in town but will pretend,
To know the cheat himself, or by his friend.
Then make no words on't, Gallants tis e'ne true,
We are condemn'd to look, and strut, like you.
Since we thus freely our hard fate confess,
Accept us these bad times in any dress.
You'l find the sweet on't, now old Pantaloons
Will go as far as formerly new Gowns,
And from your own cast Wigs expect no frowns.
The Ladies we shall not so easily please;
They'l say what impudent bold things are these
That dare provoke, yet cannot do us right,
Like men with huffing looks, that dare not fight.
But this reproach, our courage must not daunt,
The Bravest Souldier may a Weapon want,

Let Her that doubts us, still send Her Gallant.
Ladies in us, you'l Youth and Beauty find,
20   All things but one, according to your mind.
And when your Eyes and Ears are feasted here,
Rise up and make out the short Meal elsewhere.

THE PERSONS.

Queen of *Sicily*——————————— Mrs *Marshall.*

Candiope, Princess of the Blood—— Mrs *Quin.*

Asteria, the Queens Confident—— Mrs *Knep.*

Florimell, A Maid of Honour—— Mrs *Ellen Guyn.*

Flavia, another Maid of Honour—— Mrs *Frances Davenport.*

Olinda,⎫ Sisters.——————— Mrs *Rutter.*
Sabina,⎭ Mrs *Eliz. Davenport.*

Melissa, Mother to *Olinda* and *Sabina* Mrs *Cory.*

Lysimantes, first Prince of the Blood Mr. *Burt.*

Philocles, the Queens favourite—— Major *Mohun.*

Celadon, a Courtier——————— Mr. *Hart.*

Guards.

Pages of Honour.

Souldiers.

The Scene *SICILY.*

SECRET LOVE,

OR THE

MAIDEN-QUEEN.

ACT I. SCENE I.

The Scene is Walks, near the Court.

Enter Celadon, Asteria, *meeting each other: he in riding habit;
they embrace.*

Celadon. Dear *Asteria!*

Asteria. My dear Brother! welcome; a thousand welcomes: Me
thinks this year you have been absent has been so tedious! I hope
as you have made a pleasant Voyage, so you have brought your
good humour back again to Court.

Cel. I never yet knew any Company I could not be merry in,
except it were an old Womans.

Ast. Or at a Funeral.

Cel. Nay, for that you shall excuse me; for I was never merrier
10 then I was at a Creditors of mine, whose Book perished with
him. But what new Beauties have you at Court? How do *Melissa*'s
two fair Daughters?

Ast. When you tell me which of 'em you are in love with, I'le
answer you.

Cel. Which of 'em, naughty sister, what a question's there?
With both of 'em, with each and singular of 'em.

Ast. Bless me! you are not serious!

---

1   *Celadon*] Q3–6, F, D; *Celedon* Q1–2.   8   Funeral.] Q2–6, F, D; ∼ ; Q1.

Cel. You look as if it were a wonder to see a man in love: are
they not handsome?

Ast. I, but both together————

Cel. I, and both asunder; why, I hope there are but two of 'em,
the tall Singing and Dancing one, and the little Innocent one?

Ast. But you cannot marry both?

Cel. No, nor either of 'em I trust in Heaven; but I can keep
them company, I can sing and dance with 'em, and treat 'em, and
that, I take it, is somewhat better then musty marrying them:
Marriage is poor folks pleasure that cannot go to the cost of
variety: but I am out of danger of that with these two, for I love
'em so equally I can never make choice between 'em: Had I but
one mistress, I might go to her to be merry, and she, perhaps, be
out of humour; there were a visit lost: But here, if one of 'em
frown upon me, the other will be the more obliging, on purpose
to recommend her own gayety, besides a thousand things that I
could name.

Ast. And none of 'em to any purpose.

Cel. Well, if you will not be cruel to a poor Lover, you might
oblige me by carrying me to their lodgings.

Ast. You know I am always busie about the Queen.

Cel. But once or twice onely, till I am a little flush'd in my
acquaintance with other Ladies, and have learn'd to prey for my
self: I promise you I'le make all the haste I can to end your
trouble, by being in love somewhere else.

Ast. You would think it hard to be deny'd now.

Cel. And reason good: many a man hangs himself for the loss
of one Mistris; How do you think then I should bear the loss
of two; especially in a Court where I think Beauty is but thin
sown.

Ast. There's one *Florimell* the Queen's Ward, a new Beauty, as
wilde as you, and a vast Fortune.

Cel. I am for her before the world: bring me to her, and I'le
release you of your promise for the other two.

Enter a Page.

Page. Madam, the Queen expects you.

Cel. I see you hold her favour; Adieu Sister, you have a little Emissary there, otherwise I would offer you my service.

Ast. Farwel Brother, think upon *Florimell.*

Cel. You may trust my memory for an handsome woman, I'le think upon her, and the rest too; I'le forget none of 'em.

Exit Asteria *and Page.*

SCENE II.

Enter a Gentleman walking over the Stage hastily:
after him, Florimell, *and* Flavia, *Masqued.*

Fla. Phormio, Phormio, you will not leave us———
Gent. In faith I have a little business———   *Exit Gentle.*
Cel. Cannot I serve you in the Gentlemans room, Ladies?
Fla. Which of us would you serve?
Cel. Either of you, or both of you.
Fla. Why, could you not be constant to one?
Cel. Constant to one! I have been a Courtier, a Souldier, and a Traveller, to good purpose, if I must be constant to one; give me some Twenty, some Forty, some a Hundred Mistresses, I have
10 more Love than any one woman can turn her to.
Flor. Bless us, let us be gone Cousin; we two are nothing in his hands.
Cel. Yet for my part, I can live with as few Mistresses as any man: I desire no superfluities; onely for necessary change or so; as I shift my Linnen.
Flor. A pretty odd kind of fellow this: he fits my humour rarely:———   *[Aside.*
Fla. You are as unconstant as the Moon.
Flor. You wrong him, he's as constant as the Sun; he would see
20 all the world round in 24 hours.

52   *Page.* Madam,] Q4–5, D; Madam Q1–3, Q6, F.
57+   *s.d.* Asteria *and Page.*] Asteria. Q1–6, F, D.
s.d. Florimell] Florimel Q1–6, F, D.   *s.d.* Flavia,] Q4–5, F; ∼∧ Q1–3, Q6, D.
7   *Cel.*] Q2–6, F, D; ∼∧ Q1.   17   *Aside*] Q3–6, F, D; *aside* Q1–2.
18   Moon.] Q2–6, F, D; ∼ : Q1.

Cel. 'Tis very true, Madam, but, like him, I would visit and away.

Flor. For what an unreasonable thing it were to stay long, be troublesome, and hinder a Lady of a fresh Lover.

Cel. A rare Creature this! [*Aside.*] ————Besides Madam, how like a fool a man looks, when after all his eagerness of two Minutes before, he shrinks into a faint kiss and a cold complement. Ladies both, into your hands I commit my selfe; share me betwixt you.

Fla. I'll have nothing to do with you, since you cannot be constant to one.

Cel. Nay, rather then loose either of you, I'll do more; I'll be constant to an 100 of you: or, (if you will needs fetter me to one,) agree the matter between your selves; and the most handsome take me.

Flor. Though I am not she, yet since my Masque's down, and you cannot convince me, have a good faith of my Beauty, and for once I take you for my servant.

Cel. And for once, I'll make a blind bargain with you: strike hands; is't a Match Mistriss?

Flor. Done Servant.

Cel. Now I am sure I have the worst on't: for you see the worst of me, and that I do not of you till you shew your face: ————Yet now I think on't, you must be handsome.————

Flor. What kind of Beauty do you like?

Cel. Just such a one as yours.

Flor. What's that?

Cel. Such an Ovall face, clear skin, hazle eyes, thick brown Eye-browes, and Hair as you have for all the world.

Fla. But I can assure you she has nothing of all this.

Cel. Hold thy peace Envy; nay I can be constant an' I set on't.

Flor. 'Tis true she tells you.

Cel. I, I, you may slander your self as you please; then you have,————let me see.

Flor. I'll swear you shan'not see.————

Cel. A turn'd up Nose, that gives an air to your face: Oh, I find
I am more and more in love with you! a full neather-lip, an
out-mouth, that makes mine water at it: the bottom of your
cheeks a little blub, and two dimples when you smile: for your
60 stature 'tis well, and for your wit 'twas given you by one that
knew it had been thrown away upon an ill face; come you are
handsome, there's no denying it.

Flor. Can you settle your spirits to see an ugly face, and not be
frighted, I could find in my heart to lift up my Masque and
disabuse you.

Cel. I defie your Masque, would you would try the experiment.

Flor. No, I won'not; for your ignorance is the Mother of your
devotion to me.

Cel. Since you will not take the pains to convert me I'll make
70 bold to keep my faith: a miserable man I am sure you have
made me.

Fla. This is pleasant.

Cel. It may be so to you but it is not to me; for ought I see, I
am going to be the most constant *Maudlin.*————

Flor. 'Tis very well, *Celadon,* you can be constant to one you
have never seen; and have forsaken all you have seen.

Cel. It seems you know me then: well, if thou shou'dst prove
one of my cast Mistresses I would use thee most damnably, for
offering to make me love thee twice.

80   *Flor.* You are i'th' right: an old Mistriss or Servant is an old
Tune, the pleasure on't is past, when we have once learnt it.

Fla. But what woman in the world would you wish her like?

Cel. I have heard of one *Florimell* the Queens Ward, would
she were as like her for Beauty, as she is for Humour.

Fla. Do you hear that Cousin?————   [*To* Flor. *aside.*

Flor. Florimell's not handsome: besides she's unconstant; and
only loves for some few days.

---

56   Nose,] Q2–6, F, D; ~ : Q1.   62   it.] Q4–6, F, D; ~ : Q1–3.
66   experiment.] Q2–6, F, D; ~ : Q1.   83   *Florimell*] Florimel Q1–6, F, D.
85   Cousin?————] ~ :———— Q1–5; ~ˌ———— Q6; ~ ?ˌ F, D.
85   [*To* Flor. *aside.*] Q5–6, D (*Aside.*] Q6); (to *Flor.* aside.) Q1–3 (asideˌ Q3);
[to *Flor.* aside. Q4; [*Aside to* Flor. F.
87   days.] Q2–6, F, D; ~ , Q1.

Cel. If she loves for shorter time then I, she must love by
Winter daies and Summer nights ifaith.

Flor. When you see us together you shall judge: in the mean
time adieu sweet servant.

Cel. Why you won'not be so inhumane to carry away my heart
and not so much as tell me where I may hear news on't?

Flor. I mean to keep it safe for you; for if you had it, you
would bestow it worse: farwell, I must see a Lady.

Cel. So must I too, if I can pull off your Masque————

Flor. You will not be so rude, I hope.

Cel. By this light but I will.

Flor. By this leg but you shan'not.

                         [*Exeunt* Flor. & Flavia *running.*

SCENE III.

Enter Philocles, *and meets him going out.*

Cel. How! my Cousin the new Favourite!————   [*Aside.*

Phil. Dear *Celadon!* most happily arriv'd.
I hear y'have been an honour to your Country
In the *Calabrian* Wars, and I am glad
I have some interest in't.

Cel. ————————But in you
I have a larger subject for my joyes:
To see so rare a thing as rising vertue,
And merit understood at Court.

Phil. Perhaps it is the onely act that can
Accuse our Queen of weakness.

Enter Lysimantes *attended.*

———————

89 ifaith.] Q2–6, F, D; ~ : Q1.
97 hope.] Q3–5, F, D; ~ ; Q1–2; ~ ? Q6.
99 shan'not.] Q4–6, F, D; ~ : Q1–3.
SCENE] Q3–6, F, D; ~ . Q1–2.
1 [*Aside*] Q5–6, F, D; [*aside* Q1 (*some copies*), Q2–4; ∧*aside* Q1 (*some copies*).
10+ s.d. *Enter* Lysimantes] Q3–6, F, D; *Enter* Lysimantes Q1–2.

95 Lady.] Q2–6, F, D; ~ : Q1.
98 will.] Q6, F, D; ~ : Q1–5.

1 *Cel.*] Q2–6, F, D; ~∧ Q1.

Lys. O, my Lord *Philocles,* well overtaken!
I came to look you.
    Phil.   Had I known it sooner
My swift attendance, Sir, had spar'd your trouble.
[*To* Cel.] ———Cousin, you see Prince *Lysimantes*
Is pleased to favour me with his Commands:
I beg you'l be no stranger now at Court.
    Cel. So long as there be Ladies there, you need
Not doubt me.   *Exit* Celadon.
    Phil. Some of them will, I hope, make you a Convert.
20   *Lys.* My Lord *Philocles,* I am glad we are alone;
There is a busines that concerns me nearly,
In which I beg your love.
    Phil.   Command my service.
    Lys. I know your Interest with the Queen is great;
(I speak not this as envying your fortune,
For frankly I confess you have deserv'd it.)
Besides, my Birth, my Courage, and my Honour,
Are all above so base a Vice———
    Phil. I know, my Lord, you are first Prince o'th' Blood;
Your Countries second hope;
30 And that the publick Vote, when the Queen weds,
Designes you for her choice.
    Lys.   I am not worthy,
Except Love makes desert;
For doubtless she's the glory of her time;
Of faultless Beauty, blooming as the Spring,
In our *Sicilian* Groves; matchless in Vertue,
And largely soul'd, where ere her bounty gives,
As with each breath she could create new *Indies.*
    Phil. But jealous of her glory.
    Lys. You are a Courtier; and in other terms,
40 Would say she is averse from marriage

---

12 you. / *Phil.* Had] F, D; you (*Phil.*) had Q1–6 (you. Q4–6; Had Q5–6).
14 [*To* Cel.]] ∧*To Cel.*∧ Q1–5 (*Cel,* Q2–3); [*To* Cel.∧ Q6, F, D (*at right*).
18 Celadon] Q3–6, F, D; *Celadon* Q1–2.
22 love. / *Phil.*] F, D; love. (*Phil.*) Q1–6.
31 worthy,] Q4–6, D; ~ . Q1–3, F.   36 soul'd] Q6, D; sould Q1–5, F.
37 *Indies*] Q3–5, F, D; Indies Q1–2, Q6.

Least it might lessen her authority.
But, whensoe're she does, I know the people
Will scarcely suffer her to match
With any neighb'ring Prince, whose power might bend
Our free *Sicilians* to a foreign Yoke.
    Phil. I love too well my Country to desire it.
    Lys. Then to proceed, (as you well know, my Lord)
The Provinces have sent their Deputies
Humbly to move her she would choose at home:
    50 And, for she seems averse from speaking with them,
By my appointment, have design'd these walks,
Where well she cannot shun them. Now, if you
Assist their suit, by joyning yours to it,
And by your mediation I prove happy,
I freely promise you————
    Phil. Without a Bribe command my utmost in it:————
And yet, there is a thing, which time may give me
The confidence to name:————
    Lys.   'Tis yours whatever.
But tell me true; does she not entertain
    60 Some deep, and setled thoughts against my person?
    Phil. I hope not so; but she, of late, is froward;
Reserv'd, and sad, and vex'd at little things;
Which, her great soul asham'd of, straight shakes off,
And is compos'd again.
    Lys. You are still near the Queen, and all our Actions come to
Princes eyes, as they are represented by them that hold the
mirour.
    Phil. Here she comes, and with her the Deputies;————
I fear all is not right.

    Enter Queen; Deputies after her; Asteria, *Guard,* Flavia,
              Olinda, Sabina.

    Queen turns back to the Deputies, and speaks entring.

41 lessen] Q4–6, D; lesson Q1–3, F.
55 you————] Q6, D; ~ .———— Q1–5, F.
58 name:———— / *Lys.*] Q4–5, F, D; name:———— (*Lys.*) Q1–3, Q6.
69+ *s.d. Guard*] D; Guard Q1–6, F.

Qu.   And I must tell you,
70 It is a sawcy boldness thus to press
On my retirements.————
    1 *Dep.* Our business being of no less concern
Then is the peace and quiet of your Subjects————
And that delay'd————
    2 *Dep.* ——————we humbly took this time
To represent your peoples fears to you.
    Qu. My peoples fears! who made them States-men?
They much mistake their business, if they think
It is to govern:————
The Rights of Subjects and of Soveraigns
80 Are things distinct in Nature: theirs, is to
Enjoy Propriety, not Empire.
    Lys. If they have err'd, 'twas but an over-care;
An ill-tim'd Duty.————
    Qu.   Cousin, I expect
From your near Bloud, not to excuse, but check 'em.
They would impose a Ruler
Upon their Lawful Queen:
For what's an Husband else?
    Lys. Farr, Madam, be it from the thoughts
Of any who pretends to that high Honour,
90 To wish for more then to be reckon'd
As the most grac'd, and first of all your servants.
    Qu. These are th' insinuating promises
Of those who aim at pow'r: but tell me Cousin;
(For you are unconcern'd and may be Judge)
Should that aspiring man compass his ends,
What pawn of his obedience could he give me,
When Kingly pow'r were once invested in him?
    Lys. What greater pledge then Love? when those fair eyes
Cast their commanding beams, he that cou'd be
100 A Rebel to your birth, must pay them homage.

————

72 1] D; 1. Q1–6, F.   74 And] Q4–6, F, D; and Q1–3.
74 2] D; 2. Q1–6, F.   87 else?] Q2–6, F, D; ∼ ; Q1.

Qu. All eyes are fair
That sparkle with the Jewels of a Crown:
But now I see my Government is odious;
My people find I am not fit to Reign,
Else they would never———
    Lys. So far from that, we all acknowledge you
The bounty of the Gods to *Sicilie:*
More than they are you cannot make our Joyes;
Make them but lasting in a Successor.
    Phil. Your people seek not to impose a Prince;
But humbly offer one to your free choice:
And such an one he is, (may I have leave
To speak some little of his great deserts.)
    Qu. I'le hear no more———
[*To the Dep.*] For you, attend to morrow at the Council,
There you shall have my firm resolves; mean time
My Cousin I am sure will welcome you.
    Lys. Still more and more mysterious: but I have gain'd one of
her women that shall unriddle it. [*Aside.*] ———Come Gentle-
men.———
    All Dep. Heav'n preserve your Majesty.
                     [*Exeunt* Lysimantes *and Deputies.*
    Qu. Philocles you may stay.
    Phil. I humbly wait your Majesties commands.
    Qu. Yet, now I better think on't, you may go.
    Phil. Madam!
    Qu. I have no commands———or, what's all one
You no obedience.
    Phil.   How, no obedience, Madam?
I plead no other merit; 'tis the Charter
By which I hold your favour, and my fortunes.
    Qu. My favours are cheap blessings, like Rain and Sun-shine,
For which we scarcely thank the Gods, because

---

111   choice] Q2-6, F, D; chioce Q1.
115   [*To the Dep.*]] ∧~ ·∧ Q1-6, F; [~ ·∧ D (*at right margin*).
119   it. [*Aside.*]] it: Q1-6, F, D.   121+ *s.d. Deputies*] D; Deputies Q1-6, F.
122   stay.] Q6, F, D; ~ : Q1-5.
126   commands———] Q6, D; ~ .——— Q1-5, F.

We daily have them.

   Phil. Madam, your Breath which rais'd me from the dust
May lay me there again
But fate nor time can ever make me loose
The sense of your indulgent bounties to me.

   Qu. You are above them now; grown popular:
Ah *Philocles,* could I expect from you
That usage! no tongue but yours
140 To move me to a marriage?——————   [*Weeps.*
The factious Deputies might have some end in't,
And my ambitious Cousin gain a Crown;
But what advantage could there come to you?
What could you hope from *Lysimantes* Reign
That you can want in mine?

   Phil. You your self clear me, Madam, had I sought
More pow'r, this Marriage sure was not the way.
But, when your safety was in question,
When all your people were unsatisfied,
150 Desir'd a King, nay more, design'd the Man,
It was my duty then.——————

   Qu. Let me be judge of my own safety;
I am a woman,
But danger from my Subjects cannot fright me.

   Phil. But *Lysimantes,* Madam, is a person——————

   Qu. I cannot love,——————
Shall I, I who am born a Sovereign Queen,
Be barr'd of that which God and Nature gives
The meanest Slave, a freedom in my love?
160 ——————Leave me, good *Philocles,* to my own thoughts;
When next I need your counsel I'le send for you——————

   Phil. I'm most unhappy in your high displeasure;
But, since I must not speak, Madam, be pleas'd

---

132 We] Q3–6, F, D; we Q1–2.   136 me.] Q2–6, F, D; ~∧ Q1.
139 usage] Q2–6, F, D; usage I have found Q1.
140 *Weeps.*] Q3–6, F, D; *weeps*∧ Q1–2.
144 Reign] Q3–5, F, D; Reign Q1–2, Q6.
148 question,] Q2–6, F, D; ~ . Q1.
162 *Phil.*] Q2–6, F, D; ~∧ Q1.

To peruse this, and therein, read my care.
>   *He plucks out a paper, and presents it to her, but*
>   *drops, unknown to him a picture; Exit* Philocles.
Queen reads. A Catalogue of such persons———
[*Spies the box.*] What's this he has let fall? *Asteria?*
   Ast. Your Majesty———
   Qu. Take that up, it fell from *Philocles.*
>   *She takes it up, looks on it, and smiles.*
   Qu. How now, what makes you merry?
   Ast. A small discovery I have made, Madam.
   Qu. Of what?
   Ast. Since first your Majesty grac'd *Philocles,*
I have not heard him nam'd for any Mistriss
But now this picture has convinc'd me.———
   Qu. Ha! Let me see it———   (*Snatches it from her.*)
Candiope, Prince *Lysimantes* sister!
   Ast. Your favour, Madam, may encourage him———
And yet he loves in a high place for him:
A Princess of the Blood, and what is more,
Beyond comparison the fairest Lady
Our Isle can boast.———
   Qu.   How! she the fairest
Beyond comparison? 'tis false, you flatter her;
She is not fair.———
   Ast. I humbly beg forgiveness on my knees,
If I offended you: But next yours, Madam,
Which all must yield to———
   Qu.   I pretend to none.
   Ast. She passes for a beauty.
   Qu. I, She may pass.———But why do I speak of her?
Dear *Asteria* lead me, I am not well o'th sudden.———
>   [*She faints.*

---

164   care.] Q2–6, F, D; ∼ : Q1.
164+   s.d. her, but] Q4–5, F; ∼ . But Q1, Q6; ∼∧ But Q2–3; ∼ ; but D.
165   reads. A] D; reads.——— / A Q1–6, F.
166   [Spies the box.]]∧∼∧ Q1–6, F; [∼∧ D (at right margin).
170   Madam.] Q2–6, F, D; ∼ ; Q1.
182   false, you flatter] some copies of Q1 have fal se,uflatter.
185   Madam] Madam Q1–6, F, D.   186   none.] Q2–6, F, D; ∼∧ Q1.
189+   s.d. faints.] Q3–6, F, D; ∼∧ Q1–2.

190   *Ast.* Who's near there? help the Queen.

                                            The Guards are coming.

        Qu. Bid 'em away, 'twas but a qualm,
        And 'tis already going.————

          Ast. Dear Madam what's the matter?
        You are of late so alter'd I scarce know you.
        You were gay humour'd, and you now are pensive,
        Once calm, and now unquiet;
        Pardon my boldness that I press thus far
        Into your secret thoughts: I have at least
        A subjects share in you.

          Qu.   Thou hast a greater,
200   That of a friend; but am I froward, saist thou!

          Ast. It ill becomes me, Madam, to say that.

          Qu. I know I am: prithee forgive me for it.
        I cannot help it, but thou hast
        Not long to suffer it.

          Ast. Alas!

          Qu. I feel my strength each day and hour consume,
        Like Lillies wasting in a Lymbecks heat.
        Yet a few dayes————
        And thou shalt see me lie all damp and cold,
210   Shrowded within some hollow Vault, among
        My silent Ancestors.

          Ast.   O dearest Madam!
        Speak not of death, or think not, if you die
        That I will stay behind.

          Qu. Thy love has mov'd me, I for once will have
        The pleasure to be pitied; I'le unfold
        A thing so strange, so horrid of my self;————

          Ast. Bless me, sweet Heaven! So horrid, said you, Madam?

          Qu. That Sun, who with one look surveys the Globe,

190+   *s.d. coming.*] Q3–6, F, D; ~ , Q1; ~∧ Q2.
193   matter?] matter! y'are Q1 (*but errata directs to omit* "you are" [*sic*] *from this line*), Q2–6, F; matter! D.
206   each day and hour] Q2–6, F, D; insensibly Q1.
217   Heaven! So] Heaven! / So Q1–6, F, D.

Sees not a wretch like me: and could the world
20 Take a right measure of my state within,
Mankind must either pity me, or scorn me.
   Ast. Sure none could do the last.
   Qu.   Thou long'st to know it:
And I to tell thee, but shame stops my mouth.
First promise me thou wilt excuse my folly,
And next be secret.————
   Ast. —————————Can you doubt it Madam!
   Qu. Yet you might spare my labour; can you not guess?————
   Ast. Madam, please you, I'le try.
   Qu.   Hold, *Asteria:*
I would not have you guess, for should you find it
I should imagine, that some other might,
30 And then, I were most wretched.
Therefore, though you should know it, flatter me:
And say you could not guess it.————
   Ast. Madam, I need not flatter you, I cannot.
And yet,————
Might not Ambition trouble your repose?
   Qu. My *Sicily* I thank the Gods, contents me.
But since I must reveal it, know 'tis love:
I who pretended so to glory, am
Become the slave of love.————
40   *Ast.* I thought your Majesty had fram'd designes
To subvert all your Laws; become a Tyrant,
Or vex your neighbours with injurious wars;
Is this all, Madam?
   Qu.   Is not this enough?
Then, know, I love below my self; a Subject;
Love one who loves another, and who knows not
That I love him.

226 labour; can . . . guess?————] labour; / Can . . . guess———— Q1–6, F, D.
227 Hold,] Q4–6, D; ~ : Q1–3, F.
233–234 cannot. / And yet,————] cannot.————and yet, Q1–3; cannot,————
and yet, Q4–5; cannot————and yet, Q6, F, D.
243 all, Madam?] Q5, D; ~ ? ~ ? Q1; ~ ? ~ . Q2–4, F; ~ , ~ . Q6.

Ast.   He must be told it, Madam.

Qu. Not for the world, *Asteria:*
When ere he knows it I shall die for shame.

Ast. What is it then that would content you?

250   *Qu.* Nothing, but that I had not lov'd.

Ast. May I not ask without offence who 'tis?

Qu. Ev'n that confirms me I have lov'd amiss;
Since thou canst know I love, and not imagine
It must be *Philocles.*

Ast. My Cousin is indeed a most deserving person;
Valiant and wise; and handsome; and well born.

Qu. But not of Royal bloud:
I know his fate unfit to be a King.
To be his wife I could forsake my Crown;

260   But not my glory:
Yet,———would he did not love *Candiope;*
Would he lov'd me,———but knew not of my love,
Or ere durst tell me his.

Ast.   In all this Labyrinth,
I find one path conducing to your quiet.

Qu. O tell me quickly then.

Ast. Candiope, as Princess of the Bloud
Without your approbation cannot marry:
First break his match with her, by vertue of
Your Sovereign Authority.

270   *Qu.* I fear that were to make him hate me,
Or, what's as bad, to let him know I love him:
Could you not do it of your self?

Ast. Ile not be wanting to my pow'r
But if your Majesty appears not in it
The love of *Philocles* will soon surmount

---

247 world,] Q4–6, D; ~ : Q1–3, F.
250 lov'd.] Q2–6, F, D; ~ ? Q1.   254   *Philocles.*] Q2, Q4–6, F, D; ~ₐ Q1, Q3.
256 born.] Q2–6, F, D; ~ , Q1.
259–260 Crown; / But] Crown; but Q1–6, F, D.
263 his. / *Ast.*] Q4–6, F, D; his: *Ast.* Q1–3.   264 quiet.] Q2–6, F, D; ~ , Q1.
270   I fear that] Q3–5, D; *I fear. That* Q1–2, Q6, F.
270 me,] Q4–5; ~ . Q1–3, Q6, F, D.

All other difficulties.

   Qu. Then, as we walk, we'l think what means are best;
Effect but this, and thou shar'st halfe my breast.   *Exeunt.*

ACT II.

SCENE, *The Queens appartments.*

Asteria, *sola.*

   Ast. Nothing thrives that I have plotted:
For I have sounded *Philocles,* and find
He is too constant to *Candiope:*
Her too I have assaulted, but in vain,
Objecting want of quality in *Philocles.*
I'le to the Queen, and plainly tell her
She must make use of her Authority
To break the match.

Enter Celadon *looking about him.*

                        Brother! what make you here
About the Queens appartments?
Which of the Ladies are you watching for?
   Cel. Any of 'em that will do me the good turn to make me
soundly in love.
   Ast. Then I'le bespeak you one; you will be desp'rately in love
with *Florimell:* so soon as the Queen heard you were return'd
she gave you her for Mistriss.
   Cel. Thank her Majesty; but to confess the truth my fancy
lies partly another way.

277   best;] Q6; ~∧ Q1; ~ , Q2–5, F, D.
s.d. SCENE,] SCENE I. Q1–6, F, D.
s.d. and 1 Asteria, sola. / Ast.] Asteria, / Sola. [as a speech heading] Q1–6, F;
Asteria sola. [as a stage direction] D.
3   Candiope:] Q2–6, F, D; ~∧ Q1.
8   match.] match. / SCENE. II. Q1–6, F, D.
14   Florimell] Florimel Q1–6, F, D.

Ast. That's strange: *Florimell* vows you are already in love with her.

20   *Cel.* She wrongs me horribly, if ever I saw or spoke with this *Florimell.*

Ast. Well, take your fortune, I must leave you.   [*Exit* Asteria.

Enter Florimell, *sees him, and is running back.*

Cel. Nay 'faith I am got betwixt you and home, you are my pris'ner, Lady bright, till you resolve me one question.

She signs she is dumb.

Pox; I think she's dumb: what a vengeance dost thou at Court, with such a rare face, without a tongue to answer to a kind question? Art thou dumb indeed, then, thou canst tell no tales,———   [*Goes to kiss her.*

Flor. Hold, hold, you are not mad!

30   *Cel.* Oh, my miss in a Masque! have you found your tongue?

Flor. 'Twas time, I think; what had become of me, if I had not?

Cel. Methinks your lips had done as well.

Flor. I, if my Masque had been over 'em, as it was when you met me in the walks.

Cel. Well; will you believe me another time? did not I say you were infinitely handsome: they may talk of *Florimell,* if they will, but i'faith she must come short of you.

Flor. Have you seen her, then?

Cel. I look'd a little that way, but I had soon enough of her,
40 she is not to be seen twice without a surfeit.

Flor. However you are beholding to her, they say she loves you.

Cel. By fate she shan'not love me: I have told her a piece of my

---

18 *Florimell*] *Florimel* Q1–6, F, D.   21 *Florimell*] *Florimel* Q1–6, F, D.
22 Asteria] Q3–5, F, D; *Asteria* Q1–2, Q6.
22+ *s.d. Enter* Florimell] SCENE, III. / *Enter* Florimel Q1–6, F, D.
24+ *s.d. She signs she is dumb.*] *She signs. She is dumb.* [*as if a speech*] Q1–5, F; *She Signs? She is dumb?* [*as part of speech*] Q6; [*She makes signs she is dumb.*] D.
27 question?] Q4–6, D; ~ . Q1–3, F.
28 *s.d.* [*Goes to kiss her.*] Q6, D; goes to kiss her. Q1–5, F.
36 *Florimell*] *Florimel* Q1–6, F, D.

mind already: pox o' these coming women: they set a man to dinner before he has an appetite.

Flavia *at the door.*

Fla. Florimell you are call'd within.————   [*Exit.*

Cel. I hope in the Lord you are not *Florimell.*

Flor. Ev'n she at your service; the same kind and coming *Florimell* you have describ'd.

Cel. Why then we are agreed already, I am as kind and coming as you for the heart of you: I knew at first we two were good for nothing but one another.

Flor. But, without raillery, are you in Love?

Cel. So horribly much, that contrary to my own Maxims, I think in my conscience I could marry you.

Flor. No, no, 'tis not come to that yet: but if you are really in love you have done me the greatest pleasure in the world.

Cel. That pleasure, and a better too I have in store for you.

Flor. This Animal call'd a Lover I have long'd to see these two years.

Cel. Sure you walk'd with your mask on all the while, for if you had been seen, you could not have been without your wish.

Flor. I warrant you mean an ordinary whining Lover; but I must have other proofs of love ere I believe it.

Cel. You shall have the best that I can give you.

Flor. I would have a Lover, that if need be, should hang himself, drown himself, break his neck, and poyson himself for very despair: he that will scruple this is an impudent fellow if he sayes he is in love.

Cel. Pray, Madam, which of these four things would you have your Lover do? for a man's but a man, he cannot hang, and drown, and break his neck, and poyson himself, altogether.

44+   *s.d.* Flavia] [*Flavia* Q1–2; [Flavia Q3–6, F, D.
45   *Fla. Florimell*] D (*Florimel*); *Florimel* Q1–6, F.
45   *Exit.*] Q3–6, F, D; ∼∧ Q1–2.
46   *Florimell.*] *Florimel;* Q1–3; *Florimel?* Q4–6; *Florimel.* D, F.
47–48   *Florimell*] *Florimel* Q1–6, F, D.   48   describ'd.] Q4–6, F, D; ∼ : Q1–3.
62   *Flor.*] Q2–6, F, D; ∼∧ Q1.
66   and poyson] Q2, Q6, F; or poyson Q1; poison Q3–5, D.

Flor. Well then, because you are but a beginner, and I would not discourage you, any one of these shall serve your turn in a fair way.

Cel. I am much deceiv'd in those eyes of yours, if a Treat, a Song, and the Fiddles, be not a more acceptable proof of love to you, then any of those Tragical ones you have mentioned.

Flor. However you will grant it is but decent you should be pale, and lean, and melancholick to shew you are in love: and
80 that I shall require of you when I see you next.

Cel. When you see me next? why you do not make a Rabbet of me, to be lean at 24 hours warning? in the mean while we burn daylight, loose time and love.

Flor. Would you marry me without consideration?

Cel. To choose, by heaven, for they that think on't, twenty to one would never do it, hang forecast; to make sure of one good night is as much in reason as a man should expect from this ill world.

Flor. Methinks a few more years and discretion would do well:
90 I do not like this going to bed so early; it makes one so weary before morning.

Cel. That's much as your pillow is laid before you go to sleep.

Flor. Shall I make a proposition to you? I will give you a whole year of probation to love me in; to grow reserv'd, discreet, sober and faithful, and to pay me all the services of a Lover.———

Cel. And at the end of it you'll marry me?

Flor. If neither of us alter our minds before.———

Cel. By this light a necessary clause.———But if I pay in all the foresaid services before the day, you shall be obliged to take
100 me sooner into mercy.

Flor. Provided if you prove unfaithful, then your time of a Twelve-month to be prolong'd; so many services I will bate you so many dayes or weeks; so many faults I will add to your 'Prentiship, so much more: And of all this I onely to be Judg.

Enter Philocles *and* Lysimantes.

72 *Flor.*] Q2–6, F, D; ∼ , Q1.   83 love.] Q2–6, F, D; ∼∧ Q1.
86 of one] Q2–6, F, D; ∼ , Q1.   98 But] F, D; but Q1–6.
103 add] Q2–6, F, D; add more Q1 (*but corrected in Errata*).
104+ *s.d. Enter*] SCENE IV. / *Enter* Q1–6, F, D.

Lys. Is the Queen this way, Madam?

Flor. I'le see, so please your Highness: Follow me, Captive.

                             [*She pulls him.*

Cel. March on Conquerour———   [*Exeunt* Cel. Flor.

Lys. You're sure her Majesty will not oppose it?

Phil. Leave that to me my Lord.

Lys. Then, though perhaps my Sisters birth might challenge

An higher match,

I'le weigh your merits on the other side

To make the ballance even.

Phil. I go my Lord this minute.

Lys. My best wishes wait on you.   [*Exit* Lysimantes.

        Enter the Queen and Asteria.

Qu. Yonder he is; have I no other way?

Ast. O Madam, you must stand this brunt:

Deny him now, and leave the rest to me:

I'le to *Candiope*'s Mother,

And under the pretence of friendship, work

On her Ambition to put off a match

So mean as *Philocles.*

Qu. to Phil.   You may approach, Sir,

We two discourse no secrets.

Phil. I come, Madam, to weary out your royal bounty.

Qu. Some suit I warrant for your Cousin *Celadon.*

Leave his advancement to my care.

Phil. Your goodness still prevents my wishes:———

Yet I have one request

Might it not pass almost for madness, and

Extream Ambition in me.———

Qu. You know you have a favourable Judg,

It lies in you not to ask any thing

---

107   Cel. Flor.] Q3–6, F, D; *Cel. Flor.* Q1–2.   113   even.] Q2–6, F, D; ~∧ Q1.
115   Lysimantes] Q3–6, F, D; *Lysimantes* Q1–2.
115+   *s.d. Enter*] SCENE V. / *Enter* Q1–6, F, D.
122   *Qu. to Phil.* . . . Sir,] [*Qu. to* Phil.] . . . Sir, Q1–6, F (*Phil.* Q2, Q6, F);
Queen. . . . Sir: [*To* Phil. D.
127–128   wishes:——— / Yet] Q5, D; wishes:———yet Q1–4, Q6, F.

I cannot grant.

   Phil. Madam, perhaps you think me now too faulty:
But Love alone inspires me with ambition,
Though but to look on fair *Candiope,*
Were an excuse for both.

   Qu. Keep your Ambition, and let Love alone;
That I can cloy, but this I cannot cure.
140 I have some reasons (invincible to me)
Which must forbid your marriage with *Candiope.*

   Phil. I knew I was not worthy.

   Qu.   Not for that;
Philocles, you deserve all things, and to show
I think it, my Admiral I hear is dead,
His vacant place (the best in all my Kingdom,)
I here confer on you.

   Phil. Rather take back all you have giv'n before,
Then not give this.
For believe, Madam, nothing is so near
150 My soul, as the possession of *Candiope.*

   Qu. Since that belief would be your disadvantage,
I will not entertain it.

   Phil. Why, Madam, can you be thus cruel to me?
To give me all things which I did not ask,
And yet deny that onely thing I beg:
And so beg that I find I cannot live
Without the hope of it.

   Qu.   Hope greater things;
But hope not this. Haste to o'recome your love,
It is but putting a short liv'd passion to a violent death.

---

136   on] Q2–6, F, D; from Q1 (*but corrected in Errata*).
136–137   *Candiope,* / Were] *Candiope,* were Q1–6, F, D.
137   both.] Q2–6, F, D; ∼ ? Q1.
140–141   me) / Which . . . forbid your] me) which . . . forbid / Your Q1–6,
F, D.
142–143   that; / *Philocles,*] that, *Philocles,* Q1–6, F; that, *Philocles;* D.
143   things, and] things, / And Q1–6, F, D.
143–144   show / I] show I Q1–6, F, D.
144   dead,] Q2, Q4–6, F; ∼ᴧ Q1; ∼ . Q3, D.
156   so] Q2–6, F, D; to Q1 (*but corrected in Errata*).

Phil. I cannot live without *Candiope.*
But I can die without a murmure,
Having my doom pronounced from your fair mouth.
    Qu. If I am to pronounce it, live my *Philocles,*
But live without (I was about to say
Without his love, but that I cannot do)   [*Aside.*
Live *Philocles* without *Candiope.*
    Phil. Ah, Madam, could you give my doom so quickly
And knew it was irrevocable!
'Tis too apparent
You who alone love glory, and whose soul
Is loosned from your senses, cannot judg
What torments mine, of grosser mould, endures.
    Qu. I cannot suffer you
To give me praises which are not my own:
I love like you, and am yet much more wretched
Then you can think your self.
    Phil. Weak barrs they needs must be that fortune puts
'Twixt Soveraign Power, and all it can desire.
When Princes love, they call themselves unhappy,
Onely because the word sounds handsome in
A Lovers mouth.
But you can cease to be so when you please
By making *Lysimantes* fortunate.
    Qu. Were he indeed the man, you had some reason;
But 'tis another, more without my power,
And yet a subject too.
    Phil. O, Madam, say not so,
It cannot be a Subject if not he.
It were to be injurious to your self
To make another choice.
    Qu. Yet *Lysimantes,* set by him I love,
Is more obscur'd then Stars too near the Sun;
He has a brightness of his own,
Not borrow'd of his Fathers, but born with him.

---

165   *Aside*] Q4–6, F, D; *aside* Q1–3.   180–181 in / A] in a Q1–6, F, D.

Phil. Pardon me if I say, who'ere he be,
He has practis'd some ill Acts upon you, Madam;
For he, whom you describe, I see is born
But from the lees o'th people.
　　Qu. You offend me *Philocles.*
200 Whence had you leave to use those insolent terms
Of him I please to love: one I must tell you,
(Since foolishly I have gone on thus far)
Whom I esteem your equal,
And far superiour to Prince *Lysimantes;*
One who deserves to wear a Crown.————
　　Phil. Whirlwinds bear me hence before I live
To that detested day.————That frown assures me
I have offended, by my over freedom;
But yet me thinks a heart so plain and honest
210 And zealous of your glory, might hope your pardon for it.
　　Qu. I give it you; but when you know him better
You'l alter your opinion;
He's no ill friend of yours.
　　Phil.　　　　　　　　　I well perceive
He has supplanted me in your esteem;
But that's the least of ills this fatal wretch
Has practis'd.————Think, for Heavens sake, Madam, think
If you have drunk no Phylter.
　　Qu. Yes he has given me a Phylter;————
But I have drunk it onely from his eyes.
220 *Phil.* Hot Irons thank 'em for't.————　　　[*Softly or turn-
　　　　　　　　　　　　　　　　　　　　　ing from her.*
　　Qu.　　　　　　　　　　What's that you mutter?
Hence from my sight: I know not whether
I ever shall endure to see you more.
　　Phil.————But hear me, Madam.
　　Qu. I say be gone. ————See me no more this day.————
I will not hear one word in your excuse:
Now, Sir, be rude again; *And give Laws to your Queen.*

---

198 But] Q3–6, F, D; but Q1–2.　　　211 but when] but / When Q1–6, F, D.
212–213 opinion; / He's] opinion; he's Q1–6, F, D.
223 Madam.] Q5; ~ : Q1–4, Q6, F; ~∧ D.

Exit Philocles *bowing.*

Asteria, come hither.
Was ever boldness like to this of *Philocles?*
Help me to reproach him; for I resolve
Henceforth no more to love him.

   Ast. Truth is, I wondred at your patience, Madam:
Did you not mark his words, his meen, his action,
How full of haughtiness, how small respect?

   Qu. And he to use me thus, he whom I favour'd,
Nay more, he whom I lov'd?

   Ast. A man, me thinks, of vulgar parts and presence!

   Qu. Or allow him something handsome, valiant, or so———
Yet this to me!———

   Ast. The workmanship of inconsiderate favour,
The Creature of rash love; one of those Meteors
Which Monarchs raise from earth,
And people wondring how they came so high,
Fear, from their influence, Plagues, and Wars, and Famine.

   Qu. Ha!

   Ast. One whom instead of banishing a day,
You should have plum'd of all his borrow'd honours:
And let him see what abject things they are
Whom Princes often love without desert.

   Qu. What has my *Philocles* deserv'd from thee
That thou shouldst use him thus?
Were he the basest of Mankind thou could'st not
Have given him ruder language.

   Ast. Did not your Majesty command me,
Did not your self begin?

   Qu. I grant I did, but I have right to do it;
I love him, and may rail; ———in you 'tis malice;
Malice in the most high degree; for never man
Was more deserving then my *Philocles.*
Or, do you love him, ha! and plead that title?
Confess, and I'le forgive you.———
For none can look on him but needs must love.

   Ast. I love him, Madam! I beseech your Majesty
Have better thoughts of me.

Qu. Dost thou not love him then?
Good Heav'n, how stupid and how dull is she!
How most invincibly insensible!
No woman does deserve to live
That loves not *Philocles.*———

    Ast. Dear madam, recollect your self; alas
270 How much distracted are your thoughts, and how
Dis-jointed all your words;———
The Sybills leaves more orderly were laid.
Where is that harmony of mind, that prudence
Which guided all you did, that sense of glory
Which rais'd you, high above the rest of Kings
As Kings are o're the level of mankind?

    Qu. Gone, gone *Asteria,* all is gone,
Or lost within me far from any use.
Sometimes I struggle like the Sun in Clouds,
280 But straight I am o'recast.———

    Ast.   I grieve to see it.———

    Qu. Then thou hast yet the goodness
To pardon what I said.———
Alas, I use my self much worse then thee.
Love rages in great souls,———
For there his pow'r most opposition finds;
High trees are shook, because they dare the winds.   [*Exeunt.*

ACT III.

SCENE of the Act, *The Court Gallery.*

Philocles, *solus.*

    Phil. 'Tis true, she banish'd me but for a day;
But Favourites, once declining, sink apace.

---

264 then?] Q5; ~ ! Q1–4, Q6, F, D.
274 did,] ~ ! Q1–3, Q6, F, D; ~ ? Q4–5.
276 mankind?] Q4–5; ~ ! Q1–3, Q6, F, D.
s.d. Philocles] Q5, D; *Philocles* Q1–4, Q6, F.

Yet Fortune, stop,————this is the likeliest place
To meet *Asteria,* and by her convey,
My humble vows to my offended Queen.

                    Enter Queen and Asteria.

Ha! She comes her self; Unhappy man!
Where shall I hide?————   (*Is going out.*)
    Qu.   Is not that *Philocles*
Who makes such haste away? *Philocles, Philocles*————
    Philocles coming back. I fear'd she saw me.
    Qu. How now Sir, am I such a Bugbear
That I scare people from me?
    Phil. 'Tis true, I should more carefully have shun'd
The place where you might be; as, when it thunders
Men reverently quit the open Air
Because the angry Gods are then abroad.
    Qu. What does he mean, *Asteria?*
I do not understand him.
    Ast. Your Majesty forgets you banish'd him
Your presence for this day.————   [*To her softly.*
    Qu. Ha! banish'd him! 'tis true indeed;
But, as thou sayst, I had forgot it quite.————   [*To her.*
    Ast. That's very strange, scarce half an hour ago.
    Qu. But Love had drawn his pardon up so soon
That I forgot he e're offended me.
    Phil. Pardon me, that I could not thank you sooner:
Your sudden grace, like some swift flood pour'd in
On narrow bancks, o'reflow'd my spirits.
    Qu. No; 'tis for me to ask your pardon *Philocles,*

---

6 man!] Q2-6, F, D; ~ₐ Q1.   7 *Is*] Q6, F, D; *is* Q1-5.
8 Who] Q2-6, F, D; who Q1.
9 *Philocles coming back.* I] [*Philocles coming back,* [I Q1-6, F (ₐ*Philocles* F;
back.] Q3-6, F); *Phil.* I . . . [*Coming back.* D.
11 from me] Q2-6, F, D; from Q1 (*but corrected in Errata*).
18 him] Q2-6, F, D; him, Q1.   19 *To*] Q6, F, D; *to* Q1-5.
21 [*To*] Q6, F, D; ₐ*to* Q1-5.   26-27 in / On] D; in on Q1-6, F.
27 bancks, o'reflow'd] D; bancks / O'reflow'd Q1-6, F.

For the great injury I did you
30 In not remembring I was angry with you.
But I'le repair my fault,
And rowze my anger up against you yet.
　　Phil. No, Madam, my forgiveness was your Act
Of grace and I lay hold of it.
　　Qu. Princes sometimes may pass,
Acts of Oblivion in their own wrong.
　　Phil. 'Tis true; but not recall them.
　　Qu. But, *Philocles,* since I have told you there is one
I love, I will go on; and let you know
40 What passed this day betwixt us; be you judg
Whether my servant have dealt well with me.
　　Phil. I beseech your Majesty excuse me:
Any thing more of him may make me
Relapse too soon, and forfeit my late pardon.
　　Qu. But you'l be glad to know it.
　　Phil.   May I not hope then
You have some quarrel to him?
　　Qu.   Yes, a great one.
But first, to justifie my self
Know, *Philocles,* I have conceal'd my passion
With such care from him, that he knows not yet
50 I love, but onely that I much esteem him.
　　Phil. O stupid wretch
That by a thousand tokens could not guess it!
　　Qu. He loves elsewhere, and that has blinded him.
　　Phil. He's blind indeed!
So the dull Beasts in the first Paradise
With levell'd eyes gaz'd each upon their kind;
There fix'd their love: and ne're look'd up to view
That glorious Creature man, their soveraign Lord.
　　Qu. Y'are too severe, on little faults, but he
60 Has crimes, untold,

32　yet.] Q4–5, F, D; ∼ : Q1–3, Q6.
33–34　Act / Of grace and] Act of grace / And Q1–6, F, D.
36　wrong.] Q2–6, F, D; ∼ : Q1.
38–39　one / I love, I] D (love;); one I love. / I Q1–6, F (love, Q4–5).
59–60　he / Has] D; he has Q1–6, F.

Which will, I fear, move you much more against him.
He fell this day into a passion with me,
And boldly contradicted all I sed.

   Phil. And stands his head upon his Shoulders yet?
How long shall this most insolent————

   Qu. Take heed you rail not,
You know you are but on your good behaviour.

   Phil. Why then I will not call him Traytor————
But onely rude, audacious and impertinent,
To use his Soveraign so. ————I beg your leave
To wish you have, at least imprison'd him.

   Qu. Some people may speak ill, and yet mean well:
Remember you were not confin'd; and yet
Your fault was great. In short, I love him
And that excuses all; but be not jealous;
His rising shall not be your overthrow,
Nor will I ever marry him.————

   Phil. That's some comfort yet
He shall not be a King.

   Qu. He never shall. But you are discompos'd;
Stay here a little; I have somewhat for you
Shall shew you still are in my favour.

                    [*Exeunt Queen and* Asteria.

        Enter to him Candiope *weeping.*

   Phil. How now, in tears, my fair *Candiope?*
So through a watry Clowd
The Sun at once seems both to weep and shine.
For what Forefathers sin do you afflict
Those precious eyes? for sure you have
None of your own to weep.

   Cand. My Crimes both great and many needs must show
Since Heav'n will punish them with loosing you.

   Phil. Afflictions sent from Heav'n without a cause
Make bold Mankind enquire into its Laws.

---

71   him.] Q2–6, F, D; ~ₐ Q1.   77   will] Q2–6, F, D; wil! Q1.

But Heav'n, which moulding beauty takes such care
Makes gentle fates on purpose for the fair:
And destiny that sees them so divine,
Spinn's all their fortunes in a silken twine:
No mortal hand so ignorant is found
To weave course work upon a precious ground.
    Cand. Go preach this doctrine in my Mother's ears.
100   *Phil.* Has her severity produc'd these tears?
    Cand. She has recall'd those hopes she gave before,
And strictly bids me ne're to see you more.
    Phil. Changes in froward age are Natural;
Who hopes for constant weather in the fall?
'Tis in your pow'r your duty to transfer
And place that right in me which was in her.
    Cand. Reason, like foreign foes, would ne're o'recome,
But that I find I am betray'd at home.
You have a friend that fights for you within.
110   *Phil.* Let Reason ever lose so love may win.

Enter Queen and Asteria.
Queen with a Picture in her hand.

    Qu. See there, *Asteria,*
All we have done succeeds still to the worse;
We hindred him from seeing her at home,
Where I but onely heard they lov'd; and now
She comes to Court, and mads me with the sight on't.
    Ast. Dear Madam, overcome your self a little,
Or they'l perceive how much you are concern'd.
    Qu. I struggle with my heart,————but it will have some vent.
[*To* Cand.] Cousin, you are a stranger at the Court.
120   *Cand.* It was my duty I confess,
To attend oftner on your Majesty.
    Qu. Asteria, Mend my Cousins Handkerchief;
It sits too narrow there, and shows too much

---

100 tears?] Q4–6, D; ∼ : Q1–3, F.   109 within.] Q4–5, F, D; ∼ : Q1–3, Q6.
116 Madam,] Q2–6, F, D; ∼ . Q1.   119 Cand.] F, D; *Cand.* Q1–6.

The broadness of her Shoulders. ———Nay fie, *Asteria*,
Now you put it too much backward, and discover
The bigness of her breasts.

   Cand. I beseech your Majesty
Give not your self this trouble.

   Qu. Sweet Cousin, you shall pardon me;
A beauty such as yours deserves a more
Then ordinary care, to set it out.
Come hither, *Philocles,* do but observe,
She has but one gross fault in all her shape,
That is, she bears up here too much,
And the malicious Workman
Has left it open to your eye.

   Phil. Where, and't please your Majesty?
Methinks 'tis very well.

   Qu. Do not you see it? Oh how blind is love!

   Cand. And how quick-sighted malice!———   [*Aside.*

   Qu. But yet methinks, those knots of sky, do not
So well with the dead colour of her face.

   Ast. Your Majesty mistakes, she wants no red.

          The Queen here plucks out her Glass, and looks
              sometimes on her self, sometimes on her Rival.

   Qu. How do I look to day, *Asteria?*
Methinks not well.

   Ast. Pardon me, Madam, most victoriously.

   Qu. What think you, *Philocles?* come do not flatter.

   Phil. Paris was a bold man who presum'd
To judg the beauty of a Goddess.

   Cand. Your Majesty has given the reason why

---

128   trouble.] Q2–6, F, D; ~ , Q1.
130–131   yours deserves a more / Then . . . care, to] yours / Deserves a more
then . . . care, / To Q1–6, F, D.
135–136   Workman / Has left it open] Workman has left it open Q1–6, F; workman has left it / Open D.
137   and't please] Q2, Q6, F; and 'please Q1, Q3, D; and please Q4; an't please
Q5.
137–138   Majesty? / Methinks . . . well.] D; Majesty, methinks . . . well? Q1–6,
F.
139   it?] D; ~ , Q1–6, F.   144   *Asteria?*] ~ ! Q1–6, F, D.

He cannot judge; his Love has blinded him.

   Qu. Methinks a long patch here beneath her eye
Might hide that dismal hollowness.
What think you *Philocles?*

   Cand. Beseech you Madam, aske not his opinion;
What my faults are it is no matter;
He loves me with them all.

   Qu. I, he may love, but when he marries you
Your Bridal shall be kept in some dark Dungeon.
160 Farwel, and think of that, too easie Maid,
I blush, thou shar'st my bloud.———   [*Exeunt Queen,* Asteria.

   Cand.   Inhumane Queen!
Thou canst not be more willing to resign
Thy part in me, then I to give up mine.

   Phil. Love, how few Subjects do thy Laws fulfil,
And yet those few, like us, thou usest ill!

   Cand. The greatest slaves, in Monarchies, are they,
Whom Birth sets nearest to Imperial sway.
While jealous pow'r does sullenly o're spy,
We play like Deer within the Lions eye.
170 Would I for you some Shepherdess had been;
And, but each May, ne're heard the name of Queen.

   Phil. If you were so, might I some Monarch be,
Then, you should gain what now you loose by me:
Then, you in all my glories should have part,
And rule my Empire, as you rule my heart.

   Cand. How much our golden wishes are in vain!
When they are past we are our selves again.

               Enter Queen and Asteria *above.*

   Qu. Look, look *Asteria,* yet they are not gone.
Hence, we may hear what they discourse alone.

---

151 him.] Q4–5, F, D; ∼ : Q1–3, Q6.
153–154 hollowness. / What] D; hallowness, what Q1–6, F (hollowness, Q2–5, F;
hollowness; Q6).
161 *Queen*] D; Queen Q1–6, F.   161 Inhumane] Q2–6, F, D; In humane Q1.
163 mine.] Q4–6, F, D; ∼ : Q1–3.   176 vain!] Q4–5; ∼ ? Q1–3, Q6, F, D.
177+ *s.d. Queen*] D; Queen Q1–6, F (Queen Q1).

Phil. My Love inspires me with a gen'rous thought
Which you unknowing, in those wishes taught.
Since happiness may out of Courts be found
Why stay we here on this enchanted ground?
And choose not rather with content to dwell
(If Love and we can find it) in a Cell?
  Cand. Those who, like you, have once in Courts been great,
May think they wish, but wish not to retreat.
They seldom go but when they cannot stay;
As loosing Gamesters throw the Dice away:
Ev'n in that Cell, where you repose would find,
Visions of Court will haunt your restless mind;
And glorious dreams stand ready to restore
The pleasing shapes of all you had before.
  Phil. He, who with your possession once is blest,
On easie terms may part with all the rest.
All my Ambition will in you be crown'd;
And those white Arms shall all my wishes bound.
Our life shall be but one long Nuptial day,
And, like chaf't Odours, melt in Sweets away.
Soft as the Night our Minutes shall be worn,
And chearful as the Birds that wake the Morn.
  Cand. Thus hope misleads it self in pleasant way;
And takes more joyes on trust then Love can pay!
But Love, with long possession, once decayd,
That face which now you Court, you will upbraid.
  Phil. False Lovers broach these tenets, to remove
The fault from them by placing it on Love.————
  Cand. Yet grant in Youth you keep alive your Fire,
Old age will come, and then it must expire:
Youth but a while does at Loves Temple stay,
As some fair Inn to lodge it on the way.
  Phil. Your doubts are kind; but to be satisfy'd,
I can be true, I beg I may be try'd.
  Cand. Tryals of love too dear the making cost;

---

199 Sweets] Q1 *(some copies),* Q2–6, F, D; Sweats Q1 *(some copies; corrected in Errata).*
213 true] *the* r *did not print in* Q1.

For, if successless, the whole venture's lost.
What you propose, brings wants and care along.
    Phil. Love can bear both.
    Cand.   But is your love so strong?
    Phil. They do not want, who wish not to have more;
Who ever said an Anchoret was poor?
220   *Cand.* To answer gen'rously as you have done,
I should not by your arguments be wonn:
I know I urge your ruine by consent;
Yet love too well that ruine to prevent.
    Phil. Like water giv'n to those whom Feavers fry;
You kill but him, who must without it die.
    Cand. Secure me I may love without a Crime;
Then, for our flight, appoint both place and time.
    Phil. Th'ensuing hour my plighted vows shall be;
The time's not long; or onely long to me.
230   *Cand.* Then, let us go where we shall ne'r be seen
By my hard Mother.
    Phil.   Or my cruel Queen.
                      [*Exeunt* Phil. Cand.
    Queen above. O *Philocles* unkind to call me cruel!
So false *Æneas* did from *Dido* fly;
But never branded her with cruelty.
How I despise my self for loving so!
    Ast. At once you hate your self and love him too.
    Qu. No, his ingratitude has cur'd my wound:
A painful cure indeed!
    Ast.   And yet not sound.
His ignorance of your true thoughts
240 Excuses this; you did seem cruel, Madam.
    Qu. But much of kindness still was mix'd with it.
Who could mistake so grosly not to know

---

217   both. / *Cand.* But] Q4–6, F, D; both (*Cand.*) but Q1–3 (But Q2–3).
231   Mother. / *Phil.* Or] Q4–6, F, D (Mother, Q4–5); Mother (*Phil.*) or Q1–3 (Or Q2–3).
232   *Queen above.*] Q5–6, F, D; *Queen / above.* Q1–4.
233   *Æneas*] Q2–6, F, D; Æneas Q1.
238   indeed! / *Ast.* And] Q4–6, F, D; indeed! (*Ast.*) and Q1–3 (And Q2–3).

A *Cupid* frowning when he draws his Bowe?

    Ast. He's going now to smart for his offence.

    Qu. Should he without my leave depart from hence?

    Ast. No matter; since you hate him, let him go.

    Qu. But I my hate by my revenge will show:

Besides, his head's a forfeit to the State.

    Ast. When you take that I will believe you hate.

Let him possess, and then he'll soon repent:

And so his Crime will prove his punishment.

    Qu. He may repent; but he will first possess.

    Ast. O, Madam, now your hatred you confess:

If, his possessing her your rage does move,

'Tis jealousie the avarice of love.

    Qu. No more, *Asteria.*

Seek *Lysimantes* out,

Bid him set Guards through all the Court and City.

Prevent their marriage first; then stop their flight.

Some fitting punishments I will ordain,

But speak not you of *Philocles* again:

'Tis bold to search, and dangerous to find,

Too much of Heaven's, or of a Princes mind.

                          [*Qu. descends and exit.*

As the Queen has done speaking, Flavia *is going hastily
over the Stage;* Asteria *sees her.*

    Ast. Flavia, Flavia, Whither so fast?

    Flav. Did you call, *Asteria?*

    Ast. The Queen has business with Prince *Lysimantes;*

Speak to any Gentleman that's next, to fetch him.

                          [*Exit* Asteria *from above.*

    Flav. I suspect somewhat, but I'le watch you close;

Prince *Lysimantes* has not chose in me,

---

244   offence.] Q2–6, F, D; ∼ : Q1.   252   possess.] Q2–6, F, D; ∼ : Q1.

257–258   out, / Bid . . . Guards through] out, bid . . . Guards through Q1–4,
F; out, bid . . . Guards / Through Q5–6, D.

263+   *s.d. Qu.*] Q6, F, D; Qu. Q1–5.   263+   *s.d. her*] Q3–6, F, D; her Q1–2.

270 The worst Spy of the Court.———*Celadon!*
What makes he here?

> *Enter* Celadon, Olinda, Sabina; *they walk over the Stage*
> *together, he seeming to court them.*

Olind. Nay, sweet *Celadon.*———
Sab. Nay, dear *Celadon.*———
Flav. O-ho. I see his business now, 'tis with *Melissa's* two
Daughters: Look look, how he peeps about to see if the Coast be
clear; like an Hawk that will not plume if she be look'd
on.——— [*Exeunt* Cel. Ol. Sab.
So———at last he has truss'd his quarry.———

> *Enter* Florimell.

Flor. Did you see *Celadon* this way?
280 *Flav.* If you had not ask'd the question, I should have thought
you had come from watching him; he's just gone off with
Melissa's Daughters.
Flor. Melissa's Daughters! he did not Court 'em I hope?
Flav. So busily, he lost no time: while he was teaching the
one a tune, he was kissing the others hand.
Flor. O fine Gentleman!
Flav. And they so greedy of him! Did you never see two Fishes
about a Bait, tugging it this way, and t'other way? for my part, I
look'd at least he should have lost a Leg or Arm i'th service.
290 ———Nay never vex your self, but e'en resolve to break with
him.
Flor. No no, 'tis not come to that, yet; I'le correct him first,
and then hope the best from time.
Flav. From time! Believe me, there's little good to be expected
from him. I never knew the old Gentleman with the Scythe and

270–271 *Celadon!* / What] *Celadon!* what Q1–6, F, D.
271 here?] *here!* Q1–2; here! Q3–6, F, D.
277 Cel. Ol. Sab.] Q3–6, F, D; *Cel. Ol. Sab.* Q1–2.
278 truss'd] Q2–6, F, D; truss'ed Q1.
288 t'other way?] ~ ; Q1–6, F, D ('tother Q1, *some copies;* Q2–3).
289 i'th] Q2–6, F, D; i'rh Q1 (*some copies*); 'irh Q1 (*some copies*).

Hourglass bring any thing but gray hair, thin cheeks, and loss of teeth: you see *Celadon* loves others.

Flor. There's the more hope he may love me among the rest: hang't, I would not marry one of these solemn Fops; they are good for nothing but to make Cuckolds: Give me a servant that is an high Flier at all games, that is bounteous of himself to many women; and yet whenever I pleas'd to throw out the lure of Matrimony, should come down with a swing, and fly the better at his own quarry.

Flav. But are you sure you can take him down when you think good?

Flor. Nothing more certain.

Flav. What wager will you venture upon the Trial?

Flor. Any thing.

Flav. My Maydenhead to yours.

Flor. That's a good one, who shall take the forfeit?

Flav. I'le go and write a Letter as from these two Sisters, to summon him immediately; it shall be deliver'd before you. I warrant you see a strange combat betwixt the Flesh and the Spirit: if he leaves you to go to them, you'l grant he loves them better?

Flor. Not a jot the more: a Bee may pick of many Flowers, and yet like some one better then all the rest.

Flav. But then your Bee must not leave his sting behind him.

Flor. Well; make the experiment however: I hear him coming, and a whole noise of Fiddles at his heels. Hey-day, what a mad Husband shall I have!——

Enter Celadon.

Flav. And what a mad wife will he have! Well, I must goe a little way, but I'le return immediately and write it: You'l keep him in discourse the while?   [*Exit* Flav.

Cel. Where are you, Madam? what do you mean to run away thus? pray stand to't, that we may dispatch this business.

---

322 have!——] ～ ?—— Q1-5, F, D; ～ₐ—— Q6.
323 have!] ～ ? Q1-6, F, D.   325 Flav.] Q3-6, F, D; *Flav.* Q1-2.

Flor. I think you mean to watch me as they do Witches, to make me confess I love you. Lord, what a bustle have you
330 kept this Afternoon! what with eating, singing and dancing, I am so wearied, that I shall not be in case to hear of any more love this fortnight.

Cel. Nay, if you surfeit on't before Tryal, Lord have mercy upon you when I have married you.

Flor. But what Kings Revenue do you think will maintain this extravagant expence?

Cel. I have a damnable Father, a rich old Rogue, if he would once die! Lord, how long does he mean to make it ere he dies?

Flor. As long as ever he can, I'le pass my word for him.

340   *Cel.* I think then we had best consider him as an obstinate old fellow that is deaf to the news of a better world; and ne're stay for him.

Flor. But e'en marry; and get him Grandchildren in abundance, and great Grandchildren upon them, and so inch him and shove him out of the world by the very force of new Generations: ———If that be the way you must excuse me.

Cel. But dost thou know what it is to be an old Maid?

Flor. No, nor hope I sha'n't these twenty years.

Cel. But when that time comes, in the first place thou wilt be
350 condemned to tell Stories, how many men thou mightest have had; and none believe thee: Then thou growest froward, and impudently weariest all thy Friends to sollicite Man for thee.

Flor. Away with your old Common-place wit: I am resolved to grow fat and look young till forty, and then slip out of the world with the first wrinckle, and the reputation of five and twenty.

Cel. Well, what think you now of a reckoning betwixt us?

Flor. How do you mean?

Cel. To discount for so many dayes of my years service, as I
360 have paid in since morning.

Flor. With all my heart.

Cel. Inprimis, For a Treat:

---

330 Afternoon!] ∼ ? Q1-6, F, D.   338 dies?] ∼ ! Q1-6, F, D.

Item, For my Glass Coach:

Item, For sitting bare, and wagging your Fann:

And lastly, and principally, for my Fidelity to you this long hour and half.

Flor. For this I 'bate you three Weeks of your Service; now hear your Bill of Faults; for your comfort 'tis a short one.

Cel. I know it.

70 *Flor. Inprimis, Item,* and Sum totall, for keeping company with *Melissa*'s Daughters.

Cel. How the Pox came you to know of that? 'Gad I believe the Devil plays booty against himself, and tels you of my sins.

                                                        [*Aside.*

Flor. The offence being so small the punishment shall be but proportionable, I will set you back onely half a year.

Cel. You're most unconscionable: why then do you think we shall come together? there's none but the old Patriarchs could live long enough to marry you at this rate. What do you take me for some Cousin of *Methusalem*'s, that I must stay an 80 hundred years before I come to beget Sons and Daughters?

Flor. Heres an impudent Lover, he complains of me without ever offering to excuse himself; *Item,* a fortnight more for that.

Cel. So ther's another puff in my voyage has blown me back to the North of *Scotland.*

Flo. All this is nothing to your excuse for the two Sisters.

Cel. 'Faith if ever I did more then kiss 'em, and that but once————

Flor. What could you have done more to me?

90 *Cel.* An hundred times more; as thou shalt know, dear Rogue, at time convenient.

Flo. You talk, you talk; Could you kiss 'em, though but once, and ne're think of me?

Cel. Nay if I had thought of thee, I had kiss'd 'em over a thousand times, with the very force of imagination.

Flor. The Gallants are mightily beholding to you, you have

---

372   that?] Q4–6, D; ∼ : Q1–3, F.

373+   *s.d. Aside.*] Q4–6, F, D; *aside*ᴧ Q1–2; *aside.* Q3.

382   offering] *the* e *failed to print in Q1.*

found 'em out a new way to kiss their Mistresses, upon other womens lips.

Cel. What would you have? You are my Sultana Queen, the
400 rest are but in the nature of your Slaves; I may make some slight excursion into the Enemies Country for forage or so, but I ever return to my head quarters.

Enter one with a Letter.

Cel. To me?

Mess. If your name be *Celadon.*   [Celad. *reads softly.*

Flor. He's swallowing the Pill; presently we shall see the operation.

Cel. to the Page. Child, come hither Child; here's money for thee: So, be gone quickly good Child, before any body examines thee: Thou art in a dangerous place, Child.————

[*Thrusts him out.*
410 Very good, the Sisters send me word they will have the Fiddles this Afternoon, and invite me to sup there!————Now cannot I forbear and I should be damn'd, though I have scap'd a scouring so lately for it. Yet I love *Florimell* better then both of 'em together;————there's the Riddle o'nt: but onely for the sweet sake of variety.———— Well, we must all sin, and we must all repent, and there's an end on't.   [*Aside.*

Flor. What is it that makes you fidg up and down so?

Cel. 'Faith I am sent for by a very dear friend, and 'tis upon a business of life and death.

420 *Flor.* On my life some woman!

Cel. On my honour some man; Do you think I would lye to you?

Flor. But you engag'd to sup with me!

Cel. But I consider it may be scandalous to stay late in your

407   *Cel. to the Page.*] [Cel. *to the Page.*] Q1–6, F, D (ᴧCel. Q5, F; ᴧ*Cel.* D).
411   invite] Q2–6, F, D; invites Q1 (*but corrected in Errata*).
413   *Florimell*] Florimel Q1–6, F, D.
416   [*Aside.*] *at end of preceding sentence in Q1–6, F, D.*
420   woman!] ∼ ? Q1–6, F, D.

Lodgings. Adieu dear Miss if ever I am false to thee again.

                                           [*Exit* Cel.

   Flor. See what constant metal you men are made of! He begins to vex me in good earnest. Hang him, let him go and take enough of 'em: and yet methinks I can't endure he should neither. Lord, that such a Mad-Cap as I should ever live to be jealous! I must after him.

Some Ladies would discard him now, but I

A fitter way for my revenge will find,

I'le marry him, and serve him in his kind.   [*Exit* Florimell.

ACT IV. SCENE I.

SCENE, *The Walks.*

Melissa, *after her* Olinda *and* Sabina.

   Melissa. I must take this business up in time: this wild fellow begins to haunt my house again. Well, I'le be bold to say it, 'tis as easie to bring up a young Lyon, without mischief, as a Maidenhead of Fifteen, to make it tame for an Husbands bed. Not but that the young man is handsome, rich and young, and I could be content he should marry one of 'em, but to seduce 'em both in this manner!———Well, I'le examine 'em apart, and if I can find out which he loves, I'le offer him his choice.———*Olinda,* Come hither Child.———

   Olin. Your pleasure, Madam?

   Mel. Nothing but for your good *Olinda,* what think you of *Celadon?*

   Olin. Why I think he's a very mad fellow; but yet I have some obligements to him: he teaches me new ayres on the Guitarre, and talks wildely to me, and I to him.

425+ *s.d.* Cel.] Q3–6, F, D; *Cel.* Q1–2.

430 jealous! I] jealous! / I Q1–6, F, D.

433 Florimell] *Florimel* Q1–2; Florimel Q3–6, F, D.

ACT IV. SCENE I.] ACT IV. Q1–6, F, D.

1 *Melissa.*] Q4–5, F, D; ~ , Q1–3, Q6.

6–7 of 'em, . . . manner!] ~∧ . . .~ , Q1; ~∧ . . .~ . Q2–3; ~ , ...~ . Q4–5, F, D; ~ ; . . .~ ! Q6.

Mel. But tell me in earnest, do you think he loves you?

Olin. Can you doubt it? There were never two so cut out for one another; we both love Singing, Dancing, Treats and Musick. In short, we are each others counterpart.

20 *Mel.* But does he love you seriously?

Olin. Seriously! I know not that; if he did, perhaps I should not love him: but we sit and talk, and wrangle, and are friends; when we are together we never hold our tongues; then we have always a noise of Fiddles at our heels, he hunts me merrily as the Hound does the Hare; and either this is Love, or I know it not.

Mel. Well, go back, and call *Sabina* to me.

————Olinda *goes behind.*

This is a Riddle past my finding out: whether he loves her or no is the question; but this I am sure of, she loves him:————O my little Favourite, I must ask you a question concerning *Celadon:*

30 Is he in love with you?

Sab. I think indeed he does not hate me, at least if a mans word may be taken for it.

Mel. But what expressions has he made you?

Sab. Truly the man has done his part: he has spoken civilly to me, and I was not so young but I understood him.

Mel. And you could be content to marry him?

Sab. I have sworn never to marry; besides, he's a wild young man; yet to obey you, Mother, I could be content to be sacrific'd.

Mel. No, no, we wou'd but lead you to the Altar.

40 *Sab.* Not to put off the Gentleman neither; for if I have him not I am resolv'd to die a Maid, that's once, Mother.————

Mel. Both my Daughters are in love with him, and I cannot yet find he loves either of 'em.

Olin. Mother, mother, yonder's *Celadon* in the walks.

Mel. Peace wanton; you had best ring the Bells for joy. Well, I'le not meet him, because I know not which to offer him; yet he seems to like the youngest best: I'le give him opportunity with her; *Olinda,* do you make haste after me.

Olin. This is something hard though. [*Exit* Mel.

Enter Celadon.

26+ s.d. behind.] Q2–6, F, D; ∼∧ Q1.   49 Mel.] Q3–6, F, D; *Mel.* Q1–2.

50   *Cel.* You see Ladies the least breath of yours brings me to you: I have been seeking you at your Lodgings, and from thence came hither after you.

Sab. 'Twas well you found us.

Cel. Found you! Half this brightness betwixt you two was enough to have lighted me; I could never miss my way: Here's fair *Olinda* has beauty enough for one Family; such a voice, such a wit, so noble a stature, so white a skin.

Olin. I thought he would be particular at last.   [*Aside.*

Cel. And young *Sabina,* so sweet an innocence, such a Rose-60 bud newly blown. This is my goodly Pallace of Love, and that my little withdrawing Room. A word, Madam.   [*To* Sab.

Olin. I like not this. [*Aside.*]———Sir, if you are not too busie with my Sister, I would speak with you.

Cel. I come, Madam.———

Sab. Time enough Sir; pray finish your Discourse,———and as you were a saying, Sir———

Olin. Sweet Sir.———

Sab. Sister, you forget, my Mother bid you make haste.

Olin. Well, go you and tell her I am coming.———

70   *Sab.* I can never endure to be the Messenger of ill news; but if you please I'le send her word you won't come.———

Olin. Minion, Minion, remember this.———*Exit* Olinda.

Sab. She's horribly in love with you.

Cel. Lord, who could love that walking Steeple? She's so high that every time She sings to me, I am looking up for the Bell that tolls to Church.——— Ha! Give me my little Fifth-rate that lies so snug.———She, hang her, a *Dutch* built bottom: she's so tall, there's no boarding her. But we lose time———Madam, let me

---

59–60 innocence, such a Rose-bud . . . blown. This] D; innocence, / Such a Rose-bud . . . blown. / This Q1–6, F.
61   Sab.] Q6, F, D; *Sab.* Q1–3; *s.d. omitted from Q4–5.*
62   this.] Q4–5; ~∧ Q1–3, Q6, F, D.
62   [*Aside.*]———] ———[*aside.*] Q1–3, Q6, F, D (*Aside* Q6, D); (*Aside.*)∧ Q4–5.
69   Well] Q2–6, F, D; WeIl Q1.
72   Olinda] Q3–6, F, D; *Olinda* Q1–2.
74   Steeple?] Q4–5; ~ : Q1–3, Q6, F, D.
76   Church.——— . . . Fifth-rate] Q2–6, F, D (Church∧——— Q6); ~ ,——— . . .~ ! Q1.
77   *Dutch*] D; Duch Q1; Dutch Q2–6, F.

seal my love upon your mouth. [*Kiss.*] Soft and sweet by Heaven!
80 sure you wear Rose-leaves between your lips.

Sab. Lord, Lord; What's the matter with me? my breath
grows so short I can scarce speak to you.

Cel. No matter, give me thy lips again and I'le speak for thee.

Sab. You don't love me.———

Cel. I warrant thee; set down by me and kiss again.———She
warms faster then *Pygmalion's* Image. [*Aside.*]———[*Kiss.*]
———I marry sir, this was the original use of lips; talking,
eating, and drinking came in by th' by.———

Sab. Nay pray be civil; will you be at quiet?

90 *Cel.* What, would you have me sit still and look upon you like
a little Puppy-dog that's taught to beg with his fore-leg up?

Enter Florimell.

Flor. Celadon the faithful! in good time Sir.———

Cel. In very good time *Florimell;* for Heavens sake help me
quickly.

Flor. What's the matter?

Cel. Do not you see? here's a poor Gentlewoman in a swoon!
(swoon away!) I have been rubbing her this half hour, and cannot
bring her to her senses.

Flor. Alas, how came she so?

100 *Cel.* Oh barbarous! do you stay to ask questions? run for
charity.

Flor. Help, help, alas poor Lady.———   [*Exit* Flor.

Sab. Is she gone?

Cel. I thanks to my wit that helpt me at a pinch; I thank
Heaven, I never pumpt for a lye in all my life yet.

Sab. I am affraid you love her, *Celadon!*

79 *Kiss.*]] D; *kiss.*‸ Q1–6, F (*Kiss* Q4–6).
81 me?] ~ ! Q1–3, Q6, F, D; ~ , Q4–5.
86 [*Aside.*]] D; ———[*aside.*‸ Q1–6, F (*Aside* Q4–6, F).
86 *Kiss*] Q4–6, F, D; *kiss* Q1–3.   88 by th'] Q2–6, F; bith' Q1; by the D.
90 What,] Q6; ~‸ Q1–5, F, D.   90 sit] Q2–6, F, D; set Q1.
91+ *s.d.* Florimell] Q3–6, F, D; *Florimell* Q1–2.
96 see?] ~ ! Q1–6, F, D.   100 questions?] ~ , Q1–6, F, D.
102 Flor.] Q2–6, F, D; *Flor.* Q1.   104 pinch; I] D; pinch; / I Q1–6, F.

Cel. Onely as a civil acquaintance or so, but however to avoid slander you had best be gone before she comes again.

Sab. I can find a tongue as well as she————

Cel. I, but the truth is, I am a kind of scandalous person, and for you to be seen in my company———— Stay in the walks, by this kiss I'le be with you presently.————   *Exit* Sab.

Enter Florimell *running.*

Flor. Help, help!————I can find no body.

Cel. 'Tis needless now my dear, she's recover'd, and gone off, but so wan and weakly.————

Flor. Umh! I begin to smell a ratt, what was your business here, *Celadon?*

Cel. Charity, Christian charity; you saw I was labouring for life with her.

Flor. But how came you hither? not that I care this,————but onely to be satisfied————   [*Sings.*

Cel. You are jealous in my Conscience.

Flor. Who I jealous? Then I wish this sigh may be the last that ever I may draw.————   [*Sighs.*

Cel. But why do you sigh then?

Flor. Nothing but a cold, I cannot fetch my breath well.———— But what will you say if I write the Letter you had, to try your faith?

Cel. Hey-day! This is just the Devil and the Sinner; you lay snares for me, and then punish me for being taken; here's trying a man's Faith indeed: What, did you think I had the faith of a Stock, or of a Stone? Nay, and you go to tantalize a man,———— 'gad I love upon the square, I can endure no tricks to be used to me.

Olinda *and* Sabina *at the door Peeping.*

112 Sab.] Q3–6, F, D; *Sab.* Q1–2.   113 *Flor.*] Q2–6, F, D; ~ , Q1.
113 help!————] ~ , ∧ Q1–6, F, D.   120 hither?] Q4–5, D; ~ ; Q1–3, Q6, F.
121 [*Sings.*] Q6 (~∧), F, D; ∧~ ·———— Q1–5.
123 jealous?] ~ ! Q1–6, F, D.   131 What,] Q6, D; ~∧ Q1–5, F.

Ol. Sab. Celadon, Celadon!

Flor. What voices are those?

Cel. Some Camerades of mine that call me to play;————Pox on 'em, they'l spoil all————   *Aside.*

Flor. Pray let's see 'em.

140 *Cel.* Hang 'em Tatterdemallions, they are not worth your sight; 'pray Gentlemen be gone, I'le be with you immediately.

Sab. No, we'll stay here for you.

Flor. Do your Gentlemen speak with Treble-voices? I am resolv'd to see what company you keep.

Cel. Nay, good my Dear.————

> *He lays hold of her to pull her back; she lays hold*
> *of* Olinda, *by whom* Sabina *holds; so that he*
> *pulling, they all come in.*

Flor. Are these your Comerades?

[*Sings.*] 'Tis *Strephon* calls; what would my love? Why do not you roar out like a great Bass-vyal, Come follow to the Myrtle-grove. Pray Sir, which of these fair Ladies is it, for

150 whom you were to do the courtesie, for it were unconscionable to leave you to 'em both; What, a man's but a man you know.

Olin. The Gentleman may find an owner.

Sab. Though not of you.

Flor. Pray agree whose the lost sheep is, and take him.

Cel. 'Slife they'l cry me anon, and tell my marks.

Flor. Troth I pity your Highness there, I perceive he has left you for the little one: Me thinks he should have been affraid to break his neck when he fell so high as from you to her.

Sab. Well my drolling Lady, I may be even with you.————

160 *Flor.* Not this ten years by thy growth, yet.

Sab. Can flesh and blood endure this?————

Flor. How now, my *Amazon in decimo sexto!*————

Olin. Do you affront my Sister?————

Flor. I, but thou art so tall, I think I shall never affront thee.————

---

135 *Celadon, Celadon*] Q6, D; Celadon, Celadon Q1–5, F.
147 calls;] ~∧ Q1–3, Q6, F; ~ , Q4–5, D.
149 Myrtle-grove] *Myrtle-grove* Q1–6, F, D.
151 What,] Q2–6, F, D; ~∧ Q1.   161 this?————] ~ !———— Q1–6, F, D.

Sab. Come away Sister, we shall be jeer'd to Death else.

[*Exeunt* Olin. Sab.

Flor. Why do you look that way? you can'nt forbear leering after the forbidden Fruit.————But when e're I take a Wenchers word again!————

Cel. A Wenchers word! Why should you speak so contemptibly of the better half of Mankind? I'le stand up for the honour of my Vocation.

Flor. You are in no fault I warrant;————'ware my busk————

Cel. Not to give a fair Lady the lye, I am in fault;—but otherwise. ————Come let us be friends; and let me wait you to your Lodgings.

Flor. This impudence shall not save you from my Table-book. *Item.* A Month more for this fault.————

[*They walk to the door.*

1 *Souldier within.* Stand.

2 *Souldier.* Stand, give the word.

Cel. Now, whats the meaning of this trow? guards set.

1 *Souldier.* Give the word, or you cannot pass; these are they brother; let's in, and seize em.

The two Souldiers enter————

1 *Sould.* ————Down with him.

2 *Sould.* Disarm him.

Cel. How now Rascalls:————

Draws and beats one off, and catches the other.

Cel. Ask your life you villain.

2 *Sould.* Quarter, quarter.

Cel. Was ever such an Insolence?

Sould. We did but our duty; here we were set, to take a Gentleman and Lady, that would steal a marriage without the Queens

———————
166+   s.d. Olin. Sab.] Q3–6, F, D; *Olin. Sab.* Q1–2.
167   way?] D; ~ , Q1–6, F.
171   Mankind?] Q2, Q6, F; ~ . Q1; ~ ! Q3–5, D.
179–180   1 . . . 2] F, D; 1. . . . 2. Q1–6 *(and similarly below [Q3–4 have 2ʌ in line 188]).*
181   trow? . . . set.] ~ , . . . ~ . Q1–6, F, D (set? Q4–5; set! D).

consent, and we thought you had been they.   [*Exit Sould.*

  Flor. Your Cousin *Philocles* and the Princess *Candiope* on my
life! for I heard the Queen give private Orders to *Lysimantes*,
and name them twice or thrice.

  Cel. I know a score or two of Madcaps here hard by, whom I
can pick up from Taverns and Gaming-houses, and Bordells;
those I'le bring to aid him: Now *Florimell*, there's an argument
for wenching; where would you have had so many honest men
200 together upon the sudden for a brave employment?

  Flor. You'l leave me then to take my fortune?

  Cel. No; if you will, I'le have you into the places aforesaid,
and enter you into good company.

  Flor. 'Thank you Sir, here's a key will let me through this
back-door to my own Lodgings.

  Cel. If I come off with life, I'le see you this evening, if not
————Adieu *Florimell.*————

  Flor. If you come not I shall conclude you are kill'd, or taken;
to be hang'd for a Rebel to morrow morning,————and then I'le
210 honour your memory with a Lampoon instead of an Epitaph.

  Cel. No no, I trust better in my Fate: I know I am reserv'd to
do you a Courtesie.   [*Exit* Celadon.

As Florimell *is unlocking the door to go out,* Flavia
*opens it against her, and enters to her, followed by
a Page.*

  Flav. Florimell, do you hear the News?

  Flor. I guess they are in pursuit of *Philocles.*

  Flav. When *Lysimantes* came with the Queens Orders,
He refused to render up *Candiope;*
And with some few brave friends he had about him
Is forcing of his way through all the Guards.

  Flor. A gallant fellow: I'le in, will you with me?
220 Hark, the noise comes this way!

---

212   Celadon] Q3–6, F, D; *Celadon* Q1–2.
213   *Florimell,*] *Florimel.* Q1; *Florimel,* Q2–6, F, D.
219   me?] Q4–5, D; ~ . Q1–3, Q6; *failed to print in* F.

Flav. I have a message from the Queen to *Lysimantes,*
I hope I may be safe among the Souldiers.
    Flor. Oh very safe, perhaps some honest fellow in the tumult
may take pity of thy Maidenhead, or so————Adiew.

                              [*Exit* Florimell.

    Page. The noise comes nearer, Madam.
    Flav.   I am glad on't:
This message gives me the opportunity
Of speaking privately with *Lysimantes.*

    Enter Philocles *and* Candiope, *with three friends; pursued by*
                Lysimantes *and Souldiers.*

    Lys. What is it renders you thus obstinate?
You have no hope of flight, and to resist
Is full as vain.
    Phil. I'le die, rather then yield her up.
    Flav. My Lord!
    Lys.   How now, some new message from the Queen?
[*To Sould.*] Retire a while to a convenient distance.

                              Lys. *and* Flav. *whisper.*

    Lys. O *Flavia* 'tis impossible!
The Queen in love with *Philocles!*
    Flav. I half suspected it before; but now,
My ears and eyes are witnesses.————
This hour I over-heard her to *Asteria*
Making such sad complaints of her hard fate!
For my part I believe you lead him back
But to his Coronation.

224+   *s.d. on next line in Q1–6, F, D.*
224+   *s.d.* Florimell] Q3–6, F, D; *Florimell* Q1–2.
225   *Page.*] F; *Page* 1. Q1–6; 1 *Page.* D.
225–226 on't: / This] on't: this Q1–6, F, D.
226–227 opportunity / Of] opportunity of Q1–6, F, D.
228–229 obstinate? / You] obstinate? you Q1–6, F, D.
229–230 resist / Is] resist is Q1–6, F, D.
232   Lord! / *Lys.* How] Q4–6, F, D; Lord! (*Lys.*) how Q1–3 (How Q2–3).
233   [*To Sould.*]] Q4–5; ∧~] Q1–3, F; [~∧ Q6, D (*at right*).
234–235 impossible! / The] impossible! the Q1–6, F, D.
238   *Asteria*] Q4–5; ~ . Q1; ~ , Q2–3, Q6, F, D.

Lys.   Hell take him first.
Flav. Presently after this she call'd for me,
And bid me run, and with strict care command you
On peril of your life he had no harm:
But, Sir, she spoke it with so great concernment,
Me thought I saw love, anger and despair
All combating at once upon her face.
    Lys. Tell the Queen———
I know not what, I am distracted so;———
250 But go and leave me to my thoughts.———   [*Exit* Flavia.
Was ever such amazing news
Told in so strange and critical a moment?
What shall I do?
Does she love *Philocles,* who loves not her;
And loves not *Lysimantes* who prefers her
Above his life? what rests but that I take
This opportunity, which she her self
Has given me, to kill this happy Rival?
Assist me Souldiers.
    Phil.   They shall buy me dearly.
260   *Cand.* Ah me, unhappy maid!

Enter Celadon *with his Friends, unbutton'd and reeling.*

Cel. Courage my noble Cousin, I have brought
A band of Blades, the bravest youths of *Syracuse:*
Some drunk, some sober, all resolv'd to run
Your fortune to the utmost. Fall on mad Boyes———
    Lys. Hold, a little;———I'm not secure
Of victory against these desperate ruffins.
    Cel. No, but I'le secure you; they shall cut your throat for such
another word of 'em. Ruffins quoth a! call Gamesters, and

248–249 Queen——— / I] Queen———I Q1–6, F, D.
250 Flavia.] Q3–6, F, D; *Flavia*∧ Q1; *Flavia.* Q2.
252 moment?] ∼ ! Q1–6, F, D.   253 do?] ∼ ! Q1–6, F, D.
256 life?] ∼ ! Q1–6, F, D.   258 Rival?] ∼ ! Q1–6, F, D.
265–266 little;———I'm not secure / Of] little;——— / I'm not secure of Q1–
6, F, D (secur'd Q1, *but corrected in Errata*).

Whoremasters, and Drunkards, Ruffins!———

   Lys. Pray Gentlemen fall back a little———

   Cel. O ho, are they Gentlemen now with you? Speak first to your Gentlemen Souldiers to retire; and then I'le speak to my Gentlemen Ruffins. [*Cel. Signs to his party.*] There's your disciplin'd men now.———

            They sign, and the Souldiers retire on both sides.
Come Gentlemen, let's lose no time; while they are talking, let's have one merry mayn before we die———for Mortality sake.

   1. Agreed, here's my Cloak for a Table.

   2. And my Hat for a Box.———   [*They lie down and throw.*

   Lys. Suppose I kill'd him!
'Twould but exasperate the Queen the more:
He loves not her, nor knows he she loves him:
A sudden thought is come into my head———
So to contrive it, that this *Philocles,*
And these his friends shall bring to pass that for me
Which I could never compass.———True I strain
A point of honour; but then her usage to me,———
It shall be so———
Pray, *Philocles,* command your Souldiers off,
As I will mine: I've somewhat to propose
Which you perhaps may like.

   Cand.   I will not leave him.

   Lys. ———'Tis my desire you should not.

   Phil. ———Cousin, lead off your friends.

   Cel.———One word in your ear Couz. Let me advise you; either make your own conditions, or never agree with him: his men are poor sober Rogues, they can never stand before us.

            Exeunt omnes præter Lys. Phil. Cand.

   Lys. Suppose some friend, e're night,

271 you?] ∼ ! Q1–6, F, D.
271–273 *as verse in* Q1–6, F, D (. . . you! / . . . then / [. . . retire; / And then D] . . . Ruffins. / [Ruffians Q1]).
273 *party.*]] ∼ ,] Q1–2; ∼ₐ] Q3–5; ∼ ·ₐ Q6, F, D (*s.d. at right*).
274+ *s.d. sign*] Q6, D; *sing* Q1–5, F.
286–287 me,——— / It] D; me, it Q1–6; me! It F.
295+ *s.d.* Lys. Phil. Cand.] Q3–6, F, D; *Lys. Phil. Cand.* Q1–2.

Should bring you to possess all you desire;
And not so onely, but secure for ever
The Nations happiness————
    Phil.   I would think of him
300 As of some God, or Angel.
    Lys.   That God or Angel
You and I may be to one another,
We have betwixt us
An hundred men; The Cittadel you govern:
What were it now to seize the Queen?
    Phil. O impiety! to seize the Queen!
To seize her, said you?
    Lys. The word might be too rough, I meant secure her.
    Phil. Was this your proposition,
And had you none to make it to but to me?
310   *Lys.* Pray hear me out e're you condemn me:
I would not the least violence were offer'd
Her person; two small grants is all I ask,
To make me happy in her self, and you
In your *Candiope.*
    Cand. And will not you do this, my *Philocles?*
Nay now my Brother speaks but reason.
    Phil. Int'rest makes all seem reason that leads to it.
Int'rest that does the zeal of Sects create,
To purge a Church, and to reform a State.
320   *Lys.* In short, the Queen hath sent to part you two;
What more she means to her, I know not.
    Phil. To her! alas! why will not you protect her?
    Lys. With you I can; but where's my power alone?
    Cand. You know she loves me not: you lately heard her
How she insulted over me: how she
Despis'd that beauty which you say I have;
I see she purposes my death.
    Phil. Why do you fright me with it?
'Tis in your Brothers pow'r to let us 'scape,
330 And then you run no danger.

300–301 Angel / You] Angel you Q1–6, F, D.   304 Queen?] ∼ ! Q1–6, F, D.

Lys.   True, I may;
But then my head must pay the forfeit of it.
    Phil. O wretched *Philocles,* whither would love
Hurry thee headlong?
    Lys.   Cease these exclamations.
Ther's no danger on your side: 'tis but
To live without my Sister, resolve that
And you have shot the gulf.
    Phil. To live without her! is that nothing think you?
The damn'd in Hell endure no greater pain
Then seeing Heaven from far with hopeless eyes.
    Cand. Candiope must die, and die for you;
See it not unreveng'd at least.
    Phil. Ha, unreveng'd! on whom should I revenge it?
But yet she dies, and I may hinder it;
Tis I then murder my *Candiope:*
And yet should I take armes against my Queen,
That favour'd me, rais'd me to what I am?
Alas, it must not be.
    Lys. He cools again. [*Aside.*] ———True; she once favour'd
        you;
But now I am inform'd,
She is besotted on an upstart wretch;
So far, that she intends to make him Master,
Both of her Crown and person.
    Phil.   Knows he that?
Then, what I dreaded most is come to pass.———   [*Aside.*
I am convinc'd of the necessity;
Let us make haste to raze
That action from the Annals of her Reign:
No motive but her glory could have wrought me.
I am a Traytor to her, to preserve her

---

333 headlong?] ~ ! Q1–6, F, D.   345 Queen,] ~ ! Q1–6, F, D.
346 am?] ~ ! Q1–6, F, D.
348 [*Aside.*] ———] ———*aside.*] Q1–3; ———(*Aside.*) Q4–5; ———*Aside.*] Q6;
———*Aside.* F; [*Aside.* D (*s.d. at right; "True . . ." set down a line*).
352 that?] ~ ! Q1–6, F, D.   353 *Aside*] Q4–6, F, D; *aside* Q1–3.
356 from the] Q2–6, F, D; from Q1 (*but corrected in Errata*).

From Treason to her self; and yet Heav'n knows
360 With what a heavy heart
Philocles turns reformer: but have care
This fault of her strange passion take no air.
Let not the vulgar blow upon her fame.
     Lys. I will be careful, shall we go my Lord?
     Phil. Time wasts apace; Each first prepare his men.
Come my *Candiope.*——   *Exeunt* Phil. Cand.
     Lys. This ruines him forever with the Queen;
The odium's half his, the profit all my own.
Those who, like me, by others help would climb,
370 To make 'em sure, must dip 'em in their crime.   *Exit* Lys.

SCENE II.

The Queens appartments.

Enter Queen and Asteria.

     Qu. No more news yet from *Philocles?*
     Ast. None, Madam, since *Flavia's* return!
     Qu. O my *Asteria,* if you lov'd me, sure
You would say something to me of my *Philocles;*
I could speak ever of him.
     Ast.   Madam, you
Commanded me no more to name him to you.
     Qu. Then I command you now to speak of nothing else:
I charge you here, on your allegiance, tell me
What I should do with him.
10   *Ast.* When you gave orders that he should be taken,
You seem'd resolv'd how to dispose of him.
     Qu. Dull *Asteria* not to know,
Mad people never think the same thing twice.

---

364 Lord?] Q4–5, D; ~ : Q1–3, Q6, F.
366 Phil. Cand.] Q3–6, F, D; *Phil. Cand.* Q1–2.
370 Lys.] Q4–6, F, D; *Lys.* Q1–3.
5–6 you / Commanded] you commanded Q1–6, F, D (Commanded Q5, F).

Alas, I'm hurried restless up and down,
I was in anger once, and then I thought
I had put into shore!
But now a gust of love blows hard against me,
And bears me off again.
    Ast. Shall I sing the Song you made of *Philocles,*
And call'd it *Secret-love?*
    Qu. Do, for that's all kindness: and while thou sing'st it,
I can think nothing but what pleases me.

Song.

> *I feed a flame within which so torments me*
> *That it both pains my heart, and yet contents me:*
> *'Tis such a pleasing smart, and I so love it,*
> *That I had rather die, then once remove it.*
>
> *Yet he for whom I grieve shall never know it,*
> *My tongue does not betray, nor my eyes show it:*
> *Not a sigh nor a tear my pain discloses,*
> *But they fall silently like dew on Roses.*
>
> *Thus to prevent my love from being cruel,*
> *My heart's the sacrifice as 'tis the fuel:*
> *And while I suffer this to give him quiet,*
> *My faith rewards my love, though he deny it.*
>
> *On his eyes will I gaze, and there delight me;*
> *While I conceal my love, no frown can fright me:*
> *To be more happy I dare not aspire;*
> *Nor can I fall more low, mounting no higher.*

    Qu. Peace: Me thinks I hear the noise
Of clashing Swords, and clatt'ring Armes, below.

Enter Flavia.

---

20 *Secret-love?*] Q4–6, F, D; ~ . Q1–3.

Now; what news that you press in so rudely?
   Flav. Madam, the worst that can be;
Your Guards upon the sudden are supris'd,
Disarm'd, some slain, all scatter'd.
   Qu. By whom?
   Flav. Prince *Lysimantes,* and Lord *Philocles.*
   Qu. It cannot be; *Philocles* is a Prisoner.
   Flav. What my eyes saw————
   Qu. Pull 'em out, they are false Spectacles.
50   *Ast.* O vertue, impotent and blind as Fortune!
Who would be good, or pious, if this Queen
Thy great Example suffers?
   Qu. Peace, *Asteria,* accuse not vertue;
She has but given me a great occasion
Of showing what I am when Fortune leaves me.
   Ast. Philocles, to do this!
   Qu. I, *Philocles,* I must confess 'twas hard!
But there's a fate in kindness
Still, to be least return'd where most 'tis given.
60 Where's *Candiope?*
   Flav. Philocles was whispering to her.
   Qu. Hence Screech-owl; call my Guards quickly there:
Put 'em apart in several Prisons.
Alas! I had forgot I have no Guards,
But those which are my Jaylors.
Never till now unhappy Queen:
The use of pow'r, till lost, is seldom known;
Now I would strike, I find my Thunder gone.
                Exeunt Queen and Flavia.

Philocles *enters, and meets* Asteria *going out.*

   Phil. Asteria! Where's the Queen?
70   *Ast.* Ah my Lord what have you done?

---

52 suffers?] ~ ! Q1–6, F, D.
68+ s.d. *Exeunt*] Q4–5; *Exit* Q1–3, Q6, F; *Ex.* D.
70 done?] ~ ! Q1–6, F, D.

I came to seek you.
    Phil.   Is it from her you come?
    Ast. No, but on her behalf: her heart's too great,
In this low ebb of Fortune, to intreat.
    Phil. 'Tis but a short Ecclipse,
Which past, a glorious day will soon ensue:
But I would ask a favour too, from you.
    Ast. When Conquerors petition, they command:
Those that can Captive Queens, who can withstand?
    Phil. She, with her happiness, might mine create;
Yet seems indulgent to her own ill fate:
But she, in secret, hates me sure; for why
If not, should she *Candiope* deny?
    Ast. If you dare trust my knowledg of her mind,
She has no thoughts of you that are unkind.
    Phil. I could my sorrows with some patience bear,
Did they proceed from any one but her:
But from the Queen! whose person I adore,
By Duty much, by inclination more.————
    Ast. He is inclin'd already, did he know
That she lov'd him, how would his passion grow!   [*Aside.*
    Phil. That her fair hand with Destiny combines!————
Fate ne're strikes deep, but when unkindness joynes!
For, to confess the secret of my mind,
Something so tender for the Queen I find,
That ev'n *Candiope* can scarce remove,
And, were she lower, I should call it love.
    Ast. She charg'd me not this secret to betray,
But I best serve her if I disobey:
For, if he loves, 'twas for her int'rest done;
If not, he'll keep it secret for his own.————   [*Aside.*
    Phil. Why are you in obliging me so slow?
    Ast. The thing's of great importance you would know;
And you must first swear sècresie to all.

———————

Phil. I swear.

Ast.   Yet hold; your oath's too general:
Swear that *Candiope* shall never know.

Phil. I swear.

Ast.   No not the Queen her self.

Phil.   I vow.

Ast. You wonder why I am so cautious grown
In telling, what concerns your self alone:
But spare my Vow, and guess what it may be
110 That makes the Queen deny *Candiope:*
'Tis neither hate nor pride that moves her mind;
Methinks the Riddle is not hard to find.

Phil. You seem so great a wonder to intend,
As were, in me, a crime to apprehend.

Ast. 'Tis not a crime, to know; but would be one
To prove ungrateful when your Duty's known.

Phil. Why would you thus my easie faith abuse?
I cannot think the Queen so ill would chuse.
But stay, now your imposture will appear;
120 She has her self confess'd she lov'd elsewhere:
On some ignoble choice has plac'd her heart,
One who wants quality, and more, desert.

Ast. This, though unjust, you have most right to say,
For, if you'l rail against your self, you may.

Phil. Dull that I was!
A thousand things now crowd my memory
That make me know it could be none but I.
Her Rage was Love: and its tempestuous flame,
Like Lightning, show'd the Heaven from whence it came.
130 But in her kindness my own shame I see;
Have I dethron'd her then, for loving me?
I hate my self for that which I have done,
Much more, discover'd, then I did unknown.

---

104 swear. / *Ast.*] Q4–6, F, D (swear: Q4, F); swear: (*Ast.*) Q1–3.
106 swear. / *Ast.* . . . self. / *Phil.*] Q4–6, F, D (swear: Q4–5, F; self: Q4, F);
swear: (*Ast.*) . . . self: (*Phil.*) Q1–3.
117 abuse?] ∼ ! Q1–6, F, D.
121 On] Q2–6, F, D; Or Q1 (*but corrected in Errata*).
124 may.] Q2–6, F, D; ∼∧ Q1.

How does she brook her strange imprisonment?
   Ast. As great souls should, that make their own content.
The hardest term she for your act could find
Was onely this, O *Philocles*, unkind!
Then, setting free a sigh, from her fair eyes
She wip'd two pearls, the remnants of mild show'rs,
Which hung, like drops, upon the bells of flowers:
And thank'd the Heav'ns,
Which better did, what she design'd, pursue,
Without her crime to give her pow'r to you.
   Phil. Hold, hold, you set my thoughts so near a Crown,
They mount above my reach to pull them down:
Here Constancy; Ambition there does move;
On each side Beauty, and on both sides Love.
   Ast. Me thinks the least you can is to receive
This love, with reverence, and your former leave.
   Phil. Think but what difficulties come between!
   Ast. 'Tis wond'rous difficult to love a Queen.
   Phil. For pity cease more reasons to provide,
I am but too much yielding to your side;
And, were my heart but at my own dispose,
I should not make a scruple where to choose.
   Ast. Then if the Queen will my advice approve,
Her hatred to you shall expel her love.
   Phil. Not to be lov'd by her, as hard would be
As to be hated by *Candiope*.
   Ast. I leave you to resolve while you have time;
You must be guilty, but may choose your crime.   *Exit* Asteria.
   Phil. One thing I have resolv'd; and that I'le do
Both for my love, and for my honour too.
But then, (Ingratitude and falshood weigh'd,)
I know not which would most my soul upbraid.
Fate shoves me headlong down a rugged way,
Unsafe to run, and yet too steep to stay.   [*Exit* Phil.

---

161 Asteria] Q3–6, F, D; *Asteria* Q1–2.   162 I'le] Q2–6, F, D; I'le Q1.
166 down . . . way,] ~ , . . . ~ ; Q1–2, Q6, F; ~ ᴧ . . . ~ ; Q3–5, D.
167 Phil.] Q3–6, F, D; *Phil.* Q1–2.

ACT V.

SCENE, *The Court.*

Florimell *in Mans Habit.*

Flor. 'Twill be rare now if I can go through with it, to out-do this mad *Celadon* in all his tricks, and get both his Mistresses from him; then I shall revenge my self upon all three, and save my own stake into the bargain; for I find I do love the Rogue in spight of all his infidelities. Yonder they are, and this way they must come.————If cloathes and a *bon meen* will take 'em, I shall do't.————Save you *Monsieur Florimell;* Faith me thinks you are a very *janty* fellow, *poudré & ajusté* as well as the best of 'em. I can manage the little Comb,————set my Hat, shake my
10 Garniture, toss about my empty Noddle, walk with a courant slurr, and at every step peck down my Head: ————if I should be mistaken for some Courtier now, pray where's the dif-ference?————

Enter to her Celadon, Olinda, Sabina.

Olin. Never mince the matter!

Sab. You have left your heart behind with *Florimell;* we know it.

Cel. You know you wrong me; when I am with *Florimell* 'tis still your Prisoner, it onely draws a longer chain after it.

Flor. Is it e'en so? then farwell poor *Florimell,* thy Maidenhead
20 is condemned to die with thee————   [*Aside.*

Cel. But let's leave the discourse; 'tis all digression that does not speak of your beauties.————

---

s.d. SCENE,] SCENE⌄ Q1–6, F, D.   s.d. Florimell] Florimel Q1–6, F, D.
1 *Flor.* 'Twill] Q6, F; 'Twill Q1–5, D.   6 If] Q4–5, F, D; if Q1–3, Q6.
19 so?] ～ ! Q1–6, F, D.
20 *Aside*] Q6, F; *aside* Q1–2; s.d. omitted from Q3–5, D.

Flor. Now for me in the name of impudence!————

                                       [Walks with them.

They are the greatest beauties I confess that ever I beheld.————

Cel. How now, what's the meaning of this young fellow?

Flor. And therefore I cannot wonder that this Gentleman who has the honour to be known to you should admire you,———— since I that am a stranger————

Cel. And a very impudent one, as I take it, Sir.————

Flor. Am so extreamely surpriz'd, that I admire, love, am wounded, and am dying all in a moment.

Cel. I have seen him somewhere, but where I know not! prithee my friend leave us, dost thou think we do not know our way in Court?

Flor. I pretend not to instruct you in your way; you see I do not go before you! but you cannot possibly deny me the happiness to wait upon these Ladies;————me, who————

Cel. Thee, who shalt be beaten most unmercifully if thou dost follow them!————

Flor. You will not draw in Court I hope!————

Cel. Pox on him, let's walk away faster, and be rid of him.————

Flor. O take no care for me, Sir, you shall not lose me, I'le rather mend my pace, then not wait on you.

Olin. I begin to like this fellow.————

Cel. You make very bold here in my Seraglio, and I shall find a time to tell you so, Sir.

Flor. When you find a time to tell me on't, I shall find a time to answer you: But pray what do you find in your self so extraordinary, that you should serve these Ladies better then I? let me know what 'tis you value your self upon, and let them Judg betwixt us.

Cel. I am somewhat more a man then you.

Flor. That is, you are so much older then I: Do you like a man ever the better for his age Ladies?

Sab. Well said, young Gentleman.

23+   s.d. *Walks*] Q6, F, D; *walks* Q1–5.
37   who————] Q4–6, F, D; ~ . ———— Q1–3.   50   I?] F; ~ ; Q1–6, D.

Cel. Pish, thee! a young raw Creature, thou hast ne're been under the Barbers hands yet.

Flor. No, nor under the Surgeons neither as you have been.

60   *Cel.* 'Slife what wouldst thou be at? I am madder then thou art.

Flor. The Devil you are; I'le Tope with you, I'le Sing with you, I'le Dance with you,———I'le Swagger with you.———

Cel. I'le fight with you.

Flor. Out upon fighting; 'tis grown so common a fashion, that a Modish man contemns it; A Man of Garniture and Feather is above the dispensation of the Sword.

Olin. Uds my life, here's the Queens Musick just going to us; you shall decide your quarrel by a Dance.

70   *Sab.* Who stops the Fiddles?

Cel. Base and Trebble, by your leaves we arrest you at these Ladies suits.

Flor. Come on Sirs, play me a Jigg, you shall see how I'le baffle him.

Dance.

Flor. Your judgment, Ladies.

Olin. You sir, you sir: This is the rarest Gentleman: I could live and die with him.———

Sab. Lord how he Sweats! please you Sir to make use of my Handkerchief?

80   *Olin.* You and I are merry, and just of an humour Sir; therefore we two should love one another.

Sab. And you and I are just of an age Sir, and therefore me thinks we should not hate one another.

Cel. Then I perceive Ladies I am a Castaway, a Reprobate with you: why faith this is hard luck now, that I should be no less then one whole hour in getting your affections, and now must lose 'em in a quarter of it.

Olin. No matter, let him rail, does the loss afflict you Sir?

Cel. No in faith does it not; for if you had not forsaken me, I

60   at?] D; ∼ , Q1–6; ∼ : F.   61   art.] Q6, D; ∼ ? Q1–5, F.
73   Jigg, you] D; Jigg, / You Q1–6, F.

had you: so the Willows may flourish for any branches I shall
rob 'em of.

Sab. However we have the advantage to have left you; not you
us.

Cel. That's onely a certain nimbleness in Nature you women
have to be first unconstant: but if you had not made the more
haste, the wind was veering too upon my Weathercock: the
best on't is *Florimell* is worth both of you.

Flor. 'Tis like she'll accept of their leavings.

Cel. She will accept on't, and she shall accept on't; I think I
know more then you of her mind Sir.

Enter Melissa.

Mel. Daughters there's a poor collation within that waits for
you.

Flor. Will you walk, musty Sir?

Cel. No merry Sir; I won'not; I have surfeited of that old
womans face already.

Flor. Begin some frolick then; what will you do for her?

Cel. Faith I am no dog to show tricks for her; I cannot come
aloft for an old Woman.

Flor. Dare you kiss her?

Cel. I was never dar'd by any man.———By your leave old
Madam.———   [*He plucks off her Ruff.*

Mel. Help, help, do you discover my nakedness?

Cel. Peace Tiffany! no harm.   [*He puts on the Ruff.*
Now Sir here's *Florimells* health to you.———   [*Kisses her.*

Mel. Away sir:———a sweet young man as you are to abuse
the gifts of Nature so.

Cel. Good Mother do not commend me so; I am flesh and
blood, and you do not know what you may pluck upon that
reverend person of yours.———Come on, follow your leader.
                        [*Gives* Florimell *the Ruff, she puts it on.*

---

103 walk,] Q6, F, D; ∼ᴧ Q1–5.   109 her?] Q4–5; ∼ ! Q1–3, Q6, F, D.
110 By] Q4–5; by Q1–3, Q6, F, D.   111 off] Q2–6, F, D; of Q1.
113 *Ruff.*] Q4–5, F; ∼ .——— Q1; ∼ᴧ——— Q2–3, D; ∼ᴧᴧ Q6.
114 *Florimells*] Florimels Q1–6, F, D.   114 *Kisses*] Q4–6, F, D; kisses Q1–3.
119+ s.d. Florimell] Florimel Q1–6, F, D.

120   *Flor.* Stand fair, Mother.————

Cel. What with your Hat on? lie thou there;————and thou too.————

   [*Plucks off her Hat and Perruke, and discovers* Florimell.
Omnes. Florimell!

Flor. My kind Mistresses how sorry I am I can do you no further service! I think I had best resign you to *Celadon* to make amends for me.

Cel. Lord what a misfortune it was Ladies, that the Gentleman could not hold forth to you.

Olin. We have lost *Celadon* too.

130   *Mel.* Come away; this is past enduring.   [*Exeunt* Mel. Olin.

Sab. Well, if ever I believe a man to be a man for the sake of a Perruke and Feather again————   [*Exit.*

Flor. Come *Celadon,* shall we make accounts even? Lord what a hanging look was there: indeed if you had been recreant to your Mistress, or had forsworn your love, that sinners face had been but decent, but for the vertuous, the innocent, the constant *Celadon!*————

Cel. This is not very heroick in you now to insult over a man in his misfortunes; but take heed, you have robb'd me of my

140 two Mistresses; I shall grow desperately constant, and all the tempest of my love will fall upon your head: I shall so pay you.

Flor. Who, you pay me? you are a banckrupt, cast beyond all possibility of recovery.

Cel. If I am a banckrupt I'le be a very honest one; when I cannot pay my debts, at least I'le give you up the possession of my body.

Flor. No, I'le deal better with you; since you're unable to pay, I'le give in your bond.

Enter Philocles *with a Commanders Staff in his hand, Attended.*

---

120 fair,] D; ~∧ Q1–6, F.   123 *Florimell*] F, D; Florimell Q1–6.
130 Mel. Olin.] Q3–6, F, D; *Mel. Olin.* Q1–2.
132 Perruke] Q3–6, F, D; Perruks Q1–2.
132 again————] Q6, F, D; ~ .———— Q1–5.
142 Who, you] D; Who you, Q1–6, F.   142 me?] ~ ! Q1–6, F, D.

Phil. Cousin I am sorry I must take you from your company
about an earnest business.

Flor. There needs no excuse my Lord, we had dispatch'd our
affairs, and were just parting.——   [*Going.*

Cel. Will you be going Sir? sweet Sir, damn'd Sir, I have but
one word more to say to you.

Flor. As I am a man of Honour, I'le wait on you some other
time.——

Cel. By these Breeches——

Flor. Which if I marry you I am resolv'd to wear; put that
into our Bargain, and so adieu Sir.——   [*Exit* Florimell.

Phil. Hark you Cousin——   (*They whisper.*)
You'll see it exactly executed; I rely upon you.

Cel. I shall not fail, my Lord; may the conclusion of it prove
happy to you.   *Exit* Celadon.

Philocles solus. Wheree're I cast about my wond'ring eyes.
Greatness lies ready in some shape to tempt me.
The royal furniture in every room,
The Guards, and the huge waving crowds of people,
All waiting for a sight of that fair Queen
Who makes a present of her love to me:
Now tell me, Stoique!——
If all these with a wish might be made thine,
Would'st thou not truck thy ragged vertue for 'em?
If Glory was a bait that Angels swallow'd
How then should souls ally'd to sence, resist it?

Enter Candiope.

Ah poor *Candiope!* I pity her,
But that is all.——

---

153   Sir? sweet] F; ~ ; ~ Q1-2, Q6; ~ , ~ Q3-5, D.
155   I am] Q4-5, D; I Q1-3; I'm Q6, F.
157-158   Breeches—— / *Flor.* Which] Q4-6, F, D (Breeches.—— Q4-5);
Breeches.—— *Flor.* which Q1-3.
163   Celadon] Q3-6, F, D; *Celadon* Q1-2.
164   *Philocles solus.* Wheree're] *Philocles solus.* / Wheree're Q1-6, F, D.
174   it?] ~ ! Q1-6, F, D.

  Cand.   O my dear *Philocles!*
A thousand blessings wait on thee!
The hope of being thine, I think will put
Me past my meat and sleep with extasie,
180 So I shall keep the fasts of Seraphim's,
And wake for joy like Nightingals in *May.*
  Phil. Wake, *Philocles,* wake from thy dream of glory,
'Tis all but shadow to *Candiope:*
Canst thou betray a love so innocent?———   [*Aside.*
  Cand. What makes you melancholick? I doubt
I have displeased you?
  Phil. No my love, I am not displeas'd with you,
But with my self, when I consider
How little I deserve you.
190 *Cand.*   Say not so
My *Philocles,* a love so true as yours
That would have left a Court, and a Queens favour
To live in a poor Hermitage with me———
  Phil. Ha! she has stung me to the quick!
As if she knew the falshood I intended:
But, I thank Heav'n, it has recal'd my vertue.———   [*Aside.*
[*To her.*] O my dear, I love you, and you onely;
Go in, I have some business for a while;
But I think minutes ages till we meet.
  Cand. I knew you had; but yet I could not choose
200 But come and look upon you.———   [*Exit* Candiope.
  Phil. What barbarous man could wrong so sweet a vertue?

    Enter the Queen in black with Asteria.

Madam, the States are straight to meet; but why
In these dark ornaments will you be seen?

176–177 *Philocles! /* A] D; *Philocles!* A Q1–6, F.
182 Wake,] Q6, F; ~∧ Q1–5, D. 184 innocent?———] ~ !——— Q1–6, F, D.
190–191 so / My] so my Q1–6, F, D.
192 me———] ~ .——— Q1–6, F, D.
195 vertue.——— [*Aside*] ~ ;——— [aside Q1–5, F, D (*Aside* Q4–5, F, D);
~∧——— [*Aside* Q6.
196 *her.*] Q5–6, F, D; ~∧ Q1–4.   201 vertue?] ~ ! Q1–6, F, D.

Qu. ———They fit the fortune of a Captive Queen.

Phil. ———Deep shades are thus to heighten colours set;
So Stars in Night, and Diamonds shine in Jet.

Qu. True friends should so in dark afflictions shine,
But I have no great cause to boast of mine.

Phil. You may have too much prejudice for some,
And think 'em false before their trial's come.
But, Madam, what determine you to do?

Qu. I come not here to be advis'd by you:
But charge you by that pow'r which once you own'd,
And which is still my right, ev'n when unthron'd;
That whatsoe're the States resolve of me,
You never more think of *Candiope*.

Phil. Not think of her! ah, how should I obey?
Her tyrant eyes have forc'd my heart away.

Qu. By force retake it from those tyrant eyes,
I'le grant you out my Letters of Reprize.

Phil. She has, too well, prevented that design
By giving me her heart in change for mine.

Qu. Thus foolish *Indians* Gold for Glass forgo,
'Twas to your loss you priz'd your heart so low.
I set its value when you were advanc'd.
And as my favours grew, its rate inhanc'd.

Phil. The rate of Subjects hearts by yours must go,
And love in yours has set the value low.

Qu. I stand corrected, and my self reprove,
You teach me to repent my low-plac'd love:
Help me this passion from my heart to tear,
Now rail on him, and I will sit and hear.

Phil. Madam, like you, I have repented too,
And dare not rail on one I do not know.

Qu. This, *Philocles*, like strange perverseness shows,
As if what e're I said, you would oppose;
How come you thus concern'd, for this unknown?

Phil. I onely judg his actions by my own.

Qu. I've heard too much, and you too much have said,

240 O Heav'ns, the secret of my soul's betray'd!
He knows my love, I read it in his face,
And blushes, conscious of his Queens disgrace.——— [*Aside.*
[*To him.*] Hence quickly, hence, or I shall die with shame.
    Phil. Now I love both, and both with equal flame.
Wretched I came, more wretched I retire:
When two winds blow it, who can quench the fire?
                                        Exit Philocles.
    Qu. O my *Asteria,* I know not whom t'accuse;
But either my own eyes or you, have told
My love to *Philocles.*
250   *Ast.* Is't possible that he should know it, Madam?
    Qu. Me thinks you ask'd that question guiltily.
[*Her hand on* Ast. *shoulder.*] Confess, for I will know,
What was the subject of your long discourse
I'th Antichamber with him.
    Ast. It was my business to convince him, Madam,
How ill he did, being so much oblig'd,
To joyn in your imprisonment.
    Qu. Nay, now I am confirm'd my thought was true;
For you could give him no such reason
260 Of his obligements as my love.
    Ast. Because I saw him much a Malecontent,
I thought to win him to your int'rest, Madam,
By telling him it was no want of kindness
Made your refusal of *Candiope.*
And he perhaps———
    Qu.   What of him now?
    Ast. As men are apt, interpreted my words
To all th'advantage he could wrest the sence,
As if I meant you Lov'd him.

---

242 *Aside*] Q4–6, F, D; *aside* Q1–3.   245 retire:] D; ∼ , Q1–6, F.
246 it,] Q6, D; ∼∧ Q1–5, F.   246 fire?] Q6; ∼ ! Q1–5, F, D.
246+ s.d. Philocles] Q3–6, F, D; *Philocles* Q1–2.
250 Madam?] ∼ ! Q1–6, F, D.   252 [*Her*] Q6, F, D; ∧∼ Q1–5.
252–253 know, / What] know, what Q1–6, F, D.
265 perhaps——— / *Qu.*] Q4–6, F, D; perhaps——— (*Qu.*) Q1–3.
265 now?] Q4–6, D; ∼ ! Q1; ∼ . Q2–3, F.

Qu. Have I deposited within thy breast
70 The dearest treasure of my life, my glory,
And hast thou thus betray'd me?
But why do I accuse thy female weakness,
And not my own for trusting thee?
Unhappy Queen, *Philocles* knows thy fondness,
And needs must think it done by thy Command.
    Ast. Dear Madam, think not so.
    Qu. Peace, peace, thou should'st for ever hold thy tongue.
For it has spoke too much for all thy life.————   [*To her.*
Then *Philocles* has told *Candiope,*
0 And courts her kindness with his scorn of me.
O whither am I fallen?
But I must rouze my self, and give a stop
To all these ills by headlong passion caus'd;
In hearts resolv'd weak love is put to flight,
And onely conquers when we dare not fight.
But we indulge our harms, and while he gains
An entrance, please our selves into our pains.

Enter Lysimantes.

    Ast. Prince *Lysimantes,* Madam!————
    Qu. Come near you poor deluded criminal;
  See how ambition cheats you:
You thought to find a Prisoner here,
But you behold a Queen.
    Lys. And may you long be so: 'tis true this Act
May cause some wonder in your Majesty.
    Qu. None, Cousin, none; I ever thought you
Ambitious, Proud, designing.
    Lys. Yet all my Pride, Designs, and my Ambition
Were taught me by a Master
With whom you are not unacquainted, Madam.
    Qu. Explain your self; dark purposes, like yours,

---

271 me?] Q6; ~ ! Q1–5, F, D.   273 thee?] Q6; ~ ! Q1–5, F, D.
281–282 fallen? / But] D (fallen!); fallen! But Q1–6, F.

Need an Interpretation.

    Lys. 'Tis love I mean.

    Qu.   Have my low fortunes giv'n thee
This insolence, to name it to thy Queen?

    Lys. Yet you have heard love nam'd without offence.
As much below you as you think my passion,
I can look down on yours.———

    Qu.   Does he know it too?
This is th' extreamest malice of my Stars!———   [*Aside.*

    Lys. You see, that Princes faults,
(How e're they think 'em safe from publick view)
310 Fly out through the dark crannies of their Closets:
We know what the Sun does,
Ev'n when we see him not in t'other world.

    Qu. My actions, Cousin, never fear'd the light.

    Lys. Produce him then, your darling of the dark,
For such an one you have.

    Qu.   I know no such.

    Lys. You know, but will not own him.

    Qu. Rebels ne're want pretence to blacken Kings,
And this, it seems, is yours: do you produce him,
Or ne're hereafter sully my Renown
320 With this aspersion.———Sure he dares not name him.———
                                              [*Aside.*

    Lys. I am too tender of your fame; or else———
Nor are things brought to that extremity:
Provided you accept my passion,
I'le gladly yield to think I was deceiv'd.

    Qu. Keep in your error still; I will not buy
Your good opinion at so dear a rate,
As my own misery by being yours.

    Lys. Do not provoke my patience by such scornes,
For fear I break through all, and name him to you.

330   *Qu.* Hope not to fright me with your mighty looks;

---

302 mean. / *Qu.*] Q4–6, F, D; mean. (*Qu.*) Q1–3.
306 too?] ∼ ! Q1–6, F, D.   307 *Aside*] Q4–6, F, D; *aside* Q1–3.
315 have. / *Qu.*] Q4–6, F, D; have. (*Qu.*) Q1–3.
320 aspersion.———] ∼ :——— Q1–5, F, D; ∼∧——— Q6.
320+ *s.d. Aside*] Q4–6, F, D; *aside* Q1–3.

Know I dare stem that tempest in your brow,
And dash it back upon you.

   Lys. Spight of prudence it will out: 'Tis *Philocles*.
Now judge, when I was made a property
To cheat my self by making him your Prisoner,
Whether I had not right to take up armes.

   Qu. Poor envious wretch!
Was this the venome that swell'd up thy brest?
My grace to *Philocles* mis-deem'd my love!

   Lys. 'Tis true, the Gentleman is innocent;
He ne're sinn'd up so high, not in his wishes;
You know he loves elsewhere.

   Qu.   You mean your Sister.

   Lys. I wish some Sybil now would tell me
Why you refus'd her to him.

   Qu. Perhaps I did not think him worthy of her.

   Lys. Did you not think him too worthy, Madam?
This is too thin a vail to hide your passion,
To prove you love him not, yet give her him,
And I'le engage my honour to lay down my Armes.

   Qu. He is arriv'd where I would wish. [*Aside.*] ———Call in
The company, and you shall see what I will do.———

   Lys. Who waits without there?———   [*Exit* Lys.

   Qu. Now hold, my heart, for this one act of honour,
And I will never ask more courage of thee:
Once more I have the means to reinstate
My self into my glory;
I feel my love to *Philocles* within me
Shrink, and pull back my heart from this hard tryal,
But it must be when glory says it must:
As children wading from some Rivers bank
First try the water with their tender feet;

---

336 armes.] ~ ? Q1–6, F, D.   338 Was] Q3–6, F, D; was Q1–2.
344 him.] ~ ? Q1–6, F, D.   347 hide] Q4–5, D; hinder Q1–3, Q6, F.
349 Armes.] Q2–6, F, D; ~ Q1.
350–351 wish. [*Aside.*] ———Call in / The] wish———*aside.*] Call in the Q1–2;
wish———*aside.* / Call in the Q3; wish——— [*Aside.* / Call in the Q4–6, F, D.
352 *Exit* Lys.] Q2–6, F, D; *Exit Lys.* Q1.
355–356 reinstate / My] reinstate my Q1–6, F, D.

Then shuddring up with cold, step back again,
And streight a little further venture on,
Till at the last they plunge into the deep,
And pass, at once, what they were doubting long:
I'le make the same experiment;
It shall be done in haste,
Because I'le put it past my pow'r t'undo.

Enter at one door Lysimantes, *at the other* Philocles, Celadon,
Candiope, Florimell, Flavia, Olinda, Sabina; *the three
Deputies, and Soldiers.*

    Lys. In Armes! is all well, *Philocles?*
370   *Phil.* No, but it shall be.
    Qu.   He comes, and with him
The fevour of my love returns to shake me.
I see love is not banish'd from my soul,
He is still there, but is chain'd up by glory.
    Ast. You've made a noble conquest, Madam.
    Qu. Come hither, *Philocles:* I am first to tell you
I and my Cousin are agreed, he has
Engag'd to lay down Armes.
    Phil. 'Tis well for him he has; for all his party
By my command already are surpriz'd,
380 While I was talking with your Majesty.
    Cel. Yes 'faith I have done him that courtesie; I brought his
followers, under pretence of guarding it, to a straight place where
they are all coupt up without use of their Armes, and may be
pelted to death by the small infantry o'the town.
    Qu. 'Twas more then I expected, or could hope;
Yet still I thought your meaning honest.
    Phil. My fault was rashness, but 'twas full of zeal:
Nor had I e're been led to that attempt,
Had I not seen it would be done without me:
390 But by compliance I preserv'd the pow'r
Which I have since made use of for your service.

366–367 experiment; / It] experiment; it Q1–6, F, D.
369 all] Q2–6, F, D; al! Q1.   381 courtesie; I] D; courtesie; / I Q1–6, F.

Qu. And which I purpose so to recompence.————
Lys. With her Crown she means; I knew 'twould come to't.
                                             [*Aside.*

Phil. O Heav'ns, she'll own her love!
Then I must lose *Candiope* for ever,
And floating in a vast abyss of glory,
Seek and not find my self!————   [*Aside.*
Qu. Take your *Candiope;* and be as happy
As love can make you both. ————How pleas'd I am
That I can force my tongue,
To speak words so far distant from my heart!————   [*Aside.*
Cand. My happiness is more then I can utter!
Lys. Methinks I could
Do violence on my self for taking Armes
Against a Queen so good, so bountiful:
Give me leave, Madam, in my extasie
Of joy, to give you thanks for *Philocles.*
You have preserv'd my friend, and now he owes not
His fortunes onely to your favour; but
What's more, his life, and more then that, his love.
I am convinc'd, she never lov'd him now;
Since by her free consent, all force remov'd
She gives him to my Sister.
Flavia was an Impostor and deceiv'd me.————   [*Aside.*
Phil. As for me, Madam, I can onely say
That I beg respit for my thanks; for on the sudden,
The benefit's so great it overwhelmes me.
Ast. Mark but th' faintness of th' acknowledgment.
                                    [*To the Qu. aside.*
Qu. to Ast. I have observ'd it with you, and am pleas'd
He seems not satisfi'd; for I still wish

393+   s.d. Aside] Q4–6, F, D; *aside* Q1–3.
397   Aside] *aside* Q1; *s.d. omitted from* Q2–6, F, D.
398   Qu.] Q2–6, F, D; *Qu,* Q1.
399   both. ————How] both: ————*how* Q1–6, F, D (both∧———— Q6; How D).
401   Aside] Q4–6, F, D; *aside* Q1–3.
403–404   could / Do] could do Q1–6, F, D.
414   Aside] *aside* Q1; *s.d. omitted from* Q2–6, F, D.
418+   s.d. To the Qu.] D; *to the* Qu. Q1–6, F.
419   to Ast.∧] D; *to* ∼ .] Q1–6, F.

That he may love me.

 Phil. I see *Asteria* deluded me
With flattering hopes of the Queens love
Onely to draw me off from *Lysimantes:*————
But I will think no more on't.
I'm going to possess *Candiope,*
And I am ravish'd with the joy on't! ha!
Not ravish'd neither.
For what can be more charming then that Queen?
430 Behold how night sits lovely on her eye-brows,
While day breaks from her eyes! then, a Crown too:
Lost, lost, for ever lost, and now 'tis gone
'Tis beautiful!————   *Aside.*

 Ast.   How he eyes you still!————*To the Queen.*
 Phil. Sure I had one of the fallen Angels Dreams;
All Heav'n within this hour was mine!————   *Aside.*

 Cand. What is it that disturbs you Dear?
 Phil. Onely the greatness of my joy:
I've ta'ne too strong a Cordial, love,
And cannot yet digest it.
440 *Qu. Clapping her hand on Asteria.* 'Tis done!
But this pang more; and then a glorious birth.
The Tumults of this day, my loyal Subjects
Have setled in my heart a resolution,
Happy for you, and glorious too for me.
First for my Cousin, though attempting on my person,
He has incurr'd the danger of the Laws,
I will not punish him.

 Lys. You bind me ever to my loyalty.
 Qu. Then, that I may oblige you more to it,
450 I here declare you rightful successor,

429 Queen?] ∼ ! Q1–6, F, D.   433 *Aside*] Q4–6, F, D; *aside* Q1–3.
433 *To*] Q5–6, F, D; *to* Q1–4. 435 *Aside*] Q4–6, F, D; *aside* Q1–3.
440 *Qu. Clapping . . . Asteria.*] [Qu. *Clapping* . . . Asteria‸] Q1–4, Q6; Qu.
[*Clapping* . . . Asteria.] Q5; Qu. . . . [*Clapping* . . . Asteria. F, D (*s.d. at
right*).
440–441 done! / But] D; done! but Q1–6, F.
449 it,] Q3–5, D; ∼ . Q1–2, Q6, F.

And heir immediate to my Crown:

This, Gentlemen,———   [*To the Deputies.*

I hope will still my subjects discontents,

When they behold succession firmly setled.

   Deputies. Heav'n preserve your Majesty.

   Qu. As for my self I have resolv'd

Still to continue as I am, unmarried:

The cares, observances, and all the duties

Which I should pay an Husband, I will place

Upon my people; and our mutual love

Shall make a blessing more then Conjugal,

And this the States shall ratifie.

   Lys. Heav'n bear me witness that I take no joy

In the succession of a Crown

Which must descend to me so sad a way.

   Qu. Cousin, no more; my resolution's past,

Which fate shall never alter.

   Phil. Then, I am once more happy:

For since none can possess her, I am pleas'd

With my own choice, and will desire no more.

For multiplying wishes is a curse

That keeps the mind still painfully awake.

   Qu. Celadon!

Your care and loyalty have this day oblig'd me;

But how to be acknowledging I know not,

Unless you give the means.

   Cel. I was in hope your Majesty had forgot me; therefore if you please, Madam, I onely beg a pardon for having taken up armes once to day against you; for I have a foolish kind of Conscience, which I wish many of your Subjects had, that will not let me ask a recompence for my loyalty, when I know I have been a Rebel.

   Qu. Your modesty shall not serve the turn; Ask something.

---

452 *To*] Q2–6, F, D; *to* Q1.   455 *Deputies.*] F, D; [∼ .] Q1–5; ∼ .] Q6.
465 a way] Q3–5, D; away Q1–2, Q6, F.   472 keeps] D; keep Q1–6, F.
472 awake.] Q4–6, F, D; ∼ : Q1–3.   474 Your] Q2–6, F, D; You Q1.
475 I] Q3–6, F, D; *I* Q1–2.

Cel. Then I beg, Madam, you will command *Florimell* never to be friends with me.

Flor. Ask again; I grant that without the Queen: But why are you affraid on't?

Cel. Because I am sure as soon as ever you are, you'l marry me.

Flor. Do you fear it?

490 *Cel.* No, 'twill come with a fear.

Flor. If you do, I will not stick with you for an Oath.

Cel. I require no Oath till we come to Church; and then after the Priest, I hope; for I find it will be my destiny to marry thee.

Flor. If ever I say word after the black Gentleman for thee *Celadon*———

Cel. Then I hope you'l give me leave to bestow a faithful heart elsewhere.

Flor. I but if you would have one you must bespeak it, for I am sure you have none ready made.

500 *Cel.* What say you, shall I marry *Flavia?*

Flor. No, she'll be too cunning for you.

Cel. What say you to *Olinda* then? she's tall, and fair, and bonny.

Flor. And foolish, and apish, and fickle.

Cel. But *Sabina,* there's pretty, and young, and loving, and innocent.

Flor. And dwarfish, and childish, and fond, and flippant: if you marry her Sister you will get May-poles, and if you marry her you will get Fayries to dance about them.

510 *Cel.* Nay then the case is clear, *Florimell;* if you take 'em all from me, 'tis because you reserve me for your self.

Flor. But this Marriage is such a Bugbear to me; much might be if we could invent but any way to make it easie.

Cel. Some foolish people have made it uneasie, by drawing the knot faster then they need; but we that are wiser will loosen it a little.

Flor. 'Tis true indeed, there's some difference betwixt a Girdle and an Halter.

Cel. As for the first year, according to the laudable custome

513 make] Q2–6, F, D; mak Q1.

of new married people, we shall follow one another up into Chambers, and down into Gardens, and think we shall never have enough of one another.———So far 'tis pleasant enough I hope.

Flor. But after that, when we begin to live like Husband and Wife, and never come near one another———what then Sir?

Cel. Why then our onely happiness must be to have one mind, and one will, *Florimell.*

Flor. One mind if thou wilt, but prithee let us have two wills; for I find one will be little enough for me alone: But how if those wills should meet and clash, *Celadon?*

Cel. I warrant thee for that: Husbands and Wives keep their wills far enough asunder for ever meeting: one thing let us be sure to agree on, that is, never to be jealous.

Flor. No; but e'en love one another as long as we can; and confess the truth when we can love no longer.

Cel. When I have been at play, you shall never ask me what money I have lost.

Flor. When I have been abroad you shall never enquire who treated me.

Cel. Item, I will have the liberty to sleep all night, without your interrupting my repose for any evil design whatsoever.

Flor. Item, Then you shall bid me good night before you sleep.

Cel. Provided always, that whatever liberties we take with other people, we continue very honest to one another.

Flor. As far as will consist with a pleasant life.

Cel. Lastly, Whereas the names of Husband and Wife hold forth nothing but clashing and cloying, and dulness and faintness in their signification; they shall be abolish'd for ever betwixt us.

Flor. And instead of those, we will be married by the more agreeable names of Mistress and Gallant.

Cel. None of my priviledges to be infring'd by thee *Florimell,* under the penalty of a month of Fasting-nights.

---

548 nothing] F; ∼ , Q1–6, D.   553 *Florimell,*] Q2–6, F, D; ∼ . Q1.

Flor. None of my privileges to be infring'd by thee *Celadon,*
under the penalty of Cuckoldom.

Cel. Well, if it be my fortune to be made a Cuckold, I had
rather thou shouldst make me one then any one in *Sicily:* and
for my comfort I shall have thee oftner then any of thy servants.

560   *Flor.* La ye now, is not such a marriage as good as wenching,
Celadon?

Cel. This is very good, but not so good, *Florimell.*

Qu. Now set me forward to th'Assembly.
You promise Cousin your consent?

Lys. But most unwillingly.

Qu. Philocles, I must beg your voice too.

Phil. Most joyfully I give it.

Lys. Madam, but one word more; since you are so resolv'd,
That you may see, bold as my passion was,

570   'Twas onely for your person, not your Crown;
I swear no second love
Shall violate the flame I had for you,
But in strict imitation of your Oath
I vow a single life.

Qu. to Asteria. Now, my *Asteria,* my joys are full;
The pow'rs above that see
The innocent love I bear to *Philocles,*
Have giv'n its due reward; for by this means
The right of *Lysimantes* will devolve

580   Upon *Candiope;* and I shall have
This great content, to think, when I am dead
My Crown may fall on *Philocles* his head.   *Exeunt omnes.*

_____

575   *to Asteria.*ʌ] *to* Asteria.] Qı–6 (*Ast.* Q6); to *Asteria.*] F; [*To* Asteria. D *(at*
right).

EPILOGUE.

Written by a Person of Honour.

O UR *Poet something doubtful of his Fate*
    Made choice of me to be his Advocate,
    Relying on my Knowledg in the Laws,
And I as boldly undertook the Cause.
I left my Client yonder in a rant
Against the envious, and the ignorant,
Who are, he sayes, his onely Enemies:
But he contemns their malice, and defies
The sharpest of his Censurers to say
Where there is one gross fault in all his Play.
The language is so fitted for each part,
The Plot according to the Rules of Art;
And twenty other things he bid me tell you,
But I cry'd, e'en go do't your self for Nelly.
Reason, with Judges, urg'd in the defence
Of those they would condemn, is insolence;
I therefore wave the merits of his Play,
And think it fit to plead this safer way.
If, when too many in the purchase share
Robbing's not worth the danger nor the care;
The men of business must, in Policy,
Cherish a little harmless Poetry;
All wit wou'd else grow up to Knavery.
Wit is a Bird of Musick, or of Prey,
Mounting she strikes at all things in her way;
But if this Birdlime once but touch her wings,
On the next bush she sits her down, and sings.
I have but one word more; tell me I pray
What you will get by damning of our Play?
A whipt Fanatick who does not recant
Is by his Brethren call'd a suffring Saint;
And by your hands shou'd this poor Poet die

24   *Prey,*] Q4–5, F, D; ~ . Q1–3, Q6.

Before he does renounce his Poetry,
His death must needs confirm the Party more
Then all his scribling life could do before.
Where so much zeal does in a Sect appear,
'Tis to no purpose, 'faith, to be severe.
But 'tother day I heard this rhyming Fop
Say Criticks were the Whips, and he the Top;
40 *For, as a Top spins best the more you baste her,*
So every lash you give, he writes the faster.

FINIS.

EPILOGUE

Spoken by Mrs. Reeves *to the* Maiden
Queen, *in mans Cloathes.*

WHAT think you Sirs, was't not all well enough,
    Will you not grant that we can strut, and huff?
    Men may be proud, but faith for ought I see,
They neither walk, nor cock, so well as we.
And for the fighting Part we may in time,
Grow up to swagger in heroick Rhime.
For though we cannot boast of equal force,
Yet at some Weapon's men have still the worse.
Why should not then we Women act alone,
10 Or whence are men so necessary grown?
Our's are so old, they are as good as none.
Some who have tri'd em if you'l take their Oaths,
Swear they're as arrant tinsell as their Cloaths.
Imagine us but what we represent,
And we could e'ne, give you as good content.

Maiden Queen, *in mans Cloathes.*] *Maiden Queen.* O1; *Maiden Queen, in mans*
Cloathes. O2; omitted from M1.
2 huff?] ~ . O1–2; ~ᴀ M1.   10 grown?] ~ , O1–2; ~ᴀ M1.
11 none.] O2; ~ᴀ O1, M1.

Our faces, shapes, all's better than you see,
And for the rest they want as much as we!
Oh would the higher Powers be kind to us,
And grant us to set up a female house.
Wee'l make our selves to please both Sexes then,
To the Men Women, to the Women Men.
Here we presume, our Legs are no ill sight,
And they would give you no ill Dreams at night.
In Dream's both Sexes may their passions ease,
You make us then as civil as you please.
This would prevent the houses joyning too,
At which we are as much displeas'd as you.
For all our Women most devoutly swear,
Each would be rather a poor Actress here,
Then to be made a Mamamouchi there.

26 too] O2, M1; two O1.

SIR MARTIN MAR-ALL

OR

THE FEIGNED INNOCENCE

Sᵣ Martin Mar-all,

OR THE

Feign d Innocence:

A

COMEDY.

As it was Acted at

His HIGHNESSE the DUKE of *YORK'S*

THEATRE.

Writt By The Duke of New Castle
The Langbaine ascribes it to Dryden

LONDON,

Printed for *H. Herringman*, at the Sign of the *Blew Anchor* in the
Lower walk of the *New Exchange*. 1668.

TITLE PAGE OF THE FIRST EDITION (MACDONALD 71A)

The Names of the Persons

rd *Dartmouth.*	In love with Mrs. *Christian.*
. Moody.	The Swash-buckler.
Martin Mar-all.	A Fool.
irner.	His Man.
John Swallow.	A Kentish Knight.
dy Dupe.	The old Lady.
s. Christian.	Her young Niece.
s. Millisent.	The Swash-bucklers Daughter.
se.	Her Maid.
s. Preparation.	Woman to the old Lady.
her Servants, Men and Women.	
ularrier.	
yliffs.	

The SCENE Covent-Garden.

PROLOGUE.

FOOLS, *which each man meets in his Dish each day,*
    Are yet the great Regalios of a Play;
    In which to Poets you but just appear,
To prize that highest which costs them so dear:
Fops in the Town more easily will pass;
One story makes a statutable Ass:
But such in Plays must be much thicker sown,
Like yolks of Eggs, a dozen beat to one.
Observing Poets all their walks invade,
10 *As men watch Woodcocks gliding through a Glade:*
And when they have enough for Comedy,
They stow their several Bodies in a Pye:
The Poet's but the Cook to fashion it,
For, Gallants, you your selves have found the wit.
To bid you welcome would your bounty wrong,
None welcome those who bring their chear along.

EPILOGUE.

As *Country Vicars, when the Sermon's done,*
Run hudling to the Benediction;
Well knowing, though the better sort may stay,
The Vulgar Rout will run unblest away:
So we, when once our Play is done, make haste
With a short Epilogue to close your taste.
In thus withdrawing we seem mannerly,
But when the Curtain's down we peep, and see
A Jury of the Wits who still stay late,
And in their Club decree the poor Plays fate;
Their verdict back is to the Boxes brought,
Thence all the Town pronounces it their thought.
Thus, Gallants, we like Lilly *can foresee,*
But if you ask us what our doom will be,
We by to morrow will our Fortune cast,
As he tells all things when the Year is past.

THE FEIGN'D INNOCENCE:

OR,

SIR MARTIN MARRALL.

ACT I.

Enter Warner *solus.*

Warn. Where the Devil is this Master of mine? he is ever out of the way when he should do himself good. This 'tis to serve a Coxcomb, one that has no more brains than just those I carry for him. Well! of all Fopps commend me to him for the greatest; he's so opinion'd of his own Abilities, that he is ever designing somewhat, and yet he sows his Stratagems so shallow, that every Daw can pick 'em up: from a plotting Fool the Lord deliver me. Here he comes, O! it seems his Cousin's with him, then it is not so bad as I imagin'd.

Enter Sir Martin Marral, *Lady* Dupe.

10   *La. Dupe.* I think 'twas well contriv'd for your access to lodge her in the same house with you.

Sir Mart. 'Tis pretty well, I must confess.

Warn. Had he plotted it himself, it had been admirable.

[*Aside.*

La. Dupe. For when her Father *Moody* writ to me to take him Lodgings, I so order'd it, the choice seem'd his, not mine.

Sir Mart. I have hit of a thing my self sometimes, when wiser Heads have miss'd it.———But that might be meer luck.

ACT] Q4–5, F, D; ∼ . Q1–3.

La. Dupe. Fortune does more than Wisdom.

Sir Mart. Nay, for that you shall excuse me; I will not value any mans Fortune at a rush, except he have Wit and Parts to bear him out. But when do you expect 'em?

La. Dupe. This Tide will bring them from *Gravesend.* You had best let your man go as from me, and wait them at the Stairs in *Durham*-yard.

Sir Mart. Lord, Cousin, what a-do is here with your Counsel! as though I could not have thought of that my self. I could find in my heart not to send him now———stay a little———I could soon find out some other way.

Warn. A minute's stay may lose your business.

Sir Mart. Well, go then,———but you must grant, if he had stay'd, I could have found a better way,———you grant it?

La. Dupe. For once I will not stand with you.———

[*Exit* Warner.

'Tis a sweet Gentlewoman this Mrs. *Millisent,* if you can get her.

Sir Mart. Let me alone for plotting.

La. Dupe. But by your favour, Sir, 'tis not so easie, her Father has already promis'd her: and the young Gentleman comes up with 'em: I partly know the man,———but the old Squire is humoursome, he's stout, and plain in speech and in behaviour; he loves none of the fine Town-tricks of breeding, but stands up for the old *Elizabeth* way in all things. This we must work upon.

Sir Mart. Sure you think you have to deal with a Fool, Cousin!

Enter Mrs. Christian.

19   *Sir*] Q2–5, F, D; ~ . Q1.
19–21   *as in D; set as verse in Q1–5, F* (. . . / I . . . / Except . . . / But).
22–24   *as in D; set as verse in Q1–5, F* (. . . / You . . . / And).
25   a-do] Q4–5, a do Q1–3, F, D.
26   as . . . self.] *as in D; set as a line of verse in Q1–5, F* (As).
31   it?] Q3–5; ~ . Q1–2, F, D.   32+   *s.d.* Warner] Q4–5, F, D; *Warner* Q1–3.
36–41   *as in D; set as verse in Q1–5, F* (. . . / Her Father . . . / And the . . . / I . . . / He's . . . / He . . . / But . . . / This).
42   Sure] D; ~ ! Q1–5, F.   42   Cousin!] Q5; ~ ? Q1–4, F, D.
42+   *s.d. Enter Mrs.* Christian.] Q5, F, D; [*Enter Mrs. Christian.* Q1–4 (Christian Q4).

La. Dupe. O my dear Neice, I have some business with you.
                                                    [*Whispers.*

Sir Mart. Well, Madam, I'le take one turn here i'th *Piazza's;*
a thousand things are hammering in this head; 'tis a fruitful
Noddle, though I say it.   [*Exit Sir* Martin.

La. Dupe. Go thy ways for a most conceited Fool.———But
to our business, Cousin: you are young, but I am old, and have
had all the Love-experience that a discreet Lady ought to have;
50 and therefore let me instruct you about the Love this rich Lord
makes to you.

Chr. You know, Madam, he's married, so that we cannot work
upon that ground of Matrimony.

La. Dupe. But there are advantages enough for you, if you
will be wise and follow my advice.

Chr. Madam, my Friends left me to your care, therefore I will
wholly follow your Counsel with secrecy and obedience.

La. Dupe. Sweet-heart, it shall be the better for you another
day: well then, this Lord that pretends to you is crafty and false,
60 as most men are, especially in Love;———therefore we must be
subtle to meet with all his Plots, and have Countermines against
his Works to blow him up.

Chr. As how, Madam?

La. Dupe. Why, Girl, hee'l make fierce Love to you, but you
must not suffer him to ruffle you or steal a kiss: but you must
weep and sigh, and say you'l tell me on't, and that you will not
be us'd so; and play the innocent just like a Child, and seem ignorant of all.

Chr. I warrant you I'le be very ignorant, Madam.

70   *La. Dupe.* And be sure when he has tows'd you, not to appear
at Supper that night, that you may fright him.

Chr. No, Madam.

La. Dupe. That he may think you have told me.

Chr. I, Madam.

La. Dupe. And keep your Chamber, and say your head akes.

Chr. O, most extreamly, Madam.

44–46   *as in D; set as verse in* Q1–5, F (. . . / A . . . / 'Tis).
46   Martin] Q4–5, F, D; *Martin* Q1–3.
47   *La.* . . . Fool.———] *as in D; set as a line of verse in* Q1–5, F.
73   *La.*] Q2–5, F, D; ∼∧ Q1.

La. Dupe. And lock the door, and admit of no night-visits: at Supper I'le ask where's my Cousin, and being told you are not well, I'le start from the Table to visit you, desiring his Lordship not to incommode himself; for I will presently wait on him agen.

Chr. But how, when you are return'd, Madam?

La. Dupe. Then somewhat discompos'd, I'le say I doubt the Meazles or Small-pox will seize on you, and then the Girl is spoil'd; saying, Poor thing, her Portion is her Beauty and her Vertue; and often send to see how you do, by whispers in my Servants ears, and have those whispers of your health return'd to mine: if his Lordship thereupon askes how you do, I will pretend it was some other thing.

Chr. Right, Madam, for that will bring him further in suspence.

La. Dupe. A hopeful Girl! Then will I eat nothing that night, feigning my grief for you; but keep his Lordship Company at Meal, and seem to strive to put my passion off, yet shew it still by small mistakes.

Chr. And broken Sentences.

La. Dupe. A dainty Girl! And after Supper visit you again, with promise to return strait to his Lordship: but after I am gone send an Excuse, that I have given you a Cordial, and mean to watch that night in person with you.

Chr. His Lordship then will find the Prologue of his trouble, doubting I have told you of his ruffling.

La. Dupe. And more than that, fearing his Father should know of it, and his Wife, who is a Termagant Lady: but when he finds the Coast is clear, and his late ruffling known to none but you, he will be drunk with joy.

Chr. Finding my simple Innocence, which will inflame him more.

La. Dupe. Then what the Lyon's skin has fail'd him in, the Foxes sublety must next supply, and that is just, Sweet-heart, as I would have it; for crafty Folks treaties are their advantage: especially when his passion must be satisfi'd at any rate, and you keep Shop to set the price of Love: so now you see the Market is your own.

Chr. Truly, Madam, this is very rational; and by the blessing of Heav'n upon my poor endeavours, I do not doubt to play my part.

La. Dupe. My blessing and my pray'rs go along with thee.

Enter Sir John Swallow, *Mrs.* Millisent, *and* Rose *her Maid.*

Chr. I believe, Madam, here is the young Heiress you expect, 120 and with her he who is to marry her.

La. Dupe. Howe're I am Sir *Martins* Friend, I must not seem his Enemy.

Sir John. Madam, this fair young Lady begs the honour to be known to you.

Mill. My Father made me hope it, Madam.

La. Dupe. Sweet Lady, I believe you have brought all the Freshness of the Country up to Town with you.   [*They salute.*

Mill. I came up, Madam, as we Country-Gentlewomen use, at an *Easter*-Term, to the destruction of Tarts and Cheese-cakes, to 130 see a New Play, buy a new Gown, take a Turn in the Park, and so down agen to sleep with my Fore-fathers.

Sir John. Rather, Madam, you are come up to the breaking of many a poor Heart, that like mine, will languish for you.

Chr. I doubt, Madam, you are indispos'd with your Voyage; will you please to see the Lodgings your Father has provided for you?

Mill. To wait upon you, Madam.

La. Dupe. This is the door,————there is a Gentleman will wait you immediately in your Lodging, if he might presume on 140 your Commands.   [*In whisper.*

Mill. You mean Sir *Martin Marral:* I am glad he has intrusted his passion with so discreet a person.   [*In whisper.*
Sir *John,* let me intreat you to stay here, that my Father may have intelligence where to find us.

Sir John. I shall obey you, Madam.   [*Exeunt Women.*

Enter Sir *Martin.*

143 Sir] *La. Dupe.* Sir Q1–5, F, D.

Sir John. Sir *Martin Marral!* most happily encounter'd! how long have you been come to Town?

Sir Mart. Some three days since, or thereabouts: but I thank God I am very weary on't already.

Sir John. Why, what's the matter, man?

Sir Mart. My villainous old luck still follows me in gaming, I never throw the Dice out of my hand, but my Gold goes after 'em: if I go to Picquet, though it be but with a Novice in't, he will picque and repicque, and Capot me twenty times together: and which most mads me, I lose all my Sets, when I want but one of up.

Sir John. The pleasure of play is lost, when one loses at that unreasonable rate.

Sir Mart. But I have sworn not to touch either Cards or Dice this half year.

Sir John. The Oaths of losing Gamesters are most minded; they foreswear play as an angry Servant does his Mistress, because he loves her but too well.

Sir Mart. But I am now taken up with thoughts of another nature; I am in love, Sir.

Sir John. That's the worst Game you could have play'd at, scarce one Woman in an hundred will play with you upon the Square: you venture at more uncertainty than at a Lottery: for you set your heart to a whole Sex of Blanks. But is your Mistress Widdow, Wife, or Maid?

Sir Mart. I can assure you, Sir, mine is a Maid; the Heiress of a wealthy Family, fair to a Miracle.

Sir John. Does she accept your service?

Sir Mart. I am the only person in her favour.

Enter Warner.

Sir John. Is she of Town or Country?

Warn. aside. How's this?

Sir Mart. She is of *Kent,* near *Canterbury.*

Warn. What does he mean? this is his Rival————   [*Aside.*

171–172   *as in D; set as verse in Q1–5, F* (. . . / The . . . / Fair).
174+   s.d. *Enter* Warner.] D; [~ Q1–5, F (~∧ Q1–3).

Sir John. Near *Canterbury* say you? I have a small Estate lies
180 thereabouts, and more concernments than one besides.

Sir Mart. I'le tell you then; being at *Canterbury,* it was my
Fortune once in the Cathedral Church————

Warn. What do you mean, Sir, to intrust this man with your
Affairs thus?————

Sir Mart. Trust him? why, he's a friend of mine.

Warn. No matter for that; hark you a Word Sir.————

Sir Mart. Prethee leave fooling.————And as I was saying
————I was in the Church when I first saw this fair one.

Sir John. Her Name, Sir, I beseech you.

190 *Warn.* For Heaven's sake, Sir, have a care.

Sir Mart. Thou art such a Coxcomb.————Her name's *Millisent.*

Warn. Now, the Pox take you Sir, what do you mean?

Sir John. Millisent say you? that's the name of my Mistress.

Sir Mart. Lord! what luck is that now! well Sir, it happen'd,
one of her Gloves fell down, I stoop'd to take it up; And in the
stooping made her a Complement.————

Warn. The Devil cannot hold him, now will this thick-skull'd
Master of mine, tell the whole story to his Rival.————

200 *Sir Mart.* You'l say, 'twas strange Sir; but at the first glance
we cast on one another, both our hearts leap'd within us, our
souls met at our Eyes, and with a tickling kind of pain slid to
each others breast, and in one moment settled as close and warm
as if they long had been acquainted with their lodging. I follow'd her somewhat at a distance, because her Father was with
her.

Warn. Yet hold Sir————

Sir Mart. Sawcy Rascal, avoid my sight; must you tutor me?
So Sir, not to trouble you, I enquir'd out her Father's House,
210 without whose knowledge I did Court the Daughter, and both
then and often since coming to *Canterbury,* I receiv'd many
proofs of her kindness to me.

181   then;] Q4–5, F; ∼ , Q1–3, D.
181–182   *as in D; set as verse in Q1–5, F (Canterbury;* [∼ , Q3–5, F] / It).
187   fooling.————And] fooling:————and Q1–5, F, D.

Warn. You had best tell him too, that I am acquainted with her Maid, and manage your love under-hand with her.

Sir Mart. Well remember'd i'faith, I thank thee for that, I had forgot it I protest! My *Valet de Chambre,* whom you see here with me, grows me acquainted with her Woman———

Warn. O the Devil.———

Sir Mart. In fine Sir, this Maid being much in her Mistresses favour, so well sollicited my Cause, that in fine I gain'd from fair Mistress *Millisent* an assurance of her kindness, and an ingagement to marry none but me.

Warn. 'Tis very well! you've made a fair discovery!———

Sir John. A most pleasant Relation I assure you: you are a happy man Sir! but what occasion brought you now to *London?*

Sir Mart. That was in expectation to meet my Mistress here; she writ me word from *Canterbury,* she and her Father shortly would be here.

Sir John. She and her Father, said you Sir?

Warn. Tell him Sir, for Heavens sake tell him all———

Sir Mart. So I will Sir, without your bidding. Her Father and she are come up already, that's the truth on't, and are to lodge by my Contrivance in yon House; the Master of which is a cunning Rascal as any in Town———him I have made my own, for I lodge there.

Warn. You do ill Sir to speak so scandalously of my Landlord.

Sir Mart. Peace, or I'le break your Fools head.———So that by his means I shall have free egress and regress when I please Sir———without her Fathers knowledge.

Warn. I am out of patience to hear this.———

Sir John. Methinks you might do well, Sir, to speak openly to her Father.

Sir Mart. Thank you for that i'faith, in speaking to old *Moody* I may soon spoil all.

Warn. So now he has told her Father's name, 'tis past recovery.

Sir John. Is her Fathers name *Moody* say you?

216 My] D; my Q1–5, F.   230 Heavens] Q2–5, F, D; Heaven Q1.
231 bidding. Her] ~ : her Q1–5, F; ~ :———Her D.
237 head.———] ~_∧——— Q1, F, D; ~ ,——— Q2–5.

Sir Mart. Is he of your acquaintance?

Sir John. Yes Sir, I know him for a man who is too wise for
you to over-reach; I am certain he will never marry his Daughter
250 to you.

Sir Mart. Why, there's the jest on't: he shall never know it:
'tis but your keeping of my Counsel; I'le do as much for you
mun.————

Sir John. No Sir, I'le give you better; trouble not your self
about this Lady; her affections are otherwise engag'd to my
knowledge————hark in your Ear————her Father hates a
Gamester like the Devil: I'le keep your Counsel for that too.

Sir Mart. Nay but this is not all dear Sir *John.*

Sir John. This is all I assure you: only I will make bold to seek
260 your Mistress out another Lodging.————   [*Ex. Sir* John.

Warn. Your Affairs are now put into an excellent posture,
Thank your incomparable discretion————this was a Stratagem
my shallow wit could ner'e have reach'd, to make a Confident of
my Rival.

Sir Mart. I hope thou art not in earnest man! is he my Rival?

Warn. 'Slife he has not found it out all this while! well Sir
for a quick apprehension let you alone.

Sir Mart. How the Devil cam'st thou to know ont? and why
the Devil didst thou not tell me on't?

270 *Warn.* To the first of your Devil's I answer, her Maid *Rose*
told me on't: to the second I wish a thousand Devils take him
that would not hear me.

Sir Mart. O unparallell'd Misfortune!

Warn. O unparallell'd ignorance! why he left her Father at
the water-side, while he led the Daughter to her lodging, whither
I directed him; so that if you had not laboured to the contrary,

---

248–250   *as in D; set as verse in Q1–3, F* (. . . / Who . . . / I . . . / To),
partially as verse in Q4–5 (. . . / Who . . . / I).
251–253   *as in D; set as verse in Q1–5, F* (. . . / He . . . / Keeping . . . / mun).
258   Sir] *Sir Q1–5, F, D.*
259–260   *as in D; set as verse in Q1–5, F* (. . . / To).
260   *Sir]* F, D; *Sir Q1–5.*
266–267   *as in D; set as verse in Q1–3, F* (. . . / Sir), *Q4–5* (. . . / Well).
268–269   *as in D; set as verse in Q1–3, F* (. . . / Why), *Q4–5* (. . . / And).
275   led] *D;* lead *Q1–5, F.*

Fortune had plac'd you in the same House with your Mistress, without the least suspition of your Rival or of her Father: but 'tis well, you have satisfi'd your talkative humour; I hope you have some new project of your own to set all right agen: for my part I confess all my designs for you are wholly ruin'd; the very foundations of 'em are blown up.

Sir Mart. Prethee insult not over the Destiny of a poor undone Lover, I am punish'd enough for my indiscretion in my despair, and have nothing to hope for now but death.

Warn. Death is a Bug-word, things are not brought to that extremity, I'le cast about to save all yet.

Enter Lady Dupe.

La. Dupe. O, Sir *Martin!* yonder has been such a stir within, Sir *John,* I fear, smoaks your design, and by all means would have the old man remove his Lodging; pray God your man has not play'd false.

Warn. Like enough I have: I am Coxcomb sufficient to do it, my Master knows that none but such a great Calf as I could have done it, such an over-grown Ass, a self-conceited Ideot as I.———

Sir Mart. Nay, *Warner,*———

Warn. Pray, Sir, let me alone:———what is it to you if I rail upon my self? now could I break my own Loggar-head.

Sir Mart. Nay, sweet *Warner.*

Warn. What a good Master have I, and I to ruine him: O Beast!———

La. Dupe. Not to discourage you wholly, Sir *Martin,* this storm is partly over.

Sir Mart. As how? dear Cousin.

La. D. When I heard Sir *John* complain of the Landlord, I took the first hint of it, and joyn'd with him, saying, if he were such an one, I would have nothing to do with him: in short, I rattled him so well, that Sir *John* was the first who did desire they might be lodg'd with me, not knowing that I was your Kinswoman.

---

305   he] Q5, F, D; she Q1-4.

310   *Sir Mart.* Pox on't, now I think on't, I could have found out this my self.————

    Warn. Are you there agen, Sir?————now as I have a Soul————

    Sir Mart. Mum, good *Warner,* I did but forget my self a little, I leave my self wholly to you, and my Cousin; get but my Mistress for me, and claim what e're reward you can desire.

    Warn. Hope of reward will diligence beget,
Find you the money, and I'le find the wit.   [*Exeunt.*

ACT II. SCENE I.

Enter Lady Dupe, *and Mrs.* Christian.

    Chr. It happen'd Madam, just as you said it would, but was he so concern'd for my feign'd sickness?

    La. D. So much that *Moody* and his Daughter, our new Guests, took notice of the trouble, but the Cause was kept too close for Strangers to divine.

    Chr. Heav'n grant he be but deep enough in love, and then————

    La. D. And then thou shalt distill him into Gold my Girl. Yonder he comes, I'le not be seen:————you know your Lesson,
10 Child.   [*Exit.*

    Chr. I warrant you.

Enter Lord Dartmouth.

    Lord. Pretty Mistress *Christian,* how glad am I to meet you thus alone!

    Chr. O the Father! what will become of me now?

---

313 Soul————] Q2–5, D; ~ .———— Q1, F.
ACT II. SCENE I.] D; ACT II. Q1–5, F.   s.d. *Lady*] Q4–5, F, D; Lady Q1–3.
1–2 *as in D; set as verse in Q1–5, F* (. . . / But).
8–10 *as in D; set as verse in Q1–5, F* (. . . / Yonder . . . / Your).
11+ *s.d. Enter Lord*] F, D; [*Enter* Lord Q1–5 (*Lord* Q4–5).
12–13 *as in D; set as verse in Q1–5, F* (. . . / How).

Lord. No harm I warrant you, but why are you so 'fraid?

Chr. A poor weak innocent Creature as I am, Heav'n of his mercy, how I quake and tremble! I have not yet claw'd off your last ill usage, and now I feel my old fit come again, my Ears tingle already, and my back shuts and opens; I, just so it began before.

Lord. Nay, my sweet Mistress, be not so unjust to suspect any new attempt: I am too penitent for my last fault, so soon to sin agen,———I hope you did not tell it to your Aunt.

Chr. The more Fool I, I did not.

Lord. You never shall repent your goodness to me, but may not I presume there was some little Kindness in it, which mov'd you to conceal my Crime?

Chr. Methought I would not have mine Aunt angry with you for all this earthly good. But yet I'le never be alone with you agen.

Lord. Pretty Innocence! let me sit nearer to you: you do not understand what love I bear you: I vow it is so pure my Soul's not sully'd with one spot of sin: were you a Sister or a Daughter to me, with a more holy Flame I could not burn.

Chr. Nay, now you speak high words———I cannot understand you.

Lord. The business of my life shall be but how to make your Fortune, and my care and study to advance and see you settled in the World.

Chr. I humbly thank your Lordship.

Lord. Thus I would sacrifice my Life and Fortunes, and in return you cruelly destroy me.

Chr. I never meant you any harm, not I.

---

21 *Lord.*] Q2–5, F, D; ∼∧ Q1.
21–23 *as in D; set as verse in* Q1–5, F (. . . / To suspect . . . / I am . . . / So soon . . . / I hope).
25–27 *as in D; set as verse in* Q1–5, F (. . . / But . . . / Kindness . . . / Crime).
28 Aunt] Q2–5, F, D; Aunt an Q1.
29–30 But . . . agen.] *as in D; set as a line of verse in* Q1–5, F.
31–34 *as in D; set as verse in* Q1–5, F (. . . / You do . . . / I vow . . . pure ——— / My . . . / Were . . . / With a).
41–42 *as in D; set as verse in* Q1–5, F (. . . / And in).

Lord. Then what does this white Enemy so near me?

> [*Touching her hand glov'd.*

Sure 'tis your Champion, and you arm it thus to bid defiance to me.

Chr. Nay fye my Lord, in faith you are to blame.

> [*Pulling her hand away.*

Lord. But I am for fair Wars, an Enemy must first be search'd for privy Armour, e're we do ingage.   [*Pulls at her glove.*

50 *Chr.* What does your Lordship mean?

Lord. I fear you bear some Spells and Charms about you, and, Madam, that's against the Laws of Arms.

Chr. My Aunt charg'd me not to pull off my Glove for fear of Sun-burning my hand.

Lord. She did well to keep it from your Eyes, but I will thus preserve it.   [*Hugging her bare hand.*

Chr. Why do you crush it so? nay now you hurt me, nay———— if you squeeze it ne're so hard————there's nothing to come out on't————fye————is this loving one————what makes you
60 take your breath so short?

Lord. The Devil take me if I can answer her a word, all my Sences are quite imploy'd another way.

Chr. Ne're stir my Lord, I must cry out————

Lord. Then I must stop your mouth————this Ruby for a Kiss————that is but one Ruby for another.

Chr. This is worse and worse.

Lady within. Why Neece, where are you Neece?

Lord. Pox of her old mouldy Chops.

Chr. Do you hear, my Aunt calls? I shall be hang'd for stay-
70 ing with you————let me go my Lord.   [*Gets from him.*

Enter Lady Dupe.

44+ *s.d.* [*Touching*] Q2–5, F, D; ∧~ Q1.
49 *glove.*] Q3–5, F, D; ~∧ Q1–2.
51–52 *as in* D; *set as verse in* Q1–5, F (you, / And,).
56 *Hugging*] Q4–5, F, D; *hugging* Q1–3.
61–62 *as in* D; *set as verse in* Q1–5, F (. . . / All).
70+ *s.d. Lady*] Q4–5, F, D; Lady Q1–3.

La. D. My Lord, Heaven bless me, what makes your Lordship here?

Lord. I was just wishing for you Madam, your Neece and I
have been so laughing at the blunt humour of your Country
Gentleman,————I must go pass an hour with him. [*Ex. Lord.*

Chr. You made a little too much haste; I was just exchanging a
Kiss for a Ruby.

Lad. No harm done; it will make him come on the faster:
never full-gorge an Hawk you mean to fly: the next will be a
Neck-lace of Pearl I warrant you.

Chr. But what must I do next?

La. Dupe. Tell him I grew suspitious, and examin'd you
whether he made not love; which you deny'd. Then tell him how
my Maids and Daughters watch you; so that you tremble when
you see his Lordship.

Chr. And that your Daughters are so envious, that they would
raise a false report to ruine me.

La. D. Therefore you desire his Lordship, as he loves you, of
which you are confident, hence-forward to forbear his Visits to
you.

Chr. But how if he should take me at my word?

La. D. Why, if the worst come to the worst, he leaves you an
honest woman, and there's an end on't: but fear not that, hold
out his messages, and then he'll write, and that is it my Bird
which you must drive it to: then all his Letters will be such
Extacies, such Vows and Promises, which you must answer short
and simply, yet still ply out of 'em your advantages.

Chr. But Madam! he's i' th' house, he will not write.

La. D. You Fool————he'll write from the next Chamber to
you, and rather than fail, send his Page Post with it upon a
Hobby-horse:————then grant a meeting, but tell me of it, and

75 *Lord*] D; Lord Q1–5, F.
76–77 *as in D; set as verse in Q1–5, F* (. . . / I).
78–80 *as in D; set as verse in Q1–5, F* (. . . / Never . . . / The).
82–85 *as in D; set as verse in Q1–5, F* (. . . / Whether . . . / Then . . . / So).
88–90 *as in D; set as verse in Q1–5, F* (. . . / As . . . / Hence-forward).
100 you, and] you. And Q1–5, F, D.

I'le prevent him by my being there; hee'l curse me, but I care not. When you are alone, hee'l urge his lust, which answer you with scorn and anger.————

Chr. As thus an't please you, Madam? What? does he think I will be damn'd for him? defame my Family, ruine my Name, to satisfie his pleasure?

La. Dupe. Then he will be prophane in's Arguments, urge Natures Laws to you.

110 *Chr.* By'r Lady, and those are shrewd Arguments. But I am resolv'd I'le stop my Ears.

La. Dupe. Then when he sees no other thing will move you, hee'l sign a portion to you before hand. Take hold of that, and then of what you will. [*Exeunt.*

SCENE II.

Enter Sir John, *Mrs.* Millisent, *and* Rose.

Sir John. Now fair Mrs. *Millisent,* you see your Chamber, your Father will be busie a few minutes, and in the mean time permits me the happiness to wait on you.————

Mill. Methinks you might have chose us better Lodgings, this house is full; the other we saw first, was more convenient.

Sir John. For you perhaps, but not for me: you might have met a Lover there, but I a Rival.

Mill. What Rival?

Sir John. You know Sir *Martin,* I need not name him to you.

10 *Mill.* I know more men besides him.

105–107 *as in D; set as verse in Q1–5, F* (. . . / What? . . . / Defame . . . / To).
108–109 *as in D; set as verse in Q1–5, F* (. . . / Urge).
110–111 *as in D; set as verse in Q1–5, F* (. . . / But).
112–114 *as in D; set as verse in Q1–5, F* (. . . / Hee'l . . . / Take).
SCENE II. *Enter*] Enter Q1–5, F, D.
1–2 *as in D; set partly as verse in Q1–5, F* (. . . / Your Father).
4–5 *as in D; set as verse in Q1–5, F* (. . . / This).
6–7 *as in D; set as verse in Q1–5, F* (. . . / You might).

Sir John. But you love none besides him, can you deny your affection to him?

Mill. You have vex'd me so, I will not satisfie you.

Sir John. Then I perceive I am not likely to be so much oblig'd to you as I was to him.

Mill. This is Romance,———I'le not believe a word on't.———

Sir John. That's as you please: however 'tis believ'd, his wit will not much credit your choice. Madam, do justice to us both;
20 pay his ingratitude and folly with your scorn; my service with your Love. By this time your Father stays for me: I shall be discreet enough to keep this fault of yours from him; the Lawyers wait for us to draw your Joynture: and I would beg your pardon for my absence, but that my Crime is punish'd in it self.   [*Exit.*

Mill. Could I suspect this usage from a favour'd Servant?

Rose. First hear Sir *Martin* ere you quite condemn him; consider 'tis a Rival who accus'd him.

Mill. Speak not a word in his behalf:———methought too, Sir *John* call'd him Fool.

30 *Rose.* Indeed he has a rare way of acting a Fool, and does it so naturally, it can be scarce distinguish'd.

Mill. Nay, he has wit enough, that's certain.

Rose. How blind Love is!   [*Aside.*

Enter Warner.

Mill. How now, what's his business? I wonder after such a Crime, if his Master has the face to send him to me?

Rose. How durst you venture hither? If either Sir *John* or my old Master see you———

18–24 *as in D; set more or less as verse in* Q1-5, F (. . . / His wit . . . / Madam, . . . / your scorn . . . [. . . / Scorn Q4-5, F] / By . . . / to keep this . . . [. . . / This Q5, F] / The Lawyers . . . / And I . . . / But).
25 Servant?] ~ ! Q1-5, F, D.
26–27 *as in D; set as verse in* Q1-5, F (. . . / Consider).
28–29 *as in D; set as verse in* Q1-5, F (. . . / Methought).
33 is! [*Aside.*] is! Q1-5, F, D.
34–35 *as in D; set as verse in* Q1-5, F (. . . / I . . . / If).
35 me?] ~ . Q1-3, D; ~ ! Q4-5, F.
36–37 *as in D; set as verse in* Q1-5, F (. . . / If).
37 you———] ~ . Q1-5, F; ~ ? D.

Warn. Pish! they are both gone out.

Rose. They went but to the next street; ten to one but they re-
40 turn and catch you here.

Warn. Twenty to one I am gone before, and save 'um a labour.

Mill. What says that Fellow to you? what business can he have
here?

Warn. Lord, that your Ladiship should ask that question,
knowing whom I serve!

Mill. I'le hear nothing from your Master.

Warn. Never breathe, but this anger becomes your Ladiship
most admirably; but though you'l hear nothing from him, I
50 hope I may speak a word or two to you from my self, Madam.

Rose. 'Twas a sweet Prank your Master play'd us: a Lady's
well helpt up that trusts her Honour in such a persons hands: to
tell all so,———and to his Rival too.
Excuse him if thou canst.   [*Aside.*

Warn. How the Devil should I excuse him? thou knowest he
is the greatest Fop in Nature.———   [*Aside to* Rose.

Rose. But my Lady does not know it; if she did——— [*Aside.*

Mill. I'le have no Whispering.

Warn. Alas, Madam, I have not the confidence to speak out,
60 unless you can take mercy on me.

Mill. For what?

Warn. For telling Sir *John* you lov'd my Master, Madam. But
sure I little thought he was his Rival.

Rose. The witty Rogue has taken't on himself.   [*Aside.*

Mill. Your Master then is innocent.

Warn. Why, could your Ladiship suspect him guilty? Pray tell
me, do you think him ungrateful, or a Fool?

Mill. I think him neither.

45–46   *as in D; set as verse in* Q1–5, F (. . . / Knowing).
57   did——— [*Aside.*] did——— Q1–5, F, D.
59–60   *as in D; set as verse in* Q1–5, F (. . . / Unless).
62–63   *as in D; set as verse in* Q1–5, F (. . . / But).
66–67   *as in D; set as verse in* Q1–5, F (. . . / Pray . . . / Ungrateful, or
[. . . / Or Q4–5, F]).

Warn. Take it from me, you see not the depth of him. But
70 when he knows what thoughts you harbour of him, as I am faithful, and must tell him,———I wish he does not take some pet,
and leave you.

Mill. Thou art not mad I hope, to tell him on't; if thou dost,
I'le be sworn, I'le foreswear it to him.

Warn. Upon condition then you'l pardon me, I'le see what I
can do to hold my tongue.

Mill. This Evening in S. *James*'s Park I'le meet him.   [*Knock*
Warn. He shall not fail you, Madam.   *within.*
Rose. Some body knocks,———Oh Madam, what shall we do?
80 'Tis Sir *John*, I hear his voice.

Warn. What will become of me?

Mill. Step quickly behind that Door.   [*He goes out.*

To them Sir John.

Mill. You've made a quick dispatch, Sir.

Sir John. We have done nothing, Madam, our Man of Law
was not within,———but I must look some Writings.

Mill. Where are they laid?

Sir John. In the Portmanteau in the Drawing-room.   [*Is going*
Mill. Pray stay a little, Sir.———   *to the Door.*
Warn. at the Door. He must pass just by me; and if he sees me,
90 I am but a dead man.

Sir John. Why are you thus concern'd? why do you hold me?

Mill. Only a word or two I have to tell you. 'Tis of importance
to you.———

Sir John. Give me leave.———

Mill. I must not before I discover the Plot to you.

69–72 *as in D; set as verse in Q1–5, F* (. . . / But . . . / As . . . / I wish).
73–74 *as in D; set as verse in Q1–5, F* (. . . / If).
75–76 *as in D; set as verse in Q1–5, F* (. . . / I'le).
78 *within.*ʌ] Q2–5, F, D; ~ .] Q1.   79 do?] ~ ! Q1–5, F, D.
79–80 *as in D; set as verse in Q1–5, F* (. . . / 'Tis).
82 [*He goes out.*] F, D; *on line below in* Q1–5.
88 *Door.*ʌ] Q2–5, F, D; ~ .] Q1.
92–93 *as in D; set as verse in Q1–5, F* (. . . / 'Tis).

Sir John. What Plot?

Mill. Sir *Martins* Servant, like a Rogue comes hither to tempt me from his Master, to have met him.

Warn. at the Door. Now would I had a good Bag of Gun-
100 powder at my Breech to ram me into some hole.

Mill. For my part I was so startled at the Message, that I shall scarcely be my self these two days.

Sir John. Oh that I had the Rascal! I would teach him to come upon such Errands.

Warn. Oh for a gentle Composition now! an Arm or Leg I would give willingly.

Sir John. What Answer did you make the Villain?

Mill. I over-reach'd him clearly, by a promise of an appoint-ment of a place I nam'd, where I ne're meant to come: but
110 would have had the pleasure first to tell you how I serv'd him, and then to chide your mean suspicion of me.

Sir John. Indeed I wonder'd you should love a Fool. But where did you appoint to meet him?

Mill. In *Grayes-Inn* Walks.

Warn. By this light, she has put the change upon him! O sweet Woman-kind, how I love thee for that heavenly gift of lying!

Sir John. For this Evening I will be his Mistress; he shall meet another *Penelope* then he suspects.

Mill. But stay not long away.

120 *Sir John.* You over-joy me, Madam.   [*Exit.*

Warn. Is he gone, Madam?

97–98   *as in D; set as verse in Q1–5, F* (. . . / To).
101–102   *as in D; set as verse in Q1–5, F* (. . . / That).
103–104   *as in D; set as verse in Q1–5, F* (. . . / To).
105–106   *as in D; set as verse in Q1–5, F* (. . . / An).
107   you] Q1 *(corrected state)*, Q2–5, F, D; you I Q1 *(uncorrected state)*.
108–110   *as in D; set in verse in Q1–5, F* (. . . / Of an . . . / Where . . . / The).
110–111   him, and . . . me.] him. / *Sir John.* And . . . me, Q1–5, F, D.
112   *Sir John.* Indeed] Indeed Q1–5, F, D.
112–113   *as in D; set as verse in Q1–5, F* (. . . / But).
115   *Warn.* . . . him!] *as in D; set as a line of verse in Q1–5, F.*
117–118   *as in D; set as verse in Q1–5, F* (. . . / He shall).
121   Madam?] Q1 *(corrected state)*, Q2–5, F, D; Madam? / *Enter* Millisent. Q1 *(uncorrected state)*.

Mill. As far as *Grayes-Inn* Walks: now I have time to walk the other way, and see thy Master.

Warn. Rather let him come hither: I have laid a Plot shall send his Rival far enough from watching him e're long.

Mill. Art thou in earnest?

Warn. 'Tis so design'd, Fate cannot hinder it. Our Landlord where we lye, vex'd that his Lodgings should be so left by Sir *John,* is resolv'd to be reveng'd, and I have found the way. You'l
130   see th' effect on't presently.

Rose. O Heavens! the door opens agen, and Sir *John* is returned once more.

Enter Sir John.

Sir John. Half my business was forgot; you did not tell me when you were to meet him. Ho! what makes this Rascal here?

Warn. 'Tis well you're come, Sir, else I must have left untold a Message I have for you.

Sir John. Well, what's your business, Sirrah?

Warn. We must be private first; 'tis only for your ear.

Rose. I shall admire his wit, if in this plunge he can get off.

                                                              [*Aside.*
140   *Warn.* I came hither, Sir, by my Masters order.————

Sir John. I'le reward you for it, Sirrah, immediately.

Warn. When you know all, I shall deserve it, Sir; I came to sound the Vertue of your Mistress; which I have done so cunningly, I have at last obtain'd the promise of a meeting. But my good Master, whom I must confess more generous than wise, knowing you had a passion for her, is resolv'd to quit: And, Sir, that you may see how much he loves you, sent me in private to advise you still to have an eye upon her actions.

122–123   *as in D; set as verse in Q1–5, F* (. . . / To).
124   *Warn.* . . . laid] *as in D; set as a line of verse in Q1–5, F.*
124   a] D; A Q1–5, F.
127   *Warn.* . . . it.] *as in D; set as a line of verse in Q1–5, F.*
129–130   You'l . . . presently.] *as in D; set as a line of verse in Q1–5, F.*
139   off. [*Aside.*] off. Q1–5, F, D.
142   *Warn.* . . . Sir;] *as in D; set as a line of verse in Q1–5, F.*

Sir John. Take this Diamond for thy good news; and give thy
150 Master my acknowledgments.

Warn. Thus the world goes, my Masters, he that will cozen
you, commonly gets your good will into the bargain.   [*Aside.*

Sir John. Madam, I am now satisfi'd of all sides; first of your
truth, then of Sir *Martins* friendship. In short, I find you two
cheated each other, both to be true to me.

Mill. Warner is got off as I would wish, and the Knight over-
reach'd.   [*Aside.*

Enter to them the Landlord disguis'd like a Carrier.

Rose. How now! what would this Carrier have?

Warn. This is our Landlord whom I told you of; but keep
160 your Countenance.———   [*Aside to her.*

Landl. I was looking here-away for one Sir *John Swallow;* they
told me I might hear news of him in this house.

Sir John. Friend, I am the man: what have you to say to me?

Landl. Nay, faith Sir, I am not so good a Schollard to say
much, but I have a Letter for you in my Pouch: there's plaguy
news in't, I can tell you that.

Sir John. From whom is your Letter?

Landl. From your old Uncle *Anthony.*

Sir John. Give me your Letter quickly.

170 *Landl.* Nay, soft and fair goes far.———Hold you, hold you.
It is not in this Pocket.

Sir John. Search in the other then; I stand on Thorns.

Landl. I think I feel it now, this should be who.

Sir John. Pluck it out then.

Landl. I'le pluck out my Spectacles and see first.   [*Reads.*
To Mr. *Paul Grimbard*———Apprentice to———
No, that's not for you, Sir,———that's for the Son of the Brother
of the Nephew of the Cousin of my Gossip *Dobson.*

149–150 *as in D; set as verse in* Q*1–5,* F (. . . / And).
154–155 In . . . me.] *as in D; set as verse in* Q*1–5,* F (. . . / Both).
156–157 over-reach'd. [*Aside.*] over-reach'd. Q1–5, F, D.
157+ *s.d.* Landlord] D; Landlord Q1–5, F.
164–166 *as in D; set as verse in* Q*1–5,* F (. . . / But . . . / There's).

Sir John. Prithee dispatch; dost thou not know the Contents
on't?

Landl. Yes, as well as I do my *Pater noster.*

Sir John. Well, what's the business on't?

Landl. Nay, no great business; 'tis but only that your Worships
Father's dead.

Sir John. My loss is beyond expression! how dy'd he?

Landl. He went to bed as well to see to as any man in *England,*
and when he awaken'd the next morning————

Sir John. What then?

Landl. He found himself stark dead.

Sir John. Well, I must of necessity take orders for my Father's
Funeral, and my Estate; Heaven knows with what regret I leave
you, Madam.

Mill. But are you in such haste, Sir? I see you take all occasions
to be from me.

Sir John. Dear Madam, say not so, a few days will, I hope, return me to you.

To them Sir Martin.

Noble Sir *Martin,* the welcomest man alive! Let me embrace my
Friend.

Rose. How untowardly he returns the salute! *Warner* will be
found out.   [*Aside.*

Sir John. Well friend! you have oblig'd me to you eternally.

Sir Mart. How have I oblig'd you, Sir? I would have you to
know I scorn your words; and I would I were hang'd, if it be not
the farthest of my thoughts.

Mill. O cunning Youth, he acts the Fool most naturally. Were
we alone, how we would laugh together!   [*Aside.*

186–187 *as in D; set as verse in Q1–5, F* (. . . / And).
187 morning————] Q4–5, F, D; ~ .———— Q1–3.
196+ *s.d. Sir*] Q2–5, F, D; Sir Q1.
197–198 *as in D; set as verse in Q1–5, F* (. . . / Let).
200 *Aside*] Q2–5, F, D; *aside* Q1.
205–206 *as in D; set as verse in Q1–5, F* (. . . / Were).
206 together!] ~ ? Q1–5, F, D.   206 *Aside*] Q2–5, F, D; *aside* Q1.

Sir John. This is a double generosity, to do me favours and conceal 'um from me. But honest *Warner* here has told me all.

Sir Mart. What has the Rascal told you?

210 *Sir John.* Your plot to try my Mistress for me————you understand me, concerning your appointment.

Warn. Sir, I desire to speak in private with you.

Sir Mart. This impertinent Rascal, when I am most busie, I am ever troubled with him.

Warn. But it concerns you I should speak with you, good Sir.

Sir Mart. That's a good one i'faith, thou knowst breeding well, that I should whisper with a Serving-man before company.

Warn. Remember, Sir, last time it had been better————

Sir Mart. Peace, or I'le make you feel my double Fists.————

220 If I don't fright him, the sawcy Rogue will call me Fool before the Company.   [*Aside.*

Mill. That was acted most naturally again.   [*Aside.*

Sir John to him. But what needs this dissembling, since you are Resolv'd to quit my Mistress to me?

Sir Mart. I quit my Mistress! that's a good one i'faith.

Mill. Tell him you have forsaken me.   [*Aside.*

Sir Mart. I understand you, Madam, you would save a quarrel; but i'faith I'me not so base: I'le see him hang'd first.

Warn. Madam, my Master is convinc'd, in prudence he should 230 say so: but Love o'remasters him; when you are gone perhaps he may.

Mill. I'le go then: Gentlemen, your Servant; I see my presence brings constraint to the Company.   [*Exeunt* Mill. Rose.

207–208 *as in D; set as verse in Q1–5, F (. . . / To . . . / But).*
213–214 *as in D; set as verse in Q1–5, F (. . . / I am).*
219 Fists.————] ~ :∧ Q1; ~ ;∧ Q2–5, F, D.
221 Company. [*Aside.*] Company. Q1–5, F, D.
222 *Aside*] Q2–5, F, D; *aside* Q1.
223 *John to him.*] Q3–5, F; *John. to him.* Q1–2; *John. [To him.]* D.
226 *Aside*] Q2–5, F, D; *aside* Q1.
227–228 *as in D; set as verse in Q1–5, F (. . . / A . . . / I'le).*
229–231 *as in D; set as verse in Q1–5, F (. . . / He should . . . / When).*
232–233 *as in D; set as verse in Q1–5, F (. . . / I).*
233 [*Exeunt*] Q3–5, F, D; ∧~ Q1–2.

Sir John. I'm glad she's gone; now we may talk more freely; for if you have not quitted her, you must.

Warn. Pray, Sir, remember your self; did not you send me of a message to Sir *John,* that for his friendship you had left Mistress *Millisent?*

Sir Mart. Why, what an impudent lying Rogue art thou!

Sir John. How's this! has *Warner* cheated me?

Warn. Do not suspect it in the least: you know, Sir, it was not generous before a Lady, to say he quitted her.

Sir John. O! was that it?

Warn. That was all.————Say, Yes good Sir *John*————or I'le swindge you.   [*Aside.*

Sir Mart. Yes, good Sir *John.*

Warn. That's well, once in his life he has heard good counsel.
                                                        [*Aside.*

Sir Mart. Heigh, Heigh, what makes my Landlord here? he has put on a Fools Coat I think to make us laugh.

Warn. The Devil's in him; he's at it again; his folly's like a sore in a surfeited Horse; cure it in one place, and it breaks out in another.   [*Aside.*

Sir Mart. Honest Landlord i'faith, and what make you here?

Sir John. Are you acquainted with this honest man?

Landl. Take heed what you say, Sir.   [*To Sir* Martin *softly.*

Sir Mart. Take heed what I say, Sir, why? who should I be afraid of? of you, Sir? I say, Sir, I know him, Sir; and I have reason to know him, Sir, for I am sure I lodge in his House, Sir, ————nay never think to terrifie me, Sir; 'tis my Landlord here in *Charles* Street, Sir.

Land. Now I expect to be paid for the News I brought him.

Sir John. Sirrah, did not you tell me that my Father————

234-235   *as in D; set as verse in Q1-5, F* (. . . / For).
241-242   *as in D; set as verse in Q1-5, F* (. . . / It was . . . / To).
244   all.————Say] all: say Q1-5, F, D (Say D).
244   Sir] Q2, Q4-5, F, D; *Sir* Q1, Q3.   245   *Aside*] Q2-5, F, D; aside Q1.
247   counsel. [*Aside.*] Q4-5, F; counsel. Q1-3, D.
252   another. [*Aside.*] Q4-5, F; another. Q1-3, D.

Land. Is in very good health, for ought I know, Sir; I beseech you trouble your self no farther concerning him.

Sir John. Who set you on to tell this lye?

Sir Mart. I, who set you on Sirrah? this was a Rogue that would cozen us both; he thought I did not know him: down on your marribones and confess the truth: have you no Tongue you Rascal?

270   *Sir John.* Sure 'tis some silenc'd Minister: he's grown so fat he cannot speak.

Land. Why, Sir, if you would know, 'twas for your sake I did it.

Warn. For my Masters sake! why, you impudent Varlet, do you think to 'scape us with a lye?

Sir John. How was it for his sake?

Warn. 'Twas for his own, Sir; he heard you were th' occasion the Lady lodg'd not at his House, and so he invented this lye; partly to revenge himself of you; and partly, I believe, in hope

280 to get her once again when you were gone.

Sir John. Fetch me a Cudgel prithee.

Land. O good Sir! if you beat me I shall run into oyl immediately.

Warn. Hang him Rogue; he's below your anger: I'le maul him for you————the Rogue's so big, I think 'twill ask two days to beat him all over.   [*Beats him.*

Land. O Rogue, O Villain *Warner!* bid him hold and I'le confess, Sir.

Warn. Get you gone without replying: must such as you be

290 prating?   [*Beats him out.*

Enter Rose.

Rose. Sir, Dinner waits you on the Table.

Sir John. Friend will you go along, and take part of a bad Repast?

274–275   you think] Q1 (*corrected state*), Q2–5, F, D; you you think Q1 (*uncorrected state*).

287–288   *as in D; set as verse in* Q1–5, F (. . . / And).

290+   *s.d. Enter* Rose. / *Rose.* Sir] D; *Enter* Rose. Sir Q1–5, F.

292–293   Repast?] Q1 (*corrected state*), Q2–5, F, D; ~ . Q1 (*uncorrected state*).

Sir Mart. Thank you; but I am just risen from Table.

Warn. Now he might sit with his Mistress, and has not the wit
to find it out.   [*Aside.*

Sir John. You shall be very welcome.

Sir Mart. I have no stomack, Sir.

Warn. Get you in with a vengeance: you have a better stomack
than you think you have.   [*Pushes him.*

Sir Mart. This hungry *Diego* Rogue would shame me; he
thinks a Gentleman can eat like a Servingman.

Sir John. If you will not, adieu dear Sir; in any thing command
me.   [*Exit.*

Sir Mart. Now we are alone; han't I carried matters bravely
Sirrah?

Warn. O yes, yes, you deserve Sugar Plums; first for your
quarrelling with Sir *John;* then for discovering your Landlord,
and lastly for refusing to dine with your Mistress. All this is
since the last reckoning was wip'd out.

Sir Mart. Then why did my Landlord disguise himself, to
make a Fool of us?

Warn. You have so little Brains, that a Penn'orth of Butter
melted under 'um, would set 'um afloat: he put on that disguise
to rid you of your Rival.

Sir Mart. Why was not I worthy to keep your counsel then?

Warn. It had been much at one: you would but have drunk
the secret down, and piss'd it out to the next company.

Sir Mart. Well I find I am a miserable man: I have lost my
Mistress, and may thank my self for't.

Warn. You'l not confess you are a Fool, I warrant.

Sir Mart. Well I am a Fool, if that will satisfie you: but what
am I the neerer for being one?

Warn. O yes, much the neerer; for now Fortune's bound to

---

296 out. [*Aside.*] Q4–5, F; out. Q1–3, D.
298 Sir.] Q1 (*corrected state*), Q2–5, F, D; ∼ ; Q1 (*uncorrected state*).
301 Rogue] Q1 (*corrected state*), Q2–5, F, D; ∼ , Q1 (*uncorrected state*).
301–302 *as in* D; *set as verse in* Q1–5, F (. . . / He).
303–304 *as in* D; *set as verse in* Q1–5, F (. . . / In).
307–310 *as in* D; *set as verse in* Q1–5, F (. . . / Your quarrelling . . . /
Landlord, and [. . . Land- / lord Q2; . . . / And Q3–5, F] . . . / All).
322–323 *as in* D; *set as verse in* Q1–3 (. . . / What), Q4–5, F (. . . / But).

provide for you; As Hospitals are built for lame people, because they cannot help themselves. Well; I have yet a project in my pate.

Sir Mart. Dear Rogue, what is't?

Warn. Excuse me for that: but while 'tis set a working you
330 would do well to scrue your self into her Fathers good opinion.

Sir Mart. If you will not tell me, my mind gives me I shall discover it again.

Warn. I'le lay it as far out of your reach as I can possible.
        ————For secrets are edg'd Tools,
And must be kept from Children and from Fools.   [*Exeunt.*

ACT III. SCENE I.

Enter Rose *and* Warner *meeting.*

Rose. Your Worship's most happily encounter'd.

Warn. Your Ladiship's most fortunately met.

Rose. I was going to your Lodging.

Warn. My business was to yours.

Rose. I have something to say to you that————

Warn. I have that to tell you————

Rose. Understand then————

Warn. If you'l hear me————

Rose. I believe that————

10 *Warn.* I am of opinion that————

Rose. Prithee hold thy peace a little till I have done.

Warn. Cry you mercy, Mistress *Rose,* I'le not dispute your ancient priviledges of talking.

Rose. My Mistress, knowing Sir *John* was to be abroad upon business this Afternoon, has asked leave to see a Play: and Sir *John* has so great a confidence of your Master, that he will trust no body with her, but him.

326–327 Well; . . . pate.] *as in D; set as a line of verse in Q1–5, F.*
329–330 *as in D; set as verse in Q1–5, F* (. . . / You . . . / Fathers).
ACT III. SCENE I.] D; ACT III. Q1–5, F.

Warn. If my Master gets her out, I warrant her, he shall show her a better Play than any is at either of the Houses————here they are: I'le run and prepare him to wait upon her.   [*Exit.*

    Enter Old Moody, *Mistress* Millisent, *and Lady* Dupe.

Mill. My Hoods and Scarfs there, quickly.
La. Send to call a Coach there.
Mood. But what kind of man is this Sir *Martin,* with whom you are to go?
La. A plain downright Country Gentleman, I assure you.
Mood. I like him much the better for't. For I hate one of those you call a man o'th' Town, one of those empty fellows of meer outside: they've nothing of the true old *English* manliness.
Rose. I confess, Sir, a Woman's in a sad condition, that has nothing to trust to, but a Perriwig above, and a well-trim'd shoe below.

          To them Sir Martin.

Mill. This, Sir, is Sir *John*'s friend, he is for your humour, Sir, He is no man o'th' Town, but bred up in the old *Elizabeth* way of plainness.
Sir Mart. I, Madam, your Ladiship may say your pleasure of me.

          To them Warner.

Warn. How the Devil got he here before me? 'tis very un-lucky I could not see him first————   [*Aside.*
Sir Mart. But as for Painting, Musick, Poetry, and the like, I'le say this of my self————
Warn. I'le say that for him, my Master understands none of 'um, I assure you, Sir.

20+   *s.d.* Millisent] Q4–5, D; Millesent Q1–3, F.
26–28   *as in* D; *set as verse in* Q1–5, F (. . . / For . . . / One . . . / They've).
28   *English*] Q3–5, F, D; English Q1–2.   37   me?] ~ ! Q1–5, F, D.
38   first———— [*Aside.*] first———— Q1–5, F, D.

Sir Mart. You impudent Rascal, hold your Tongue: I must rid my hands of this fellow; the Rogue is ever discrediting me before Company.

Moody. Never trouble your self about it, Sir, for I like a man that————

Sir Mart. I know you do, Sir, and therefore I hope you'll think never the worse of me for his prating: for though I do not boast
50 of my own good parts————

Warn. He has none to boast of, upon my faith, Sir.

Sir Mart. Give him not the hearing, Sir; for, if I may believe my friends, they have flatter'd me with an opinion of more————

Warn. Of more than their flattery can make good, Sir;———— 'tis true he tells you, they have flatter'd him; but in my Conscience he is the most downright simple natured creature in the world.

Sir Mart. I shall consider you hereafter Sirrah; but I am sure in all Companies I pass for a *Vertuoso.*

60 *Mood. Vertuoso!* what's that too? is not *Vertue* enough without *O so?*

Sir Mart. You have Reason, Sir!

Mood. There he is again too; the Town Phrase, a great Compliment I wiss; you have Reason, Sir; that is, you are no beast, Sir.

Warn. A word in private, Sir; you mistake this old man; he loves neither Painting, Musick, nor Poetry; yet recover your self, if you have any brains.   [*Aside to him.*

Sir Mart. Say you so? I'le bring all about again I warrant
70 you————   [*Aside.*
I beg your pardon a thousand times Sir; I vow to Gad I am not Master of any of those perfections; for in fine, Sir, I am wholly ignorant of Painting, Musick, and Poetry; only some rude escapes————but, in fine, they are such, that, in fine, Sir————

Warn. This is worse than all the rest.   [*Aside.*

68 *Aside*] Q4–5, F, D; *aside* Q1–3.
70–71 you———— [*Aside.* / I] you————I Q1–5, F, D.
71–74 I am not . . . that, in fine, Sir————] *as in D; set as verse in* Q1–5, F
(. . . for in fine, / Sir . . . / Only . . . / In fine, Sir————).
75 *Aside*] Q4–5, F, D; *aside* Q1–3.

Mood. By Coxbones one word more of all this Gibberish,
and old *Madge* shall fly about your ears: what is this *in fine* he
keeps such a coil with too?

Mill. 'Tis a Phrase *a-la-mode,* Sir, and is us'd in conversation
now, as a whiff of Tobacco was formerly, in the midst of a discourse, for a thinking while.

La. In plain *English, in fine,* is in the end, Sir.

Mood. But by Coxbones there is no end on't me thinks: if thou
wilt have a foolish word to lard thy lean discourse with, take
an *English* one when thou speakest *English;* as So Sir, and Then
Sir, and so forth; 'tis a more manly kind of nonsense: and a Pox
of In fine, for I'le hear no more on't.

Warn. He's gravell'd, and I must help him out.   [*Aside.*
Madam, there's a Coach at Door to carry you to the Play.

Sir Mart. Which House do you mean to go to?

Mill. The Dukes, I think.

Sir Mart. It is a damn'd Play, and has nothing in't.

Mill. Then let us to the Kings.

Sir Mart. That's e'ne as bad.

Warn. This is past enduring.   [*Aside.*
There was an ill Play set up, Sir, on the Posts, but I can assure
you the Bills are altered since you saw 'um, and now there are
two admirable Comedies at both Houses.

Mood. But my Daughter loves serious Plays.

Warn. They are Tragi-Comedies, Sir, for both.

Sir Mart. I have heard her say she loves none but Tragedies.

Mood. Where have you heard her say so, Sir?

Warn. Sir you forget your self, you never saw her in your life
before.

Sir Mart. What not at *Canterbury,* in the Cathedral Church
there? this is the impudentest Rascal————

Warn. Mum, Sir————

Sir Mart. Ah Lord, what have I done? as I hope to be sav'd

---

77 *Madge*] Madge Q1-5, F, D.
82 *English, in fine*] Q3, D; English, in fine Q1; English, *in fine* Q2, Q4-5, F.
85 *English . . . English*] Q3-5, F, D; English . . . English Q1-2.
88 *Aside*] Q2, Q4-5, F, D; *aside* Q1, Q3.
95 *Aside*] Q4-5, F, D; *aside* Q1-3.   108 done?] ~ ! Q1-5, F, D.

Sir, it was out before I was aware; for if ever I set Eyes on her be-
110 fore this day———I wish———

Mood. This fellow is not so much fool, as he makes one believe he is.

Mill. I thought he would be discovered for a wit: this 'tis to
over-act ones part!   [*Aside.*

Mood. Come away Daughter, I will not trust you in his hands;
there's more in't than I imagin'd.

[*Exeunt* Moody, Mill. *Lady,* Rose.

Sir Mart. Why do you frown upon me so, when you know
your looks go to the heart of me; what have I done besides a
little *lapsus linguæ?*

120 *Warn.* Why, who says you have done any thing? you, a meer
Innocent.

Sir Mart. As the Child that's to be born in my intentions; if
I know how I have offended my self any more than in one
word———

Warn. But don't follow me however———I have nothing to
say to you.

Sir Mart. I'le follow you to the worlds end, till you forgive me.

Warn. I am resolv'd to lead you a Dance then. [*Exit running.*

Sir Mart. The Rogue has no mercy in him, but I must mollifie
130 him with money.   [*Exit.*

SCENE II.

Enter Lady Dupe.

La. Truly my little Cousin's the aptest Scholar, and takes out
loves lessons so exactly that I joy to see it: she has got already the

109   out before] before Q1–5, F, D.   114   *Aside*] Q4–5, F, D; *aside* Q1–3.
116+   s.d. [*Exeunt*] Q3–5, F, D; ∧~ Q1–2.
116+   s.d. *Lady*] D; Lady Q1–5, F.
122   Child that's to] Q3–5, F; Child's that Q1–2, D.
124   word———] Q3–5, F; ~ .——— Q1–2, D.
SCENE II. / *Enter Lady* Dupe. / *La.* Truly] *Enter old La.* Truly Q1–3; *Enter*
La. *Dupe.* Truly Q4–5, F; *Enter Lady* Dupe. / *L. Dupe.* Truly D.

Bond of two thousand pounds seal'd for her Portion, which I keep for her; a pretty good beginning: 'tis true, I believe he has enjoy'd her, and so let him; *Mark Anthony* wooed not at so dear a price.

To her Christian.

Chr. O Madam, I fear I am a breeding!

La. A taking Wench! but 'tis no matter; have you told any body?

Chr. I have been venturing upon your foundations, a little to dissemble.

La. That's a good Child, I hope it will thrive with thee, as it has with me: Heaven has a blessing in store upon our endeavours.

Chr. I feign'd my self sick, and kept my bed; my Lord, he came to visit me, and in the end I disclos'd it to him in the saddest passion.

La. This frighted him, I hope, into a study how to cloak your disgrace, lest it should have vent to his Lady.

Chr. 'Tis true; but all the while I subt'ly drove it, that he should name you to me as the fittest instrument of the concealment; but how to break it to you, strangely does perplex him: he has been seeking you all o're the house; therefore I'le leave your Ladiship, for fear we should be seen together.   [*Exit.*

La. Now I must play my part;
Nature, in Women, teaches more than Art.

Enter Lord.

Lord. Madam, I have a Secret to impart, a sad one too, and have no Friend to trust but only you.

La. Your Lady or your Children sick?

Lord. Not that I know.

6+   *s.d. To her* Christian. / *Chr.* O] D (*Enter to*); *To her Chr.* O Q1–5, F.
26+   *s.d. Lord*] D; Lord Q1–5, F.
27–28   *as in* D; *set as verse in* Q1–5, F (. . . / A sad).

La. You seem to be in health.

Lord. In body, not in mind.

La. Some scruple of Conscience, I warrant; my Chaplain shall resolve you.

Lord. Madam, my Soul's tormented.

La. O take heed of despair, my Lord!

Lord. Madam, there is no Medicine for this sickness, but only you; your friendship's my safe Haven, else I am lost and ship-wrack'd.

40   *La.* Pray tell me what it is.

Lord. Could I express it by sad sighs and groans, or drown it with my self in Seas of tears, I should be happy, would, and would not tell.

La. Command whatever I can serve you in, I will be faithful still to all your ends, provided they be just and vertuous.

Lord. That word has stopt me.

La. Speak out, my Lord, and boldly tell what 'tis.

Lord. Then in obedience to your Commands; your Cousin is with Child.

50   *La.* Which Cousin?

Lord. Your Cousin *Christian* here ith' house.

La. Alas then she has stoln a Marriage, and undone her self: some young Fellow, on my Conscience, that's a Beggar; youth will not be advis'd; well, I'le never meddle more with Girls; one is no more assur'd of 'um than Grooms of Mules, they'l strike when least one thinks on't: but pray your Lordship, what is her choice then for an Husband?

Lord. She is not married that I know of, Madam.

La. Not married! 'tis impossible, the Girl does sure abuse you.

60 I know her Education has been such, the flesh could not prevail; therefore she does abuse you, it must be so.

Lord. Madam, not to abuse you longer, she is with Child, and I the unfortunate man who did this most unlucky act.

41–43 *as in D; set as verse in Q1–5, F* (. . . / Or . . . / I should).
44 *La.* . . . in,] *as in D; set as a line of verse in Q1–5, F.*
52–57 *as in D; set mostly as verse in Q1–4* (. . . / Some . . . / Youth . . . /
One is . . . [*prose to end*]), *entirely as verse in Q5, F* (. . . / One is . . . /
They'll . . . / But).

La. You! I'le never believe it.

Lord. Madam, 'tis too true; believe it, and be serious how to hide her shame; I beg it here upon my knees.

La. Oh, oh, oh.——————   [*She faints away.*

Lord. Who's there? who's there? help, help, help!

Enter two Women, Rose, Millisent.

1 Wom. O merciful God, my Lady's gone!

2 Wom. Whither?

1 Wom. To Heaven, God knows, to Heaven.

Rose. Rub her, rub her; fetch warm Cloaths.

2 Wom. I say, run to the Cabinet of Quintessence; *Gilberts* Water, *Gilberts* Water.

1 Wom. Now all the good Folks of Heaven look down upon her.

Mill. Set her in the Chair.

Rose. Open her mouth with a Dagger or a Key; pour, pour, where's the Spoon?

2 Wom. She stirs, she revives, merciful to us all, what a thing was this! speak, Lady, speak.

La. So, so, so.

Mill. Alas, my Lord, how came this fit?

Lord. With Sorrow, Madam.

La. Now I am better: *Bess,* you have not seen me thus.

1 Wom. Heav'n forefend that I should live to see you so agen.

La. Go, go, I'm pretty well; withdraw into the next Room, but be near I pray, for fear of the worst.   [*They go out.*

——————My Lord, sit down near me I pray, I'le strive to speak a few words to you, and then to bed,——————nearer——————, my voice is faint.——————My Lord, Heaven knows how I have ever lov'd you; and is this my reward? had you none to abuse but me in that unfortunate fond Girl that you know was dearer to me than my life? this was not Love to her, but an inveterate malice to poor me. Oh, oh.——————   [*Faints again.*

---

68   help!] ～ . Q1–5, F, D.   68+   *s.d.* Millisent.] Penelope. Q1–5, F, D.
86   forefend] Q2–5, F, D; foresend Q1.

Lord. Help, help, help!

All the Women again.

1 Wom. This fit will carry her: alas it is a Lechery!

2 Wom. The Balsom, the Balsom!

1 Woman. No, no, the Chymistry Oyl of Rosemary: hold her
100 up, and give her Air.

Mill. Feel whether she breathes, with your hand before her
Mouth.

Rose. No, Madam, 'tis Key-cold.

1 Wom. Look up, dear Madam, if you have any hope of Salvation!

2 Wom. Hold up your finger, Madam, if you have any hope of
Fraternity. O the blessed Saints that hear me not, take her Mortality to them.

La. Enough, so, 'tis well,————withdraw, and let me rest a
110 while; only my dear Lord remain.

1 Wom. Pray your Lordship keep her from swebbing.

[*Exeunt Women.*

Lord. Here humbly once again, I beg your pardon and your
help.

La. Heaven forgive you, and I do: stand up, my Lord, and sit
close by me: O this naughty Girl! but did your Lordship win her
soon?

Lord. No, Madam, but with much difficulty.

La. I'm glad on't; it shew'd the Girl had some Religion in her,
all my Precepts were not in vain: but you men are strange tempt-
120 ers; good my Lord, where was this wicked act then first committed?

Lord. In an out-room upon a Trunk.

La. Poor Heart, what shift Love makes! Oh she does love you
dearly, though to her ruine! and then what place, my Lord?

Lord. An old waste Room, with a decay'd Bed in't.

La. Out upon that dark Room for deeds of darkness! and that
rotten Bed! I wonder it did hold your Lordships vigour: but you

---
96   help!] ~ . Q1–5, F, D.

dealt gently with the Girl. Well, you shall see I love you: for I
will manage this business to both your advantages, by the assistance of Heaven I will; good my Lord help, lead me out.

[*Exeunt.*

SCENE III.

Warner, Rose.

Rose. A mischief upon all Fools! do you think your Master
has not done wisely? first to mistake our old mans humour, then
to dispraise the Plays; and lastly, to discover his Acquaintance
with my Mistress: my old Master has taken such a Jealousie of
him, that he will never admit him into his sight again.

Warn. Thou mak'st thy self a greater Fool than he, by being
angry at what he cannot help.————I have been angry with him
too; but these friends have taken up the quarrel.————

[*Shews gold.*

Look you he has sent these Mediators to mitigate your wrath:
here are twenty of 'um have made a long Voyage from *Guinny* to
kiss your hands: and when the Match is made, there are an hundred more in readiness to be your humble Servants.

Rose. Rather then fall out with you, I'le take 'um; but I confess it troubles me to see so loyal a Lover have the heart of an
Emperour, and yet scarce the brains of a Cobler.

Warn. Well, what device can we two beget betwixt us, to separate Sir *John Swallow* and thy Mistress?

Rose. I cannot on the sudden tell; but I hate him worse than
foul weather without a Coach.

Warn. Then I'le see if my project will be luckier than thine.
Where are the Papers concerning the Joynture I have heard you
speak of?

Rose. They lye within in three great Bags, some twenty Reams
of Paper in each Bundle, with six lines in a sheet: but there is a
little Paper where all the business lyes.

SCENE III. / Warner, Rose.] Q4–5, F, D; *Warner, Rose.* Q1–3.

Warn. Where is it? canst thou help me to it?

Rose. By good chance he gave it to my custody before he set out for *London.* You came in good time, here it is, I was carrying it to him; just now he sent for it.

30   *Warn.* So, this I will secure in my Pocket: when thou art ask'd for it, make two or three bad faces, and say, 'twas left behind: by this means he must of necessity leave the Town, to see for it in *Kent.*

Enter Sir John, *Sir* Martin, *Mrs.* Mill.

Sir John. 'Tis no matter, though the old man be suspicious; I knew the story all beforehand; and since then you have fully satisfi'd me of your true friendship to me.————Where are the Writings?   [*To* Rose.

Rose. Sir, I beg your pardon; I thought I had put 'um up amongst my Ladys things, and it seems in my haste I quite for-
40 got 'um, and left 'um at *Canterbury.*

Sir John. This is horribly unlucky! where do you think you left 'um?

Rose. Upon the great Box in my Ladys Chamber; they are safe enough I'me sure.

Sir John. It must be so————I must take Post immediately: Madam, for some few days I must be absent; and to confirm you, friend, how much I trust you, I leave the dearest Pledge I have on Earth, my Mistress, to your care.

Mill. If you lov'd me, you would not take all occasions to leave
50 me thus!

Warn. aside. Do, go to *Kent,* and when you come again, here they are ready for you.   [*Shows the Paper.*

Sir Mart. What's that you have in your hand there, Sirrah?

Warn. aside. Pox, what ill luck was this! what shall I say?

---

36 to me.————] ~ˌ———— Q1–5, F, D.
45–48 *as in D; set as verse in Q1–5, F* (. . . / Madam, . . . / And . . . / I leave . . . / My).
51–52 *as in D; set as verse in Q1–5, F* (. . . / Here).
54 *Warn. aside.*] Q4–5, F; *Warn.* Q1–3, D.

Sir Mart. Sometimes you've tongue enough, what, are you silent?

Warn. 'Tis an Accompt, Sir, of what Money you have lost since you came to Town.

Sir Mart. I'm very glad on't: now I'le make you all see the severity of my Fortune,———give me the Paper.

Warn. Heaven! what does he mean to do? it is not fair writ out, Sir.

Sir John. Besides, I am in haste, another time, Sir.———

Sir Mart. Pray, oblige me, Sir,———'tis but one minute: all people love to be pity'd in their Misfortunes, and so do I: will you produce it, Sirrah?

Warn. Dear Master!

Sir Mart. Dear Rascal! am I Master or you? you Rogue!

Warn. Hold yet, Sir, and let me read it:———you cannot read my hand.

Sir Mart. This is ever his way to be disparaging me,———but I'le let you see, Sirrah, that I can read your hand better than you your self can.

Warn. You'l repent it, there's a trick in't, Sir.———

Sir Mart. Is there so, Sirrah? but I'le bring you out of all your Tricks with a Vengeance to you.———   [*Reads.* How now! what's this? A true particular of the Estate of Sir *John Swallow* Knight, lying and scituate in, &c.

Sir John. This is the very Paper I had lost: [*Takes the Paper.*] I'm very glad on't, it has sav'd me a most unwelcome Journey, ———but I will not thank you for the Courtesie, which now I find you never did intend me———this is Confederacy, I smoak it now.———Come, Madam, let me wait on you to your Father.

Mill. Well, of a witty man, this was the foolishest part that ever I beheld.   [*Exeunt Sir* John, Millisent, *and* Rose.

Sir Mart. I am a Fool, I must confess it, and I am the most miserable one without thy help,———but yet it was such a mistake as any man might have made.

55 what,] Q2–5, D; ~ₐ Q1, F.   61 do?] Q2–5, F, D; ~ , Q1.
62 Sir.] Q4–5, F, D; ~ ? Q1; ~ ; Q2–3.
65 love] Q1 (*corrected state*), Q2–5, F, D; are Q1 (*uncorrected state*).
83 now.———] ~ₐ———Q1–5, F, D.

Warn. No doubt on't.

90 *Sir Mart.* Prethee chide me! this indifference of thine wounds me to the heart.

Warn. I care not.

Sir Mart. Wilt thou not help me for this once?

Warn. Sir, I kiss your hands, I have other business.

Sir Mart. Dear *Warner!*

Warn. I am inflexible.

Sir Mart. Then I am resolv'd I'le kill my self.

Warn. You are Master of your own Body.

Sir Mart. Will you let me damn my Soul?

100 *Warn.* At your pleasure, as the Devil and you can agree about it.

Sir Mart. D'ye see the point's ready? will you do nothing to save my life?

Warn. Not in the least.

Sir Mart. Farewel, hard-hearted *Warner.*

Warn. Adieu soft-headed Sir *Martin.*

Sir Mart. Is it possible?

Warn. Why don't you dispatch, Sir? why all these Preambles?

Sir Mart. I'le see thee hang'd first: I know thou wou'dst have
110 me kill'd, to get my Cloaths.

Warn. I knew it was but a Copy of your Countenance; people in this Age are not so apt to kill themselves.

Sir Mart. Here are yet ten Pieces in my Pocket, take 'em, and let's be friends.

Warn. You know the Eas'ness of my Nature, and that makes you work upon it so. Well, Sir,———for this once I cast an Eye of pity on you,———but I must have ten more in hand, before I can stir a foot.

Sir Mart. As I am a true Gamester, I have lost all but these,
120 ———but if thou'lt lend me them, I'le give 'em thee agen.

Warn. I'le rather trust you till to morrow, once more look up, I bid you hope the best.

Why should your folly make your Love miscarry,

Since men first play the Fools, and then they marry? [*Exeunt.*

---

102 point's] Q3–5, F, D; points Q1–2.
121–122 *as in D; set as verse in* Q1–5, F (. . . / Once).

ACT IV.

Enter Sir Martin *and* Warner.

Sir Mart. But are they to be married this day in private, say you?

Warn. 'Tis so concluded, Sir, I dare assure you.

Sir Mart. But why so soon, and in private?

Warn. So soon, to prevent the designs upon her; and in private, to save the effusion of Christian Money.

Sir Mart. It strikes to my heart already; in fine, I am a dead man.————*Warner.*

Warn. Well, go your ways, I'le try what may be done. Look if he will stir now; your Rival and the Old man will see us together, we are just below the Window.

Sir Mart. Thou can'st not do't.

Warn. On the peril of my twenty pieces be it.

Sir Mart. But I have found a way to help thee out, trust to my wit but once.

Warn. Name your wit, or think you have the least grain of wit once more, and I'le lay it down for ever.

Sir Mart. You are a sawcy masterly Companion, and so I leave you.   [*Exit.*

Warn. Help, help, good People, Murther, Murther!

Enter Sir John *and* Moody.

Sir John & Mood. How now, what's the matter?

Warn. I am abus'd, I am beaten, I am lam'd for ever.

Mood. Who has us'd thee so?

Warn. The Rogue my Master.

Sir John. What was the Offence?

Warn. A trifle, just nothing.

Sir John. That's very strange.

ACT IV.] Q4-5, F, D; ACT. IV. Q1-3.

Warn. It was for telling him he lost too much at Play; I meant him nothing but well, Heaven knows, and he in a cursed damn'd
30 humour would needs revenge his losses upon me: A' kick'd me, took away my money, and turn'd me off; but if I take it at his hands————

Mood. By Cox nowns it was an ill-natur'd part, nay, I thought no better could come on't, when I heard him at his Vow to Gads, and In fines.

Warn. But if I live I'le cry quittance with him: he had engag'd me to get Mrs. *Millisent* your Daughter for him; but if I do not all that ever I can to make her hate him, a great Booby, an over-grown Oafe, a conceited *Bartlemew*————

40 *Sir John.* Prethee leave off thy Choler, and hear me a little: I have had a great mind to thee a long time; if thou think'st my Service better than his, from this minute I entertain thee.

Warn. With all my heart, Sir, and so much the rather, that I may spight him with it.————This was the most propitious Fate.————

Mood. Propitious! and Fate! what a damn'd *Scander-bag* Rogue art thou to talk at this rate! hark you, Sirrah, one word more of this Gibberish, and I'le set you packing from your new Service; I'le have neither Propitious nor Fate come within my
50 doors.————

Sir John. Nay, pray Father————

Warn. Good old Sir be pacified: I was pouring out a little of the dregs that I had left in me of my former Service, and now they are gone, my stomach's clear of 'em.

Sir John. This Fellow is come in a happy hour; for now, Sir, you and I may go to prepare the Licence, and in the mean time he may have an Eye upon your Daughter.

Warn. If you please I'le wait upon her till she's ready, and then bring her to what Church you shall appoint.

60 *Mood.* But, Friend, you'l find she'l hang an Arse, and be very

---

35 In] D; in Q1–5, F.   39 *Bartlemew*————] Q4–5, F; ~ .———— Q1–3, D.
41 time;] ~ , Q1–5, F, D.
46–47 *Scander-bag* Rogue] Scander-bag-Rogue Q1–2; Scander-bag Rogue Q3–5, F, D.
51 Father————] ~ .———— Q1–2, D; ~ .ᴧ Q3–5, F.

loth to come along with you, and therefore I had best stay behind, and bring her my self.

Warn. I warrant you I have a trick for that, Sir: she knows
nothing of my being turn'd away: so I'le come to her as from Sir
Martin, and under pretence of carrying her to him, conduct her
to you.

Sir John. My better Angel————

Mood. By th' mess 'twas well thought on; well Son, go you
before, I'le speak but one word for a Dish or two at Dinner, and
follow you to the Licence-Office. Sirrah————stay you here
————till my return.   [*Ex. Sir* John *and* Moody.

Warn. solus. Was there ever such a lucky Rogue as I! I had
always a good opinion of my wit, but could never think I had so
much as now I find. I have now gained an opportunity to carry
away Mistress *Millisent* for my Master, to get his Mistress by
means of his Rival, to receive all his happiness, where he could
expect nothing but misery: after this exploit I will have *Lilly*
draw me in the habit of a Hero, with a Lawrel on my Temples,
and an Inscription below it, *This is* Warner *the flower of
Serving-men.*

Enter Messenger.

Mess. Pray do me the favour to help me to the speech of Mr.
Moody.

Warn. What's your business?

Mess. I have a Letter to deliver to him.

Warn. Here he comes, you may deliver it your self to him.

Re-enter Moody.

Mess. Sir, a Gentleman met me at the corner of the next
Street, and bid me give this into your own hands.

Mood. Stay friend, till I have read it.

Mess. He told me, Sir, it required no Answer.   [*Ex. Mess.*

80+   *s.d. Messenger*] D; Messenger Q1–5, F.
85   him. / *Re-enter* Moody.] him. Q1–3; him. / [*Re-enter* Moody. Q4–5, F;
him. / *Enter* Moody. D.
89   *Ex. Mess.*] D; *Ex.* Mess. Q1–5, F.

90 *Mood. reads. Sir, permit me, though a stranger, to give you
counsel; some young Gallants have had intelligence, that this
day you intend privately to marry your Daughter, the rich Heiress; and in fine, above twenty of them have dispersed themselves
to watch her going out: therefore put it off, if you will avoid
mischief, and be advised by*

Your unknown Servant.

Mood. By the Mackings, I thought there was no good in't,
when I saw *in fine* there; there are some Papishes, I'le warrant,
that lye in wait for my Daughter, or else they are no *Englishmen,*
100 but some of your *French Outalian* Rogues; I owe him thanks
however, this unknown Friend of mine, that told me on't.
Warner, no Wedding to day, *Warner.*

Warn. Why, what's the matter, Sir?

Mood. I say no more, but some wiser than some, I'le keep my
Daughter at home this Afternoon, and a fig for all these *Outalians.* [*Exit* Moody.

Warn. So, here's another Trick of Fortune as unexpected for
bad, as the other was for good. Nothing vexes me, but that I had
made my Game Cock-sure, and then to be back-gammon'd: it
110 must needs be the Devil that writ this Letter, he ow'd my Master
a spight, and has paid him to the purpose: and here he comes as
merry too, he little thinks what misfortune has befal'n him, and
for my part I am asham'd to tell him

Enter Sir Martin *laughing.*

Sir Mart. Warner, such a Jest, *Warner.* [*Laughs agen.*

Warn. What a Murrain is the matter, Sir? Where lyes this Jest
that tickles you?

90 *Mood. reads.*] Mood. reads. Q1–5, F, D.
99 *Englishmen*] D; Englishmen Q1–5, F.
100 *French Outalian* Rogues] French Outalion-Rogues Q1–2; French Outalian
Rogues Q3–5, F; *French* Outalian-Rogues D.
105–106 *Outalians*] Outalians Q1–5, F, D.
113+ *s.d. Enter Sir* Martin *laughing.*] *as in D; in preceding speech, at right
margin in two lines in Q1–2 ([~]), run in after "thinks" in Q3 ([~]), at right
margin in Q4–5, F ([~).
115–116 *as in D; set as verse in Q1–5, F (. . . / Where).*

Sir Mart. Let me laugh out my laugh, and I'le tell thee.

[*Laughs agen.*

Warn. I wish you may have cause for all this mirth.

Sir Mart. Hereafter, *Warner*, be it known unto thee, I will
endure no more to be thy May-game: thou shalt no more dare
to tell me, I spoil thy projects, and discover thy designs; for I
have play'd such a Prize, without thy help, of my own Mother-
wit ('tis true I am hasty sometimes, and so do harm; but when I
have a mind to shew my self, there's no man in *England*, though
I say't, comes near me as to point of imagination) I'le make thee
acknowledge I have laid a Plot that has a soul in't.

Warn. Pray, Sir, keep me no longer in ignorance of this rare
Invention.

Sir Mart. Know then, *Warner*, that when I left thee, I was
possest with a terrible fear, that my Mistress should be married:
well, thought I to my self, and mustring up all the Forces of my
Wit, I did produce such a Stratagem.

Warn. But what was it?

Sir Mart. I feign'd a Letter as from an unknown Friend to
Moody, wherein I gave him to understand, that if his Daughter
went out this Afternoon, she would infallibly be snapt by some
young Fellows that lay in wait for her.

Warn. Very good.

Sir Mart. That which follows is yet better; for he I sent assures me, that in that very nick of time my Letter came, her Father was just sending her abroad with a very foolish rascally fellow that was with him.

Warn. And did you perform all this a' Gods name? could you
do this wonderful miracle without giving your soul to the Devil
for his help?

Sir Mart. I tell thee man I did it, and it was done by the help
of no Devil, but this familiar of my own brain; how long would
it have been e're thou couldest have thought of such a project?
Martin said to his man, *Who's the fool now?*

---

120 shalt] Q2–5, F, D; shall Q1.   143 a' Gods] Q4–5, F; a'gods Q1–3, D.
144 without giving] Q5, F; without Q1–4, D.

150   *Warn.* Who's the fool? why, who us'd to be the fool? he that ever was since I knew him, and ever will be so!

Sir Mart. What a Pox? I think thou art grown envious, not one word in my commendations?

Warn. Faith Sir, my skill is too little to praise you as you deserve; but if you would have it according to my poor ability, you are one that had a knock in your Cradle, a conceited lack-wit, a designing Ass, a hair-brain'd Fop, a confounded busie-brain, with an eternal Wind-mill in it; this in short, Sir, is the Contents of your Panegyrick.   .

160   *Sir Mart.* But what the Devil have I done, to set you thus against me?

Warn. Only this, Sir, I was the foolish rascally fellow that was with *Moody,* and your Worship was he to whom I was to bring his Daughter.

Sir Mart. But how could I know this? I am no Witch.

Warn. No, I'le be sworn for you, you are no conjurer. Will you go Sir?

Sir Mart. Will you hear my justifications?

Warn. Shall I see the back of you? speak not a word in your
170 defence.   *[Shoves him.*

Sir Mart. This is the strangest luck now————   *[Exit.*

Warn. I'm resolv'd this Devil of his shall never weary me, I will overcome him, I will invent something that shall stand good in spight of his folly. Let me see————

Enter Lord.

Lord. Here he is————I must venture on him, for the tyranny of this old Lady is unsupportable, since I have made her my confident, there passes not an hour but she has a pull at my Purse-strings; I shall be ruin'd if I do not quit my self of her suddenly: I find now, by sad experience, that a Mistress is much more
180 chargeable than a Wife, and after a little time too, grows full as

---

150 us'd] Q4–5, F; use Q1–3; uses D.
157 busie-brain] Q3–5, F; busie brain Q1–2, D.
166–167 *as in* D; *set as verse in* Q1–5, F (. . . / Will).
174+ *s.d. Lord*] D; Lord Q1–5, F.

dull and insignificant. Mr. *Warner!* have you a mind to do your self a courtesie, and me another?

Warn. I think, my Lord, the Question need not be much disputed, for I have always had a great service for your Lordship, and some little kindness for my self.

Lord. What, if you should propose Mistress *Christian* as a Wife to your Master? you know he's never like to compass t'other.

Warn. I cannot tell that my Lord———

Lord. 500 *l.* are yours at day of marriage.

Warn. 500 *l.*! 'tis true, the temptation is very sweet, and powerful; the Devil I confess has done his part, and many a good Murder and Treason have been committed at a cheaper rate; but yet———

Lord. What yet?

Warn. To confess the truth, I am resolv'd to bestow my Master upon that other Lady (as difficult as your Lordship thinks it) for the honour of my wit is ingag'd in it: will it not be the same to your Lordship were she married to any other?

Lord. The very same.

Warn. Come my Lord, not to dissemble with you any longer, I know where it is that your Shoe wrings you: I have observ'd something in the House, betwixt some parties that shall be nameless: and know that you have been taking up Linnen at a much dearer rate, than you might have had it at any Drapers in Town.

Lord. I see I have not danc'd in a Net before you.

Warn. As for that old Lady, whom Hell confound, she is the greatest Jill in Nature, cheat is her study, all her joy to cosen, she loves nothing but her self, and draws all lines to that corrupted centre.

Lord. I have found her out, though late: first, I'le undertake I n'ere enjoy'd her Neice under the rate of 500 *l.* a time; never was womans flesh held up so high: every night I find out for a new maidenhead, and she has sold it me as often as ever mother

---

191   *l*!] D; *l.*ₐ Q1–5, F.   195   yet?] ∼——— Q1–5, F, D.
197   difficult] Q2–5, F, D; difficultly Q1.

Temple, Bennet, or *Gifford,* have put off boil'd Capons for
Quails and Partridges.

Warn. This is nothing to what Bills you'l have when she's
brought to bed, after her hard bargain, as they call it; then
cram'd Capons, Pea-hens, Chickens in the grease, Pottages, and
220 Frigacies, Wine from *Shatling,* and *La-fronds,* with New River,
clearer by six pence the pound than ever God Almighty made it;
then Midwife—Dry-Nurse—Wet-Nurse—and all the rest of
their Accomplices, with Cradle, Baby-Clouts, and Bearing-
Cloaths————Possets, Cawdels, Broth, Jellies, and Gravies; and
behind all these, Glisters, Suppositers, and a barbarous Pothe-
cary's Bill, more inhumane than a Taylors.

Lord. I sweat to think on't.

Warn. Well my Lord! chear up! I have found a way to rid you
of it all, within a short time you shall know more; yonder ap-
230 pears a young Lady whom I must needs speak with, please you
go in and prepare the old Lady and your Mistress.

Lord. Good luck, and 500 *l.* attend thee.   [*Exit.*

Enter Millisent *and* Rose *above.*

Mill. I am resolv'd I'le never marry him!

Rose. So far you are right, Madam.

Mill. But how to hinder it, I cannot possibly tell! for my Father presses me to it, and will take no denial: wou'd I knew some
way————

Warn. Madam, I'le teach you the very nearest, for I have just
now found it out.

240 *Rose.* Are you there, Mr. Littleplot?

Warn. Studying to deserve thee, *Rose,* by my diligence for thy
Lady; I stand here, methinks, just like a wooden *Mercury,* to
point her out the way to Matrimony.

Rose. Or, Serving-man-like, ready to carry up the hot meat for
your Master, and then to fall upon the cold your self.

242 *Mercury*] Q3–5, F, D; Mercury Q1–2.
244 Serving-man-like] Q2, Q4–5, F; Serving-man like Q1, D; Serving man-like
Q3.

Warn. I know not what you call the cold, but I believe I shall
find warm work on't: in the first place then I must acquaint you,
that I have seemingly put off my Master, and entred my self into
Sir *John*'s service.

50   *Mill.* Most excellent!

Warn. And thereupon, but base————

Enter Moody.

Mill. Something he would tell us, but see what luck's here!

Mood. How now, Sirrah? are you so great there already?

Mill. I find my Father's jealous of him still!

Warn. Sir, I was only teaching my young Lady a new Song,
and if you please you shall hear it.

SINGS.

Make ready fair Lady to night,
*   And stand at the Door below,*
For I will be there
*   To receive you with care,*
*   And to your true Love you shall go.*

Mood. Ods Bobs this is very pretty.

Mill. I, so is the Lady's Answer too, if I could but hit on't.

SINGS.

And when the Stars twinckle so bright,
Then down to the Door will I creep,
*   To my Love I will flye,*
*   E're the jealous can spye,*
And leave my old daddy asleep.

251+   s.d. Enter Moody.] *as in* D; *at right on line above in* Q1-4 ([~); *after*
next line in Q5, F.

Mood. Bodikins I like not that so well, to cosen her old Father;
270 it may be my own case another time.

Rose. Oh Madam! yonder's your Persecutor return'd.

Enter Sir John.

Mill. I'le into my Chamber to avoid the sight of him as long
as I can; Lord! that my old doting Father should throw me away
upon such an Ignoramus, and deny me to such a Wit as Sir
Martin.   [*Ex.* Mill. *and* Rose *from above.*

Mood. O Son! here has been the most villainous Tragedy
against you.

Sir John. What Tragedy? has there been any blood shed since I
went?

280 *Mood.* No blood shed, but, as I told you, a most damnable
Tragedy.

Warn. A Tragedy! I'le be hang'd if he does not mean a Stratagem.

Mood. Jack Sawce! if I say it is a Tragedy, it shall be a Tragedy
in spight of you; teach your Grandam how to piss———what
———I hope I am old enough to spought *English* with you
Sir?

Sir John. But what was the reason you came not after me?

Mood. 'Twas well I did not, I'le promise you, there were those
290 would have made bold with Mistress Bride; an' if she had stir'd
out of doors, there were Whipsters abroad i'faith, Padders of
Maiden-heads, that would have truss'd her up, and pick'd the
lock of her affections, e're a man could have said, what's this?
but by good luck I had warning of it by a friends Letter.

Sir John. The remedy for all such dangers is easie, you may
send for a Parson, and have the business dispatch'd at home.

Mood. A match, i'faith, do you provide a *Domine,* and I'le go
tell her our resolutions, and hearten her up against the day of
battel.   [*Exit.*

---

285 you;] Q4–5, F; ∼ , Q1–3, D.   285 Grandam] Q2–5, F, D; Grandham Q1.
286 *English*] D; English Q1–5, F.   293 this?] Q3–5, F; ∼ : Q1–2, D.

Sir John. Now I think on't, this Letter must needs come from
Sir *Martin;* a Plot of his, upon my life, to hinder our marriage.

Warn. I see, Sir, you'l still mistake him for a Wit; but I am
much deceiv'd, if that Letter came not from another hand.

Sir John. From whom I prithee?

Warn. Nay, for that you shall excuse me, Sir, I do not love to
make a breach betwixt persons that are to be so near related.

Sir John. Thou seem'st to imply that my Mistress was in the
Plot.

Warn. Can you make a doubt on't? do you not know she ever
lov'd him, and can you hope she has so soon forsaken him? you
may make your self miserable, if you please, by such a marriage.

Sir John. When she is once mine, her Vertue will secure me.

Warn. Her Vertue!

Sir John. What, do you make a mock on't?

Warn. Not I, I assure you, Sir, I think it no such jesting matter.

Sir John. Why, is she not honest?

Warn. Yes in my Conscience is she, for Sir *Martin's* Tongue's
no slander.

Sir John. But does he say to the contrary?

Warn. If one would believe him, which for my part I do not,
he has in a manner confess'd it to me.

Sir John. Hell and Damnation!———

Warn. Courage, Sir, never vex your self, I'le warrant you 'tis
all a Lye.

Sir John. But how shall I be 'sur'd 'tis so?

Warn. When you are married you'l soon make tryal, whether
she be a Maid or no.

Sir John. I do not love to make that Experiment at my own
cost.

Warn. Then you must never marry.

Sir John. I, but they have so many tricks to cheat a man, which
are entayl'd from Mother to Daughter through all Generations,
there's no keeping a Lock for that Door for which every one has
a Key.

Warn. As for Example, their drawing up their breaths with

Oh! you hurt me, can you be so cruel? then the next day she steals a Visit to her Lover, that did you the Courtesie before-hand, and in private tells him how she cozened you; twenty to
340 one but she takes out another Lesson with him to practice the next night.

Sir John. All this while miserable I must be their May-game.

Warn. 'Tis well if you escape so; for commonly he strikes in with you, and becomes your friend.

Sir John. Deliver me from such a friend that stays behind with my Wife, when I gird on my Sword to go abroad.

Warn. I, there's your man, Sir; besides he will be sure to watch your haunts, and tell her of them, that if occasion be, she may have wherewithal to recriminate: at least she will seem to be
350 jealous of you, and who would suspect a jealous Wife?

Sir John. All manner of ways I am most miserable.

Warn. But if she be not a Maid when you marry her, she may make a good Wife afterwards, 'tis but imagining you have taken such a mans Widow.

Sir John. If that were all; but the man will come and claim her again.

Warn. Examples have been frequent of those that have been wanton, and yet afterwards take up.

Sir John. I, the same thing they took up before.

360 *Warn.* The truth is, an honest simple Girl that's ignorant of all things, maketh the best Matrimony: There is such pleasure in instructing her, the best is, there's not one Dunce in all the Sex; such a one with a good Fortune——

Sir John. I, but where is she, *Warner?*

Warn. Near enough, but that you are too far engag'd.

Sir John. Engag'd to one that hath given me the earnest of Cuckoldom before-hand?

Warn. What think you then of Mrs. *Christian* here in the house? There's 5000 *l.* and a better penny.

370 *Sir John.* I, but is she Fool enough?

Warn. She's none of the wise Virgins, I can assure you.

339–340 you; . . . one] Q2–5, F, D; ~ʌ. . . ~ ; Q1.
359 thing] Q1 *(corrected state)*, Q2–5, F, D; ~ , Q1 *(uncorrected state)*.
369 *l.*] Q4–5, F; l. Q1–3; Pounds D.

Sir John. Dear *Warner,* step into the next Room, and in-
veigle her out this way, that I may speak to her.

Warn. Remember above all things, you keep this Wooing
secret; if it takes the least wind, old *Moody* will be sure to hinder
it.

Sir John. Do'st thou think I shall get her Aunts Consent?

Warn. Leave that to me.   [*Exit* Warner.

Sir John. How happy a man shall I be, if I can but compass
80 this! and what a Precipice have I avoided! then the revenge too
is so sweet to steal a Wife under her Fathers nose, and leave 'um
in the lurch who has abus'd me; well, such a Servant as this
Warner is a Jewel.

Enter Warner *and Mrs.* Christian *to him.*

Warn. There she is, Sir, now I'le go to prepare her Aunt.

Sir John. Sweet Mistress, I am come to wait upon you.

Chr. Truly you are too good to wait on me.

Sir John. And in the Condition of a Suitor.

Chr. As how, forsooth?

Sir John. To be so happy as to marry you.

90 *Chr.* O Lord, I would not marry for any thing!

Sir John. Why? 'tis the honest end of Woman-kind.

Chr. Twenty years hence, forsooth: I would not lye in bed
with a man for a world, their beards will so prickle one.

Sir John. Pah,———what an innocent Girl it is, and very
child! I like a Colt that never yet was back'd; for so I shall make
her what I list, and mould her as I will: Lord! her innocency
makes me laugh my Cheeks all wet.———   [*Aside.*
Sweet Lady———

Chr. I'm but a Gentlewoman, forsooth.

)0 *Sir John.* Well then, sweet Mistress, if I get your Friends consent, shall I have yours?

Chr. My old Lady may do what she will, forsooth, but by my
truly, I hope she will have more care of me, then to marry me

387 Suitor.] Q2-5, F, D; ~ : Q1.   393 beards] D; beards it Q1-5, F.
397-398 [*Aside.* / Sweet Lady———] Sweet Lady.——— [*Aside.* Q1-5, F, D
(Lady∧——— Q2-5, F, D).

yet; Lord bless me, what should I do with a Husband?

Sir John. Well, Sweet-heart, then instead of wooing you, I must wooe my old Lady.

Chr. Indeed, Gentleman, my old Lady is married already: cry you mercy forsooth, I think you are a Knight.

Sir John. Happy in that Title only to make you a Lady.

410   *Chr.* Believe me, Mr. Knight, I would not be a Lady, it makes Folks proud, and so humerous, and so ill Huswifes, forsooth.

Sir John. Pah,————she's a Baby, the simplest thing that ever yet I knew; the happiest man I shall be in the world; for should I have my wish, it should be to keep School, and teach the bigger Girls, and here in one my wish it is absolv'd.   [*Aside.*

Enter Lady Dupe.

La. Dupe. By your leave, Sir: I hope this noble Knight will make you happy, and you make him.

Chr. What should I make him?   [*Sighing.*

La. Dupe. Marry, you shall make him happy in a good Wife.

420   *Chr.* I will not marry, Madam.

La. Dupe. You Fool!

Sir John. Pray, Madam, let me speak with you, on my Soul 'tis the pretti'st innocent'st thing in the world.

La. Dupe. Indeed, Sir, she knows little besides her Work and her Prayers; but I'le talk with the Fool.

Sir John. Deal gently with her, dear Madam.

La. Dupe. Come, *Christian,* will not you marry this noble Knight?

Chr. Yes, yes, yes.————   [*Sobbingly.*

430   *La. Dupe.* Sir, it shall be to night.

Sir John. This innocence is a Dowry beyond all price.

            [*Exeunt Old Lady and Mrs.* Christian.

Enter Sir Martin; *Sir* John *musing.*

---

415   absolv'd. [*Aside.*] absolv'd. Q1-5, F, D.   424   *La.*] Q2-5, F, D; *La* Q1.
431+   *s.d.* Martin; *Sir* John] Martin, and *Sir* John, Q1-5, F (Martin∧ Q1-2);
Martin, *to Sir* John D.

Sir Mart. You are very melancholy methinks, Sir.

Sir John. You are mistaken, Sir.

Sir Mart. You may dissemble as you please, but Mrs. *Millisent* lyes at the bottom of your Heart.

Sir John. My Heart, I assure you, has no room for so poor a Trifle.

Sir Mart. Sure you think to wheadle me, would you have me imagine you do not love her?

Sir John. Love her! why should you think me such a Sot? love a Prostitute, and infamous person!

Sir Mart. Fair and soft, good Sir *John.*

Sir John. You see I am no very obstinate Rival, I leave the field free to you: go on, Sir, and pursue your good Fortune, and be as happy as such a common Creature can make thee.

Sir Mart. This is *Hebrew-Greek* to me; but I must tell you, Sir, I will not suffer my Divinity to be prophan'd by such a Tongue as yours.

Sir John. Believe it, whate're I say I can quote my Author for.

Sir Mart. Then, Sir, whoever told it you, ly'd in his Throat, d'you see, and deeper than that d'ye see, in his stomach and his guts d'ye see: tell me she's a common person! he's a Son of a Whore that said it, and I'le make him eat his words, though he spoke 'em in a privy-house.

Sir John. What if *Warner* told me so? I hope you'l grant him to be a competent Judge in such a business.

Sir Mart. Did that precious Rascal say it?————Now I think on't I'le not believe you: in fine, Sir, I'le hold you an even Wager he denies it.

Sir John. I'le lay you ten to one, he justifies it to your face.

Sir Mart. I'le make him give up the Ghost under my fist, if he does not deny it.

Sir John. I'le cut off his Ears upon the Spot, if he does not stand to't.

Enter Warner.

---

446 *Hebrew-Greek*] D; Hebrew-Greek Q1–5, F.
449 it,] Q1 *(corrected state)*, Q3–5, F, D; ~ ; Q1 *(uncorrected state)*, Q2.
453 I'le make] F, D; make Q1–5.
454 privy-house] Q2–5, F, D; privy house Q1.

Sir Mart. Here he comes in Pudding-time to resolve the question: come hither, you lying Varlet, hold up your hand at the Bar of Justice, and answer me to what I shall demand.

Warn. What a Goodier is the matter, Sir?

Sir Mart. Thou Spawn of the old Serpent, fruitful in nothing
470 but in Lyes!

Warn. A very fair beginning this.

Sir Mart. Didst thou dare to cast thy Venom upon such a Saint as Mrs. *Millisent,* to traduce her Vertue, and say it was adulterate?

Warn. Not guilty, my Lord.

Sir Mart. I told you so.

Sir John. How, Mr. Rascal! have you forgot what you said but now concerning Sir *Martin* and Mrs. *Millisent?* I'le stop the Lye down your Throat, if you dare deny't.

480 *Sir Mart.* Say you so? are you there agen i'faith?

Warn. Pray pacifie your self, Sir, 'twas a Plot of my own devising.   [*Aside to Sir* Martin.

Sir Mart. Leave off your winking and your pinking, with a Horse-pox t'ye, I'le understand none of it; tell me in plain *English* the truth of the business: for an' you were my own Brother, you should pay for it: belye my Mistress! what a Pox, d'ye think I have no sense of Honour?

Warn. What the Devil's the matter w'ye? either be at quiet, or I'le resolve to take my heels, and be gone.

490 *Sir Mart.* Stop Thief there! what, did you think to scape the hand of Justice?   [*Lays hold on him.*
The best on't is, Sirrah, your heels are not altogether so nimble as your tongue.   [*Beats him.*

Warn. Help! Murder! Murder!

Sir Mart. Confess, you Rogue, then.

Warn. Hold your hands, I think the Devil's in you,———I tell you 'tis a device of mine.

---

480 so?] ~ ! Q1–5, F, D.
481–482 devising. [*Aside to Sir* Martin.] devising. Q1–5, F, D.
484–485 *English*] Q3–5, D; English Q1–2, F.   486 Pox,] ~∧ Q1–5, F, D.
490 what,] D; ~∧ Q1–5, F.

Sir Mart. And have you no body to devise it on but my Mistress, the very Map of Innocence?

Sir John. Moderate your anger, good Sir *Martin.*

Sir Mart. By your patience, Sir, I'le chastise him abundantly.

Sir John. That's a little too much, Sir, by your favour, to beat him in my presence.

Sir Mart. That's a good one i'faith, your presence shall hinder me from beating my own Servant.

Warn. O Traytor to all sense and reason! he's a going to discover that too.   [*Aside.*

Sir Mart. An' I had a mind to beat him to Mummy, he's my own, I hope.

Sir John. At present I must tell you he's mine, Sir.

Sir Mart. Hey-day! here's fine Jugling!

Warn. Stop yet, Sir, you are just upon the brink of a Precipice.

Sir Mart. What is't thou meanest now?————a Lord! my mind mis-gives me I have done some fault, but would I were hang'd if I can find it out.

Warn. There's no making him understand me.   [*Aside.*

Sir Mart. Pox on't, come what will, I'le not be fac'd down with a Lye; I say he is my man.

Sir John. Pray remember your self better; did not you turn him away for some fault lately, and laid a Livery of black and blew on his Back before he went?

Sir Mart. The Devil of any fault, or any black and blew that I remember: either the Rascal put some Trick upon you, or you would upon me.

Sir John. O, ho! then it seems the cudgelling and turning away were pure invention; I am glad I understand it.

Sir Mart. In fine, it's all so damn'd a Lye————

Warn. Alas! he has forgot it, Sir, good Wits, you know, have bad Memories.

Sir John. No, no, Sir, that shall not serve your turn, you may return when you please to your old Master, I give you a fair dis-

---

507   too. [*Aside.*] too. Q1–5, F, D.
516   [*Aside.*] *on last line of preceding speech in* Q1–5, F, D.
527   Lye————] D; ~.———— Q1–5, F.

charge, and a glad man I am to be so rid of you: were you thereabouts i'faith? what a Snake had I entertain'd into my bosom!
fare you well, Sir, and lay your next Plot better between you, I
advise you.   [*Exit Sir* John.

Warn. Lord, Sir, how you stand! as you were nip'd i'th' head:
have you done any new piece of Folly, that makes you look so
like an Ass?

Sir Mart. Here's three pieces of Gold yet; if I had the heart
540 to offer it thee.   [*Holds the Gold afar off trembling.*

Warn. Noble Sir, what have I done to deserve so great a Liberality? I confess if you had beaten me for your own fault, if you
had utterly destroyed all my projects, then it might ha' bin expected that ten or twenty pieces should have been offer'd by way
of recompence and satisfaction.————

Sir Mart. Nay, an' you be so full o' your Flowts, your Friend
and Servant; who the Devil could tell the meaning of your signs
and tokens, an' you go to that?

Warn. You are no Ass then?

550 *Sir Mart.* Well, Sir, to do you service, d'ye see, I am an Ass in
a fair way; will that satisfie you?

Warn. For this once produce those three pieces, I am contented to receive that inconsiderable tribute, or make 'em six
and I'le take the fault upon my self.

Sir Mart. Are we Friends then? if we are, let me advise
you————

Warn. Yet advising!————

Sir Mart. For no harm, good *Warner:* but pray next time make
me of your Counsel, let me enter into the business, instruct me
560 in every point, and then if I discover all, I am resolv'd to give
over affairs, and retire from the world.

Warn. Agreed, it shall be so; but let us now take breath a
while, then on agen.

For though we had the worst, those heats were past,

Wee'l whip and spur, and fetch him up at last.   [*Exeunt.*

ACT V. SCENE I.

Enter Lord, Lady Dupe, *Mistress* Christian, Rose,
and Warner.

Lord. Your promise is admirably made good to me, that Sir *John Swallow* should be this night married to Mrs *Christian;* instead of that, he is more deeply engag'd than ever with old *Moody.*

Warn. I cannot help these ebbs and flows of fortune.

La. D. I am sure my Neice suffers most in't, he's come off to her with a cold Complement of a mistake in his Mistress's Vertue, which he has now found out, by your Masters folly, to be a Plot of yours to separate them.

Chr. To be forsaken when a woman has given her consent!

Lord. 'Tis the same scorn, as to have a Town render'd up, and afterwards slighted.

Rose. You are a sweet youth, Sir, to use my Lady so, when she depended on you; is this the faith of *Valet de Chambre?* I would be asham'd to be such a dishonour to my profession; it will reflect upon us in time, we shall be ruin'd by your good example.

Warn. As how my dear Lady Embassadress?

Rose. Why, they say the women govern their Ladies, and you govern us: so if you play fast and loose, not a Gallant will bribe us for our good wills; the gentle *Guiny* will now go to the Ordinary, which us'd as duly to steal into our hands at the stair-foot as into Mr. Doctors at parting.

Lord. Night's come, and I expect your promise.

La. D. Fail with me if you think good, Sir.

Chr. I give no more time.

Rose. And if my Mistress go to bed a Maid to night———

Warn. Hey-day! you are dealing with me, as they do with the Banquers, call in all your debts together; there's no possibility

ACT V. SCENE I.] D; ACT. V. Q1–4; ACT V. Q5, F.
s.d. *Lord*] D; Lord Q1–5, F.

of payment at this rate, but I'le coin for you all as fast as I can, I
30 assure you.

La. Du. But you must not think to pay us with false Money,
as you have done hitherto.

Rose. Leave off your Mountebank tricks with us, and fall to
your business in good earnest.

Warn. Faith, and I will *Rose;* for to confess the truth, I am a
kind of a Mountebank, I have but one Cure for all your Dis-
eases, that is, that my Mr. may marry Mistress *Millisent,* for then
Sir *John Swallow* will of himself return to Mrs. *Christian.*

Lord. He says true, and therefore we must all be helping to
40 that design.

Warn. I'le put you upon something, give me but a thinking
time. In the first place, get a Warrant and Bailifs to arrest Sir
John Swallow upon a promise of marriage to Mistress *Christian.*

Lord. Very good.

La. D. We'll all swear it.

Warn. I never doubted your Ladiship in the least, Madam
————for the rest we will consider hereafter.

Lord. Leave this to us.   [*Ex. Lord, La.* D. Chr.

Enter Millisent *above.*

Warn. Rose where's thy Lady?
50 *Mill.* What have you to say to her?

Warn. Only to tell you, Madam, I am going forward in the
great work of projection.

Mill. I know not whether you will deserve my thanks when
the work's done.

Warn. Madam, I hope you are not become indifferent to my
Master.

Mill. If he should prove a fool after all your crying up his wit,
I shall be a miserable woman.

---

48 *Lord, La.* D.] Lord, La. D. Mill. Q1; Lord. La. *Du.* Mill. Q2; Lord, *Lady*
Dupe, Mill. Q3–5; Lord, *Lady* Dupe, F; *Lord, L.* Dupe. Mill. D.
48 Chr. / *Enter* Millisent *above.*] Chr. Q1–5, F, D.

Warn. A fool! that were a good jest i'faith: but how comes
your Ladiship to suspect it?

Rose. I have heard, Madam, your greatest wits have ever a
touch of madness and extravagance in them; so perhaps has he.

Warn. There's nothing more distant than wit and folly, yet
like East and West, they may meet in a point, and produce actions that are but a hairs breadth from one another.

Rose. I'le undertake he has wit enough to make one laugh at
him a whole day together: He's a most Comical person.

Mill. For all this I will not swear he is no fool; he has still discovered all your plots.

Warn. O Madam, that's the common fate of your Machivili-
ans, they draw their Designs so subtile, that their very fineness
breaks them.

Mill. However I'm resolv'd to be on the sure side, I will have
certain proof of his wit before I marry him.

Warn. Madam, I'le give you one, he wears his cloaths like a
great sloven, and that's a sure sign of wit, he neglects his outward parts; besides, he speaks *French,* sings, dances, plays upon
the Lute.

Mill. Does he do all this, say you?

Warn. Most divinely, Madam.

Mill. I ask no more, then let him give me a Serenade immediately; but let him stand in the view, I'le not be cheated.

Warn. He shall do't Madam.————But how, the Devil knows
————for he sings like a Scritch-Owle, and never touch'd the
Lute.   [*Aside.*

Mill. You'le see't perform'd?

Warn. Now I think on't, Madam, this will but retard our enterprise.

Mill. Either let him do't, or see me no more.

Warn. Well, it shall be done, Madam; but where's your Father? will not he over-hear it?

---

62   them;] ~ , Q1–5, F, D.   65   one another] Q2–5, F, D; another Q1.
77   *French*] Q3–5, F, D; French Q1–2.
83   Madam.————But] Madam: but Q1–3; Madam: But Q4–5, F, D.
85   Lute. [*Aside.*] Q4–5, F; Lute. Q1–3, D.

Mill. As good hap is, he's below stairs, talking with a Seaman, that has brought him news from the *East-Indies.*

Warn. What concernment can he have there?

Mill. He had a Bastard-Son there, whom he lov'd extreamly: but not having any news from him these many years, concluded him dead; this Son he expects within these three days.

Warn. When did he see him last?

Mill. Not since he was seven years old.

100 *Warn.* A sudden thought comes into my head to make him appear before his time; let my Master pass for him, and by that means he may come into the House unsuspected by your Father, or his Rival.

Mill. According as he performs his Serenade, I'le talk with you————make haste————I must retire a little.

[*Ex.* Mill. *from above.*

Rose. I'le instruct him most rarely, he shall never be found out; but in the mean time, what wilt thou do for a Serenade?

Warn. Faith, I am a little non-plus'd on the sudden, but a warm consolation from thy lips, *Rose,* would set my wits a work-
110 ing again.

Rose. Adieu, *Warner.*   [*Exit* Rose.

Warn. Inhumane *Rose,* adieu.
Blockhead *Warner,* into what a *premunire* hast thou brought thy self? this 'tis to be so forward to promise for another————
but to be Godfather to a Fool, to promise and vow he should do any thing like a Christian————

Enter Sir Martin.

Sir Mart. Why, how now Bully, in a Brown Study? for my good I warrant it; there's five shillings for thee, what, we must encourage good wits sometimes.

120 *Warn.* Hang your white pelf: sure, Sir, by your largess you mistake me for *Martin Parker,* the Ballad-Maker; your covetous-ness has offended my Muse, and quite dull'd her.

102 your] Q4-5, F; her Q1-3, D.   107 for] D; with Q1-5, F.
111 *Exit* Rose.] Q3-5, F; *Exit.* Rose. Q1-2; *Exit.* D.
113 *premunire*] Q3-5, F; premunire Q1-2, D.

Sir Mart. How angry the poor Devil is! in fine thou art as cholerick as a Cook by a Fire side.

Warn. I am over-heated, like a Gun, with continual discharging my wit: 'slife, Sir, I have rarifi'd my brains for you, till they are evaporated; but come, Sir, do something for your self like a man, I have engag'd you shall give to your Mistress a Serenade in your proper person: I'le borrow a Lute for you.

Sir Mart. I'le warrant thee, I'le do't man.

Warn. You never learn't, I do not think you know one stop.

Sir Mart. 'Tis no matter for that, Sir, I'le play as fast as I can, and never stop at all.

Warn. Go to, you are an invincible Fool I see; get up into your Window, and set two Candles by you, take my Land-lords Lute in your hand, and fumble on't, and make grimmaces with your mouth, as if you sung; in the mean time, I'le play in the next Room in the dark, and consequently your Mistress, who will come to her Balcone over against you, will think it to be you; and at the end of every Tune, I'le ring the Bell that hangs between your Chamber and mine, that you may know when to have done.

Sir Mart. Why, this is fair Play now, to tell a man before-hand what he must do; Gramercy i'faith, Boy, now if I fail thee————.

Warn. About your business then, your Mistress and her Maid appear already: I'le give you the sign with the Bell when I am prepar'd, for my Lute is at hand in the Barbers shop. [*Exeunt.*

Enter Millisent, Rose, *with a Candle by 'em above.*

Rose. We shall have rare Musick.

Mill. I wish it prove so; for I suspect the Knight can neither play nor sing.

Rose. But if he does, you're bound to pay the Musick, Madam.

Mill. I'le not believe it, except both my Ears and Eyes are Witnesses.

---

123   is!] Q4–5, F; ∼ ? Q1–3, D.   138   who] Q2–5, F, D; who who Q1.
148+   *s.d.* Millisent,] Q2–5, F, D; Millesent, Q1.

Rose. But 'tis night, Madam, and you cannot see 'em; yet he may play admirably in the dark.

Mill. Where's my Father?

Rose. You need not fear him, he's still employ'd with that same Sea-man, and I have set Mrs. *Christian* to watch their dis-
160 course, that betwixt her and me *Warner* may have wherewithal to instruct his Master.

Mill. But yet there's fear my Father will find out the Plot.

Rose. Not in the least, for my old Lady has provided two rare disguises for the Master and the Man.

Mill. Peace, I hear them beginning to tune the Lute.

Rose. And see, Madam, where your true Knight Sir *Martin* is plac'd yonder like *Apollo,* with his Lute in his hand and his Rays about his head.

> *Sir* Martin *appears at the adverse window,*
> *a Tune play'd; when it is done,* Warner
> *rings, and Sir* Martin *holds.*

Did he not play most excellently, Madam?
170   *Mill.* He play'd well, and yet methinks he held his Lute but untowardly.

Rose. Dear Madam, peace; now for the Song.

The SONG

Blind Love to this hour
Had never like me, a slave under his power.
    Then blest be the Dart
    That he threw at my heart,
      For nothing can prove
A joy so great as to be wounded with love.

My Days and my Nights
180   *Are fill'd to the purpose with sorrows and frights;*
    From my heart still I sigh
    And my Eyes are ne're dry,
      So that Cupid *be prais'd,*
I am to the top of Love's happiness rais'd.

---

160 me] Q1 *(corrected state),* Q2–5, F, D; ~ , Q1 *(uncorrected state).*

My Soul's all on fire,
So that I have the pleasure to doat and desire,
  Such a pretty soft pain
  That it tickles each vein;
    'Tis the dream of a smart,
Which makes me breath short when it beats at my heart.

Sometimes in a Pet,
When I am despis'd, I my freedom would get;
  But streight a sweet smile
  Does my anger beguile,
    And my heart does recall,
Then the more I do struggle, the lower I fall.

Heaven does not impart
Such a grace as to love unto ev'ry ones heart;
  For many may wish
  To be wounded and miss:
    Then blest be loves Fire,
And more blest her Eyes that first taught me desire.

               [*The Song being done,* Warner *rings agen; but Sir*
                 Martin *continues fumbling, and gazing on his*
                 Mistress.

Mill. A pretty humour'd Song:————but stay, methinks he plays and sings still, and yet we cannot hear him.————Play louder, Sir *Martin,* that we may have the fruits on't.

Warn. peeping. Death! this abominable Fool will spoil all agen. Dam him, he stands making his Grimaces yonder, and he looks so earnestly upon his Mistress, that he hears me not.

                                 [*Rings agen.*

Mill. Ah, ah! have I found you out, Sir? now as I live and breathe, this is a pleasant, *Rose,*————his man play'd and sung for him, and he, it seems, did not know when he should give over.

                         [Millisent *and* Rose *laugh.*

Warn. They have found him out, and laugh yonder as if they would split their sides. Why, Mr. Fool, Oafe, Coxcomb, will you hear none of your names?

202+   *s.d.* [*The*] Q4–5, F; ∧~ Q1–3, D.   213   Why,] Q4–5, F, D; ~∧ Q1–3.

Mill. Sir *Martin,* Sir *Martin,* take your mans counsel, and keep time with your Musick.

Sir Mart. peeping. Ha! what do you say, Madam? how does your Ladiship like my Musick?

Mill. O most heavenly! just like the Harmony of the Spheres
220 that is to be admired, and never heard.

Warn. You have ruin'd all by your not leaving off in time.

Sir Mart. What the Devil would you have a man do when my hand is in? well o' my conscience I think there is a Fate upon me.
[*Noise within.*

Mill. Look, *Rose,* what's the matter.

Rose. 'Tis Sir *John Swallow* pursu'd by the Bailiffs, Madam, according to our plot; it seems they have dog'd him thus late to his Lodging.

Mill. That's well! for though I begin not to love this Fool; yet I am glad I shall be rid on him.   [*Ex.* Millisent, Rose.

Enter Sir John *pursu'd by three Bailiffs over the Stage.*

230   *Sir Mart.* Now I'le redeem all agen, my Mistress shall see my Valour, I'm resolv'd on't. Villains, Rogues, Poultroons! what? three upon one? in fine, I'le be with you immediately.   [*Exit.*

Warn. Why, Sir, are you stark mad? have you no grain of sense left? he's gone! now is he as earnest in the quarrel as *Cokes* among the Poppits; 'tis to no purpose whatever I do for him.
[*Exit* Warner.

Enter Sir John *and Sir* Martin (*having driven away the Bailiffs*) *Sir* Martin *flourisheth his Sword.*

Sir Mart. Victoria! Victoria! what heart, Sir *John,* you have received no harm, I hope?

Sir John. Not the least, I thank you Sir for your timely assistance, which I will requite with any thing but the resigning of my
240 Mrs.————Dear Sir *Martin,* a good night.

223 in?] ~ ! Q1–5, F, D.   234 *Cokes*] F, D; Cokes Q1–5.
235+ *s.d.* [*Exit*] Q3–5, F, D; ∧~ Q1–2.

Sir Mart. Pray let me wait upon you in Sir *John*.

Sir John. I can find my way to Mrs. *Millisent* without you, Sir, I thank you.

Sir Mart. But pray, what were you to be arrested for?

Sir John. I know no more than you; some little debts, perhaps, I left unpaid by my negligence: once more good night, Sir. [*Exit.*

Sir Mart. He's an ungrateful Fellow; and so in fine, I shall tell him when I see him next————

Enter Warner.

Monsieur *Warner*, A propos! I hope you'l applaud me now, I have defeated the Enemy, and that in sight of my Mistress; Boy, I have charm'd her, i'faith, with my Valour.

Warn. I, just as much as you did e'ne now with your Musick; go, you are so beastly a Fool, that a Chiding is thrown away upon you.

Sir Mart. Fool in your face, Sir; call a man of Honour, Fool, when I have just atchieved such an Enterprise————Gad now my blood's up, I am a dangerous person, I can tell you that, *Warner*.

Warn. Poor Animal, I pity thee.

Sir Mart. I grant I am no Musician, but you must allow me for a Sword-man, I have beat 'em bravely; and in fine, I am come off unhurt, save only a little scratch i'th' head.

Warn. That's impossible, thou hast a Scull so thick, no Sword can pierce it; but much good may't d'ye, Sir, with the fruits of your Valour: you rescu'd your Rival when he was to be arrested on purpose to take him off from your Mistress.

Sir Mart. Why, this is ever the Fate of ingenious men; nothing thrives they take in hand.

Enter Rose.

248–249 next———— / *Enter* Warner. / Monsieur *Warner*] next————Monsieur
———— [*Enter* Warner. / *Warner* Q1–5, F, D (/ ∧*Enter* D).
268+   *s.d. Enter*] Q5, F, D; [∼ Q1–4.

Rose. Sir *Martin,* you have done your business with my Lady,
270 she'l never look upon you more; she says, she's so well satisfied
of your Wit and Courage, that she will not put you to any further
tryal.

Sir Mart. *Warner,* is there no hopes, *Warner?*

Warn. None that I know.

Sir Mart. Let's have but one civil plot more before we part.

Warn. 'Tis to no purpose.

Rose. Yet if he had some golden Friends that would engage for
him the next time———

Sir Mart. Here's a *Jacobus* and a *Carolus* will enter into Bonds
280 for me.

Rose. I'le take their Royal words for once.

                        [*She fetches two disguises.*

Warn. The meaning of this, dear *Rose?*

Rose. 'Tis in pursuance of thy own invention, *Warner;* a child
which thy wit hath begot upon me: but let us lose no time, help,
help, dress thy Master, that he may be *Anthony,* old *Moody*'s
Bastard, and thou his Servant, come from the *East-Indies.*

Sir Mart. Hey-tarockit———now we shall have *Roses* device
too, I long to be at it, pray let's hear more on't.

Rose. Old *Moody* you must know in his younger years, when
290 he was a *Cambridge*-Scholar, made bold with a Towns-mans
Daughter there, by whom he had a Bastard whose name was
Anthony, whom you Sir *Martin,* are to represent.

S. Mart. I warrant you, let me alone for *Tony:* but pray go on,
Rose.

Rose. This Child in his Fathers time he durst not own, but
bred him privately in the Isle of *Ely,* till he was seven years old,
and from thence sent him with one *Bonaventure* a Merchant for
the *East-Indies.*

Warn. But will not this over-burden your memory, Sir?

300 *Sir Mart.* There's no answering thee any thing, thou think'st
I am good for nothing.

---

279 *Jacobus* . . . *Carolus*] Q3–5, F, D; *Jacobus* . . . Carolus Q1–2.
281+ *s.d. disguises.*] Q3–5, F, D; ~ₐ] Q1; ~ .] Q2.
284–285 help, help,] Help! Help! Q1; Help! help! Q2, D; help! help! Q3–5, F.
286 his Servant,] his Q1; his, Q2–5, F, D.

Rose. Bonaventure dy'd at *Surat* within two years, and this *Anthony* has liv'd up and down in the *Moguls* Country unheard of by his Father till this night, and is expected within these three days: now if you can pass for him, you may have admittance into the house, and make an end of all the business before the other *Anthony* arrives.

Warn. But hold, *Rose,* there's one considerable point omitted; what was his Mother's name?

Rose. That indeed I had forgot; her name was *Dorothy,* Daughter to one *Draw-water* a Vintner at the *Rose.*

Warn. Come, Sir, are you perfect in your Lesson? *Anthony Moody* born in *Cambridge,* bred in the Isle of *Ely,* sent into the *Moguls* Country at seven years old with one *Bonaventure* a Merchant, who dy'd within two years; your Mother's name *Dorothy Draw-water* the Vintners Daughter at the *Rose.*

Sir Mart. I have it all *ad unguem*————what, do'st think I'm a Sot? but stay a little, how have I liv'd all this while in that same Country?

Warn. What Country?————Pox, he has forgot already————

Rose. The *Moguls* Country.

Sir Mart. I, I, the *Moguls* Country! what a Devil, any man may mistake a little; but now I have it perfect: but what have I been doing all this while in the *Moguls* Country? He's a Heathen Rogue, I am afraid I shall never hit upon his name.

Warn. Why, you have been passing your time there, no matter how.

Rose. Well, if this passes upon the Old man, I'le bring your business about agen with my Mistress, never fear it; stay you here at the door, I'le go tell the Old man of your arrival.

Warn. Well, Sir, now play your part exactly, and I'le forgive all your former errours.————

Sir Mart. Hang 'em, they were only slips of Youth————how peremptory and domineering this Rogue is! now he see's I have need of his service: would I were out of his power agen, I would make him lye at my feet like any Spaniel.

Enter Moody, *Sir* John, *Lord, Lady* Dupe, Millisent, Christian, Rose.

Mood. Is he here already, say'st thou? which is he?

Rose. That Sun-burn'd Gentleman.

Mood. My dear Boy *Anthony,* do I see thee agen before I dye?
340 welcome, welcome.

Sir Mart. My dear Father, I know it is you by instinct; for methinks I am as like you as if I were spit out of your mouth.

Rose. Keep it up I beseech your Lordship. [*Aside to the Lord.*

Lord. He's wond'rous like indeed.

La. Dupe. The very image of him.

Mood. Anthony, you must salute all this Company: this is my Lord *Dartmouth,* this my Lady *Dupe,* this her Niece Mrs. *Christian.* [*He salutes them.*

Sir Mart. And that's my Sister, methinks I have a good re-
350 semblance of her too: honest Sister, I must need kiss you Sister.

Warn. This fool will discover himself, I foresee it already by his carriage to her. [*Aside.*

Mood. And now *Anthony,* pray tell's a little of your Travels.

Sir Mart. Time enough for that, forsooth Father, but I have such a natural affection for my Sister, that methinks I could live and dye with her: give me thy hand sweet Sister.

Sir John. She's beholding to you, Sir.

Sir Mart. What if she be Sir, what's that to you Sir?

Sir John. I hope, Sir, I have not offended you?

360 *Sir Mart.* It may be you have, and it may be you have not, Sir; you see I have no mind to satisfie you, Sir: what a Devil! a man cannot talk a little to his own flesh and blood, but you must be interposing with a murrain to you.

Mood. Enough of this, good *Anthony,* this Gentleman is to marry your Sister.

Sir Mart. He marry my Sister! ods foot, Sir, there are some Bastards, that shall be nameless, that are as well worthy to marry her, as any man; and have as good blood in their veins.

Sir John. I do not question it in the least, Sir.

370 *Sir Mart.* 'Tis not your best course, Sir; you marry my Sister! what have you seen of the world, Sir? I have seen your Hurricanoes, and your Calentures, and your Eclipticks, and your Tropick Lines, Sir, an' you go to that, Sir.

---

352 her. [*Aside.*] her. Q1–5, F, D.

Warn. You must excuse my Master, the Sea's a little working in his brain, Sir.

Sir Mart. And your *Prester Johns* o'th' *East-Indies,* and your Great *Turk* of *Rome* and *Persia.*

Mood. Lord, what a thing it is to be Learned, and a Traveller! Bodikins it makes me weep for joy; but, *Anthony,* you must not bear your self too much upon your Learning, Child.

Mill. Pray Brother be civil to this Gentleman for my sake.

Sir Mart. For your sake, Sister *Millisent,* much may be done, and here I kiss your hand on't.

Warn. aside. Yet again stupidity?

Mill. Nay, pray Brother hands off, now you are too rude.

Sir Mart. Dear Sister, as I am a true *East-India* Gentleman———

Mood. But pray, Son *Anthony,* let us talk of other matters, and tell me truly, had you not quite forgot me? and yet I made woundy much of you when you were young.

Sir Mart. I remember you as well as if I saw you but yesterday: A fine grey-headed———grey-bearded old Gentleman as ever I saw in all my life.

Warn. aside. Grey-bearded old Gentleman! when he was a Scholar at *Cambridge.*

Mood. But do you remember where you were bred up?

Sir Mart. O yes, Sir, most perfectly, in the Isle———stay ———let me see, oh———now I have it———in the Isle of *Silly.*

Mood. In the Isle of *Ely,* sure you mean?

Warn. Without doubt he did, Sir, but this damn'd Isle of *Silly* runs in's head ever since his Sea-Voyage.

Mood. And your Mothers name was———come pray let me examine you———for that I'm sure you cannot forget.

Sir Mart. Warner! what was it *Warner?*   [*Aside to him.*

Warn. Poor Mrs. *Dorothy Draw-water,* if she were now alive, what a joyful day would this be to her!

---

377   *Turk*] D; Turk Q1–5, F.   384   *Warn. aside.*] *Warn.* Q1–5, F, D.
394   *Warn.*] Q2–5, F, D; *Warn* Q1.
405   *Warner? [Aside to him.*] *Warner?* Q1–5, F, D.
407   her!] ∼ ? Q1–5, F, D.

Mood. Who the Devil bid you speak, Sirrah?

Sir Mart. Her name, Sir, was Mrs. *Dorothy Draw-water.*

410 *Sir John.* I'le be hanged if this be not some Cheat.

Mill. He makes so many stumbles, he must needs fall at last.

Mood. But you remember, I hope, where you were born?

Warn. Well, they may talk what they will of *Oxford* for an University, but *Cambridge* for my Money.

Mood. Hold your tongue you *Scanderbag* Rogue you, this is the second time you have been talking when you should not.

Sir Mart. I was born at *Cambridge,* I remember it as perfectly as if it were but yesterday.

Warn. How I sweat for him! he's remembring ever since he

420 was born.

Mood. And who did you go over withall to the *East-Indies?*

Sir Mart. Warner!   [*Aside to him.*

Warn. 'Twas a happy thing, Sir, you lighted upon so honest a Merchant as Mr. *Bonaventure,* to take care of him.

Mood. Sawcy Rascal! this is past all sufferance.

Rose. We are undone *Warner,* if this discourse go on any further.

Lord. Pray, Sir, take pity o'th' poor Gentleman, he has more need of a good Supper, than to be ask'd so many Questions.

430 *Sir John.* These are Rogues, Sir, I plainly perceive it; pray let me ask him one question——which way did you come home Sir?

Sir Mart. We came home by Land, Sir.

Warn. That is, from *India* to *Persia,* from *Persia* to *Turkey,* from *Turkey* to *Germany,* from *Germany* to *France.*

Sir John. And from thence, over the narrow Seas on Horse-back.

Mood. 'Tis so, I discern it now, but some shall smoke for't. Stay a little *Anthony,* I'le be with you presently.   [*Ex.* Mood.

440 *Warn.* That wicked old man is gone for no good, I'm afraid, would I were fairly quit of him.   [*Aside.*

---

415   *Scanderbag*] scanderbag Q1; Scanderbag Q2–5, F, D.

422   *Warner!* [*Aside to him.*] *Warner!* Q1–5, F, D.

441   *Aside*] Q3–5, F, D; *aside* Q1–2.

Mill. aside. Tell me no more of Sir *Martin, Rose,* he wants natural sence, to talk after this rate; but for this *Warner,* I am strangely taken with him, how handsomly he brought him off!

Enter Moody *with two Cudgels.*

Mood. Among half a score tough Cudgels I had in my Chamber, I have made choice of these two as best able to hold out.

Mill. Alas! poor *Warner* must be beaten now for all his wit, would I could bear it for him. 　　　　　　　　　　　　　*[Aside.*

Warn. But to what end is all this preparation, Sir?

Mood. In the first place, for your Worship, and in the next, for this *East-Indian* Apostle, that will needs be my Son *Anthony.*

Warn. Why, d'ye think he is not?

Mood. No, thou wicked Accomplice in his designs, I know he is not.

Warn. Who, I his Accomplice? I beseech you, Sir, what is it to me, if he should prove a Counterfeit? I assure you he has cozen'd me in the first place.

Sir John. That's likely, i'faith, cozen his own Servant?

Warn. As I hope for mercy, Sir, I am an utter stranger to him, he took me up but yesterday, and told me the story word for word as he told it you.

Sir Mart. What will become of us two now? I trust to the Rogues wit to bring me off. 　　　　　　　　　　　　　　　*[Aside.*

Mood. If thou wou'dst have me believe thee, take one of these two Cudgels, and help me to lay it on soundly.

Warn. With all my heart.

Mood. Out you Cheat, you Hypocrite, you Imposter! do you come hither to cozen an honest man? 　　　　　　　　*[Beats him.*

Sir Mart. Hold, hold, Sir.

Warn. Do you come hither with a lye to get a Father, Mr. *Anthony* of *East-India?*

Sir Mart. Hold you inhumane Butcher.

444　off!] Q3–5, F; ∼ ? Q1–2, D.　　　444+　*s.d. Enter]* Q3–5, F, D; [∼ Q1–2.
448　him. [*Aside.*] Q4–5, F; him. Q1–3, D.
456　Counterfeit?] Q4–5, F; ∼ ; Q1–3, D.
463　off. [*Aside.*] Q4–5, F; off. Q1–3, D.

Warn. I'le teach you to counterfeit again, Sir.

Sir Mart. The Rogue will murder me.

[*Ex. Sir* Mart. *and* Warn.

Mood. A fair riddance of 'em both: let's in and laugh at 'em.

[*Exeunt.*

Enter again Sir Martin, *and* Warner.

Sir Mart. Was there ever such an affront put upon a man, to be beaten by his Servant?

Warn. After my hearty salutations upon your back-side, Sir, may a man have leave to ask you, what news from the *Moguls*
480 Country?

Sir Mart. I wonder where thou hadst the impudence to move such a question to me, knowing how thou hast us'd me.

Warn. Now, Sir, you may see what comes of your indiscretion and stupidity: I always gave you warning of it, but for this time I am content to pass it by without more words, partly, because I have already corrected you, though not so much as you deserve.

Sir Mart. Do'st thou think to carry it off at this rate, after such an injury?

Warn. You may thank your self for't; nay 'twas very well I
490 found out that way, otherwise I had been suspected as your Accomplice.

Sir Mart. But you laid it on with such a vengeance, as if you were beating of a Stock-fish.

Warn. To confess the truth on't, you had anger'd me, and I was willing to evaporate my choler; if you will pass it by so, I may chance to help you to your Mistress: no more words of this business, I advise you, but go home and grease your back.

Sir Mart. In fine, I must suffer it at his hands; for if my shoulders had not paid for this fault, my purse must have sweat blood
500 for't: the Rogue has got such a hank upon me——   [*Aside.*

Enter Rose.

474+   *s.d.* Mart. *and* Warn.] Mart. Q₁–₅, F, D.
500   me—— [*Aside.*] me—— Q₁–₅, F, D.
500+   *s.d.* Enter] D (*but after next speech*); [~ Q₁–₅, F (*at end of next line*).

Warn. So, so, here's another of our Vessels come in after the storm that parted us: what comfort, *Rose,* no Harbour near?

Rose. My Lady, as you may well imagine, is most extreamly incens'd against Sir *Martin;* but she applauds your ingenuity to the Skies. I'le say no more, but thereby hangs a Tale.

Sir Mart. I am considering with my self about a Plot, to bring all about agen.

Rose. Yet again plotting! if you have such a mind to't, I know no way so proper for you as to turn Poet to *Pugenello.*

Warn. Hark! is not that Musick in your house? [*Musick plays.*

Rose. Yes, Sir *John* has given my Mistress the Fiddles, and our Old man is as jocund yonder, and does so hug himself to think how he has been reveng'd upon you.

Warn. Why, he does not know 'twas we, I hope?

Rose. 'Tis all one for that.

Sir Mart. I have such a Plot; I care not, I will speak an' I were to be hang'd for't———shall I speak, dear *Warner?* let me now; it does so wamble within me, just like a Clyster, i'faith law, and I can keep it no longer for my heart.

Warn. Well, I am indulgent to you; out with it boldly in the name of Non-sense.

Sir Mart. We two will put on Vizards, and with the help of my Landlord, who shall be of the party, go a Mumming there, and by some device of dancing, get my Mistress away unsuspected by 'em all.

Rose. What if this should hit now, when all your projects have fail'd, *Warner?*

Warn. Would I were hang'd if it be not somewhat probable: nay, now I consider better on't———exceeding probable, it must take, 'tis not in Nature to be avoided.

Sir Mart. O must it so, Sir? and who may you thank for't?

Warn. Now am I so mad he should be the Author of this device. How the Devil, Sir, came you to stumble on't?

Sir Mart. Why should not my brains be as fruitful as yours or any mans?

---

523 Landlord] Q3-5, F, D; Lordland Q1-2.   531 Sir?] ~ ! Q1-5, F, D.

Warn. This is so good, it shall not be your Plot, Sir, either dis-own it, or I will proceed no further.

Sir Mart. I would not lose the credit of my Plot to gain my Mistress: the Plot's a good one, and I'le justifie it upon any
540 ground of *England;* an' you will not work upon't, it shall be done without you.

Rose. I think the Knight has reason.

Warn. Well, I'le order it however to the best advantage: hark you, *Rose.*   [*Whispers.*

Sir Mart. If it miscarry by your ordering, take notice 'tis your fault, 'tis well invented I'le take my Oath on't.

Rose. I must in to 'em, for fear I should be suspected; but I'le acquaint my Lord, my old Lady, and all the rest who ought to know it, with your design.

550 *Warn.* We'll be with you in a twinkling: you and I, *Rose,* are to follow our Leaders, and be pair'd to night———

Rose. To have, and to hold, are dreadful words, *Warner;* but for your sake I'le venture on 'em.   [*Exeunt.*

SCENE II.

Enter Lord, Lady Dupe, *and* Christian.

La. Dupe. Nay! good my Lord be patient.

Lord. Does he think to give Fiddles and Treatments in a house where he has wrong'd a Lady? I'le never suffer it.

La. Dupe. But upon what ground will you raise your quarrel?

Lord. A very just one, as I am her Kinsman.

La. Dupe. He does not know yet why he was to be arrested; try that way agen.

Lord. I'le hear of nothing but revenge.

Enter Rose.

---

544   *Whispers*] Q3–5, F, D; *whispers* Q1–2.
SCENE II. / *Enter*] *Enter* Q1–5, F, D.   s.d. *Lord*] Q3, D; Lord Q1–2, Q4–5, F.
8+   s.d. *Enter*] Q5, D; [∼ Q1–4, F.

Rose. Yes, pray hear me one word, my Lord, Sir *Martin* him-
0 self has made a Plot.
Chr. That's like to be a good one.
Rose. A Fool's Plot may be as lucky as a Fool's Handsel; 'tis
a very likely one, and requires nothing for your part, but to get
a Parson in the next room, we'll find work for him.
La. Dupe. That shall be done immediately; *Christian,* make
haste, and send for Mr. *Ball* the Non-conformist, tell him here
are two or three Angels to be earn'd.
Chr. And two or three Possets to be eaten: may I not put in
that, Madam?
0 *La. Dupe.* Surely you may.   [*Exit* Christian.
Rose. Then for the rest—'tis only this—Oh! they are here!
pray take it in a whisper; my Lady knows of it already.

Enter Moody, *Sir* John, Millisent.

Mill. Strike up agen, Fiddle, I'le have a *French* Dance.
Sir John. Let's have the Brawls.
Mood. No, good Sir *John,* no quarreling among Friends.
La. Dupe. Your Company is like to be increas'd, Sir; some
Neighbors that heard your Fiddles are come a mumming to you.
Mood. Let 'em come in, and we'l be Jovy; an' I had but my
Hobby-horse at home————
0 *Sir John.* What, are they Men or Women?
La. Dupe. I believe some Prentices broke loose.
Mill. Rose! go and fetch me down two *Indian* gowns and
Vizard-masks————you and I will disguise too, and be as good
a Mummery to them as they to us.   [*Exit* Rose.
Mood. That will be most rare.

Enter Sir Martin, Warner, *Landlord disguised like a Tony.*

Mood. O here they come! Gentlemen Maskers you are welcome———— [*Warner signs to the musick for a Dance.*] He signs
———
23   *French*] D; French Q1–5, F.
32   *Indian* gowns] Q2–5, F, D; Indian-gowns Q1.
35+   s.d. *Landlord*] D; Landlord Q1–5, F.
37   *stage direction at right margin in Q1–5, F, D.*

for a Dance I believe; you are welcome, Mr. Musick, strike up,
I'le make one as old as I am.

40   *Sir John.* And I'le not be out.   [*Dance.*

Lord. Gentlemen Maskers, you have had the Frolick, the next
turn is mine; bring two Flute-glasses and some stools, Ho, we'll
have the Ladies health.

Sir John. But why stools, my Lord?

Lord. That you shall see: the humour is, that two men at a
time are hoysted up; when they are above, they name their
Ladies, and the rest of the Company dance about them while
they drink: this they call the Frolick of the Altitudes.

Mood. Some High-lander's invention, I'le warrant it.

50   *Lord.* Gentlemen-maskers, you shall begin.

[*They hoyst Sir* Mart. *and* Warn.

Sir John. Name the Ladies.

Lord. They point to Mrs. *Millisent* and Mrs. *Christian,* Allons, Touche! Touche!

[*While they drink the Company dances*
and sings: they are taken down.

Mood. A rare toping health this: come Sir *John,* now you and
I will be in our altitudes.

Sir John. What new device is this tro?

Mood. I know not what to make on't.

[*When they are up, the Company dances about*
'em: then dance off. Tony dances a Jig.

Sir John to Tony. Pray, Mr. Fool, where's the rest o' your
Company? I would fain see 'em again.

60   *Landl.* Come down and tell 'em so, *Cudden.*

Sir John. I'le be hang'd if there be not some plot in't, and this
Fool is set here to spin out the time.

Mood. Like enough: undone! undone! my Daughter's gone,
let me down, Sirrah.

50+   *s.d. and* Warn.$_\wedge$] Q3–5, F, D; *and* Warn.] Q1–2.
52–53   Allons,] A Lou's$_\wedge$ Q1–2, D; A Lon's$_\wedge$ Q3–5, F.
53+   *s.d.* [While . . . down.] *as in D; at right margin of next three speeches and*
continuous with next stage direction, which is similarly arranged, in Q1–3 ($_\wedge$ ~);
after following speech in Q4–5, F.
57+   *s.d.* [When . . . Jig.] F, D; $_\wedge$ ~ Q1–3; { ~ Q4–5.

Landl. Yes, *Cudden.*

Sir John. My Mistress is gone, let me down first.

Landl. This is the quickest way, *Cudden.*

                            [He offers to pull down the stools.

Sir John. Hold! Hold! or thou wilt break my neck.

Landl. And you will not come down, you may stay there,

 0 *Cudden.*   *[Exit Landlord dancing.*

Mood. O *Scanderbag* Villains!

Sir John. Is there no getting down?

Mood. All this was long of you Sir *Jack.*

Sir John. 'Twas long of your self to invite them hither.

Mood. O you young Coxcomb, to be drawn in thus!

Sir John. You old Sot you, to be caught so sillily!

Mood. Come but an inch nearer, and I'le so claw thee.

Sir John. I hope I shall reach to thee.

Mood. And 'twere not for thy wooden breast-work there.

    Sir John. I hope to push thee down from *Babylon.*

    Enter *Lord, La.* Dupe, *Sir* Mart. Warn. Rose, Mill. *vail'd,*

                        Landl.

Lord. How, Gentlemen! what, quarrelling among your selves?

Mood. Coxnowns! help me down, and let me have fair play, he shall never marry my Daughter.

Sir Mart. leading Rose. No I'le be sworn that he shall not, therefore never repine, Sir, for Marriages you know are made in Heaven: in fine, Sir, we are joyn'd together in spight of Fortune.

Rose pulling off her mask. That we are indeed, Sir *Martin,* & these are Witnesses; therefore in fine never repine, Sir, for marriages you know are made in Heaven.

Omn. Rose!

Warn. What, is *Rose* split in two? sure I ha' got one *Rose!*

67+   *s.d. stools.*ʌ] Q4–5, F, D; ~ .] Q1–3.

71   *Scanderbag*] Scanderbag Q1–5, F, D.

75   Coxcomb] Q4–5, F, D; Coxcombs Q1–3.

80+   *s.d. Lord*] Q3, D; Lord Q1–2, Q4–5, F.

80+   *s.d. Dupe,*] Q2–5, F, D; ~ . Q1.

80+   *s.d. Landl.*] Q3, D; Landl. Q1–2, Q4–5, F.

81   what,] Q3–5, D; ~ʌ Q1–2, F.   81   your selves?] ~ ! Q1–5, F, D.

Mill. I, the best *Rose* you ever got in all your life.
                            [*Pulls off her Mask.*
Warn. This amazeth me so much, I know not what to say or think.

Mood. My Daughter married to *Warner!*

Sir Mart. Well, I thought it impossible any man in *England* should have over-reach'd me: sure *Warner* there was some mistake in this: prithee *Billy* let's go to the Parson to set all right
100 again, that every man may have his own before the matter go too far.

Warn. Well, Sir! for my part I will have nothing farther to do with these Women, for I find they will be too hard for us, but e'ne sit down by the loss, and content my self with my hard fortune: But, Madam, do you ever think I will forgive you this, to cheat me into an Estate of 2000 *l.* a year?

Sir Mart. And I were as thee, I would not be so serv'd *Warner!*

Mill. I have serv'd him but right for the cheat he put upon me, when he perswaded me you were a Wit————now there's a
110 trick for your trick, Sir.

Warn. Nay, I confess you have out-witted me.

Sir John. Let me down, and I'le forgive all freely.
                            [*They let him down.*
Mood. What am I kept here for?

Warn. I might in policy keep you there, till your Daughter and I had been in private, for a little consummation: But for once, Sir, I'le trust your good nature.   [*Takes him down too.*

Mood. And thou wert a Gentleman it would not grieve me!

Mill. That I was assur'd of before I married him, by my Lord here.

120 *Lord.* I cannot refuse to own him for my Kinsman, though his Father's sufferings in the late times have ruin'd his Fortunes.

Mood. But yet he has been a Serving-man.

Warn. You are mistaken, Sir, I have been a Master, and besides there's an Estate of 800 *l.* a year, only it is mortgaged for 6000 *l.*

93+   *s.d.* [*Pulls*] Q3-5, F, D; ∧ ~ Q1-2.   121   have] Q5, F, D; hath Q1-4.

Mood. Well, we'll bring it off, and for my part, I am glad my
Daughter has miss'd *in fine,* there.

Sir John. I will not be the only man that must sleep without
a Bedfellow to night, if this Lady will once again receive me.

30   *La. D.* She's yours, Sir.

Lord. And the same Parson, that did the former execution, is
still in the next Chamber; what with Cawdels, Wine, and Quidding, which he has taken in abundance, I think he will be able
to wheadle two more of you into matrimony.

Mill. Poor Sir *Martin* looks melancholly! I am half afraid he
is in love.

Warn. Not with the Lady that took him for a wit, I hope.

Rose. At least, Sir *Martin* can do more than you, Mr. *Warner,*
for he can make me a Lady, which you cannot my Mistress.

40   *Sir Mart.* I have lost nothing but my man, and in fine, I shall
get another.

Mill. You'll do very well, Sir *Martin,* for you'll never be your
own man, I assure you.

Warn. For my part I had lov'd you before if I had follow'd
my inclination.

Mill. But now I am afraid you begin of the latest, except your
love can grow up like a Mushroom at a nights warning.

Warn. For that matter never trouble your self, I can love as
fast as any man, when I am nigh possession; my love falls heavy,

50 and never moves quick till it comes near the Centre; he's an ill
Falconer that will unhood before the quarry be in sight.

Love's an high mettal'd Hawk that beats the Air,
But soon grows weary when the Game's not near.

FINIS.

---

153   near.] Q1 *(corrected state),* Q2–5, **F, D;** ~∧ Q1 *(uncorrected state),*

COMMENTARY

List of Abbreviated References

Allen: Ned Bliss Allen, *The Sources of John Dryden's Comedies,* Ann Arbor, 1935

Day: *Songs of John Dryden,* ed. C. L. Day, Cambridge, Mass., 1935

Downes: John Downes, *Roscius Anglicanus,* 1708

ELH: A Journal of English Literary History

HLQ: Huntington Library Quarterly

JEGP: Journal of English and Germanic Philology

Ker: *Essays of John Dryden,* ed. W. P. Ker, Oxford, 1926

Langbaine: Gerard Langbaine, *An Account of the English Dramatick Poets,* 1691

Macdonald: Hugh Macdonald, *John Dryden: A Bibliography of Early Editions and Drydeniana,* Oxford, 1939

MLN: Modern Language Notes

MP: Modern Philology

Nicoll: Allardyce Nicoll, *A History of Restoration Drama, 1660–1700,* 4th ed., Cambridge, 1952

OED: Oxford English Dictionary

PMLA: Publications of the Modern Language Association

PQ: Philological Quarterly

RES: Review of English Studies

SB: Studies in Bibliography

S-S: *The Works of John Dryden,* ed. Sir Walter Scott and George Saintsbury, 1882–1893

Strype: John Strype's revision of *Stow's Survey of London,* 1720

Summers: Dryden's *Dramatic Works,* ed. Montague Summers, London, 1931

Tilley: M. P. Tilley, *A Dictionary of Proverbs,* Ann Arbor, 1950

Van Lennep: *The London Stage, 1660–1800,* Part 1: 1660–1700, ed. William Van Lennep, with Critical Introduction by Emmett L. Avery and Arthur H. Scouten, Carbondale, Ill., 1965

Ward: Charles E. Ward, *The Life of John Dryden,* Durham, N.C., 1961

Wilson: John Harold Wilson, *All The King's Ladies,* Chicago, 1958

W&M: Gertrude L. Woodward and James G. McManaway, *A Checklist of English Plays, 1641–1700,* Chicago, 1945

Works: Dryden's works in the present edition

The Indian Emperour

The Indian Emperour was first performed by the King's Company in the Theatre Royal, Bridges Street, Drury Lane, in the spring, very likely in April, 1665. It was entered in the *Stationers' Register* by Herringman on 26 May and such registration usually followed soon after a play was acted. An allusion in the prologue to the use of costumes from *The Indian Queen* confirms the fact that it was produced the year after that play, which had first appeared in January, 1664; and a date in 1665 is consistent with an allusion in the epilogue to the wits' hostility to the Dutch, against whom the English went to war that year. Downes records the names of the principal actors: among others, Mohun as Montezuma, Kynaston as Guyomar, Hart as Cortes, and one of the Marshall sisters, presumably Anne, as Almeria.[1] He lists Nell Gwyn in the role of Cydaria, but from a remark of Pepys's about a later performance of the play on 22 August 1667, it seems uncertain whether or not she was in the original cast.[2] Presumably most of the actors in the play had previously appeared in *The Indian Queen;* certainly Anne Marshall had had a major role in the earlier play, probably that of Zempoalla.[3] It is impossible to say how many times the play was performed during the spring of 1665, before the theaters were closed by order of the Lord Chamberlain on 5 June because of the spread of the plague.

Assuming that *The Indian Emperour* was first acted in April, it would have appeared in opposition to the Earl of Orrery's most popular heroic play, *Mustapha,* first performed that month by the Duke's Company. When Pepys saw *Mustapha* on 3 April, the King as well as two actresses from the King's Company, Rebecca Marshall and Nell Gwyn, were present, a circumstance suggesting that this was the première.[4] Handsomely mounted,

---

[1] Downes, p. 9. He also lists Wintersel as Odmar, Cartwright as the Priest (not specifying whether the Indian or the Christian one), and Burt as Vasquez.

[2] The relevant passage, in an exact transcription by Professor William Matthews, is as follows (the crossings-out are Pepys's; italicized words appear in longhand in the text): "After dinner with my Lord *Br*[ouncker] and his mistress, to the ~~DYs~~ *King's* playhouse and there saw ~~again St Martin Marrall~~ the *Indian Emperour,* where I find *Nell* come again, which I am glad of but was most infinitely displeased with her being put to *act* the *Emperours* daughter, which is a great and serious part, which she doth most basely." This is not without ambiguity. As Pepys apparently did not see the *Emperour* before the theaters were closed because of the plague, he may not have known whether or not Nell Gwyn was in the original cast.

[3] Pepys, 1 February 1664. Cf. Wilson, p. 168.

[4] W. S. Clark, ed., *The Dramatic Works of Roger Boyle* (1937), I, 226. Pepys did not like the play when he first saw it; but he later changed his mind and in fact praised it on both occasions when he saw it in 1667, 5 January and 4 September.

with new costumes for the actors and new stage properties, the play was well performed, and it brought Davenant and his company a large profit.[5] The play provided, at least in theatrical terms, stern competition for *The Indian Emperour,* which nevertheless achieved its own success. The near simultaneity of the two initial runs suggests the current vogue of plays in rhymed couplets.

The theaters remained closed until late in the autumn of 1666,[6] and like many patrons of the theaters Dryden resided in the country, at his father-in-law's seat at Charlton, Wiltshire. We first hear of the reappearance of *The Indian Emperour* from Pepys, who alluded to, though he did not attend, a performance on 15 January 1667. Even in this first reference to the play, Pepys implies that it was well enough known for roles to be associated with individuals: "Knipp," he says, "acts Mrs. Weaver's great part." [7] A week later the Theatre Royal performed it before royalty; [8] and probably the company performed it a number of other times that season. When Pepys first saw it on 22 August, he thought it "pretty good," but "not well acted by most of them." He saw the play three times the following season, on 11 November 1667 ("a good play, but not so good as people cry it up"), 28 March 1668 ("a very good play indeed"), and on 21 April; and it must have been acted a number of other times. It was certainly acted at least once that season before royalty, on 20 January.[9] In *Of Dramatick Poesie* (1668) Dryden alluded to its popularity (in defending the use of rhyme in drama): "no serious Playes written since the Kings return have been more kindly receiv'd by them ["the noblesse"], then the Siege of *Rhodes,* the *Mustapha,* the *Indian* Queen, and *Indian* Emperour." [10] It was his first unaided play to achieve a considerable success.

The success was lasting: for more than seventy years the play maintained a place in the repertories of the London theaters. It survived the satirical thrusts in *The Rehearsal* to sustain the similar thrusts of a later age in *The Tragedy of Tragedies.* We may infer that it was performed frequently in the later seventeenth century because it was often reprinted and because in the early eighteenth century (when daily theatrical notices began to appear in the newspapers) it was still popular.[11] From the beginning of the new century, in fact, until 1737 it was performed most years: in 1702 and 1705 and beginning in 1707 every year through 1721 except 1716 and 1719; in 1724 and then again every year from 1729 until

---

[5] Downes, p. 26.   [6] Van Lennep, p. 93.

[7] Probably the role of Alibech (Wilson, p. 144).

[8] P.R.O., L.C. 5/139, p. 129 (cited in Nicoll, p. 343).

[9] Nicoll, p. 344.   [10] P. 66; Ker, I, 100.

[11] For the years after 1668 records exist of performances in London in 1674, 1675, 1691, and 1692 (Cf. Van Lennep, *passim*). In 1697 George Farquhar had the role of Guyomar in a performance at Smock Alley, Dublin—a momentous occasion since he was led to abandon the stage and take up writing plays by an accident in which he wounded a fellow actor with his sword (Willard Connely, *Young George Farquhar* [1949], pp. 46–48).

1737, after which it seems to have dropped out of the repertory.[12] One notable amateur performance of the play about 1731, by children of the nobility at the house of Conduitt, Master of the Mint, is the subject of a painting by Hogarth, which shows both the youthful actors and the small audience, including three of George II's children.[13] The play was last performed professionally in London, so far as available records indicate, at Lincoln's Inn Fields on 7 May 1737, the month before Parliament passed the Stage Licensing Act.

Although Herringman had entered *The Indian Emperour* in the *Stationers' Register* in 1665, he did not publish it until October 1667, the delay presumably having been caused by the national disasters, the plague and the fire. Dryden dated his dedication to the Duchess of Monmouth 12 October; Pepys bought the play, "newly printed," on 28 October.

In his dedicatory epistle to Anne, Duchess of Monmouth, the first of many in which Dryden indulged his vein of extravagant flattery, he attributed the "favour which Heroick Plays have lately found upon our Theaters" to the "countenance and approbation they have receiv'd at Court." Over-statement perhaps, but only that. The courtiers liked the heroic plays,[14] and the Duchess of Monmouth in particular liked this one. The young and beautiful wife of the King's son, she would have been an influential advocate for it. Some years later the author of *The Medal of John Bayes* (1682) asked sarcastically how Dryden could have failed to succeed when he had enjoyed the Duchess' patronage;[15] and Dryden himself in the final decade of his life described her as "my first and best Patroness."[16] The Duchess, her Duke, and their friends in fact liked the play well enough to act in a performance of it at court, on 13 January 1668. Pepys reported the following day with his usual candor what he had heard of the performance: "they told me these things most remarkable: that not any woman but the Duchesse of Monmouth and Mrs. Cornwallis did any thing but like fools and stocks, but that these two did do most extraordinary well." Dryden had reason to be grateful to the Duchess.

Herringman brought out a second edition of the play in 1668, probably late in the summer, for Pepys had a copy of it by 20 September. It was prefixed to this second edition that Dryden's *A Defence of an Essay of Dramatick Poesie* first appeared, his answer to Sir Robert Howard's preface to *The Duke of Lerma,* published, also by Herringman, in the summer of 1668. For reasons that are considered below, the *Defence* was canceled from most copies of the second edition and not reprinted in the seventeenth century. The continuing popularity of the play is attested by the

---

[12] Emmett L. Avery, ed., *The London Stage, 1660–1800,* Pt. 2: 1700–1729 (1960); Arthur H. Scouten, ed., *The London Stage, 1660–1800,* Pt. 3: 1729–1747 (1961).
[13] Frederick Antal, *Hogarth and His Place in European Art* (1962), pp. 65–66.
[14] Cf. Dryden's statement quoted above (p. 294) from *Of Dramatick Poesie* on the fondness of "the noblesse" for heroic plays.
[15] Pp. 9–10.
[16] Dedication (to Lord Halifax) of *King Arthur* (1691), sig. A3v; S-S, VIII, 136.

fact that a total of twelve editions of it appeared before 1700.[17] Dryden must have known even from the initial performances in the spring of 1665 that the play was a considerable success, and perhaps for that reason he took unusual care in revising it. In any event, he seems to have revised it several times. A surviving manuscript, not holograph, which may date from 1665 and thus precede by two years the publication of the play, includes readings that do not appear in the first edition.[18] It would thus suggest that Dryden made changes in the period while the theaters were closed because of the plague. He made further changes in the second and third editions but apparently not in any of the subsequent ones.[19]

If superior in quality to *The Indian Queen, The Indian Emperour* nevertheless resembles it in theme, locale, and characters; and indeed its dramatic action fulfills prophecies alluded to in the prologue of the earlier play that the Mexican world would "be subdu'd by one more old." This early allusion to the prophecies introduces a graceful compliment to the theatrical audience, and it may have been written with nothing else in mind; but it at least raises the possibility that Dryden made plans for the later play at the time he worked on *The Indian Queen. The Indian Emperour* offered him an opportunity for further exploitation of reading done for the earlier play, and it offered the King's Company an opportunity for further profitable use of costumes and stage properties on hand.

> *The Scenes are old, the Habits are the same,*
> *We wore last year, before the* Spaniards *came,*

goes a candid acknowledgment in the prologue; and we may surmise that the actors would have encouraged Dryden to undertake the play, which is described in the *Stationers' Register* as "the sequall of the Indian Queene." The marked superiority of *The Indian Emperour* is at least in part to be explained by the fact that it was Dryden's unaided work, whereas *The Indian Queen* had been a collaborative effort with Sir Robert Howard.[20]

Prefixed to the play was the "Connexion of the *Indian Emperour, to the Indian Queen,*" in which Dryden, with a humorous acknowledgment of the dramatist's right to manipulate events to his advantage, briefly recounts the political and family history of the twenty years separating the imagined times of the two plays. The interval was just long enough for a new generation to reach marriageable age: two sons and a daughter of Montezuma and his deceased wife Orazia, and two daughters and a son of Zempoalla, the usurping Indian Queen of the earlier play, and her general Traxalla. A satirical remark in *The Rehearsal* has sometimes been taken to mean that this "Connexion" was printed separately in advance and distributed among the first audiences "to insinuate the plot into the

---

[17] See Textual Notes, below, pp. 381–382.

[18] *Ibid.*

[19] *Ibid.*

[20] On the collaboration, see *Works*, VIII, 283, where Dryden is credited with the dominant role. For rebuttal of the claims made there for him, see H. J. Oliver, *Sir Robert Howard* (1963), pp. 63–67.

boxes."[21] Perhaps so, but there is no other evidence that it was so distributed, and in any event it would not have been necessary, for the continuity between the two plays is of the slenderest. Leaving several ghosts out of account, Montezuma alone of the characters appears in both plays; and although the other Indian characters in the later play are sons and daughters of characters who appear in the earlier, little apart from remembered resentments is made of the relationships. For the central action of *The Indian Emperour*, the conquest of Mexico by Cortes, there is precedent in the earlier play only in the warfare between Peruvians and Mexicans; and thus there is no precedent at all for the most distinctive feature of the later play, the confrontation of sophisticated Europeans and semi-civilized yet eminently rational Indians. This aspect of the play, Dryden says in the "Connexion," he took from history; and in fact he says of the interesting passages in the first and fifth acts, "touching the sufferings and constancy of *Montezuma* in his Opinions, I have only illustrated, not alter'd from those who have written of it."

If there is little continuity in plot between the two plays, there is a close formal similarity. Both are heroic plays in the special sense in which Dryden used the term; in *The Indian Emperour* he explores more fully and more successfully a dramatic vein that he and Howard had opened in *The Indian Queen*. Again in heroic couplets he dramatizes a series of conflicts between "love" and "honor" (complex terms which are considered below), emphasizing at once the noble and villainous traits in his characters; he exploits the ceremonial and the spectacle of the exotic Mexican civilization; he employs character types resembling those in the earlier play;[22] and even more than in the earlier play he conceives of his dramatic action in a manner reminiscent of epic. The action of *The Indian Emperour* is, to be sure, more ample and complex than that of *The Indian Queen*, which has a sharp focus in a single love intrigue. It is extended over a longer period of time, four days rather than the one day of the earlier play;[23] and it encompasses three different though interrelated love affairs, as well as the historical events of the conquest. These latter, as already noted, fulfill the prophecy alluded to in the prologue of *The Indian Queen*.

Because the heroic play is patently a summation of a group of Renaissance literary themes, it has been the subject of a large body of investigation devoted to an assessment of its sources. Scholars have emphasized, and justly emphasized, the formative influence of Renaissance chivalric epic, French drama, French prose romance, and English romantic drama of the Caroline and Commonwealth periods; and they have pointed to mid-seventeenth-century theoretical developments affirming close affinities between epic and tragedy. All this is explained in Volume VIII of this edi-

---

[21] *The Rehearsal*, I, ii. Bayes addresses Johnson: "Besides, sir, I have printed above a hundred sheets of paper to insinuate the plot into the boxes."

[22] Herbert Wynford Hill, *La Calprenède's Romances and the Restoration Drama* (1910), pp. 65–69.

[23] Cf. *Works*, VIII, 293.

tion [24] and need not be repeated here. It will be enough to comment on
those aspects of the subject which have special relevance to *The Indian
Emperour.*

In his prefatory essay to *The Conquest of Granada* (1672), Dryden iso-
lates Davenant as the author of the first heroic play, *The Siege of Rhodes*
(significantly performed first as an opera and only later, after the Restoration, as a "just drama"); and he suggests also sources for two of the most
distinctive qualities of the heroic play: Corneille for the heightening in
characterization and Ariosto for the subject matter and theme. Happening
to read the opening lines of *Orlando Furioso* as he thought about Davenant's experiments, he arrived at a conception of what the heroic play
should attempt: that it "ought to be an imitation, in little of an Heroick
Poem: and, consequently, that Love and Valour ought to be the Subject of
it." [25] Whether or not this is, as has been argued, [26] a defensive definition
formulated after the plays themselves were written to defend them from
the satirical attack of *The Rehearsal,* it well suggests their scope and
achievement and gives us assistance in interpreting and evaluating them. [27]

Yet if relevant to *The Indian Emperour,* Dryden's essay *Of Heroique
Playes* was written some seven years after the play itself; a more nearly
contemporary discussion of the literary theory that shaped the play appears
in *Of Dramatick Poesie,* not published until 1668 but written, at least in
a preliminary draft, in 1665 and 1666, only a few months after the first
performance of *The Indian Emperour* and before the play was published. [28] We may view the play as an experiment in the application of
some of the ideas Dryden's interlocutors express in *Of Dramatick Poesie;*
both the play and the essay convey the impression of having been con-
ceived in a time of active and fluid critical speculation. If almost everything in the essay has some bearing on *The Indian Emperour,* three major
attitudes or opinions expressed in it would seem to be particularly relevant to our understanding of the play: the familiarity with and admiration shown for Corneille, the qualified approval expressed for the doctrine of the unities, and the strong argument advanced for the use of
rhyme in serious drama.

The several references to Corneille and acknowledged borrowings from
him suggest that the French dramatist was much in Dryden's mind in
1665. [29] Corneille had published in 1660 a collected edition of his works—
the twenty-five plays he had by then written, *Examens* of each of them,
and his three *Discours*—and we may assume that Dryden was familiar

[24] *Works,* VIII, 284–289.   [25] 1672, sig. a3r; Ker, I, 150.
[26] W. S. Clark, "The Sources of the Restoration Heroic Play," *RES,* IV (1928),
52–53.
[27] Cecil V. Deane, *Dramatic Theory and the Rhymed Heroic Play* (1931),
pp. 5–6n. The relationship of the heroic play to the Renaissance epic will be
considered in Volume XI of the present edition, in the commentary on Dryden's prefatory essay to *The Conquest of Granada.*
[28] Cf. *Works,* I, 260.
[29] John M. Aden, "Dryden, Corneille, and the *Essay of Dramatic Poesy*,"
RES, n.s., VI (1955), 147–156.

with the edition.[30] Much more than was usual with literary Englishmen of that time, he perceived the greatness of Corneille's achievement; [31] and in *Of Dramatick Poesie* he employs the character Lisideius (a name that may be a pun on the title of Corneille's most famous play) [32] to present a warm appreciation of Corneille's work and a defense of the doctrine of the unities embodied in it.

It is in the remarks on the unities that the debt to Corneille appears most clearly, in Neander's approbatory quotation of Corneille's complaint that observation of the unities excludes many beauties from the stage.[33] Rather than a strict observation of the unities of time and place in *The Indian Emperour*, there is a crowding of events and an impression of epic action compressed into a short span of time and into a narrow place, not unlike that produced by Corneille's *Le Cid*. Dryden acknowledged in the dedication of his play that it is "an irregular piece if compar'd with many of *Corneilles.*" We recall that in Corneille's later plays the unities are more scrupulously observed than in *Le Cid*. The locale of *The Indian Emperour*, "MEXICO and two Leagues about it," represents a very liberal interpretation of the unity of place; and the interpretation of the unity of time, four days, is equally liberal. References to the passage of time suggest that Dryden was at pains to defend the credibility of his time scheme. Montezuma (III, iv, 1–2) says: "It moves my wonder that in two days space, / This early Famine spreads so swift a pace." And Odmar explains why the famine came on so quickly: because the city, never having undergone siege before, was unprepared to feed its millions of inhabitants when its supply routes across the lake were cut off. When Guyomar early in the play describes to his father the landing of the Spaniards, he may be assumed to be talking about an event that took place earlier; and Cortes' opening description of the New World is not to be taken as his first impression of it.

We may read Dryden's remarks in the *Defence of an Essay* on the unities of place and time as a commentary on problems he had encountered in writing *The Indian Emperour*. Sir Robert Howard in the preface to *The Duke of Lerma* had criticized the effort to discover rules that might guide authors in writing plays; [34] and in a passage marked by his failure to perceive that it is not truth but the impression of truth which the dramatist attempts to achieve, he had sarcastically alluded to Dryden's remarks in *Of Dramatick Poesie* on the unities.[35] In his rejoinder in the *Defence*

---

[30] Pierre Legouis, "Corneille and Dryden as Dramatic Critics," in *Seventeenth Century Studies Presented to Sir Herbert Grierson* (1938), pp. 269–291; Frank Livingstone Huntley, *On Dryden's "Essay of Dramatic Poesy"* (1951), pp. 6–8. Laurence E. Padgett ("Dryden's Edition of Corneille," *MLN*, LXXI [1956], 173–174) has pointed out that Dryden used the edition of 1660 rather than one of the subsequent revised editions.

[31] Legouis, "Corneille and Dryden as Dramatic Critics," p. 287.

[32] Huntley, *On Dryden's "Essay,"* p. 11.   [33] 1668, p. 44; Ker, I, 75–76.

[34] 1668, sig. A4r. See below, p. 304.

[35] 1668, sig. A4v. For further discussion of the distinction, see below, p. 305.

of an Essay, Dryden enunciates the principle that it is the imagination, not literal truth, with which the dramatist is concerned, though he fails to draw the conclusion reached by Samuel Johnson a century later that the imagination could make big leaps as easily as small.[36] Rather, Dryden argues that the imagination is aided by the observation of the unities, even by a loose observation of them. He explains how much imagined time he would allow the dramatist:

> In Comedy I would not exceed 24 or 30 hours: for the Plot, Accidents, and Persons of Comedy are small, and may be naturally turn'd in a little compass: But in Tragedy the Design is weighty, and the Persons great, therefore there will naturally be required a greater space of time in which to move them.[37]

And he cites in support of his opinion the example of Ben Jonson, who had allowed only twenty-four hours to his comedies but a longer time to his two tragedies, "though he draws both of them into as narrow a compass as he can." [38] So then with *The Indian Emperour:* Dryden drew the events of the conquest into as narrow a compass as he could achieve without sacrificing the magnitude and complexity of his plot.

The plot is indeed so complex that it is consistent only with a liberal conception of the unity of action. Having resemblances in its elaboration to the structure of the romances of La Calprenède (from which Dryden and Howard had drawn suggestions for *The Indian Queen*),[39] the dramatic action conveys an impression of diversity as several pairs of lovers alternately become the focus of attention. Yet despite the multiplicity of events, everything that occurs has a clear relationship to "the conquest of Mexico" and thus is consistent with at least a liberal interpretation of the unity of action. The largeness and complexity of design notwithstanding, the play exhibits a tidiness of construction founded on a symmetrical arrangement of characters. The central dramatic movement, that of the conquest, turns on a succession of changes in the states of mind of a few persons. Military success or failure follows as a matter of course from decisions made by the Spanish leaders (who possess irresistible weapons), and these decisions are influenced if not determined by their fortunes in love. Cortes' sudden infatuation with Cydaria assumes crucial military significance. All aspects of the action are thus responsive to love and to the complications and inhibitions with which it is hedged about by honor.

If "love" and "honor," and the conflicts they engender, provide a principal theme of *The Indian Emperour* as of other heroic plays, we are not to assume that that theme is explained merely by reference to those two

---

[36] "Preface to Shakespeare," *Works,* ed. Arthur Murphy (1792), II, 97. David Nichol Smith (*Shakespeare in the Eighteenth Century* [1928], pp. 71–75) considers the background in earlier criticism for Johnson's comments on the unities.

[37] See above, p. 20.   [38] *Ibid.*   [39] *Works,* VIII, 289–293.

words in their usual meanings.⁴⁰ The love that leads Almeria to her extravagant cruelty is not identical with that responsible for the tender compassion of Cydaria, nor is Guyomar's conception of honor identical with that of his brother. Dryden was familiar with Hobbes's anatomy of the personality, and he used it, though not uncritically, in his dramatic characterizations.⁴¹ His villains, here Almeria and Pizarro, act on Hobbesian principles, but his heroes temper the naturalistic impulses which they too feel to achieve an ideal of behavior which may be called heroic.

In his elaboration of the ideal of behavior to which his admirable characters aspire, Dryden may well have been influenced by Corneille—and here, in the standard of conduct which he celebrates, we may recognize a possible contribution of the French dramatist to the heroic play. This standard of conduct has strong resemblances to Hobbesian naturalism; but it is not from Hobbes but from Corneille that Dryden took the conception of self-aggrandizement which shapes many of his characters.⁴² Climactic scenes in *The Indian Emperour,* as in Dryden's other rhymed plays, provide opportunities for characters to display grandeur and magnanimity, qualities that approximate the *gloire* for which the Cornélian heroes strive.⁴³ These qualities are achieved when the characters most fully realize the needs of their own personalities. Yet if the characters seek self-fulfillment, they nevertheless exhibit their magnanimity, their *gloire,* in Dryden as in Corneille, in a manner compatible with the good of the group to which they owe allegiance. The fortitude in adversity of Cortes, Montezuma, and Guyomar, the adherence to an ideal of duty or of love, provides them with opportunities to test and reveal their capacities, but not in an antisocial way. Episodes in *The Indian Emperour,* as

⁴⁰ Scott C. Osborn ("Heroical Love in Dryden's Heroic Drama," *PMLA,* LXXIII [1958], 480–490) has examined the conception of love in these plays (emphasizing affinities with themes in Burton's *Anatomy of Melancholy*); Jean Gagen ("Love and Honor in Dryden's Heroic Plays," *PMLA,* LXXVII [1962], 208–220) has examined the conception of honor as well.

⁴¹ Hobbes's influence on Dryden has been much investigated. Mildred E. Hartsock ("Dryden's Plays: A Study in Ideas," *Seventeenth Century Studies,* 2d ser. [1937], pp. 71–176) demonstrates Dryden's extensive use of Hobbesian ideas, though without carefully examining the implied evaluations of them. Louis Teeter ("The Dramatic Use of Hobbes's Political Ideas," *ELH,* III [1936], 140–169) shows that only Dryden's villains are thoroughgoing Hobbesians. John A. Winterbottom ("The Place of Hobbesian Ideas in Dryden's Tragedies," *JEGP,* LVII [1958], 665–683) similarly emphasizes the use of Hobbes for purposes of characterization. He points out that although Montezuma, Odmar, and Cortes are characterized in a manner consistent with Hobbesian psychology, Guyomar is not so characterized, and Dryden emphasizes the fact by the prominence he gives him. Dryden, in brief, used Hobbes as needed for specific dramatic purposes but without revealing any comprehensive commitment to him.

⁴² Cf. Arthur C. Kirsch, *Dryden's Heroic Drama* (1965), pp. 46–65.

⁴³ Paul Bénichou, *Morales du Grand Siècle* (1948), pp. 13–76, examines the

in Corneille's plays, seem to have been constructed to demonstrate the strength of the characters' devotion to their ideals; and again as in Corneille a conversational dialectic elucidates the subtleties of the characters' achievements. The resistance of Montezuma to the torture inflicted by Pizarro and the Christian priest provides the outstanding instance of fortitude (an episode ironically reminiscent of Polyeucte's defiance of his pagan persecutors in Corneille's play), but there are others, including several involving Cortes. Characters act with a resolution approaching fanaticism. Odmar and Guyomar reveal the kind of deference to commands imposed by their beloved (Alibech) which Corneille's Cinna shows to those of his (Émilie). The result of all this, as in plays of the French dramatist, is an emphasis on the capacity of the personality to subdue momentary instinctual needs in favor of sustained ideals of love or duty.

By the example it provides of the dramatic use of the heroic couplet as well as by the circumstance that the *Defence of an Essay of Dramatick Poesie* appeared as a preface to its second edition, *The Indian Emperour* assumes a prominent place in Dryden's controversy with Howard on the appropriateness of rhyme in serious plays. We may be sure that the two men (who had collaborated in writing *The Indian Queen* in couplets) often discussed the subject in conversation, and we may assume that at least in the early stages of their published debate,[44] before tempers grew heated, they merely expressed divergent opinions on a topic of wide contemporary interest. For the topic had been a lively one in literary circles at least since the first year of the Restoration when the King, who remembered the French Alexandrine, commanded the Earl of Orrery to write an English play in rhyme.[45]

Not until Howard replied to *Of Dramatick Poesie* in the preface to *The Duke of Lerma*, published late in the summer of 1668,[46] does personal antagonism appear in the debate between the brothers-in-law (though an allusion to unsuccessful poets in Dryden's dedicatory epistle to his essay might have been intended or interpreted as a slight);[47] and that it then

ethos of the Cornélian hero. Although he does not allude to Dryden, his discussion (as Kirsch, *Dryden's Heroic Drama*, pp. 51–53, points out) suggests the relevance of Corneille's standard of conduct to Dryden's.

[44] The origins and early stages of the controversy will be considered in *Works*, XVII, in the commentary on *Of Dramatick Poesie*.

[45] Thomas Morrice, *Memoirs of Roger, Earl of Orrery*, in Orrery's *State Letters* (1742), p. 39.

[46] Ward, pp. 62–63.

[47] Dryden wrote in his dedication addressed to Buckhurst (1668, sig. A2v; Ker, I, 24): "For your Lordship may easily observe that none are very violent against it [rhyme], but those who either have not attempted it, or who have succeeded ill in their attempt." Oliver (*Howard*, ch. vi) suggests that this statement may have given affront to Howard and thus have led to the animosity he expressed in the preface to *The Duke of Lerma*. Yet it should be remembered that in view of the success of *The Indian Queen*, which was known as Howard's play, he had no special reason for sensitivity on the subject, notwithstanding the relative failure of his subsequent rhymed play, *The Vestal Virgin*.

appeared is perhaps to be explained not so much by their differences of
opinion on rhyme and the unities—scarcely subjects to engender passion—
as by the fact that harsh satire had been directed at Howard, for which he
may have thought Dryden responsible. Dryden in a prologue to a revival
in February 1668 of a Jacobean play, Thomas Tomkis' *Albumazar,*
referred scornfully to plagiarism,[48] a tender subject with Howard because
of his free use of another dramatist's play in writing *The Duke of Lerma.*
This would have been at most a glancing blow; a more telling one
followed in May when Thomas Shadwell's *The Sullen Lovers* was acted
by the Duke's Company. The play includes a harsh caricature of Howard
in the person of Sir Positive At-all, "A foolish Knight, that pretends to
understand every thing in the world, and will suffer no man to understand
any thing in his Company," and we have it on the very dubious authority
of a pamphlet published five years later that Dryden supplied Shadwell
with the idea for the character.[49] In any event, Sir Positive has at least
a generic resemblance to Crites in *Of Dramatick Poesie* (who has some
resemblances to Howard, though the character in his literary opinions is a
composite [50]): "a person of a sharp judgment, and somewhat too delicate
a taste in wit, which the world have mistaken in him for ill nature." [51]
There was much laughter that season at Howard's expense,[52] and his
temper was understandably short when in the late spring or early summer
he wrote the preface to *The Duke of Lerma.*[53]

Like other indifferent poets before and after him, Howard takes refuge
in an appeal to taste in opposition to systematic literary theory; and he
exhibits more than a trace of anti-intellectualism. With contemptuous
brevity he dismisses Dryden's effort in *Of Dramatick Poesie* to arrive at a

---

[48] Perhaps Dryden had in mind merely *Albumazar,* in which theft and plagiarism are discussed (cf. *Works,* I, 344). But *The Duke of Lerma* was first performed (by the other company, the King's) only a few days before *Albumazar*
was revived (James Kinsley, *The Poems of John Dryden* [1958], IV, 1854), and
whatever Dryden's intention the passage in the prologue could have been interpreted as an attack on Howard.
[49] *The Friendly Vindication of Mr. Dryden from the Censure of the Rota by
His Cabal of Wits* (1673), p. 8. Oliver (*Howard,* p. 112) points out that there
is some support for the charge in the fact that similar jibes at a poem by
Howard appear in both *The Sullen Lovers* and the *Defence of an Essay* (see
below, pp. 322–323). Yet relations between Shadwell and Dryden could scarcely
have been cordial even at this time: in the preface to the play Shadwell censures
current fashions in comedy in a passage that would seem to glance at *Secret
Love.*
[50] G. R. Noyes, " 'Crites' in Dryden's *Essay of Dramatic Poesy,*" *MLN,* XXXVIII
(1923), 333–337.
[51] 1668, p. 2; Ker, I, 29.
[52] Pepys, 8 May 1668: "But, Lord! to see how this play of Sir Positive At-All,
in abuse of Sir Robert Howard, do take, all the Duke's and everybody's talk
being of that, and telling more stories of him, of the like nature, that it is now
the town and country talk, and, they say, is most exactly true."
[53] Entered in *Stationers' Register* on 24 June 1668 (Ward, p. 63).

tentative statement of rules for writing and judging drama, and he insists that any such effort is foredoomed to failure. "I rather blame the unnecessary understanding of some that have labour'd to give strict rules to things that are not Mathematical," he writes, recommending a psychological relativism as the only basis for literary criticism. Taking the pose of a gentleman above pedantry, he opposes Dryden's arguments in defense of the unities of place and time. It is as impossible, he argues, "for one stage to present two Houses, or two Roomes truely, as two Countreys or Kingdomes," and similarly as impossible for twenty-four hours as for a thousand to be comprehended in the two hours and a half of a play's presentation. In replying to Dryden's defense of the rhymed couplet in serious plays, he resorts to the argument he had earlier used in his preface to *Four New Plays* (1665): rhyme in drama is unnatural, meaning very different from actual conversation. This argument, like the one he used against the unities, turns on the relationship between drama and what it purports to imitate. "For 'tis not the question," he writes, "whether Rhime or not Rhime be best, or most Natural for a grave and serious Subject, but what is neerest the nature of that which it presents." And since rhymed verse differs more obviously than blank verse from the actual conversation that the poet pretends to represent, Howard concludes that it is less suitable for drama. Thus a literal conception of poetic imitation as dependent on correspondences of detail between drama and its subject lies at the heart of his argument.

Dryden is as superior to Howard in aesthetic sophistication as he is in controversial finesse, and he perceives and wittily exposes the ambiguities and the fallacies of Howard's argument. He clarifies the conception of imitation on which his dramatic theory rests, and at the same time sustains a devastating raillery, scoring easily on Howard's imprecise diction, faulty Latinity, and pomposity. Driven to a reconsideration of his critical assumptions, Dryden rejects as inadequate Howard's criterion of audience reaction as a guide to literary judgment, reaffirming his own support for systematic literary theory. He makes a careful distinction between the possibility of valid rules for drama, which he regards as demonstrable, and the specific rules themselves, which he regards as merely problematical and not demonstrable.[54] In doing so he uses an illuminating analogy with religious thought: just as the existence of order implies the existence of a deity who should be worshiped though not the manner of the worship, so also the existence of nature as the object to be imitated implies the existence of dramatic rules though not the specific rules themselves. Dryden's argument for the rules derives from his conception of the dramatist's objective: "if Nature be to be imitated, then there is a Rule for imitating Nature rightly, otherwise there may be an end, and no means conducing to it." His dogmatism stops at this point. He refuses to defend the individual rules as more than tentative formulations.

Dryden follows in the *Defence* the sequence of topics in Howard's

[54] Hoyt Trowbridge. "The Place of Rules in Dryden's Criticism," *MP*, XLIV (1946), 84–96.

preface (though not to the exclusion of sarcastic and personal digressions). By doing so, he can move from discussion of a critical position, the use of rhyme in serious plays, in which he was something of an innovator, to a position, the observation of the unities, in which he followed long precedent. And thus he can employ a steadily rising tone of contempt for the opinions of his antagonist.

He acknowledges that the use of rhyme removes dialogue from the conventions of conversation; and in a discussion of the basis of dramatic imitation he explains that dialogue is to be judged, not by the degree of its correspondence to empirical reality, but by its effect on the audience. His is a rhetorical conception of imitation,[55] grounded on an understanding of drama as literary artifice; and it is a conception that takes into account the differing rhetorical demands of separate genres. Hence he can urge the right of the tragic dramatist to use the resources of language, rhyme as well as metaphor, to intensify and heighten the sentiments of his characters. " 'Tis true," he writes, "that to imitate well is a Poets work; but to affect the Soul, and excite the Passions, and above all to move admiration (which is the delight of serious Plays) a bare imitation will not serve." In answer to Howard he argues that rhyme is to be preferred to prose (and he would identify blank verse with prose) [56] because of the very fact of its greater difference from actual conversation. The difference aids the dramatist in reaching the emotional objectives of the serious play.

Dryden's argument for the unities of time and place is again based on a rhetorical consideration: not that they lead to a closer approximation of reality but that they aid the spectator in his imaginative response to the play. Dryden finds it easy to dispose of Howard's argument that the doctrine of the unities implies degrees in impossibilities because Howard had not taken sufficiently into account the dramatist's concern, not with a truthful representation of reality, but with the illusion of it. Dryden is at his best in his analysis of the reasons for observing the unities, an analysis that turns on the nature of the imagination itself.[57] "Imagination in a man, or reasonable Creature," he writes, "is supposed to participate of reason, and when that governs, as it does in the belief of fiction, reason is not destroyed, but misled, or blinded: that can prescribe to the reason, during the time of the representation, somewhat like a weak belief of wʰ it sees and hears; and reason suffers it self to be so hood-wink'd, that it may better enjoy the pleasures of the fiction. . . ." Acknowledging that his arguments for the unities are derivative, he assumes an air of shocked incredulity that Howard could make assertions in flagrant contradiction to the opinions of Aristotle, Horace, Jonson, and Corneille, the most respected theorists of ancient and modern times. He thus concludes his carefully reasoned *Defence* in a conventional appeal to authorities.

---

[55] Huntley, *On Dryden's "Essay,"* pp. 66–67. [56] See below, pp. 336–337.
[57] John M. Aden ("Dryden and the Imagination: The First Phase," *PMLA,* LXXIV [1959], 28–40) examines Dryden's theory of the imagination at length.

Howard did not reply to the *Defence of an Essay,* though some supporter
who signed himself "R.F." and who may have been Flecknoe did with
venom. Dryden omitted it in subsequent editions of *The Indian Emperour*
(according to the malicious testimony of *The Medal of John Bayes* [1682]
because Howard forced him to do so under threat of a duel).[58] On the issue
of rhyme, Dryden, of course, changed his mind, and after *Aureng-Zebe*
(1675) no longer used the couplet in drama.

Dryden describes in his dedicatory epistle the use he made in the play
of historical accounts of the conquest of Mexico: "In it I have neither
wholly follow'd the truth of the History, nor altogether left it: but have
taken all the liberty of a Poet, to adde, alter, or diminish, as I thought
might best conduce to the beautifying of my work; it being not the
business of a Poet to represent Historical truth, but probability." He says
substantially the same thing in the "Connexion": "as near as I could, [I]
have traced the Native simplicity and ignorance of the *Indians,* in relation
to *Europæan* Customes: The Shipping, Armour, Horses, Swords, and Guns
of the *Spaniards,* being as new to them as their Habits and their Language
were to the Christians." In those portions of the first and the fifth acts,
he adds, in which he depicts the character and opinions of Montezuma,
he has been particularly faithful to historical sources. What those sources
are he does not say, and it is important for us to know, for an examination
of them would help us to understand what is historical, or pseudohistorical
literary convention, and what distinctive in his version of the Spanish
conquest of the New World.

The dramatic action taken up with the several love affairs that complicate the conquest derives to some extent from the conventions of the French
romances. The lovers, in the abruptness and the intensity with which they
conceive their passions, are typical of the heroic play, and their changing
allegiances are conventional. In a general way they, like their predecessors
in *The Indian Queen,* resemble characters in the romances, and the code of
conduct of the sympathetic characters has much in common with that cele-
brated by La Calprenède, Scudéry, and others.[59]

It has been argued, however, that in addition to this generalized literary
debt Dryden owes a more specific one to Calderón de la Barca's *El Príncipe
Constante,* written in 1628 or 1629 and printed three times before 1665,
though apparently not translated into English. Several situations in it resemble ones in *The Indian Emperour:* those in which the Spaniards describe
Mexico, the princesses are courted ceremonially, Guyomar reports his sight-
ing of the fleet, and Cortes captures Guyomar and then releases him.[60] Guyo-

---

[58] " 'Gainst him a scandalous Preface dist thou write, / Which thou dist soon
expunge, rather than fight [p. 9]."

[59] Cf. Hill, *La Calprenède's Romances,* pp. 65–69.

[60] See N. D. Shergold and Peter Ure, "Dryden and Calderón: A New Spanish
Source for 'The Indian Emperour,'" *Modern Language Review,* LXI (1966),
369–383. The resemblances between the two plays would seem to constitute less
than proof that Dryden borrowed from the Spanish one. In each instance the
resemblances appear amid much that is very different, and in fact the plays are

mar's description of the approaching fleet includes similarities of descriptive detail to the parallel passage in Calderón, though perhaps not more than can be accounted for by the circumstance that the two dramatists were writing about a similar subject.

It is difficult to feel certainty in assessing Dryden's sources. Probably he made some use of historical fiction. For the Peruvian and Mexican background of *The Indian Queen,* he and Howard had drawn on a digression in Gomberville's *Polexandre,* a story entitled (in the English translation which they perhaps used) *The History of Zelmatida, Heir to the Empire of the Incas;*[61] and in writing *The Indian Emperour* Dryden would have remembered, whether or not he made conscious use of it, this highly colored account of the Incas and also the Aztecs. In the story, to illustrate the nature of the material available to him, the Inca King's first impression of the environs of the Mexican capital is not unlike Cortes' first impression of them as related in the opening scene of the play. When after many days of pleasant travel the King saw the city at a distance, "he began to take notice of the marvelous scituation of Mexico, and before hee came on that long causeway, which crosseth the marshes where it is built, stay'd in a Playne so covered with flowres and trees, compassed with so many channells, and watered with so many sources of living fountaines, that he confest there was nothing more delightfull to be seen."[62] Here is a response to the beauty of the place resembling Cortes', as well as an allusion to the causeway, to which Cortes' Indian guide refers. These details, however, and a number of others appearing both in the story and the play, were commonplaces of history and historical fiction alike, and it is therefore impossible to say what specific sources Dryden used for them.

Even in late sixteenth- and early seventeenth-century drama, allusions to America in the idealized vein of *The Indian Emperour* are not uncommon. Captain Seagull, for example, in Chapman, Jonson, and Marston's *Eastward Hoe,* refers to the abundant gold in Virginia, and describes the country as "temperate and full of all sorts of excellent viands"; and Rodomont, the King of Cuba in Greene's *Orlando Furioso,* describes his country as bounteously endowed with natural wealth.[63] The proverbial wealth of the New World is the subject of four important allusions in Shakespeare, in *The Comedy of Errors, Twelfth Night, 1 Henry IV,* and *Henry VIII;*[64] and the proverbial fruitfulness and temperateness of America would seem to pervade the island that provides the setting of *The Tempest,* though it is nominally in the Old World.

The indefiniteness of the island's location notwithstanding, *The*

---

strikingly unlike in total impact. For another possible source of Guyomar's description, see below, pp. 309–310. Gerard Langbaine's account of the sources of *The Indian Emperour* (pp. 165–166) is not specific enough to be very helpful.

[61] Clark, "The Sources of the Restoration Heroic Play," pp. 55–57; *Works,* VIII, 289–292.

[62] *The History of Polexander,* trans. William Browne (1647), Pt. I, Bk. ii, p. 53.

[63] Robert Ralston Cawley, *The Voyagers and Elizabethan Drama* (1938), p. 291.

[64] *Ibid.,* pp. 297–298.

Tempest bears the impress of the chronicles of American travel,[65] and it embodies literary themes that had been emphasized by the voyages: the contrast of art and nature, civilization and primitive society, sophisticated manners and morals and their untaught native equivalents. More than any other Shakespearian or indeed Renaissance English play, it anticipates the American themes of *The Indian Emperour.* In *The Tempest,* as later in Dryden's play, a group of Europeans are brought into association with a primitive against whose conduct their own is measured, and if the brutish Caliban is in personal accomplishments utterly different from Montezuma, the dramatic function of the two characters as standards for the measurement of civilized behavior is similar. The themes of *The Tempest* lack the clarity of outline observable in *The Indian Emperour;* Caliban, bearing resemblances to the wild man of literary tradition,[66] represents a version of man in his natural state and as such serves as an agent by which the achievements of civilization, represented by the virtuous characters, and the liabilities, represented by the wicked, can be demonstrated,[67] but he is no such philosophical construct as is Montezuma, who intermittently at least seems to possess an uncontaminated natural reason. Shakespeare characteristically refuses to simplify and clarify issues and contrasts, preferring an ambiguity of implied evaluation, with the result that we do not find in the play such neat, schematic judgments as in Dryden's. *The Tempest* reveals a searching interest in the comparative examination of natural and civilized morality—but not the interpretation of the native in terms of a rationalistic primitivism.

Dryden in collaboration with Davenant produced an adaptation of *The Tempest* in 1667,[68] two years after *The Indian Emperour,* and there is some evidence that he had Shakespeare in mind when he wrote the earlier play. In the beginning he apparently called the Indian High Priest by the name Caliban: the character is consistently so called throughout the manuscript that precedes the first edition and he is once so called in the first edition (the speech heading "Callib." appears in I, ii, 13, as though in this one instance the person correcting the manuscript copy had neglected to make the change to "*High Pr.*").[69] Shakespeare's source for the name, beyond his own imagination, is not known beyond dispute, but the name would seem to be related to the word *carib,* meaning an American savage or, more specifically, a cannibal; perhaps it is merely an anagram of this word.[70] In any event, the one undisputed source of *The Tempest* is Montaigne's essay "Of the Canibales"

---

[65] E. K. Chambers, *William Shakespeare: A Study of Facts and Problems* (1930), I, 491–492; Frank Kermode, ed., *The Tempest* (Arden Edition, 1954), pp. xxv–xxxiv.

[66] Cf. Richard Bernheimer, *Wild Men in the Middle Ages* (1952), p. 11.

[67] Kermode, ed., *The Tempest,* pp. xxxiv–xliii.

[68] Arthur H. Nethercot, *Sir William D'Avenant* (1938), pp. 398–403.

[69] See Textual Notes, p. 389. Dryden retained the separate name Kalib in II, i, for the spirit called up by the High Priest; perhaps he omitted the Priest's name to avoid confusion.

[70] Kermode, ed., *The Tempest,* p. xxxviii.

in Florio's translation (1603); [71] and, as shown below, there is good reason to believe that Dryden drew on another essay by Montaigne, if not on this one as well, for *The Indian Emperour*. Dryden, like Shakespeare before him, would have found in Montaigne a concise assessment of the impact of the voyages of discovery on moral philosophy,[72] a subject with which both dramatists in their separate ways are preoccupied.

The resemblances between *The Indian Emperour* and *The Tempest* are important but subtle; those between Dryden's play and two by Sir William Davenant are more obvious. In 1658 Davenant produced two "operas" about Spanish atrocity in the New World, *The Cruelty of the Spaniards in Peru* and *The History of Sir Francis Drake,* and after the Restoration, in 1663, he used them as "acts" in his *The Play-house To Be Let.*[73] On grounds of probability we may assume Dryden was familiar with these works, at least in their later versions, which were part play, part tableau, performed with songs, dances, and recitative against painted scenes; and certain passages in *The Indian Emperour* suggest that he borrowed from the former [74] if not from both of them. The theme of the former, the earlier of the two, is summarized by its title; Davenant's conception of the theme must have been influenced by his principal source, Bartolomé de Las Casas (in English translation),[75] the most influential critic of Spanish exploitation of America. Like Dryden, Davenant establishes a contrast between the state of the Indians before the conquest and their misery under the Spaniards, who in *The Cruelty of the Spaniards in Peru* as in *The Indian Emperour* resort to cruel and sadistic torture.[76] Dryden would thus have learned of Las Casas' interpretation of the conquest, implying as it did the existence of an idyllic age in pre-conquest America, even if he had not himself read the envenomed account, which was readily available in English translation as well as in the original Spanish. His play resembles Davenant's entertainment in certain details as well as in theme. Guyomar's account of the Spanish ships arriving on the coast (I, ii), to take a notable instance, may have been suggested by the painted scenes and the pantomime of Davenant's "Second

---

[71] Chambers, *Shakespeare*, I, 494; Kermode, ed., *The Tempest*, p. xxxiv.

[72] Gilbert Chinard, *L'Amérique et le Rêve Exotique dans la Littérature Française au XVIIe et au XVIIIe Siècle* (1913), p. v.

[73] Nethercot, *D'Avenant*, pp. 325-328, 331-334, 377-381.

[74] Dougald MacMillan, "The Sources of Dryden's *The Indian Emperour*," *HLQ*, XIII (1950), 355-370. For my account of the literary and historical background of *The Indian Emperour*, I am heavily indebted to MacMillan's review of the subject, though I disagree in important details with his conclusions.

[75] Nethercot (*D'Avenant*, p. 325) asserts that Davenant used J. Phillips' translation *The Tears of the Indians* (1656). MacMillan (*HLQ*, XIII [1950], 359) argues that it is more likely he used the translation by "M.M.S." reprinted in *Purchas his Pilgrimes* (1625).

[76] Davenant emphasized the contrast in the "Argument" prefixed to his libretto. Here he implies that the Indians' degeneracy had its beginning even before the arrival of the Spaniards.

Entry," [77] in which "a Fleet is discern'd at distance . . . and on the right side are seen some Natives of *Peru*, pointing with amazment to the Fleet, (as never having had the view of Ships before) and in a mourning condition take their leaves of their wives and children; because of an antient Prophecy amongst them, which did signifie, That a Bearded People . . . should spring out of the Sea, and conquer them." [78] Here are several details that reappear in *The Indian Emperour.* If Davenant was merely working with historical commonplaces, he gave them striking dramatic expression in a work we may assume Dryden knew.

Yet if Dryden drew from imaginative renderings of the conquest, there is no reason to doubt him when he states that he went to the histories themselves. To judge by his own assertions [79] as well as by his use of untranslated materials,[80] he could read Spanish; and he may well have read some of the chronicles in the original language. He could have read them in English translation in a single convenient compilation, *Purchas his Pilgrimes,* published by Samuel Purchas in 1625. This work, it has been argued,[81] was his chief source for the historical scenes, and in fact this compilation of travel narratives would have provided a source for all the historical material in the play except for the striking passage of dialogue in the torture scene in which Montezuma chides the Indian Priest for faintheartedness. "Think'st thou I lye on Beds of Roses here," says Montezuma (V, ii, 103), echoing a passage in Francisco López de Gómara's *La Istoria de las Indias y Conquista de Mexico* (1552) which was omitted from the selection of the work included in Purchas.[82] For this passage Dryden could have gone to the original Spanish of Gómara,[83] or, much more likely, to the translation and adaptation of it in Montaigne's *Essays,* which in Florio's translation into English was one of his favorite books.[84]

---

[77] MacMillan, *HLQ,* XIII [1950], 359–360. But see above, pp. 306–307.

[78] *The Cruelty of the Spaniards in Peru* (1658), pp. 6–7.

[79] Dryden often referred to Spanish authors and in at least two instances implied that he read them in the original language: in the letter to Howard prefixed to *Annus Mirabilis,* in which he alluded to Spanish practices in rhyming (*Works,* I, 51); and in the preface to *The Hind and the Panther,* in which he identified the portions of a Spanish book from which a recent English tract was translated (S-S, X, 114–115; cf. also S-S, XVII, 253–254n).

[80] James Urvin Rundle, "The Source of Dryden's 'Comic Plot' in *The Assignation,*" *MP,* XLV (1947), 111n.

[81] MacMillan, *HLQ,* XIII [1950], 355–370.

[82] *Ibid.,* pp. 367–369. MacMillan is mistaken in assuming that this passage was not available to Dryden elsewhere in French or English translation.

[83] The passage in Gómara, not about Montezuma but about his successor, occurs in a chapter entitled "Como dieron tormento a Quahutimoc para saber del tesoro." It is as follows (1552; Pt. II, lxxxvi verso): "Quando lo quemavan mirava mucho al rey para que, aviendo compassion del [that is, of his companion], le diesse licencia como dizen, de manifestar lo que sabia. O lo dixesse el. Quahutimoc le miro con ira. Y lo trato vilissimamente como muelle, y de poco, diziendo si estava el en algun deleyte, o baño."

[84] Louis I. Bredvold, *The Intellectual Milieu of John Dryden* (1934), p. 118. Bredvold is primarily concerned with a later period of Dryden's career. The ap-

Two of Montaigne's essays include discussion of American Indians, "Of the Canibales" (which as noted was a source for *The Tempest*) and "Of Coaches," and in them may be found anticipations of much that is distinctive in Dryden's interpretation of the conquest: an idealized conception of the Indians as rational primitives, a conception of the Spaniards as cruel and bigoted, a use of the contrast between the races to emphasize at once the liabilities of civilization, and the relativity of social, moral, and even by implication religious beliefs.[85] The essay "Of Coaches" is of the two the more relevant to *The Indian Emperour;* in it occurs the passage that may well be Dryden's source for the torture scene:

> After which victory [over the King of Mexico, not identi-
> fied by name], the Spaniards not finding that quantitie of
> gold they had promised themselves, when they had
> ransacked and ranged all corners, they by meanes of the
> cruellest tortures and horriblest torments they could
> possibly devise, beganne to wrest and draw some more
> from such prisoners as they had in keeping. But unable
> to profit any thing that way, finding stronger hearts
> than their torments, they in the end fell to such moody
> outrages, that contrary to all law of nations, and against
> their solemne vowes and promises, they condemned
> the King himselfe and one of the chiefest Princes of his
> Court, to the Racke, one in presence of another: The
> Prince environed round with hot burning coales, being
> overcome with the exceeding torment, at last in most
> pitous sort turning his dreary eyes toward his Master,
> as if hee asked mercy of him for that hee could endure
> no longer: The king fixing rigorously and fiercely his
> lookes upon him, seeming to upbraid him with his
> remisnesse and pusilanimity, with a sterne and setled
> voyce uttered these few words unto him; "What? sup-
> posest thou I am in a cold bath? am I at more ease
> than thou art?" Whereat the silly wretch immediately
> fainted under the torture, and yeelded up the ghost.
> The king half rosted, was carried away. . . .[86]

The torture scene of *The Indian Emperour* obviously resembles this passage (though with the substitution of an Indian priest for a prince), and the circumstance that Montezuma's spirited and vivid retort to his follower, preserved with a modification of the metaphor in the play, does not occur in any other English or French version prior to 1665, so far as is known, would suggest that Montaigne was here Dryden's source.

---

parent use of *The Essays* in *The Indian Emperour* would suggest Dryden's familiarity with Montaigne at this earlier period.

[85] Gilbert Chinard (*L'Exotisme Américain dans la Littérature Française au XVI*e *Siècle* [1911], pp. 193–218) examines at length Montaigne's treatment of the Indians.

[86] Trans. Florio, Tudor Translations (1893), III, 147–148.

The apparent borrowing from Montaigne in this detail raises the possibility that Dryden may owe him a more extensive debt for his version of the Spanish conquest. An assessment of that debt must be tentative, for, as will already be apparent, Dryden had access to many historical, pseudohistorical, and fictional narratives and interpretations of the conquest, and in composition he would have followed as they came ideas derived from years of reading. Yet it is not implausible that he should have given special attention to Montaigne, a writer for whom he always expressed admiration.

The dramatization of historical materials is largely confined to two scenes in *The Indian Emperour,* the torture scene (V, ii) and the arrival scene (I, ii); and each corresponds rather closely to a paragraph in the essay "Of Coaches." Montaigne begins his digression on the Spaniards in the New World with an exchange between them and the Indians which anticipates most of the distinctive features of the comparable exchange in the arrival scene. Dryden's Vasquez thus explains the conditions under which the Spaniards hold out friendship to the Indians:

> *Spain's* mighty Monarch, to whom Heaven thinks fit
> That all the Nations of the Earth submit,
> In gracious clemency, does condescend
> On these conditions to become your Friend,
> First, that of him you shall your Scepter hold,
> Next, you present him with your useless Gold:
> Last, that you leave those Idols you adore
> And one true Deity with prayers implore.

And in answer to Montezuma's question as to the grounds of the Spanish King's claim of sovereignty, Pizarro replies that the Pope has given the empire of Mexico to him. Montaigne's Spaniards had told the Indians

> That they were quiet and well-meaning men, comming
> from farre-countries, being sent from the King of Castile,
> the greatest King of the habitable earth, unto whom the
> Pope, representing God on earth, had given the prin-
> cipality of all the Indies. That if they would become
> tributaries to him, they should bee most kindly used and
> courteously entreated: They required of them . . . some
> gold for the behoofe of certaine Physicall experiments.
> Moreover, they declared unto them, the beleeving in one
> onely God, and the trueth of our religion. . . .[87]

The Indians' reply is substantially the same in both versions. First Montaigne's:

> As concerning their King, since he seemed to beg, he
> shewed to be poore and needy: And for the Pope, who
> had made that distribution, he expressed himselfe a man
> loving dissention, in going about to give unto a third
> man, a thing which was not his owne: so to make it ques-

---

[87] *Ibid.*, III, 145.

tionable and litigious amongst the ancient possessors of
it. . . . And for gold, they had but little, and that it was
a thing they made very small accoumpt of, as meerely
unprofitable for the service of their life, . . . and therefore, what quantity soever they should finde, that onely
excepted which was employed about the service of their
Gods, they might bouldly take it. As touching one onely
God, the discourse of him had very well pleased them:
but they would by no meanes change their religion, under
which they had for so long time lived so happily: . . .[88]

Dryden's Montezuma:

You speak your Prince a mighty Emperour,
But his demands have spoke him Proud, and Poor;
He proudly at my free-born Scepter flies,
Yet poorly begs a mettal I despise.
Gold thou may'st take, what-ever thou canst find,
Save what for sacred uses is design'd.

And when Montezuma is told that the Spanish King bases his claim on a
grant from the Pope, he, like Montaigne's Indians, charges the Pope
with fomenting trouble:

Ill does he represent the powers above,
Who nourishes debate not Preaches love;
Besides what greater folly can be shown?
He gives another what is not his own.

He too resolves to keep his own gods, even while disavowing an intention
to slight the Christian God.

Montaigne's paragraph recounting this dialogue, then, could have
provided Dryden's source for the arrival scene just as his next paragraph
but one could have provided the source for the torture scene. There
cannot be certainty that Dryden did so use Montaigne; the essayist
himself used a source to which Dryden had access, at least in Spanish.[89]
He could have based the dialogue of the arrival scene on the translations
in Purchas of the chroniclers' accounts of Pizarro's first meeting with
the Inca Atabalipa (sometimes rendered Atahuallpa). In particular, the
account by Jerome Benzo in Purchas anticipates certain details of the
scene. "As for the Pope, he must needs appeare to be a foole, and a
shamelesse man," says the Inca in Benzo's version in anticipation of the
Aztec of the play, "which was so bountifull in giving that which is none

[88] *Ibid.*, III, 145–146.
[89] Montaigne followed López de Gómara very closely (Pierre Villey, *Les Sources
et L'Évolution des Essais de Montaigne* [1908], I, 393). Since the passage in
Gómara corresponding to Montezuma's "Beds of Roses" speech was omitted from
the French translation by S. de Genillé Mart. Fumée (1584) (cf. MacMillan, *HLQ*,
XIII [1950], 368–369), presumably Montaigne drew from the Italian translation
by Agostino di Cravalix (1576). Villey asserts (I, 138) that he apparently made
use of this translation in the years before 1588, when the essay "Of Coaches"
first appeared.

of his owne." [90] Yet close as is the resemblance of Montezuma's rejoinder to this statement, the resemblance to the rejoinder of Montaigne's Indians is yet closer, for the latter includes also the idea of the Pope as not only foolish but litigious. And in general Dryden would seem to be closer to Montaigne than to Purchas' *Pilgrimes*.

He felt no obligation to confine himself to historical truth, as he acknowledged in his dedication, and indeed, as will already have been suggested, he used episodes from the chronicles of Peru along with those from the chronicles of Mexico. (It is perhaps significant that Montaigne, in the paragraph anticipating the arrival scene, does not allude to the nationality of the Indians whom the Spaniards meet, nor in the subsequent paragraph does he identify the Mexican king whom the Spaniards torture.) The dramatic character Montezuma is in fact a composite of at least three historical ones: Montezuma himself, the Inca Atabalipa, and Montezuma's successor Quahutimoc,[91] whose resolute resistance to the Spaniards' torture as reported by López de Gómara provided Dryden's (and Montaigne's) source in the relevant episode. Dryden's most conspicuous interpolation from Peruvian history is his portrayal of Pizarro as Cortes' lieutenant. Pizarro's treachery in Peru to the Inca King who had fulfilled the terms of his ransom may have suggested the characterization of him as a villain. In any event, the characterization serves a useful dramatic function: it makes possible a contrast between Pizarro and the noble Cortes. If the idealized conception of Cortes is a necessity of a plot turning on love and honor, it is supported in a general way by the chronicles, which interpret his character favorably.

The sequence of events in the play approximates in telescoped form that of history. In the opening scene the Spaniards have marched from the coast to the environs of Mexico City, and already they have formed their alliance with the tribe of Tlaxcalans, the enemies of the Aztecs. The Spaniards meet Montezuma, and there is a ceremonial exchange of courtesies—followed by an Indian revolt, and this by a Spanish victory. Dryden justly claimed that he had followed history with a poet's license.

If the events of the play represent an abbreviated and simplified version of the conquest, they also provide a framework for the dramatic elucidation of a series of the significant ideas of the Restoration: on primitivism, religion, and political theory. It is one of the distinctive achievements of *The Indian Emperour* that it suggests the intellectual dimension of exploration, that it conveys something of the impetus provided by the discoveries of new lands and cultures to the review of long-held and fundamental convictions. Like other theorists Dryden found primitive characters to be useful agents to employ in examining the validity of traditional assumptions; and in fact he used Montezuma in a manner that anticipated the familiar eighteenth-century convention of the "citizen of the world," the rational yet unprejudiced and uncommitted commentator on European affairs such as Montesquieu's Persian, Swift's King of Brobdingnag, Voltaire's Micromégas, and Goldsmith's Chinese.

[90] Quoted in MacMillan, *HLQ*, XIII [1950], 366.   [91] *Ibid.*, p. 369.

Like those later characters Montezuma has the combination of strong natural reason and emotional distance needed to expose with devastating logic irrationalities in European beliefs. The fact that Voltaire in the following century admired and borrowed from *The Indian Emperour* provides a measure of its intellectual vigor.[92]

It will be apparent that Dryden's conception of preconquest Mexican civilization as a pastoral golden age and of the Spanish conquistadors as avaricious, hypocritical, and sadistically cruel has extensive ancestry, in the Spanish chroniclers and in subsequent writers of history and imaginative literature. Las Casas was the most influential of the early expositors of Spanish atrocity and Indian innocence, and Dryden had some knowledge of his ideas. Dryden knew Gómara too, and if Gómara was less harsh in his version of the conquest, he nevertheless provided details that Dryden used in his indictment of the Spaniards and in his idealized portrait of the Indians. And quite apart from the histories of the conquest there was an extensive literature of primitivism, more precisely of cultural in contrast with chronological primitivism, on which Dryden drew.[93] For the Indians of the play, though nominally Aztecs, are idealized primitives having a closer kinship to the savages of literary tradition than to those of Mexico. Whatever concessions Dryden makes to anthropological accuracy, such as the allusion to human sacrifice (I, ii), are sufficiently casual not to destroy the impression of the Indians as noble primitives.[94] Like the chroniclers of geographical discovery before him, he fuses traditional ideas concerning the golden age, some of them inherited from the classical writers of antiquity, with ideas deriving from the observations of the explorers.[95] Probably he, like Montaigne earlier, was attracted to Las Casas, Gómara, and the other historians because of the readiness with which their work lent itself to a primitivistic interpretation, and thus to an arraignment of dogmatism, intolerance, and bigoted cruelty.

[92] Trusten Wheeler Russell (*Voltaire, Dryden & Heroic Tragedy* [1946], pp. 81, 96) points out that Voltaire borrowed from the play for his *Alzire* (1736), and further included in his *Essai sur les moeurs* (1750) an episode based on the torture scene. Merle L. Perkins ("Dryden's *The Indian Emperour* and Voltaire's *Alzire*," *Comparative Literature,* IX [1957], 229–237) considers at length the relationship between the two plays.

[93] Lois Whitney (*Primitivism and the Idea of Progress* [1934], pp. 7–41) provides a comprehensive survey of this literature of primitivism. Arthur O. Lovejoy, in a foreword to her book, distinguishes between cultural and chronological primitivism.

[94] Because of the advanced state of their civilization, Dryden's Aztecs are not primitives in a rigorous sense (cf. Whitney, *Primitivism and the Idea of Progress,* pp. 79–81). Davenant had differentiated, in the "Argument" prefixed to *The Cruelty of the Spaniards in Peru,* between the idyllic state of the Indians anciently, "when their inclinations were govern'd by Nature," and the troubled state they reached with the progress of their civilization, even before the Spaniards came; and some such distinction concerning different stages in the development of the Aztec civilization may have been in Dryden's mind. Yet he makes no explicit allusion to the distinction, and it is at most latent in the play.

[95] Arthur O. Lovejoy and George Boas consider at length "The Noble Savage in

It is in the use of the theory of primitivism and its derivative religious conceptions in conjunction with the history of the conquest as a means of condemning Spanish atrocity that the play in its intellectual dimension is most impressive. Other Englishmen before Dryden, notably Davenant in *The Cruelty of the Spaniards in Peru* and *The History of Sir Francis Drake,* had contrasted the state of the Indians prior to the conquest with the wretchedness to which they were reduced by Spanish cruelty practiced in the name of religion. Dryden added to that contrast logical argument which by implication undercut the religious basis on which the superstructure of persecution rested. Like Voltaire's philosophical tales of a century later, *The Indian Emperour* employs the arguments of a modified skepticism in defense of a humanity suffering under the fanaticism of zealots. Montezuma's strategy in argument is not unlike that of Micromégas, and it is directed to the same noble ends.

Montezuma's debate with the Christian priest (carried on while he undergoes torture) takes the form of a confrontation of revealed and natural religion, and the fact that the revealed religion is in this instance Roman Catholicism provides a justification for the implied judgment against it. The debate includes a summary of the principles of natural religion as variously expressed earlier by many writers: among others, Montaigne, Hooker, Grotius, and Lord Herbert of Cherbury.[96] "All under various names," explains the Christian priest (V, ii, 63 ff.),

> Adore and Love
> One power Immense, which ever rules above.
> Vice to abhor, and Virtue to pursue,
> Is both believ'd and taught by us and you.

And to that point Montezuma agrees with him; but when the priest adds that Christians learn more about the Divinity through revelation, Montezuma objects on grounds that to assume so would be to accuse God of partiality. If the argument is not resolved, the moral superiority of Montezuma to his opponent gives him an advantage in the mind of the reader. The locale of this striking debate reminds us of the importance in the development of religious thought of comparative studies stimulated by the voyages of discovery.[97]

Antiquity," in *Primitivism and Related Ideas in Antiquity* (1935), pp. 287–367. Bernheimer (*Wild Men in the Middle Ages,* pp. 106–107) discusses the discoverers' use of classical and medieval theories of the golden age.

[96] Since the ideas concerning natural religion expressed in the debate were commonplaces of religious thought, it is vain to look for specific sources for them. Influential formulations of the ideas are to be found in Montaigne, trans. Florio (1893), II, 220–222; Hooker, *Ecclesiastical Polity* (Everyman Edition), I, 174–187; Grotius, *De Jure Belli Ac Pacis Libri Tres,* trans. Kelsey (1925), II, 13–14, 510–514; Herbert, *De Veritate,* trans. Carré (1937), pp. 289–307.

[97] Basil Willey (*The Seventeenth Century Background* [1934], pp. 122–123) describes the impact of the enlargement of the known world upon Lord Herbert's religious thought: "It must be remembered that the old simple situation, in which Christendom pictured itself as the world, with only the foul paynim

If Montezuma reveals an independence from European religious dogmas, he nevertheless accepts the European doctrine of monarchy. It is a measure of Dryden's political conservatism that he tacitly assumes kingship as a form of government sanctioned in nature,[98] and not even by indirection does he suggest an alternative to it. However audacious Montezuma may be in his criticism of Spanish Catholicism and of the territorial aggression it encourages, his criticism of the Spanish government is confined to its relations with the Catholic church: in reply to the Spaniards' proposal to send priests to each Mexican town, he argues (I, ii, 317–318), "That Monarch sits not safely on his Throne, / Who suffers any pow'r, to shock his own." The objection is that of a monarchist, and indeed Montezuma expresses a conception of his kingly office consistent with the royalist opinions of the Stuarts. His own crown was bestowed by heaven, he insists; it "is absolute, and holds of none" (I, ii, 324). He regards it as inalienable, disdainfully rejecting the possibility of outliving the independence of his nation (V, ii). His heroic son Guyomar shares his political convictions. When out of a sense of desperation Alibech suggests disobedience to Montezuma, using an argument for revolution (IV, ii), Guyomar reprimands her, reminding her that "impious Rebels" use such arguments to justify their dark ambitious schemes. All this is what we would expect in a play written by a Royalist a few years after the Restoration.

However remarkable the play may be as an imaginative version of a decisive historical event, it remains a qualified success, more impressive in its parts than in its entirety, and revealing an incomplete assimilation of its themes into the conventional form of the heroic play. The tension between themes and form appears most openly in the depiction of Montezuma, the exigencies of separate dramatic situations forcing an emphasis on different qualities in his personality which ill accord with one another. It is, to say the least, difficult to reconcile the clarity of mind and the resolution of will he intermittently displays with his abject submission to Almeria. He recognizes, in his pathetic outburst against Almeria's demand that he execute Cortes (III, iv), the malignity of his passion, and yet he is powerless to free himself from it. Like other protagonists of heroic plays he experiences emotional turmoil arising from the conflicting demands of love and honor, and like them he vacillates. But unlike the other protagonists he appears in the quite different role of spokesman for a critical rationality. At times the middle-

---

outside and the semi-tolerated Jews within the gates, had passed away for ever. Exploration and commerce had widened the horizon, and in many writers of the century one can see that the religions of the East, however imperfectly known, were beginning to press upon the European consciousness. It was a pioneer-interest in these religions, together with the customary preoccupation of Renaissance scholars with the mythologies of classical antiquity, which led Lord Herbert to seek a common denominator for all religions."

[98] Cf. John Loftis, *The Politics of Drama in Augustan England* (1963), pp. 11–14.

aged lover suffering under the tyranny of a youthful beauty, he is at other times the audacious and perceptive critic of irrational institutions; and the two roles are not made consistent with any show of plausibility.

The inconsistency in the characterization of Montezuma is symptomatic of Dryden's incomplete reconciliation of his philosophic argument with his dramatic form. An arraignment of Spanish atrocity in America provides a principal theme of the play, and yet that theme is conveyed by way of dramatic action turning on a series of formalized love intrigues conducted within literary conventions shared by the French romances. To be sure, the complications in the love intrigues derive from the opposition of Aztecs and Spaniards, and they are all related to the conquest of Mexico. But the connection between certain episodes—those, for example, having to do with the rivalry of Odmar and Guyomar for the love of Alibech— and the conquest is not very close. Like most heroic plays *The Indian Emperour* is less notable for its thematic coherence than for the rhetoric of its isolated scenes, which at their best achieve a kind of operatic formality.

The formality derives from the rhymed verse used in the play. That verse is uneven. Brilliant lines, couplets, passages are followed by unimpressive and even awkward passages. In Cortes' opening speech, for example, a couplet combining rhetorical sophistication with imaginative insight is followed abruptly by a couplet turning on an obstetrical metaphor of embarrassing vividness. Yet the dialogue is largely free of the bombast that marks *Tyrannick Love* and *The Conquest of Granada,* and it is consequently less vulnerable to parody.

The rhymed couplet is used throughout except in the songs and in the first exchange between Cortes and Cydaria (I, ii), a passage of twenty-four lines set off like a lyrical interlude by the substitution of heroic quatrains for couplets. The uninterrupted couplets of the rest of the play, in which as always in English poetry stress reinforces rhyme, have seemed overemphatic and monotonous to most readers since Dryden's time. Yet if the verse may be judged a limited success, it nevertheless exhibits the qualities for which Dryden's poetry, nondramatic as well as dramatic, became famous: rapidity of movement, dignity without pomposity, boldness of metaphor, and the assimilation into vigorous heroic couplets of stretches of complex and abstract argument. The conquistadors' description of the New World and Montezuma's disputations with them remain in the mind of the reader as remarkable expressions of themes given importance by the voyages of discovery.

DEFENCE OF AN ESSAY

P. 3 *The Great Favourite.* Sir Robert Howard's *The Great Favourite, Or, the Duke of Lerma* was first acted by the King's Company at Drury Lane, 20 February 1668. Herringman entered it in the *Stationers' Register* on 24 June 1668, and published it during the summer—probably early in the summer since Pepys had Dryden's published reply by 20 September (H. J. Oliver, *Sir Robert Howard* [1963], p. 138; Ward, p. 63).

4:1 *Dimock.* A reference to the Lord of the Manor of Scrivelsby (in Lincolnshire), who was the hereditary Champion of England.

4:5–6 *one, who has the reputation of understanding all things.* A sarcastic allusion to the caricature of Howard as Sir Positive At-all in Shadwell's *The Sullen Lovers,* first produced at Lincoln's Inn Fields on 2 May 1668.

4:7–8 *the Philosopher . . . to the Emperour.* Ker: "*Favorinus to Hadrian.* Cf. Aelius Spartianus, *Hadrian,* c. 15. Malone has further pointed out that the story is given in Barclay, *Icon Animorum,* c. 10. Dryden had been reading Barclay. . . ." Dryden refers again to the story in the preface to *All for Love.*

4:21–23 *Repulse upon repulse . . . detraction do its worst.* An ironical comment on the opening lines of *The Duke of Lerma* and on Howard's explanation in his preface that he had so extensively reworked an unpublished play that he had made it his own.

4:24 *distributive Justice.* "One of the two divisions of Justice, according to Aristotle (the other being COMMUTATIVE); that which consists in the distribution of something in shares proportionate to the deserts of each among the several parties" (*OED*).

4:25 *those advantages,* etc. Howard wrote (1668, sig. A2r): "I most gratefully acknowledge to have receiv'd some advantage in the opinion of the sober part of the World. . . ."

4:33–5:2 *The Author of a Dramatique Essay . . . The Author of the Duke of Lerma.* Dryden overstates his literary debt, though he had borrowed from other writers (notably Corneille) and probably also from friends whose opinions he learned in conversation. The passage includes a sly allusion to the charge that Howard was guilty of plagiarism in *The Duke of Lerma.*

5:6–7 *Natural in a wrong application.* After his preliminaries, Dryden settles to the central critical issue under debate: the relationship between a play and the empirical reality it purports to represent. Thus the meaning attached to the word "natural" assumes crucial importance.

5:25–29 *what Gentleman that was . . . three hundred persons.* Howard wryly remarks that he wonders Dryden should have troubled himself twice to prove that "nothing may seeme something, by the help of a Verse. . . ." And he continues: "But I have heard that a Gentleman in Parliament going to speak twice, and being interrupted by another Member, as against the Orders of the House, he was excused by a third, assuring the House he had not yet spoken to the Question" (1668, sig. A4r). Dryden suggests that the butt of the story is Howard himself, who was a member of Parliament.

6:1–2 *to imitate well is a Poets work.* Cf. Aristotle, *Poetics,* I–III.

6:3–4 *to move admiration . . . a bare imitation will not serve.* In this important statement of the effect to be sought in the serious play, Dryden implies a relationship between epic and dramatic poetry. In his letter to Howard prefixed to *Annus Mirabilis* he had referred to admiration, i.e., wonder, as the proper object of heroic poetry (*Works,* I, 56).

6:26–30 *Vt pictura Poesis . . . relinquit.* Horace, *Ars Poetica,* 361–364,

149–150 (Loeb trans.): "A poem is like a picture: one strikes your fancy more, the nearer you stand; another, the farther away. This courts the shade, that will wish to be seen in the light, and dreads not the critic insight of the judge.

"And what he fears he cannot make attractive with his touch he abandons."

7:5 *Lazar.* The lazar (meaning "leper" or perhaps merely "the diseased and filthy poor of a city") is in Dryden's criticism a recurrent image, used to convey an analogy between poetry and painting. Here the image seems to imply a correspondence between Jonson's comedy and such work as Dutch genre painting. Dryden's use of the image is discussed in *Works,* I, 274–276.

7:7–8 *he sometimes ascends to Verse.* Dryden here means rhymed verse, as often when he uses the word without a modifier. See below, pp. 336–337, for further discussion of his distinction between rhymed and blank verse.

8:1–2 *I am not so fitted by Nature to write Comedy.* In the preface to *An Evening's Love* (1671, sig. A4r; Ker, I, 135), Dryden refers again to his temperamental incapacity to write and appreciate low comedy.

8:18 *Reserate Clusos,* etc. Seneca, *Hippolytus,* l. 863 (Loeb trans.): "Unbar the closed portals of the royal house." Ker observes that both Dryden and Howard print *clusos* for *clausos.* Howard had of course mistranslated *reserate,* yet, as Frank Livingstone Huntley points out (*On Dryden's "Essay of Dramatic Poesy"* [1951], pp. 58–59), this mistake was at least understandable, since in his preface to *Four New Plays* Howard had used a command to shut a door as an example of an idea especially unsuited to expression in rhymed verse. It was as a response to this example that Dryden had used the quotation from Seneca in *Of Dramatick Poesie.*

8:27 *Delectus verborum est origo Eloquentiæ.* Cicero, *Brutus,* LXXII.

9:5 *Errata.* George Watson (*Of Dramatic Poesy and Other Critical Essays* [1962], I, 117n) has pointed out that the only known surviving copy of the errata leaf, bound as an addition with *The Duke of Lerma* (1668), is in the Pepys Library, Magdalene College, Cambridge. The leaf reads as follows:

ERRATA.

Though there be many Errors in the play it self, yet I will neither give my self nor the Reader any trouble in the Correcting; but [in] the Epistle to the Reader, containing matter of Argument, I would not have my Sense, which possibly, may not be very strong, rendred weaker by mistakes in Printing.

Page 4. l.20. for like, r. likes; l.ult. for shutting, r. opening; p. 5. l.5. for so, r. As; to make the Sense entire, as I intended it; which was, That the shutting of a door shou'd be as loftily exprest by the Author there mentioned, as he fanci'd the opening a door was by Seneca. P. 6. l.24. for than, r. then; p.ult. l.12. the word Fancy is by a Comma made the end of a Sentence, which shou'd have begun the next.

9:10 *Barach.* This Hebrew word means either "bless" or "curse," depending on context.

10:10–22 *last farewel of the Muses . . . false Grammar.* In mocking Howard's pompous farewell to literary studies in the preface to *The Duke of Lerma,* Dryden glances maliciously at his reputation for conceit and overassurance, the subject of current gossip because of Shadwell's caricature of him as Sir Positive At-all.

10:23 *now fetter'd in business.* In referring to his unpleasant business, Howard probably had in mind his legal difficulties with his second wife, as Dryden would have known (Oliver, *Howard,* p. 111). Dryden was perhaps consciously misinterpreting Howard's remarks, though the tone of the preface to *The Duke of Lerma* is indeed that of a gentleman of affairs who has condescended to take a passing interest in literature.

10:25 *corruption of a Poet . . . Generation of a Statesman.* Watson (*Of Dramatic Poesy and Other Critical Essays,* I, 118–119n) observes that the antithesis stems from Aristotle and calls attention to Browne's remark about "that axiom in Philosophy, that the generation of one thing, is the corruption of another" (*Pseudodoxia Epidemica,* III.ix). Dryden was to employ the locution again in the *Dedication* to *Examen Poeticum:* "Thus the corruption of a Poet, is the Generation of a Critick" (1693, sig. A4r; Ker, II, 2–3). Inasmuch as even Richard Flecknoe was familiar with it, there can be little doubt that the phrasing was commonplace. In the preface to his *Farrago of several Pieces* (1666), Flecknoe wrote that most of the pieces in the book had been written in the country when he fled the city to escape the plague, and he added that it was not strange "that the Corruption of one, shu'd be the Generation of another."

10:27 *nullos habitura triumphos.* Lucan, *Pharsalia,* I, 12 (Loeb trans.): "[To wage wars] that could win no triumphs."

10:34–35 *However, he condemns not,* etc. Howard wrote (1668, sig. A3r): ". . . nothing cou'd appear to me a ruder folly, than to censure the satisfaction of others; I rather blame the unnecessary understanding of some that have labour'd to give strict rules to things that are not Mathematical, and with such eagerness, pursuing their own seeming reasons, that at last we are to apprehend such Argumentative *Poets* will grow as strict as *Sancho Pancos* Doctor was to our very Appetites; for in the difference of *Tragedy* and *Comedy,* and of *Fars* it self, there can be no determination but by the Taste; nor in the manner of their Composure. . . ." Doctor Pedro Recio de Agüero appears briefly in *Don Quixote,* Pt. II, ch. xlvii, prescribing delicacies for Sancho.

11:26 *the Comedies of my Lord L.* An obscure reference. Ker plausibly suggests that the lord was "John Maitland, second Earl and [later] first Duke of Lauderdale, 1616–1682." Presumably Dryden refers to Lauderdale's well-known debaucheries.

11:28 *Chère Entière.* "Grand repas qu'on fait suivre de divertissements" (*Grand Dictionnaire Universel*).

12:27 *Ficta voluptatis causâ sint proxima veris.* Horace, *Ars Poetica,* 338 (Loeb trans.): "Fictions meant to please should be close to the real."

12:34–36 *A great Wits . . . Berkenhead.* Dryden quotes a line from a eulogistic poem ("In Memory of Mr. William Cartwright") by Sir John Berkenhead published in a collection of *Comedies, Tragi-Comedies, With other Poems, by Mr. William Cartwright, late Student of Christ-Church in Oxford and Proctor of the University* (1651). Berkenhead (1616–1679) was a Fellow of All Souls College, Oxford, and a member of the Royal Society. In the work cited Berkenhead wrote (sig. *8r–v):

> For thy Imperial Muse at once defines
> Lawes to *arraign* and *brand* their weak *strong lines:*
> Unmask's the Goblin-Verse that fright's a page
> As when old time brought Devills on the Stage.
> Knew the right mark of things, saw how to choose,
> (For the great Wit's great work is to *Refuse,*)
> And smil'd to see what shouldering there is
> To follow *Lucan* where he trod amiss.

13:7 *And now I come to the boldest part of his Discourse.* The turning point in Dryden's argument, in which, following the sequence of topics in Howard's preface, he moves from rebuttal of specific objections raised by his opponent to rebuttal of the more fundamental objections to rules in dramatic theory.

13:19 Στῆ . . . &c. *Iliad,* VIII, 267.

14:2 *my definition of a Play. Of Dramatick Poesie* (1668, p. 8; Ker, I, 35–36): "Lisideius . . . conceiv'd a Play ought to be, *A just and lively Image of Humane Nature, representing its Passions and Humours, and the Changes of Fortune to which it is subject; for the Delight and Instruction of Mankind.*"

15:7–11 *my whole Discourse was Sceptical . . . the Royal Society.* Dryden often writes in this vein of admiration for the methods and achievements of natural scientists, the members of the Royal Society in particular. Cf. *Of Dramatick Poesie* (1668, p. 9; Ker, I, 36–37); and the preface to *An Evening's Love* (1671, sig. a1r; Ker, I, 138): ". . . why should there be any *ipse dixit* in our Poetry, any more than there is in our Philosophy?" The subject is considered at length by Richard Foster Jones, "Science and Criticism in the Neo-Classical Age of English Literature," in *The Seventeenth Century* (1951), pp. 41–74.

15:16 *Lord Buckhurst.* Charles Sackville (1638–1706), later Earl of Dorset, was a generous patron to Dryden throughout the poet's life. Cf. Brice Harris, *Charles Sackville, Sixth Earl of Dorset, Patron and Poet of the Restoration* (1940).

16:1 *a positive or self-conceited person.* Malone observed that Dryden is here alluding to Sir Robert's reputation for dogmatism. Cf. Shadwell's characterization of him as a man "so foolishly Positive, that he will never be convinced of an Error, though never so grosse."

16:18 *two hours.* Howard wrote (1668, sig. A4v): "two houres and a halfe."

16:25–26 *in obedience to him, I will abbreviate.* Presumably a sarcastic allusion to the brevity with which Howard in the preface to *The Duke of Lerma* dismisses the arguments for the dramatic unities of time and place.

16:36–17:1 *as great a Secret, as that we are all mortal.* A derisive allu-

sion to a platitudinous poem by Howard, "Against the Fear of Death."
The poem does not appear in either edition of Howard's poems in the
seventeenth century, but was said by Giles Jacob (*The Poetical Register*
[1723], II, 80) to have "gained him no small Reputation." The quality of
the poem may be judged from the following lines quoted by Jacob:
    We all must pass thro' Death's dead-sea of Night
    To reach the Haven of Eternal Light.
Satirical reference to this poem is made also in *The Sullen Lovers* (I, i)
where Sir Positive At-all declares, "I find you may be a Poet, a Musitian, a
Painter, a Divine, a Mathematician, a States-man; but betwixt you and I,
let me tell you, we are all Mortal."

17:10–11 *if strictly and duely weighed.* Howard uses this clause to qual-
ify the statement quoted on 21:16 ff., but not with the remainder of the
sentence here cited.

18:23–25 *If Ben. Johnson himself will remove the Scene from Rome into
Tuscany . . . and from thence return to Rome.* An allusion to *Catiline*,
Act V. Cf. *Of Dramatick Poesie* (1668, p. 43; Ker, I, 75):
    . . . though in the latter [*Catiline*] I cannot but observe
    one irregularity of that great Poet: he has remov'd the
    Scene in the same Act, from *Rome* to *Catiline's* Army,
    and from thence again to *Rome;* and besides, has allow'd
    a very inconsiderable time, after *Catilines* Speech, for the
    striking of the battle, and the return of *Petreius*, who is
    to relate the event of it to the Senate.

19:23–24 *the comparison of a Glass.* This old and important similitude
in aesthetics is discussed authoritatively by M. H. Abrams, *The Mirror
and the Lamp* (1953), pp. 31–35.

19:36 *so many years as the favour of the Duke of Lerma continued.* I.e.,
from 1598, when Lerma was entrusted with the conduct of state affairs
by Philip III, soon after that monarch succeeded his father, until 1618,
when he resigned his offices and became a cardinal. As Dryden says, Howard's play encompasses this full span of time.

20:10–11 *cites the words of Corneille himself.* Of *Dramatick Poesie*
(1668, p. 44; Ker, I, 75–76): "[Neander:] I will alledge *Corneille's* words,
as I find them in the end of his Discourse of the three Unities; *Il est facile
aux speculatifs d'estre severes, &c.* ' 'Tis easie for speculative persons to
judge severely; but if they would produce to publick view ten or twelve
pieces of this nature, they would perhaps give more latitude to the Rules
then I have done, when by experience they had known how much we are
bound up and constrain'd by them, and how many beauties of the Stage
they banish'd from it.' "

21:4 *I prefer the Silent Woman.* Cf. the *Examen* of this play in *Of
Dramatick Poesie* (1668, pp. 50–54; Ker, I, 83–87).

DEDICATION

P. 23. *Anne, Dutchess of Monmouth.* For discussion of the Duchess'
patronage of Dryden, see above, p. 295.

23:16–19 *High Objects . . . greens to entertain it.* The passage illustrates with remarkable succinctness and clarity the general lack of appreciation for mountains before the eighteenth century. The relevant aesthetic attitudes and subsequent changes in them are considered at length by Marjorie Hope Nicolson, *Mountain Gloom and Mountain Glory: The Development of the Aesthetics of the Infinite* (1959). Miss Nicolson (p. 68) points out that Dryden's remark, even though it shows him indifferent to "barren mountains," foreshadows the psychological response to them common in the following century.

25:25–26 *not the business of a Poet to represent Historical truth, but probability.* Cf. Aristotle, *Poetics*, XXIII, XXV.

25:28 *if compar'd with many of Corneilles.* For discussion of Dryden's admiration for Corneille, see above, pp. 298–299.

25:29 *written with more Flame then Art.* The metaphor is burlesqued in *The Rehearsal* (I, ii): "*Bayes:* . . . but I write for some persons of Quality, and peculiar friends of mine, that understand what Flame and Power in writing is: and they do me the right, Sir, to approve of what I do."

CONNEXION

For discussion of the "Connexion," see above, pp. 296–297.

NAMES OF THE PERSONS

Alibech. As Summers notes, the name is taken from Madeleine de Scudéry's *Ibrahim* (Pt. I, Bk. I). In English translation (ed. of 1674, pp. 4–11): *"The History of Osman and Alibech."*

Pizarro. In historical fact, Francisco Pizarro (1470?–1541), the conqueror of Peru, did not take part in the conquest of Mexico. His reputation for cruelty perhaps suggested the introduction of him into this play as a villain.

PROLOGUE

5–6 *The Scenes are old . . . before the Spaniards came.* Referring to the use in the play of scenery and costumes used the year before in *The Indian Queen,* the dramatic action of which is supposed to have taken place before the Spanish conquest.

7–9 *Our Prologue, th' old-cast too . . . ingenious Bird or Beast.* I.e., our prologue is of the old, familiar kind and is not spoken "by some ingenious Bird or Beast." These lines, which were omitted after the first edition, were presumably a scornful allusion to current theatrical practices. A reference to one such attempt at novelty occurs in Downes, p. 23, where a production of Davenant's *The Rivals,* 10 September 1664, is said to have included "Mr. Price introducing the Dancing, by a short Comical Prologue." (The editors are grateful to Emmett L. Avery for information included in this note.)

I, i

The opening description of the New World as a primitivistic paradise repeats themes that often appear in earlier poetry and drama. Dryden himself had written in a similar vein in *To My Lord Chancellor* (ll. 73–78, 135–142) and *To My Honored Friend, Dr. Charleton* (ll. 9–20). So had Davenant, even earlier, in *The Cruelty of the Spaniards in Peru* and *The History of Sir Francis Drake* (see above, pp. 315n, 316). In the former work, Davenant suggests a distinction, which would seem to be implied in the *Emperour*, between true primitives, as the Indians were anciently, and such modified primitives as the Indians had become with the advance of their civilization.

3–4 *As if our old world . . . brought forth a new!* Rochester derided this vulnerable simile in *Timon* (*Rochester's Poems on Several Occasions*, ed. James Thorpe [1950], p. 109):

There are Two *Lines!* who but he durst presume
To make the old *World*, a new withdrawing Room,
Where of another *World* she's brought to *Bed!*
What a brave *Midwife* is a *Laureats* head!

15–20 *In Spain our Springs . . . often dy'd appears.* Reflecting the widespread belief in the decay of nature. For consideration of this belief, see Richard Foster Jones, *Ancients and Moderns* (2d ed., 1961), ch. ii.

Richard N. Ringler ("Two Sources for Dryden's *The Indian Emperour*," *PQ*, XLII [1963], 423–424) plausibly suggests that Dryden had in mind several passages from Donne's *First Anniversary*:

And now the Springs and Sommers which we see,
Like sonnes of women after fiftie bee. (ll. 203–204)

The cloudes conceive not raine, or doe not powre,
In the due birth time, downe the balmy showre;
Th'Ayre doth not motherly sit on the earth,
To hatch her seasons, and give all things birth. (ll. 381–384)

. . . summers robe growes
Duskie, and like an oft dyed garment showes. (ll. 355–356)

33–48 *four hundred foot . . . noon of day.* For discussion of Dryden's historical sources, see above, pp. 306–314. His account of Cortes' approach to the Aztec capital coincides in certain important details with the account in Gómara, *The Pleasant Historie of the Conquest of the Weast India, now Called New Spayne* (trans. Thomas Nicholas [1578], pp. 169–170):

From *Iztacpalapan* to *Mexico* is two leagues all upon a fayre calsey, upon the which eight horsemen may passe on ranke, and so directly straight as though it had bene made by line. And who soever hath good eiesight might discerne the gates of *Mexico* from thence. . . .
Cortes passed this calsey with .400. Spaniardes, & .6000.

> *Indians* his friends: theyr passage was with much ado,
> by reason of the great multitude of *Indians* which came
> to see him. . . .

37 *Taxallan.* Tlascalan. An independent Indian nation, surrounded
by the Aztec empire. A modern scholar, Francis Augustus MacNutt (*Letters of Cortes* [1908], Introduction, I, 32), has thus described the crucial
importance to Cortes of his alliance with the Tlascalans:

> They were from a military point of view the equals, if
> not the superiors, of the Aztecs in the field, fighting with
> the same weapons and employing like tactics; hence one
> hundred thousand Tlascalans, captained by Cortes, who
> came as the fulfiller of prophecies, almost a supernatural
> being with demigods in his train, commanding thunder
> and lightning, and mounted upon unknown and for-
> midable beasts, were invincible. The Tlascalans had long
> bided the time for their vengeance, and in the alliance
> with Cortes they saw their opportunity. In two poten-
> tial moments Tlascala held the balance of victory or
> defeat, and a hair would have tipped it either way. . . .
> Throw the weight of Tlascala on the Aztec side, and the
> history of the conquest of Mexico would have to be re-
> written.

46 *the City on the Lake.* Cortes (*Letters*, I, 256) thus described the
Aztec capital: "This great city of Temixtitan is built on the salt lake, and
from the mainland to the city is a distance of two leagues, from any side
from which you enter. It has four approaches by means of artificial cause-
ways, two cavalry lances in width. The city is as large as Seville or Cor-
doba. Its streets (I speak of the principal ones) are very broad and straight,
some of these, and all the others, are one half land, and the other half
water on which they go about in canoes."

I, ii

5 *Five hundred Captives.* The early authorities on the conquest are in
agreement that the Aztecs annually sacrificed some thousands of captives.
Dryden's figure for a single ceremony is not excessive.

71–74 *To prove the lasting torment . . . his dissembled joys.* One of
the several cynical attacks on marriage which occur in Dryden's writings.
Cf. 2 *The Conquest of Granada*, III, i (1672, p. 100; S-S, IV, 155); IV, iii
(1672, p. 138; S-S, IV, 199); *Aureng-Zebe*, II, i (1676, pp. 21–26; S-S, V,
226–232).

95–112 *To that Sea shore . . . cut the yielding Seas.* Dougald Mac-
Millan ("The Sources of Dryden's *The Indian Emperour*," *HLQ*, XIII
[1950], 360) plausibly suggests that Dryden might have taken suggestions
from the painted scenery used in staging Davenant's *The Cruelty of the
Spaniards in Peru* for visual details in Guyomar's account of the ocean
and the Spanish ships. But see above, pp. 306–307.

123 *Old Prophecies.* The prophecies are widely mentioned in earlier

literature: among other places, in the prologue to *The Indian Queen* (ll. 11–12), and in Davenant's *The Cruelty of the Spaniards in Peru* (1658), pp. 7–8.

148 *Yours first set out, mine reach'd her in the race.* An allusion to the race of Nisus and Euryalus, *Aeneid*, V, 294–361 (Reuben Arthur Brower, "Dryden's Epic Manner and Virgil," *PMLA*, LV [1940], 122).

192–194 *Behind the covert . . . Of ambush'd men.* Brower (*ibid.*) notes that this passage is in the manner of Virgil.

232 *Patron of Mexico and god of Wars.* William H. Prescott (*History of the Conquest of Mexico* [1886], I, 63) thus describes this god:

> At the head of all stood the terrible Huitzilopotchli, the Mexican Mars; although it is doing injustice to the heroic war-god of antiquity to identify him with this sanguinary monster. This was the patron deity of the nation. His fantastic image was loaded with costly ornaments. His temples were the most stately and august of the public edifices; and his altars reeked with the blood of human hecatombs in every city of the empire.

240 *mild and gentle god.* Quetzalcoatl, a god whose residence on earth was supposed to have been marked by a golden age of peace and of progress in the arts and crafts. Prescott (*Conquest of Mexico*, I, 64) describes the significance of this god for the Mexicans:

> He was said to have been tall in stature, with a white skin, long, dark hair, and a flowing beard. The Mexicans looked confidently to the return of the benevolent deity; and this remarkable tradition, deeply cherished in their hearts, prepared the way . . . for the future success of the Spaniards.

250–336 *Ambassadour of Peace . . . yet have no Enemy.* For discussion of the sources of this first exchange between Montezuma and the Spaniards, see above, pp. 312–313.

280–288 *But, by what right . . . what is not his own.* Dryden had earlier, in *Heroique Stanzas*, spoken of the Pope as "That old unquestion'd Pirate of the Land" (*Works*, I, 15, and Commentary, p. 205).

349–372 *My Father's gone . . . as I am true.* The tenderness of this first exchange between Cydaria and Cortes is emphasized by a modification of the verse form from couplets to quatrains. Dryden and Howard had used occasional quatrains (fifteen in all) in *The Indian Queen*. Cf. *Works*, VIII, 299.

II, i

This scene in the magician's cave resembles that in *The Indian Queen* (III, ii) in which Zempoalla goes to Ismeron's cell seeking an interpretation of a dream.

75+, 84+ *s.d. Traxalla and Acacis . . . the Indian Queen.* Characters in the *Queen* who met their deaths because of Montezuma. The queen, like Dido with whose fate hers seems to be compared, killed herself out of frustrated love.

95 *early Cocks.* Cf. *Hamlet,* I, i, 149–156.

96 *a meeting place below.* As Summers points out, Dryden seems to have had in mind the Mourning Fields (*Aeneid,* VI, 440–474), where Aeneas saw the ghost of Dido.

II, ii

101 *For Liberty. For Love.* The passage is burlesqued in Fielding, *The Tragedy of Tragedies,* III, ix (ed. Hillhouse [1918], pp. 138–139, 183n).

II, iii

29 *I kill'd a double Man.* Reflecting the Indian belief that a horse and his rider were one. Prescott (*Conquest of Mexico,* I, 179–180) emphasizes the importance of cavalry to Cortes in frightening the Indians.

93 *'Tis true I Lov'd, but she is Dead.* Perhaps an allusion to Cortes' marriage in Cuba before coming to Mexico (Gómara, *The Pleasant Historie of the Conquest,* trans. Thomas Nicholas, pp. 7–9). His wife, however, was not dead at the time of the conquest.

III, i

94 *Drown'd in his Sleep.* Reminiscent of a metaphor in the *Aeneid,* II, 265. A similar metaphor appears again in IV, iii, 68. (Brower, *PMLA,* LV [1940], 122.)

III, ii

1–5 *All things are hush'd . . . Ev'n Lust and Envy sleep.* Thomas Rymer ("Preface to Rapin," *The Critical Works of Thomas Rymer,* ed. Curt A. Zimansky [1956], p. 15) praised this passage extravagantly, preferring it to descriptions of the night by poets writing in other languages: "In this description, four lines yield greater variety of matter, and more choice thoughts than twice the number of any other Language. Here is something more *fortunate* than the boldest fancy has yet reached, and something more *just,* than the severest reason has observed."

III, iv

2 *This early Famine.* In historical fact, the prolonged siege of the Aztec capital, lasting seventy-five days, occurred after Montezuma's death, when his nephew Guatemozin (also spelled Quahutimoc) had become emperor. Cortes (*Letters,* II, 126) described the effects of the siege: "It appears they had perished to the number of more than fifty thousand, from the salt water which they drank, or from starvation, and pestilence."

81 *place.* Plaza or public square.

IV, ii

21–22 *If either Death or Bondage . . . my life I lose.* Montezuma's resolution suggests that of Cato the Younger as described by Plutarch (MacMillan, *HLQ,* XIII [1950], 369–370).

39–44 *As Callow Birds . . . people in their misery.* Brower (*PMLA,* LV [1940], 122) notes that this passage is in the manner of Virgil, even to the use of a hemistich, which Dryden considered Virgilian.

IV, iii

1 *Ah fading joy.* Day, p. 143: "There is an attractive musical setting by the gifted composer Pelham Humphrey in *Choice Ayres, Songs, & Dialogues,* 1675, I, 70–71; 1676, I, 66–67. 'I. Tyndall' made a glee for four voices of it in 1785 (British Museum: Addit. MS 31811, ff. 29–32), and Charles Lucas, Principal of the Royal Academy of Music from 1859 to 1866, set it to music as a madrigal for five voices in 1857 [British Museum: H. 1775. v. (27)]." The Bodleian Library possesses a probably unique manuscript version of this song containing two additional couplets. See Textual Notes, p. 383.

5 *And follow Fate which would too fast pursue.* This metaphor was severely criticized in the pamphlet written by "R. F." (possibly Richard Flecknoe), *A Letter from a Gentleman to the Honourable Ed. Howard Esq.* (1668, p. 5). Dryden replied to the criticism in a paragraph added to the preface in the second edition of *Tyrannick Love* (1672, sig. A3v; S-S, III, 381–382), saying that the metaphor was borrowed from a line in the *Aeneid* (XI, 695): *Eludit gyro interior, sequiturque sequentem.*

16+ *s.d. Dance a Saraband.* *The Rehearsal* (III, i) glances satirically at Dryden's introduction of dances into his heroic plays.

68 *Buried in their Sleep or Joy.* Reminiscent of a metaphor in the *Aeneid,* II, 265. A similar metaphor appears in III, i, 94. (Brower, *PMLA,* LV [1940], 122.)

IV, iv

94–100 *All hopes of safety . . . much less to do.* Dryden's remark in *The Grounds of Criticism in Tragedy* (1679, sig. b2r; Ker, I, 223) that "no man is at leisure to make sentences and similes, when his soul is in an Agony," is, as Ker notes, a relevant criticism of this passage. Cf. *The Rehearsal* (II, iii): "*Bayes:* . . . That's a general Rule: you must ever make a *simile,* when you are surpris'd; 'tis the new way of writing."

132 *As Halcyons Brooding.* For discussion of Dryden's use of the symbol of the halcyon, see *Works,* I, 206–207.

V, ii

s.d. a Christian Priest. Prescott (*Conquest of Mexico,* I, 193) writes that there were "two ecclesiastics who attended the expedition,—the licentiate Juan Diaz and father Bartolomé de Olmedo."

1 *discover'd all thy store.* For discussion of the sources of the torture scene, see above, pp. 310–311.

39–97 *Those Pains . . . short step of life to make.* For discussion of this debate on natural religion, see above, p. 316. Cf. the debate between Apollonious and St. Catharine in Act II of *Tyrannick Love* (1670, pp. 16–17; S-S, III, 403–404). Cf. also the exposition of the deist's creed in *Religio Laici,* ll. 42–61.

The passage in the *Emperour* attracted a satirical comment in *A Letter from a Gentleman to the Honourable Ed. Howard Esq.* (p. 7): ". . . we may justly presume that when his *Indian Emperour* was first acted, he intended to instruct and reform all Churches in Polemical Divinity, by his admirable Dispute between a Christian and a Heathen Priest; which also shows how great a loss the Church had of him, when he was diverted from entering into Orders."

77–80 *If in this middle way . . . in uncertain way.* Ringler (*PQ*, XLII [1963], 425n) points out a parallel in Donne's "Satyre III" (ll. 77–79):

> doubt wisely; in strange way
> To stand inquiring right, is not to stray;
> To sleepe, or runne wrong, is.

192+ *s.d. Zoty.* From the Spanish word *azotea*, meaning "the flat roof of a house."

200–205 *As when upon the sands . . . like Waves renew'd.* In *Grounds of Criticism in Tragedy* (1679, sig. b2r; Ker, I, 224), Dryden criticises this passage: "My Indian Potentate was well skill'd in the Sea for an Inland Prince, and well improv'd since the first Act, when he sent his son to discover it. The Image had not been amiss from another man, at another time: *Sed nunc non erat hisce locus:* he destroy'd the concernment which the Audience might otherwise have had for him; for they could not think the danger near, when he had the leisure to invent a Simile."

Brower (*PMLA*, LV [1940], 122–123) notes that the passage is in the manner of Virgil.

234 *But I'm a King while this is in my Hand.* As MacMillan points out (*HLQ*, XIII [1950], 369–370), Montezuma's remark is reminiscent of that reported by Plutarch of Cato the Younger when his sword is brought to him. MacMillan plausibly suggests that Dryden in depicting Montezuma's noble resolution in face of death also had in mind the death of Brutus as it was portrayed by Shakespeare. In any event, Stoical commonplaces similar to this one occur earlier in the play: cf. II, i, 3–4, and II, iii, 54. John A. Winterbottom ("Stoicism in Dryden's Tragedies," *JEGP*, LXI [1962], 868–883) discusses Dryden's use of Stoical doctrine.

EPILOGUE

19–20 *the Coffee-wits . . . to Damn the Dutch.* England declared war against the Dutch (the Second Dutch War) in March 1665, though in the preceding year there were acts of hostility. The war had wide popular support in England.

Secret Love

Produced by the King's Company acting in the theater at Bridges Street, Drury Lane, *Secret Love* appeared in the first season after the theaters were reopened following the plague. The first performance that can be dated precisely was the one on 2 March 1667, when Pepys saw it, but the play had been acted in February and perhaps as early as January. The epilogue of Buckingham's adaptation of Fletcher's *The Chances*, which Pepys saw on 5 February, contains what may be an allusion to *Secret Love,* and thus provides uncertain evidence for a January date of first production.[1] Pepys wrote of the play on 2 March as "mightily commended for the regularity of it," implying that it had been known long enough to have a reputation with the critics.

Such theatrical records as have survived establish the fact that *Secret Love* was unusually successful in its first few seasons. The King, who liked it so much as to give it "the Title of His Play," [2] saw it on 2 and 5 March and 18 April (the latter time at court) 1667; and on 4 and 27 January (again at court) 1668.[3] Pepys saw it four times its first season (2 and 25 March, 24 May, and 23 August 1667), twice its second (18 and 24 January 1668), and twice its third (1 and 13 January 1669); and he regularly praised it, as when he wrote on 24 January 1668, that the more he saw it the more he loved it, and thought it "one of the best plays I ever saw, and is certainly the best acted of any thing ever the House did, and particularly Becke Marshall [as the queen] to admiration." It is impossible to say much more about its stage history in the later seventeenth century than that it was occasionally revived, as it was in the summer of 1672,[4] on 5 December 1676, and on 15 December 1686.[5] Printings of the play in 1679 and 1691 suggest that it may have been acted in those years. The more comprehensive records of the eighteenth century reveal performances in 1704, 1705, and 1706, after which *Secret Love* seems to have disappeared from the stage.[6]

If a very good play, the initial success of *Secret Love* came in part from the skill of the actors, as we may assume from Pepys's comments and from Dryden's tribute to them in his preface: "the chief parts of it both

---

[1] John Harrington Smith, "Dryden and Buckingham: The Beginnings of the Feud," *MLN,* LXIX (1954), 242–245.

[2] In his preface Dryden explains the absence of a dedication by reference to this title given by the King.

[3] P.R.O., L.C. 5/139, p. 129; P.R.O. 5/12, p. 17. (Cited in Nicoll, pp. 343–344).

[4] Van Lennep, p. 195. See below, p. 346.

[5] Van Lennep, *passim.*

[6] Emmett L. Avery, ed., *The London Stage, 1660–1800,* Pt. 2: 1700–1729 (1960), *passim.*

serious and comick, being performed to that height of excellence, that nothing but a command which I could not handsomely disobey, could have given me the courage to have made it publick." It was in this play that Nell Gwyn achieved her greatest success: "there is a comical part done by Nell, which is Florimell," wrote Pepys of the performance on 2 March 1667, "that I never can hope ever to see the like done again, by man or woman. . . . But so great performance of a comical part was never, I believe, in the world before as Nell do this, both as a mad girle, then most and best of all when she comes in like a young gallant; and hath the motions and carriage of a spark the most that ever I saw any man have. It makes me, I confess, admire her."

Since Nell Gwyn and her fellow actors and actresses seem to have influenced Dryden's conception of his dramatic characters, it is profitable to consider them in relation to their roles (which, perhaps significantly, are identified in the dramatis personae of the first edition). At the time he wrote the play Dryden knew the members of the company well, and he must have had individuals in mind for certain roles or he would not have ventured such precise descriptions—as of the queen as a brunette (V, i). Rebecca Marshall had the part, and that she had dark hair and eyes is corroborated by a description of a character she subsequently portrayed in Nathaniel Lee's *Nero* (I, ii).[7] Dryden makes an extended joke of the contrast in height between the two sisters, Sabina and Olinda (IV, i), as he would scarcely have done had not the company included actresses suitably short and tall. Elizabeth Davenport had the former role; Margaret Rutter the latter. Certainly Celadon's description of Florimell (I, ii) seems to be a description of Nell herself: "Such an Ovall face, clear skin, hazle eyes, thick brown Eye-browes, and Hair. . . . A turn'd up Nose, that gives an air to your face: . . . a full neather-lip, an out-mouth, . . . the bottom of your cheeks a little blub, and two dimples when you smile: for your stature, 'tis well, and for your wit 'twas given you by one that knew it had been thrown away upon an ill face." All this fits the portraits of Nell Gwyn, and what we know of her personality would suggest that her wit was of the irreverent and effervescent kind that Florimell displays.[8] It has indeed been plausibly suggested that Dryden and his fellow dramatists, searching for a new style in comedy in that first decade of the professional actress, found in Nell a living model for their quick-witted and saucy heroines,[9] those anti-Platonic coquettes who influence if they do not establish the tone of the plays. Nell had in *Secret Love* a suitable partner in the role of Celadon, the debonair and experienced actor Charles Hart. Together they provided the first consummate embodiment of the Restoration "gay couple," and it may not be too much to say that they thus left a permanent mark on English comedy.[10]

Herringman entered *Secret Love* in the *Stationers' Register* on 7 August 1667, along with *Of Dramatick Poesie* and *The Wild Gallant*. The title page bears the date 1668; Pepys bought a copy of it "newly printed" on

[7] Wilson, p. 172.   [8] Cf. S-S, II, 416; Allen, p. 41; Wilson, p. 100.
[9] Wilson, pp. 99–100.   [10] *Ibid.*

18 January 1668, noting that Dryden in his preface boasts, justifiably, Pepys thought, of the play. Dryden had reason indeed to be pleased with the direction his career was taking.

Along with *Of Dramatick Poesie* and *Annus Mirabilis, Secret Love* belongs in its composition to the prolific period of Dryden's residence at his father-in-law's estate at Charlton in Wiltshire, where with his wife he took refuge during the plague. He apparently had considerable leisure for writing, and, judging from the breadth of detailed allusions to other authors in his writings of this period, he had access to a large number of books.[11] A passage in the letter to Sir Robert Howard prefixed to *Annus Mirabilis* establishes the approximate time of composition: dating the letter 10 November 1666, Dryden mentions a recent request that Howard read a play that must have been *Secret Love.*[12] (It was the only new play he had ready when the theaters reopened.) Probably he wrote it before *Annus Mirabilis* and after the first draft of *An Essay of Dramatick Poesie:* most likely in the winter and spring of 1665–66.[13] He thus wrote it at approximately the time he was taken up with the speculations recorded in the essay, a circumstance that helps to explain the obvious relevance of the theories examined there to the dramatic practice embodied in the play.

It has been well suggested that the prologue of *Secret Love,* with its adroit allusions to the French and English dramatic traditions, provides an epilogue to the essay; [14] and in fact both the prologue and the short preface testify to Dryden's preoccupation in writing the play according to the neoclassical rules of drama. He begins the prologue with a boast that he has followed the rules: that he has observed the unities and maintained *liaison des scènes;* and that he has adapted to his own needs Jonson's theory of humours characterization and Corneille's employment of rhyme. Again in the preface Dryden asserts that the play "is regular, according to the strictest of Dramatick Laws," at some length defending himself against the imputation of violating the critical principle of decorum in the treatment of the queen. His extended discussion of decorum suggests that in the interval between the first performance of the play in January or February 1667 and its publication in January 1668, it had been the subject of critical conversation—of the kind, we may surmise, that Dryden portrays in *Of Dramatick Poesie.* To this conversation the King himself had been a party, as is implied by Dryden's allusion to an objection, in which he had concurred, to the conduct of the final scene, a theoretical objection grounded in neoclassical theory: that Celadon

---

[11] Presumably Dryden's statement in the note "To the Reader" prefixed to *Of Dramatick Poesie* (1668, sig. A4v; Ker, I, 27) that the essay was written "without the help of Books" is merely a conventional disclaimer. Certainly in the essay as well as in *Secret Love* there is internal evidence that he drew from a wide range of books.

[12] *Works,* I, 49.   [13] *Works,* I, 260n; Ward, p. 46.

[14] Ker, I, xlix. Frank Harper Moore (*The Nobler Pleasure* [1963], p. 41), emphasizing the close connection between the essay and the play, writes that *Of Dramatick Poesie* could be considered the preface to *Secret Love.*

and Florimell discuss their marriage in too light a vein in the presence of their sovereign, who stands idle while the main action is still unresolved. Yet if Dryden acknowledges that the play has not escaped censure, his tone in the preface, as Pepys noted, is distinctly one of pride. We recall that Pepys nearly a year before reported that the play "was mightily commended for the regularity of it."

The reputation of *Secret Love* for "regularity" would at first seem paradoxical. If we form our conception of that quality, as did Lisideius in Dryden's essay, on the best drama of mid-seventeenth-century France, we will conclude that the play lacks unity of action and even unity of emotional effect. It is after all a tragicomedy in the specialized sense of combining serious and comic plots, each largely independent of the other. Although Dryden at the time regarded this kind of tragicomedy as consistent with the rules, he understood well enough that some critics, including his brother-in-law, disagreed with him. Howard in 1665, in the preface to *Four New Plays,* had censured the English dramatists for "mingling and interweaving Mirth and Sadness through the whole Course of their Plays," asserting that the audience could not change moods quickly enough to follow the turns of their plots.[15] On this subject Lisideius in the essay argues in a similar vein: "There is no Theatre in the world has any thing so absurd as the English Tragi-comedie, . . . here a course of mirth, there another of sadness and passion; a third of honour, and fourth a Duel."[16] Neander's arguments in rebuttal, in defense of tragicomedy, would seem to reflect Dryden's current thoughts as he was soon to give them dramatic expression in *Secret Love* (though he later changed his mind, or at least the tenor of his critical pronouncements).[17] Probably he wrote this defense of the combination of a serious and a comic plot, which has been called "the first real defense of tragicomedy in English criticism,"[18] with his plans for the play in mind. "A continued gravity keeps the spirit too much bent," he wrote with obvious relevance to the play; "we must refresh it sometimes, as we bait upon a journey, that we may go on with greater ease."[19] Neander expresses dissatisfaction with French drama precisely because of its narrow focus on a single action and consequent lack of variety. In the same vein, and with similar relevance to *Secret Love,* he defends the English habit of depicting

---

[15] Sig. [a2]*v.*

[16] 1668, p. 28; Ker, I, 57–58.

[17] Cf. *Grounds of Criticism in Tragedy* (1679, sig. a2r; Ker, I, 208). Fred G. Walcott ("John Dryden's Answer to Thomas Rymer's *The Tragedies of the Last Age,*" *PQ,* XV [1936], 194–214) plausibly suggests that the conservatism of this later essay may be attributable to Dryden's response to Rymer's *Tragedies of the Last Age* (1677).

[18] Frank Humphrey Ristine, *English Tragicomedy, Its Origin and History* (1910), p. 169. Ristine summarizes other contemporary comment on the subject, notably that by Milton and Edward Phillips (pp. 168–169n). For discussion of the earlier history of tragicomedy, see Marvin T. Herrick, *Tragicomedy: Its Origin and Development in Italy, France, and England* (1955).

[19] 1668, p. 39; Ker, I, 70.

violence upon the stage, provided incredible actions are removed. "If we are to be blam'd for showing too much of the action," Neander concludes, "the French are as faulty for discovering too little of it." [20] Dryden may already have planned the scenes of military action that bring the serious plot to its climax.

Although he made himself vulnerable to charges of violating the unity of action and the doctrine of kinds by employing the two-part form of tragicomedy, Dryden found the form an aid in satisfying the demands imposed by the neoclassical conception of decorum. By mingling the serious and comic scenes he could produce a varied dramatic action, which included episodes of effervescent and irreverent wit, and yet observe the strict rules of decorum which forbade the infringement of the courtesies due a dramatic sovereign.[21] "All crown'd heads by *Poetical right* are *Heroes*," Thomas Rymer later wrote in *The Tragedies of the Last Age* (1677),[22] and it is an opinion with which Dryden implicitly concurred throughout his career. However rebellious he was toward the rules concerning the unity of action and the mixture of kinds, he acknowledged the claims of those pertaining to the treatment of characters of exalted rank, even if, as in *Secret Love,* the exigencies of dramatic situations sometimes led him to interpret them loosely.[23] It would appear from the preface to the play that despite all his care his first critics found more to censure in his infringements—or alleged infringements—of decorum than in his employment of a double plot. The very sensitivity of critics to the dramatic treatment of royalty (a subject that had political implications in that first decade after the Restoration) suggests why it was useful to Dryden in writing the play to be able to keep the banter of his gay young lovers out of the scenes in which the queen appeared.

Quite apart from the arguments of seventeenth-century critics, a case can be made for the success of Dryden's juxtaposition of the serious and the comic plots. If they are largely independent of each other, they nevertheless coexist harmoniously and in fact complement each other in producing the distinctive tone of the play, which is neither pompous nor trivial, as it might have been if one or the other existed in isolation. The two plots in conjunction produce an effect not unlike that of Madeleine de Scudéry's *Cyrus*, Dryden's principal source, in which also there is a juxtaposition of love plots in different moods.[24] In some of them lofty idealism predominates and in others laughing passion. Whatever their differences in seriousness, both plots in the play turn on the court-ship of young lovers, and they have love in different moods as their themes: sensual, gay, frank, and uninhibited; idealized, sublimated, and repressed. The plots reveal certain parallels of detail: dialogue in praise of the queen's beauty (I, iii) follows similar dialogue in praise of

---

[20] 1668, p. 43; Ker, I, 75.   [21] Moore, *The Nobler Pleasure*, pp. 43–45.
[22] *The Critical Works of Thomas Rymer*, ed. Curt A. Zimansky (1956), p. 42.
[23] Cf. John Loftis, *The Politics of Drama in Augustan England* (1963), pp. 11–14.
[24] Allen, pp. 100 ff.

Florimell's (I, ii); depiction of the queen's jealousy and petulant criticism
of the appearance of her rival Candiope (III, i) precedes a similar depiction
of Florimell's jealousy and criticism of her two rivals Sabina and Olinda,
the one because she is too short and the other because she is too tall
(IV, i). In the earlier part of the play the two plots follow the double
pattern familiar to us in later Restoration comedy.[25] The love banter of
a gay couple provides contrast for the love intrigue of a serious couple,
which is impeded by an outside authority, in this instance the queen.
The violent and heroic dimension of the serious plot does not fully
emerge until the fourth act. It is the natural compatibility of the different
plots much more than the mechanical devices such as *liaison des scènes*
and the use of certain minor characters in both of them which brings
about the harmonious union. Still, the fact that Dryden could maintain
liaison des scènes (except once in the fourth act) testifies to his success in
achieving the union.

Secret Love came at a time when Dryden's thoughts were engaged with
the theory of the heroic play and the language appropriate to it, at a time
in fact when he was engaged in the extended debate with Howard on the
subject of rhyme in drama. The serious plot understandably bears the
impress of the heroic play: in the characterization and the standard
of honor by which the characters regulate, or attempt to regulate, their
conduct and in the occasional use of rhyme. We could plausibly interpret
the serious plot of *Secret Love* as a heroic play humanized by the fact
that it is accompanied and in a measure paralleled by a plot taken up
with the deeds of such eminently credible characters as Celadon and
Florimell.

The movement from the one plot to the other is accompanied by changes
in the nature of the language employed: colloquial but metaphorical and
very witty prose in the comic plot, and verse, or something approximating
verse, in the serious. The serious scenes are set as verse, but frequently
nothing but typographical convention identifies them as such. Dryden
extends to its utmost limits the process of relaxation in the structure
of blank verse observable in the comedies and tragicomedies of Beaumont
and Fletcher, plays that were much in his thoughts in the 1660's.[26] In
doing so he had ample precedent among the mid-century cavalier
dramatists, whose blank verse had frequently been so irregular as to lead
compositors mistakenly to set it as prose.[27] Dryden did not in fact regard
blank verse as verse at all: "Now measure alone in any modern Language,
does not constitute verse," says his spokesman Neander in *Of Dramatick
Poesie*, but only measure accompanied by rhyme.[28] Hence he could
without any theoretical inconsistency treat it as loosely as he wished:

---

[25] John Harrington Smith (*The Gay Couple in Restoration Comedy* [1948],
passim) describes many of these double plots.

[26] See below, pp. 342–343.

[27] Alfred Harbage, *Cavalier Drama* (1936), pp. 38–39.

[28] 1668, pp. 62–63; Ker, I, 96.

"blank verse being properly but measured prose," as Neander put it.[29]

Dryden believed he had found in the plays of antiquity a precedent for his variations in the form of dramatic language. "Neither is that other advantage of the Ancients to be despis'd," says Neander in the essay, "of changing the kind of verse when they please with the change of the Scene, or some new entrance"; [30] and the remark has obvious relevance to *Secret Love* (even if in Dryden's opinion only the passages in couplets were in verse). Elsewhere in the essay Neander alludes, again in a passage of relevance to the play, to Ben Jonson's *The Sad Shepherd*, "which goes sometimes upon rhyme, sometimes upon blanck Verse, like an Horse who eases himself upon Trot and Amble." [31] The metaphor implies caprice in the movement from the one form to the other, somewhat more caprice than exists in the modulations from the one to the other in Dryden's serious scenes, for the couplets do come at intervals of reflection and of emotional intensity: as in the third act, when for the first time in the play Candiope and Philocles meet, and in the fourth act when Asteria reveals the queen's "secret love" to Philocles. The division between blank verse and couplets does not correspond to a precise plan, and yet there is some logic in it. Along with the couplets comes a lyrical and meditative mood, a slowing down of the dramatic action as the characters ponder its significance in a verse form that lends itself to the aphoristic summary of experience. The movement from one verse form to another, and from verse to prose and back again, is never obtrusive. The dramatic language is consistently graceful and appropriate to the tone of the play.[32]

Dryden's debt to the French romances is to be observed in the tone of *Secret Love*, as already suggested, the tone that is the gay and yet courtly effect of the juxtaposed scenes of love in varying moods. The setting of the play in the Sicily of antiquity and the use of pastoral names for the characters have precedents in the French romances as well as in English Renaissance drama, and both setting and names help to differentiate the tone even of the comic plot from that of the comedies of London life which Etherege and lesser dramatists were already writing. Their determination to avoid romantic clichés notwithstanding, Celadon and Florimell

---

[29] *Ibid.* In the dedication to *The Rival Ladies* (*Works*, VIII, 99), Dryden had written about blank verse in a similar vein:

> *Shakespear* (who with some Errors not to be avoided in that Age, had undoubtedly a larger Soul of Pœsie than ever any of our Nation) was the first, who to shun the pains of continual Rhyming, invented that kind of Writing, which we call Blanck Verse, but the *French* more properly, *Prose Mesurée:* into which the *English* Tongue so naturally Slides, that in writing Prose 'tis hardly to be avoided.

[30] 1668, p. 63; Ker, I, 97.   [31] 1668, p. 46; Ker, I, 78.

[32] Dryden had a recent precedent for the intermixture of blank verse and rhyme in Sir Robert Howard's *The Vestal Virgin* (printed in 1665; H. J. Oliver, *Sir Robert Howard* [1963], p. 81). If it is unlikely he could have learned much from his brother-in-law's example, he may well have profited from conversations with him on the subject.

retain (in the phrase of John Harrington Smith) "a certain aura of the ideal,"[33] a certain distance from the realities even of love life which reminds us of the French romances.

However languid these romances may seem to us, to Dryden they were an important source of inspiration, in their disguised renderings of the intrigues of famous people (some of whom were still alive), as well as in their narrative manner. In the preface he acknowledged his debt to the story of Cleobuline in Madeleine de Scudéry's *Artamène, ou Le Grand Cyrus* (published under her brother's name; hence Dryden's use of the masculine pronoun): "the Play is founded on a story in the *Cyrus,* which he calls the Queen of *Corinth;* in whose Character, as it has been affirm'd to me, he represents that of the famous *Christina,* Queen of *Sweden.*" From this story Dryden took his serious plot in rather close detail: in the characterization of the queen, the relationships of the characters, the principal events (with the single important exception of the episode of the armed rebellion), and the final resolution. All the major characters and character relationships are anticipated in the story. The young and accomplished queen loves one of her subjects, whom she has advanced at court without revealing her love. Inhibited by the difference in their qualities, he does not return her affection but rather loves the sister of the queen's kinsman and heir. The queen reveals her secret to a confidante, who first tries herself to break off the projected match between the young couple and, when she has failed, persuades the queen's heir, the brother of the young woman, to forbid it. Ultimately the queen undergoes a change of heart and removes her objection to the young couple's love. She declares her resolve not to marry and expresses the hope that her heir similarly will not marry, so that ultimately the crown will devolve, through the prince's sister, upon the man whom she has secretly loved. Dryden used all this, and in fact made few departures from the *Cyrus.*[34]

His only major addition to the story is the episode of the armed rebellion against the queen, which serves the dramatic function of providing an exciting climax for the serious plot. Yet however useful, the episode required delicate management. Dryden after all depicts Philocles, a man of honor who is the leading character of the serious plot, in open rebellion against his sovereign. Yet without seeming to do violence to poetic justice or to the principle of decorum, he rewards him with marriage to his beloved and with the hope even of eventual succession to the crown [35]

---

[33] *The Gay Couple,* p. 58.

[34] Allen (pp. 80–106) presents a comprehensive account of the literary background of the play.

[35] Langbaine (p. 143), however, considered Dryden's treatment of the character to be a breach of decorum: "As to Mr. *Fletcher,* should we grant that he understood not the *Decorum* of the Stage, as Mr. *Dryden,* and Mr. *Flecknoe* before him in his Discourse on the English Stage, observe; his Errors on that account, are more pardonable than those of the former, who pretends so well to know it, and yet has offended against some of its most obvious and established Rules. Witness . . . *Philocles* joining with Prince *Lisimantes* in taking the Queen Prisoner, who rais'd him to be her chief Favourite."

—all this in a play produced seven years after the Restoration. Several passages reveal Dryden's sensitivity to political implications. While Candiope argues for the rebellion led by her brother, Philocles hesitates, even though he knows she is in danger; and in an obvious allusion to the recent English civil wars he speaks most cynically of the motives that impell men to revolutionary action (IV, i, 317–319):

> Int'rest makes all seem reason that leads to it.
> Int'rest that does the zeal of Sects create,
> To purge a Church, and to reform a State.

After this analysis of the revolutionists' motives, Philocles does indeed join them, but only for the most compelling personal reasons: to protect Candiope from physical danger and to protect the queen from the consequences of her secret love for a man of inferior station (himself, though he does not know it). The rebellion itself is of a cautious kind, involving merely the brief confinement of the queen to her palace; [36] and the rebels are properly contrite after they have submitted themselves to her authority. Celadon's humorous request for forgiveness passes a judgment against the rebellion—and glances at English politics (V, i, 478–482):

> . . . Madam, I onely beg a pardon for having taken up
> armes once to day against you; for I have a foolish kind
> of Conscience, which I wish many of your Subjects had,
> that will not let me ask a recompence for my loyalty,
> when I know I have been a Rebel.

King Charles would have understood Celadon well enough.

The fact that the story of Queen Cleobuline was a version of Queen Christina's romantic if eccentric career would have given the play an added dimension of interest in the seventeenth century. Madeleine de Scudéry had incorporated into *Le Grand Cyrus*, in transparent allegory, an account of great events and famous personalities of the first half of the seventeenth century,[37] with the result that the romance must have seemed to Dryden and to others of his time a lively rendering of the careers of fascinating people.

One of the most fascinating of all was Queen Christina. Born in 1626, reigning as child and woman from 1632 to 1654 (and thus still queen at the time the *Cyrus* was published from 1649 to 1653 though not when *Secret Love* was acted in 1667), Christina abdicated in favor of her cousin Charles Gustavus (Basilides in the story; Lysimantes in the play) and thereafter lived mainly in Paris and Rome. Although a brilliant and accomplished woman and a patron of learned men, she became increasingly eccentric and unstable as she grew older. She attracted attention throughout Europe, in her youth sympathetic interest, which in the years after

---

[36] Yet it was not a bloodless rebellion: some of the queen's guards were killed (IV, ii).

[37] Victor Cousin (*La Société Française au XVIIe Siècle d'après Le Grand Cyrus de Mlle de Scudéry* [1858]) explicates the allegory at length, using a near contemporary "key." Cyrus, the principal character of the romance, is to be identified with Prince Condé.

her abdication (and especially after her murder of one of her followers in 1657) turned into hostility. Dryden alludes in his preface to her fame. She was, in fact, so well known, the subject of so many pamphlets and books in the major European languages including English, that we may assume Dryden and his audience would have known the major events in her career. Her reputation had become tarnished indeed in the interval between the publication of the *Cyrus* and the performance of *Secret Love,* but Dryden nevertheless follows Scudéry's idealized portrait of her.

Dryden's borrowings for his serious plot are obvious; those for his comic plot are much less so. For the comic plot he took suggestions from many authors and elaborated them with the inventiveness of genius. It is worse than futile to try to identify his sources precisely except for a few passages of dialogue in which he followed some previous author closely. Apart from his borrowings in these passages, we can at best hope to describe the literary background against which he worked.

The most remarkable achievement of the comic plot, as indeed of the play, is the characterization of the gay couple, Celadon and Florimell; as already suggested, that characterization may bear the impress of the personalities of Charles Hart and Nell Gwyn, who first acted the roles. Yet even in 1667 the gay couple had important literary ancestors. Celadon and Florimell, in their linguistic virtuosity and their attitudes toward each other, toward love, and toward matrimony, belong to a literary tradition.[38] They could in fact be considered the most influential members of the tradition, for they represent the first instance after the Restoration of the assimilation of elements from a variety of literary sources, non-dramatic as well as dramatic, into characters who in artistic maturity exemplify the attitudes and the wit subsequently shown by many couples of Restoration comedy. They were to have a numerous progeny, of whom Congreve's Mirabel and Millamant are the most distinguished.[39]

Even in his first comedy, *The Wild Gallant,* Dryden had experimented with such characters.[40] The title character of that play, Loveby, is a more boisterous rendering of the gay lover than the later Celadon. Already in love with Constance when the play begins, he courts her in what becomes a contest of wits, an uneven one since she has an able second in her cousin Isabelle, and the result is comic dialogue in the vein of *Secret Love*—as when early in the second act the young women interrogate Loveby concerning his pretended estate. Already there is a well-developed theme of anti-Platonic sex antagonism. The pattern of the gay couple is not yet fully established (among other reasons, the cousin Isabelle rather than Constance is the more witty and aggressive conversationalist); yet the nature if not the quality of the comic dialogue approximates that in the later play.

---

[38] Smith (*The Gay Couple*) provides a comprehensive account of the establishment and development of this tradition.

[39] Kathleen Lynch, ed., Congreve's *The Way of the World* (1965), pp. xiv–xv, describes the evolution of the gay couple from Dryden to Congreve.

[40] *Works,* VIII, 238–239.

In the interval between the first performances of *The Wild Gallant* and *Secret Love,* Sir George Etherege's *The Comical Revenge* appeared (March 1664), and in it too are anticipations of Celadon and Florimell's banter. So popular was Etherege's play [41] that we may assume Dryden knew it and that indeed he had it in mind when he wrote Neander's remarks in *Of Dramatick Poesie* on the English invention of tragicomedy.[42] His departures in *Secret Love* from his own earlier comedies *The Wild Gallant* and *The Rival Ladies* (a tragicomedy but in the different form in which potentially tragic action is brought to a happy conclusion) [43] may owe something to the structure of *The Comical Revenge,* in which also there is an alternation of scenes in verse portraying love in a noble mood and comic scenes in prose portraying love of a more fleshly kind. Yet he achieved a thematic relationship between the serious and the comic in *Secret Love* unlike anything in *The Comical Revenge,* which has not two but four plots and groups of characters.[44]

Dryden and Etherege were the two most able dramatists experimenting in those early years of the Restoration with comedy of gay sex antagonism, but others were doing the same thing less skillfully. As early as 1663 James Howard, one of Dryden's brothers-in-law, had written a comedy, *The English Monsieur,*[45] which includes a fully developed duel of wits between reluctant lovers, Welbred and Lady Wealthy, the latter a widow possessing wit as well as wealth and determination not to be won easily. However maladroit James Howard may have been, his play merits at least passing attention because it incorporates important aspects of the emerging tradition of Restoration comedy: notably, the distinctive attitude toward love and the preoccupation with social affectation which we see fully developed in, say, Etherege's *The Man of Mode.* The play was produced four years before *Secret Love;* James Howard's *All Mistaken; or The Mad Couple* was produced some seven months later than Dryden's play, in September 1667, and it too includes a gay couple, Philidor and Mirida, so close indeed to Celadon and Florimell in conception that they would seem to be imitations of them.[46] Still another such couple, in this instance

---

[41] Downes (p. 25) wrote that this play "got the Company more Reputation and Profit than any preceding Comedy."

[42] 1668, pp. 38–39; Ker, I, 69–70. Cf. Allen, pp. 78–80.

[43] *Works,* VIII, 265–267.

[44] Cf. Dale Underwood, *Etherege and the Seventeenth-Century Comedy of Manners* (1957), p. 44.

[45] The comedy was not printed until 1674, but it was apparently seen by traveling Dutch students in July 1663 (Ethel Seaton, *Literary Relations of England and Scandinavia in the Seventeenth Century* [1935], p. 337).

[46] Philidor and Mirida execute a mock legal proviso ensuring their mutual rights to inconstancy (II) which closely resembles the proviso of Celadon and Florimell. One item in Howard's proviso (Mirida: "Thou shalt drown'd thy self when Thou wilt, or hang thy self when thou Wilt, or go to the Devil when thou wilt") apparently echoes a passage in *Secret Love,* not in the proviso scene but earlier (Florimell: "I would have a Lover, that if need be, should hang himself, drown himself, break his neck, or poyson himself for very despair . . ." [II, i]).

Colonel Boldman and the Lady Pleasant, appeared in *The Humorous Lovers* by William Cavendish, Duke of Newcastle (soon to be Dryden's collaborator in writing *Sir Martin Mar-all*), acted by the Duke's Company at about the time that *Secret Love* was acted by the King's. By 1667, it will be apparent, the banter of reluctant lovers had become a commonplace of comedy.[47]

Even in Renaissance drama there are notable instances of verbal duels between witty lovers who are attracted to each other but who are nevertheless, sometimes on one side and sometimes on both, reluctant to submit to the restrictions imposed by matrimony. Shakespeare repeatedly provides glimpses of the sex antagonism that accompanies courtship, and in at least two comedies, *Love's Labour's Lost* and *Much Ado About Nothing*, explores it at length in witty repartee. Berowne and Rosaline of the former play and Benedick and Beatrice of the latter have in fact the combination of conversational pugnacity and emotional ambivalence toward matrimony which we associate with the Restoration gay couple. Love is a game that all are playing in *Love's Labour's Lost,* and the antagonism between the sexes is resolved in something approximating a formal proviso when the ladies enunciate the conditions under which they will receive their suitors—after the lapse of a year (the term of probation that Florimell initially establishes for Celadon). In Fletcher's comedies too there are reluctant lovers—Mirabel the "wild goose," for example, of *The Wild Goose Chase*—wit duels, and at least one proviso: that between Leon and Margarita of *Rule a Wife and Have a Wife* (II, iii).[48] The example of Fletcher more than that of Shakespeare seems to have been in Dryden's mind as he fashioned the exchanges between Celadon and Florimell, as would appear from Neander's admiring reference in *Of Dramatick Poesie* to Fletcher's comic dialogue, the "chase of wit" carried on by his characters.[49] Beaumont and Fletcher, said Neander, "understood and imitated the conversation of Gentlemen much better [than Shakespeare]; whose wilde debaucheries, and quickness of wit in reparties, no Poet can ever paint as they have done." [50] If we are to look for precedents in earlier seventeenth-century drama for Dryden's comic vein, we find our

James R. Sutherland ("The Date of James Howard's 'All Mistaken, or The Mad Couple,'" *Notes & Queries*, CCIX [1964], 339–340) has suggested the possibility that *All Mistaken* may be the earlier play, and thus Celadon and Florimell may derive from Philidor and Mirida. The present editors do not agree; in the instance cited above of close verbal similarity between the two plays, Dryden, but not Howard, is borrowing from the *Cyrus* (cf. below, pp. 344, 347).

[47] Shadwell's complaint in the preface to *The Sullen Lovers* (dedication dated 1 September 1668) about the chief characters of current comedy would suggest that the banter of the gay couple was a recognized convention: ". . . in the *Playes* which have been wrote of late, there is no such thing as perfect Character, but the two chief persons are most commonly a Swearing, Drinking, Whoring, Ruffian for a Lover, and an impudent ill-bred *tomrig* for a Mistress, and these are the fine people of the *Play*."

[48] Kathleen M. Lynch, "D'Urfé's *L'Astrée* and the 'Proviso' Scenes in Dryden's Comedy," *PQ*, IV (1925), 302.

[49] 1668, p. 41; Ker, I, 72.   [50] 1668, p. 48; Ker, I, 81.

most convincing ones in the comedies that Fletcher wrote alone or in collaboration with Beaumont.[51] It has been well suggested that the theory of
comedy which finds expression in *Secret Love* represents Dryden's adaptation of Jonson's theory of humours (to which he alludes in his prologue) to
comedy of fashionable life enlivened by witty dialogue in the manner of
Fletcher.[52] Thus we could interpret Celadon and Florimell as male and
female versions of a single humour, that of the inconstant, and their sustained banter as modeled on that in Fletcher's plays.[53]

For the famous "proviso" between Celadon and Florimell, however,
Dryden had a specific source: the marriage articles between a pair of anti-
Platonic lovers, Hylas and Stelle, in Honoré D'Urfé's famous pastoral
romance, *L'Astrée*,[54] published originally in parts between 1602 and 1627
and in English translation in 1657 and 1658.[55] Hylas and Stelle, like their
counterparts in Dryden's play, are intolerant of courtly conventions of
lovemaking and fearful too of an emotional disillusionment in the stifling
bonds of matrimony. Most candidly they set down in pseudolegal terminology, employing a fellow shepherd as a scribe, twelve conditions to
which they mutually agree as a preliminary to marriage. The first four
of them (in the English translation Dryden probably used) will suggest at
once their tenor and their resemblance to Dryden's proviso:

> *That the one shall not usurp over the other, that*
> *soveraigne authority which may truly be called Tyranny.*
> *That both of us shall be at one and the same time,*
> *both the lover and the loved.*
> *That our affection shall be eternally without con-*
> *straint.*
> *That we shall love one another as long as we please.*[56]

As Kathleen Lynch points out, this contract agrees with that in *Secret
Love* in its "essential regulations (1) prohibiting jealousy, (2) sanctioning
inconstancy, (3) safe-guarding liberty of speech and action, and (4) abol-
ishing terms of endearment. . . ."[57] In substance then, as well as in
tone and mock legal form, Dryden's proviso follows D'Urfé's,[58] a circum-

---

[51] Arthur Colby Sprague, *Beaumont and Fletcher on the Restoration Stage*
(1926), and John Harold Wilson, *The Influence of Beaumont and Fletcher on
Restoration Drama* (1928), describe the high popularity of their plays in Dryden's
time. In the first three or four years of the Restoration, at least twenty-one of
the plays were presented (Sprague, p. 24; Wilson [p. 8] puts the figure even
higher).

[52] Moore, *The Nobler Pleasure*, ch. iii.   [53] *Ibid.*

[54] Lynch, *PQ*, IV (1925), 302–308.

[55] Inconclusive evidence suggests that Dryden himself may have written the
prefaces for the three volumes of the English translation (James M. Osborn,
John Dryden: Some Biographical Facts and Problems [1940], pp. 168–180).

[56] Honoré D'Urfé, *Astrea* (1657), Vol. II, Pt. 3, Bk. I, pp. 193–194.

[57] Lynch, *PQ*, IV (1925), 307.

[58] Allen (pp. 93–94) suggests that Dryden may have borrowed from D'Urfé by
way of some unidentified French intermediary. He points out that Dryden's
proviso contains no *verbal* echoes of D'Urfé's.

stance emphasizing yet again the formative influence of the French romances on the play.

The *précieuse* code of love embodied in *L'Astrée,* against which Hylas and Stelle protest in their articles of marriage, appears also in Madeleine de Scudéry's *Cyrus,* and in modified form in a number of French and English plays, some of which include borrowings from D'Urfé. A character in Thomas Corneille's *L'Amour à la Mode* (printed in 1651), for example, is based on the anti-Platonic Hylas,[59] a literary relationship that assumes a relevance to *Secret Love* because Dryden had read the French play and in fact describes it in some detail in *Of Dramatick Poesie.*[60] From French dramatists as well as from English ones, including Fletcher who also borrowed from D'Urfé,[61] Dryden could have drawn hints for the distinctive conception of love, which has some resemblance to the *précieuse* code, against which Celadon and Florimell are so gaily in rebellion.

For some details of this couple's banter as for other characters and situations in the comic plot, Dryden borrowed from Madeleine de Scudéry, as Langbaine noted (with his customary oversimplification): "The Characters of *Celadon, Florimel, Olinda,* and *Sabina,* are borrow'd from the Story of *Pisistrates* and *Cerintha* in the *Grand Cyrus,* Part 9. Book 3. and from the Story of the *French Marquess* in *Ibrahim,* Part 2. Book 1." [62] Dryden took details of Celadon's and Florimell's banter—for example, that about a lover's proving his devotion by killing himself in a variety of ways (II, i)— from passages of banter between Pisistrate and Cerinthe in the *Cyrus;* [63] and he took the idea of having Celadon simultaneously in love with both Sabina and Olinda from *Ibrahim.*[64] The borrowing from the latter work is most obvious perhaps in the first scene of the fourth act: in the resemblance of Melissa's interrogation in turn of her two daughters about Celadon to an episode in which a brother (Marsé) interrogates in turn his four sisters about their love for a gallant marquis.[65] Yet if Dryden's gay couple borrow from the conversation of others who came before them, we may nevertheless assume that the primary source of their sprightliness and charm is Dryden's imagination.

PREFACE

115:19 *regular, according to the strictest of Dramatick Laws.* See above, pp. 333–336, for discussion of the play's conformity to neoclassical precepts.

115:25–26 *whether an Author may be allowed as a competent judg of his own works.* Samuel Johnson praised Dryden's conclusions on this subject (*Lives of the English Poets,* ed. George Birkbeck Hill [1905], I, 340).

---

[59] Lynch, *PQ,* IV (1925), 304.   [60] 1668, pp. 44–45; Ker, I, 76–77.
[61] In *Monsieur Thomas* and *Valentinian* (*Cambridge Bibliography of English Literature,* I, 334).
[62] P. 170.   [63] Allen, pp. 82 ff.   [64] *Ibid.,* pp. 86 ff.
[65] *Ibrahim,* trans. Henry Cogan (1674), pp. 97–98.

115:32–116:1 *judgment . . . Fancy.* Dryden had made a similar distinction between these two faculties in his dedicatory epistle to the Earl of Orrery prefixed to *The Rival Ladies* (*Works*, VIII, 95): "This worthless Present was design'd you, long before it was a Play; When it was only a confus'd Mass of Thoughts, tumbling over one another in the Dark: When the Fancy was yet in its first Work, moving the Sleeping Images of things towards the Light, there to be Distinguish'd, and then either chosen or rejected by the Judgment. . . ."

117:34–35 *story in the Cyrus, which he calls the Queen of Corinth.* For discussion of the source of the serious plot in Madeleine de Scudéry's *Le Grand Cyrus*, see above, p. 338.

PROLOGUE

Like the preface, the prologue reflects Dryden's pride in the neoclassical regularity of the play. Unlike most of his prologues and epilogues (which are rhymed in couplets), this one is in its first eighteen lines rhymed in triplets, a pattern Dryden used also in the epilogue to *The Tempest*, the prologue to *The Kind Keeper*, and the *Prologue to the King and Queen at the Opening of their Theatre* (1682) (Mark Van Doren, *John Dryden: A Study of his Poetry* [1946], p. 133).

10–12 *Plays are like, Towns . . . Defendant unespy'd.* As Langbaine pointed out (p. 169), the metaphor in this stanza is borrowed from the last paragraph of the preface to Madeleine de Scudéry's *Ibrahim. The Rehearsal* (I, i) includes a satirical allusion to this stanza as an example of Dryden's "transversion"—that is, turning borrowed prose into verse.

SECOND PROLOGUE

Sharply different in tone from the first prologue, this second one is remarkable for its pugnacious attack on the critics in the audience. Dryden was perhaps encouraged to take the offensive against them by his confidence in the merit of the play, which he knew to be both lively and "correct" (cf. James Sutherland, "Prologues, Epilogues and Audience in the Restoration Theatre," in John Butt, ed., *Of Books and Humankind: Essays and Poems Presented to Bonamy Dobrée* [1964], pp. 41–42).

45 *Judgment.* Critic. Cf. Dryden's epilogue to *An Evening's Love*, l. 3: "First, looking for a Judgement or a Wit."

PROLOGUE SPOKEN BY MRS. BOUTELL

This prologue and the *Epilogue Spoken by Mrs. Reeves* (pp. 202–203, above) were first printed anonymously in *Covent Garden Drollery* in 1672. Scott reprinted them and they have remained in the Dryden canon ever since. G. Thorn-Drury (*Covent Garden Drollery* [1928], p. 113) first called attention to a seventeenth-century manuscript version (see Textual Notes, p. 421) where they are ascribed to Dryden.

Secret Love was performed by the women in the summer of 1672, possibly as early as June (cf. Van Lennep, p. 195), more probably after 4 July (cf. Epilogue, l. 30n). Whatever the precise date, the play was acted while the King's Company was using the inadequate theater in Lincoln's Inn Fields (cf. *Works,* I, 345–347). The company had taken refuge there after a fire on the preceding 25th of January destroyed their old playhouse as well as their costumes. They were to continue in Lincoln's Inn Fields until March 1674.

The competition of the Duke's Company in their splendid new theater in Dorset Garden was difficult to meet. One expedient, apparently, was to mount productions acted entirely by women. The records suggest that Elizabeth Boutell was both fetching and successful in "breeches parts" (cf. Wilson, p. 76).

9 *sweet.* "Something that affords enjoyment or gratifies desire" (*OED*).

I, ii

9 *a Hundred Mistresses.* Dryden comments on this extravagance in his preface to *An Evening's Love* (1671, sig. B2v; Ker, I, 142): "In the *Silent Woman, Dauphine,* (who with the other two Gentlemen, is of the same Character with my *Celadon* in the *Maiden Queen,* and with *Wildblood* in this) professes himself in love with all the Collegiate Ladies. . . ."

16 *humour.* The allusion in the prologue to "Johnsons *humour*" would suggest that the word is here used in the Jonsonian sense.

48 *Such an Ovall face.* The portraits of Nell Gwyn suggest that this description of Florimell is an accurate description of the actress herself (cf. Wilson, p. 100).

58 *out-mouth.* Protruding mouth.

59 *blub.* Protrusion.

74 *Maudlin.* "A penitent resembling Mary Magdalen" (*OED*).

I, iii

36–37 *And largely soul'd . . . Indies.* And as generous as if she could create new Indies.

81 *Propriety.* Property.

165 *A Catalogue of such persons.* Presumably Philocles has drawn up a catalogue of appropriate husbands for the queen.

207 *Lymbecks.* Limbics, or alembics, were used by chemists and alchemists in distillation. Cf. *Annus Mirabilis,* ll. 49–52:

> He, first, survey'd the charge with careful eyes,
> Which none but mighty Monarchs could maintain;
> Yet judg'd, like vapours that from Limbecks rise,
> It would in richer showers descend again.

II, i

1 *Nothing thrives that I have plotted.* In depicting the efforts made by the queen and her confidante to frustrate Philocles' courtship of

Candiope, Dryden follows closely the story of Queen Cleobuline in Scudéry's *Cyrus* (Tome VII, Livre ii).

47 *coming.* "Inclined to make or meet advances" (*OED*).

65–66 *I would have a Lover . . . should hang himself.* Dryden follows closely the story of Pisistrate and Cerinthe in Scudéry's *Cyrus* (Tome IX, Livre iii). Cf. the following from the English translation by F. G. (1655; Vol. V, Pt. IX, p. 138): "Do not think Sir, said she [Cerinthe] being excellent at Rallary, that when I say I long to see a Lover, I mean such Lovers as say they are in Love, but are not, for I have no desire to see such a one: But on the contrary, I mean such a Lover as is able to do all that the most violent passion in the world can make one do: What do you mean Madam, said he? I mean, said she, that he should (if occasion present it self) kill himself, throw himself down a precipice, and poyson himself for very dispair. But Madam, replied *Pisistrates,* I pray tell me which one of these three testimonies of Love would you have a man give you, if you should make him in Love? For, said he and laughed, a man cannot kill himself, throw himself down a Precipice, and poyson himself all at once."

81 *Rabbet.* A reference to the proverb "He is like a Rabbit, fat and lean in twenty-four hours" (Tilly, R2).

86 *forecast.* "Forethought; prudence" (*OED*).

92 *That's much as your pillow is laid before you go to sleep.* Perhaps a proverb, though it has not been traced.

167–168 *Ah, Madam, could you give my doom so quickly / And knew it was irrevocable.* Saintsbury: "This is a little obscure; 'and knew' probably = 'when you knew.'"

239 *The workmanship of inconsiderate favour.* This speech of Asteria's is reminiscent in several details of the exchange between Gloucester and Edmund in *King Lear,* I, ii, 112–145. Cf. the allusions in both passages to ingratitude, "rash love," heavenly portents, and fear of disasters.

272 *The Sybills leaves.* Summers refers to the *Aeneid,* III, 443–452. The leaves on which the Sybil has written her prophecies are scattered by the wind.

286 *High trees are shook, because they dare the winds.* Proverbial. Tilley (C208) cites Davenant's *The Cruel Brother* (1630): "The Shrub Securely grows. The tallest tree stands Most in the wind."

III, i

13–15 *as, when it thunders . . . are then abroad.* Cf. *Annus Mirabilis,* ll. 91–92:

> So reverently men quit the open air
>   When thunder speaks the angry Gods abroad.

The similarity between the two passages provides a reminder that the poem and the play were written at about the same time.

22 *scarce half an hour ago.* Cf. II, i, 224. An allusion to the pretended interval of time between the second and third acts.

36 *Acts of Oblivion.* Presumably a reference to Charles II's Act of Oblivion. Cf. David Ogg, *England in the Reign of Charles II* (1934), I, 154–155:

"The Bill of Indemnity received the royal assent on August 29, 1660. It bestowed a general pardon for all treasons, felonies, and numerous other offences committed since January 1, 1637, by any 'colour of command' from the late king Charles, or from the present king, or by any pretended authority derived from either or both Houses. All acts of hostility between king and parliament were to be consigned to perpetual oblivion."

55–58 *So the dull Beasts . . . their soveraign Lord.* Although the passage is suggestive of *Paradise Lost,* which was published later in the same year that *Secret Love* was first acted, there is no reason to assume that either work influenced the other. In Milton there are no beasts at all "dull," but rather frolic to entertain Adam and Eve (IV, 340–347).

141 *knots of sky.* Bows of sky-blue ribbon.

228 *Th'ensuing hour my plighted vows shall be.* My vows shall be plighted [in] the ensuing hour.

276–278 *an Hawk that will not plume . . . truss'd his quarry.* Saintsbury: "In falconry the hawk 'trusses' the quarry, in securing it and carrying it off, 'plumes' or 'deplumes' it by tearing out the feathers."

321 *noise.* "A company or band of musicians" (*OED*).

328 *watch me as they do Witches.* A reference to a test for witchcraft: the suspected woman was watched for twenty-four hours while she was tied in some uncomfortable position (Summers).

331 *in case.* Prepared; ready.

363 *Glass Coach.* Coach with glass windows. Cf. Ogg, *England in the Reign of Charles II,* I, 67: "Glass works were established near London, and in Restoration England the glass window was to be found . . . in the 'gilt coaches' of the rich."

373 *plays booty.* "*To play booty:* To join with confederates in order to 'spoil' or victimize another player" (*OED*).

399 *Sultana Queen.* "The favourite concubine of a sultan; hence, a favourite mistress" (*OED,* which cites this line from *Secret Love* as the first example of this usage).

417 *fidg.* Cf. *The Wild Gallant,* IV, i, 151 (*Works,* VIII, 59): "How Loveby fidges up and down."

IV, i

7 *Well, I'le examine 'em apart.* In the interrogation scene Dryden borrows from Scudéry's *Ibrahim,* trans. Henry Cogan (1674), pp. 97–98 (cf. Allen, pp. 86–92).

13–15 *Why I think . . . I to him.* Cf. *Ibrahim,* p. 98: "She replyes laughing, that the obligation which she had unto him for having taught her so many excellent airs, for having taken such pains to make her sing well, and to tune her Lute to her voice, deserved that her answer should be favourable to him."

17–19 *Can you doubt it? . . . each others counterpart.* Cf. *Ibrahim,* p. 98: "Can you doubt of it, said she? and see you not that the conformity which is between us must needs produce a fair affection? He is merry, I am not melancholick; he understands musick, and I can sing; he plays on the

Lute, and so do I; he daunces admirably, and I do not dance with an ill grace; in conclusion, there is a kind of I know not what invisible thing, called, as I think, Sympathy, which makes us that we cannot hate one another."

41 *that's once*. Once for all. *OED* cites this line as the last example of the usage.

76 *Fifth-rate*. A nautical metaphor, referring to the classification of naval vessels according to size or strength. Ships of the British navy were divided into six rates.

77 *a Dutch built bottom: she's so tall*. Cf. *Annus Mirabilis*, ll. 233–236:
On high-rais'd Decks the haughty *Belgians* ride,
Beneath whose shade our humble Fregats go:
Such port the Elephant bears, and so defi'd
By the *Rhinocero's* her unequal foe.

86 *Pygmalion's Image*. Cf. Ovid, *Metamorphoses*, X, 243–297.

105 *pumpt for a lye*. I.e., had to strain to invent a lie.

120–121 *not that I care this, —— but onely to be satisfied*. Perhaps phrases from a popular song.

131–132 *the faith of a Stock, or of a Stone*. "Stock: . . . Applied contemptuously to an idol or a sacred image. Chiefly in the phrase *stocks and stones* = 'gods of wood and stone'" (*OED*).

133 *I love upon the square*. Cf. *Sir Martin Mar-all*, I, i, 167–168 (see above, p. 215): "scarce one Woman in an hundred will play with you upon the Square."

147 *'Tis Strephon calls; what would my love?* Perhaps an impromptu parody of a song.

155 *cry me anon, and tell my marks*. As a town crier gives notice of a strayed animal that can be claimed upon proper identification of it by its owner.

164–165 *thou art so tall, I think I shall never affront thee*. A pun on the literal meaning of "affront."

173 *busk*. Scott: "The now almost forgotten *busk* was a small slip of steel or wood, used to stiffen the stays. Florimel threatens to employ it as a rod of chastisement."

262 *Syracuse*. One of the few reminders that *Secret Love* has a setting in the Sicily of antiquity.

276 *mayn*. "In the game of hazard, a number (from five to nine inclusive) called by the 'caster' before the dice are thrown" (*OED*). Cf. Dorset's "Song: Written at Sea, in the First Dutch War, 1665, The Night before an Engagement" (ll. 43–44):
To pass our tedious Hours away,
We throw a merry Main.

317–319 *Int'rest makes all . . . to reform a State*. For the political implications of this passage, see above, pp. 338–339.

336 *shot the gulf*. A common figurative phrase for accomplishing a decisive act.

338–339 *The damn'd in Hell . . . with hopeless eyes*. For discussion of this theological commonplace, see John M. Steadman, "Milton and Wolleb

Again (*Paradise Lost*, I, 54–55, 777)," *Harvard Theological Review*, LIII (1960), 155–156.

IV, ii

The Queens appartments. A break in *liaison des scènes,* inconsistent with the boast in the prologue of *"Scenes unbroken."*

23–38 *I feed a flame . . . mounting no higher.* Day, p. 143: "This exquisite song never attained great popularity, and the music would appear to be irrevocably lost."

V, i

7 *Save you Monsieur Florimell.* Cf. Portia's boast in *The Merchant of Venice* of how well she will imitate a man (III, iv, 60–78). Pepys wrote (2 March 1667), with reference to this scene, that Nell Gwyn had "the motions and carriage of a spark the most that ever I saw any man have."

9 *the little Comb.* Cf. Newcastle, *The Humorous Lovers*, Lincoln's Inn Fields, March 1667 (I, i): "Prithee, what Airy Coxcomb's this? he prates, and combs his Perriwig so briskly."

10–11 *courant slurr.* Summers: "The fashionable courant or coranto was a dance characterized by a gliding step as distinguished from a leaping step."

74+ *s.d. Dance.* Pepys (7 March 1667): "Thence to the Duke's playhouse . . . and saw 'The English Princesse, or Richard the Third;' a most sad, melancholy play, and pretty good; but nothing eminent in it, as some tragedys are; only little Mis. Davis did dance a jig after the end of the play, and there telling the next day's play; so that it come in by force only to please the company to see her dance in boy's clothes; and, the truth is, there is no comparison between Nell's dancing the other day at the King's house in boy's clothes and this, this being infinitely beyond the other."

90–91 *so the Willows . . . rob 'em of.* The metaphor alludes to the willow as a symbol of grief for unrequited love.

107–108 *come aloft.* "To have an erection" (Partridge, *Dictionary of Slang*).

113 *Tiffany.* "A kind of thin transparent silk" (*OED*).

172 *truck.* "To barter away (what should be sacred or precious) *for* something unworthy" (*OED*).

220 *Letters of Reprize.* The metaphor alludes to royal authorizations for naval reprisals against acts of piracy.

500 *shall I marry Flavia?* Kathleen M. Lynch writes ("D'Urfé's *L'Astrée* and the 'Proviso' Scenes in Dryden's Comedy," *PQ*, IV [1925], 304): "The 'proviso' scenes in *L'Astrée* and in *Secret Love* are similarly prefaced. In *L'Astrée* Hylas, debating with Silvandre in an assemblage of shepherds, repudiates other attractive shepherdesses before acknowledging his preference for Stelle and making his covenant with her."

514–562 *Some foolish people . . . but not so good, Florimell.* For discussion of this famous scene, see above, pp. 343–344.

EPILOGUE SPOKEN BY MRS. REEVES

Gossip had it that Anne Reeves, an actress of small achievement, was Dryden's mistress.

4 *cock.* "To play the 'cock,' behave boastfully or defiantly; to swagger, strut. . . ." Also, quoting Johnson, "to set up the hat with an air of petulance and pertness" (*OED*).

26–27 Thorn-Drury (*Covent Garden Drollery*, pp. 114–115) notes that these lines suggest negotiations regarding the joining of the two companies some ten years before the union took place.

30 *Mamamouchi.* A reference to Ravenscroft's play, *The Citizen Turn'd Gentleman,* which began a successful run at Dorset Garden on 4 July 1672 (Macdonald, p. 197). The play is an adaptation of Molière's *Bourgeois Gentilhomme,* in which M. Jourdain is gulled into thinking that the son of the Grand Turk confers upon him the exalted title of *Mamamouchi.* Dryden attacked Ravenscroft's Mamamouchi episode in the prologue to *The Assignation* a few months later (*Works,* XI).

Sir Martin Mar-all

Since Pepys liked *Sir Martin Mar-all,* somewhat more information about its early stage history is available than about that of most Restoration plays. He went to Lincoln's Inn Fields to see it on 15 August 1667, the first recorded performance and probably the première; but arriving late he found the King and his retinue present and the theater full.[1] Hence it was not until 16 August that he was able to see it and record his delighted response:

> To the Duke's playhouse, where we saw the new play acted yesterday, "The Feign Innocence, or Sir Martin Marr-all;" a play made by my Lord Duke of Newcastle, but, as everybody says, corrected by Dryden. It is the most entire piece of mirth, a complete farce from one end to the other, that certainly ever was writ. I never laughed so in all my life. I laughed till my head [ached] all the evening and night with the laughing; and at very good wit therin, not fooling. The house full. . . .

Pepys went two other times during the play's initial run, on 19 August and 20 August, and frequently during the next several seasons, as he did on 22 May 1668, when he wrote that he thought he had seen it ten times, "yet the pleasure I have is yet as great as ever, and is undoubtedly the best comedy ever was wrote." After an initial run of at least five performances (15, 16, 19, 20, and 21 August), and probably several more,[2] the play was acted a total of some thirty times at Lincoln's Inn Fields and more than four times at court in the little more than four years until the Duke's Company, on 9 November 1671, moved into Dorset Garden, inaugurating the theater with a run of three more performances of the play.[3] According to Downes, it brought the company more money than any preceding comedy except Etherege's *Love in a Tub.*[4] It would appear from Cibber's *Apology* that the popularity of the comedy persisted until about 1690,[5] though the scarcity of theatrical records in the later seventeenth century allows us to list only a few specific performances after 1671: on 31 August 1672, 21 October 1673, 21 and 22 January 1675, and, at court, 20 October 1686.[6] The more abundant theatrical records of the

---

[1] Pepys's phrasing would suggest that this was the first performance, and the fact that the King attended supports the assumption. This is the earliest performance of the play listed among the Lord Chamberlain's papers as having been attended by royalty (P.R.O., L.C. 5/139, p. 125 [cited in Nicoll, p. 346]).
[2] Van Lennep, p. 189. [3] Downes, p. 31. [4] Downes, p. 28.
[5] Cibber implies, in the appreciative description of Nokes in the role of Sir Martin (quoted below), that the play was still popular when his own career in the theater began in 1690.
[6] Van Lennep, *passim.*

eighteenth century reveal that the play was occasionally acted until 1728, when the company at Drury Lane last presented it on 22 April.[7]

The great initial success derived in part from the skill of the actor James Nokes, to whose special abilities Dryden had adapted the role of Sir Martin.[8] By good fortune we have a detailed account by Colley Cibber (whose career in the theater began just as the older actor's was ending) of the way in which he played the part, an account that goes far in explaining why the play had so considerable a success:

> When he debated any matter by himself, he would shut
> up his Mouth with a dumb studious Powt, and roll his
> full Eye into such a vacant Amazement, such a palpable
> Ignorance of what to think of it, that his silent Per-
> plexity (which would sometimes hold him several Min-
> utes) gave your Imagination as full Content as the most
> absurd thing he could say upon it. In the Character
> of Sir *Martin Marr-all,* who is always committing Blun-
> ders to the Prejudice of his own Interest, when he had
> brought himself to a Dilemma in his Affairs by vainly
> proceeding upon his own Head, and was afterwards
> afraid to look his governing Servant and Counsellor in
> the Face, what a copious and distressful Harangue have
> I seen him make with his Looks (while the House has
> been in one continued Roar for several Minutes) before
> he could prevail with his Courage to speak a Word to
> him! [9]

Downes too testified to Nokes's success in the role; [10] and so much later did Thomas Davies, who though he could not have known the actor personally would have known him from theatrical tradition. "This play," Davies wrote in the middle of the eighteenth century about *Sir Martin Mar-all,* "owed its Theatrical life to the excellent action of Nokes—for since his death I do not find it ever was revived." [11] Davies was mistaken in saying that it was not acted after the death of Nokes (in 1696); [12] but there seems no reason to question the essential truth of his assertion that the success of the play came in considerable measure from Nokes's performance.

The original cast also included Henry Harris as Warner, William Smith as Sir John Swallow, Young as Lord Dartmouth, Cave Underhill as Old Moody, Mrs. Norris as Lady Dupe, and Mary Davis as Millisent.[13] Of this group Underhill remained on the stage in 1690 when Cibber's career be-

[7] Emmett L. Avery, ed., *The London Stage, 1660–1800,* Pt. 2: 1700–1729 (1960), *passim.*

[8] Downes, p. 28.

[9] *An Apology for the Life of Mr. Colley Cibber,* ed. Robert W. Lowe (1889), I, 143–144.

[10] Downes, p. 28.

[11] Manuscript note in the handwriting of Davies on a blank sheet interleaved in a copy of Downes, now in the Huntington Library (HEH 32292, facing p. 28).

[12] Nicoll, p. 290n.   [13] Downes, p. 28.

gan, and again there is in the *Apology* an account of his style of acting—
not specifically in the role of Old Moody though its suitability to that
character is apparent:

> . . . his particular Excellence was in Characters that
> may be called Still-life, I mean the Stiff, the Heavy, and
> the Stupid; to these he gave the exactest and most expres-
> sive Colours, and in some of them look'd as if it were
> not in the Power of human Passions to alter a Feature
> of him. . . . His Face was full and long; from his Crown
> to the end of his Nose was the shorter half of it, so that
> the Disproportion of his lower Features, when soberly
> compos'd, with an unwandering Eye hanging over them,
> threw him into the most lumpish, moping Mortal that
> ever made Beholders merry! [14]

So appropriate would this style of acting be to the character of Moody,
the bluff old admirer of Elizabethan times, that we wonder if the Duke
of Newcastle and Dryden might not have had the actor in mind as they
prepared the play for the stage.[15] We know less about the special abilities and styles of the other actors and actresses but yet enough to believe
that they were well cast. Thus the prominent and popular Henry
Harris, accomplished as a stage lover,[16] was Warner. Mrs. Norris, who
specialized in elderly "humours" characters,[17] was Lady Dupe. Mary
Davis, the Millisent of the play, reputed to be the illegitimate daughter
of Dryden's father-in-law, the Earl of Berkshire,[18] was a young woman of
unusual charm—as we may be sure from the fact that less than a year
after she acted the role she became the mistress of Charles II.[19] Probably
she sang the song of "Blind Love" (V, i), and in the general merriment
accompanying "the Frolick of the Altitudes" (V, ii, 48 ff.) she sang and
danced with Priest,[20] who had a minor role, presumably that of the landlord of the inn.

Herringman entered *Sir Martin Mar-all* in the *Stationers' Register* on
24 June 1668,[21] as "A Comedy written by the Duke of Newe Castle," and
when later in the summer he published it, the title page bore neither
Newcastle's nor Dryden's name. Pepys had referred to the play the preceding year, in a passage already quoted, as "made by my Lord Duke of
Newcastle, but, as everybody says, corrected by Dryden." [22] Downes is
more specific (but, as will be argued below, he is wrong in important details): "Sir *Martin Marral*, The Duke of *New-Castle*, giving Mr. *Dryden* a
bare Translation of it, out of a Comedy of the Famous *French* Poet Mon-

---

[14] *Apology*, I, 154–155.
[15] Underhill survived until the time of Steele, who paid a tribute to him in
The Tatler, no. 22.
[16] Arthur H. Nethercot, *Sir William D'Avenant* (1938), pp. 350–351.
[17] Wilson, p. 174.   [18] Pepys, 14 January 1668.
[19] *Ibid.*; Downes, p. 24. Cf. Wilson, pp. 139–141.   [20] Downes, p. 28.
[21] The play was listed in the Term Catalogues for Michaelmas (November)
1668.
[22] 16 August 1667.

seur Moleiro: He Adapted the Part purposely for the Mouth of Mr. *Nokes,* and curiously Polishing the whole; . . ." [23] Not until 1691, fifteen years after Newcastle's death, did Dryden claim *Sir Martin Mar-all* by placing his name on the title page of a new edition and by including it in a published list of his plays.[24] Earlier, the play was not generally regarded as his literary property. Unlike his preceding four plays it was not produced by the King's Company with which he had close though not yet contractual relations,[25] but by the Duke's Company, led by Davenant, long a close friend of Newcastle's. This would suggest that the play was considered the Duke's, and such fragmentary evidence of early opinion on the subject as exists conveys a similar impression. When in 1671 Francis Kirkman printed a catalogue of published plays he listed *Sir Martin Mar-all* anonymously, although he placed Dryden's name by six of his plays.[26] And— a mere straw in the wind—when in 1672 Edward Ravenscroft expressed his hostility to Dryden in the prologue of his *The Citizen Turn'd Gentleman* by alluding scornfully to *The Conquest of Granada,* he referred in quite a different tone to *Sir Martin Mar-all,* perhaps because he did not regard it as Dryden's.[27] The earliest published attribution of the comedy to Dryden seems to be that of 1688 by Gerard Langbaine in *Momus Triumphans: Or, The Plagiaries of the English Stage,* in which it is listed without comment on the authorship under the entry for Dryden in the "Catalogue of Plays." [28] Three years later, in *An Account of the English Dramatick Poets,* Langbaine is more explicit: "This Play is generally ascrib'd to Mr. *Dryden,* tho' his Name be not affix'd to it." [29] He refrains from any mention of Newcastle's share in the play, though he could scarcely have been ignorant of it, presumably because he was accusing Dryden of plagiarism, and he would have regarded it as indecorous to associate a ducal author with that literary crime.

Unlike Dryden's contemporaries, most modern writers on the subject have emphasized his part in the play almost to the exclusion of the Duke's.[30] Yet if there is reason to assume that the radical superiority of

---

[23] P. 28.

[24] Advertisement prefixed to *King Arthur: Or, The British Worthy.*

[25] The formal agreement by which Dryden promised to provide the King's Company with three plays a year in exchange for a share of the company's profits was not made until 1668 (Ward, p. 57).

[26] *A True, perfect, and exact Catalogue of all the Comedies, Tragedies, Tragi-Comedies . . . that were ever yet Printed.*

[27] Macdonald, p. 197 and n.   [28] P. 7.   [29] P. 170.

[30] Cf. Henry T. E. Perry, *The First Duchess of Newcastle and Her Husband as Figures in Literary History* (1918), pp. 151–152; John Wilcox, *The Relation of Molière to Restoration Comedy* (1938), pp. 35–46; Douglas Grant, *Margaret the First: A Biography of Margaret Cavendish Duchess of Newcastle, 1623–1673* (1957), p. 226; Ward, p. 49. Frank Harper Moore (*The Nobler Pleasure* [1963], pp. 55–58), who made the important discovery that the "feigned innocence" subplot of *Sir Martin Mar-all* derives from Newcastle's *The Humorous Lovers,* would allow the Duke somewhat more: "I believe that Dryden deserves the credit for *Sir Martin* as a finished product, and that Newcastle was either directly or indirectly responsible for the raw material from which it was manufactured."

Sir Martin Mar-all to the Duke's unaided plays is owing to the genius of Dryden, there is also reason to assume that much of the comedy did indeed originate with Newcastle. The play reveals signs of revision, major ones occurring even after printing had begun; [31] and it reveals other signs of incomplete revision, as in the too abrupt announcement by Warner in the last act that he is a gentleman and hence an appropriate husband for Millisent. All this suggests that the play was completed in haste, without undergoing the kind of close and critical review that *Secret Love*, Dryden's preceding play, had received. We may surmise that Dryden had a limited time for his work of revision. What he added and how thoroughly he rewrote the material given to him cannot be determined with precision. Yet he did not rewrite it so thoroughly as to remove all evidence of the Duke's hand.

The circumstances of the collaboration by two men so different from each other in age and social position are obscure. How did Dryden become acquainted with the Duke, the old Cavalier general, seventy-four years old in 1667, who had been the governor of Charles II when he was a boy? Presumably Davenant, who had been on Newcastle's staff in 1642 as lieutenant general of ordnance and who had subsequently seen much of him when they were both in exile on the Continent, was the intermediary between the dramatist and the elderly Duke.[32] At any rate that same year Dryden collaborated with Davenant as well as Newcastle, joining him in writing an adaptation of *The Tempest*, produced, also by the Duke's Company at the theater in Lincoln's Inn Fields, in November 1667; and it would seem likely that the two collaborations were somehow related. When in 1671 Dryden dedicated *An Evening's Love* to the Duke (who survived until 1676 though Davenant died in 1668), he alluded to his patronage of Davenant, as also to his earlier patronage of Ben Jonson, taking an understandable pride in associating himself with those two earlier dramatists as a recipient of the Duke's favors. We may surmise that Davenant at about the beginning of 1667 introduced Dryden to Newcastle as a brilliantly successful dramatist who could help him prepare for the stage a comedy he had written, with liberal borrowings from the French.

Only one modern scholar, André de Mandach (*Molière et la Comédie de Moeurs en Angleterre* [1946], pp. 69–80), has assigned Newcastle primary responsibility for the comedy. If he overstates his case his arguments nevertheless suggest a new approach to the problem. Although he wrote before Moore's discovery of the source of the subplot in *The Humorous Lovers*, he demonstrated that *Sir Martin Mar-all* shares important characteristics with Newcastle's plays which are absent in Dryden's.

[31] Several of the original leaves were canceled (see Textual Notes, p. 433). A copy of the first quarto now in the Folger Shakespeare Library includes a page of dialogue (reprinted in Textual Notes, p. 436), occurring before the end of Act I, between Sir John Swallow and Old Moody; in the play as otherwise known, Old Moody does not appear until the third act. In several speeches of this canceled dialogue, indication of speaker is missing, a further sign of haste in preparation of copy.

[32] Ward, pp. 48–49.

Living quietly in the country after the Restoration, the Duke had turned again to the drama, in which he had been interested before the war, when he had written, or written part of, two plays, *The Country Captain* and *The Varietie*. The former and much the better of the two was the result of a collaboration with James Shirley;[33] the latter was probably Newcastle's unaided work. They were not printed until 1649, though according to a statement on the title page which they shared they had been "Lately presented by His Majesties Servants, at the Black-Fryers," presumably a short time before Parliament in 1642 closed the theaters.[34] After the Restoration *The Country Captain* was revived, in 1661, 1667, and 1668;[35] it was in fact acted by the King's Company in May 1667,[36] only three months before the other company first acted *Sir Martin Mar-all*. In March of that year Davenant's company had acted a new comedy by Newcastle, *The Humorous Lovers,* described by Pepys, who thought that Newcastle's wife had written it, as "the most silly thing that ever come upon a stage."[37] Overstatement, but the judgment had some basis. At any rate the Duke apparently wrote the play without professional assistance. Then came *Sir Martin Mar-all* and after it, in 1674, *The Triumphant Widow,* in which Thomas Shadwell had a major share.[38] Thus of the five surviving plays associated with Newcastle's name, only two, *The Varietie* and *The Humorous Lovers,* seem largely to have been written by him alone, without the aid of an experienced dramatist. It is therefore with reference to them that we should undertake an examination of *Sir Martin Mar-all* in attempting to form an estimate of Newcastle's probable contribution in the collaboration with Dryden.

Such an examination yields useful results. Both *The Varietie* and *The Humorous Lovers* are "humours" comedies in the Jonsonian sense, plays in which a slender thread of plot holds together an assortment of characters broadly drawn as embodiments of particular aberrations. In them as in Jonson the causal relationship between episodes is reduced to a minimum, and attention is focused on a succession of episodes in which characters exhibit their humours. Newcastle had been the patron of Ben Jonson,[39] and obviously he formed his conception of comedy on a close study of that great dramatist's plays. In them he would have found precedent for the broad tone of his own comedies, the matter-of-fact treatment of commonplace and occasionally sordid subjects, and the outspoken sexuality; and he would have found precedent too for his detailed rendering of the minutiae of English life. Thus when we encounter in *Sir Martin Mar-all* a strong Jonsonian strain, a much stronger and more obvious one

---

[33] Gerald Eades Bentley, *The Jacobean and Caroline Stage* (1956), III, 145–148.
[34] *Ibid.,* III, 145–151. [35] Grant, *Margaret the First,* p. 224.
[36] Van Lennep, p. 108. [37] 30 March 1667.
[38] A fragment of this comedy survives in the Duke's handwriting and has been printed: *A Pleasante & Merrye Humor off A Roge,* ed. Francis Needham (*Welbeck Miscellany No. 1,* 1933). Passages present in the fragment, which represent only a small fraction of the whole, have been revised and amplified but not substantially changed in the published play.
[39] Bentley, *Jacobean and Caroline Stage,* III, 143.

than in Dryden's *Secret Love,* first produced only a few months earlier, we
have reason to suspect the hand of Newcastle. Several of the major characters in *Sir Martin Mar-all* resemble Jonsonian humours: Sir Martin himself, Old Moody, and Lady Dupe. The tone and especially the frank sexuality of the subplot are much more in Jonson's and Newcastle's customary
manner than in Dryden's; and again the kind of literal exactitude in rendering the contemporary English scene is more in their manner than in
his (though something of it appears in his first play, *The Wild Gallant*).

Yet there is much more specific evidence of Newcastle's hand in *Sir
Martin Mar-all* than these qualities of the Jonsonian comedy which he so
much admired: the presence in it of characters who so closely resemble
others in his unaided plays as to seem to be reworkings of them. Thus
Old Moody has a close relationship to the character Manly in *The Varietie;* and Lady Dupe and Mrs. Christian have equally close relationships
to Mistresses Hood and Dameris of *The Humorous Lovers.* Certainly it is
much more probable that Newcastle would have drawn on his own earlier
comedies than that Dryden would have done so.

Moody, the father of Millisent, is described in the dramatis personae
as a "Swash-buckler," a term applied to persons who (as Scott put it) "retained the old blunt manners of Queen Elizabeth's time, when sword and
buckler were the common weapons." [40] The most obvious example of a
Jonsonian humour among the characters, he does not appear until the
third act and he does not contribute to the advancement of the action except in the passive sense that he is the parent whom Sir Martin and
Warner attempt to outwit; his dramatic function is largely that of ex-
hibiting his humour, his fondness for the manners of a long-passed age.
As Millisent explains in introducing her father to Sir Martin (III, i, 33–
34): "He is no man o'th' Town, but bred up in the old *Elizabeth* way of
plainness," and he promptly shows the accuracy of his daughter's characterization when he objects to Sir Martin's foppish use of Frenchified expressions. (It is perhaps relevant to recall that Newcastle, born in 1593,
would have remembered the reign of Queen Elizabeth.) Now Manly in
Newcastle's *The Varietie* has just such a fondness for the blunt manners of
the Queen's reign, and he too objects to Frenchified affectations. Wearing
an outmoded suit of clothes, described as "Leisters habit" because it was
copied from the clothes the Earl of Leicester wore in a portrait, he pays
his court in his own idiosyncratic way to Lady Beaufield, a widow (III, i):

> I am bold to present a sute to you, I confesse it was
> not made by a French Tailor, I can make a leg and kisse
> my hand too after the fashion of my cloaths, this serv'd
> in those honest dayes, when Knights were Gentlemen,
> and proper men tooke the walls of dwarfes. . . .

And a moment later he complains that "It was never a good time since
these cloaths went out of fashion," a sentiment in which Mr. Moody
could have heartily concurred. The characters are, then, variants of the
same humour, and since Dryden obviously had nothing to do with *The*

---

[40] S-S, III, 4.

Varietie it would seem reasonable to conclude that at least the conception for Moody, and probably his conversation in a preliminary version, came from Newcastle.

This fondness for old times appears also in the character of Mistress Hood, "An old School-mistris, and a match maker," in Newcastle's *The Humorous Lovers*, though her similarity to Mr. Moody in *Sir Martin Mar-all* is much less striking than her similarity to Lady Dupe. Her mother, Mistress Hood explains, was "a Waiting Gentlewoman of the Mother of the Maids in Queen *Elizabeth*'s time" (III, i), and she speaks nostalgically of the manners of that reign. But it is in her role of instructress to Mistress Dameris, "a young Countrey Gentlewoman," that she provides the clearest anticipation of a character in *Sir Martin Mar-all*, for she offers Dameris the same shrewd, unscrupulous, and frank advice on the most advantageous means to market her youthful beauty as Lady Dupe offers Mrs. Christian.[41] Here would seem to be the source of, or at least the origin of the conception for, the subplot of *Sir Martin Mar-all*. Mistresses Hood and Dameris undertake just such a calculated campaign to gain money from a wealthy man as do Lady Dupe and Mrs. Christian, though with the difference that since the victim in *The Humorous Lovers* is unmarried, the objective sought for and gained is matrimony rather than mere extortion. "You know, Madam, he's married," Mrs. Christian says about Lord Dartmouth as she and Lady Dupe make their plans (I, i, 52–53), "so that we cannot work upon that ground of Matrimony." The two plays, then, depict similar characters pursuing similar tactics except for the minor variations required as matrimony or extortion is the objective. Again, since Dryden had nothing to do with *The Humorous Lovers,* it is probable that the subplot of *Sir Martin Mar-all* came, at least in a preliminary draft, from Newcastle.

We have the more reason to think so because the calculating sexuality of the Lady Dupe–Mrs. Christian scenes sounds like the parallel scenes in *The Humorous Lovers.* Consider the similarities in tone as well as in detail between the advice given by Mistress Hood and by Lady Dupe.

> *Hood.* . . . give a careless look sometimes to put a man in doubt whether it be chance or kindness, and if you find him coming, then is your time, be coy, hold off, and if he press your hand seem to be angry, but give him good words again quickly, if he tread on your foot at dinner, or at cards, take no notice of it, but pull it away, and tread on his again, as if it were by chance. (III, i)
>
> *La. Dupe.* Why, Girl, hee'l make fierce Love to you, but you must not suffer him to ruffle you or steal a kiss: but you must weep and sigh, and say you'l tell me on't, and that you will not be us'd so; and play the innocent just like a Child, and seem ignorant of all. (I, i, 64–68)

---

[41] Moore (*The Nobler Pleasure,* pp. 57–58) notes this similarity between the two plays.

Dryden perhaps tightened the syntax and sharpened the phrases of the latter, but the substance must have come from Newcastle.

Still another detail of the play can on grounds of probability be assigned to Newcastle: the "Frolick of the Altitudes" (V, ii, 48 ff.), the episode in which Mr. Moody and Sir John Swallow are hoisted onto tall stools and before they can get down are deserted by the others. As Langbaine pointed out,[42] the episode is borrowed from a comedy by Schackerley Marmion, *A Fine Companion* (IV, i), printed in 1633 with the statement on the title page that it had been "Acted before the King and Queene at White-hall, And sundrie times with great applause at the private House in Salisbury Court, By the Prince his Servants." The best available evidence would suggest that the play was produced sometime between the beginning of 1632 and the middle of the following year,[43] a time when, though Dryden was an infant, Newcastle was already a prominent courtier. More specifically, he was in association with Ben Jonson,[44] of whose Tribe Marmion was himself a member.[45] Probably Newcastle knew Marmion and saw his play, and when much later he came to write his share of *Sir Martin Mar-all* he took over the farcical trick involving the high stools. Dryden could have found the episode in the published play, to be sure, but farcical episodes are not for the most part effective on the printed page, even assuming that he might have read the old and obscure comedy. There is no evidence of any performance of *A Fine Companion* on the Restoration stage [46] (beyond the survival of a copy of the 1633 quarto marked in seventeenth- or eighteenth-century handwriting as if for theatrical production),[47] though the fragmentary nature of the surviving records makes it impossible to say that there was no performance.

If probability would suggest Newcastle's responsibility for this detail, it would suggest Dryden's responsibility for another: the extended joke about the daughter of the vintner at the Rose Tavern in Cambridge (V, i, 289 ff.), a tavern Dryden must have known in his undergraduate days.[48] Some authentic bit of student merriment apparently lies back of the passage. Rose, the clever maidservant of the play, explains that "Old *Moody* . . . in his younger years, when he was a *Cambridge*-Scholar, made bold with a Towns-mans Daughter there, by whom he had a Bastard." And when it is agreed that Sir Martin should impersonate that bastard, who has long been in the East Indies, Rose tells him that his supposed mother "was *Dorothy*, Daughter to one *Draw-water* a Vintner at the *Rose*." Now Pepys, who had known Dryden at Cambridge,[49] wrote in

---

[42] P. 170.   [43] Bentley, *Jacobean and Caroline Stage*, IV, 742–743.

[44] *Ibid.*, III, 143.   [45] *Ibid.*, IV, 737–738.

[46] Van Lennep records no performance.

[47] W. W. Greg, *A Bibliography of the English Printed Drama to the Restoration* (1939–1959), II, 628.

[48] There were apparently two Rose taverns at Cambridge in Dryden's time: one in Rose Crescent and the other, the "Little Rose," on Trumpington Street almost opposite the garden of the Fellows of Peterhouse College (Royal Commission on Historical Monuments, England, *An Inventory of the Historical Monuments in the City of Cambridge* [1959], Pt. Two, pp. 330, 352).

[49] Cf. entry for 3 February 1664.

his diary on 8 October 1667, less than two months after the first performance of the play: "away to Cambridge, it being foul, rainy weather, and there did take up at the Rose, for the sake of Mrs. Dorothy Drawwater, the vintner's daughter, which is mentioned in the play of Sir Martin Marrall. Here we had a good chamber, and bespoke a good supper." [50] Presumably Dorothy was a young woman who had been prodigal of her favors when Dryden and Pepys were at Cambridge, and hence would have been an appropriate mother for the vacuous Sir Martin to claim. Whatever the true facts, we have reason to assume that the passage alludes to a Cambridge joke of the 1650's, and thus that it was original with Dryden.

Apart from the appearance of variations on characters and themes from earlier comedies by Newcastle, perhaps the strongest evidence of his hand in *Sir Martin Mar-all* is to be found in the impression of improvisation conveyed by the play, of unresolved difficulties in its construction. The impression is intensified when the play is contrasted with Dryden's *Secret Love*, first acted earlier in the same year. Dryden had written the tragicomedy, as already noted, at approximately the time that he wrote the first draft of his *Essay of Dramatick Poesie*, revealing in the play the same kind of respectful preoccupation with the neoclassical rules of drama which appears in the essay.[51] The first audiences commended the play for its regularity, we know from Pepys, and Dryden himself boasted in his prologue that he had followed *"Th' exactest Rules"*; indeed he had carefully observed the unities and, with a single exception, had maintained continuity of scenes. When against a background of this critical fastidiousness, we find that *Sir Martin Mar-all* flouts not only the precepts of seventeenth-century neoclassicism but also principles of dramatic construction having more general applicability, we have reason to suspect Newcastle's responsibility.

The most blatant instance of violation of the rules, and even of simple possibility, lies in the time scheme—or more accurately the double time scheme—of the play.[52] The main plot, taken up with Warner's series of frustrated stratagems to help Sir Martin win Millisent, would seem to require only a few hours of the day on which Millisent arrives in London with her father and Sir John; there is no particular indication of the passage of time as one episode follows hard on another. Yet the subplot of the "Feigned Innocence" would require at least several weeks. At the outset, as Lady Dupe and Mrs. Christian make their plans to entrap Lord Dartmouth, he has not yet enjoyed Mrs. Christian. Yet midway through the play she confides to Lady Dupe that she has become pregnant by him; and still later, some time after the lord makes his humiliating confession to Lady Dupe, he tells Warner that he has bought the young woman's maidenhead as often as the hardened procuresses of the town have passed off their stale wares for fresh virgins (IV, i, 211–216). All this would have required time, much more time than can be reconciled with the events of the main plot or with the doctrine of the

---

[50] Summers (II, 483) noted the relevance of the passage to Dryden's play.
[51] See above, pp. 333–336. [52] Moore, *The Nobler Pleasure*, p. 57.

unities. It is in fact a tribute to the liveliness of the separate episodes of the comedy that the incongruity is not more apparent and more damaging.

The doctrine of decorum in characterization is, to say the least, treated casually in *Sir Martin Mar-all*. Against the background of sensitive awareness in *Secret Love*, and indeed in most of Dryden's other plays, of social proprieties in characterization, there is in this comedy a blurring of considerations of social rank, unlike Dryden's usual practice though having some precedent in his apprentice work, *The Wild Gallant*.[53] The neoclassical assumption that a character's rank should correlate with the personal qualities he displays and the deference he is accorded by other characters is ignored in this play, in which the son of a peer is a dupe, a titled lady (presumably the wife of a knight) is a procuress, and two knights are fools. The characters live familiarly together, showing a minimum of concern for distinctions of rank. Even before Warner reveals that he is a distressed gentleman, he feels no reluctance in berating his foolish master in the most downright manner, and he enjoys the confidence of Lord Dartmouth on the intimate and embarrassing subject of his relations with Mrs. Christian. Warner's and Sir Martin's reversal of roles in the marriages that terminate the plot represents a curious departure from the usual social conservatism of Restoration comedy, even when allowance is made for the belated revelation of Warner's status as an impoverished gentleman. Conceptions of decorum in characterization which in their implications were both social and literary usually prevented departures from class relationships in matching couples at the end of comedies. Whatever liberties Dryden may have taken in depicting a lord as a fool in *The Wild Gallant*, he nevertheless followed class lines in pairing his couples off. Here, however, not only is an heiress married to a "gentleman" servingman but a knight is married to a lady's maid, and one who has no claim to quality except the considerable one of a ready and engaging wit.

Quite apart from considerations of neoclassical theory, aspects of *Sir Martin Mar-all* suggest inexperience or inexpertness in the author, notably the abundant use of asides and soliloquies for exposition. Characters interpret events or reflect upon them in asides, as when (II, ii, 206 ff.) Millisent in a whole series of them explains to the audience her otherwise inexplicable admiration for Sir Martin: she thinks his foolish behavior is calculated and not spontaneous. Repeatedly, in fact, Millisent uses asides to express her changing attitudes toward him, admiration for his supposed cleverness giving way to bewilderment and then to contempt. There is a similar reliance upon soliloquies to convey essential information to the audience. Warner opens the play with one of them, in which he characterizes his master and succinctly describes his own predicament. Such expository soliloquies recur several times. Thus Lady Dupe (at the beginning of III, ii) describes the success Mrs. Christian has had in bilking Lord

---

[53] Lord Nonsuch of that play is if anything treated with less respect than is Lord Dartmouth of this.

Dartmouth; and a little later (IV, i, 72–80, 107–113) Warner in rapid succession indulges in two such soliloquies, the first of self-congratulation as a stratagem seems to have succeeded and the second of complaint as he perceives that it has failed. The expository soliloquy (as distinguished from the reflective soliloquy in the manner of *Hamlet*) is at best a clumsy device, and the frequent employment of it would seem to suggest haste, carelessness, or inexperience. In any event Dryden used it only sparingly in his other plays, and, although there can be no certainty in the matter, the heavy use of it here would seem to suggest the inexpert hand of the Duke of Newcastle. (His holograph fragment of a comedy, *A Pleasante & Merrye Humor off A Roge*, begins with just such an expository soliloquy as does *Sir Martin Mar-all*.[54])

The casual handling of dramatic construction appears also in the absence of psychological realism in characters' responses to the events depicted. It requires a willing suspension of disbelief, to say the least, to believe that Millisent could ever have thought Sir Martin a witty man, and her delay in reaching the conclusion that he is an absolute fool is hard to reconcile with the evidence of intelligence she usually displays. Other characters, too, fail to follow normal human patterns of behavior. Sir John Swallow's reaction to the news of the supposed death of his father is callous even for a character in seventeenth-century comedy; the emotional implications of the reported death are ignored, and the event becomes the occasion for merely another display of Sir Martin's stupidity. Psychological probability is again strained in the rapidity of the realignments of affection, Millisent and Warner to each other rather than to Sir Martin and Rose, which make possible the denouement, though to object on naturalistic grounds to such realignments would be to ignore dramatic convention. Any conclusion must be tentative. We can merely say that there is less attention paid to psychological realism in *Sir Martin Mar-all* than is usual in Dryden's plays.

Barring the discovery of new manuscripts (such as Newcastle's worksheets for the play [55]), a detailed account of the nature of the collaboration is hardly possible. Yet there are reasons enough to assume that Newcastle was responsible for most of a preliminary draft of *Sir Martin Mar-all*: the use of materials from his earlier comedies, the borrowing from an obscure comedy presented at court when he was a young man, the departures from Dryden's customary dramatic practices. There remains one major reason for assuming that Dryden's share was substantial, aside from the fact that he ultimately put his name on the title page: the play's excellence. This is in part to be attributed to the French plays by Quinault and Molière from which it is adapted, but only in part. The success of *Sir Martin Mar-all* in the theater, the greatest success perhaps achieved by any of

---

[54] Cf. n. 38 above.

[55] A large number of Newcastle's manuscripts, including both notes for and fair copies of a variety of nondramatic and dramatic works, are preserved in the library of the University of Nottingham. A search of them has revealed nothing that can be associated with *Sir Martin Mar-all*.

Dryden's plays in his lifetime, provides evidence of an experienced and skillful hand. Dryden must at the least have given the play a thorough revision. We return to Pepys's account of the collaboration, the one strictly contemporary account we have. The comedy, he wrote in his diary on 16 August 1667, was "made by my Lord Duke of Newcastle, but, as everybody says, corrected by Dryden." Like most of what Pepys wrote, this would seem to be accurate.

As has already been suggested, Newcastle and Dryden in *Sir Martin Mar-all* follow their literary sources closely, more closely than Dryden did in his unaided plays. Much that is distinctive about the comedy derives from the two French comedies on which it is based, to such an extent indeed that it could almost be considered an adaptation from them rather than an original play; and therefore an examination of its relationship to these French plays, and to the Italian play on which both of them are in turn based, must be a preliminary to an assessment of it. Whether he knew it or not, Samuel Pepys in applauding *Sir Martin Mar-all* was responding to a comedy having a close and direct ancestry in Italian *commedia dell'arte,* a dramatic form of which it is—in its stylized characters and in its series of disjunctive, farcical scenes dominated by a clever servant—a rather close English approximation.

Downes's statement that Dryden based the play on a translation of *L'Étourdi* made by Newcastle is misleading as to sources as well as to the nature of the collaboration, for *Sir Martin Mar-all* owes if anything more to Philippe Quinault's *L'Amant Indiscret* than to Molière. Approximately the first half of the English play, apart from the subplot, derives in close detail of episode and occasionally even of language from Quinault's comedy; the remainder, from Molière's.[56] Newcastle may well have seen one or both of the plays performed in Paris before the Restoration (though while on the Continent he lived mainly in Antwerp). *L'Amant Indiscret* was first acted in Paris about 1654 and was published there in 1656;[57] *L'Étourdi* was acted in Lyon in 1655 and in Paris in 1658, where it was published in 1663.[58] Whether or not Dryden knew the plays before his collaboration with Newcastle, it is impossible to say. He mentioned both the French dramatists favorably in *Of Dramatick Poesie,* published in 1668, the year after *Sir Martin Mar-all* was first performed. He had written a preliminary draft of the essay in 1665 and 1666, but the passage about French comedy could be a later interpolation. "But of late years," says his spokesman Neander, "*de Moliere,* the younger *Corneille, Quinault,* and some others, have been imitating of afar off the quick turns and graces

---

[56] The sources of *Sir Martin Mar-all* are described with precision and in detail by L. Albrecht, *Dryden's "Sir Martin Mar-all" in Bezug auf seine Quellen* (1906). The subject is reviewed by Allen, pp. 211–225. Both writers erroneously assume that the subplot was original with Dryden.

[57] Henry Carrington Lancaster, *A History of French Dramatic Literature in the Seventeenth Century* (1929–1942), Pt. Three, I, 95.

[58] *Ibid.,* p. 105; Eugène Despois, ed., *Oeuvres de Molière* (1907), I, 86–87.

of the English Stage." [59] A grudging tribute from a dramatist who owed so much to two of them.

Dryden and Newcastle could easily splice together their borrowings from *L'Amant Indiscret* and *L'Étourdi* because those plays had similar characters and plots, taken from their common source, Niccolò Barbieri's *L'Inavvertito*, first printed in Venice in 1630.[60] Barbieri was a prominent actor of the *commedia dell'arte*, who also wrote plays—generally only synopses, since the dialogue in these plays was impromptu. He wrote *L'Inavvertito* as a synopsis in the beginning, though in published form it has dialogue in full. It is a farcical comedy elaborated from the situation central to *Sir Martin Mar-all:* that of a clever servant devising a succession of stratagems to help his master win his sweetheart, only to have them frustrated by his master's ineptitude. Here the setting is Venetian and the institution of slavery provides important complications: the sweetheart is herself a slave, and the clever servant (a *zanni* in the terminology of the Italian comedy [61]), who resembles the resourceful and knavish slaves of Plautus' comedies of antiquity, attempts to arrange for his master to buy her. *L'Inavvertito* is made up of a lively succession of boisterous episodes, variations on the single comic situation, with little causal relationship between them and only the slenderest thread of continuity. This structural pattern, typical of the *commedia dell'arte* and arising from its dependence on the virtuosity of trained actors in the impromptu elaboration of a succession of farcical episodes, appears in the French plays as well as in *Sir Martin Mar-all.*

If both of the French dramatists borrow from Barbieri, they do so in very different ways, Molière following him much more closely than Quinault. *L'Étourdi* was Molière's first five-act comedy, written during his extended period of touring the provinces, at a time when he was strongly under the influence of the Italian actors and their improvised comedy, and before he developed his own mature dramatic style. One of the closest approximations to the form of *commedia dell'arte* in French literature, the play has, in the words of a modern authority on Molière, "the incessant activity of the Italian farces, their sudden

---

[59] 1668, p. 38; Ker, I, 68–69. Several years later, in the preface to *An Evening's Love,* Dryden refers harshly to the French dramatists and to his own borrowing from them (1671, sig. A4v–B1r; Ker, I, 136–137):

> After all, it is to be acknowledg'd, that most of those Comedies, which have been lately written, have been ally'd too much to Farce: and this must of necessity fall out till we forbear the translation of *French Plays:* for their Poets wanting judgement to make, or to maintain true characters, strive to cover their defects with ridiculous Figures and Grimaces. While I say this, I accuse myself as well as others.

[60] *L'Inavvertito* is reprinted as an appendix to *L'Étourdi,* in *Oeuvres de Molière,* ed. Despois, I.

[61] The type character of the *zanni* is considered at length in K. M. Lea, *Italian Popular Comedy* (1934), I, 54 ff.

reversals of situation, their unfailing gaiety, their spontaneous fun, and their exaggeration almost to caricature, but never to burlesque." [62] The vaguely realized Italian setting and the use of the institution of slavery to complicate the plot derive from *L'Inavvertito,* and so do the attempts of the stupid master with the aid of his servant to purchase the slave girl he loves; about half of Molière's scenes have an equivalent in the Italian play.[63] On the other hand, Quinault modernizes Barbieri's central situation, adapting his characters and plot to the institutions of contemporary France. No longer is there any question of a master-slave relationship but rather that of a suitor and his beloved who is his social equal; and no longer a remote locale but rather a contemporary Parisian one, as fully exploited in its picturesque details as is the London of *Sir Martin Mar-all.*

It will be apparent that Dryden and Newcastle's version of the central relationships resembles that of Quinault more than it does that of Molière; they merely anglicize Quinault's locale and characters. As already noted, about the first half of *Sir Martin Mar-all* follows *L'Amant Indiscret* closely, until the episode (III, iii, 21 ff.) in which Warner schemes to get Sir John Swallow out of the way by pretending that the legal documents needed for the marriage settlement have been left in the country. The corresponding stratagem in Quinault succeeds, with the result that the rival is removed from the competition and the mother of the young woman takes his place as the antagonist to be outwitted. The stratagem fails in the English play, as always because of the stupidity of Sir Martin; and, beginning at this point, with Sir Martin's threat to commit suicide (III, iii, 97), the play follows Molière. The events of the subplot represent, of course, a departure from *L'Étourdi,* and so do the episodes of the lute playing [64] and the frolic of the altitudes. In Molière, as also in Quinault and Barbieri, the master despite his stupidity finally wins his sweetheart, as he does not in the English play.

This difference has as a corollary a difference in the interpretations of the master. If in much of their play Newcastle and Dryden merely adapt characters, situations, and episodes from one or the other of the two French plays, they interpret the stupid master in a new way. Sir Martin is after all a vain and vapid fool, an impossible husband for so spirited a young woman as Millisent; Quinault's Cleandre and Molière's Lélie are both of them generous and honorable young men, less stupid than impetuous and maladroit. As Voltaire observed, citing critical commonplace, Molière's subtitle of *Les Contre-Temps* is more appropriate to the play than the principal title of *L'Étourdi,* for Lélie is rather the victim of his own generosity and of his servant's failure to give him advance warning

[62] Brander Matthews, *Molière: His Life and His Works* (1910), p. 61.
[63] Lancaster, *French Dramatic Literature,* Pt. Three, I, 105.
[64] The famous episode of Sir Martin's pretended playing upon the lute is borrowed, as Langbaine noted (p. 170), from Charles Sorel (who used the pseudonym M. de Moulines, sieur de Parc), *Histoire comique de Francion,* which was published in an English translation in 1655. In this translation the relevant passage occurs in Book VII, pp. 16–17. See below, pp. 373–374.

of his successive stratagems than of stupidity.[65] We are pleased that Cleandre and Lélie win their loves in marriage; we are similarly pleased that Warner saves Millisent from the contemptible Sir Martin.

The closeness with which Newcastle and Dryden followed their sources accounts in part for the impression conveyed by the play of improvisation, of movement from one amusing instance of a stratagem by Warner foiled by Sir Martin to another, with little planned relationship between them. They appropriated episodes from the two French plays, from Newcastle's earlier plays, from Schackerley Marmion's *A Fine Companion*, from Charles Sorel's *The Comical History of Francion*, linking them only loosely together. For their casual handling of continuity, they had the precedent of the French plays, and back of those plays the tradition of the *commedia dell'arte*. Yet if the transitions are casual only one of them is abrupt: when Warner, late in the final act, after having shown pride in his skill as ingenious servingman, announces that he is in fact a distressed gentleman whose estate was ruined in the civil wars and thus is a suitable husband for Millisent. Throughout the play he is portrayed as cleverer and less knavish than his counterparts in the French plays, just as his master is portrayed as more of a dolt than his counterparts. The transformation is necessary to provide a suitable husband for Millisent. The fact that it is so abruptly accomplished, however, would suggest that it was an afterthought, made during a late revision of the play.

Of theme in the sense of thesis (in the manner of Molière's later and more famous comedies), this comedy is singularly lacking. Sir Martin's folly is incurable and thus no profitable subject for a didactic satirist to undertake, and his series of blunders leads the audience to laughter rather than to improved understanding of any aspect of human nature. If the vices of the characters in the subplot might be considered curable they are scarcely reprehended in the play. On the contrary, Lady Dupe and Mrs. Christian find their sordid scheme extraordinarily profitable, the latter indeed winning marriage to a wealthy knight as well as a dowry from Lord Dartmouth. The lord suffers for his lechery, to be sure, since he is bilked of his money, but his loss is merely financial and it is one that he can easily sustain. The moral structure of *Sir Martin Mar-all* is in fact as casual as the exposition and characterization, and as remote from any close and calculated design. The play is incidentally satirical of abnormalities of behavior, of Old Moody's excessive admiration for the manners of a bygone age and of Sir Martin's intermittent gallicisms, but it has no central satirical focus in the follies of Restoration society. Sir Martin is in the first instance a fool rather than a would-be wit, and so in lesser degree is Sir John Swallow. The comic episodes provide glimpses of the everyday life of London in the first decade after Charles II's return, but not an ordered critique of the life of the town.

Perhaps in part because of its very improvised quality and its lack of studied design, its relative lack even of artistic sophistication, the play

---

[65] Voltaire, *Sommaire de L'Étourdi* (reprinted in *Oeuvres de Molière*, ed. Despois, I, 100–101).

conveys an impression of authenticity in its rendering of the bustle of everyday London life. With a locale in a house on Charles Street, just off Covent Garden, it proceeds in a matter-of-fact tone of social realism in the depiction of events in Pepysian London. For the London of the play is that of the famous diary, and the places referred to—the piazzas in Covent Garden, the steps in Durham Yard, Gray's Inn Walks, St. James Park—are authentic ones that Pepys knew. The first performance followed by only a year the great fire that had swept London just to the east of Covent Garden; and together with other suburbs of Westminster this one in 1667 was swollen with persons who had been burned out of their former residences. The mingling of social classes observable in the play seems to have been typical of Covent Garden, a rapidly growing part of the town in which lords and their families lived near their social inferiors.[66] The recording of social history is not the noblest function of comedy, but it is a legitimate function, and it is one vividly performed by this play.

The preoccupation with the texture of London life had been anticipated in the comedies of Ben Jonson. So had the unflinching realism of tone and language characteristic of *Sir Martin Mar-all.* The tone is as unromantic as is that of *Bartholomew Fair,* as objective and matter-of-fact; and the language is as imitative of unstudied conversation and as colloquial. The high frequency of obsolete slang words suggests the play's approximation to the language of the streets. Where an obvious rhetorical heightening of language occurs, for example in Lord Dartmouth's confession to Lady Dupe that Mrs. Christian is pregnant by him (III, ii, 27 ff.), the effect is likely to be that of affectation—in this instance, of sanctimoniousness—just as it is in Jonson's comedies.[67] Here the heightened diction shades into the blunt diction more usual in the play, as Lord Dartmouth describes to Lady Dupe the places where he seduced Mrs. Christian: "In an out-room upon a Trunk," the first time, he explains, and later in "An old waste Room, with a decay'd Bed in't." This is the convincing idiom of familiar speech. The dialogue will not bear comparison with the carefully elaborated dialogue of Ben Jonson, but it would nevertheless appear that Newcastle and Dryden shared an antirhetorical ideal with their great predecessor.

The Jonsonian strain is strong in *Sir Martin Mar-all* notwithstanding the fact of its continental ancestry. The structural pattern of the play derives, as has been said, from *commedia dell'arte,* but the pattern has precedent in Jonson, who as well as Barbieri emphasized single comic episodes at the expense of relationships between them. The English comic model and the

---

[66] "And if we consider this Parish [St. Paul's Covent Garden], as to its fine, streight, and broad Streets, replenished with such good Buildings, and so well inhabited by a Mixture of Nobility, Gentry, and wealthy Tradesmen, here seated since the Fire of *London* 1666, scarce admitting of any Poor, not being pestered with mean Courts and Alleys; likewise its open and large Piazza or Garden, so delightful to walk in: It may deservedly be reckoned for one of the best Parishes in the Cities of *London* and *Westminster,* or Parts adjacent" (Strype, Bk. VI, p. 87).

[67] Cf. Jonas Barish, *Ben Jonson and the Language of Prose Comedy* (1960), p. 2.

continental materials were in fact so thoroughly compatible that Newcastle and Dryden could bring them together harmoniously even in a play as casually written and revised as this one seems to have been. Largely ignoring considerations of neoclassical theory, they addressed themselves pragmatically to the construction of a series of entertaining scenes, joining them loosely together on two strands of plot, and endowing them with a unity of tone rather than of theme. Close attention to dramatic construction is scarcely to be expected in a farcical comedy of situation, patterned, even if indirectly, on the Italian popular comedy, and providing like that comedy a vehicle for the virtuoso performances of skilled actors. It is finally irrelevant to complain of inadequacies of motivation or implausibilities of event in a play that was so frankly—and so successfully—adapted to the skills of Nokes and his fellow members of Davenant's company.

CAST OF CHARACTERS

Lord Dartmouth. Few lords appear in Restoration comedy and fewer still with names, such as this one, which sound authentic. The choice of so plausible a name would have been audacious, and we may at least surmise that it was made by the Duke of Newcastle. At the time the play was first performed, no peerage of this title existed, though one was created in 1675 when the King gave a barony to his illegitimate son Charles Fitz-Charles (*Complete Peerage,* IV, 87).

PROLOGUE

2 *Regalios.* "Regalo. A present, especially of choice food or drink" (*OED*). *Cf.* "Epilogue to the Wild Gallant reviv'd," l. 12.

10 *Woodcocks.* Because of the ease with which the woodcock can be deceived and captured, it serves as a symbol for credulity and folly. As Summers notes, one of the characters in Shadwell's *The Sullen Lovers* has the name Woodcock. Cf. *The Wild Gallant,* III, i, 209–210, and *Works,* VIII, 253n.

EPILOGUE

13 *Lilly.* William Lilly (1602–1681), thought of today primarily as an astrologer and almanac maker, did not think of himself in so narrow a light, as is evidenced by his own choice of a pseudonym, Merlinus Anglicanus Junior. Many of his most sensational "successes" came not from astrological prognostication but from the revival of ancient prophecies plus, in at least one instance, the devising of "hieroglyphics." He was much given to making ex post facto claims of having precisely predicted, in such riddling and cryptic utterances, the whole course of the Civil War (or, minimally, the execution of Charles I), the Plague, the Fire, and so on. (The editors are grateful to Hugh G. Dick for the information in this note).

I, i

24 *Durham-yard.* Strype, Bk. VI, p. 75: "Thus having spoken of the North Side of the *Strand,* next the South Side is to be perambulated. . . . *Salisbury-street,* better built than inhabited, by Reason of its Narrowness, and steep Descent towards the Water Side, where there is a Pair of Stairs to take Water at. *Ivy Bridge,* now very bad, and scarce fit for Use, by Reason of the Unpassableness of the Way. It hath an Inlet into *Durham Yard. Durham Yard,* anciently *Duresme House,* as being the Residence of the Bishops of *Durham.*"

39 *humoursome.* The word is used in the Jonsonian sense.

44 *Piazza's.* Strype, Bk. VI, p. 89: "On the North and East Sides [of Covent Garden] are Rows of very good and large Houses, called the *Piazzo's,* sustained by Stone Pillars, to support the Buildings. Under which are Walks, broad and convenient, paved with Freestone. The South Side lieth open to *Bedford Garden,* where there is a small Grotto of Trees, most pleasant in the Summer Season; and in this Side there is kept a Market for Fruits, Herbs, Roots, and Flowers. . . . And on the West Side is the Church of St. *Paul's Covent Garden.*"

70 *tows'd.* "Touse. To pull (a woman) about rudely, indelicately, or in horse-play" (*OED*).

109–110 *the Lyon's skin . . . the Foxes sublety.* Proverbial (Tilley, L319).

154 *picque.* "In *Piquet,* the winning of thirty points on cards and play, before one's opponent begins to count, entitling the player to begin his score at sixty" (*OED*).

154 *repicque.* ". . . the winning of thirty points on cards alone before beginning to play (and before the adversary begins to count), entitling the player to begin his score at ninety" (*OED*). Cf. *The Wild Gallant,* IV, i, 4–32 and explanation of the game of piquet, *Works,* VIII, 255.

154 *Capot.* Charles Cotton, *The Compleat Gamester* (1674), pp. 86–87: "He that wins more than his own Cards reckons Ten, but he that wins all the Cards reckons Forty, and this is called *Capet*" (Summers).

155–156 *want but one of up.* Summers: "Want one point to win the game."

161 *The Oaths of losing Gamesters are most minded.* Saintsbury: "This seems contrary to the proverb and to what Sir John means. One would expect 'least,' not 'most.'"

167–168 *upon the Square.* Cf. *Secret Love,* IV, i, 133 (see above, p. 167): "I love upon the square."

286 *Bug-word.* "A word meant to frighten or terrify" (*OED*).

289 *smoaks.* Suspects.

297 *Loggar-head.* A disproportionately large head.

II, i

17 *claw'd off.* "To claw off. To get rid of (as an itch by clawing)" (*OED*).

II, ii

114 *Grayes-Inn Walks.* Strype, Bk. III, p. 253: "The chief Ornament belonging to this Inn [Gray's], is its spacious Garden, with curious Walks, as well those that are shady by the lofty Trees, as those that are raised higher, and lie open to the Air, and the enjoyment of a delightful prospect of the Fields. And this Garden hath been, for many Years, much resorted unto, by the Gentry of both Sexes."

117–118 *He shall meet another Penelope then he suspects.* An ironical allusion to the faithfulness of Penelope, the wife of Ulysses.

170 *soft and fair goes far.* Proverbial (Tilley, S601).

260 *Charles Street.* Strype, Bk. VI, p. 63: "Behind this North Side of *King's-street,* is *Charles's-street,* a fine large Street, not many Years built, with good Houses well inhabited: And *Duke-street,* new built, with good Houses and well inhabited, especially that Side towards St. *James's* Park."

270 *silenc'd Minister.* A reference to clergymen ostracized by the Act of Uniformity of 1662.

301 *Diego.* A Spaniard. Cf. *Of Dramatick Poesie* (1668, p. 38; Ker, I, 69); in speaking of French drama, Neander alludes to the comic servant in Sir Samuel Tuke's *Adventures of Five Hours* (1663): "Most of their new Playes are like some of ours, deriv'd from the Spanish Novells. There is scarce one of them without a vail, and a trusty *Diego,* who drolls much after the rate of the *Adventures.*"

III, i

62 *You have Reason.* That is, *avoir raison.* Cf. Wycherley, *The Gentleman Dancing-Master* (1673), V, i: "The Fool has reason, I find" (cited by Summers).

73–74 *escapes.* Unstudied or artless performances. This is the only example of the usage cited in *OED.*

76 *Coxbones.* A very old oath, used in Chaucer (Manciple's prologue, l. 9): "for cokkes bones." Mr. Moody repeatedly uses old oaths.

77 *old Madge.* Moody refers to his cane. Presumably a figurative use of the word "madge," meaning a "leaden hammer covered thickly with stout woollen cloth" (*OED*).

77–78 *keeps . . . a coil.* Makes a fuss (*OED*).

91 *The Dukes.* The Duke's Company, acting in the theater in Lincoln's Inn Fields.

93 *the Kings.* The King's Company, acting in the theater on Bridges Street, Drury Lane.

96 *on the Posts.* Referring to the theatrical announcements posted in the center of London. Cf. Emmett L. Avery, ed., *The London Stage, 1660–1800,* Pt. 2:1700–1729 (1960), pp. lxxxix-xciii.

III, ii

73 *Cabinet of Quintessence.* Medicine chest.

73–74 *Gilberts Water.* A stimulant, named for Queen Elizabeth's physician, William Gilbert.

97 *a Lechery.* Saintsbury: "Of course a malapropism for 'lethargy.'" So also below, "fraternity" for "eternity."
103 *Key-cold.* Proverbial. Cf. *Richard III*, I, ii, 5: "Poor key-cold figure of a holy king" (Tilley, K23).
111 *swebbing.* From *sweb*, meaning "to faint."

III, iii

111 *Copy of your Countenance.* Mere outward show of what you would do (*OED*).

IV, i

33 *Cox nowns.* Cf. "Coxbones" (III, i, 76), also used by Moody. The fondness for old oaths is an expression of his humour.
39 *Bartlemew.* Summers: "Warner is going to say 'a conceited Bartlemew Cokes,' a common term applied to a ninny. Cokes = a fool occurs as early as 1567, and the term largely became general owing to Squire Cokes, the simpleton in *Bartholomew Fair*." Cf. V, i, 234.
46 *Scander-bag.* A favorite oath of Moody's, derived from the name of the Albanian national hero, Scanderbeg (*c.* 1404–1468). Cf. V, i, 414; V, ii, 71.
72–80 *Was there ever . . . the flower of Serving-men.* Cf. *L'Étourdi*, II, viii, 786–794 (Eugène Despois, ed., *Oeuvres de Molière* [1907], I, 157):
Fut-il jamais au monde un plus heureux garçon?
Oh! que dans un moment Lélie aura de joie!
Sa maîtresse en nos mains tomber par cette voie!
Recevoir tout son bien d'où l'on attend le mal,
Et devenir heureux par la main d'un rival!
Après ce rare exploit, je veux que l'on s'apprête
A me peindre en héros un laurier sur la tête,
Et qu'au bas du portrait on mette en lettres d'or:
Vivat Mascarillus, fourbum imperator!
77 *Lilly.* Sir Peter Lely (1618–1680).
97 *Mackings.* A term formed from *mack* plus a suffix. Cf. *OED* under *Mack:* "An unmeaning word suggested either by 'by Mary' or by 'by the Mass.'" Again Moody uses an old oath. Cf. III, i, 76; IV, i, 33.
206 *danc'd in a Net.* Proverbial, meaning to believe mistakenly that one is undetected in doing something (Tilley, N130).
214–215 *mother Temple, Bennet, or Gifford.* Notorious procuresses. It was Mother Bennett to whom Wycherley addressed his ironical dedication of *The Plain Dealer* (1677).
220 *Wine . . . with New-River.* I.e., wine adulterated with water from the canal called the "New River."
220 *Shatling, and La-fronds.* Well-known and expensive taverns. Summers calls attention to references in Pepys and Shadwell. Cf. Pepys, 22 April 1668: "To the fishmonger's, and bought a couple of lobsters, and over to the 'sparagus garden, thinking to have met Mr. Pierce, and his wife and Knepp; but met their servant coming to bring me to Chatelin's, the French house, in Covent Garden, and there with musick and good

company, Manuel and his wife, and one Swaddle, a clerk of Lord Arlington's, who dances, and speaks French well, but got drunk, and was then troublesome, and here mighty merry till ten at night. . . . This night the Duke of Monmouth and a great many blades were at Chatelin's, and I left them there, with a hackney-coach attending him." Cf. also Shadwell in Act II of *The Sullen Lovers* (1668, p. 26): "One, that but the other day, could eat but one meal a day, and that at a three-penny Ordinary; now struts in State, and talks of nothing but Shattellin's and Lefronds."

257 *Make ready fair Lady to night.* Day, p. 143: "The tune is preserved in two ballad-operas: *The Village Opera*, 1729, air XLV, by Charles Johnson; and *The Chamber-Maid*, 1730, air XXIII, by Edward Phillips. The words are in *The New Academy of Complements*, 1671 and 1713, p. 200; *Westminster-Drollery*, 1671 and 1672, p. 47; and *Windsor-Drollery*, 1672, p. 140."

284 *Jack Sawce.* "A saucy or impudent fellow" (*OED*).

342 *May-game.* "An object of sport, jest, or ridicule" (*OED*).

415 *absolv'd.* Accomplished. *OED* cites *Paradise Lost*, VII, 94: "The work begun, how soon Absolved."

465 *Pudding-time.* Seasonably, i.e., at a time when the pudding is ready (Tilley, P634).

468 *Goodier.* A meaningless expletive (perhaps derived from a Dutch idiom), used chiefly in interrogative phrases.

V, i

61–62 *your greatest wits have ever a touch of madness and extravagance in them.* Cf. the famous line in *Absalom and Achitophel* (l. 163): "Great Wits are sure to Madness near ally'd."

113 *premunire.* A loose use of a legal term, here meaning merely "predicament."

120 *white pelf.* Silver money (Summers) and thus of little value.

121 *Martin Parker.* A mid-seventeenth-century author of ballads, the most famous of which is "When the king enjoyes his owne again." Warner apparently refers to the fact that the ballads, often printed on single sheets, cost very little.

124 *cholerick as a Cook.* Proverbial (Tilley, C634). Cf. *The Alchemist*, III, i:

> Beside, we should giue somewhat to mans nature,
> The place he liues in, still about the fire,
> And fume of mettalls, that intoxicate
> The braine of man, and make him prone to passion.
> Where haue you greater *Atheists*, then your Cookes?
> Or more prophane, or cholerick then your Glasse-men?

128 *you shall give to your Mistress a Serenade.* See above, p. 366. Cf. Sorel, *The Comical History of Francion* (English translation, 1655), Bk. VII, pp. 16–17: "It so came to passe that there was a Gentleman with him who played very well upon the Lute, he intreated him to give him a Lesson or two, and that he might not be seen, he did conceal him in a con-

venient place hard by the window. In the mean time he did take another Lute into his own hand, and standing at the window he' so fingered it, that it might be believed by those who stood in the window over against him, that it was he who played, hoping that his Mistresse would be the more inamoured on him, having made it apparent to her that he was indued with so Gentlemanlike a quality; but as it fell out most unfortunately for him, one of the Companions of the Daughter of the Physician, who could play well on that Instrument, perceiving by his stops, and his unskilfull touching of the strings, that it was not he who made the harmony, did goe into a Room which was a pair of stairs higher, where they plainly discovered who it was that played. To make sport therefore with the Count, sometimes they told him that his Lute was out of Tune, sometimes that he did touch the strings too rudely, sometimes that he had broke his Trebble; Neverthelesse for all that the Musick continued a long time."

173 *Blind Love to this hour.* Day, pp. 144–145: "This is an adaptation of a song by Voiture. . . . Dryden has reproduced Voiture's meter, and his first, second, fourth, and fifth stanzas are based upon the first, second, seventh, and fourth stanzas of his model. His third stanza is original."

190 *breath.* A seventeenth-century spelling of the verb "to breathe."

219 *Harmony of the Spheres.* For an authoritative discussion of this ancient notion, see John Hollander, *The Untuning of the Sky: Ideas of Music in English Poetry, 1500–1700* (1961), pp. 28–30.

234–235 *Cokes among the Poppits.* A reference to the foolish squire Bartholomew Cokes of Jonson's *Bartholomew Fair,* who responds to a group of puppets as though they were living persons. The same character is alluded to above (IV, i, 39).

279 *Jacobus and a Carolus.* Gold coins, struck in the reigns of James I and Charles I respectively.

287 *Hey-tarockit.* A meaningless exclamation, apparently derived from "tarocs" or "tarots," as old playing cards were called.

310–311 *Dorothy, Daughter to one Draw-water.* See above, pp. 360–361.

317 *ad unguem.* To a nicety, exactly.

342 *spit out of your mouth.* "The very spit of, the exact image, likeness, or counterpart of" (*OED*).

438 *smoke.* "To smart, to suffer severely" (*OED*)

493 *beating of a Stock-fish.* Proverbial: "To beat one like a Stockfish" (Tilley, S867).

500 *hank.* Here used in the figurative sense of "a restraining or curbing hold" (*OED*).

509 *to turn Poet to Pugenello.* I.e., to write plays to be performed by the puppet Punchinello.

V, ii

12 *as lucky as a Fool's Handsel.* Proverbial (Tilley, F517).

16 *Mr. Ball the Non-conformist.* Presumably a satirical reference to some nonconformist minister, perhaps Nathaniel Ball (1623–1681), who after resigning his post in consequence of the Act of Uniformity served

as an evangelist in a number of towns (*Dictionary of National Biography*). A nonconformist minister was apparently considered to be more appropriate for a tricked marriage, such as this one of the pregnant Mrs. Christian to Sir John Swallow. Cf. Gellert Spencer Alleman, *Matrimonial Law and the Materials of Restoration Comedy* (1942), p. 43.

24 *the Brawls.* "Brawl. A kind of French dance resembling a cotillon" (*OED*).

28 *Jovy.* Jovial.

35+ *s.d. Tony. A New Dictionary of the Terms . . . of the Canting Crew* [*c.* 1699]: "a silly Fellow, or Ninny."

42 *Flute-glasses.* Saintsbury: "'Flute' in this sense is of French origin = a long narrow glass."

48 *the Frolick of the Altitudes.* This episode was suggested by a similar one in Schackerley Marmion, *A Fine Companion* (1633), IV, i (see above, p. 360).

53 *Touche.* Referring to the clinking of wine glasses.

57+ *s.d. Tony dances a Jig.* Downes, p. 28: "This Comedy was Crown'd with an Excellent Entry: In the last Act at the Mask, by Mr. *Priest* [the landlord] and Madam *Davies* [Millisent]."

60 *Cudden.* "A born fool, a dolt" (*OED*).

74 *long of.* "Attributable to" (*OED*).

80 *down from Babylon.* I.e., from the Tower of Babel (the high stool).

132–133 *Quidding.* Presumably "chewing tobacco," though *OED* records no such usage before 1727.

TEXTUAL NOTES

Introduction

CHOICE OF THE COPY TEXT

The copy text is normally the first printing, on the theory that its accidentals are likely to be closest to the author's practice; but a manuscript or a
subsequent printing may be chosen where there is reasonable evidence
either that it represents more accurately the original manuscript as finally
revised by the author or that the author revised the accidentals.

REPRODUCTION OF THE COPY TEXT

The copy text is normally reprinted *literatim,* but there are certain classes
of exceptions. In the first place, apparently authoritative variants found
in other texts are introduced as they occur, except that their purely acci-
dental features are made to conform to the style of the copy text. These
substitutions, but not their minor adjustments in accidentals, are recorded in footnotes as they occur. In the second place, the editors have introduced nonauthoritative emendations, whether found in earlier texts or
not, where the sense seems to demand them. These emendations are also
listed in the footnotes. In the third place, accidentals, speech headings,
stage directions, scene headings, and so forth, are introduced or altered
where it seems helpful to the reader. All such changes also are recorded in
footnotes as they occur. In the fourth place, turned b, q, d, p, n, and u are
accepted as q, b, p, d, u, and n, respectively, and if they result in spelling
errors are corrected in the text and listed in the footnotes. The textual
footnotes show the agreements among the texts only with respect to the
precise variation of the present edition from the copy text; for example,
in *The Indian Emperour* at V, ii, 187, the footnote "Make haste] Q2–12, F,
D, M2; Haste then Q1, M1" has reference to the change and repositioning
of "make" and "then"; M1 and M2 actually read "hast."

Certain purely mechanical details have been normalized without special
mention. Long "s" has been changed to round "s," "VV" to "W"; swash
italics have been represented by plain italics; head titles and any accompanying rules, act and scene headings, and display initials and any
accompanying capitalization, have been made uniform with the style of
the present edition; when a speech begins in the middle of a verse line, it
has been appropriately indented; the position of speech headings and
stage directions and their line division have been freely altered (braces in
the speech tags have been omitted; those in the stage directions have been
replaced by brackets; erratic uses of capitals in stage directions have been
normalized); wrong font, and turned letters other than q, b, p, d, u, and
n have been adjusted; medial apostrophes that failed to print have been
restored; italicized plurals in -'s have been distinguished (by italic final
"s") from possessives (roman final "s"); quotations have been marked with
inverted commas at the beginning and end only and always; spacing be-

tween words and before and after punctuation has been normalized when
no change in meaning results; the common contractions have been counted
as single words, but otherwise words abbreviated by elision have been sep-
arated from those before and after if the apostrophe is present; if the
elided syllable is written out as well as marked by an apostrophe, the
words have been run together (*"speak'it"*).

TEXTUAL NOTES

The textual notes list the relevant manuscripts and printings, assign them
sigla, and give references to the bibliographies where they are more fully
described. Normally only the seventeenth-century manuscripts and the
printed editions through Congreve's (1717) [1] are cited, since there is normally no likelihood that authoritative readings will be found in any later
manuscripts or editions. The textual notes also outline the descent of the
text through its various manuscripts and printings, indicate which are
the authorized texts, and explain how the copy text was selected in each
instance. A list of copies collated follows. If the differences between variant copies are sufficient to warrant a tabular view of them, it will follow
the list of copies collated.

The sigla indicate the format of printed books (F = folio, Q = quarto,
O = octavo, etc.) and the order of printing, if this is determinable, within
the format group (F may have been printed after Q1 and before Q2). If
order of printing is in doubt, the numbers are arbitrary, and they are
normally arbitrary for the manuscripts (represented by M).

Finally the variants in the texts collated are given. The list is not ex-
haustive, but it records what seemed material, viz.:

All variants of the present edition from the copy text except in the
mechanical details listed above.

All other substantive variants and variants in accidentals markedly
affecting the sense. The insertion or removal of a period before a
dash has sometimes been accepted as affecting the sense; other punc-
tuational variants before dashes have been ignored. Failure of letters
to print, in texts other than the copy text, has been noted only when
the remaining letters form a different word or words, or when a word
has disappeared entirely.

All errors of any kind repeated from one edition to another, except
the use of -'s instead of -s for a plural.

Spelling variants where the new reading makes a new word (e.g.,
then and *than* being in Dryden's day alternate spellings of the conjunction, a change from *than* to *then* would be recorded, since the
spelling *then* is now confined to the adverb, but a change from *then*
to *than* would be ignored as a simple modernization).

In passages of verse, variants in elision of syllables normally pronounced (except that purely mechanical details, as *had'st, hadst,* are

---

[1] How much Congreve had to do with this edition beyond writing the dedication, and how much the text represents Dryden's last thoughts, is questionable
(see Macd, p. 151), but it has seemed wiser to include its variant readings always.

ignored). Thus *heaven, heav'n* is recorded, but not *denied, deny'd.*
Relining, except when passages printed as prose are reprinted as
prose.

When texts generally agree in a fairly lengthy variation, but one or two
differ from the rest in a detail that would be cumbrous to represent in the
usual way, the subvariations are indicated in parentheses in the list of
sigla. For example:

> Gate.——— [*Exit* Indian.] Q2–12, F, D, M2 (Gate∧——— D);
> Gate∧——— Q1, M1.

This means that D agrees with Q2–12, F, and M2 in all respects except
that it omits the period after "Gate"; Q1 and M1 omit this period as
well as the stage direction following the dash.

When variants in punctuation alone are recorded, the wavy dash is
used in place of the identifying word before (and sometimes after) the
variant punctuation.

As in the previous volumes, no reference is made to modern editions
where the editor is satisfied that reasonable care on his part would have
resulted in the same emendations, even if he collated these editions before beginning to emend.

Mechanical aids to accuracy were developed while this volume was being
prepared (e.g., Vinton A. Dearing, "The Poor Man's Mark IV or Ersatz Hin-
man Collator," *PBSA,* LX [1966], 149–158), but were not used throughout.

The Indian Emperour

The earliest known text of *The Indian Emperour* is Trinity College MS
R.3.10 (M1), which is dated 1665. The first edition of the play (Q1, Macd
69a) was published in October 1667 (Ward, p. 53). Fredson Bowers ("Current Theories of Copy Text, with an Illustration from Dryden," *MP,*
XLVIII [1950–51], 12–20) identified variant forms in outer B, D, and H,
inner E, and inner and outer I, and recognized Dryden's correcting hand
in inner I; the readings of the uncorrected and corrected forms are shown
in the apparatus as Q1a and Q1b respectively.

The second edition, dated 1668 (Q2, Macd 69b), was printed from a copy
of Q1 probably having uncorrected inner I (the two changes in the text
in inner I are made, but not the two changes in the stage directions). Professor Bowers (*ibid.*) identified variant forms in inner B of Q2 and recognized Dryden's correcting hand there; the readings of the uncorrected
and corrected forms are shown in the apparatus as Q2a and Q2b respectively. Some copies of Q2 have uncanceled "A Defence of an Essay of
Dramatique Poesie" as the first item in the preliminaries. There Dryden
remarks that he has made some corrections in the text, but not all he
might have.

Dryden continued his corrections in the third edition, dated 1670 (Q3,
Macd 69c), which was printed from a copy of Q2 with corrected inner B.
There were, in all, three "third" editions, all with the same date. The
second of these (Q4) was printed from a copy of Q3 and was in turn the

copy for the last (Q5, Macd 69d). Q4 has the first gathering unsigned, like Macd 69c, and reads "was new! too too late," in the last line on p. 46, like Macd 69d; other variations are noted in the apparatus. Subsequent editions are not numbered on their title pages. The sixth edition, dated 1681 (Q6, Macd 69e), was printed from a copy of Q2 with corrected inner B. The seventh edition, dated 1686 (Q7, Macd 69f), was printed from a copy of Q6. The eighth edition, dated 1692 (Q8, Macd 69g), was printed from a copy of Q7. The ninth edition, dated 1694 (Q9, Macd 69h), was printed partly from a copy of Q7 and partly from a copy of Q8. The last three seventeenth-century editions, all dated 1696, descend serially from Q9 (these are Q10, Macd 69k; Q11; and Q12, Macd 69i).

The text in Dryden's *Comedies, Tragedies, and Operas* (1701), I, 107–149 (F, Macd 107ai–ii [two issues, the differences not affecting this play]), was set from a copy of Q10. The text in Congreve's edition of Dryden's *Dramatick Works* (1717), I, 295–371 (D, Macd 109ai–ii [two issues, the differences not affecting this play]), was set from a copy of Q6, except for "A Defence of an Essay," here first reprinted and so set necessarily from a copy of Q2. The "Defence" was inserted after the dedication by canceling N7 and inserting a sheet signed NO in its place.

Professor Bowers ("Variants in Early Editions of Dryden's Plays," *Harvard Library Bulletin*, III [1949], 278) first distinguished Q4, and he first correctly ordered Q10–12 (*A Supplement to the Woodward & MacManaway Check List* [Charlottesville, Va., 1949]). Edward Hooker first distinguished Q11 (James M. Osborn, "Macdonald's Bibliography of Dryden," *MP*, XXXIX [1941], 80–81). The relationships of Q1–10 and F were first set out by James S. Steck ("Dryden's *Indian Emperour:* The Early Editions and their Relation to the Text," *SB*, II [1949–1950], 139–152).

Another manuscript of the play, probably belonging to the mid-1690's, is the Douai Bibliothèque Publique MS 7.87, fols. 252*v*–286*v* (M2). G. B. Evans ("The Douai Manuscript—Six Shakespearean Transcripts [1694–1695]," *PQ*, XLI [1962], 158–172) believes the plays in this volume were prepared for school performances at one of the English religious foundations at Douai. They are not bound in order as dated by the copyist, and *The Indian Emperour* is not dated at all, but the hand is the same throughout. The text of *The Indian Emperour* has been cut in various places, most notably where Dryden reflects upon the Catholic church. It was copied from Q6.

M1 is a more important manuscript, and Professor Bowers ("The 1665 Manuscript of Dryden's *Indian Emperour*," *SP*, XLVIII [1951], 738–760) regards it as in many respects superior to Q1, with which it has a common ancestor. Professor Bowers' conclusion that this common ancestor was the printer's copy, his discussion of the nature of the printer's copy, and his explanation of the cancellation of G1 in Q1 (which he was the first to notice) seem not to be provable. His preference for M1 over Q1 rests upon the mistaken impression that M1 has more of Dryden's spellings than Q1 (see Vinton A. Dearing, "The Use of a Computer in Analyzing Dryden's Spelling," *Literary Data Processing Conference Proceedings, September 9, 10, 11, 1964,* [Armonk, N.Y.: IBM, 1964]).

Professor Bowers' contributions to the study of *The Indian Emperour* have been so considerable that it seems almost supererogatory to disagree with him once more, but this does seem to be the place to argue the point he raised in his "Current Theories of Copy Text" in connection with the play. As edition follows edition, errors creep into a text even when the author is correcting and proofreading. Bowers follows Greg in advocating that the modern editor should therefore feel free to reject variant readings found in authoritatively revised texts when the readings themselves are not certainly authoritative. The question arises not over the variants that are certainly not authoritative, but over the uncertain ones. The older policy of accepting the doubtful variants as authoritative appears to be more satisfactory than that advocated by Greg and Bowers whenever the number of certain corrections exceeds the number of certain errors, because the compositor follows copy more often than not, and therefore is more probably doing so than not in any doubtful variant. In some instances the probability will not be in accord with the fact, or it would not be a probability, but it is impossible to determine which instances these are, and there will be more mistakes if the Greg-Bowers policy is followed than otherwise.

The present text of the play is based on the Clark copy of Q1a (*PR3417.L1), modified where the sense is affected to agree with Q3, and otherwise emended as seemed necessary (in the dedication, the use of romans and italics in Q1 has been reversed). The two variants in the stage directions in corrected inner I of Q1 have been retained, as it appears likely that they did not carry over into Q2 because Dryden revised for the press a copy with uncorrected inner I and did not remember (rather than rejected) these two earlier changes. The copy text for the "Defence of an Essay" is the Folger copy of Q2 (D2206h, v. 1).

Kalib's song (II, i, 53–62) occurs in a music manuscript in Henry Purcell's hand, now in the Guildhall Library, London (Gresham College MS VI.5.6, fols. 10*v*–11*v*; M3). The small variants in lines 54 and 60 suggest that Purcell copied from some printed text between Q6 and Q9 inclusive. The song that opens IV, iii, occurs in two seventeenth-century manuscripts, Bodleian MS Rawl. poet. 65, fol. 38*v* (M4), and Folger MS V. a. 226, pp. 27–28 (M5). M4 is a collection of poetry compiled by an Oxford man (St. John's College) in the last quarter of the century. M5 was compiled by William Deedes from contemporary plays; when the volume is read in one direction the selections deal with love; with the volume reversed the topics are miscellaneous. Besides the song, Deedes quotes from the play thirteen passages on love (pp. 26–28) and twenty-seven on miscellaneous subjects (pp. 22–24, volume reversed). The source of M4 cannot be determined, except that it is not Q1, M1, or M2; the text is interesting because it contains two couplets not found elsewhere. M5 was probably copied from Q2 or Q6; the variants are of no interest, and are not noted except for the song in IV, iii. The passages quoted are as follows: I, ii, 140, 163–166, 200–201, 285–286; II, ii, 8, 68–71, 90–91; II, iii, 121–122; III, i, 39–40, 43–44; III, ii, 1–6; III, iii, 35–38; IV, iii, 1–16; IV, iv, 139–140 (all on love); I, ii, 67–68, 305–308, 317–318; II, i, 41–46, 108–109; II, ii, 30–31, 38–41; II, iii,

54, 117–118, 159–160; III, i, 98–103; IV, i, 38, 43, 78, 105–114; IV, ii, 21–22, 131; IV, iii, 24, 48–50; V, i, 94, 97, 109; V, ii, 27, 69–70, 108–109, 226–227, 318–319.

The following additional copies of the several editions have also been examined: Q1: Huntington (123014), Folger (D2206h, v. 1), Texas (Wj.D848.667i), Harvard (*EC65.D8474.667i); Q2: Clark (*PR3417.L1.1668), Huntington (151877), Folger (D2206h, v. 1), Texas (Aj.D848.667ib), Harvard (*EC65.D8474.667ib); Q3: Clark (*PR3417.L1.1670), Folger (D2290), Texas (Aj.D848.667ic), Harvard (*EC65.D8474.667ic); Q4: Huntington (122829), Texas (Aj.D848.667ica), Chicago (PR3418.I4.1670); Q5: Clark (*PR3417.L1.1670a [cop. 1]), Folger (D2291), Yale (Ij.D848.667cb); Q6: Clark (*PR3417.L1.1681), Huntington (122830), Folger (D2292); Q7: Clark (*PR3417.L1.1686), Huntington (122831), Folger (D2293); Q8: Clark (*PR3417.L1.1692), Huntington (122832), Folger (D2325); Q9: Clark (*PR3417.L1.1694), Folger (D2210, v. 1), Texas (Aj.D848.667ig); Q10: Clark (*PR3417.L1.1696b, *PR3410.C95a. v. 1), Texas (Aj.D848.667ih); Q11: Clark (*PR3417.L1.1696a); Q12: Clark (*PR3417.L1.1696), Folger (D2296); F: Clark (*fPR3412.1701 [2 cop.]); D: Clark (*PR3412.1717 [2 cop.]). The textual apparatus does not normally record corrections in M1–2 made *currente calamo*. In M2, the stage directions at V, i, 25, seem to be in another hand from the rest of the play.

Press Variants by Form

Q1
Sheet B (outer form)
Uncorrected (?): Clark, Huntington, Folger
Corrected (?): Harvard, Texas
Sig. B3
  I, ii, 75 shown] ~,
Sheet D (outer form)
Uncorrected: Yale (examined only for this form)
Corrected: Clark, Folger, Harvard, Huntington, Texas
Sig. D
  II, ii *s.d.* Alibeck] Alibech
Sig. D3
  II, iii, 23 in] on
Sheet E (inner form)
Uncorrected: Harvard, Texas
Corrected: Clark, Huntington, Folger
Sig. E3v
  III, ii, 19 The] *Orb.* The
Sheet E (outer form)
Uncorrected: Texas
Corrected: Clark, Folger, Harvard, Huntington
Sig. E2v
  III, i, 92 known] ~,

Sig. E4*v*
   III, iii, 16 appear:] ∼.
Sheet F (outer form)
Uncorrected (?): Clark, Folger, Harvard, Texas
Corrected (?): Huntington
Sig. F2*v*
   catchword: The] Then
Sheet G (outer form)
Uncorrected: Harvard
Corrected: Clark, Folger, Huntington, Texas
Sig. G3
   IV, iii, 7 *In the*] *In their*
Sheet H (inner form)
Uncorrected (?): Clark, Folger
Corrected (?): Huntington, Harvard, Texas
Sig. H2
   IV, iv, 124 *Vsq* .] *Vasq.*
Sheet H (outer form,
Uncorrected: Clark, Folger
Corrected: Huntington, Harvard,* Texas
Sig. H2*v*
   IV, iv, 175+ *s.d.* Spaniards] ∼,
Sig. H3
   IV, iv, 179 to her] her to
   V, i, 2 blame] ∼,
   V, i, 21 elsewher] elsewhere:
Sheet I (inner form)
Uncorrected: Clark
Corrected: Huntington, Folger, Harvard, Texas
Sig. I3*v*
   V, ii, 172 that] who
        173 He] Him
        178–180 *s.d. walk*] *walk and*
Sig. I4
   V, ii, 192+ *s.d. Balcone*] Zoty
Sheet I (outer form)
Uncorrected: Clark, Folger
Corrected: Huntington, Harvard, Texas
Sig. I
   V, i, 128+ *s.d. falls*] ∼.
Sig. I2*v*
   V, ii, 117 *s.d.* M] Montezuma.
Sig. I3
   V, ii, 132 free] ∼,
        134 Gold . . . crimes:] ∼, . . . ∼;
        135 climes] Climes

---

* The Harvard copy also wants the catchword on H3.

136 brought] ~,
137+ *s.d. to] by*
154–155 *s.d.* Montezu] Montezuma.
Sig. I4*v*
V, ii, 218 e stte] estate

Q2
Sheet B (inner form)

Uncorrected: Clark
Corrected: Folger, Harvard, Huntington, Texas
Sig. B1*v*
I, i, 23 season] seasons
29 pour,] ~∧
30 bowels] ~,
40 fit] just
45 fair] far
Sig. B3*v*
I, ii, 110 blow.] ~:
Sig. B4
I, ii, 133 pa rt] part.
144 that] which
163 know,] ~:

Sheet B (outer form)

Uncorrected: Clark
Corrected: Folger, Harvard, Huntington, Texas
Sig. B3
I, ii, 82 'le] I'le

A Defence of an Essay of Dramatique Poesie: Found in some copies of Q2 and in D only.   3:5 some gross] Q2; some D.   3:14 Lerma, the] Lerma. The Q2, D.   3:24 and so,] and, so Q2, D.   5:17–18 Conversation?] Q2; ~ . D.   5:25–26 what Gentleman that was] *what Gentleman that was* Q2, D.   6:11 *spoken:*] Q2; ~ . D.   6:34 and] D; and Q2.   8:5 reparties, so] reparties. So Q2, D.   8:12–18 *Our . . . Laris*] romans and italics reversed from Q2, D, except for "Latine" (*bis*).   8:19 that] *That* Q2, D.   8:28, 29 *Latine*] D; Latine Q2.   9:33 *Latine*] D; Latine Q2.   9:34 *English*] D; English Q2.   10:23 Well] *Well* Q2, D.   11:1 says he] D; *says he* Q2.   11:18 familiar;] Q2; ~ . D.   11:21 he] *he* Q2, D.   11:24 that] *that* Q2, D.   11:27 Fricassés] Fricasses Q2, D.   11:28 *Chère Entière*] Chere Entiere Q2, D.   11:31 errour] D; errrour Q2.   12:14 that] *That* Q2, D.   12:32 Poets:] Q2; ~ . D.   13:17 *Trojans*] Trojans Q2, D.   13:19 Αἴαντος σάκεϊ Τελαμωνιάδαο, &c.] Ἀίαντος σακέϊ Τελαμωνιάδαω, &c. Q2, D (*D* omits &c.).   14:2–3 *a just . . . [italics] . . . &c.*] a just . . . [romans] . . . &c. Q2, D.   15:19 Dialogue:] ~ . Q2, D.   15:19–22 'Tis true . . . [italics] . . . reasonable] *'Tis true . . . [romans] . . . reasonable* Q2, D.   15:23–28 *The drift . . . my self*] romans and italics reversed from Q2, D, except for "English" and "French".   16:13 whom] *whom* Q2, D.   16:16 that]*That* Q2, D.   16:32 place:] Q2; ~ . D.   17:10 which]

which Q2, D.   17:35   chocqu'd] Q2; choak'd D.   20:8, 35   *French*]
D;   French Q2.   21:1   *Englishmen*] D;   English   men   Q2.   22:5
Frenchman] D;   French man Q2.
Dedication: *Completely omitted from M1–2.   caption: and Countess
of* Bucclugh, *Wife to the most Illustrious and High-born Prince* James
Duke of Monmouth.] Q2–12, F, D (Prince, Q5; *Monmouth*, Q4); Countess
of *Bucclugh*, &c. Q1.   23:5   Court, the] ~. *The* Q1–12, F, D.   23:6
having so] Q1–11, F, D; have so Q12.   23:8   passion.] Q1–11, F, D;
~∧ Q12.   23:15–16   goodness   only   could]   Q3–5;   *goodness*   Q1–2,
Q6–12, F, D.   23:16   them:] Q1; ~. Q2–12, F, D.   23:16   Objects
may] Q3–5; *Objects, 'tis true,* Q1–2, Q6–12, F, D.   23:18   on] Q1–9,
Q11–12, F, D; no Q10.   23:21   there to] Q2–12, F, D; *there* Q1.   23:
21   on] Q2–12, F, D; *upon* Q1.   24:2   once it is] Q1–7, D; it is once
Q8–12, F.   24:4   farther] Q1–10, F, D; further Q11–12.   24:4   from
us.] Q3–5; *off.* Q1–2, Q6–12, F, D.   24:4–5 This, Madam] *This,* Madam
Q1–12, F, D (*This∧* Q5).   24:7   in which to flourish] Q2–12, F, D; *to
flourish in* Q1.   24:10   Wines] Q1–10, F, D; Vines Q11–12.   24:11
nature] Q3–5; *natures* Q1–2, Q6–12, F, D.   24:15   only to] Q2–12,
F, D; *only* Q1.   24:22   are] Q1–12, D; and F.   24:25   many] Q2–12,
F, D; *many* Q1.   24:28   Virtue] Q3–5; *Virtue of your Graces* Q1–2, Q6–
12, F, D.   24:30   Court Favours] Q1; Court-Favours Q2–12, F, D.   25:2
way] Q1–6, Q8–12, F, D; *may* Q7.   25:7–8   can give it better Education]
Q3–5; *will better breed it up* Q1–2, Q6–12, F, D.   25:11   a] Q1–4, Q6,
Q8, D; an Q5, Q7, Q9–12, F.   25:12   than] Q1–3, Q5–12, F, D; *then*
Q4.   25:13   Native *Indies*] Q3–5, Q8–12, D; *Native Indies* Q1–2, Q6–7;
Native *India* F.   25:16   he is] Q3–5; *him as* Q1–2, Q6–12, F, D.
25:17   *Indian* Prince] Indian Prince Q1–12, F, D.   25:18   that, with
which . . . him] Q3–5 (*that∧* Q5); *what . . . him withal* Q1–2, Q6–12,
F, D.   25:24   work; it] Q4–5, Q9–12, F, D (It Q4–5); ~. *It* Q1–3, Q6–8.
25:25   Historical truth] Q2–12, F, D; *truth* Q1.   26:1 intentions] Q1–12,
D; Intention F.   date: October *the*] Q1–4, Q6; October Q5, Q7–12,
F, D.

Connexion: *Completely omitted from M1–2.   27:2   writ*] Q1–12, D;
write F.   27:3   on it] Q3–5; on Q1–2, Q6–12, F, D.   27:4   *(viz.)* . . .
Orazia;] Q1–3, Q6–12, F, D; (viz. . . . *Orazia,* Q4; (viz. . . . *Orazia)*
Q5.   27:6   those two; and considering that] Q3–5; the old ones; and
considering Q1–2, Q6–12, F, D.   27:6   Queen] *Queen* Q1–12, F, D.
27:8   he has rais'd from them] Q3–5; from those two, he has rais'd Q1–2,
Q6–12, F, D.   27:12   Mens] Q1–12, D; Men F.   27:16   in] Q3–5;
and in Q1–2, Q6–12, F, D.   27:18   joyning] Q1–7, D; joyned Q8–12, F.
27:19   *Taxallan-Indians*]   Q1,   D;   *Tlaxcallan-Indians* Q2–3,   Q6–7;
Traxallan Indians Q4–5; *Traxallan-Indians* Q8–11, F; *Taxallian-Indians*
Q12.   27:26   Habits] Q2–12, F, D; ~, Q1.   27:26–27   Language
were to the Christians] Q2–12, F, D; Language Q1.

Names of the Persons: *Completely omitted from M1.   The Names
of the Persons Represented.*] Q1–12, F; Dramatis Personae. D; The Persons
Represented M2.   *Indians* Men,] Indians Men, Q1–12, F; INDIAN
MEN D; *omitted from M2.   his Eldest Son. . . . his Younger Son.*]

Q1–12, F, D; { his Sons M2.   *Orbellan,* Son to] Q1–12, M2; *Orbellam,*
Son to F; *Orbellan,* Son of D.   Queen] M2; *Queen* Q1–12, F,
D.   *Traxalla*] Q1–12, F, D; Truxalla M2.   High Priest of the Sun]
M2; *High Priest* of the *Sun* Q1–6, D; *High Priest of the Sun* Q7–12, F
(*Priests* Q12).   *M2 puts the Spaniards next, and omits* "Women".   Sis-
ters; and Daughters to the late] Q6–12, F, D (Sisters∧ Q9–12, F); Sisters; and
Daughter to the late Q1–5 (Sister, Q4; Sister∧ Q5); Daughters to the M2.
Queen.] *Queen.* Q1–10, F, D; *Queen*∧ Q11–12; queen∧ M2.   *Spaniards*]
Spaniards Q1–12, F, D; *omitted from M2.*   *M2 adds* "Indians / Spaniards
/ Souldiers / Messengers".   The Scene] Q1–12, F; *Scene* D, M2.   two
Leagues about it.] Q1–12, F, D; yᵉ Adjacent Country M2.
     Prologue: Completely omitted from M1–2.   2   *fear;*] D; ~ . Q1–12, F.
4 *Play.*] Q1–7, Q10–12, F, D; ~ , Q8–9.   5 *same*] Q6–12, F, D; ~ ,
Q1–5.   7–9 *omitted from Q2–12, F, D.*   13 *too:*] Q1–10, F, D; ~ .
Q11–12.   14 *you,*] Q1–9, D; ~∧ Q10–12, F.   16 *observes,*] Q5, D;
~∧ Q1–4, Q6–12, F.   20 Phœbus,] Q6–12, F, D; ~∧ Q1–5.   23
Play;] Q6–12, F, D; ~ . Q1–5.   24 *arrogantly,*] Q1–4, Q6–12, F, D; ~∧
Q5.   26 *about*] Q1–4, Q6; ~ , Q5, Q7–9, F, D; ~ . Q10–12.

I, i

     Caption: THE INDIAN EMPEROUR.] Q1–12, D, M1; THE Indian
Emperour: OR, THE CONQUEST of *MEXICO.* F; The Conquest of
Mexico By yᵉ Spaniards. M2.   ACT I. SCENE I.] Q1–12, F, D (ACT I∧
Q4); ACT: 1ˢᵗ Sc: 1ˢᵗ M1; Act I M2.   s.d.   *The Scene*] Q1–12, F; SCENE
D; The Scene is M2; *line omitted from M1.*   s.d.   Indians *of their
party.*] Q1–12, F, D; Indians M1–2.   1 new happy] Q1–12, F, D, M1;
new M2.   2 lately known;] Q1–6, D; ~ ? Q7, Q9–12, F; ~ ! Q8;
~∧ M1; late unknowne M2.   4 new!] Q1–7, Q9–12, F, D; ~ . Q8,
M2; ~∧ M1.   10 does] Q1–12, F, D, M1; doth M2.   12 differing]
Q1–12, F, D, M1; different M2.   13 wrought,] Q2–11, F, D; ~ . Q12;
~∧ M1–2; taught, Q1.   14 we] Q1–12, F, D, M2; wee M1.   15
Children, be] Q1, Q3–5, Q7–9, M1; ~∧~∧ Q2, Q6, D, M2; ~∧~, Q10–12,
F.   16 Infancy:] Q1–12, F, D, M1; ~ . M2.   18 seasons] Q1–3,
Q6–12, F, D, M1–2; season Q4–5.   18 birth.] Q1–12, F, D, M2; ~∧ M1.
22 ground.] Q1–12, F, D, M1; ~∧ M2.   23 Here . . . the] Q1–12,
F, D, M2; the . . . their M1.   23 seasons] Q2b–12, F, D, M1–2; season
Q1–2a.   24 see:] Q1–12, F, D; ~∧ M1; ~ . M2.   26 makes] Q1–12,
F, D, M1; make M2.   27 walk] Q1–12, F, D, M1; talk M2.   28
Ore] Q1–12, F, D, M2; Oare M1.   28 common] Q1–10, F, D, M1–2;
command Q11–12.   30 shower] Q1–12, F, D, M1; Showr M2.   31
provide] Q1–12, F, D, M2; ~ . M1.   32 hide,] Q1–4, Q6–7, Q9–12, F,
D; ~ . Q5, M1; ~ ; Q8; ~∧ M2.   34 Dare] Q2–12, F, D, M1–2; We
Ql.   34 New found] Q1–2, Q6–12, F, D, M1–2; New-found Q3–5.
36 subdue,] Q1; ~ ; Q2–12, F, D, M2; ~ . M1.   37 *Taxallan*] Q1–12,
F, D, M1; Truxalla M2.   37 powers] Q1–12, F, D, M2; pow'rs M1.
38 Has,] Q5, Q8; ~∧ Q1–4, Q6–7, Q9–12, F, D, M1–2.   39 King]
Q1–3, Q6, M1–2; ~ . Q4–5; ~ , Q7–12, F, D.   40 just] Q2b–12, F, D,
M1–2; fit Q1–2a.   40 bring] Q1–12, F, D, M2; ~ . M1.   42 our]

Q1–12, F, D, M2; and M1.   43   *Cort.* My self] Q2–12, F, D, M1–2; My self Q1.   43   go;] Q1–12, F, D; ~∧ M1–2.   44 Speak,] Q7–12, F, M1; ~∧ Q1–6, D, M2.   44   *Mexico?*] Q1–12, F, D; ~ . M1–2.   45 far] Q1, Q2b–12, F, D, M1–2; fair Q2a.   45 make] Q1–12, F, D, M2; take M1.   46 Lake.] Q1–12, F, D; ~ ; M1; ~∧ M2.   50 charge] Q1–4, Q6–12, F, D, M1–2; ~ , Q5.   50 scout;] Q1–12, F, D; ~∧ M1–2. 51 prepare,] Q1–12, F, D; ~ . M1; ~∧ M2.   52 war. *Exeunt.*] Q1–12, F, D, M1; war. M2.

I, ii

SCENE II] Q1–12, F, D, M2; 2ᵈ Scene M1.   *s.d.   Temple, and the*] Q1–12, F; *Temple. The* D, M2; temple and Caliban the M1.   *s.d. with other Priests.*] Q1–12, F, D; and other Preists appeareing in it. M1; and other priest M2.   1 Haste] Q1–12, F, D, M1; hast M2.   1 Priest,] Q2–12, F, D; ~∧ Q1, M1–2.   2 *High Pr.*] Q1–12, F, D, M2; Calib—M1 *(and similarly below).*   2 sets] Q2–12, F, D, M1–2; gets Q1.   2 He is] Q1–12, F, D, M2; hee's M1.   5 Sun,] Q1–3, Q6–12, F, D, M1; ~ . Q4–5; ~∧ M2.   6 ere] Q1–3, Q6–12, F, D, M1–2; e're, Q4–5.   6 run] Q1–12, F, D, M2; done M1.   10 pray'rs.] Q1–12, F, M1; ~ , D; prayers, M2.   11 stay,] Q1–11, F, D; ~ . Q12; ~∧ M1–2. 12 rites] Q2–12, F, D, M1; rights Q1, M2.   12 day.] Q2–7, Q9–11, F, D, M1–2; ~ : Q1; ~∧ Q8, Q12.   12+   *s.d. his Daughter* Cydaria;] Q8, D; ~ , Q1–7, Q9–12, F; ~ : M1; Cydaria∧ M2.   12+   *s.d.* Almeria,] Q1–11, F, D, M1–2; ~ . Q12.   12+   *s.d.* Orbellan, *and Train. They place themselves.*] Q1–12, F, D, M1 (*Train, they* Q4–5; traine they M1; themselves∧ Q12, M1); and Orbellan; they sit down. M2.   13 *High Pr.*] Q2–12, F, D, M2; *Callib.* Q1, M1.   13 birth day] Q1–2, Q6–7, Q9–12, F, D; birth-day Q3–5, Q8; birth M1; birthday M2.   18 Crown the] Q3–5; Crown her Q1–2, Q6–12, F, D, M1–2.   18 year,] D; ~ . Q1–12, F, M2; ~∧ M1.   19 Of] Q1–12, F, D, M2; Chorus———— Of M1.   19 day,] Q1–12, F, D, M2; day∧ / ————Crowne her Queen, whome you obey / ————Crowne her Queen Crowne her Queene M1.   22 suspect. [*Aside.*] suspect. Q1–12, F, D, M2; suspect∧ M1.   22+   *s.d. rises, goes about*] Q1–12, F, D, M1; Looks upon M2.   22+   *s.d. stays at* Almeria *and bows.*] Q1–12, F, D; stayes at Almeria, & kneels. M1; bowes to Almeria. M2.   24 Queen] Q1–3, Q6–7, Q9–12, F, D, M1; ~ . Q4–5, M2; ~ , Q8.   25–26 *s.d. omitted from M1.*   26 owe,] Q1–4, Q6–7, Q9–12, F, D, M2; ~∧ Q5, Q8; ~ . M1.   26 *s.d.* Sister] Q1–4, Q6–12, F, D, M2; Sisters Q5.   27 To whom not only he his] Q3–5; Whom his hard heart not only Q1–2, Q6–12, F, D, M1–2.   28 sufferings] Q1–4, Q6–12, F, D, M1; suff'rings Q5; suffering M2.   30 you,] Q1–3, Q6–7, Q9–12, F, D, M1–2; ~ . Q4–5, Q8.   32 bed. [*Aside to her.*] bed. Q1–5, Q8–12, F, D, M1–2; bed, Q6–7.   35 who] Q2–12, F, D, M2; that Q1, M1. 35 pay. [*Aside.*] pay. Q1–12, F, D, M1; pay∧ M2.   36 way. [*Aside.*] way. Q1–12, F, D, M1–2.   36+   *s.d. omitted from M1.*   36+   *s.d. him who is kneeling . . . while*] Q1–12, F, D (*kneeliug* Q1); him kneeling . . . time M2.   37 is] Q1–11, F, D, M1–2; if Q12.   37 design'd, [*Kneeling.*] Q1–12, F, D; design'd, M1–2.   38 Heaven] Q1–12, F, M1–

2; Heav'n D.   40   forgive.] Q1–12, F, D, M2; ~∧ M1.   41   both my]
Q1–3, Q6–12, F, D, M1–2; both by Q4–5.   41   dy'd;] Q1–12, F, D; ~ .
M1; ~∧ M2.   42   thy sword] Q1–8, D, M1; the sword Q9–12, F, M2.
44   who] Q2–12, F, D, M2; that Q1, M1.   44   now:] Q1–7, Q9–12, F,
D; ~ ; Q8; ~ . M1; ~∧ M2.   45   sufferings] Q1–12, F, D, M2; suffrings
M1.   46   found] Q1–12, F, D, M1; felt M2.   49   He] Q1–12, F, D,
M2; Hee M1.   50   pow'r] Q1–12, F, D, M1; power M2.   52   pow'r-
ful . . . soul] Q1–12, F, D, M1; powerful . . . heart M2.   52   weak?] Q1–4,
Q6–12, F, D, M1–2; ~ ; Q5.   53   it.——— [*Aside.* / Madam] it, Madam
Q1–2, Q6–7, Q9, F, M2; it. Madam Q3, Q8, Q10–12, D; it; Madam Q4–5;
it? Madam M1.   57   these.] Q1–6, Q8–12, F, D; ~∧ Q7, M1–2.   58
and] Q1–12, D, M1–2; an F.   58   please.] Q1–12, F, D, M2; ~∧ M1.
60   do] Q1–12, F, D; doe M1–2.   62   I] Q1–12, D, M1–2; I'll F.   66
Not] Q1–4, Q6–12, F, D, M1–2; Nor Q5.   68+   *s.d. omitted from M1.*
68+   *s.d. are this while*] Q1–12, F, D; are M2.   69   always] Q1–12, F,
D, M1; never M2.   71   torment] Q1–11, F, D, M1–2; torments Q12.
72   Wife.] Q1–12, D, M1; ~ , F; ~∧ M2.   73   care] Q1–12, F, D, M2;
cares M1.   73   an] Q1–12, F, D, M1; a M2.   73   destroys,] Q1–12,
D, M1–2 (~ . Q5; ~∧ M1–2); destroy, F.   74   and] Q1–12, F, D, M2;
or M1.   75   mark] Q1–12, F, D, M2; markes M1.   75   shown,] Q1b–
10, F, D; ~∧ Q1a, Q11–12, M2; ~ ? M1.   76   lose] Q1–12, F, D, M1;
loose M2.   76   own?] Q1–5, Q8, Q10–12, F, M1–2; ~ ! Q6–7, Q9, D.
77   love relies] Q1–12, F, D, M1; kindness lies M2.   78   do] Q1–12, F,
D, M1; doe M2.   78   eyes:] Q1–7, Q9–12, F, D, M2; ~ . Q8, M1.   80
find?] Q2–12, F, D, M1; ~ . Q1, M2.   82   I'le] Q1, Q2b–12, F, D, M1–2;
'le Q2a.   82   King;] Q1–12, F, D; ~ . M1; ~∧ M2.   85   you,] Q1–
10, F, D, M1–2; ~ . Q11–12.   85   *s.d. omitted from M1.*   85   [*To*]
Q3–5, Q8–12, F, D; ∧*to* Q1–2; [*to* Q6–7, M2.   90   eye] Q1–12, F, D,
M1; eyes M2.   95   Sea shore] Q1, M1–2; Sea-shore Q2–12, F, D.   96
breaking] Q1–12, F, D, M1; beating M2.   96   ground,] Q1–2, Q6–12,
F, D; ~ ; Q3–5; ~ . M1; ~∧ M2.   97   for] Q1–12, F, D, M1; fore M2.
99   low hung] Q1–2, Q6–12, F, D, M1–2; low-hung Q3–5.   99   clouds]
Q1–12, F, D, M1; clowd clouds M2.   99   rain] Q1–12, M1–2; ~ , D;
~ . F.   101   my] Q1–12, F, D, M2; mine M1.   102   methought,] Q3–
5; ~∧ Q1–2, Q6–12, F, D, M1–2.   102   rise] Q1–12, F, D, M2; ~ . M1.
105   represent?] Q1–12, F, D; ~∧ M1–2.   106   than] Q1–12, F, D, M1;
then M2.   106   wonder] Q1–12, D, M1–2; wonders F.   108   flew,]
Q1–12, F, D; ~ . M1; ~∧ M2.   110   winds] Q1–12, F, D, M1; wind M2.
110   blow.] Q1–2a, M1; ~ : Q2b–12, F, D; ~∧ M2.   112   out-bow'd]
Q1, Q3–5, M1; out-blow'd Q2, Q6–12, F, D; out blowd M2.   113   ye]
Q1–12, F, D, M2; yea M1.   113   are] Q3–5; were Q1–2, Q6–12, F, D,
M1–2.   114   Seas!] Q1–12, F, D; ~ ? M1; ~∧ M2.   115   shore?] Q1–
12, F, D; ~∧ M1–2.   116   them roar:] Q1–12, F, D (~ ; Q11–12); um
roare. M1; em roare. M2.   118   smoke.] Q1–11, F, D, M2; ~ , Q12; ~∧
M1.   120   these the] Q1–12, F, D, M1; these are M2.   122   support]
Q1–12, F, D, M1; sustaine M2.   123   Prophecies] Q1–12, F, D, M1;
Prophesies M2.   124   in] Q1–12, F, D, M1; on M2.   124   Land,] Q1–
12, F, D, M1 (~ . D, M1); stand M2.   126   fore-shows] Q1–12, F, D, M1;

portends M2.   126 decree. *Exit High Pr.*] decree. Q1–12, F, D, M1–2.
127 remain;] Q3–5; ~ , Q1–2; ~ . Q6–12, F, D; ~∧ M1–2.   129 most]
Q1–12, F, D, M2; not M1.   129 fair.] Q1–12, F, D; ~∧ M1–2.   131–
132 *s.d. omitted from M1–2*.   132 am sure] Q1–12, F, D, M2; am M1.
133 part.] Q1, Q2b–4, Q6–12, F, D, M2; ~∧ Q2a, M1; ~ : Q5.   134 a
heart:] Q1–12, F, D; an heart. M1; my heart. M2.   138 due.] Q1–12,
F, D, M1; ~∧ M2.   143 from her] Q1–12, F, D, M2; from my M1.
144 wounds which first] Q3–5; first wounds that Q1–2a, M1; first wounds
which Q2b, Q6–12, F, D, M2.   145 glories] Q1–12, D, M1–2; Glorious
F.   146 day break] Q1, M1; day-break Q2–12, F, D; daybreake
M2.   147 pace,] Q1–12, F, D, M1; ~∧ M2.   151 suit] Q1–
12, F, D, M1; suite M2.   154 begun:] Q1–12, F, D, M2; ~ ; M1.   155
I can no] Q3–5; should I a Q1–2, Q6–12, F, D, M1–2.   156 ere] Q1–3,
Q6, D, M1–2; e're Q4–5, Q7–12, F.   156 awake:] Q1–12, F, D; ~ . M1–
2.   158 refuse] Q2–12, F, D, M1–2; refufe Q1.   159 owe] Q1–12,
F, D, M1; ow M2.   160 reward,] Q1–2, Q6, M1; ~ ; Q3–5; ~ : Q7–12,
F; ~ . D; ~∧ M2.   161–162 services . . . service] Q1–11, F, D, M1–2;
service . . . services Q12.   162 past.] Q1–3, Q6–12, F, D; ~ , Q4; ~ :
Q5; ~∧ M1–2.   163 know:] Q2b–12, F, D, M1; ~ , Q1–2a; ~∧ M2.
165 decay,] Q1–6, Q9–12, F, D; ~ . Q7–8; ~∧ M1–2.   167 birth.]
Q1–6, D, M2; ~ ; Q7–12, F; ~∧ M1.   169 cease,] Q1–4, Q6–12, F, D;
~ ; Q5; ~∧ M1–2.   170 friendship] Q1, M2; ~ , Q2–12, F, D, M1.
171 wreath.] Q1–4, Q6–12, F, D, M2; ~ , Q5, M1.   172 not, ev'n] Q1–
2, Q6, D, M1; not ev'n Q3, Q7–12, F, M2; ev'n Q4; even Q5.   173 any
thing.] Q2–12, F, D; ~ : Q1; ~∧ M1–2.   174 King.] Q2–12, F, D, M1;
~ ? Q1; ~∧ M2.   175 gone?] Q1–12, F, D; ~ . M1; ~∧ M2.   176
Traxalla's] Q1–9, F, D, M1–2; *Taxalla's* Q10–12.   178 dead!] Q1–12,
F, D; ~ . M1; ~∧ M2.   179 enemy,] Q1–3, Q6, D, M1; ~∧ Q4–5; ~ ;
Q7–12, F; ~ . M2.   180 *Traxalla's*] Q1–3, Q6–11, F, D, M1–2; *Tax-
alla's* Q4–5, Q12.   181 strive,———] ~ ,∧ Q1–12, F, D; ~ : ———
M1; ~∧——— M2.   182 Loves] Q1–12, D, M2; Love F, M1.   186
an] Q1–2, Q6–12, F, D, M1; a Q3–5, M2.   189 you?] Q1–12, F, D, M2;
~ . M1.   190 *Mont.* You] Q2–12, F, D, M2; *Mont.* How now——— /
You Q1, M1 (now. M1).   190 amaz'd] Q1–12, F, D, M1; amazdly M2.
192 1 *Guard*] Q1–12, F, D, M1 (1. Q4); G: M2.   192 where this] Q1–
12, F, D, M1; where the M2.   194 ambush'd . . . whom] Q1–12, F, D,
M1; ambush . . . who M2.   195 *Taxallan*] Q10–12, D, M1; *Taxcallan* Q1–5; *Traxallan* Q6–9, F, M2.   195+ *s.d. Another Enters.*] Q1–5;
enter another M2; *omitted from Q6–12, F, D, M1*.   196 2 *Guard.*] Q1–
12, F, D, M2; 2d——— M1.   196 round.] Q2–4, Q6–12, F, D, M2;
~ , Q1; ~∧ Q5, M1.   201 Than] Q1–12, F, D, M1; Then M2.   201
Love. *Exeunt omnes.*] M1; Love. Q1–12, F, D; love (Exeunt M2.   201+
s.d. within.] Q2–4, Q6–12, F, D; ~ , Q1, Q5, M1; ~∧ M2.   201+ *s.d.*
Enter Montez. Odm. Guy. Alib. Orb. Cyd. Alm.] Q1–12, F, D; Enter Montezuma, Odmar, Guyomar, Orbellan, behind them Cydaria, Almeria, Alibech, M1; then enter all again M2.   201+ *s.d. by*] Q2–12, F, D; by Q1,
M1–2.   201+ *s.d.* Taxallans] Q1–12, D, M1; Traxallans F; the traxallans
M2.   202 None] Q1–12, F, D, M1; No M2.   204 revenge] Q1–4,

Q6–12, F, M2; ∼ , Q5, D; ∼ : M1.   204   past,] Q1–12, F; ∼ ; D; ∼∧
M1–2.   205+   *s.d.* Pizarro, *to the* Taxallans, Cort. *stays them*] Q1–12,
F, D, M1 (Traxallans F); and Piz: Cortez stays the traxallans M2.   206–
207   sight! [*To his* Indians.] Q1–12, F, D (Indians∧ Q1–3, Q6); sight∧
M1–2.   207   charge . . . fight?] Q1–12, F, D, M2; ∼ ; . . .∼ . M1.
209   your Enemies] Q1–12, F, D, M2; their Enemies M1.   211   these]
Q1–12, F, D, M1; those M2.   211   would ignorantly] Q1–12, F, D, M1;
most ignorantly would M2.   211   save;] Q3–5, M1; ∼ , Q1–2, Q6–12,
F; ∼ . D; ∼∧ M2.   214   Where,] Q8–12, F, D, M1; ∼∧ Q1–7, M2.
215   thy] Q1–12, F, D, M2; the M1.   215   race!] Q1–5, M2; ∼ ? Q6–12,
F, D, M1.   218   shown] Q1–12, F, D, M1; showd M2.   218   distrest!]
Q1–12, F, D; ∼∧ M1–2.   221   Friends:] Q1–12, F, D; ∼ . M1–2.   222
s.d. omitted from M1–2.   223   who do] Q2–12, F, D, M2 (doe M2);
that do Q1, M1.   224   *Ind.* O] Q1–12, F, D, M2; O M1.   224
s.d. omitted from M1–2.   226   *The* Taxallans *retire.*] Q1–12, F, D, M1
(Traxallans F; *M1 as* 227+); (they retire. M2 (*on* 227).   227   silent,]
Q1–12, F, D, M1; ∼∧ M2.   227   dye.] Q1–3, Q6–12, F, D, M1; ∼∧ Q4–
5, M2.   228   *Taxallans*] Q1–12, D, M1; *Traxallans* F, M2.   231
come] Q1–12, F, D, M2; some M1.   231   Mont. *kneels to* Cort.] Q1–12,
F, D, M1; Kneeling M2 (*on* 232).   233   Stars———] M1; ∼ . Q1–12,
F, D, M2.   234   misplace.] Q1–12, F, D; ∼∧ M1–2.   235   Thy] Q1–
9, F, D, M1–2; They Q10–12.   235   Race.] Q1–6, D; ∼ , Q7–12, F; ∼∧
M1–2.   238   I with Slaves will] Q1–12, F, D, M2; I'll with Captives M1.
239   hot] Q1–12, F, D, M2; that M1.   242   I] Q2–12, F, D, M2; we Q1,
M1.   242   heart;] Q2–9, D; ∼ , Q1, M1; ∼ : Q10–12, F; ∼∧ M2.   244
rarest] Q3–5; choicest Q1–2, Q6–12, F, D, M1–2.   251   Herauld] Q1–11,
F, D, M1–2; Heralds Q12.   257   *Mexico;*] Q1–12, F, D; ∼ . M1; ∼∧
M2.   260   know,] Q1–9, D; ∼ . Q10–12, F; ∼∧ M1–2.   261   wide] Q1–
12, F, D, M1; vast M2.   262   so] Q1–12, F, D, M1; such M2.   265
King?] Q1–12, F, D, M2; ∼ . M1.   265+   *s.d. omitted from M1–2.*
265+   *s.d.* them,] Q2–12, F, D; ∼∧ Q1.   266   *Spain's*] Q1–12, F, D,
M1; Spains M2.   269   Friend,] Q1; ∼ . Q2–12, F, D, M1; ∼∧ M2.
271   him with . . . Gold:] Q1–12, F, D, M1; to him . . .∼ . M2.   272
adore] Q3–5; implore Q1–2, Q6–12, F, D, M1–2.   273   prayers implore]
Q3–5 (Pray'rs Q4–5); him adore Q1–2, Q6–12, F, D, M1–2.   274   speak]
Q1–2, F, D, M2; spoke M1.   277   mettal] Q1–12, F, D, M1; mettle M2.
280   your . . . be] Q1–12, F, D, M2; thy . . . bee M1.   281   This]
Q1–5, M1–2; The Q6–12, F, D.   283   pow'r] Q1–12, F, D, M1; power
M2.   284   to our] Q1–3, Q6–12, F, D, M1–2; to your Q4–5.   285
Ill] Q1–12, F, D, M2; I'll M1.   286   love;] Q1–12, F, D, M2; ∼∧ M1.
287   shown?] Q1–12, F, D; ∼∧ M1–2.   290   an] Q1–11, F, D, M1–2;
and Q12.   291   Heaven] Q1–12, F, D, M2; Heav'n M1.   291   give,]
Q1–12, F, D; ∼ . M1; ∼∧ M2.   292   less] Q2–12, F, D, M1–2; least Q1.
292   receive;] Q1–12, F, D; ∼ . M1; ∼∧ M2.   295   power] Q1–12, F,
D, M2; pow'r M1.   295   our end] Q1–12, F, D, M1; his end M2.   301
who] Q1–12, F, D, M1; that M2.   303–323   *omitted from M2.*   303
Fasts] Q1–8, M1; Fast Q9–12, F.   304   the] Q1–12, F, D; their M1.
309   these] Q1–12, F, D; those M1.   310   some;] Q1–7, Q9–12, F,

D; ~. Q8, M1.　312 on] Q1-5, Q7-12, F, D, M1; one Q6.　313 none!] Q1-12, F, D. ~? M1.　313 them] Q1-7, Q9-12, F, D, M1; 'em Q8.　315 Those] Q1-12, F, D; These M1.　316 my] Q1-12, F, D; the M1.　318 suffers any pow'r, to shock] Q3-5 (pow'r∧ Q4-5); bears, within, a power that shocks Q1-2, Q6-12, F, D, M1.　318 own.] Q3-12, F, D; ~, Q1-2; ~∧ M1.　321 accuse,] Q1-9, Q11-12, D; ~. Q10, F; ~∧ M1.　324 none;] Q1-12, F, D; ~. M1; ~∧ M2.　327 Prince,] Q1-10, F, D; ~∧ Q11-12, M1-2.　329 but, . . . man] Q1-7, Q9-12, F, D; ~∧ . . . ~, Q8; ~∧ . . . ~∧ M1; ~∧ . . . ~. M2.　331 Honour requir'd that act, ev'n from a Foe,] Q3-5; It was an act my Honour bound me to, Q1-2, Q6-12, F, D, M1-2 (too M2).　332 But] Q1-12, F, D, M2; But I M1.　332 again to do,] Q1-12, F, D, M1 (do. Q4-5; doe∧ M1); to doe again∧ M2.　333-334 That reason which inclin'd my will before / Would urge it now, for Love has fir'd it] Q3-5; I could not do it on my Honours score, / For Love would now oblige me to do Q1-2, Q6-12, F, D, M1-2 (I would . . . doe . . . doe M2).　335 Is] Q1-12, F, D, M2; *Mont.* Is M1.　337 *Vasq.* He] Q1-12, F, D, M2; Hee M1.　338 *Mont.* Since] Q1-12, F, D, M2; Since M1.　338 Heav'n] Q3-5; Heavens Q1-2, Q6-12, F, D; Heav'ns M1; heaven M2.　338 make,] Q1-12, F, D; ~∧ M1-2.　340 decree,] Q1-12, F, D, M2; ~; M1.　341 shown,] Q1-4, Q6-12, F, D; ~. Q5; ~∧ M1-2.　343 than] Q1-12, F, D, M1; then M2.　343 do] Q1-12, F, D; doe M1-2.　344 you;] Q1-12, F, D; ~∧ M1-2.　345 stay,] Q1-12, F, D; ~∧ M1-2.　347-348 *omitted from M1.*　347 to *Cyd.*] Q9-12, F; to *Cyd.* Q1-8, D; Going M2.　347 shown.] Q6-12, F, D; ~, Q1-5; ~∧ M2.　348 his] Q1-12, F, D; the M2.　348 *s.d. omitted from M1.*　348+ *s.d. Exeunt.* . . . *Alm. and Alib.*] in *Q1-12*, F, D, *M1-2 follows l. 346* (Almeria, Alibech M1).　348+ *s.d.* Cyd. . . . *while.] omitted from* M2.　348+ *s.d.* upon] Q1-12, F, D; on M1.　348+ *s.d.* Cortez,] Q1-10, F, D, M1; ~. Q11-12.　348+ *s.d.* looking] Q2-12, F, D, M1; loooking Q1.　349 Father's] Q1-12, F, D, M1; fathers M2.　350 behind! *Aside.*] Q1-12, F, D; behind——— M1; behind∧ M2.　351 who] Q2-12, F, D, M2; that Q1, M1.　352 blind. *Aside.*] Q1-12, F, D (blind, F); blind——— M1; blind∧ M2.　356 would] Q1-12, F, D, M1; should M2.　357 storms within] Q1-5, M1-2; torments in Q6-12, F, D.　361 swear,] Q6-12, F, D; ~∧ Q1-5, M1-2.　361 those] Q1-12, F, D, M2; these M1.　364 to] Q2-12, F, D, M2; by Q1, M1.　364 here.] Q1-12, F, D; ~∧ M1-2.　366 lies.] Q1-12, F, D; lyes∧ M1-2.　369 me,] M1; ~? Q1-12, F, D; ~! M2.　371 *Cort.* Mine] Q1-12, F, D, M2; Mine M1.　372 so just] Q1-12, F, D, M2; as kind M1.　372+ *s.d.* Orbellan.] Q2-12, F, D, M1-2 (~∧ Q4, M2); Orb. Q1.　375 go.] Q1-12, F, D; ~∧ M1-2.　378 high plac'd] Q1-3, Q6-12, F, D, M1-2; high-plac'd Q4-5.　379 That] Q3-5; Dares———that Q1-2, Q6-12, F, D, M2; Dares!——— / that M1.　379 spoke] Q1-12, F, D, M2; spake M1.　380 who] Q2-12, F, D, M2; that Q1, M1.　380 it;] Q1-12, F, D, M2; ~. M1.　382 guilt's] Q1-12, F, D, M1; guilts M2.　383 born] Q1-12, F, D, M2; borne M1.　384 morn!] Q1-12, F, D, M2; ~. M1.　385 those] Q1-12, F, D, M2; these M1.　386 within] Q3-5; beneath Q1-2,

Q6–12, F, D, M1–2.   386 those] Q1–12, F, D, M2; their M1.   387–
388 *both lines have parens before and after (and no other end punctuation) in M1.*   388 *Exeunt omnes.*] Q1–12, F, D; Exeunt severally M1;
Exeunt M2.

II, i

ACT II. SCENE I.] D; ACT II. Q1–12, F; Act: 2ᵈ: M1; *omitted from M2.*
s.d. SCENE, *The*] Q1–12, F, D, M1; The M2   *s.d. Enter* Montezuma,
High Priest] Q1–12, F, D (*and High* D); Montezuma, Caliban M1 (*and so
throughout the scene*); Montezuma and the High-priest M2.   1 do]
Q1–12, F, D; doe M1–2.   2 th'] Q1–12, F, D, M1; the M2.   2
event] Q1–12, F, D, M2; events M1.   4 content;] Q1–12, F, D, M2;
~ . M1.   5 search does . . . motive] Q3–5; motive . . . cause does
Q1–2, Q6–12, F, D, M1–2.   6 rules] Q1–5, Q7–12, F, D, M1–2; rule
Q6.   6 heart] Q1–12, D, M1–2; Heatt F.   6 King;] Q1–12, F, D, M2;
~ . M1.   7 I more] Q1–12, F, D, M2; more M1.   8 state] Q1–12,
F, D, M1; fate M2.   10+ *s.d. Charm.*] Q4–5, D; ~ , Q1–3, Q6–12,
F; ~∧ M1–2.   12 ye] Q2–12, F, D, M2; yea Q1, M1.   13 your] Q1–
3, Q6–12, F, D, M2; you Q4–5; these M1.   17 who] Q2–12, F, D, M2;
that Q1, M1.   19 Who] Q2–12, F, D, M2; That Q1, M1.   20 do;]
Q1–12, F, D; doe. M1; doe∧ M2.   22+ *s.d. Earthy*] Q1–12, D, M1–2;
earthly F.   24 which] Q2–12, F, D, M2; that Q1, M1.   24 more:]
Q1–12, F, D, M2; ~ . M1.   25 commands,] Q1–3, Q6–12, F, D; ~ . Q4–
5; ~∧ M1–2.   26 Lands;] Q1–12, F, D; ~ . M1; ~∧ M2.   29 their
. . . they] Q3–5; our . . . we Q1–2, Q6–12, F, D, M1–2.   29 slept,]
Q1–12, F, D, M2; ~ . M1.   30 Heaven] Q1–12, F, D, M2; Heav'n M1.
30 a long] Q1–9, D, M1–2; along Q10–12, F.   31–34 *omitted from
M1.*   33 horn-feet] Q1–12, F, D; horn feet M2.   34 cry.] Q1–8, D,
M2; ~ : Q9–12, F.   35 rule] Q1–12, F, D, M1; have M2.   36
Deface:] Q1–12, F, D; ~ . M1; ~∧ M2.   42 who] Q2–12, F, D; that
Q1, M1–2.   44 e're . . . I'le scorn] Q1–12, F, D, M1; ere . . . I
scorn M2.   45 please] Q1–9, D, M1–2; please with Q10–12, F.   45
stand,] Q1–6, D; ~ . Q7–12, F; ~∧ M1–2.   46 with] Q1–12, F, D, M2;
in M1.   47 Those] Q1–12, F, D, M1; These M2.   49 Colours]
Q1–5, M1–2; colour Q6-12, F, D.   50 hide] Q1–9, Q11–12, D, M1;
hid Q10, F, M2.   50 ill.] Q1–6, D, M1–2; ~ , Q7–8; ~ : Q9–12, F.
52+ *s.d. ascends*] Q1–12, F, D, M2; ascends to a Light ayrie time, [*sic*]
M1.   52+ *s.d. White in the shape of a Woman and Sings.*] Q1–12, F, D
(*in shape* Q6–12, F, D; *Woman,* Q2–12, F, D); White, in the shape of a
Woman. M1; White and Sings M2.   53 *Kalib.*] Q1–12, F, D, M2;
Kalib—sings M1.   54 lower,] Q1–3; *lowr,* Q6–12, F, D; *lower.* Q4–5;
lowre∧ M1, M3; lower∧ M2.   55 When] Q1–12, D, M1–3; *Where* F.
57 power] Q1–12, F, D, M2; pow'r M1, M3.   58 be] Q1–12, F, D,
M2–3; bee M1.   59 thy] Q1–10, F, D, M1–3; *the* Q11–12.   60
shalt] Q2–12, F, D, M3; shall Q1, M1–2.   60 Raign:] Q1–5; ~ . Q6–12,
F, D, M1; ~∧ M2–3.   61 O] Q1–12, F, D, M1–2; Oh! M3.   63
deserve my] Q1–12, F, D, M2; deserveing M1.   66 Love's] Q2–12, F, D;
Lov's Q1; loves M1–2.   67 Arise] Q1–12, F, D, M2; Arise—— /

Arise M1.   67   ye subtle] Q1–12, F, D, M1; ye M2.   67   that] Q1,
Q3–12, F, D, M1–2; than Q2.   67   spy] Q8, M1–2; ~ , Q1–7, Q9–12,
F, D.   69   read it] Q1–3, Q6–12, F, D, M1–2; read Q4–5.   71   that
can] Q1–12, F, D, M1; that M2.   72   Womans] Q1–12, F, D, M2;
Womens M1.   72   fancie] Q6–12, F, D, M1–2; ~ , Q1–5.   74   heart,]
Q1–6, D, M2; ~ . Q7–12, F, M1.   75   Arise.———] Q1; ~∧———
Q2–4, Q6–12, F, D; ~ ∧∧ Q5; ~ ·∧ M2; *omitted from M1*.   75+   *s.d.*
The] Q1–12, F, D, M2; Two M1.   75+   *s.d.* *Ghosts*] Q1–6, D, M1–2;
Ghost Q7–12, F.   75+   *s.d.* Traxalla] Q1–10, F, D, M1–2; Taxalla
Q11–12.   75+   *s.d. arise, they stand still*] Q1–12, F, D, M1; rise M2.
77   portend.———] ~ :∧ Q1–5, M2; ~ ,∧ Q6–12, F; ~ ·∧ D; ~∧∧ M1.
78   begon.——— They] M1 (they); begon,———they Q1–12, F, D, M2
(begon∧——— Q7–12, F).   78   dis-appear,] Q1–12, F, D; ~ . M1; ~∧
M2.   80   fright,] Q1–12, F, D; ~ . M1; ~∧ M2.   81   these] Q1–12,
F, D; their M1; those M2.   81   night;] Q1–8, D, M2; ~ . Q9–12, F; ~∧
M1.   82   and] Q1–11, F, D, M1–2; an Q12.   82   sport? *They smile.*]
Q1–12, F, D, M2; sport? M1.   83   you] Q1–12, F, D, M2; ye M1.   83
flesh———] Q1–12, F, D; ~ .——— M1; ~ . M2.   84+   *s.d.* *Queen*]
Queen Q1–12, F, D, M1–2.   84+   *s.d. betwixt the Ghosts*] Q1–12, F, D,
M1; between the other two M2.   84+   *s.d. in*] Q2–12, F, D, M1–2;
into Q1.   88–103   *in italics in* Q2–*12*, F, D.   89   mine;] Q1–12,
F, D; ~ . M1; ~∧ M2.   90   who] Q2–12, F, D, M2; that Q1, M1.
90   show,] Q1–3, Q7–9, M2; ~ . Q4–5; ~∧ Q10–12, F, D, M1.   92
doest] Q1–3; *dost* Q4–12, F, D, M1–2.   92   Arms?] Q1–12, F, D,
M2; ~ , M1.   93   Charms?] M1; ~ ! Q1–12, F, D, M2.   95   away:]
Q1–12, F, D, M2; ~ . M1.   96   a] Q1–12, F, D, M2; some M1.   96
below,] Q1–3, Q6–9, D; ~∧ Q4–5, M2; ~ . Q10–12, F; ~ ; M1.   97
there] Q1–12, F, D, M2; the M1.   97   o're] Q1–12, F, D, M1; ore M2.
100   Fields] Q1–8, D, M1–2; *Field* Q9–12, F.   101   grow,] Q1–12, F, D,
M2 (~∧ Q2, *some copies*); ~ . M1.   103   thou doest] Q1–3; *thou dost*
Q4–12, F, D, M1; it does M2.   104   Fate,] Q1; ~ : Q2–12, F, D; ~ .
M1; ~∧ M2.   107   hope] Q1–12, F, D, M2; hopes M1.   107   fear;]
Q1–9, D; ~ : Q10–12, F; ~ . M1; ~∧ M2.   108   War,] Q1–7, Q9–12,
F, D, M1; ~ . Q8; ~∧ M2.   109   Feavers] Q1–11, F, D, M1–2; Fears
Q12.

II, ii

SCENE II.] Q1–12, F, D, M2 (SCENE, Q4); Second Scene M1.   *s.d.*
Cydaria *and* Alibech, *Betwixt the two Armies.*] Q1–12, F, D, M2 (Cydaria,
Alibeck Q1a; Cydaria, Alibech Q1b; between M2); Cydaria. Alibech. M1.
8   command;] Q1–12, F, D, M2; ~ . M1.   9   here.———] ~ ·∧ Q1–12,
F, D, M1–2.   9+   *s.d.* Cort. *and* Vasq. *to them.*] Q1–12, F, D, M1; to
them Cortez and Vasques M2.   11   *Indians*] Q1–12, F, D, M1; Indian
M2.   11   stand;] Q1–12, D, M2; ~ . M1; stands; F.   12   betwixt]
Q1–12, F, D, M1; between M2.   12   Clouds] Q1–9, D, M1–2; Cloud,
Q10–12, F.   13   day, . . . both] Q1–7, Q9–12, F, D (both, Q10–12, F);
~∧ . . . ~ , Q8; ~∧ . . . ~∧ M1–2.   13   loose] Q1–12, F, M1–2; lose
D.   17   ruine] Q2–12, F, D, M2; scatter Q1, M1.   18   power] Q1–2,

Q6–12, F, D, M2; pow'r Q3–5, M1.   21 off'ring] Q1–7, Q9–12, F, D,
M2; offering Q8, M1.   21 refuse;] Q1–9, D; ∼ : Q10–12, F; ∼ . M1; ∼∧
M2.   25 blame.] Q1; ∼ : Q2–12, F, D, M2; ∼∧ M1.   28 blindly]
Q1–12, F, D, M1; boldly M2.   28 obey,] Q1–12, F, D; ∼∧ M1–2.   29
away.] Q1–3, Q6–12, F, D, M1–2; ∼ , Q4–5.   30–31 *omitted from* M2.
33 me;] Q1–12, F, D; ∼ . M1; ∼∧ M2.   36 obey,] Q1–12, F, D; ∼∧
M1–2.   37 Honour] Q1–4, Q6–12, F, D, M2; ∼ , Q5, M1.   38
which] Q2–12, F, D, M2; that Q1, M1.   38 controul?] Q1–6, Q8,
Q10–12, F, D; ∼ ; Q7, Q9; ∼ . M1; ∼∧ M2.   39 Soul;] Q1–12, F,
D; ∼ . M1; ∼∧ M2.   42 *Cyd.* Lay] Q1–12, F, D, M2; Lay M1.   44
Cort.] Q1–12, F, D, M2; *Mont.* M1.   45 Crown'd:] Q1–5; ∼ . Q6–12,
F, D; ∼∧ M1–2.   46 Flood,] Q1–12, D; ∼ . F; ∼∧ M1–2.   47, 49
Father's] Q1–12, F, D, M1; fathers M2.   51 us'd;] Q1–7, Q9–12, F,
D; ∼ . Q8, M1; ∼∧ M2.   53 her] Q1–8, D, M1–2; a Q9–12, F.   53
breast?] Q2–12, F, D, M1–2; ∼ ! Q1.   57 more;] Q1–12, F, D, M2; ∼ .
M1.   59 Fight] Q4–5, Q8, M2; ∼ , Q1–3, Q6–7, Q9–12, F, D, M1.
59 there,] Q1; ∼ : Q2–12, F, D, M2; ∼ . M1.   62 Battel, but I'le]
Q1–12, F, D, M1 (Battel; Q7–12, F); fight but I will M2.   63 Bow;]
Q1–7, Q9–12, F, D; ∼ : Q8; ∼∧ M1–2.   64 strife,] Q1–3, Q6–12, F, D,
M1; ∼ . Q4–5; ∼∧ M2.   65+ *s.d. omitted from Q1, M1–2.*   66
more,] Q1–12, F, D, M2; ∼∧ M1.   66 death,] Q1–6, M1; ∼ ; Q7–12,
F, D; ∼ . M2.   67 breath?] Q2–12, F, D, M1–2; ∼ ! Q1.   69 name;]
Q1–12, F, D; ∼∧ M1; ∼ . M2.   70 Men] Q1–4, Q6–12, F, D, M1–2;
Man Q5.   71 mind.] Q2–12, F, D, M2; ∼ , Q1, M1.   72 off]
Q1–12, F, D; of M1–2.   72 Men,] Q1–6, D, M2; ∼ . Q7–12, F; ∼∧ M1.
72 War's] Q1–12, F, D, M1; wars M2.   72 done. *To* Piz.] done.
Q1–12, F, D, M1–2.   73 orders] Q1–4, Q6–12, F, D, M1–2; Order's Q5.
74 gives] Q1–12, D, M1; drives F; comes M2.   75 their] Q1–12, F,
D, M1; the M2.   77 to] Q1–12, F, D, M1; for M2.   77 Love;]
Q1–12, F, D; ∼ . M1; ∼∧ M2.   78 I] Q2–12, F, D, M2; I'le Q1, M1.
79 but] Q1–12, F, D, M2; and M1.   79+ *s.d. Exeunt* Cort. Vasq. Piz.]
Q1–12, F, D; Exeunt; M1; Exeunt Spaniards M2.   79+ *s.d.* Guy. *to*
Alib. *and* Cyd.] Q1–12, F, D, M1 (*Cyd.* Q1); Guiomar. M2.   84 Live,]
Q1–12, F, D; ∼∧ M1–2.   85 give;] Q1–12, F, D; ∼ . M1; ∼∧ M2.   86
it.] M1–2; ∼ ? Q1–12, F, D.   89 know;] Q1–12, F, D; ∼ . M1; ∼∧ M2.
92 who] Q2–12, F, D, M2; that Q1, M1.   94 all] Q1–10, F, D, M1–2;
last Q11–12.   95 That] Q2–12, F, D, M1–2; that Q1.   95 Merits,]
Q1–12, F, D, M1; ∼ . M2.   95 give:] Q1–12, F, D, M1; ∼ . M2.   97
alone,] Q1–5, M2; ∼ . Q6–12, F, D, M1.   101 Liberty.] Q3–12, F,
D; ∼ , Q1–2, M1; ∼∧ M2.   101+ *s.d. Exeunt, the Women following.*]
Q1–12, F, D, M1 (*Exeunt*∧ Q1, M1); Exeunt M2.

II, iii

SCENE III. / SCENE] SCENE Q1–12, F, D, M1–2.   *s.d. Country.*]
Q1–9, Q11–12, F, D; ∼∧ Q10, M1–2.   *s.d. Enter* Mont. *attended by
the* Indians.] Q1–12, F, D (*by his* Q1); Montezuma enters at the doore
behind M1; Enter Mont. M2.   1 *Taxallans* yield,] Q1–12, F, D, M1;
traxallans fly∧ M2.   2 Field:] Q1–12, F, D, M2; ∼ . M1.   4+ *s.d.*

Alarm,] Q1–6, D, M1–2; ~ . Q7–12, F.　5　*Taxallans*] Q1–12, F, D, M1;
Traxallans M2.　7–8 *omitted from M2.*　7　be, . . . hopes] Q1–12,
F, D; be? . . . hope M1.　8　who] Q2–12, F, D, M1; that Q1.　8
where] Q1–11, F, D, M1; were Q12.　8　fear?] M1; ~ ! Q1–12, F, D.
8+ *s.d.* Piz.] Q1–12, F, M1; Pizarro *and* D, M2.　9　now] Q1–12, F, D,
M1; still M2.　14　rear.] M1; ~ ; Q1–6, D; ~: Q7–12, F; ~∧ M2.　14
To Vasq.] Q3–5; *To* Piz. Q1–2, Q6–12, F, D; *omitted from M1–2.*　15
retire,] Q1–12, F, D, M2; ~∧ M1.　15　*To* Piz.] Q3–5; *To* Vasq. Q1–2,
Q6–12, F, D; *omitted from M1–2.*　16+ *s.d.* Guy. *meeting each other*
in the Battel.] Q2–12, F, D; Guy. *meeting each other.* Q1; Guy. *meeting*
M1; Guiomar M2.　17　since first] Q1–8, F, D, M1–2; since Q9–12.
18　Man?] Q1–3, Q6–12, F, D; ~ ; Q4–5; ~ . M1; ~∧ M2.　20　Love.]
Q2–12, F, D, M1–2; ~ : Q1.　21　*Taxallans*] Q1–12, F, D, M1; traxallans
M2.　23　on] Q1b–12, F, D, M1–2; in Q1a.　24　Slain;] Q1–12, F,
D; ~ . M1; ~∧ M2.　26　case:] Q1–10, F, D, M1–2; ~ ? Q11–12.　28
Flint] Q1–12, F, D, M1; steel M2.　29　one] Q1–10, Q12, F, D, M1–2;
on Q11.　30　*Guns go off within.*] Q1–12, F, D, M2 (of M2); *omitted*
from M1.　30+ *s.d.* with him] Q1–12, F, D, M1; with M2.　31
lost———] Q1–12, F, D; ~ . M1–2.　32　Fight,] Q1–12, F, D; ~∧
M1–2.　33　Flight;] Q1–10, F, D, M1; ~ ? Q11–12; ~∧ M2.　34
deaths] Q2–6, D, M2; death's Q1, Q7–12, F, M1.　34　Invisible come]
Q1–6, D, M1–2; invisible, comes Q7–12, F.　34　Fire,] Q1–12, F, D; ~ .
M1; ~∧ M2.　36　ye] Q1–12, F, D, M1; you M2.　37　made]
Q1–12, F, D, M2; make M1.　37　unfortunate:] Q1–12, F, D,
M2; ~ . M1.　38　Ill] Q1–12, F, D, M2; I'll M1.　39　Pride,]
Q1; ~ : Q2–12, F, D; ~ . M1; ~∧ M2.　40　your] Q1–4, Q6–
12, F, D, M1–2; our Q5.　40　god-heads] Q1–12, F, D, M2;
Godhead M1.　41　You'r] Q1–12, F, D, M1; you are M2.　41
you] Q1–12, F, D, M2; ye M1.　42　to day] Q6–12, F, D, M1–2; ~ ,
Q1–5.　43　the prey;] Q1–12, F, D, M1; our prey. M2.　44　on]
Q1–12, F, D, M2; you M1.　44　Prisoner] Q1–12, F, D, M1; prisner
M2.　45+ *s.d.* with two goes to *Attaque*] Q1–12, F, D, M1; goes to
attach M2.　45+ *s.d.* King] Q2–12, F, D; King Q1, M1–2.　45+
s.d. Vasq. *with another to seize*] Q1–12, F, D, M1; Vas: M2.　47+ *s.d.*
retreats *from* Vasq. *with* Alib. *off the Stage,*] Q1–12, F, D, M1 (Alib∧ Q1;
Stage. M1); carries of *Alibech* M2.　48　gave,] Q1–12, F, D; ~∧ M1–2.
49+ *s.d.* Mont. *Fights off,* Guy. *making his retreat, stays.*] Q1–12, F, D,
M1; *Montezuma escapes.* M2.　50　do] Q1–12, F, D, M1; doe M2.
51+ *s.d.* He *runs*] Q1–12, F, D, M1; runs M2.　51+ *s.d.* Vasq.,]
Q2–12, F, D; Vasq.∧ Q1; Pizarro M1; vasq:∧ M2.　51+ *s.d. behind*
and taken.] Q1–12, F, D, M1; behind M2.　52　off,———] off,∧ Q1–12,
F, D; off;∧ M1; of∧∧ M2.　53　guarded be] Q1–12, F, D, M1; guarded
M2.　54+ *s.d.* Guy.] Guy∧ Q1, M1; Guyomar Q2–12, F, D; *Gui:* M2.
55　day!] Q1–12, F, D; ~∧ M1–2.　56　dangers] Q1–6, D, M2; Danger
Q7–12, F, M1.　57　Arm] Q1–12, F, D, M2; Armes M1.　57　run,]
Q1–12, F, D; ~ . M1; ~∧ M2.　58　th'] Q1–12, F, D, M1; the M2.
58+ *s.d.* Cydaria, *who seems weeping, and begging of him.*] Q1–12, F, D,
M1 (Cidaria Q1; *seems crying,* Q1–2, Q6–12, F, D, M1); Cydaria M2.　62

had once] Q1–12, F, D, M2; once had M1.   62 given] Q1, M1–2;
giv'n Q2–12, F, D.   64 power] Q1–3, Q5–12, F, D, M2; pow'r Q4, M1.
67 Heart,] Q1–12, F, D, M1; ~ . M2.   70 customs] Q1–12, D, M1–2;
custom F.   70 severe;] Q1–5; ~ . Q6–12, F, D, M1; ~∧ M2.   71–82
omitted from M2.   72 ere] Q1–2, Q6–12, F, D, M1; e're Q3–5.   72
we] Q1–12, F, D; wee M1.   74 delay] Q1–12, F, D; delayes M1.   77
believ'd,] Q1–11, F, D, M1; ~ . Q12.   84 Failing] Q1–12, F, D, M1;
Falling M2.   84 they Court] Q1–12, F, D, M2; the Court M1.   84
Sence:] Q2–12, F, D; ~ , Q1; ~ . M1; ~∧ M2.   85 Pomp] Q2–12, F, D;
Pomps Q1, M1–2.   86 two;] Q1–12, F, D, M2; ~ . M1.   87–88 *omit-
ted from M2.*   87 passion move?] Q1–12, F, D; passions move∧ M1.   90
use;] Q1–12, F, D; ~ . M1; ~∧ M2.   92 Love!] Q1–12, F, D, M1; ~ ?
M2.   92 have you] Q1–12, F, D, M1; you have M2.   92 before?]
Q3–5, M1; ~ ! Q1–2, Q6–12, F, D, M2.   93 but she is] Q1–3, Q6–12,
F, D, M1–2; but she's Q4–5.   94 Fled,] Q2–12, F, D, M1; ~ ; Q1; ~∧
M2.   96 my] Q1–12, F, D, M1; yr M2.   97 art!] Q1–12, F, D, M1;
~∧ M2.   98 keep'st] Q1–12, F, D, M2; keeps M1.   98 Heart;]
Q1–12, F, D; ~ . M1; ~∧ M2.   99 mak'st] Q1–12, F, D, M1; makest
M2.   100 Memory;] Q1–12, F, D, M2; ~ . M1.   101 Memory, . . .
so,] Q1–12, F, D; ~ ! . . . ~ ! M1; ~∧ . . . ~∧ M2.   103 breast,]
Q1–12, F, D; ~ ! M1; ~∧ M2.   104 Inhumane . . . rest!] Q1–12, F, D,
M2; too cruell . . . rest. M1.   105 Heart! She slumbers in . . . Tomb,]
Q2–12, F, D, M2 (Heart, Q5; heart∧ M2); Heart! / She slumbers deep,
deep in . . . Tomb. Q1, M1.   107 Poor-heart] Q1–2, Q6; Poor heart,
Q3–5, Q7, Q9–12, F, M2; Poor Heart! Q8, D, M1.   107 death!] Q3–5,
D; ~ , Q1–2, Q6–7, Q9–12, F; ~ . Q8; ~ : M1; ~∧ M2.   108 breath]
Q1–6, M2; ~ , Q7–12, F, D; ~. M1.   109 thee;] D; ~ , Q1–12, F,
M1–2.   109 be,] Q1–12, F, D; ~ . M1; bee∧ M2.   110 for but]
Q1–12, F, D, M1; But for M2.   112 would not] Q1–12, F, D, M1;
cannot M2.   112 bear?] Q1–4, Q6–12, F, D; ~ : Q5; ~ ! M1; ~∧ M2.
113–114 *omitted from M2.*   114 Love.] Q1–4, Q8; ~ , Q5–7, Q9–12,
D, M1; ~ ; F.   116 me not] Q2–12, F, D, M2; not me Q1, M1.   117
Passions] Q1–11, F, D, M1–2; passion Q12.   117 Breast,] Q1–12, F,
D; ~ . M1; ~∧ M2.   119 brings] Q1–10, F, D, M1–2; bring Q11–12.
122 which] Q2–12, F, D; that Q1, M1–2.   124 Grave;] Q1–12, F,
D; ~ . M1; ~∧ M2.   125 meant] Q1–11, F, D, M1–2; mean Q12.
125 you when] Q1–12, F, D; when M1; me when M2.   126 beside,]
Q1–12, F, D; ~ . M1–2.   129 Heaven] Q1–12, F, D, M2; Heav'n M1.
129 does] Q1–12, F, D, M1; doth M2.   129 Swear,] Q1–7, Q9–12, F,
D; ~ . Q8; ~∧ M1–2.   133–134 *omitted from M2.*   133 grief.]
Q1–11, F, D, M1; ~ ? Q12.   135 account.] Q1–12, F, D; ~∧ M1–2.
136 which could] Q1–12, F, D, M1; that could M2.   136 surmount:]
Q1–12, F, D; ~ . M1–2.   137–140 *omitted from M2.*   138 Love]
Q1–6, D, M1; lov'd Q7–12, F.   141 ye gods] Q1–12, F, D; yea pow'rs
M1; you gods M2.   141 him] Q1–12, F, D, M2; wht M1.   141 you
hear,] Q1–7, Q9–12, F, D; ~ . Q8; ~∧ M1–2.   142 the] Q1–12, F, D;
this M1–2.   142 hold] Q1–12, F, D, M1; love M2.   143 me;] ~ ,
Q1–12, F, D, M1; ~∧ M2.   144 dread.] Q1–10, F, D, M1–2; ~ , Q11–

12.　147　off] Q1–12, F, D; of M1–2.　147　go.] Q1–6, D, M2; ~ ,
Q7–12, F, M1.　148　show?] Q1–6, Q8, D, M1–2; ~ . Q7, Q9–12, F.
149　do] Q1–12, F, D, M1; doe M2.　150　keep me ever] Q1–12, F, D,
M2; ever keep me M1.　152　then] Q1–3, Q5–12, F, D, M1–2; them Q4.
152　Conqu'rours] Q1–5, Q7–11, F, D; Conqu'rous Q6, Q12; Conquerors
M1–2.　154　Th'] Q1–12, F, D, M1; the M2.　155　sin!] Q6–12, F,
D; ~ ; Q1–4; ~ : Q5; ~∧ M1–2.　157　bear, [*To* Guyomar.] Q1; bear.
[*To* Guyomar. Q2–12, F, D; bear∧ M1–2.　159　Fortune's] Q1–12, F, D,
M1; Fortunes M2.　160　should] Q1–12, F, D, M1; would M2.　162
thee;] Q1–7, Q9–12, F, D; ~ . Q8, M1; ~∧ M2.　164　These . . . those]
Q1–12, F, D, M1; Those . . . these M2.　164　bear;] Q1–7, Q9–10, F,
D; ~ . Q8, M1; ~ : Q11–12; ~∧ M2.　165　I'm] Q1–12, F, D, M1; I
am M2.　168　should] Q1–12, F, D, M2; could M1.　168　rest;] Q1–
12, F, D, M2; ~ . M1.　169　lose] Q1–12, F, D, M1; loose M2.　169
Free,] Q1–5, Q8–12, F; ~ . Q6–7, D; ~ : M1; ~∧ M2.　171　still] Q1–
12, F, D, M1; all M2.　173　Brother (that] Q2–12, F, D, M2; Brother,
that Q1; Brother; that M1.　173　own,] Q1–12, F, D; ~∧ M1–2.
173–174　*s.d. omitted from M1–2.*　174　Foe] Q1–12, F, D, M2; ~ ,
M1.　174　be] Q1–7, Q9–12, F, D, M1–2; is Q8.　174　known;)] Q2–
12, F, D; known;∧ Q1; ~∧∧ M1; ~∧) M2.　176　seem] Q1–12, D, M1–
2; seems F.　176　fear;] Q1–5, M2; ~ : Q6–7, Q9–12, F, D; ~ . Q8; ~∧
M1.　177　be] Q1–12, F, D, M2; ~ . M1.　178　Courted] Q1–12, F,
D, M1; courtsied M2.　178　Adversity.] Q1–12, F, D, M1; ~∧ M2.
179　tell.] Q1–4, Q6–12, F, D, M2; tell∧ Q5, M1.　180　time———]
Q6–12, F, D, M2; ~ .——— Q1–5; ~ . M1.　180+ · *s.d. Exeunt*] Q1–2,
Q6–12, F, D, M1–2; *Ex.* Q3–4; *Exit* Q5.

III, i

ACT III. SCENE I.] D; ACT III. Q1–12, F, M2 (Act. Q4; III∧ M2);
Act: 3ᵈ: M1.　*s.d. Chamber*] Q1–12, F, M1; a *Chamber* D; The Chamber
M2.　*s.d. Enter* Odmar *and*] Q1–12, F, D, M2; Odmar. M1.　1
gods, fair *Alibech*,] Q2–12, F, D; gods∧ fair *Alibech*∧ Q1, M2; Gods∧ fair
Alibech, M1.　4　come:] Q1–7, Q9–12, M1; ~ ; Q8; ~ . M2.　5–6　re-
gard, . . . Courage] Q1–12, F, D, M2; ~∧ . . . ~ , M1.　6　hope] Q1–12, F,
D, M1; find M2.　7–8　*s.d. omitted from M1.*　8　lost.] Q1–3, Q6–12, F,
D, M1; ~∧ Q4–5, M2.　10　thee;] Q1–9, D; ~ : Q10–12, F; ~ , M1; ~∧
M2.　12　vanquisht] Q1–12, F, D, M1; conquerd M2.　13　dispute]
Q8, M2; ~ , Q1–7, Q9–12, F, D, M1.　16　known] Q8, M2; ~ , Q1–7, Q9–
12, F, D, M1.　16　fled;] Q1–12, F, D; ~ . M1; ~∧ M2.　19　*Odm.*
Freedom] Q2–12, F, D, M1–2; Freedom Q1.　19　remain,] Q2–7, Q9–
12, F, D; remains, Q1; remain. Q8; remains∧ M1; remain∧ M2.　20
thy] Q1–12, F, D, M1; the M2.　20　Chain?] Q2–7, Q9–12, F, D, M2;
Chains? Q1, M1; Chain. Q8.　21　No, no,] Q1–4, Q6–12, F, D, M1; No.
no Q5; no no M2.　21　him] Q1–4, Q6–12, F, D, M1–2; me Q5.　21
Crown,] Q1–12, F, D; ~∧ M1–2.　22　Renown.] Q1–12, F, D; ~∧ M1–
2.　25　were] Q1–12, F, D, M2; were very M1.　26　Enemies:] Q1–
12, F, D, M1; ~ . M2.　31　your] Q1–4, Q6–12, F, D, M1–2; our Q5.
32　But] Q1–12, F, D, M1; and M2.　33　prefer,] Q1–9, D; ~∧ Q10–

12, F, M1–2.   34 her;] Q1–12, F, D; ~∧ M1–2.   37 You aiding]
Q1–12, F, M1–2; Your aiding D.   39 more;] Q8; ~, Q1–7, Q9–12, F,
D; ~∧ M1–2.   40 Crime;] Q1–12, F, D; ~∧ M1; ~. M2.   41 to
her] Q1–12, F, D, M1; to yᵉ M2.   42 word;] Q1–12, F, D; ~. M1; ~∧
M2.   43 prefer] Q1–9, Q12, F, D, M1–2; perfer Q10–11.   46 desire,]
Q1–12, F, D; ~∧ M1–2.   49 a more] Q1–12, F, D, M1; amore M2.
50 or was] Q1–12, F, D, M1; or else M2.   50 none;] Q1–12, F, D; ~,
M1; ~∧ M2.   51 breast,] Q1–6, D, M1–2; ~. Q7–12, F.   52 best:]
Q1–12, F, D, M2; ~. M1.   54 plain;] Q1–7, Q9–12, F, D; ~. Q8; ~∧
M1–2.   56+ s.d. To them, Enter] Q2–12, F, D; Enter Q1, M1–2.
56+ s.d. talking with Almeria] Q1–12, F, D, M1; Almeria M2.   58
of the] Q1–12, F, D, M2; of this M1.   60 does his Arms] Q1–12, F, D,
M1; doth his arm M2.   60 with-hold,] Q1–7, Q9–12, F, D; ~. Q8, M1;
~∧ M2.   61 offering] Q1–12, F, D, M1; offring M2.   61 Peace,]
Q1–4, Q6–12, F; ~∧ Q5, D, M1–2.   62 take;] Q1–12, F, D; ~: M1;
~∧ M2.   63 those,] Q1–12, F, D, M2; ~! M1.   64 o'recome what
could they worse] Q1–12, F, D, M1; ore come wᵗ worse could they M2.
66 Masters] Q1–10, Q12, F, D, M1–2; Master Q11.   66 Feet.] Q1–5,
Q8, F, M2; ~, Q6–7, Q9–12, D, M1.   67 Mines,] Q1–4, Q6–12, F, D,
M1; ~. Q5; ~∧ M2.   68 Temples] Q1–12, F, D, M2; Temple M1.
68 shines;] Q1–12, F, D; shine∧ M1; shines∧ M2.   69 shameful] Q1–
12, F, D, M1; shamfull M2.   70 and] Q1–12, F, D, M2; but M1.   74
War.] Q1–12, F, D, M2; ~: M1.   75 exasperate] Q1–3, Q8, M2; exas-
p'rate Q4–7, Q9–12, F, D, M1.   76 warm:] Q1–7, Q9–12, F, D, M1; ~.
Q8; ~∧ M2.   77 which] Q1–12, F, D, M1; who M2.   78 Victory,]
Q2–3, Q6–12, F, D; ~; Q1, M1; ~. Q4–5; ~∧ M2.   79 cries,] Q1;
~; Q2–12, F, D, M2; ~∧ M1.   80 fearful,] Q1–12, F, D; ~; M1; ~∧
M2.   81 killing] Q1–12, F, D, M1; yᵗ from M2.   83 Fight,] Q1–12,
F, D; ~∧ M1–2.   84 decreases] Q1–10, F, D, M1–2; discreases Q11–12.
85 does] Q1–12, F, D; doth M1–2.   86 ——And so am I.] Q1–12, F,
D, M1; I am for war. M2.   88+ s.d. Exeunt Mont. Odm. Guy. Alib.
Almeria stays Orbellan.] Q2–12, F, D (Guyomar and D); Exeunt Mont.
Odm. Guy. Alib. Q1, M1; Exeunt Manent Alm: et Orbellan. M2.   89
Alm. to Orb.] Q2–12, F, D; Alm. Q1, M1–2.   89 allow,] Q1–8, D, M1–2;
~. Q9–12, F.   90 brow;] Q1–12, F, D; ~∧ M1–2.   91–92 s.d. omitted
from M1–2.   92 known,] Q1b–12, F, D; ~∧ Q1a; ~) M1–2.   95 the
Guards] Q1–12, F, D, M2; his Guards M1.   96 back:] Q1–12, F, D,
M2; ~. M1.   100 minds;] Q1–12, F, D, M2; ~. M1.   101 judge-
ment] D, M1–2; ~, Q1–12, F.   101 doubtful] Q1–12, F, D, M1; wak-
ing M2.   101 still,] Q1–4, Q6–12, F, D, M1; ~∧ Q5, M2.   102
good] Q1–3, Q6–12, F, D, M1–2; ~, Q4–5.   102 can of] Q1–12, F, D,
M1; can doe M2.   102 ill;] Q1–3, Q6–12, F, D; ~? Q4–5; ~. M1; ~∧
M2.   104 Blood;] Q1–12, F, D; ~. M1; ~∧ M2.   105 Alm. Orb.]
Q1–12, F, M1–2; Alm. and Orb. D.   106 way?] M1–2; ~! Q1–12, F,
D.   108 it so;] Q1–12, F, D; it soe. M1; him so; M2.   110 consent-
ing] Q2–12, F, D, M1–2; confenting Q1.   110 deed.] Q1–4, Q6–12, F,
D, M2; ~, Q5; ~! M1.   111 led] Q1–12, F, D, M1; lead M2.   111
way,] Q1–12, F, D, M2; ~, M1.   112–113 they; / Something] Q1–12, F,

D, M2; ~, / ——— ~ M1.　114　*Exit* Guyomar.] Q1–12, F, D, M1;
Exit M2.

III, ii

SCENE II] Q1–12, F, D, M2; 2ᵈ Scene. M1.　　*s.d.　Enter* Cortez *alone*]
Q1–12, F, D; Cortez alone M1; Enter Cortez M2.　　*s.d.　Night-gown*]
Q1–12, F, D; night Gowne M1–2.　　2　head;] Q1–12, F, D, M2; ~ . M1.
3　dreams their Songs] Q1–12, F, D, M1; Songs their Dreams M2 (*marked
for transposition*).　　4　Flowers,] Q1–12, M2; Flow'rs F, D, M1.　　4
night-dew] Q1–12, F, D, M1; night dew M2.　　4　sweat;] Q1–12, F, D,
M2; ~ . M1.　　5　Ev'n] Q1–12, F, D, M1; Even M2.　　8　come.] M1;
~ : Q1–12, F, D, M2.　　9　Fight, *Noyse within*] Q1–12, F, D; fight∧ M1–2
(*M2 has* "noyse" *on line above*).　　10+　*s.d.* Orbellan *flying in the dark,*]
Q1–12, F, D, M1; *Orbellan* M2.　　11　Oh] Q1–12, F, D, M1; o M2.
11　flye?] Q1–12, F, D; ~ ! M1; ~∧ M2.　　12　Treachery;] Q1–12, F,
D, M2; ~ ! M1.　　13　I'm . . . where,] Q1–12, F, D, M1; I am . . . ~∧
M2.　　15　say?] M2; ~ ! Q1–12, F, D, M1.　　16　*Taxallan . . . his
way, To him.*] Q1–12, F, D, M1; traxallan . . . the way M2.　　17　the
terrours of the] Q1–12, F, D, M2; this blind, and moonelesse M1.　　18
thy] Q1–10, F, D, M1–2; this Q11–12.　　18　fright] Q2–12, F, D, M1–2;
flight Q1.　　19　*Orb.* The] Q1b–12, F, D, M1–2; The Q1a.　　21
Crimes] Q1–12, F, D, M2; crime M1.　　23　worse. *Aside.*] Q1–12,
F, D; worse! M1; worse∧ M2.　　23　me,] Q1–12, F, D; ~ . M1; ~∧ M2.
24　set] Q2–12, F, D, M1–2; let Q1.　　24　thee] Q1–12, F, D, M1; the
M2.　　25　Heaven] M1–2; ~ , Q1–12, F, D.　　28　*Guyomar*] Q7–12,
F, D, M2; ~ , Q1–6, M1.　　31　Murtherer:] Q2–12, F, M2; ~ , Q1; ~ .
D; ~∧ M1.　　32　I] Q1–12, F, D, M2; wee M1.　　36　hated] Q1–12,
F, D, M2; hatefull M1.　　39　his] Q1–3, Q6–12, F, D, M1–2; this Q4–5.
41　with] Q1–7, F, D, M1–2; which Q8–12.　　42　again.] Q1–3, Q6–12,
F, D, M1; ~ , Q4–5; ~∧ M2.　　42+　*s.d. Exeunt* Vasquez, Pizarro.] Q1–
7, M2; *Exeunt* Vasq. *and* Piz. Q8–12, F, D; Exit: Vas: Piz: &c. M1.　　42+
s.d. omitted from M2.　　43　gone,] Q1–7, D, M1; ~ . Q8–12, F; ~∧ M2.
44　alone;] Q1–12, F, M2; ~∧ D; ~ . M1.　　46　who] Q2–12, F, D, M2;
that Q1, M1.　　46　aid?] Q1–8, D, M1; ~ . Q9–12, F; ~ : M2.　　46+　*s.d.
omitted from M1.*　　46+　*s.d. Enter* Orbellan] Q1–12, F, D; Orb: enters
M2.　　48　Skies,] Q1–12, F, D; ~ . M1; ~∧ M2.　　49　In] Q1–12, F, D,
M1; I M2.　　50–51　hide; / . . . Rival] Q1–7, D; ~ ; / . . . ~ , Q8–12,
F; ~∧ / . . . ~ , M1; ~∧ / . . . ~∧ M2.　　53　say] Q1–12, F, D, M1;
sway M2.　　54　have taken a much nobler] Q3–5; how e're have took a
fairer Q1–2, Q6–12, F, D, M1–2.　　55　'Tis true] Q1–12, F, D, M2; Although M1.　　56　sake;] Q1–12, F, D; ~∧ M1–2.　　57　set me] Q1–
11, F, D, M1–2; set Q12.　　60　death———] Q1–12, F, D; ~ . M1–2.
62　do] Q1–12, F, D, M1; doe M2.　　62　thee;] Q1–8, D, M1–2; thee?
Q9–12, F.　　63　Tent,] Q1–12, F, D; ~∧ M1–2.　　64　prevent;] Q1–7,
D, M1–2; ~∧ Q8–12, F.　　65　haste] Q1–12, F, D; hast M1–2.　　65
[*They go out.*] They go out, Q1–7, D, M1–2; [*Exeunt.* Q8–12, F.

III, iii

SCENE III. / *The*] the Q1-7, D, M1-2; *The* Q8-12, F.   *s.d. they
return*] Q1-12, F, D, M1; the returne M2.   3 go,] Q1-10, F, D; ~ .
Q11-12, M1; ~∧ M2.   5 haste] Q1-12, F, D, M1; hast M2.   5
Breast.————] Q1, M2; ~∧———— Q2-7, D; ~ . Q8-12, F, M1.   5 *s.d.
omitted from M1.*   6 Dye,] Q1-6, D, M1-2; ~ . Q7-12, F.   7 high;]
Q1-11, F, D; ~ : Q12; ~ . M1; ~∧ M2.   9 Man;] Q1-7, D; ~ . Q8-12,
F, M1; ~∧ M2.   10-15 *omitted from M1.*   11 flint-edg'd] Q1-12,
F, D; flint edgd M2.   11 by;] Q1-7, D; ~ . Q8-12, F; ~∧ M2.   14
tell,] Q1-12, F, D; ~∧ M2.   16 appear.] Q1b-12, F, D; ~ : Q1a; ~∧
M1-2.   17 fear:] Q1-12, F, D; ~ . M1; ~∧ M2.   20 time] Q3-5;
let's Q1-2, Q6-12, F, D, M1; letts M2.   21 day.] Q1-3, Q6-12, F, D,
M1-2; ~ , Q4-5.   21+ *s.d. his Sword falls out of it.*] Q1-12, F, D, M1;
drops his sword M2.   23 you;] Q1-8, D; ~ : Q9-12, F; ~ . M1; ~∧
M2.   23-24 *s.d. Throws his Sword again.*] Q1-12, F, D; *gives his sword*
M2; *omitted from M1.*   25 you Fought] Q1-12, F, D, M2; thou
foughs't M1.   26-27 requite, / . . . not] Q1-12, F, D; ~∧ / . . .~ ,
M1; ~∧ / . . .~∧ M2.   27 Fight;] Q1-9, D, M2; ~ : Q10-12, F; ~ .
M1.   28 its] Q1-12, F, D, M1; a M2.   28-29 *s.d. He strives . . .
cannot*] Q1-12, F, D; *strives . . . can not* M2; *omitted from M1.*   29
ill] Q1-12, F, D, M1; not M2.   30 that] Q1-12, F, D, M1; thou M2.
30 will!] Q1-12, F, D, M1; ~∧ M2.   31 vanquish'd] Q1-12, F, D,
M2; Conquer'd M1.   31 Kill?] Q1-4, Q6-12, F, D, M1-2; ~ ; Q5.
34 do] Q1-12, F, D, M1; doe M2.   35 cannot] Q1-12, F, D, M1; can
not M2.   35 less;] Q1-7, D, M2; ~ . Q8-12, F; ~ : M1.   36 were
but] Q1-12, F, D, M1; is in M2.   37 again;] Q1-12, F, D; ~ . M1; ~∧
M2.   41 I'le] Q2-12, F, D, M1-2; i'le Q1.   42 thee] Q1-12, F, D,
M2; the M1.   43 free;] Q1-5, Q7-12, F; ~ , Q6, D; ~ . M1; ~∧ M2.
46 To . . . Arms,] Q1-8, F, D; ~ . . .~∧ Q9-12, M2; ———— ~ . . .~ ,
M1.   46 way,] Q1-12, F, D; ~∧ M1-2.

III, iv

SCENE IV. / *Mexico.*] SCENE III. *Mexico.* Q1-4, Q6-12, F, D, M2
(SCENE, Q4); SCENE III. Q5; Scene Mexico. M1.   3 seems] Q1-12, F,
D, M1; is M2.   4 change;] Q1-3, Q6-12, F, D, M2; ~ : Q4-5; ~ . M1.
9 shame.] Q1-12, F, D; ~∧ M1-2.   12 happy!] Q1-8, D; ~ . Q9-12,
F, M2; ~∧ M1.   12 Yet] Q3-5, Q7-12, F, D; yet Q1-2, Q6, M1-2.
12 so,] Q1-7, D; ~ . Q8-12, F, M1-2.   13 slain?] Q1-12, F, D, M1;
~ . M2.   14 other-ways] Q1-3; other ways Q4-9, D; otherways Q10-
12, F, M2; otherwise M1.   14 ordain.] Q2-12, F, D, M1-2; ~ , Q1.
14 *s.d. omitted from Q4-5, M1.*   15 should mourn] Q3-5; lament
Q1-2, Q6-12, F, D, M1-2.   15+ *s.d. his Sister*] Q1-12, F, D; *to his
Sister* M1; *Almeria* M2.   16 breath] Q1-12, F, D, M1; breathe M2.
17 hear,] Q1-3, Q6-12, F; ~ . Q4-5, D; ~∧ M1-2.   18 looks]
Q1-12, F, D, M1; eyes M2.   18+ *s.d. omitted from M2.*   19 Be-
tray'd!] Q1-12, F, D, M2; ~ ? M1.   20 there;] Q1-12, F, D; ~ . M1;
~∧ M2.   22 makes] Q3-12, F, D; make Q1-2, M1-2.   22+ *s.d. Ali-*

bech,] Q1-12, F, M1; Alibech, *and* D, M2.   23   Sir,] Q1-7, D, M1; ~ !
Q8-10, F; ~ ? Q11-12; ~∧ M2.   24   your own] Q1-12, F, D, M1; yʳ
M2.   24   exprest:] Q1-12, F, D; ~ . M1; ~∧ M2.   27   I strict] Q1-
11, F, D, M1-2; strict Q12.   28   show;] Q1-12, F, D; ~ , M1; ~∧ M2.
29   Eyes,] Q1-8, D; ~ . Q9-12, F; ~∧ M1-2.   34   you;] Q1-7, D; ~ .
Q8-12, F; ~ : M1; ~∧ M2.   36   you] Q1-12, F, D, M2; yoʳ M1.   36+
s.d. Messenger] D; Messenger Q1-12, F, M1-2.   37   *Mess.* Arm] Q3-5,
D; Arm Q1-2, Q6-12, F, M1-2.   37   King,] Q1-7, D; ~ ! Q8-12, F; ~∧
M1-2.   39   Their] Q1-7, D, M1-2; The Q8-12, F.   39   Murdering]
Q1-12, F, D, M1; murdring M2.   40   calls.] Q2-12, F, D, M1; ~ ,
Q1; ~∧ M2.   42+   *s.d. omitted from M1.*   43   defend:] Q2-12, F,
D, M2; ~∧ Q1; ~ ; M1.   44   end;] Q1-7, D, M2; ~ . Q8-12, F, M1.
46   'till] Q1-2; till Q3-12, F, D, M1-2.   47   him] Q1-12, F, D, M2;
her M1.   48   he] Q1-12, F, D, M2; shee M1.   48+   *s.d. Second
Messenger*] D; Second Messenger Q1-12, F; 2ᵈ Messengᵗ M1; 2 Messenger
M2.   49   *Mess.* 2. From] Q3-5, D (2 *Mess.* D); From Q1-2, Q6-12, F,
M1-2.   50   yield.] Q1-10, F, D, M1-2; ~ , Q11-12.   50+   *s.d. Third
Messenger*] D; Third Messenger Q1-12, F; 3ᵈ Messengᵗ M1; 3 Mess: M2.
51   *Mess.* 3. Some] Q3-5, D (3 *Mess.* D); Some Q1-2, Q6-12, F, M1-2.
52   They only Death] Q1-12, F, D, M2; that they but death M1.   53
shout!———] Q8-12, F; ~ !∧ Q1-7, D, M1; ~∧∧ M2.   54   rules]
Q1-12, F, D, M1; Rule M2.   54   do] Q3, Q5-12, F, D, M1; do, Q1-2;
doe Q4, M2.   55   Courage] *some copies of Q4 read* Conrage.   55
deserve. [*Exit.*] D, M1-2 (*Exit*∧ M1-2); deserve. Q1-12, F.   57+   *s.d.
within.*] Q1-3, Q6-12, F, D; ~ , Q4-5, M1; ~ : M2.   57+   *s.d.* Orbellan,
Indians *driven in*] Q2-12, F, D; Orbell. Indians *driven in* Q1; Orbellan &
Indians driven in M1; *Orbellan,* M2.   57+   *s.d. them, and one or two
Spaniards.*] Q1-12, F, D, M1; him. M2.   58-59   *thus in M1:* hees
found, hees found——— / Cort— that loue thou didst usurp thy life
shall pay; / thus thy night Treason I reward by day.   59   once,] Q2-12,
F, D; ~∧ Q1, M2.   59   shalt] Q1-12, F, D; can M2.   59   day. [*Kills
Orbellan.*] Q1-12, F, D; day. M1; day. kills him. M2.   60   [*Dyes.*]
∧Dyes. Q1, M1; ∧*Dyes.* Q2-12, F, D, M2.   61-62   *s.d. He is beset.*]
Q1-12, F, D; Cortez is beset. M2; *omitted from M1.*   62+   *s.d. omitted
from M1-2.*   62+   *s.d. seem to weep over*] Q3-5; *falls on* Q1; *fall on*
Q2, Q6-12, F, D.   63   could] Q1-12, F, D, M1; can M2.   63   meet?]
D; ~ , Q1-12, F, M2; ~∧ M1.   64   reveng'd, and] Q1-12, F, D, M1
(~∧ Q10-12); revenged M2.   64   feet.] D, M1; ~ ? Q1-12, F; ~∧ M2.
64+   *s.d. They fall on him and bear him down, Guyomar takes his Sword.*]
Q1-12, F, D (*him,* Q3-5); *Cortez is taken prisoner. Alm: and Alli: fall on
Orbellan.* M2; *omitted from M1.*   65   Brother's] Q1-12, F, D, M1;
Brothers M2.   65   Slain:] Q1-7; ~ ; Q8-12, F; ~ , D; ~∧ M1; ~ . M2.
66   hand] Q2-12, F, D, M1-2; head Q1.   66   is vain] Q1-6, D, M1;
was vain Q7-12, F, M2.   67   complaints] Q1-10, F, D, M1-2; complaint
Q11-12.   67   wast] Q1-12, F, D, M1; loose M2.   68   Death,] Q1-12,
F, D; ~ . M1; ~∧ M2.   69   Dead.] Q2-12, F, D, M1-2; ~ : Q1.   72
beg,———] Q1-6; ~∧——— Q7-8, D; ~∧∧ Q9-11, F, M1; ~ .∧ Q12; ~ .
——— M2.   72   Live?] Q1-12, F, D; ~ . M1; ~∧ M2.   76   which

was] Q2–12, F, D, M1–2; that was Q1.　76　Love?] Q1–12, F, D, M2; ∼.
M1.　78　Wife;] Q1–12, F, M1–2; ∼. D.　79　once] Q3–12, F, D,
M1–2; ∼, Q1–2.　83　were] Q1–12, D, M1–2; was F.　84　s.d.
omitted from M1–2.　85　divide] Q1–12, F, D, M2; divides M1.　85
breast!] Q1–8, D, M2; ∼; Q9–12, F; ∼ₐ M1.　86　rest.] Q1–12, F, D,
M1; ∼ₐ M2.　87　give?] Q1–12, F, D; ∼! M1; ∼ₐ M2.　88
Ungrateful,] Q2–4, Q6–12, F, D; ∼ₐ Q1, Q5, M1–2.　88　Live?] Q1–12,
F, D, M2; ∼! M1.　89　Tears] Q1–12, F, D, M1; tear's M2.　89
deny?] Q9–12, F; ∼! Q1–8, D, M1; ∼ₐ M2.　92　Pris'ner] Q1–12, F, D,
M1; prisoner M2.　92　Sword; [*Gives his Sword.*] Q1–12, F, D; Sword.
M1; Sword; M2.　95　Rebel,] Q6–12, F, D; ∼ₐ Q1–5, M2; ∼! M1.
95　degenerate] Q1–6, Q9–12, F, D, M1–2; degen'rate Q7–8.　95　Boy?]
Q2–12, F, D; ∼, Q1; ∼ₐ M1–2.　96+　s.d. *omitted from M1.*　98
ill:] Q1–12, F; ∼. D, M1; ∼ₐ M2.　103　Breast] Q1–12, F, D, M1;
heart M2.　104　e're . . . for you.] Q1–12, F, D, M1; ere . . . from
youₐ M2.　107　Gen'rous] Q1–6, D; Generous Q7–12, F, M1–2.　107
Youths] Q1–12, F, D, M2; youth M1.　108　see,] Q1–6; ∼; Q7–12,
F; ∼: D; ∼. M1; ∼ₐ M2.　110　your Father's] Q1–3, Q7–12, F, D;
your Fathers Q4–6, M2; your M1.　110　make:] Q1–8, D; ∼; Q9–12,
F, M2; ∼. M1.　111–112　s.d. *omitted from M1–2.*　112　revenge]
Q1–12, F, D, M1; reward M2.　112　General.] Q1–11, F, D, M1–2; ∼!
Q12.　113　resign,] Q1–8, D, M1; ∼. Q9–12, F, M2.　114　mine!]
Q1–12, F, D; ∼. M1; ∼ₐ M2.　116　Live;] Q1–3, Q6–12, F, D; ∼:
Q4; ∼ₐ Q5, M2; ∼. M1.　117　wears,] Q1–4, Q6–12, F, D; ∼ₐ Q5,
M1–2.　119　haste . . . haste] Q1–12, F, D, M1; hast . . . hast M2.
121　Brother's] Q1–12, F, D, M1; Brothers M2.　121　hovering] Q1–12,
F, D, M1; hovring M2.　122　O're] Q1–12, F, D, M1; ore M2.　122
Air,] Q1–12, F, D, M2; ∼. M1.　125　prove] Q1–12, F, D, M1; grow M2.
126　how well I Love] Q1–12, F, D, M1; wᵗ love I owe M2.　127
'Till] Q1–12, F, D, M1; till M2.　127　when,] D, M1; ∼ₐ Q1–12, F, M2.
127　Pris'ner] Q1–12, F, D, M1; prisoner M2.　128　Lake:] Q1–12,
F, D; ∼. M1; ∼ₐ M2.　130　these] Q1–12, F, D, M2; those M1.
130　which] Q2–12, F, D, M2; that Q1, M1.　130　remain:] Q1–5; ∼;
Q6–12, F, D; ∼. M1; ∼ₐ M2.　131　head-long] Q1–12, F, D, M1; head
long M2.　132　and] Q1–12, F, D, M1; but M2.

IV, i

ACT IV. SCENE I] D; ACT IV. Q1–12, F, M2 (ACT. Q4); Act 4ᵗʰ
1ˢᵗ Sc: M1.　s.d.　SCENE, A] Q1–12, F, D, M2; a M1.　s.d. *Enter
Almeria and an* Indian, *they speak entring.*] Q1–12, F, D (Almeria, Q4–5;
Indianₐ Q1); Almeria and an Indian speake entring M1; Enter Almeria
and an Indian M2.　2　not,] Q1–12, F, D; ∼. M1; ∼ₐ M2.　2
know:] Q1–12, F, D, M1; ∼ₐ M2.　4　doest] Q1–12, F, D, M1; dost
M2.　5　Without,] ∼ₐ Q1–12, F, D, M1; with outₐ M2.　5　coming]
Q1–4, Q6–12, F, D, M1–2; ∼, Q5.　5+　s.d. *omitted from M1.*　5+
s.d. *Chain'd and laid asleep.*] Q1–12, F, D (*asleep,* Q4; *asleep*ₐ Q8);
*asleep*ₐ M2.　6　Gate.——— [*Exit* Indian.] Q2–12, F, D, M2 (Gateₐ
——— D); Gateₐ——— Q1, M1.　6+　s.d. *omitted from M1–2.*　8

shalt] Q1–9, Q11–12, F, D, M1–2; shall Q10.   8 such ease] Q1–10, F, D, M1–2; thy ease Q11–12.   9 pac'd,] Q1–10, F, M1; plac'd, Q11–12; pac'd: D; pac'd∧ M2.   11 Revenge?] Q1–11, F, D, M2; ∼! Q12; ∼, M1.   13 nigh] Q2–12, F, D, M2; near Q1, M1.   14 Whence] Q1–12, F, D, M2; whence then M1.   14 come?] Q1–12, F, D; ∼∧ M1–2.   15 Innocence?] Q1–12, F, D; ∼, M1; ∼! M2.   15 part,] Q1–12, F; ∼. D, M2; ∼∧ M1.   16 assur'd,] Q1–12, F, M2; ∼? M1; ∼∧ D.   16 Heart:] Q1–8; ∼∧ Q9–12, M2; ∼. F, M1; ∼! D.   16+ *s.d. omitted from M1*.   16+ *s.d. Holds*] Q2–12, F, D, M2; *Hold* Q1.   17 *s.d. omitted from M2*.   19 do] Q1–12, F, D, M1; doe M2.   19 Bleed,] Q1–12, F; ∼? D, M1; ∼∧ M2.   19 *s.d. omitted from M1–2*.   21 I've . . . off] Q1–12, F, D, M1; I have . . . of M2.   21 *s.d. omitted from M1–2*.   21 Comes] Q1–7, Q9–12, F, D; Come Q8.   22 here:] Q1–3, Q6–8, D; here. Q4; here, Q5; here∧ Q9–12, F; heere. M1; there. M2.   23 does] Q1–12, F, D, M1; doth M2.   23 move!] Q1–4, Q6–12, F, D, M1–2; ∼? Q5.   24 could] Q1–12, F, D, M2; would M1.   24 *s.d. omitted from M1–2*.   25 command,] Q1–12, F, D, M2; ∼? M1.   26 hand:] Q1–12, F, D; ∼! M1; ∼∧ M2.   27 late] Q1–12, F, M1–2; ∼ : D.   28 Mothers Fate:] Q1–5; Mothers Fate. Q6–12, F, D, M1; fathers hate. M2.   29 Foe, . . . Brother's Murtherer,] Q1–12, F, D; foe! . . . Brothers murderer. M1; foe∧ . . . Brothers murderer∧ M2.   30 forbear:] Q1–12, F, D, M2; ∼. M1.   31 It] Q2–12, F, D, M1–2; I Q1 (*some copies of Q1 may have* It).   31 w'onnot] Q1–12, F, D, M2; cannot M1.   31 on, [*Coming on again.*] Q1–12, F, D (*coming* Q1–2, Q6); on M1–2.   32+ *s.d. omitted from M1–2*.   34 by] Q1–12, F, D, M1; with M2.   35 or strike,] Q1–6, Q10–12, F, D, M1; or strike. Q7–9; to strike∧ M2.   36 Fore-seen] Q1–12, F, D, M1; fore seen M2.   38 They have most] Q1–12, F, D, M1; The most have M2.   38 passions] Q1–12, F, D, M2; passion M1.   38 *s.d. omitted from M1*.   40 could . . . neglect;] Q1–12, F, D, M2 (neglect∧ M2); would . . . neglect. M1.   47 given] Q1–12, F, D, M1; giv'n M2.   47 refuse] Q2–12, F, D, M1–2; refufe Q1.   50 find,] Q1–12, F, D; ∼. M1; ∼∧ M2.   52 Love,] Q1–12, F, D; ∼. M1; ∼∧ M2.   53 desire] Q1–2, Q6, M2; ∼, Q3–5, Q7–12, F, D; ∼? M1.   54 Nobler] Q1–11, F, D, M1–2; Noble Q12.   54 Fire?] Q1–12, F, D, M2; ∼. M1.   55 found,] Q1–12, F, D; ∼∧ M1–2.   58 could] Q1–12, F, D, M2; would M1.   59 ignorance,] Q1–12, F; Ignorance! D, M1; ∼∧ M2.   60 *s.d. omitted from M1*.   61 you,] Q5; ∼∧ Q1–4, Q6–12, F, D, M1–2.   61 even] Q1–12, F, D, M1; ev'n M2.   61 *s.d. omitted from M2*.   61 him.] Q2–12, F, D; ∼∧ Q1, M1.   62 restore,] Q1–12, F, D; ∼. M1; ∼∧ M2.   64 her,] Q1–4, Q6, D; ∼∧ Q5, Q7–12, F, M1–2.   66 could not] Q1–12, F, D, M1; should M2.   66 vow'd,] Q2–6, D, M1; ∼∧ Q1, Q7–12, F, M2.   67 has] Q1–6, D, M1–2; hath Q7–12, F.   68 disgrace? [*Aside.*] disgrace? Q1–12, F, D, M1; ∼. M2 ("(Aside" *on line above*).   69 Love,——— . . . be, [*To him.*] Love,∧ . . . be, Q1–12, F, D, M1–2 (Love? M1; be∧ M2).   70 me———] ∼. Q1–12, F, D, M1; ∼∧ M2.   72 hand] Q1–11, F, D, M1–2; had Q12.   72 slew? ———] Q1–2, Q6–12, F, D; ∼∧——— Q3–5; ∼.——— M1; ∼?∧ M2.

74 farther] Q1–12, F, D, M2; further M1.   74 do:] Q1–12, F, D; do.
M1; doe. M2.   76 or] Q1–12, F, D; nor M1–2.   79 so,] Q1–12,
F, D, M1; ~∧ M2.   79 could I] Q1–4, Q6–12, F, D, M1–2; I could Q5.
80 what] Q1–12, F, D, M2; that M1.   80 *s.d. omitted from M1.*
81 shook. [*Aside.* / ———Suppose] shook; ———suppose Q1–12, F, D,
M1–2 (shook∧——— M1; shook:∧ M2).   81–82 speak, / . . . break?]
Q1–12, F, D; ~∧ / . . .~ . M1; ~∧ / . . .~? M2.   86 dangerously]
Q1–10, F, D, M1–2; generously Q11–12.   86 try'd:] Q1–12, F, D; ~ .
M1; ~∧ M2.   88 live:] Q1–12, F, D, M2; ~ . M1.   89 mankind,]
Q1–12, F, D, M1; ~∧ M2.   91 who] Q1–12, F, D, M2; that M1.
96 could] Q1–12, F, D, M1; should M2.   100 worth] Q1–12, F, D,
M2; love M1.   100 improve.] Q1–12, F, D, M1; ~∧ M2.   102 me:]
Q1–2, Q6–12, F, D, M2; ~ ; Q3–5; ~ . M1.   104 offers] Q1–8, D, M1–2;
offer Q9–12, F.   104 *s.d. omitted from M1.*   105 *Cort.*] Q1–12,
F, D, M2; Cortez / Solus M1.   105 left,] Q1–12, F; ~ ? D; ~ ! M1; ~∧
M2.   105 *s.d. omitted from M1–2.*   106 I wish bereft!] Q1–12, F,
D, M1; bereft. M2.   107–110 *omitted from M2.*   108 is] Q4–5,
Q7–12, F, M1; ~ , Q1–3, Q6, D.   110 up] Q2–12, F, D; of Q1, M1.
110 Fire:] Q1–12, F, D; ~ . M1.   111 We . . . our] Q1–12, F, D,
M1; I . . . my M2.   111 Feaverish] Q1–12, F, D, M2; feav'rish M1.
112 our] Q1–12, F, D, M1; my M2.   112 still:] Q1–12, F, D, M2; ~ .
M1.   114+ *s.d. Goes . . . him.*] Q1–12, F, D, M1; Exit M2.

IV, ii

SCENE II. / *Chamber Royal.*] Q1–12, F, D, M2 (II∧ M2); 2d: Scene
Mexico. M1.   *s.d. Enter* Montezuma, Odmar, Guyomar, Alibech.] M1–2
(*Enter omitted from M1;* Enter . . . and Alibech M2); Enter *Montezuma,
Odmar, Guyomar, Alibech.* Q1–12, F, D (*and* Alibech. D).   1 crowd.]
Q2–12, F, D; ~ : Q1; ~∧ M1–2.   2 are now grown] Q1–12, F, D, M1;
grow now both M2.   2 loud:] Q1–12, F, D; ~ . M1; ~∧ M2.   3
General's] Q1–8, D, M1–2; Gen'ral's Q9–12, F.   5 hour] F, D, M1–2; ~ ,
Q1–12.   6 power] Q1–3, Q6–12, F, D, M2; pow'r Q4–5, M1.   8
do] Q1–12, F, D, M1; doe M2.   9 oft] Q1–11, F, D, M1–2; often Q12.
10 prevail'd:] Q1–12, F, D, M2; ~ . M1.   12 Peace:] Q1–12, F, D; ~ .
M1; ~ ; M2.   14 obey:] Q1–7, Q9–12, F, D, M2; ~ ; Q8; ~ . M1.
16 before:] Q1–12, F, D; ~ . M1; ~∧ M2.   17 could] Q1–12, F, D,
M2; must M1.   18 These] Q1–9, D, M1; Those Q10–12, F, M2.   18
must] Q1–12, F, D, M2; could M1.   18 not] Q1–12, F, D, M1; or M2.
19 back:] Q1–12, F, D; ~∧ M1; ~ . M2.   20 desp'rate] Q1–7, Q9–12,
F, D; desperate Q8, M1–2.   20 take?] Q5, Q8, M2; ~ ! Q1–4, Q6–7,
Q9–12, F, D; ~ . M1.   22 lose] Q1–4, Q6–12, F, D, M1; loose Q5, M2.
24 us'd:] Q1–11, F, D, M2; ~ . Q12; ~∧ M1.   26 who] Q1–12, F, D,
M1; that M2.   26+ *s.d.* Montezuma, Odmar.] Q1–12, F; Mont. *and*
Odm. D, M2; Mont. M1.   27 Ah] Q1–12, F, D, M1; Ay M2.   27
heard!] Q1–12, F, D; ~ ? M1; ~∧ M2.   27 stay,] Q9–12, F; ~∧ Q1–8,
D, M1–2.   28 you prepare?] Q1–12, F, D, M1; to prepare, M2.   29
with] Q1–11, F, D, M1–2; which Q12.   30 And to that use] Q3–5; A
death, to which Q1–2, Q6–12, F, D, M1–2.   30 design'd] Q1–12, F, D,

M2; destin'd M1.   31   well] Q1–11, F, D, M1–2; will Q12.   32
oppress:] Q1–12, F, D; ∼ . M1–2.   33–36 *omitted from* M2.   33
use,] Q2–12, F, D; ∼∧ Q1; ∼) M1.   34   Even] Q1–8, D, M1; E'en
Q9–12, F.   34   pois'nous] Q1–12, F, D; poysonous M1.   36   death:]
Q1–12, F, D; ∼ . M1.   38   Ghosts, not Men,] Q4–5, Q7–12, F, D, M1;
Ghosts not Men Q1–3, Q6, M2.   38   the] Q1–7, Q9–12, F, D, M1–2;
our Q8.   40   Mother's] Q1–12, F, D, M1; Mothers M2.   40   the]
Q2–12, F, D; their Q1, M1–2.   42   blast] Q1–12, F, D, M2; whist M1.
47   General] Q1–8, D, M1–2; Gen'ral Q9–12, F.   47   know:] Q1–7,
Q9–12, F, D, M2; ∼ . Q8, M1.   50   hear:] Q1–4, Q6–7, Q9–12, F, D,
M2; ∼ ; Q5; ∼ ! Q8; ∼∧ M1.   51   you spoke] Q1–12, F, D, M1; I
spoke M2.   51   believe;] Q1–7, Q9–12, F, D; ∼ ! Q8; ∼ . M1; ∼∧ M2.
52   do . . . once thought] Q1–12, F, D, M1; doe . . . thought once M2.
53   Enslave?] Q1–12, F, D, M2; ∼ ! M1.   56   should] Q2–12, F, D,
M1; should Q1; shou'd M2.   56   do] Q1–12, F, D; doe M1–2.   57
lose your Love,] Q1–12, F, D, M1; loose y^r love! M2.   57   then]
Q1–10, F, D, M1–2 (M2 *has* "and" *before and* "th" *after, both crossed
out*); that Q11–12.   57   to] Q1–12, F, D, M1; too M2.   59   it:]
Q1–12, F, D, M2; ∼ . M1.   61   ——I]∧∼ Q1–12, F, D, M1–2.   61
Mind;] Q1–12, F, D, M2; ∼ . M1.   62–73 *omitted from* M2.   63
serve:] Q1–7, Q9–12, F, D; ∼ . Q8; ∼∧ M1.   65   Blood:] Q1–7, Q9–12,
F, D; ∼ . Q8, M1.   67   fame;] Q1–12, F, D; ∼ . M1.   74 *Alib.*
When] Q1–12, F, D, M1; When M2.   74   grow stubborn, slothful]
Q1–12, F, D, M2 (∼∧∼ Q10, M2); are slothfull, stubborn M1.   75
Each private man for publick good] Q1–12, F, D, M2; for publique good
each private man M1.   75   should] Q1–12, F, D, M1; may M2.   75
rise.] Q2–12, F, D; rise∧ M2; rise; / As when the Head distempers does
endure, / Each several part must join t'effect the cure. Q1; rise; / Virtue
though straight, doth of loose folds consist / which larger Soules can can
[*sic*] widen as they list. M1.   77   impious] Q1–12, F, D; sawcy M1;
monstrous M2.   77   use:] Q1–7, Q9–12, M2; ∼ . Q8, M1.   79
desire;] Q1–12, F, D, M2; ∼ . M1.   81   make;] Q1–12, F, D, M2; ∼ .
M1.   82   what e're] Q1–12, F, D, M1; w^t ere M2.   82   faults]
Q1–12, F, D, M2; fault M1.   82   time] Q1–12, F, D, M1; times M2.
83   Judge where can be no] Q1–12, F, D, M1; judges where none can M2.
84   plainly let me] Q1–12, F, D, M1; lett me plainly M2.   85   me:]
Q1–3, Q6–12, F, D, M2; ∼ . Q4–5, M1.   87   you;] Q1–7, Q9–12, F,
D; ∼ . Q8; ∼ : M1; ∼∧ M2.   91   kind:] Q1–12, F, D, M2; ∼ ; M1.
92   But] Q1–12, F, D, M1; For M2.   93   Bleeding] Q1–12, F, D, M1;
broken M2.   93   Heart:] Q1–12, F, D; ∼ . M1–2.   95   forsake:]
Q1–7, Q9–12, F, D; ∼ . Q8, M1; ∼∧ M2.   97+   *s.d. Enter*] Q2–12,
F, D, M2 (*Enter*, Q5); *Enter a* Q1, M1.   97+   *s.d. Messenger*] D;
Messenger Q1–12, F, M1–2.   98   Fate;] Q1–12, F, D; ∼∧ M1–2.   99
Watch-Tower] Q1–12, F, D, M1; watch tower M2.   99   Gate,] Q1–12,
F, D; ∼ . M1; ∼∧ M2.   102   run,] Q1–12, F, D; ∼ . M1; ∼∧ M2.
103   Bowers] Q1–12, F, D, M2; Bow'rs M1.   103   them] Q1–12, F, D,
M1; 'em M2.   103   Sun.] Q1–3, Q6–12, F, D, M1–2; ∼ , Q4–5.   105+
s.d. both s.d. omitted from M1.   105+   *s.d. Messenger*] D; Messenger

Q1–12, F, M2.   106 Eye,] Q1; ~ : Q2–7, Q9–12, F, D; ~ ; Q8; ~∧
M1; ~ . M2.   108 *Odmar*] Q1; *Odmar*, Q2–8, F, D, M1–2; *Odmar*.
Q9–10; *Odm*. Q11–12.   108 come] Q1–12, F, D, M2; came M1.
109 beg'd] Q2–12, F, D, M1–2; beg Q1.   110 *Odm*.] Q1–11, F,
D, M1–2; *Alib*. Q12.   111 to] Q1–12, F, D, M1; by M2.   111
you:] Q1–7, Q9–12, F, D; ~ . Q8, M1; ~∧ M2.   112 who] Q2–12,
F, D, M2; that Q1, M1.   114 *Alib*. What] Q1–11, F, D, M1–2; What
Q12.   114 bestow,] Q1–4, Q6–12, F, D, M2; ~ . Q5; ~∧ M1.   117
Love.] Q1–12, F, D; ~ , M1; ~∧ M2.   118 receive] Q1–12, F, D,
M2; receives M1.   119 want;] Q1–7, Q9–12, F, D, M2; ~ . Q8,
M1.   120 hope] hopes Q1–12, F, D, M1–2.   120 is] Q1–12,
F, D, M1; are (*written over* "is") M2.   121 haste;] Q1–12, F, D (hast
Q4–5); haste∧ M2; hast. M1.   123 General's] Q1–12, F, D, M1;
generalls M2.   125 Brother's] Q1–12, F, D, M1; brothers M2.   125
Murderer] Q1–2, Q6–12, F, D, M1–2; Murd'rer Q3–5.   126 Brother,]
Q1–2, Q6–8, Q11–12, D; ~∧ Q3–5, Q9–10, F, M1–2.   127 treacherous]
Q1–4, Q6–12, F, D, M1–2; treach'rous Q5.   128 spilt] Q1–10, F, D,
M1–2; split Q11–12.   133 will obey;] Q1–12, F, D, M2; must obey.
M1.   135 *Exit* Odmar.] Q1–12, F, D, M1; Exit M2.   136 *Alib*.]
Q1–12, F, D, M2; Alib— / sola. M1.   137 how,] Q1–12, F, D;
~∧ M1–2.   137 want:] Q1–7, Q9–12, F, D, M2; ~ , Q8; ~ . M1.
138 mind,] Q1–12, F, D; ~∧ M1–2.   139 find:] Q1–12, F, D; ~ .
M1–2.   140 one, denying,] Q1–12, F, D; ~∧~∧ M1–2.   141 this,
obeying, . . . more:] Q1–12, F, D; ~∧~∧ . . .~ . M1; ~∧~∧ . . . ~∧
M2.   142 refuse,] Q1–12, F, D, M1; ~∧ M2.   143 haste] Q1–12,
F, D, M1; hast M2.   143 use:] Q1–12, F, D, M2; ~ . M1.   145 of
the . . . undone:] Q1–12, F, D, M2; of his . . .~ . M1.   147 Town:]
Q1–12, F, D; ~ . M1–2.   149 more——] Q1–12, F, D, M2; ~ . M1.
152 fram'd a] Q1–10, F, D, M1–2; fram'd Q11–12.   153 *Exit*
Alibech.] Q1–12, F, D, M1; Exit M2.

IV, iii

SCENE III.] Q1–12, F, D, M2; 3d: Scene M1.   s.d. *in it a Fountain
spouting; round about it*] Q1–12, F, D, M2 (spouting∧ M2); a Fountaine
spouting in it, Indian rarities round about. M1.   s.d. *other* Spaniards]
Q1–12, F, D, M1; others M2.   s.d. *un-arm'd, and*] Q1–12, F, D; disarm'd, M1 (*M1 omits the rest of this s.d. and runs in 16+ as shown below*);
unarmd, M2.   s.d. *the following*] Q1–12, F, D; a M2.   1–16 *and
heading* "SONG." *omitted from M1–2*.   1 joy,] Q1–5, Q8–12, F; ~∧
Q6–7, M4–5; ~ ſ D.   1 past?] Q1–4, Q6–12, F, D, M4; ~∧ Q5, M5.
2 ruine] Q1–12, F, D, M5; ruines M4.   2 haste:] Q1–5, M4 (hast Q4–
5); ~ . Q6–12, F, D; ~∧ M5.   *After line 2 M4 has*: And what too soon
would dye / Help to destroy.   3 cares] Q1–12, F, D, M5; care M4.
4 new:] Q1–3, Q6–12, F, D, M4–5; ~ . Q4; ~ , Q5.   5 follow Fate]
Q1–12, F, D, M5; draw fate on M4.   5 which would] Q2–12, F, D,
M4–5; that does Q1.   6 on] Q1–12, F, D, M4; in M5.   7 In their]
Q1b–12, F, D, M4–5; In the Q1a.   7 happiness.] Q1–3, Q6–12, F, D,
M5; ~∧ Q4–5, M4.   9 lay their] Q1–12, F, D, M5; lay the M4.   9

care:] Q1–3, Q6–12, F, D, M5; ~ , Q4; ~ . Q5; ~∧ M4.   10 *below,*]
Q7–12, F, D; ~∧ Q1–6, M4–5.   *After line 12 M4 has:* For vain doth natures
bounteous hands supply / What peevish mortalls to themselves deny.   13
Hark, hark] Q2–12, F, D, M4–5; *Hark, bark* Q1.   16+   *s.d. After the Song
two* Spaniards *arise and Dance a Saraband with Castanieta's: at the end of
which,* Guyomar *and his* Indians *enter, and e're the* Spaniards *can recover their Swords, seize them.*] Q1–12, F, D (*Song,* Q5, Q7, Q9–12, F;
Saraband Q1–7, Q9–12, F, D; Sarabrand Q8; Castanieta's Q1–8, D; Castanieta's Q9–12, F; Indian's Q1); two Spaniards dancing a Sarabrand, at
the end of which Guyomar enters and ere they can recover their Swords
seizes them. M1; *After which Enter Guyomar and his Indians, who seize
upon the Spaniards ere thy can recover their swords.* M2.   17 without,]
D; ~∧ Q1–12, F, M1–2.   19 in these] Q1–12, F, D, M1; these M2.
21 our] Q1–12, F, D, M2; youre M1.   24 out-live] Q1–12, F, D, M1;
out live M2.   24+ *s.d. omitted from M1.*   24+ *s.d. are led out.*]
Q1–12, F, D; led of M2.   25 1] Q1, M2; ~ . Q2–12, F, D, M1.   25
quickly] Q1–12, F, D, M2; swiftly M1.   26+ *s.d.* Montezuma; Alibech;] ~ ,
~ , Q1–12, F, D; ~ , ~ . M1; *Mont:* ~ , M2.   27 *s.d. omitted from M2.*
28 out-done] Q1–12, F, D, M1; out done M2.   29 all] Q2–12, F, D,
M2; such Q1, M1.   29 shower,] Q1–12, F, D, M2; Show're M1.   32
Deity:] Q1–12, F, D; ~ . M1; ~∧ M2.   33 neither] Q1–12, F, D, M1;
nether M2.   33 Fame,] Q1–5, Q10–12, F, D, M1; ~ . Q6–9; ~∧ M2.
36+ *s.d.* A Guyomar, &c.] *A* Guyomar, &c. Q1–4, Q6–12, F, D; Guyomar,
&c. Q5; A Guyomar. M1; *A Guiomar* M2.   38 Fate:] Q1–12, F, D, M2;
~ . M1.   39 them] Q1–12, F, D, M1; em M2.   41 Conquest] Q1–
12, F, D, M2; Conquests M1.   43 day,] Q1–12, F, D, M2; ~ . M1.   44
delay:] Q1–12, F, D, M2; ~ . M1.   47 do] Q1–12, F, D, M1; doe M2.
47 same:] Q1–12, F, D; ~ . M1; ~∧ M2.   49 and what e're] Q1–12,
F, D, M1; what ever M2.   50+ *s.d. and* Alibech] Q1–12, F, D, M2;
Alibech M1.   51 voice,] Q1–12, F, D, M2; ~ ! M1.   53 was not]
Q1–3, Q6–12, F, D, M1–2; was Q4–5.   53 new!] Q1–12, F, D; ~ , M1;
~∧ M2.   53 too] Q1–3, Q6–12, F, D, M1–2; too too Q4–5.   54
that it must] Q1–12, F, D, M1; it must needs M2.   54 me.———] Q1–
5; ~·∧ Q6–12, F, D, M1; ~∧——— M2.   55 feel] Q1–12, F, D, M2;
see M1.   56 do] Q1–12, F, D, M1; doe M2.   56 ill:] Q1–12, F, D,
M2; ~ . M1.   58 led:] Q1–12, F, D, M2; ~ . M1.   60 well!] Q1–
12, F, D, M2; ~ . M1.   62 all.] Q1–12, F, D, M1; ~∧ M2.   63 in
———] Q1–12, F, D, M1; ~ . M2.   63+ *s.d. omitted from M1.*   63+
s.d. Vasquez,] Q1, Q4–12, F; Vasquez. Q2–3; Vasquez, *and* D, M2.   65,
66 do] Q1–12, F, D, M1; doe M2.   67 show:] Q1–12, F, D; ~ . M1–2.
69 Destroy;] Q1–12, F, D, M2; ~ . M1.   70 my own] Q3–12, F, D,
M1–2; my one Q1–2.   71 Honours] Q1–5, M1–2; Honour Q6–12, F,
D.   72 request] Q1–10, F, D, M1–2; ~ . Q11–12.   74 given] Q1–
12, F, D, M2; giv'n M1.   74 me.] Q1–3, Q6–12, F, D, M1–2; ~ , Q4–5.
75 who e're] Q1–12, F, D, M1 (whoe're Q4–5); who ere M2.   77
———I] ∧~ Q1–12, F, D, M1–2.

IV, iv

SCENE IV. *A*] Q1–12, F, D, M2 (Scene, Q4); 4th Scene M1. *s.d. dis-cover'd, bound:*] Q2–12, F, D; *discovered, bound by one Foot,* Q1; discover'd bound by the feet M1; *Bound:* M2.   1–2 prove, / . . . me]
Q1–12, F, D; ∼∧ / . . . ∼ , M1; ∼∧ / . . . ∼∧ M2.   5 unbelief,] Q1–12, F, D; ∼∧ M1; ∼. M2.   6 grief:] Q1–12, F, D, M2; ∼. M1.   7 Love,] Q1–12, F, D; ∼! M1; ∼∧ M2.   8 know:] Q1–12, F, M2; ∼ ; D; ∼. M1.   9 not,] Q1–12, F, M1; ∼ ; D; ∼∧ M2.   9–10 *s.d. omitted from M1.*   10 Brother's] Q1–12, F, D, M1; Brothers M2.   16 falls,] Q3–12, F, D, M1; ∼∧ Q1–2, M2.   17 appear] Q1–4, Q6–12, F,· D, M1–2; ∼ , Q5.   23 a way] Q1–3, Q5–12, F, D, M1–2; away Q4.
24 guilt] Q1–3, Q6–12, F, D, M1–2; ∼ , Q4–5.   24 betray:] Q1–3, Q6–12, F, D; ∼ , Q4–5; ∼. M1; ∼∧ M2.   26 Condemn;] Q1–12, F, D, M2; ∼. M1.   28 ne're . . . I will] Q2–12, F, D, M2; not . . . I'le still Q1, M1.
28 adore;] Q1–12, F, D, M2; ∼. M1.   30 hand.] Q1–12, F, D; ∼∧ M1–2.   30+ *s.d.* Cydaria.] Q1–4, Q6–12, F, D, M2; Cydaria, Q5; Cydaria and sees it. M1.   31 Eyes!] Q1–12, F, D, M2; ∼? M1.   31 do] Q1–12, F, D, M1; doe M2.   32 me!] Q1–12, F, D, M2; ∼? M1.   34 Faith?] Q1–12, F, D, M1; ∼∧ M2.   34 *s.d. omitted from M2.*   35 words, dear Saint, are these] Q1–12, F, D; words are these deare Saint, M1–2 (are those M2).   36 those] Q2–12, F, D, M1–2; these Q1.   37 o're] Q1–12, F, D, M1; ore M2.   37–38 spoyl; / . . . Crocodile:] Q1–12, F, D; ∼! / . . . ∼! M1; ∼∧ . . . ∼∧ M2.   40 which] Q1–12, F, D, M1; that M2.   43 accus'd?] Q1–12, F, D, M1; ∼∧ M2.   44 Life,] Q1–12, F, D, M1; ∼∧ M2.   45 thousand times] Q1–12, F, D, M2; thousands time M1.   46 have . . . find] Q1–12, F, D, M1; find . . . have M2.   46 true;] Q1–12, F, D; ∼. M1; ∼∧ M2.   47 therefore] Q1–12, F, D, M1; therefor M2.   48 *s.d. at head of next line in M1; omitted from M2.*   49 *s.d. omitted from M2.*   54 blush? . . . hand.] Q1–12, F, D; ∼ , . . . ∼? M1; ∼! . . . ∼. M2.   55 not, . . . Love's] Q1–12, F, D, M1; ∼∧ . . . Loves M2.   56 aside;] Q1–12, F, D; ∼. M1; ∼ , M2.   58 boast:] Q1–12, F, D, M2; ∼. M1.   59 true] Q1–3, Q6, M1; ∼ , Q4–5, Q7–12, F, D; ∼. M2.   61 words!] Q1–4, Q6–10, F, D, M2; ∼? Q5, Q11–12, M1.   61–62 needs / . . . deeds?] Q1–12, F, D, M2; ∼? / . . . ∼. M1.   63 say?] Q11–12; ∼! Q1–10, F, D; ∼∧ M1–2.   64 That] Q2–12, F, D, M2; As Q1, M1.   64 it . . . much.] Q1–12, F, D, M1; is . . . much∧ M2.   67 prepare:] Q1–7, Q9–12, F, D; ∼ , Q8; ∼∧ M1–2.   68 is] Q1–12, F, D, M2; shee's M1.   72 while] Q1–12, F, D, M1; whilst M2.   74 my] Q1–12, F, D, M1; the M2.   76 Pride:] Q1–7, Q9–12, F, D; ∼ , Q8; ∼. M1; ∼∧ M2.   77 Fears,] Q1–12, F, D; ∼∧ M1–2.   81 Nat'rally] Q1–12, F, D; naturally M1–2.   83 constancy;] Q1–12, F, D, ∼∧ M1–2.   85 him;] Q1–7, Q9–12, F, D; ∼ , Q8; ∼∧ M1–2.   87 malicious Beauty,] Q2–12, F, D, M2; Inhumane Creature∧ Q1, M1.   87 be:] Q1–7, D, M2; ∼ ; Q8; ∼? Q9–12, F, M1.   89 Swords] Q1–3, Q6–12, F, D, M1–2; Sword Q4–5.   89 way.] Q1–3, Q6–12, F, D, M1; ∼∧ Q4–5, M2.   89+ *s.d.*, 90 *Within.*]

Q9–12, F; *within.* Q1–8, D; *omitted from M1–2.* 90 cannot . . . o're-
powr'd] Q1–12, F, D, M1; can not . . . ore powerd M2. 90 betray.]
Q1–3, Q6–12, F, D, M1–2; ~∧ Q4–5. 92 General] Q1–8, D, M1–2;
Gen'ral Q9–12, F. 92 Free:] Q1–7, Q9–12, F, D, M2; ~. Q8, M1.
92 *Within.*] Q9–12, F; *within.* Q1–8, D, M2; *omitted from M1.* 94
hopes . . . are] Q1–12, F, D, M2; hope . . . is M1. 94 gone:] Q1–7,
Q9–12, F, D; ~. Q8, M1; ~ ; M2. 95 As when . . . Thunder-clap]
Q1–12, F, D, M1; As . . . thunder clap M2. 95–96 nigh, / . . . Fire]
Q1–12, F, D; ~∧ / . . .~, M1; ~∧ / . . . ~∧ M2. 96 shoots
swiftly] Q1–12, F, D, M1; shouts quickly M2. 96 Skie,] Q1–12, F, D;
~. M1; ~∧ M2. 97 e're scarce] Q1–12, F, D, M1; before M2. 98
ill] Q1–9, Q11–12, F, D, M1–2; I'll Q10. 98 fear:] Q1–7, Q9–12, F, D;
~ ; Q8; ~. M1; ~∧ M2. 99 wo;] Q1–5; ~ , Q6–11, F, D, M1; ~.
Q12; ~∧ M2. 100 pow'r] Q1–12, F, D, M1; power M2. 100 do:]
Q1–7, Q9–12, F; ~. Q8, D, M1; doe: M2. 101 Live,] Q1–7, D; live?
Q8–12, F, M1; life∧ M2. 102 destroy? [*Aside.*] Q1–12, F, D; destroy.
M1; destroy? M2. 105 jealousie] Q2–12, F, D, M2; jealous Thoughts
Q1, M1. 108+ *s.d. omitted from M1.* 108+ *s.d. towards her.*]
Q1–11, D, M2 (*her*∧ M2); *towards him.* Q12; *toward her.* F. 109–110
omitted from M1. 109 ah] Q1–12, F, D; O M2. 109 Barbarous]
Q1–8, F, D, M2; barb'rous Q9–12. 109 oh] Q1–12, F, D; o M2. 110
pity! is . . . nigh?] Q9–12, F; pity, is . . . nigh! Q1–8, D; pitty! is . . .
nigh! M2. 112+ *s.d. omitted from M1.* 113 any where:] Q1–7,
Q9–12, F, D, M1; anywhere. Q8, M2. 113+ *s.d. omitted from M1.*
115 part:] Q1–7, Q9–12, F, D; ~ ! Q8; ~∧ M1; ~. M2. 117 Ah!]
Q1–7, Q9–12, F, D; ~∧ Q8, M1–2. 117 Woman,] Q1–7, Q9–12, F,
D; ~ ! Q8, M1; ~∧ M2. 117 design!] Q1–7, D, M1; ~? Q8–12, F;
~∧ M2. 118 This Weapons point shall mix that blood with mine!]
Q2–12, F, D, M2; At least this Weapon both our Blood shall joyn. Q1,
M1 (blouds M1). 118+ *s.d. omitted from M1.* 118+ *s.d. and
being within*] Q1–12, F, D; *but being in* M2. 120+ *s.d. omitted
from M1.* 120+ *s.d. with drawn Swords*] Q1–6, Q8–12, F, D; *with
drawn Sword* Q7; *drawn swords* M2. 122 bleed:] Q1–7, Q9–12, F,
D, M2; ~. Q8, M1. 124 *Vasq.*] Q1b–12, F, D, M1; *Vsq.* Q1a; V: M2.
124 led;] Q1–7, Q9, D; ~. Q8, M1; ~ : Q10–12, F; ~∧ M2. 125
Men,] Q8; ~∧ Q1–7, Q9–12, F, D, M1–2. 127 came] Q1–12, F, D,
M1; come M2. 128 March along] Q1–12, F, D, M1; walk a long M2.
129 fear: [*To* Cydaria.] Q1–12, F, D, M1 (fear; Q8; fear∧ M1); fear∧
M2. 130 Swords, no] Q1–12, F, D, M2 (Swords∧ M2); Swords nor M1.
132 Halcyons] Q1–3, Q6–12, F, D, M1–2; Halcyon Q4–5. 132
Winter] Q1–7, Q9–12, F, D, M1–2; Winter's Q8. 133 fright,] Q1–3,
Q6–7, Q9–12, F, D; ~∧ Q4–5, M1–2; ~. Q8. 134 night:] Q1–7,
Q9–12, F, D; ~. Q8, M1; ~∧ M2. 136 alone:] Q1–7, Q9–12, F, D,
M2; ~. Q8, M1. 137 Feet.———] Q1–3, Q6–7, D, M1; ~∧———
Q4–5, Q8–12, F, M2. 138 meet.] Q1–12, F, D, M2; ~ , M1. 139
Th'] Q1–12, F, D, M1; The M2. 143 bear:] Q1–7, Q9–12, F, D; ~ ,
Q8, M1; ~∧ M2. 147 Life;] ~ , Q1–12, F, D, M1; ~∧ M2. 150
Yet, leaving it,] Q2–6, D; Yet leaving it Q1, M2; Yet Leaving it, Q7–12,

F; Leaving mee Life M1. 150 inhumane] Q1–12, F, D, M1; in
humane M2. 150 prove:] Q1–12, F; ~ . D, M1; ~∧ M2. 151
some] Q1–6, D, M1–2; soft Q7–12, F. 152 kind.] Q1–12, F, D,
M2; ~ ! M1. 153 *Cort.*] Q1–12, F, D, M2; Cort to / Cydaria M1.
153 do] Q1–12, F, D, M1; doe M2. 154 your] Q2–12, F, D, M2;
thy Q1, M1. 154 return.] Q1–12, F, D, M2; ~ : M1. 154 *s.d.*
omitted from M1–2. 155 Your] Q2–12, F, D, M2; Thy Q1, M1.
155 Father's] Q1–12, F, D, M1; fathers M2. 156 your] Q2–12, F, D,
M2; thy Q1, M1. 158 more:] Q1–7, Q9–12, F, D; ~ . Q8, M1; ~∧ M2.
159 Dead] Q1–5, M1–2; ~ , Q6–12, F, D. 162 Dear.] Q1–10, F, D,
M1; ~ , Q11–12, ~∧ M2. 162 farewel:] Q1–12, F, D, M2; ~ ! M1.
164 not one, not one last] Q1–3, Q6–12, F, D, M1–2; not one last
Q4–5. 164 afford?] M1–2; ~ ! Q1–12, F, D. 165 stay,] Q1–3,
Q6–12, F, D; ~ ; Q4–5; ~∧ M1–2. 166 betray;] Q1–7, Q9, D; ~ .
Q8; ~ : Q10–12, F; ~∧ M1–2. 167 Yon] Q1–10, F, D, M1–2; Your
Q11–12. 169 me there——— [He leads her.] Q1–12, F, D (her∧
Q4); mee——— M1; me there M2. 171 go] Q1–7, Q9–12, F, D,
M1–2; ~ , Q8. 171+ *s.d. omitted from M1.* 171+ *s.d.* Pizarro,]
Q1–12, F; Piz. *and* D, M2. 172 much Lov'd,] Q1–12, F, D; ~ ! M1;
~∧ M2. 172 vain!] Q1–11, F, D, M1; ~∧ Q12, M2. 172 *s.d.*
Sola.] Q1–3, Q6–12, F, D, M1 (*at head of next line in M1*); *sola*∧ Q4–5;
omitted from M2. 173 remain!] Q1–12, F, D, M2; ~ . M1. 175
give the] Q1–12, F, D, M1; give that M2. 175+ *s.d.* Cortez, . . .
Spaniards, *return again.*] Q1–12, F, D, M1 (Spaniards∧ Q1a, M1; returnes
M1); Enter Cort . . . Spaniards M2. 176 *Cort.* All] Q1–12, F, D,
M2; All M1. 176 *s.d. omitted from M1.* 177+ *s.d. and* Vasquez]
Q1–12, F, D, M2; Vasquez M1. 178 *Piz.* I'le] Q1–12, F, D, M2; I'le
M1. 179 her to] Q1b–12, F, D, M1–2; to her Q1a. 180 *Exit*] Q1–12,
F, D, M2; stalks of and Exit M1.

V, i

ACT V. SCENE I.] Q1–12, F, D, M2 (Scene, Q4); Act: 5th 1:st Scene
M1. *s.d. The Chamber Royal, an* Indian *Hamock discover'd in it.*
/ *Enter* Odmar *with Souldiers,* Guyomar, Alibech, *bound.*] Q1–12, F, D,
M1 (SCENE *a Chamber* D; Hamock Q1–4, Q6–12, F, D, M1; it, M1;
Odmar, Q12; Soldjers. M1; *and* Alibech D); the Royall Chamber. Odmar
Guy: and Ali: Bound: M2. 2 blame,] Q1b–12, F, D, M1; ~∧ Q1a,
M2. 3 provide?] Q1–12, F, D; ~ ! M1; ~∧ M2. 4 of] Q1–12,
F, D, M1; on M2. 4 Conquering] Q1–8, D, M1–2; Conq'ring Q9–12,
F. 7 contemn] Q1–12, F, D, M2; Contemn'd M1. 7 thee] Q1–12,
F, D, M1; the M2. 8 refusing] Q1–12, F, D, M1; rejecting M2.
12 a] Q2–12, F, D, M2; most Q1, M1. 16 'twas] Q1–12, F, D, M1;
was M2. 16 you:] Q1–12, F, D, M2; ~ . M1. 17 Fear:] Q1–12,
F, D; ~∧ M1–2. 21 elsewhere,] Q2–12, F, D; elsewher∧ Q1a;
elsewhere: Q1b; else where∧ M1–2. 22 Fear.] Q1–12, F, D, M2;
~∧ M1. 25 wish.——— [Offers to stab.] M2 (wish∧———offers—
"stab" *written above* "strike"; *which is crossed out*); wish.——— Q1;
wish,——— Q2–8; Wish∧——— Q9–12, F, D, M1. 26 Hold] Q1–12,

F, D, M1; then M2.   26 hold:―――― [*Stops his hand.*] M2 (hold_∧――――
stops); hold:―――― Q1–9; hold_∧―――― Q10–12, F, M1; hold:_∧ D.   27
resign;] Q1–12, F, D; ～ , M1; ～_∧ M2.   29 thou would'st] Q1–12, F,
D, M1; you would M2.   30 Even] Q1; Ev'n Q2–12, F, D, M1–2.   30
thee:] Q1–12, F, D, M2; ～. M1.   33 way:] Q1–12, F, D, M2; ～. M1.
34 betray. [*Aside.*] Q1–12, F, D (betray:); betray.―――― M1; betray: M2.
35 Wife; [*To her.*] Q1–12, F, D, M1 (Wife: Q10–12; Wife, M1); Wife.
M2.   36 in your] Q1–9, Q11–12, F, D, M1–2; in you Q10.   36
power] Q1–12, F, D, M1; pow'r M2.   36 Life:] Q1–12, F, D, M2; ～.
M1.   41 only threatn'd . . . could not] Q1–12, F, D, M2; threatn'd
. . . thinke not I could M1.   42 Love:] Q1–12, F, D, M2; ～. M1.
45 that . . . Breath] Q1–12, F, D, M1; yʳ . . . breathe M2.   46
Life:] Q1–12, F, D; ～ , M1; ～. M2.   46 if not,] Q2–12, F, D, M1–2
(not_∧ M2); I'le not Q1.   46+ *s.d. omitted from M1–2.*   47 do?]
M1; ～! Q1–12, F, D; doe_∧ M2.   47 What, are] Q6–12, F, D; What
are Q1–5, M1–2.   49 Interest] Q1–12, F, D, M1; intrest M2.   52
which] Q2–12, F, D; that Q1, M1–2.   53+ *s.d. omitted from M1–2.*
54 yet e're] Q1–10, F, D, M2; e're yet Q11–12; ere M1.   59+ *s.d.*
omitted from M1.   59+ *s.d.* her Husband.] Q1–12, F, D; *Guyom:* M2.
60 No,] Q1–3, Q6–12, F, D; ～. Q4; ～_∧ Q5, M1–2.   60 embrace:
[*He turns from her.*] Q1–12, F, D, M2 (embrace_∧ M2); embrace_∧ M1.
61 do] Q1–12, F, D, M1; doe M2.   63 Voice.] Q1–4, Q6–12, F, D,
M1; ～ : Q5; ～_∧ M2.   64 pretence] Q2–12, F, D, M1–2; prctence Q1.
69 could give] Q1–12, F, D, M1; would doe M2.   69 you.] Q1–12,
F, D, M2; ～ : M1.   70 Jealousie,] Q1–3, Q6–12, F, D; ～ . Q4–5; ～_∧
M1–2.   71 Dye:] Q1–12, F, D; ～. M1; ～_∧ M2.   73 be thought
fearful, or, what's worse,] Q2–12, F, D, M2 (or_∧ Q8, D, M2); worse_∧ M2);
think the other fearful, or Q1, M1.   75 *Embracing him.*] Q1–12, F, D,
M1 (*her.* Q8; *s.d. at head of line in M1*); embraces him_∧ M2.   77
Faith which] Q2–12, F, D, M2 (Faith, D); Faith that Q1, M1.   80
Souldiers.――――] Q1–4, Q6, M1–2; ～_∧―――― Q5, Q7–12, F, D.   80+
s.d. omitted from M1.   80+ *s.d.* Vasquez,] Q1–12, F; Vasquez, *and*
D, M2.   81 hold! I] M1; ～ , ～ Q1–12, F, D; ～_∧～ M2.   83 *Odm.*
You] Q1–12, F, D, M2; You M1.   84 say] Q1–8, D, M1–2; ～ , Q9–12,
F.   84 *Spaniard*] Q1–12, F, D, M2; Spaniards M1.   84 be gone.]
Q1–6, Q11–12, F, D, M1; be gone, Q7–10; begone. M2.   85 design:]
Q1–12, F, D; ～. M1; ～_∧ M2.   86 who] Q1–12, F, D, M1; wᶜʰ M2.
87 Your'e] Q1–12, F, D, M1; you are M2.   88 Father's] Q1–12, F,
D, M1; fathers M2.   93 you cannot] Q1–12, F, D, M1; thou canst
not M2.   94 Face:] Q1–12, F, D; ～. M1–2.   95 Laws.] Q1–12,
F, D; ～_∧ M1–2.   97 undergo.] Q1–12, F, D; ～_∧ M1–2.   100
shame.] Q1–12, F, D, M1; ～_∧ M2.   102 Ravisher:] Q1–12, F, D; ～.
M1; ～_∧ M2.   103 our] Q1–12, F, D, M2; the M1.   105 rests]
Q1–12, F, D, M2; rest M1.   106 this] Q1–12, F, D, M2; his M1.
106 prize,] Q1–12, F, D; ～ ; M1; ～_∧ M2.   107 haste,――――] haste,_∧
Q1–12, F, D; haste_{∧∧} M2; hast_∧―――― M1.   108 cannot] Q1–12, F,
D, M1; cannot not M2.   108 perplext:] Q1–12, F, D; ～ , M1; ～. M2.
109 my next] Q1–12, F, D, M1; the next M2.   109+ *s.d. Fight,* . . .

Indians *Fight.*] Q1–12, F, D; ~∧ . . . ~~ . M1; *Fight, as also* . . .
Indians M2.   111   too! [*Unbinds her Husband.*] Q1–12, F, D; too.
M1–2.   112   mine;] Q1–12, F, D; ~∧ M1–2.   112   *s.d. omitted from*
M2.   114   yet!———] ~ !∧ Q1–12, F, D, M2; ~∧——— M1.   116
Earth-born-brethren] Q1–2, Q6; Earth-born Brethren Q3–5, Q7–12, F,
D; Earth borne brethren M1–2 (born M2).   117   afford,] Q1–12, F,
D; ~∧ M1–2.   118   My Cause is more advantage then your] Q1–12,
F, D, M2; I have enough advantage in my M1.   121   kill!] Q1–12, F,
D; ~ ; M1; ~∧ M2.   124   hast] Q1–8, D, M1–2; has Q9–12, F.
124+   *s.d. a little and*] Q1–12, F, D, M1; & M2.   125   the] Q1–12,
F, D, M1; this M2.   126   Life:] Q1–12, F, D, M2; ~∧ M1.   126
s.d. omitted from M2.   127   thy] Q1–12, F, D, M2; this M1.   127
gain,] Q1–12, F, D; ~ : M1; ~∧ M2.   128+   *s.d. back, they Fight*
again,] Q1–12, F, D, M1 (back∧ M1); *back. Fight again.* M2.   128+
s.d. falls.] Q1b–12, F, D, M1–2; ~∧ Q1a.   130   'Twere vain] Q2–12,
F, D, M2; I scorn Q1, M1.   132   adore. [*Dyes.*] Q1–12, F, D, M2;
adore.——— M1.   133   remove:] Q1–12, F; ~ . D; ~∧ M1–2.   136
The Vanquish'd Crying, and] Q1–12, F, D, M2 (vanquish'd, Q5); the
cryes of vanquisht men M1.   136   Victor's] Q1–11, F, D; Victor Q12,
Victors M1–2.   137   Father's] Q1–12, F, D, M1; fathers M2.   137
flye;] Q1–6, D, M1; ~ . Q7–8; ~ , Q9–12, F; ~∧ M2.   138   Ruine]
Q1–10, F, D, M1–2; Ruines Q11–12.   138   *Exeunt.*] Q1–11, F, D; ~∧
Q12, M1; ~ : M2.

V, ii

SCENE II.] Q1–12, F, D, M2 (SCENE, Q4); 2ᵈ: Scene. M1.   *s.d.*
Indian *High Priest*] Indian High Priest Q1–12, F, D, M2; Caliban M1.
s.d. Spaniards] Q1–12, F, D, M1; and Spaniards M2.   *s.d. drawn, a*
Christian Priest.] *drawn, a* Christian Priest. Q1–12, F, D (*drawn.* Q12);
drawn, a Jesuite, M1; drawn. M2.   2   more:] Q1–12, F, D; ~ . M1–2.
5–10   *omitted from M2.*   5   *Chr. Priest.*] Q1–12, F, D; Jes— M1 (*and*
similarly below).   6   denies:] Q1–3, Q6–10, F, D; ~∧ Q4; ~ ; Q5; ~ .
M1.   8   stealth:] Q1–12, F, D; ~ ! M1.   10   *Ind. High Pr.*] Q1–12,
F, D; Calib— M1 (*and so throughout*).   10   Cruelty] Q1–3, Q5–12,
F, D, M1; Cruely Q4.   12   assail;] Q1–12, F, D, M2; ~ . M1.   14+
s.d. racks] M1; *rack* Q1–12, F, D, M2.   14+   *s.d. and then*] Q1–12,
F, D; and M1–2.   16   so:] Q1–12, F, D, M2; ~ . M1.   17   now the]
Q1–12, F, D, M2; the M1.   17   Tyranny] Q1–12, F, D, M1; cruelty M2.
18   me.] Q1–3, Q6–12, F, D, M1; ~ , Q4–5; ~∧ M2.   19   Gold,]
Q1–12, F, D, M1; ~∧ M2.   21–99   *omitted from M2, which has here*
only a s.d., "They pull them more and more."   21   rack] Q1–11, F,
D, M1; Race Q12.   23   Barb'rous] Q1–7, Q9–12, F, D; Barbarous Q8,
M1.   25   bring:] Q1–7, Q9–12, F, D; ~ . Q8; ~ , M1.   28   my]
Q1–12, F, D; theire M1.   28   art:] Q1–7, Q9–12, F, D; ~ . Q8, M1.
31   *High*] Q2–12, F, D, M1; ~ . Q1.   32   down;] Q1–12, F, D; ~ .
M1.   33   it's] Q1–10, F, D, M1; it Q11–12.   34   use:] Q1–12, F,
D; ~ . M1.   39   sufferest] Q1–6, D; suffer'st Q7–12, F, M1.   42   cure.]
Q1–4, Q6, Q8–12, F, D, M1; ~ , Q5, Q7.   45   there,] Q1–11, F, D; ~ .

Q12; ~_∧_ M1. 46 Air:] Q1-7, Q9-12, F, D; ~ . Q8, M1. 49
man, . . . misled,] Q1-12, F, D; ~ ! . . . ~ ! M1. 50 Dead:] Q1-7,
Q9-12, F, D; ~ . Q8, M1. 54 the search] Q1-12, F, D; that search
M1. 54 different be,] Q1-12, F, D; diff'rent bee. M1. 56 Right.]
Q1-9, D, M1; ~ , Q10-12, F. 59 eternally,] Q8; ~_∧_ Q1-7, Q9-12,
F, D, M1. 62 receive:] Q1-7, Q9-12, F, D; ~ ; Q8; ~ . M1. 63-64
omitted from M1. 64 above.] Q1-10, F, D; ~_∧_ Q11-12. 66 you:]
Q1-7, Q9-12, F, D; ~ . Q8, M1. 67 another] Q1-12, F, D; a
severall M1. 67 way.] Q1; ~ .———— Q2-5; ~_∧_———— Q6-12, D; ~
————. F; ~ , M1. 68 stay:] Q1-12, F, D; ~ . M1. 71-80 *omitted*
from M1. 79 'tis] Q2-12, F, D; 'twas Q1. 80 in uncertain] Q1-7,
Q9-12, F, D; in an unknown Q8. 81 *Chr.*] Q2-12, F, D; ~_∧_ Q1;
Jes— M1. 82 now.] Q1, M1; ~ , Q2-12, F, D. 83 Religion]
Q1-12, F, D; Religions M1. 84 Suff'rings] Q1-5, D, M1; sufferings
Q6-12, F. 85 All Faiths] Q1-12, D; All Faith F; they all M1. 85
Wise:] Q1-7, Q9-12, F, D; ~ ; Q8; ~ . M1. 88 *Pr.*] Q2-12, F, D;
Pr.. Q1; *omitted from M1.* 89 your self] Q1-12, F, D; your faith M1.
90 erre!] Q1-6, D; ~ ? Q7-12, F; ~_∧_ M1. 92 betray,] Q1-4, Q6-12,
F, D; ~ ? Q5; ~_∧_ M1. 94-97 *omitted from M1.* 95 to go] Q1-7,
Q9-12, F, D; you go Q8. 99 *Pr.*] Q2-12, F, D; *Pr.*. Q1; *omitted from*
M1. 100 more:] Q1-12, F, D; ~_∧_ M1-2. 101 thy store,] Q1-12,
F, D, M2; your store. M1. 104 ease?] Q1-12, F, D, M2; ~ , M1.
105+ *s.d. High Priest*] M2; High Priest Q1-12, F, D; Caliban M1.
105+ *s.d. attended by* Spaniards, *he speaks entring.*] Q1-12, F, D; attended. M1; *attended by* Spaniards. M2. 106-112 *omitted from M1.*
106 who] Q2-12, F, D, M2; that Q1. 109 Massacre] Q1-12, F, D;
Massacree M2. 109 War:] Q1-7, Q9-12, F, D, M2; ~ . Q8. 111-
112 Love. / Ha————] Q1-12, F, D (Ha! Q5; Ha!———— Q8); love: M2.
113 What] Q6-12, F, D, M2 (————w^t M2); *Cort.* What Q1-5, M1.
114 Victory!] Q1-12, F, D; ~ . M1; ~ ? M2. 114+ *s.d. off*] Q1-12,
F, D; of M1-2. 115-116 *omitted from M2.* 115 haste:] Q1-
12, F, D; hast! M1. 115 frown?] *the* ? *pulled out during printing in*
Q6. 116 Haste_∧_] Q1-12, F, D; hast, M1. 117 Ah Father, Father,]
Q1-12, F, D, (Ah, Q9-12, F; Father, Father! Q8); Ah! Father! Father! M1;
Ah Father M2. 117 do] Q1-12, F, D, M1; doe M2. 117 endure]
Q1-8, D, M2; ~ , Q9-12, F; ~ ? M1. 117 *s.d. omitted from M2.*
117 Montezuma.] Q1b-12, F, D, M1; M Q1a. 118 these] Q1-12, F,
D; those M1-2. 118 Cure!] Q1-12, F, D, M2; ~ . M1. 120 King?]
Q1-12, F, D, M2; ~ ! M1. 123-124 *Cort.* . . . hence? [*To* Pizarro.]
Q1-12, F, D; Cort to Piz— . . . hence_∧_ M1; C: . . . hence. M2. 125-
130 *for these lines M2 has:* W^t devill led thee on? 125 you,————]
Q8; ~ , _∧_ Q1-7, Q9-12, F, D; ~_∧_———— M1. 125 *the Chr. Priest.*]
Q1-12, F, D; Jes— M1. 127 sway;] Q1-12, F, D; ~ . M1. 128
power,] Q1-12, F, D; pow'r M1. 129 Viper-like] Q1-7, D; Viper like,
Q8-12, F, M1. 129 devour,] Q1-7, Q9-12, F, D; ~ . Q8, M1. 130
Crowns————] ~ . Q1-12, F, D; ~ ! M1. 130 *Chr. Pr.*] Q1-12, F,
D; Jes— M1; Piz: M2. 130 away,] Q1-12, F, D; ~ . M1; ~_∧_ M2.
132-137 *omitted from M1.* 132 free,] Q1b-12, F, D; ~_∧_ Q1a, M2.

416   *Textual Notes*

133 shine:] Q1–12, F, D; ~$_\Lambda$ M2.   134 Gold,] Q1b–12, F, D; ~$_\Lambda$ Q1a, M2.   134 crimes;] Q1b–4, Q6–11, F, D; ~ : Q1a, Q12; ~ ! Q5; ~$_\Lambda$ M2.   135 Parent] Q1–12, F, D; proper M2.   135 Climes] Q1b– 12, F, D; climes Q1a, M2.   136 brought,] Q1b–12, F, D; ~$_\Lambda$ Q1a, M2. 137+ *s.d. omitted from M2.*   137+ *s.d. Exeunt Priest and* Pizarro.] Q1–12, F, D (Priest Q1–12, F); Exit Jes M1 (*on line 131*).   137+ *s.d. by*] Q1b–12, F, D; *to* Q1a.   138 forget] Q1–12, F, D, M2; forgive M1. 138 commit?] Q1–12, F, D, M1; commit? (to Monte: M2.   139 do] Q1–12, F, D; doe M1–2.   139 is] Q2–12, F, D, M1–2; it Q1.   139 fit:] Q1–12, F, D, M2; ~ . M1.   141 Tears:] Q1–12, F, D, M2; ~ . M1. 142 you?] Q1–12, F, D, M2; ~ ! M1.   142 ——Ah] $_\Lambda$~ Q1–12, F, D, M1–2.   142 to] Q1–4, Q6–12, D, M2; too Q5, F, M1.   143 shame,] Q1–7, Q9–12, F, D, M2; ~ . Q8, M1.   144 lost] Q1–7, Q9–12, F, D, M1–2; last Q8.   145 weep not you,] Q2–4, Q7–12, F, D; weep not, you$_\Lambda$ Q1; weep you, Q5; weep not$_\Lambda$ you$_\Lambda$ Q6, M1–2.   145 King.] Q1–12, F, D, M1; ~$_\Lambda$ M2.   147 mind:] Q1–7, Q9, D, M2; ~ . Q8, M1; ~ ; Q10–12, F.   148 Dye.] Q1–12, F, D; ~$_\Lambda$ M1–2.   151 retreat] Q1–11, F, D, M2; retreats Q12, M1.   154–155 Montezuma.] Q1b–6, D; Montezu Q1a; Montez. Q7–12, F; Mont. M1–2.   155 Friend.] Q1–3, Q6–12, F, D, M2; ~ , Q4–5; ~$_\Lambda$ M1.   156 Man!——] Q8; ~ ! $_\Lambda$ Q1– 7, Q9–12, F, D, M1; man$_{\Lambda\Lambda}$ M2.   156 *s.d. omitted from M1.*   156 *Exit* Cortez, &c.] Q1–12, F, D; Exit M2.   160 meet:] Q1–12, F, D, M2; ~ . M1.   161 are and Misery!] Q2–12, F, D, M2; are! / Such is th' infectious strength of Misery, Q1, M1.   163 *Almeria's*] Q1–12, F, D, M1; Almeria M2.   163 here:] Q1–7, D; ~ ; Q8; ~ , Q9–12, F; ~ ! M1–2. 163 Face!] Q1–12, F, D, M1; ~$_\Lambda$ M2.   166 that . . . you:] Q1–12, F, D, M2; the . . . ~ . M1.   167 me;] Q1–12, F, D; ~ ! M1; ~$_\Lambda$ M2. 168 Victory:] Q1–12, F, D, M1; ~$_\Lambda$ M2.   169 While] Q1–12, F, D, M1; Whilst M2.   171 who] Q2–12, F, D, M2; that Q1, M1.   171 thee lose?] Q1–12, F, D; the loose? M1; thee loose$_\Lambda$ M2.   172 who] Q1b–12, F, D, M2; that Q1a, M1.   172 refuse:] Q1–12, F, D; ~ , M1; ~$_\Lambda$ M2.   173 Him who] Q2–12, F, D, M2; He that Q1a, M1; Him that Q1b.   174 me.] Q1–10, F, D, M1; ~$_\Lambda$ Q11–12, M2.   177 do] Q1–12, F, D, M1; doe M2.   177 streight?] M1; ~ ! Q1–12, F, D; ~$_\Lambda$ M2.   178 weight:] Q1–4, Q6–12, F, D; ~ , Q5; ~ . M1; ~$_\Lambda$ M2. 178–180 *s.d. omitted from M1–2.*   179 *walk and*] Q1b; *walk* Q1a, Q2–3, Q6; *walk,* Q4–5, Q7–12, F, D.   181 I've] Q1–12, F, D, M1; I have M2. 181 *Alm. I've . . . below,* [Alm. *musing.*] Q1–12, F, D (below$_\Lambda$ Q9); Alm— musing I've . . . below$_\Lambda$ M1; Alm: I have . . . below$_\Lambda$ M2.   181 upon't:] Q1–12, F, D; ~ ! M1; ~$_\Lambda$ M2.   182 go.] M1; ~ : Q1–12, F, D; ~$_\Lambda$ M2.   183 *s.d. at head of line in M1, omitted from M2.*   184 free:] Q1–12, F, D, M2; ~ . M1.   185 the Tower] Q1–12, F, D, M2; this Tow'r M1.   186 power,] Q1–8, D; power. Q9–12, F; pow'r$_\Lambda$ M1; power; M2.   187 prevail,——] Q1–6; ~$_\Lambda$—— Q7–12, F, M2; ~ . —— D, M1.   187 Make haste] Q2–12, F, D, M2 (hast M2); Haste then, Q1, M1 (hast M1).   187 call;] Q1–12, F, D; ~ . M1; ~$_\Lambda$ M2. 189 own,] Q1–12, F; ~ . D; ~$_\Lambda$ M1–2.   190 *s.d. Almeria steps behind.*] Q1–12, F, D; Almeria absconds M1; *She goes behind* M2.   191

Cydaria!] Q1-4, Q6-12, F, D, M1-2; ~ . Q5. 192 Father's] Q1-12, F, D; fathers M1-2. 192 forget.] Q1-12, F, D; ~ ? M1; ~∧ M2. 192+ *s.d. at last* Cydaria *looks over*] Q1-12, F, D, M1 (looks. Q11); *Cydaria comes to* M2. 192+ *s.d.* Zoty] *Balcone* Q1a, Q2-12, F, D, M1-2; Zoty Q1b. 195 fear] Q1-12, F, D, M2; ~ . M1. 197 *Cydaria!*————] ~ ! ∧ Q1-12, F, D; ~∧———— M1; ~ . ∧ M2. 198 Sure] M2; ———— ~ Q1-12, F, D, M1. 198 haste] Q1-12, F, D; hast M1-2. 199 past:] Q1-12, F, D; ~ . M1; ~∧ M2. 200 when upon the sands the] Q2-12, F, D, M2 (Sands, D; sand's M2); on the sand the frighted Q1, M1 (Sands M1). 202 The] Q1-12, F, D, M2; and M1. 203 place:] Q1-12, F, D; ~ . M1; ~∧ M2. 204 mis-fortunes] Q1-12, F, D, M2; misfortune M1. 206 alone? / *Mont.* ————I am. / *Cyd.*———— I'le] Q1-12, F, D, M2; alone? here Almeria beckens earnestly to him. / ————I am. / ————I'll M1. 207+ *s.d.* Cydaria *descends and . . . betwixt with* Montezuma.] Q1-12, F, D, M1; *Descends . . . betwixt* M2. 208 *Cyd. Almeria . . . again.*] Q1-12, F, D, M2 (again∧ M2); Almeria . . . ~ ! M1. 209 vain:] Q1-5, M2; ~ . Q6-12, F, D; ~∧ M1. 210 haste] Q1-12, F, D; hast M1-2. 210+ *s.d.* Cortez] M1; [~ Q1-12, F, D, M2. 210+ *s.d.* Spaniards . . . *the other end.*] Q1-12, F, D, M1 (*end*∧ F); *others . . . yᵉ end of yᵉ Stage*∧ M2. 211 do] Q1-12, F, D; doe M1-2. 211+ *s.d. over-powers*] Q2-12, F, D; *oevr-powers* Q1; *over powers* M1-2. 211+ *s.d.* shuts.] Q1-3, Q6-12, F, D, M1; *shuts*———— Q4-5; *shuts the door.* M2. 212 *Cort.*] Q2-12, F, D, M2; *Cyd.* Oh Heavens! / *Cort.* Q1; *Cyd*— within Oh heav'ns! / *Cort*— M1. 212 face,] Q1-12, F, D, M1 (~ . Q5, *some copies*); ~∧ M2. 213 Vision] Q2-12, F, D, M1-2; ~ , Q1. 213 place:] Q1; ~ . Q2-12, F, D, M1; ~∧ M2. 214 find] Q1-4, Q6-12, F, D; ~ , Q5, M1-2. 215 hopes] Q1-4, Q6-12, F, D, M1-2; hope, Q5. 215 *s.d. knocks a little, then*] Q1-12, F, D, M1; *knoks* M2. 215+ *s.d.* Cydaria, Almeria] Q1-12, F (Almeria. Q4; Cydaria. Q7); Cydaria *and* Almeria D, M2; Alm, Cydaria M1. 218 estate] Q1b-12, F, D, M1-2; e stte Q1a. 219 Fate.] Q1-10, F, D, M1; ~∧ Q11-12, M2. 221 there.] Q1-12, F, D, M1; near∧ M2. 222 Conquering] Q1-8, D, M1-2; Conqu'ring Q9-12, F. 223 May . . . again?] Q1-12, F, D; My . . . ~ . M1; May . . . ~ . M2. 224 No,] Q1-3, Q6-12, F, D; ~∧ Q4-5, M1-2. 224 know,] Q1-8, D, M1-2; ~ ; Q9-12, F; ~∧ M2. 224 who] Q1-12, F, D, M2; that M1. 224 born] Q1-12, F, D; borne M1-2. 228 these!] Q1-12, F, D, M2; ~ ? M1. 230 dye] Q1-12, F, M2; ~ . D, M1. 233 gone:] Q1-12, F, D; ~ . M1; ~∧ M2. 234 [*His Sword.*] Q1-12, F, D; sword M1; (*Draws* M2). 235 who] Q1-12, F, D, M1; that M2. 235 Command:] Q1-12, F, D; ~ . M1; ~∧ M2. 236 t'have] Q1-6, Q9-12, F, D, M1-2; to have Q7-8. 238 Haste] Q1-12, F, D, M2; hast M1. 238 ope] Q1-10, F, D, M1-2; open Q11-12. 239 *omitted from Q1.* 239 remain] Q2-12, F, D, M2; remaines M1. 239+ *s.d. omitted from M1.* 239+ *s.d. The* Soul-diers] Q1-12, F, D; Soldiers M2. 239+ *s.d. the first*] Q1-4, Q6-12, F, D, M2; *first the* Q5. 241 stay.] Q1-3, Q6-12, F, D, M1-2; ~ , Q4-5. 245 Scorn!] Q1-12, F, D; ~ . M1; ~∧ M2. 247 decays.] Q1-4, Q6-12, F, D, M1; ~ : Q5; ~∧ M2. 249 do:] Q1-12, F, D; doe.

M1; doe~∧~ M2.   250   Farewel] Q1-6, Q10-12, F, D, M1; ~ , Q7-8, M2;
~ . Q9.   250   s.d. omitted from Q3-5.   252   so:] Q1-7, Q9-12, F, D;
~ ; Q8; ~∧ M1-2.   254   Oh] Q1-8, D, M1-2 (O M1); ~ ! Q9-12, F.
254   me;] Q1-6, D; ~ , Q7-12, F; ~ ! M1; ~∧ M2.   255   blow:] Q1-
12, F, D; ~ . M1; ~∧ M2.   258   Blood?] Q8, F; ~ , Q1-7, Q9-12, D;
~∧ M1-2.   259   Barb'rous Woman!] Q9-12, F; Barb'rous Woman?
Q1-7, D; Barbarous Woman! Q8, M1; Barbarous Woman? M2.   259
Woman! that's] Q1-12, F, D, M2; ~ ∧ ~ M1.   259   good,] Q1-12, F,
D, M1; ~∧ M2.   263   smart. [Going to kill her.] M1; smart. Q1-12,
F, D, M2.   264   hand!] Q1-5, Q7-12, F; ~ , Q6, D, M1; ~∧ M2.
266   e're . . . e're] Q1-12, F, D; ere . . . ere M1-2.   267   Sweet
———] Q1-10, F, D, M2; ~∧ Q11-12; ~ . M1.   267   ———This but
offends] This but offends Q2-12, F, D, M2; ∧These words offend Q1, M1.
267   more,] Q1; ~ ; Q2-12, F, D; ~∧ M1-2.   270   Fool, . . . alone
. . . Live:] Q1-12, F, D (Fool∧ Q4-5, Q8); ~∧ . . . ~ , . . . ~ . M1; ~∧
. . . ~∧ . . . ~∧ M2.   272   ne're shall] Q1-12, F, D, M1; shall not M2.
274   approve.] Q1-12, F, D; ~∧ M1-2.   277   Tender,] Q1-12, F, D,
M1; ~∧ M2.   281   more.] Q1-12, F, D; ~∧ M1-2.   282+   s.d.
haste] Q1-12, F, D; hast M1-2.   283   Eyes:] Q1-12, F, D; ~∧ M1-2.
284   lose] Q1-12, F, D; loose M1-2.   286   Live:] Q1-12, F, D; ~ . M1-
2.   287   stay?] Q9-12, F, M2; ~ ! Q1-8, D; ~∧ M1.   288   save,]
Q1-7, D, M1; ~∧ Q8, M2; ~ ; Q9-12, F.   289   hard-hearted] Q1-12,
F, D; hard hearted M1-2.   293   Throne:] Q1-12, F, D; ~∧ M1-2.
294   are] Q8; is Q1-7, Q9-12, F, D, M1-2.   294   gone.] Q1-12, F, D,
M2; ~ ; M1.   295   Death:] Q1-4, Q6-7, Q9-12, F, D; ~ ; Q5, Q8; ~∧
M1-2.   300   you . . . refuse:] Q1-12, F, D; thee . . . ~ . M1; you
. . . ~ . M2.   301   pain, it is not] Q2-12, F, D, M2 (pain∧ M2; no
Q8); pain 'twill not be Q1, M1.   302   no] Q1-12, F, D, M2; not M1.
303   hark!] Q1-12, F, D, M1; ~∧ M2.   304   design'd:] Q1-12, F, D,
M2; ~ . M1.   305   Take there] Q2, Q6-12, F, D, M1-2; Take, there's
Q1; Take, there Q3-5.   305   gift.———] Q1-6, D; ~∧——— Q7-12,
F, M1; ~ .∧ M2.   305   her.] Q1-12, F, D, M1; Cyd: M2.   306
Deed.] Q1-8, Q11-12, D; ~ , Q9-10, F; ~ ; M1; ~∧ M2.   307   which]
Q2-12, F, D, M1-2; that Q1.   308   her self.] Q1-12, F, D; her selfe∧
M1-2.   309   Heart-blood] Q1-12, F, D; heart blood M1; hearts blood
M2.   309   thee] Q2-12, F, D, M1-2; the Q1.   309+   s.d. [Cortez
here goes in as to her.] M1; omitted from Q1-12, F, D, M2.   310   me
in] Q1-3, Q6-12, F, D, M1-2; in Q4; within Q5.   310   Light;] Q1-12,
F, D; ~ . M1; ~∧ ·M2.   311   too] Q1-12, F, D, M2; soe M1.   312
leav'st me,] Q1-12, F, D, M1; leavest me∧ M2.   312   part,] Q1-12, F,
D; ~ . M1; ~∧ M2.   313   Heart:] Q1-10, F, D; ~ ; Q11-12; ~ . M1-2.
315   Love!] Q1-4, Q6-9, D, M2; ~ . Q5, M1; ~ ; Q10-12, F.   316
strike:] Q1-4, Q6, D, M2; ~ ; Q5, Q7-12, F; ~∧ M1.   316   thought,]
Q7-12, F, D, M1; ~∧ Q1-6, M2.   316   Breast.] Q1-4, Q6-12, F, D;
~ : Q5; ~∧ M1-2.   317   differing . . . prest!] Q1-12, F, D; diff'rent
. . . ~ . M1; different . . . ~ ! M2.   318   off] Q1-12, F, D; of M1-2.
320   O] Q1-12, F, D, M1; oh M2.   320   Rival, . . . kill;] Q1-12, F,
D; ~ ! . . . ~ ! M1; ~∧ . . . ~∧ M2.   321   has] Q1-5, M1-2; hath

Q6–12, F, D. 321 will:] Q1–12, F, D; ~ . M1; ~∧ M2. 324 the Victory,] Q1–12, F, D; that Victory, M1; the victory∧ M2. 325 thee.] Q8, M1–2; ~ : Q1–7, Q9–12, F, D. 325+ *s.d. Enter Souldiers above.*] *Enter Souldjers.* M1; *omitted from Q1–12, F, D, M2.* 326 down. ———] ~ .∧ Q1–12, F, D; ~ ∧∧ M1; ~ : ∧ M2. 326+ *s.d. Exeunt*] Q3–5, Q7–12, F, D; Exeunt Q1–2, Q6, M1–2 (*Ex:* M2). 326+ *s.d. Souldiers*] M2 (*Soldiers*); Souldiers Q1–12, F, D, M1. 326+ *s.d. enter*] Q1–4, Q6–12, D, M1; *enter,* Q5, F; enter below M2. 327 *s.d. at head of line in M1; omitted from M2.* 327 fear] Q1–12, F, D, M2; ~ . M1. 328 near.] Q1–12, F, D; ~∧ M1–2. 329 give:] Q1–5; ~ ; Q6–12, F, D; ~ . M1; ~∧ M2. 329 *s.d. omitted from M2.* 330 you, if] Q1–12, F, D, M2 (you∧ M2); youres, so M1. 331 Enough,] Q1–12, F, D, M1; ~∧ M2. 332 Mind.] M1; ~ : Q1–12, F, D, M2. 333 near,] Q1–12, F, D; ~∧ M1–2. 333 Crime.] Q1–10, F, D, M2; ~ , Q11–12; ~∧ M1. 335 bathe] Q1–12, F, D; bath M1–2. 335 Wound] M1–2; Wounds Q1–12, F, D. 335 Offence:] Q1–12, F, D; ~∧ M1–2. 336 Recompence.] Q1–12, F, D, M1; ~∧ M2. 336+ *s.d. their hands. Shoves her back.*] M1; *their hands.* Q1–12, F, D; *hands* M2. 337 high:] Q1–12, F, D; ~ . M1; ~∧ M2. 339 past!] Q1–12, F, D; ~ . M1; ~∧ M2. 340 breathe] Q1–12, F, D; breath M1–2. 340 last.] Q1–12, F, D; ~∧ M1–2. 341 in this] Q1–12, F, D, M2; I in M1. 341 Live,] Q1–5, Q8, Q11–12, F, D; ~ . Q6–7, Q9–10; ~∧ M1–2. 342 I have] Q1–12, F, D, M2; Enjoy M1. 342 what e're] Q1–3, Q5–12, F, D; what ever Q4; what ere M1–2. 342 give.———] Q1–4, Q6, M2; ~ ,——— Q5; ~∧——— Q7–12, F, D; ~ .∧ M1. 343 ev'n] Q1–12, F, D, M1; even M2. 344 Glad] Q1–11, F, D, M1–2; Glast Q12. 344 lend] Q1–12, F, D, M1; send M2. 344 thee.] M1; ~ : Q1–10, F, D, M2; ~ ! Q11–12. 345 lest] Q1–12, F; least D, M1–2. 345 believe] Q2–12, F, D, M1–2; ~ ——— Q1. 345 *s.d. omitted from M1–2.* 347 dead?———] ~ ?∧ Q1–10, F, D, M2; ~ :∧ Q11–12; ~ !∧ M1. 349 no:] Q1–12, F, D; ~ . M1–2. 351 can shew no sorrow now.] Q1–12, F, D, M2; I cannot shedd one now. / both kissing. M1. 351+ *s.d. bound, with*] Q2–9, D; *bound with* Q1, Q10–12, F, M1; *bound.* M2. 352 O Friendship's shame!] Q1–12, F, D; O freindshipps shame∧ M1; oh friendships shame∧ M2. 353+ *s.d. him, and Cydaria, Alibech.*] M1 (him∧ Cydaria∧); *him, Cydaria, Alibech.* Q1–12, F, D; *him.* M2. 354 See,] Q1–3, Q6–12, F, D; ~∧ Q4–5, M1–2. 354 there:] Q1–12, F, D; ~ ! M1; ~∧ M2. 355 do] Q1–12, F, D; doe M1–2. 355+ *s.d. her Dead Sister.*] Q1–12, F, D, M1 (*Sister∧* Q1); *Almeria∧* M2. 356 Live,] Q1–8, D; ~∧ Q9–12, F, M1–2. 357 power.] Q1–12, F, D, M2; Pow'r∧ M1. 359 take:] Q1–12, F, D; ~ . M1; ~∧ M2. 361 maintain:] Q1–12, F, D; ~ . M1; ~∧ M2. 362 decreed] Q1–12, F, D, M2; decrees M1. 363 Ruines] Q1–12, F, D, M2; ruine M1. 364 leaves] Q1–9, Q12, D, M1–2; leave Q10–11, F. 365 chuse:] Q1–12, F, D; ~ . M1; ~∧ M2. 367 see] Q1–12, F, D, M2; be M1. 369 Snow;] Q1, Q9; ~ , Q2–8, D; ~ : Q10–12, F; ~ . M1–2. 370 Plains] Q1–11, F, D, M1–2; Plants Q12. 371 Mine . . . yields:] Q1–12, F, D; mynes . . .~ . M1; Mine . . .~ . M2. 376 Father's . . . provide:] Q1–12, F, D; ffathers . . .~ , M1; fathers

. . . ~ₐ M2.   377   done, in Peace] Q1-12, F, D; done in Peace, M1;
done in peace M2.   377   your] Q1-12, F, D, M1; the M2.   377
guide;] D; ~ . Q1-9, F, M1-2; ~ , Q10-12.   378   While . . . above,]
Q1-12, F, D, M1; whilst . . . ~ₐ M2.   379   *s.d. omitted from Q9-12,
F.*
    Epilogue: *Completely omitted from M1-2; in Q8-12, follows immedi-
ately after the prologue.*   2   me] Q1-7, D; *you* Q8-12, F.   2   *greeting,*] ~ . Q1-12, F, D.   8   Who] Q2-12, F, D; *That* Q1.   14   *farther*]
Q1-12, D; *further* F.   20   Dutch:] Q1-7, D; ~ . Q8-12, F.   21   *Dons*]
Q9-12, F; *Dons* Q1-8, D.   23   own.] Q1-3, Q6-12, F, D; ~ : Q4-5.
25   *pow'r*] Q1; *power* Q2-12, F, D.

Secret Love

The first edition of *Secret Love* was published in 1668 (Q1, Macd 70a) and
is found with B4 (I, iii, 39-104) canceled or uncanceled (the differences are
given separately below and not repeated elsewhere), as well as with or without a list of errata below the dramatis personae. Other editions followed,
dated 1669 (Q2, W&M 446), 1669 (Q3, W&M 447), 1679 (Q4, Macd 70c), 1691
(Q5, Macd 70d), and 1698 (Q6, Macd 70e). The play was reprinted in Dryden's *Comedies, Tragedies, and Operas* (1701), I, 150-189 (F; Macd 107ai-ii
[two issues, the differences not affecting this play]), and in Congreve's edition of Dryden's *Dramatick Works* (1717), II, 5-83 (D; Macd 109ai-ii [two
issues, with a cancel title for Vol. I in the second]). Q2 was printed from a
copy of Q1 with cancel B4, Q3 from a copy of Q2, Q4 from a copy of Q3, Q5
from a copy of Q4, Q6 from a copy of Q2, F from a copy of Q2, and D from a
copy of Q3.
    The cancelandum B4 of Q1 found unremoved in the Bodleian copy reads
as follows (all changes are in I, iii; line references below are to the present
edition):   45   Our free] Our   49   home:] ~ₐ   63   soul] Soul
63-64   straight shakes off, / And is compos'd again.] shakes them off, / And
straight composes.———   70-71   thus to press [*catchword* On] / On]
you assume [*catchword* To] / to press on   75   to you.] and dangers.
79   Soveraigns] Sovereigns   82   Lys.] Lysim.   82   over-care] over care
83   ill-tim'd] ill tim'd   84   Bloud] bloud   85   They] By all the Gods
they   90   more then] more, than   93   Of] of   95   man compass]
man, / Compass
    Except for the list of errata and the cancel in Q1, Dryden does not seem
to have revised the text, unless perhaps casually at the beginning of the
copy for Q2 (e.g., I, iii, 139, 206), and therefore the Clark copy of Q1, with
errata and cancel B4 (*PR3418.F1), has been chosen for the copy text.
Emendations have been made where it seemed desirable, except at II, i,
85, where no emendation suggested itself; the sentence has been perforce
accepted as an uncharacteristic anacoluthon.

The prologue "Spoken by Mrs. Boutell" and the epilogue "Spoken by Mrs. Reeves" were printed in *Covent Garden Drollery* (1672), pp. 1–3 of both editions, O1 (Macd 54a–b [two issues, the differences not affecting these poems]), and O2 (Macd 54c). British Museum MS Egerton 2623, a collection of sixteenth- and seventeenth-century manuscripts formed by J. P. Collier, includes a folio sheet, fols. 43–44, containing this prologue and epilogue in a seventeenth-century hand (M1). M1 appears to be a copy of O2. *Covent Garden Drollery* contains still another epilogue, beginning "The Prologue durst not tell, before 'twas seen," which has been thought to be Dryden's and to belong to *Secret Love;* it belongs to *The Knight of the Burning Pestle* and is probably not Dryden's (see Macd, p. 96).

There are two seventeenth-century manuscript copies of the song in IV, ii, in miscellaneous collections in the British Museum, MS Harley 3991, fol. 82r–v (M2), and MS Harley 7332, fol. 198 (M3), and another in the Bodleian Library in a volume of poetry compiled by an Oxford man, MS Rawl. poet. 65, fol. 29v (M4). The three are independent; their source is not clear.

The following copies of the various editions have also been examined: Q1: Huntington (122936), Folger (D2353; G3 from a copy of Q2), Texas (Aj.D848.668s), Harvard (*EC65.D8474.668sa), Bodleian (4°.O.29 Art.); Q2: Clark (*PR3418.F1.1669, cop. 1), Huntington (122935), Folger (D2354; sigs. C, E–F, I from a copy of Q3); Q3: Clark (*PR3418.F1.1669a), Huntington (32200), Folger (D2354a); Q4: Clark (*PR3418.F1.1679), Huntington (123052), Folger (D2327, cop. 3); Q5: Clark (*PR3418.F1.1691); *PR3412. 1679, v. 1; *PR3410.C91); Q6: Clark (*PR3418.F1.1698 [2 cop.]; *PR3410. C95a, v. 1); F: Clark (*fPR3412.1701 [2 cop.]); D: Clark (*PR3412.1717 [2 cop.]); O1, *first issue:* Harvard (15437.2.9*); O1, *second issue:* Clark (*PR1213.C87); O2: Folger (C6624B).

Preface: 115:1   *French*] D; French Q1–6, F.   115:11   more] Q1; most Q2–6, F, D.   115:28   he may] D; may Q1–6, F.   116:6   as] Q1–3, Q5–6, F, D; at Q4.   116:10   predominates.] Q1–6, F; ~ : D.   116:18 *Indian Emperour*] Q6, F, D; Indian Emperour Q1–5.   116:35   objects.] Q1–2, Q4–6, F; ~ , Q3; ~ ; D.   117:23   impulsion] Q1–2, Q6, F; impulsions Q3–5, D.   117:31   divertising] Q1–6, D; diverting F.   118:1 *Maiden-Queen*] Q6, F, D; Maiden-Queen Q1–5.
First Prologue: 3 *wrought:*] ~ . Q1–6, F, D.   10   *howe're*] Q1, D; *how e're* Q2–6, F.   12   *o'reseen*] Q1; *o'r-seen* Q2–6, D; *o'er-seen* F.   17 *Souldier-like*] Q1–6, D; *Soldier like* F.
Second Prologue: 30   should] Q1–2, Q6, F; shall Q3–5, D.   30 him] Q1, D; them Q2–6, F.   40   e're] Q1–4, Q6, F, D; ere Q5.   45 Brother] Q1–6, D; Brother's F.   48   Bear;] Q1–4, Q6, F, D; ~ . Q5.   50 trade:] Q1–2, Q6, F; ~ , Q3–4; ~ . Q5.
Prologue Spoken by Mrs. Boutell: title: *M1* has "Prologue" only. Maiden Queen, in mans Cloathes.] Maiden Queen. O1; Maiden Queen, in mans Cloathes. O2.   4   friend.] O1; ~ , O2; ~ ∧ M1.   6   We] O1–2; Wee M1 (and so throughout).   9   Pantaloons] M1; ~ , O1–2.   10 far] M1; ~ , O1–2.   11   Wigs] M1; ~ , O1–2.   12   please;] O2; ~ .

O1; ~∧ M1.   13   these] M1; ~ . O1–2.   14   do] O1–2; doe M1.   15
fight.] O1; ~ ! O2; ~∧ M1.   20   mind.] O1; ~ : O2; ~∧ M1.
   *The Persons: D and F head instead "Dramatis Personae". F heads the two
sections "WOMEN" and "MEN" and inserts "and" between "Olinda" and
"Sabina" on a line with "Sisters".* Q2–3 *have "Candiope,* Princes*" and Q4–
6 have "Mrs Queen" in the same line.*

I, i

   S.d.   habit; they] Q1–5, F; ~ . *They* Q6; ~ , ~ D.   1   *Celadon]* Q3–6,
F, D; *Celedon* Q1–2.   8   Funeral.] Q2–6, F, D; ~ ; Q1.   29   between
'em:] Q1, Q6, F, ~ , Q2–3; ~ . Q4–5, D.   41   self:] Q1–6, F; ~ . D.
41   haste] Q1, Q3–6, D; hast Q2, F.   41   end your] Q1–2, Q6, F; end
the Q3–5, D.   47   sown.] Q1–3, Q6, F; ~ ? Q4–5, D.   52   *Page.*
Madam] Q4–5, D; *Madam* Q1–3, Q6, F.   57+   *s.d.* Asteria *and Page.]*
Asteria. Q1–6, F, D.

I, ii

   S.d.   Florimell] Florimel Q1–6, F, D.   *s.d.   Flavia,]* Q4–5, F; ~∧ Q1–3,
Q6, D.   6   Why] Q1–2, Q6, F; Who Q3–5, D.   7   *Cel.]* Q2–6, F, D;
~∧ Q1.   10   any one] Q1–2, Q6, F; any Q3–5, D.   17   *Aside]* Q3–6,
F, D; *aside* Q1–2.   18   Moon.] Q2–6, F, D; ~ : Q1.   20   round in]
Q1–2, Q6, F; in Q3–5, D.   25   this! *[Aside.]* ———Besides] this!
———besides Q1–6, F, D (Besides F, D).   30   do] Q1–2, Q5–6, F, D; doe
Q3–4.   32   do] Q1, Q3–6, F, D; doe Q2.   39   *Cel.]* Q4–6, F, D; *Cell.*
Q1–3.   41   Servant.] Q2–6, F, D; ~ : Q1.   44   handsome.———]
Q1–5, D; ~∧——— Q6, F.   51   an'] Q1–2, Q6, F; an Q3–5, D.   55
see.———] Q1–5; ~∧——— Q6, F; ~.∧ D.   56   Nose,] Q2–6, F, D; ~ :
Q1.   57   neather-lip] Q1–2, Q6, F; neather Lip Q3–5, D.   62   it.]
Q4–6, F, D; ~ : Q1–3.   64   frighted,] Q1–3, Q6, F; ~ ? Q4–5, D.   66
experiment.] Q2–6, F, D; ~ : Q1.   74   to be] Q1; to Q2–6, F, D.   83
heard] Q1, Q3–6, F, D; herd Q2.   83   *Florimell]* Florimel Q1–6, F, D.
85   Cousin?———] ~ :——— Q1–5; ~∧——— Q6; ~?∧ F, D.   85   [*To*
Flor. *aside.]* Q5–6 *(Aside* Q6), D; (to Flor. aside.) Q1–3 (aside∧) Q3); [to
Flor. aside. Q4; [*Aside to* Flor. F.   87   days.] Q2–6, F, D; ~ , Q1.   89
ifaith.] Q2–6, F, D; ~ : Q1.   92   inhumane] Q1, Q3–6, F, D; in humane
Q2.   95   Lady.] Q2–6, F, D; ~ : Q1.   96   Masque———] Q1; ~ .
Q2–6, F, D.   97   hope.] Q3–5, F, D; ~ ; Q1–2; ~ ? Q6.   98   will.]
Q6, F, D; ~ : Q1–5.   99   shan'not.] Q4–6, F, D; ~ : Q1–3.

I, iii

   SCENE] Q3–6, F, D; ~ . Q1–2.   1   *Cel.]* Q2–6, F, D; ~∧ Q1.   1
Favourite!———] Q1–5, D; ~∧——— Q6, F.   1   [*Aside]* Q5–6, F, D;
[*aside* Q1 *(some copies),* Q2–4; ∧*aside* Q1 *(some copies).*   4   glad] Q1–3,
Q6, F, D; ~ . Q4–5.   5   in't] Q1–6, F; in it D.   10+   *s.d.* Enter Lysi-
mantes] Q3–6, F, D; Enter *Lysimantes* Q1–2.   12   you. / *Phil.* Had] F, D;
you *(Phil.)* had Q1–6 (you. Q4–6; Had Q5–6).   14   [*To* Cel.]] ∧*To Cel.*∧
Q1–5 *(Cel,* Q2–3); [*To* Cel.∧ Q6, F, D *(at right).*   18   Celadon] Q3–6, F,
D; *Celadon* Q1–2.   22   love. / *Phil.]* F, D (love, F); love. *(Phil.)* Q1–6.

31 worthy,] Q4-6, D; ~. Q1-3, F. 36 soul'd] Q6, D; sould Q1-2; sold Q3-5, F. 37 breath] Q1-5, F, D; Breathe Q6. 37 *Indies*] Q3-5, F, D; Indies Q1-2, Q6. 40 say] Q1; you say Q2-6, F, D. 41 lessen] Q4-6, D; lesson Q1-3, F. 49 choose] Q1, Q3-5, F, D; chose Q2, Q6. 50 them,] Q1, Q4-5, D; ~∧ Q2-3, Q6, F. 55 you————] Q6, D; ~.———— Q1-5, F. 58 name:———— / *Lys.*] Q4-5, F, D; name: ———— (*Lys.*) Q1-3, Q6. 63 straight] Q1, Q4-5; strait Q2-3, Q6, F, D. 67 mirour] Q1-6, D; Miter F. 69+ *s.d. Guard*] D; Guard Q1-6, F. 69+ *s.d.* Olinda,] Q1-6, F; Olinda *and* D. 72 1] D; 1. Q1-6, F. 74 And] Q4-6, F, D; and Q1-3. 74 2] D; 2. Q1-6, F. 75 peoples] Q1, Q3-6, F, D; people Q2. 82 over-care] Q1-5, F, D; over care Q6. 87 else?] Q2-6, F, D; ~; Q1. 92 th'] Q1-2, Q6, F; the Q3-5, D. 111 choice] Q2-6, F, D; chioce Q1. 112 an one] Q1; a one as Q2-6, F, D. 115 [*To the Dep.*]] ∧~·∧ Q1-6, F; [~ ·∧ D (*at right margin*). 119 it. [*Aside.*]] it: Q1-6, F, D. 121+ *s.d. Deputies*] D; Deputies Q1-6, F. 122 stay.] Q6, F, D; ~ : Q1-5. 126 commands————] Q6, D; ~.———— Q1-5, F. 132 We] Q3-6, F, D; we Q1-2. 136 me.] Q2-6, F, D; ~∧ Q1. 139 usage] Q2-6, F, D; usage I have found Q1. 140 *Weeps.*] Q3-6, F, D; *weeps*∧ Q1-2. 144 Reign] Q3-5, F, D; *Reign* Q1-2, Q6. 148 question,] Q2-6, F, D; ~. Q1. 157 I, I] Q1-4, Q6, F, D; I Q5. 157 am born] Q1-2, Q6, F; born Q3-5; was born D. 160 thoughts;] Q1-5, F, D; ~! Q6. 162 *Phil.*] Q2-6, F, D; ~∧ Q1. 164 care.] Q2-6, F, D; ~ : Q1. 164+ *s.d.* her, but] Q4-5, F; ~ . But Q1, Q6; ~∧ *But* Q2-3; ~ ; *but* D. 164+ *s.d.* picture;] Q1-2; ~. Q3-6, F, D. 165 reads.] A] D; reads.———— / A Q1-6, F. 166 [*Spies the box.*]] ∧~·∧ Q1-6, F; [~ ·∧ D (*at right margin*). 166 Asteria?] Q1-2, Q6, F; ~ : Q3-5, D. 170 Madam.] Q2-6, F, D; ~ ; Q1. 176 *Lysimantes* sister] Q1-6, D; ~ , Sister F. 182 comparison?] Q1; ~ : Q2-3, Q6, F; ~ ! Q4-5, D. 182 false, you flatter] *some copies of Q1 have* fal se,uflatter. 185 Madam] *Madam* Q1-6, F, D. 186 none.] Q2-6, F, D; ~∧ Q1. 188 do] Q1, Q3-6, F, D; doe Q2. 189+ *s.d.* faints.] Q3-6, F, D; ~∧ Q1-2. 190+ *s.d. coming.*] Q3-6, F, D; ~ , Q1, ~∧ Q2. 193 matter?] matter! y'are Q1 (*but errata directs to omit* "you are" [*sic*] *from this line; and see next variation*), Q2-6, F; matter! D. 194 You are of] Q1; Of Q2-6, F; You're of D. 200 thou!] Q1-3, Q6, F, D; ~ ? Q4-5. 206 each day and hour] Q2-6, F, D; insensibly Q1. 217 Heaven! So] Heaven! / So Q1-6, F, D. 222 know it] Q1; know't Q2-6, F, D. 223 to] Q1, D; do Q2-6, F. 226 labour; can . . . guess?————] labour; / Can . . . guess———— Q1-6, F, D. 227 Hold, *Asteria:*] Q4-6, D; ~ : ~ : Q1-3; ~ : ~ . F. 230 wretched.] Q1-2, Q6, F; ~ ; Q3-5, D. 233-234 cannot. / And yet,————] cannot.————and yet, Q1-3; cannot,————and yet, Q4-5; cannot————and yet, Q6, F, D. 236 me.] Q1-3, Q6, F, D; ~ : Q4-5. 243 all, Madam?] Q5, D; ~ ? ~ ? Q1; ~ ? ~ . Q2-4, F; ~ , ~ . Q6. 244 Subject;] Q1-5, F, D; ~ ! Q6. 247 world,] Q4-6, D; ~ : Q1-3, F. 250 lov'd.] Q2-6, F, D; ~ ? Q1. 252 amiss;] Q1-4, Q6, F, D; ~ ? Q5. 254 *Philocles.*] Q2, Q4-6, F, D; ~∧ Q1, Q3. 256 born.] Q2-6, F, D; ~ , Q1. 259-260 Crown; / But] Crown; but Q1-6, F, D. 263 his. / *Ast.*] Q4-6, F, D; his: *Ast.* Q1-3.

264   quiet.] Q2–6, F, D; ∼ , Q1.   270   I fear that] Q3–5, D; *I fear.* That
Q1–2, Q6, F.   270   me,] Q4–5; ∼ . Q1–3, Q6, F, D.   277   best;] Q6;
∼∧ Q1; ∼ , Q2–5, F, D.

II, i

S.d.   SCENE,] SCENE I. Q1–6, F, D.   *s.d.   appartments*] Q1–2, F;
Apartment Q3–6, D.   s.d. *and* 1   Asteria, *sola. / Ast.*] *Asteria, / Sola.* [*as a
speech heading*] Q1–6, F (*sola* Q4, Q6); Asteria *sola.* [*as a stage direction*] D.
3   *Candiope:*] Q2–6, F, D; ∼∧ Q1.   7–8   Authority / To] Q1–6, D;
Authority to F.   8   match.] match. / SCENE. II. Q1–6, F, D.   13–14
one; . . . with] Q1–6, F; ∼ , . . . ∼ ; D.   14   *Florimell*] *Florimel* Q1–6,
F, D.   18   *Florimell*] *Florimel* Q1–6, F, D.   21   *Florimell.*] *Florimel.*
Q1–2, Q6; *Florimel.*——— Q3–5; *Florimel*∧——— D, F.   22   Asteria]
Q3–5, F, D; *Asteria* Q1–2, Q6.   22+   *s.d. Enter* Florimell] SCENE III.
/ *Enter* Florimel Q1–6, F, D (SCENE, Q1).   23   'faith] Q1–2, Q6, F;
y'faith Q3–5, D.   24+   *s.d. She signs she is dumb.*] *She signs.* She is
dumb. [*as if a speech*] Q1–5, F; She Signs? She is dumb? [*as part of speech*]
Q6; [*She makes signs she is dumb.*] D.   27   question?] Q4–6, D; ∼ . Q1–
3, F.   27   indeed, then,] Q1–4, F; ∼ , ∼∧ Q5; ∼ ; ∼∧ Q6; ∼ ? ∼∧ D.
28   *s.d.* [*Goes to kiss her.*] Q6, D; goes to kiss her. Q1–5, F.   36   *Florimell*] *Florimel* Q1–6, F, D.   44+   *s.d.* Flavia] [*Flavia* Q1–2; [Flavia Q3–6,
F, D.   45   *Fla. Florimell*] D (*Florimel*); *Florimel* Q1–6, F.   45   *Exit.*]
Q3–6, F, D; ∼∧ Q1–2.   46   *Florimell.*] *Florimel;* Q1–3; *Florimel?* Q4–6;
Florimel. D, F.   47–48   *Florimell*] *Florimel* Q1–6, F, D.   48   describ'd.] Q4–6, F, D; ∼ : Q1–3.   62   *Flor.*] Q2–6, F, D; ∼∧ Q1.   63
have other] Q1–2, Q4–6, F, D; other Q3.   63   ere] Q1; e'r Q2–6, F, D.
66   and poyson] Q2, Q6, F; or poyson Q1; poison Q3–5, D.   71   alto-
gether] Q1–3, Q6, F; all together Q4–5, D.   72   *Flor.*] Q2–6, F, D; ∼ , Q1.
73   any one] Q1–2, Q6, F; any Q3–5, D.   80   see] Q1–5, F, D; seen Q6.
83   love.] Q2–6, F, D; ∼∧ Q1.   86   do] Q1–2, Q5–6, F, D; doe Q3–4.
86   of one] Q2–6, F, D; ∼ , Q1.   98   clause.———But] F, D; ∼ .———
but Q1–3; ∼ , ———but Q4–5; ∼∧———but Q6.   103   add] Q2–6, F, D;
add more Q1 (*but corrected in Errata*).   104+   *s.d. Enter*] SCENE IV. /
Enter Q1–6, F, D.   107   Cel. Flor.] Q3–6, F, D; *Cel. Flor.* Q1–2.   113
even.] Q2–6, F, D; ∼∧ Q1.   115   Lysimantes] Q3–6, F, D; *Lysimantes*
Q1–2.   115+   *s.d. Enter*] SCENE V. / *Enter* Q1–6, F, D.   121   off]
Q1–6, D; of F.   122   *Qu. to Phil.* . . . Sir,] [*Qu. to* Phil.] . . . Sir, Q1–6,
F (*Phil.* Q2, Q6, F); *Queen.* . . . Sir: [*To* Phil. D.   127–128   wishes:
——— / Yet] Q5; wishes:———yet Q1–4, F; wishes∧ ———yet Q6;
wishes.——— / Yet D.   128   request] Q1–2, F; ∼ . Q3, Q6; ∼ , Q4–5, D.
134   me now] Q1; me Q2–6, F, D.   136   on] Q2–6, F, D; from Q1 (*but
corrected in Errata*).   136–137   Candiope, / Candiope] *Were*] Candiope, were Q1–
6, F, D.   137   both.] Q2–6, F, D; ∼ ? Q1.   140–141   me) / Which . . .
forbid your] me) which . . . forbid / Your Q1–-6, F, D.   142–143   that;
/ *Philocles,*] that, *Philocles,* Q1–6, F; that, *Philocles;* D.   143   things,
and] things, / And Q1–6, F, D.   143–144   show / I] show I Q1–6, F, D.
144   dead,] Q2, Q4–6, F; ∼∧ Q1; ∼ . Q3, D.   147   have] Q1; had Q2–6,
F, D.   156   so] Q2–6, F, D; to Q1 (*but corrected in Errata*).   158

Haste] Q1, Q3–5, D; Hast Q2, Q6, F.   164   I] Q1–6, D; as I F.   164
say] Q1–2, Q6, F; ~) Q3–5, D.   165   do)] Q1–2, Q6, F; ~ ; Q3–5, D.
165   *Aside*] Q4–6, F, D; *aside* Q1–3.   167   Ah, Madam] Q1–2, Q6, F;
Madam Q3–5, D.   180–181   in / A] in a Q1–6, F, D.   195   Pardon
me] Q1; Pardon Q2–6, F, D.   195   who'ere] Q1; who e'r Q2–6, F, D.
198   But] Q3–6, F, D; but Q1–2.   202   gone on] Q1; gone Q2–6, F, D.
208   over freedom] Q1–2, Q6; over-freedom Q3–5, F, D.   211   but
when] but / When Q1–6, F, D.   212–213   opinion; / He's] opinion; he's
Q1–6, F, D.   216   Think] Q1–5, F, D; Thing Q6.   216   Heavens] Q1–
6, F; Heav'n's D.   220   Irons] Q1, Q4–6, F, D; Irnos Q2–3.   223
Madam.] Q5; ~ : Q1–4, Q6, F; ~∧ D.   225   excuse:] Q1–3, Q6, F, D;
~ . Q4–5.   228   *Philocles?*] Q1–2, Q4–6, F, D; *Poilocles:* Q3.   231
wondred] Q1–5, F, D; wonder Q6.   253   me,] Q1–6, F; ~ ? D.   257
high] Q1–6, D; highest F.   263   of] Q1–2, Q6, F, D; on Q3–5.   264
then?] Q5; ~ ! Q1–4, Q6, F, D.   271   words;———] Q1–3, F; ~ !———
Q4–5; ~ ;∧ Q6; ~∧——— D.   274   did,] ~ ! Q1–3, Q6, F, D; ~ ? Q4–5.
276   mankind?] Q4–5; ~ ! Q1–3, Q6, F, D.   285   pow'r] Q1–6, F; Power
D.   286   winds. [*Exeunt.*] Q1–5, F; winds. Q6; Winds. / [*Exeunt omnes.*
D.

III, i

S.d.   SCENE of the Act,] Q1–6, F (~∧ Q2; ~ . F); SCENE I. / SCENE D.
s.d. Philocles] Q5, D; *Philocles* Q1–4, Q6, F.   1   me] Q1–2, Q4–6, F, D;
him Q3.   6   man!] Q2–6, F, D; ~∧ Q1.   7   *Is*] Q6, F, D; *is* Q1–5,   8
Who] Q2–6, F, D; who Q1.   9   *Philocles coming back.* I] [*Philocles coming back,* [I Q1–6, F (∧*Philocles* F; back.] Q3–6, F); *Phil. I . . . [Coming
back.* D.   11   from me] Q2–6, F, D; from Q1 (*but corrected in Errata*).
16   *Asteria?*] Q1; ~ ! Q2–6, F, D.   18   him] Q2–6, F, D; ~ , Q1.   19
To] Q6, F, D; *to* Q1–5.   21   [*To*] Q6, F, D; ∧*to* Q1–5.   26–27   in /
On] D; in on Q1–6, F.   27   bancks, o'reflow'd] D (o'er-flow'd); bancks /
O'reflow'd Q1–2, Q4–6, F (O'r-flow'd Q2–3, Q6, F; O'r flow'd Q4–5).   30   not]
Q1–2, Q4–6, F; my Q3, D.   32   yet.] Q4–5, F, D; ~ : Q1–3, Q6.   33–34
Act / Of grace and] Act of grace / And Q1–6, F, D.   36   wrong.] Q2–6,
F, D; ~ : Q1.   38–39   one / I love, I] D (love;); one I love. / I Q1–6, F
(love, Q4–5).   40   you] Q1; our Q2–6, F, D.   47   self] Q1–3, Q6; ~ ,
Q4–5, F; ~ . D.   59–60   he / Has] D; he has Q1–6, F.   71   him.] Q2–
6, F, D; ~∧ Q1.   77   will] Q2–6, F, D; wil! Q1.   87   eyes?] Q1–2, F;
~ ! Q3–5, D; ~ ; Q6.   100   tears?] Q4–6, D; ~ : Q1–3, F.   109   within.] Q4–5, F, D; ~ : Q1–3, Q6.   110+   *s.d.* D has "*Enter Queen with a
Picture in her Hand, and* Asteria."   116   Madam,] Q2–6, F, D; ~ . Q1.
119   Cand.] F, D; *Cand.* Q1–6.   124   of her] Q1–3, Q6, F, D; of the Q4–
5.   128   trouble.] Q2–6, F, D; ~ , Q1.   130–131   yours deserves a
more / Then . . . care, to] yours / Deserves a more then . . . care, / To
Q1–6, F, D.   135–136   Workman / Has left it open] Workman has left it
open Q1–6, F; workman has left it / Open D.   137   and't please] Q2,
Q6, F; and 'please Q1, Q3, D; and please Q4; an't please Q5.   137–138
Majesty? / Methinks . . . well.] D; Majesty, methinks . . . well? Q1–6, F.
139   it?] D; ~ , Q1–6, F.   144   *Asteria?*] ~ ! Q1–6, F, D.   151   him.]

426   *Textual Notes*

Q4–5, F, D; ~ : Q1–3, Q6.   153–154   hollowness. / What] D; hallowness, what Q1–6, F (hollowness, Q2–5, F; hollowness; Q6).   155   opinion;] Q1–2, Q6, F; ~ . Q4–5; ~ : Q3, D.   161   *Queen*,] Queen, Q1–6, F; *Queen and* D.   161   Inhumane] Q2–6, F, D; In humane Q1.   163 mine.] Q4–6, F, D; ~ : Q1–3.   167   sway.] Q1–2, Q6, F; ~ ; Q3–5, D. 174   glories] Q1–3, Q5–6, F, D; glorious Q4.   176   vain!] Q4–5; ~ ? Q1– 3, Q6, F, D.   177+   *s.d. Queen*] D; Queen Q1–6, F (*Queen* Q1).   180 gen'rous] Q1–3, Q6, F, D; generous Q4–5.   183   ground?] Q1–2, Q6, F; ~ : Q3–5, D.   199   melt in] Q1–5, F, D; melting Q6.   199   Sweets] Q1 (*some copies*), Q2–6, F, D; Sweats Q1 (*some copies; corrected in Errata*). 199   away.] Q1; ~ ; Q2–6, F, D.   202   misleads] Q1–5, F, D; mislards Q6.   203   takes] Q1–5, F, D; take Q6.   213   true] *the* r *did not print in Q1.*   217   both. / *Cand.* But] Q4–6, F, D; both (*Cand.*) but Q1–3 (But Q2–3).   220   gen'rously] Q1; generously Q2–6, F, D.   231 Mother. / *Phil.* Or] Q4–6, F, D (Mother, Q4–5); Mother (*Phil.*) or Q1–3 (Or Q2–3).   231+   *s.d.* Phil.] Q1–6, F; Phil. *and* D.   232   *Queen above.*] Q5–6, F, D; *Queen / above.* Q1–4.   233   *Æneas*] Q2–6, F, D; Æneas Q1. 238   indeed! / *Ast.* And] Q4–6, F, D; indeed! (*Ast.*) and Q1–3 (And Q2–3). 244   offence.] Q2–6, F, D; ~ : Q1.   252   possess.] Q2–6, F, D; ~ : Q1. 257–258   out, / Bid . . . Guards through] out, bid . . . Guards through Q1–4, F; out, bid . . . Guards / Through Q5–6, D.   261   again:] Q1–5, F, D; ~ . Q6.   263   Heaven's] Q1–3, F; Heavn's Q4–5, D; Heaven Q6. 263+   *s.d. Qu.*] Q6, F, D; Qu. Q1–5.   263+   *s.d. her*] Q3–6, F, D; her Q1–2.   265   *Asteria?*] Q1, Q4–5, D; ~ . Q2–3, Q6, F.   271–272   Court. ——*Celadon!* / What] Court.——*Celadon!* what Q1–6, F; Court—— / *Celadon!* what D.   271   here?] *here!* Q1–2; here! Q3–6, F, D.   275 O-ho.] Q1–4; O ho. Q5; O ho: Q6; O-ho; F; O-ho! D.   277   plume] Q1, Q3–6, D; plum Q2, F.   277   Cel. Ol. Sab.] Q3–6, F, D (*and* Sab. D); *Cel. Ol. Sab.* Q1–2.   278   truss'd] Q2–6, F, D; truss'ed Q1.   288 t'other way?] ~ ; Q1–6, F, D ('tother Q1, *some copies;* Q2–3).   289   i'th] Q2–6, F, D; i'rh Q1 (*some copies*); 'irh Q1 (*some copies*).   302   whenever] Q1–2, Q6, F, D; when ever Q3–5.   314   strange] Q1, Q3–5, F, D; strang Q2; strong Q6.   318   yet like] Q1–3, Q6, F, D; like Q4–5.   322   have! ——] ~ ? —— Q1–5, F, D; ~ʌ —— Q6.   323   have!] ~ ? Q1–6, F, D.   325   Flav.] Q3–6, F, D; *Flav.* Q1–2.   330   Afternoon!] ~ ? Q1– 6, F, D.   333   mercy] Q1–2, Q5–6, F, D; mery Q3–4.   338   ere] Q1; e'r Q2–6, F, D.   338   dies?] ~ ! Q1–6, F, D.   348   hope] Q1–6, D; I hope F.   353   Common-place wit] Q1, Q6; Common place-wit Q2–5, F; Common-place-wit D.   362   Treat:] Q1–6; ~ . F, D.   363   *Item,*] Q1– 2, D; ~ . Q3–6, F.   363   Coach:] Q1–6; ~ . F, D.   364   *Item,*] Q1, Q3, D; ~ . Q2, Q4–6, F.   364   Fann:] Q1–6; ~ . F, D.   367   'bate] Q1–2, Q6; bate Q3–5, F, D.   372   that?] Q4–6, D; ~ : Q1–3, F.   372   'Gad] Q1–2; Gad Q3–6, F, D.   373+   *s.d. Aside.*] Q4–6, F, D; asideʌ Q1–2; aside. Q3.   376   why] Q1–3, Q6; when Q4–5, F, D.   378   What do] Q1–5, F, D; What, no Q6.   379   for] Q1–3, Q6, F, D; ~ , Q4–5.   382 offering] *the* e *failed to print in Q1.*   401   excursion] Q1–6, F; Excursions D.   407   Cel. to the Page.] [Cel. *to the Page.*] Q1–6, F, D (ʌCel. Q5, F; *Cel.* D).   411   invite] Q2–6, F, D; invites Q1 (*but corrected in Errata*).

411 there!] Q1–4, F, D; ~ ; Q5; ~∧ Q6. 413 *Florimell*] *Florimel* Q1–6, F, D. 414 of 'em] Q1, F, D; 'em Q2–6. 416 [*Aside.*] *at end of preceding sentence in Q1–6, F, D.* 417 fidg] Q1–5, F, D; fig Q6. 420 woman!] ~ ? Q1–6, F, D. 425 Lodgings.] Q1–5, F, D; ~ , Q6. 425+ *s.d. Cel.*] Q3–6, F, D; *Cel.* Q1–2. 430 jealous! I] jealous! / I Q1–6, F, D. 433 *Florimell*] *Florimel* Q1–2; *Florimel* Q3–6, F, D.

IV, i

ACT IV. SCENE I.] ACT IV. Q1–6, F, D. 1 *Melissa.*] Q4–5, F, D; ~ , Q1–3, Q6. 6–7 of 'em, . . . manner!] ~∧ . . . ~ , Q1; ~∧ . . . ~ . Q2–3; ~ , . . . ~ . Q4–5, F, D; ~ ; . . . ~ ! Q6. 9 *Olinda,* Come] Q1, D; *Olinda.* Come Q2–4 [*as a speech by Olinda in Q4*], Q6, F; Come . . . [*To* Olinda. Q5. 11 *Olinda,* what] Q1–5, F; ~ . What Q6; ~ ; what D. 14 on] Q1–2, Q6, F; of Q3–5, D. 23 then] Q1; and then Q2–6, F, D. 26+ *s.d. behind.*] Q2–6, F, D; ~∧ Q1. 35 him.] Q1–6, D; ~ ? F. 38 could] Q1; would Q2–6, F, D. 41 die] Q1–6, D; dye F. 48 her;] Q1–6, F; ~ . D. 49 Mel.] Q3–6, F, D; *Mel.* Q1–2. 59–60 innocence, such a Rose-bud . . . blown. This] D; innocence, / Such a Rose-bud . . . blown. / This Q1–6, F. 61 Madam. [*To* Sab.] Madam. [*To* Sab. Q1–3 (Madam.——— Q2–3); Madam. ——— Q4–5; Madam.——— [*To* Sab. Q6, F, D. 62 this.] Q4–5; ~∧ Q1–3, Q6, F, D. 62 [*Aside.*]———] ———[*aside.*] Q1–3, Q6, F, D (*Aside* Q6, D); (*Aside.*)∧ Q4–5. 64 Madam.———] Q1–5, F, D; ~∧——— Q6. 65 your] Q1–2, Q4–6, F, D; you Q3. 65 Discourse, ———] Q1; ~ .——— Q2–4, F, D; ~∧——— Q5–6. 68 forget] Q1–6, D; forgot F. 68 haste] Q1–5, F, D; hast Q6. 69 Well] Q2–6, F, D; Well Q1. 72 Olinda] Q3–6, F, D; *Olinda* Q1–2. 74 Steeple?] Q4–5; ~ : Q1–3, Q6, F, D. 76 Church.——— ... Fifth-rate] Q2–6, F, D (Church∧——— Q6); ~ ,——— . . . ~ ! Q1. 77 *Dutch*] D; Duch Q1; Dutch Q2–6, F. 78 her] Q1–6, D; of her F. 79 *Kiss.*]] D; *kiss.*∧ Q1–6, F (*Kiss* Q4–6). 81 me?] ~ ! Q1–3, Q6, F, D; ~ , Q4–5. 86 [*Aside.*]———] D; ———[*aside.*∧ Q1–6, F (*Aside* Q4–6, F). 86 *Kiss*] Q4–6, F, D; *kiss* Q1–3. 88 by th'] Q2–6, F; bith' Q1; by the D. 90 What,] Q6; ~∧ Q1–5, F, D. 90 sit] Q2–6, F, D; set Q1. 91+ *s.d. Florimell*] Q3–6, F, D (*Elorimel* Q3); *Florimell* Q1–2. 96 see?] ~ ! Q1–6, F, D. 97 (swoon away!)] Q1–4, Q6, F, D; (*swoons away!*) Q5. 100 questions?] ~ , Q1–6, F, D. 102 Flor.] Q2–6, F, D; *Flor.* Q1. 104 thanks] Q1–2, Q6, F; thanks be Q3–5, D. 104 pinch; I] D; pinch; / I Q1–6, F. 108 be gone] Q1–6, D; begone F. 112 Sab.] Q3–6, F, D; *Sab.* Q1–2. 113 *Flor.*] Q2–6, F, D; ~ , Q1. 113 help!———] ~ ,∧ Q1–6, F, D. 120 hither?] Q4–5, D; ~ ; Q1–3, Q6, F. 121 [*Sings.*] Q6, F, D (~∧ Q6); ∧~ .———Q1–5. 123 jealous?] ~ ! Q1–6, F, D. 127 write] Q1; wrote Q2–6, F, D. 131 What,] Q6, D; ~∧ Q1–5, F. 131 did] Q1; do Q2–6, F, D. 135 *Celadon, Celadon*] Q6, D; Celadon, Celadon Q1–5, F. 141 'pray] Q1–2, Q6, F; pray Q3–5, D. 147 calls;] ~∧ Q1–3, Q6, F; ~ , Q4–5, D. 149 *Myrtle-grove*] *Myrtle-grove* Q1–6, F, D (*Myrtle grove* Q4–5). 151 What,] Q2–6, F, D; ~∧ Q1. 160 thy] Q1–2, Q6, F; the Q3–5, D. 161 this?

428 Textual Notes

———] ～ !——— Q1; ～ !∧ Q2–6, F, D.   163 Sister?] Q1–2, Q6, F; ～ !
Q3–5, D.   166+ s.d. Olin. Sab.] Q3–6, F, D (Olin. and Sab. D); Olin. Sab.
Q1–2.   167 way?] D; ～, Q1–6, F.   168, 170 Wenchers] Q1–6, D;
Wenches F.   170 word!] Q1, Q4–5, D; ～, Q2–3, Q6, F.   171 Man-
kind?] Q2, Q6, F; ～ . Q1; ～ ! Q3–5, D.   175 wait] Q1–2, F; wait on
Q3–5, D; wait upon Q6.   179–180 1 . . . 2] F, D; 1. . . . 2. Q1–6 (and
similarly below [Q3–4 have 2∧ in line 188]).   181 trow? . . . set.] ～ ,
. . . ～ . Q1–6, F, D (set? Q4–5; set! D).   183 let's in,] Q1; let's, in Q2,
Q6, F; let's in∧ Q3–5, D.   186 Rascalls:———] Q1–3, Q6; ～ !———
Q4–5; ～ .——— F; ～ ?∧ D.   192 Sould.] Q1–3, Q6, F, D; Souldier. Q4–
5.   204 'Thank] Q1–5, D; Thank Q6, F.   212 Celadon] Q3–6, F, D;
Celadon Q1–2.   213 Florimell,] Florimel. Q1; Florimel, Q2–6, F, D.
219 me?] Q4–5, D; ～ . Q1–3, Q6; failed to print in F.   224+ s.d. on
next line in Q1–6, F, D.   224+ s.d. Florimell] Q3–6, F, D; Florimell Q1–
2.   225 Page.] F; Page 1. Q1–6; 1 Page. D.   225–226 on't: / This]
on't: this Q1–6, F, D.   226–227 opportunity / Of] opportunity of Q1–6,
F, D.   228–229 obstinate? / You] obstinate? you Q1–6, F, D.   229–230
resist / Is] resist is Q1–6, F, D.   232 Lord! / Lys. How] Q4–6, F, D; Lord!
(Lys.) how Q1–3 (How Q2–3).   232 Queen?] Q1–6, D; ～ . F.   233
[To Sould.]] Q4–5; ∧To Sould.] Q1–3, F; [To the Souldiers. Q6, D (at right).
234–235 impossible! / The] impossible! the Q1–6, F, D.   236 half]
Q1–2, Q6, F; have Q3–5, D.   238 Asteria] Q4–5; ～ . Q1; ～ , Q2–3, Q6,
F, D.   245 so] Q1–6, D; such F.   248–249 Queen——— / I] Queen
———I Q1–6, F, D.   250 Flavia.] Q3–6, F, D; Flavia∧ Q1; Flavia. Q2.
252 moment?] ～ ! Q1–6, F, D.   253 do?] ～ ! Q1–6, F, D.   256
life?] ～ ! Q1–6, F, D.   257 which she] Q1, D; which Q2–6, F.   258
Rival?] ～ ! Q1–6, F, D.   265–266 little;———I'm not secure / Of] little;
——— / I'm not secure of Q1–6, F, D (secur'd Q1, but corrected in Errata).
267 I'le] Q1–2, Q6, F; I' Q3, D; I Q4–5.   268 Gamesters, and] Q1–2,
Q6, F; Gamesters, Q3–5, D.   271 you?] ～ ! Q1–6, F, D.   271–273 as
verse in Q1–6, F, D (. . . you! / . . . then / [. . . retire; / And then D]
. . . Ruffins. / [Ruffians Q1]).   273 party.]] ～ ,] Q1–2; ～∧] Q3–5; ～ ·∧
Q6, F, D (s.d. at right).   274+ s.d. sign] Q6, D; sing Q1–5, F.   276
die] Q1–2, Q5–6, F, D; dye Q3–4.   286–287 me,——— / It] D; me, it
Q1–6; me! It F.   293 ear Couz.] Q1–2, F; ear. Couz. Q3; Ear, Couz. Q4–
5; Ear Cousin. Q6; Ear.———Couz, D.   295+ s.d. Lys. Phil. Cand.]
Q3–6, F, D; Lys. Phil. Cand. Q1–2.   297 all you] Q1–3, Q6, F, D; all
your Q4–5.   300 As of] Q1; As Q2–6, F, D.   300–301 Angel / You]
Angel you Q1–6, F, D.   301 and . . . another,] Q1–6, D; or . . . ～ . F.
304 Queen?] ～ ! Q1–6, F, D.   309 but to] Q1–3, Q6; but Q4–5, F, D.
310 me:] Q1; ～ ! Q2–6, F, D.   312 two] Q1–2, Q5–6, F, D; too Q3–4.
322 why] Q1–3, Q6, F; ～, Q4–5, D.   324–325 not: you . . . me: how]
Q1–6, D; not: How F.   332 Philocles, whither] Q1–6, D; ～ ! Whither
F.   333 headlong?] ～ ! Q1–6, F, D.   333 exclamations] Q1–2, Q6, F,
D; acclamations Q3–5.   334–335 but / To live] Q1–2, Q6, F; but to /
Live Q3–5, D.   339 Heaven] Q1–6, F; Heav'n D.   345 Queen,] ～ !
Q1–6, F, D.   346 what I] Q1–2, Q5–6, F, D; what Q3–4.   346 am?]

~ ! Q1–6, F, D.   348 again.] Q1–4, F; ~∧ Q5–6; ~ , D.   348 [*Aside.*]
———] ———aside.] Q1–3; ———(*Aside.*) Q4–5; ———*Aside.*] Q6; ———
Aside. F; [*Aside.* D (*s.d. at right;* "True . . ." *set down a line*).   350
wretch;] Q1–6, F; ~∧ D.   352 that?] ~ ! Q1–6, F, D.   353 *Aside*]
Q4–6, F, D; *aside* Q1–3.   355 haste] Q1, Q3–5, D; hast Q2, Q6, F.
356 from the] Q2–6, F, D; from Q1 (*but corrected in Errata*).   364
Lord?] Q4–5, D; ~ : Q1–3, Q6, F.   366 Phil. Cand.] Q3–6, F, D; *Phil.
Cand.* Q1–2.   367 forever] Q1–2, Q6; for ever Q3–5, F, D.   370 Lys.]
Q4–6. F, D; *Lys.* Q1–3.

IV, ii

2 return!] Q1–3, Q6, F, D; ~ . Q4–5.   4 *Philocles;*] Q1–2, Q6, F; ~ ?
Q3–5; ~ ! D.   5–6 you / Commanded] you commanded Q1–6, F, D
(Commanded Q5, F).   7 now to] Q1–2, Q6, F; now Q3–5, D.   20
Secret-love?] Q4–6, F, D; ~ . Q1–3.   22+ Song.] Q1–6, F, D; Secret Love
M2; Grideline, or Secret Love. M3; *no title* M4.   23 *which*] Q1–6, F, D,
M2–3; that M4.   26 *die*] Q1–6, F, D; Dye M2–4.   27 *Yet*] Q1–6,
F, D, M2–3; But M4.   27 *he for whom I grieve*] Q1–6, F, D, M2,
M4; she whom I adore M3.   27 *shall never*] Q1–6, F, D, M2–3;
never shall M4.   28 *tongue does not betray . . . eyes*] Q1–6, F,
D, M2; eyes shall not betray . . . tongue M3; tongue shall ne're
disclose . . . eye M4.   29 *pain*] Q1–6, F, D, M2; griefe M3; heart M4.
30 *on*] Q1–6, F, D, M3–4; of M2.   31 *Thus*] Q1–6, F, D, M3–4; But
M2.   32 *heart's*] Q1–6, F, D, M2–3; hearts M4.   33 *while . . . this*]
Q1–6, F, D, M2–3; whilst . . . it M4.   33 *him*] Q1–6, F, D, M2, M4; her
M3.   34 *faith . . . he*] Q1–6, F, D, M2, M4; truth . . . she M3.   35
his] Q1–6, F, D, M2, M4; her M3.   35 *will I*] Q1–6, F, D, M3–4; I will
M2.   35 *and there*] Q1–6, F, D, M3; there to M2; & shal M4.   36
While] Q1–6, F, D, M3; Whilst M2, M4.   36 *frown*] Q1–6, F, D, M3;
frownes M2; fears M4.   37 *To*] Q1–6, F, D, M3–4; Nor to M2.   38
can I fall more low] Q1–6, F, D, M2–3; lower can I fall M4.   39 Peace:]
Q1–5, D; ~ ! Q6, F.   47 Prisoner] Q1–5, F, D; Pris'ner Q6.   52 suffers?] ~ ! Q1–6, F, D.   64 forgot] Q1–5, F, D; ~ , Q6.   65 Jaylors.]
Q1, D; ~ , Q2–6, F.   66, 67 till] Q1–6, F; 'till D.   68 would] Q1–2,
Q6, F; should Q3–5, D.   68+ *s.d. Exeunt*] Q4–5; *Exit* Q1–3, Q6, F; *Ex.*
D.   70 done?] ~ ! Q1–6, F, D.   80 Yet] Q3–6, D; 'Yet Q1–2, F.
90 *Aside*] Q4–6, F, D; *aside* Q1–3.   97 this] Q1–5, F, D; the Q6.   98
disobey:] Q1–2, Q6, F; ~ . Q3–5, D.   100 *Aside*] Q4–6, F, D; *aside* Q1–
3.   102 thing's] Q1–2, Q4–6, F, D; things Q3.   104 swear. / *Ast.*]
Q4–6, F, D (swear: Q4, F); swear: (*Ast.*) Q1–3.   104 general:] Q1–4, Q6,
F, D; ~ . Q5.   106 swear. / *Ast.* . . . self. / *Phil.*] Q4–6, F, D (swear:
Q4–5, F; self: Q4, F); swear: (*Ast.*) . . . self: (*Phil.*) Q1–3.   117 abuse?]
~ ! Q1–6, F, D.   121 On] Q2–6, F, D; Or Q1 (*but corrected in Errata*).
122 more,] Q1, Q3–5, D; ~∧ Q2, Q6, F.   124 may.] Q2–6, F, D; ~∧
Q1.   127 make] Q1–6, D; makes F.   139 remnants] Q1; remnant
Q2–6, F, D.   139 mild] Q1; wild Q2–6, F, D.   140 flowers] Q1–2,
Q6, F; flow'rs Q3–5, D.   155 where to] Q1–2, Q6, F; to Q3, D; then to

Q4–5.   161 Asteria] Q3–6, F, D; *Asteria* Q1–2.   162 I'le] Q2–6, F,
D; Itle Q1.   166 down . . . way,] ~ , . . .~ ; Q1–2, Q6, F; ~∧ . . .
~ ; Q3–5, D.   167 Phil.] Q3–6, F, D; *Phil.* Q1–2.

V, i

S.d. SCENE,] SCENE∧ Q1–6, F; SCENE I. SCENE∧ D.   *s.d.* Flori-
mell] Florimel Q1–6, F, D.   1 *Flor.* 'Twill] Q6, F; 'Twill Q1–5, D.   4
I do] Q1–6, D; I F.   6 If] Q4–5, F, D; if Q1–3, Q6.   8 *poudré &
ajusté*] Q1 (*ajusté*), Q6; *poudrè & ajustè* Q2, Q4–5, F; *poudrê & ajustê* Q3,
D.   13+ *s.d.* Olinda,] Q1–6, F; Olinda *and* D.   19 so?] ~ ! Q1–6, F,
D.   20 thee——— [*Aside.*] Q1–2, Q6, F (*aside* Q1–2); thee——— Q3–5,
D.   23 name of] Q1–5, F, D; name Q6.   23+ *s.d. Walks*] Q6, F, D;
walks Q1–5.   25 this] Q1–6, D; ~ , F.   35 way] Q1–3, Q5–6, F, D;
may Q4.   37 who———] Q4–6, F, D; ~ .——— Q1–3.   50 I?] F; ~ ;
Q1–6, D.   57 thee!] Q1–3, Q6, F, D; ~ ? Q4–5.   60 at?] D; ~ , Q1–6;
~ : F.   61 art.] Q6, D; ~ ? Q1–5, F.   73 Jigg, you] D; Jigg, / You
Q1–6, F.   78 to make] Q1–6, D; make F.   81 one] Q1, Q3–6, F, D;
on Q2.   87 lose] Q1, Q4–6, D; loose Q2–3, F.   93 us.] Q1–6, F; ~
———D.   103 walk,] Q6, F, D; ~∧ Q1–5.   104 merry] Q1–2, Q6, F;
marry Q3–5, D.   109 her?] Q4–5; ~ ! Q1–3, Q6, F, D.   110 By] Q4–
5; by Q1–3, Q6, F, D.   111 *off*] Q2–6, F, D; *of* Q1.   113 *Ruff.*] Q4–5,
F; ~ .——— Q1; ~∧——— Q2–3, D; ~∧∧ Q6.   114 *Florimells*] *Flori-
mels* Q1–6, F, D.   114 you.———] Q1–5; ~∧——— Q6, F, D.   114
Kisses] Q4–6, F, D; *kisses* Q1–3.   116 gifts] Q1; gift Q2–6, F, D.   119+
s.d. Florimell] Florimel Q1–6, F, D.   120 fair,] D; ~∧ Q1–6, F.   123
Florimell] F, D; *Florimell* Q1–6.   130 *Mel. Olin.*] Q3–6, F, D (Mel. *and*
D); *Mel. Olin.* Q1–2.   132 Perruke] Q3–6, F, D; Perruks Q1–2.   132
again——— [*Exit.*] again.———[*Exit.* Q1; again.——— Q2–5; again———
Q6, F, D.   134 hanging look was there:] Q1–6, F; Hanging-look was there!
D.   138 you now] Q1–6; you, now F; you now, D.   139 robb'd] Q1–
6, D; rob'd F.   141 you.] Q1–2, Q6, F; ~ .——— Q3–5; ~∧——— D.
142 Who, you] D; Who you, Q1–6, F.   142 me?] ~ ! Q1–6, F, D.
147 you're] Q1; you are Q2–6, F, D.   152 parting.——— [*Going.*] Q1;
parting. Q2–6, F, D.   153 Sir? sweet] F; ~ ; ~ Q1–2, Q6; ~ , ~ Q3–5, D.
155 I am] Q4–5, D; I Q1–3; I'm Q6, F.   155 I'le] Q1–2, Q6, F, D; (I'l
Q3–5.   157–158 Breeches——— / *Flor.* Which] Q4–6, F, D (Breeches.
——— Q4–5); Breeches.——— *Flor.* which Q1–3.   163 Celadon] Q3–6,
F, D; *Celadon* Q1–2.   164 *Philocles solus.* Wheree're] *Philocles solus.* /
Wheree're Q1–6, F, D (Philocles F, D).   165 me.] Q1–3, Q6, F, D; ~ ,
Q4–5.   174 it?] ~ ! Q1–6, F, D.   176 that] Q1–5, F, D; this Q6.
176–177 *Philocles!* / A] D; *Philocles!* A Q1–6, F.   177 blessings] Q1–2,
Q5–6, F, D; blessing Q3–4.   178 think] Q1–6, F; ~ , D.   182 Wake,]
Q6, F; ~∧ Q1–5, D.   184 innocent?———] ~ !——— Q1; ~ !∧ Q2–6, F,
D.   190–191 so / My] so my Q1–6, F, D.   192 me———] ~ .———
Q1–6, F, D.   195 vertue.——— [*Aside*] ~ ;——— [*aside* Q1–5, F, D
(*Aside* Q4–5, F, D); ~∧——— [*Aside* Q6.   196 her.]] ~∧] Q1–4; her.)
Q5; Her.∧ Q6, F, D (*s.d. at right*).   196 O] Q1–6, F; Oh D.   198 till]

Q1–6, F; 'till D.   201 vertue?] ~! Q1–6, F, D.   202 States] Q1–2, Q4–6, F, D; Sates Q3.   207 so] Q3–5, D; ~, Q1–2, Q6, F.   210 trial's] Q1–6, F; Tryals D.   212 come] Q1; came Q2–6, F, D.   217 obey?] ~! Q1–6, F, D.   223 *Indians*] D; Indians Q1–6, F.   225 advanc'd.] Q1; ~, Q2–4, Q6, F, D; ~∧ Q5.   230 low-plac'd] Q1–2. Q6, F, D; low plac'd Q3–5.   234 do] Q1–2, Q4–6, F, D; doe Q3.   238 actions] Q1–5, F, D; Action Q6.   239 said,] Q1; ~. Q2–6, F, D.   242 *Aside*] Q4–6, F, D; aside Q1–3.   245 retire:] D; ~, Q1–6, F.   246 it,] Q6, D; ~∧ Q1–5, F.   246 fire?] Q6; ~! Q1–5, F, D.   246+ *s.d.* Philocles] Q3–6, F, D; *Philocles* Q1–2.   247 t'accuse] Q1–2, Q6, F; to accuse Q3–5, D.   250 possible] Q1, Q4–6, F, D; possibly Q2–3.   250 Madam?] ~! Q1–6, F, D.   252 [*Her*] Q6, F; ∧*Her* Q1–5; [*Lays her* D.   252 shoulder.]] Q1–5; ~ ∙∧ Q6, F, D (*s.d. at right*).   252–253 know, / What] know, what Q1–6, F, D.   255 was my] Q1; was Q2–6, F, D.   262 int'rest] Q1; interest Q2–6, F, D.   265 perhaps——— / *Qu.*] Q4–6, F, D; perhaps——— (*Qu.*) Q1–3.   265 now?] Q4–6, D; ~! Q1; ~. Q2–3, F.   271 me?] Q6; ~! Q1–5, F, D.   273 thee?] Q6; ~! Q1–5, F, D.   277 tongue.] Q1–5, F; ~; Q6; ~: D.   281–282 fallen? / But] D (fallen!); fallen! But Q1–6, F (fall'n! Q6).   283 caus'd;] Q1–5, F; ~: Q6; ~. D.   288 Madam!——————] Q1–5, F, D; ~∧ ——— Q6.   302 mean. / *Qu.*] Q4–6, F, D; mean. (*Qu.*) Q1–3 (mean∧ Q2–3).   304 offence.] Q1, D; ~, Q2–3, F.   306 too?] ~! Q1–6, F, D.   307 *Aside*] Q4–6, F, D; aside Q1–3.   314 your] Q1, Q4–5, D; you Q2–3, Q6, F.   315 have. / *Qu.*] Q4–6, F, D (have∧——— Q6); have. (*Qu.*) Q1–3.   320 aspersion.———] ~ :——— Q1–5, F, D; ~∧——— Q6.   320+ *s.d. Aside*] Q4–6, F, D; aside Q1–3.   327 misery] Q1–6, F; ~, D.   336 armes.] ~? Q1–6, F, D.   338 Was] Q3–6, F, D; was Q1–2.   339 love!] Q1–3, Q6, F, D; ~. Q4–5.   344 him.] ~? Q1–6, F, D.   347 hide] Q4–5, D; hinder Q1–3, Q6, F.   349 Armes.] Q2–6, F, D; ~∧ Q1.   350–351 wish. [*Aside.*] ———Call in / The] wish———*aside.*] Call in the Q1–2; wish———*aside.* / Call in the Q3; wish——— [*Aside.* / Call in the Q4–6, F, D.   352 there?———] Q1–5, F, D; ~∧——— Q6.   352 *Exit* Lys.] Q2–6, F, D; *Exit Lys.* Q1.   355–356 reinstate / My] reinstate my Q1–6, F, D.   366 haste] Q1–5, F, D; hast Q6.   366–367 experiment; / It] experiment; it Q1–6, F, D.   369 all] Q2–6, F, D; al! Q1.   381 'faith] Q1–5, F, D; faith Q6.   381 courtesie; I] D; courtesie; / I Q1–6, F.   384 o'the] Q1–2, Q6, F; o're the Q3–5, D.   392 recompence.———] Q1–5, F; ~∧——— Q6, D.   393+ *s.d. Aside*] Q4–6, F, D; aside Q1–3.   394 Heav'ns] Q1–2, Q5–6, F; Heaven's Q3–4; Heav'n's D.   397 self!——— [*Aside.*] Q1 (aside); self!——— Q2–6, F, D (self!∧ Q5; self∧——— Q6).   398 *Qu.*] Q2–6, F, D; *Qu*, Q1.   399 both. ———How] both:———how Q1–6, F, D (both∧——— Q6; How D).   401 heart!———] Q1–5, F, D; ~∧——— Q6.   401 *Aside*] Q4–6, F, D; aside Q1–3.   403–404 could / Do] could do Q1–6, F, D.   407 Philocles.] Q1–6, D; ~, F.   414 me.——— [*Aside.*] Q1 (aside); me.——— Q2–5, F, D; me∧——— Q6.   416 the] Q1–2, Q6, F; a Q3–5, D.   418 but th'] Q1–3, Q6, F; but the Q4–5, D.   418+ *s.d. To the Qu. aside.*] D;

to the Qu. *aside.* Q1–5, F; *Aside to the* Queen. Q6.   419   *to Ast.*∧] D;
to Ast.] Q1–6, F.   429   that] Q1–6, D; the F.   429   Queen?] ~ ! Q1–
6, F, D.   431   too:] Q1–6, D; ~ ! F.   433   beautiful!———] Q1; ~ .
——— Q2–6, F, D.   433   *Aside*] Q4–6, F, D; *aside* Q1–3.   433   still!
———] Q1–6; still!∧ F; ~∧——— D.   433   *To*] Q5–6, F, D; *to* Q1–4.
435   *Aside*] Q4–6, F, D; *aside* Q1–3.   440   *Qu. Clapping . . . Asteria.*]
[Qu. *Clapping . . .* Asteria∧] Q1–4, Q6; Qu. [*Clapping . . .* Asteria.] Q5;
Qu. . . . [*Clapping . . .* Asteria. F, D (*s.d. at right*).   440–441   done! /
But] D; done! but Q1–6, F.   449   it,] Q3–5, D; ~ . Q1–2, Q6, F.   452
Gentlemen,———]   Q1–5; ~ .∧Q6; ~ .——— F; ~∧——— D.   452
To] Q2–6, F, D; *to* Q1.   455   *Deputies.*] F, D; [~.] Q1; [~∧] Q2–
5; ~ .] Q6.   461   Conjugal,] Q1; ~ . Q2–6, F, D.   465   a way] Q3–5,
D; away Q1–2, Q6, F.   468   happy:] Q1–6, D; ~ ! F.   472   keeps]
D; keep Q1–6, F.   472   awake.] Q4–6, F, D; ~ : Q1–3.   473   *Celadon!*] Q1–2, Q6, F; ~ , Q3–5, D.   474   Your] Q2–6, F, D; You Q1.
474   me;] Q1–2, Q6, F; ~ ! Q3–5, D.   475   I] Q3–6, F, D; *I* Q1–2.
478   I] Q1; *I'l* Q2–6, F, D.   513   make] Q2–6, F, D; mak Q1.   518
an Halter] Q1–2, Q6; a Halter Q3–5, F, D.   529   alone:] Q1; ~ , Q2–
3; ~ . Q4–6; ~ ; F, D.   548   nothing] F; ~ , Q1–6, D.   553   priv-
iledges] Q1–3, Q6, F, D; priviledge Q4–5.   553   *Florimell,*] Q2–6, F,
D; ~ . Q1.   554   Fasting-nights] Q1–4, Q6, D; Fasting nights Q5, F.
560   ye] Q1–6, D; you F.   568   more; since] Q1; ~ ;——— Q2–6, F;
~ ;——— / Since D.   575   *to Asteria.*∧] *to* Asteria.] Q1–6 (*Ast.* Q6); *to*
Asteria.] F; [*To* Asteria. D (*s.d. at right*).

      Epilogue: 22   Poetry;] Q1; ~ , Q2–3, Q6, F, D; ~ . Q4–5.   24   *Prey,*]
Q4–5, F, D; ~ . Q1–3, Q6.   25   way;] Q1–2, Q6, F; ~ . Q3–5, D.   35
before.] Q1–2, Q6, F; ~ : Q3–5, D.   40   spins best] Q1–2, Q6, F; spins
Q3–5; *spins more,* D.

      Epilogue Spoken by Mrs. Reeves: title M1 has "Epilogue" only.
Maiden Queen, *in mans Cloathes.*] Maiden Queen. O1; Maiden Queen, *in
mans Cloathes.* O2.   2   we] O1–2; wee M1 (*and so throughout*).   2
huff?] ~ . O1–2; ~∧ M1.   4   we.] O1; ~ ; O2; ~∧ M1.   9   alone,]
O1; ~ ? O2; ~∧ M1.   10   grown?] ~ , O1–2; ~∧ M1.   11   so] O1–2;
too M1.   11   none.] O2; ~∧ O1, M1.   16   than] O1; then O2; that
M1.   17   we!] O1; ~ . O2; ~∧ M1.   19   house.] O1; ~ ; O2; ~∧
M1.   23   would . . . night.] O1; will . . .~ : O2; will . . . ~∧ M1.
26   too] O2, M1; two O1.   27   you.] O1; ~ : O2; ~∧ M1.

Sir Martin Mar-all

The first edition of *Sir Martin Mar-all* was published in 1668 (Q1; Macd
71a); the second is dated 1668 or 1669 in different copies (Q2; Macd 71b);
the third, 1678 (Q3; Macd 71c); the fourth, 1691 (Q4; Macd 71d); and the
fifth, 1697 (Q5; Macd 71e). The play was reprinted in Dryden's *Comedies,
Tragedies, and Operas* (1701), I, 190–225 (F; Macd 107ai–ii [two issues,

the differences not affecting this play]), and in Congreve's edition of Dryden's *Dramatick Works* (1717), II, 85–161 (D; Macd 109ai–ii [two issues, with a cancel title page for Vol. I in the second]).

Dryden made considerable revisions in Q1 after it had begun to go through the press: from I, i, 278 to II, i, 29, where C1,2 (pp. 9–12) were replaced by a single leaf, C1 (pp. 9–10), on the conjugate of which the prologue and the epilogue were printed; in V, i, from line 107 through the stage direction after line 202, where two conjugate leaves (pp. 55–58, first count) were substituted for the original H4 (when Macdonald, p. 98, says the second of these leaves "shows no evidence of being a cancel" he means a cancel of a cancel, a disjunct leaf); and in V, ii, from line 89 to the end of the play, where a single leaf (pp. 69–70), printed on the same stock as the cancel C1, was substituted for the original K3,4. One of the Folger copies has uncanceled C2, pp. 11–12 (this is the copy referred to by Macdonald). It shows that the opening of Act II was reprinted without change, and that Act I was first intended to end differently, but suggests that this ending was never fully prepared for the press. In addition, Dryden may have ordered corrections in inner and outer D and inner F of Q1. Q2 was printed from a copy of Q1 with Dryden's revisions, Q3 from a copy of Q2, Q4 from a copy of Q3, Q5 from a copy of Q4, F partly from Q1 and, partly from Q5, and D from a copy of Q2. As there is no evidence that Dryden revised the text after the first edition, one of the Clark copies of Q1(b), *PR3418.G1, copy 1, has been chosen as the copy text, with revisions from the other copy when the first has uncorrected forms (see below). A great deal of the text was printed as verse, and some was printed in lines of verse length but without initial capitalization of the lines. Some of this "verse" is obviously prose; some scans very well; some of what was printed as prose could be divided into pentameters. The solution adopted here, as in Congreve's edition, is to set the whole as prose. The notes generally record these normalizations only when the lines begin with a capital in Q1. The stage directions in Q1 tend to drift in from the right margin, but this peculiarity has always been silently normalized.

Francis Needham has suggested that one change in V, i, of Q1 was the substitution of the song, "Blind Love," which occupies the whole of pp. 57–58 (first count), for "A song made by Sr Marten Marall & his man Warner to the Lady falklands tune," which Needham printed from a manuscript in *Welbeck Miscellany No. 2* ([Bungay, Suffolk], 1934), pp. 46–47. The present editors agree with Macdonald, p. 98, that the Welbeck song does not seem to be Dryden's.

The following copies of the various editions have also been examined: Q1: Clark (*PR3418.G1 [cop. 2]); Folger (D2206h, v. 1, D2359 [3 cop.]); Q2: Clark (*PR3418.G1.1668 [2 cop.]), Yale (Ij.D848.668saf); Q3: Clark (*PR3418.G1.1678), Folger (D2362), Huntington (122920); Q4: Clark (*PR3418.G1.1691 [cop. 1]), Huntington (122930), Folger (D2363); Q5: Clark (*PR3418.G1.1697 [cop. 1]), Huntington (28645), Folger (D2364); F: Clark (*fPR3412.1701 [2 cop.]); D: Clark (*PR3412.1717 [2 cop.]).

Press Variants by Form

Q1
Sheet D (inner form)
Uncorrected: Clark cop. 1, Folger (D2359, cop. 2)
Corrected: Clark cop. 2, Folger (3)
Sig. D1*v*
    II, ii, 107 you I] you
        121 *Warn.* . . . Madam? / *Enter* Millisent.] *Warn. entring.* . . .
        Madam?
Sig. D2
    II, ii, 126–127 (to "it.") *on* D2, *catchword* "Our"] *on* D1*v, catchword*
    "*Mill.*"
                Sheet D (outer form)
Uncorrected: Clark cop. 1, Folger (D2359, cop. 2)
Corrected: Clark cop. 2, Folger (3)
Sig. D3
    II, ii, 274–275 you you think] you think
        292–293 Repast.] ~ ?
        298 Sir;] ~ .
        301 Rogue,] ~∧
                Sheet F (inner form)
Uncorrected: Folger (D2359, cop. 1)
Corrected: Clark (2), Folger (3)
Sig. F1*v*
    III, iii, 65 are] love
                Sheet G (inner form)
Uncorrected: Clark cop. 2, Folger (3)
Corrected: Clark cop. 1, Folger (D2359, cop. 3)
Sig. G3*v*
    IV, 359 thing,] ~∧
                Sheet G (outer form)
Uncorrected? Clark cop. 1, Folger (D2359, bd. w. D2206h, v. 1)
Corrected? Clark cop. 2, Folger (3)
Sig. G4*v*
    IV, 449 it;] ~ ,
             χ [cancel for H4] (inner form)
Uncorrected? Clark cop. 2.
Corrected? Clark cop. 1, Folger (4)
Sig. χ1*v*
    V, i, 160 me,] ~∧
             χ [cancel for H4] (outer form)
Uncorrected: Folger (D2359, bd. w. D2206h, v. 1)
Corrected: Clark (2), Folger (3)
Sig. χ1
    V, i, 142 *no catchword*] *Sir*

Sheet K (inner form)
Uncorrected: Folger (D2359, cop. 2)
Corrected: Clark (2), Folger (3)
Sig. K3*v*
V, ii, 153 near] ~ .

The Names of the Persons: headed "Dramatis Personae" *in Q5, F, D.*
Prologue: 4 costs] Q1, F; *cost* Q2-5, D.

I, i

ACT] Q4-5, F, D; ~. Q1-3.   I.] Q1-5, F; I. SCENE I. D.   13+   *s.d.*
Aside] Q1, Q4-5, F, D; *aside* Q2-3.   19   *Sir]* Q2-5, F, D; ~∧ Q1.
19-21   *as in D; set as verse in Q1-5, F* (. . . / I . . . / Except . . . / But).
22-24   *as in D; set as verse in Q1-5, F* (. . . / You . . . / And).   25
a-do] Q4-5, a do Q1-3, F, D.   26   as . . . self.] *as in D; set as a line of*
verse in Q1-5, F (As).   31   stay'd] Q1-5, F; staid D.   31   it?] Q3-5;
~ . Q1-2, F, D.   32+   *s.d.* Warner] Q4-5, F, D; *Warner* Q1-3.   36-
41   *as in D; set as verse in Q1-5, F* (. . . / Her Father . . . / And the
. . . / I . . . / He's . . . / He . . . / But . . . / This).   42   Sure] D;
~ ! Q1-5, F.   42   Cousin!] Q5; ~ ? Q1-4, F, D.   42+   *s.d. Enter*
Mrs. Christian.] Q5, F, D; [*Enter Mrs. Christian.* Q1-4 (Christian Q4).
44-46   *as in D; set as verse in Q1-5, F* (. . . / A . . . / 'Tis).   46
Martin] Q4-5, F, D; *Martin* Q1-3.   47   La. . . . Fool.————] *as in*
D; set as a line of verse in Q1-5, F (Fool∧———— Q4-5, F, D).   73   *La.*]
Q2-5, F, D; ~∧ Q1.   77   night-visits] Q1-2, Q4-5, F, D; night visits
Q3.   78   ask where's] Q1-3, D; ask, Where's Q4-5, F.   83   say] Q1;
~ , Q2-5, F, D.   90   further] Q1-5, D; farther F.   140, 142   *In*
whisper] Q1-3, D; *Whispers* Q4-5, F.   143   *Sir] La.* Dupe. Sir Q1-5,
F, D.   156   of up] Q1-5, D; up F.   162   as] *some copies of Q4 read*
sa.   162   does] Q1-2, F, D; doth Q3-5.   171-172   *as in D; set as*
verse in Q1-5, F (. . . / The . . . / Fair).   174+   *s.d. Enter* Warner.]
D; [~ Q1-5, F (~∧ Q1-3).   180   thereabouts] Q1-4, F, D; there about
Q5.   181   then;] Q4-5, F; ~ , Q1-3, D.   181-182   *as in D; set as*
verse in Q1-5, F (Canterbury; [~ , Q3-5, F] / It).   184   Affairs] Q1,
F; Affair Q2-5, D.   187   fooling.————And] fooling:————and Q1-5,
F, D.   189   beseech you] Q1-3, F, D; beseech Q4-5.   216   My] D;
my Q1-5, F.   230   Heavens] Q2-5, F, D; Heaven Q1.   231   bidding.
Her] ~ : her Q1-5, F; ~ :———— Her D.   233   yon] Q1-3, F, D; yon'
Q4-5.   237   head.————] ~∧———— Q1, F, D; ~ ,———— Q2-5.   248-
250   *as in D; set as verse in Q1-3, F* (. . . / Who . . . / I . . . / To),
partially as verse in Q4-5 (. . . / Who . . . / I).   251-253   *as in D;*
set as verse in Q1-5, F (. . . / He . . . / Keeping . . . / mun).
257   like the] Q1, F; like a Q2-5, D.   258   *Sir] Sir* Q1-5, F, D.   259-
260   *as in D; set as verse in Q1-5, F* (. . . / To).   260   *Sir]* F, D; Sir
Q1-5.   266-267   *as in D; set as verse in Q1-3, F* (. . . / Sir), Q4-5
(. . . / Well).   268-269   *as in D; set as verse in Q1-3, F* (. . . /
Why), Q4-5 (. . . / And).   275   led] D; lead Q1-5, F.   278   Father:] Q1-2, Q5, F; ~ , Q3-4; ~ . D.   286   Bug-word] Q1-5, D; Bug-bear

word F.   305   he] Q5, F, D; she Q1–4.   313   Soul————] Q2–5, D;
~ .———— Q1, F.

Note: Cancel C1 of Q1 begins with the second syllable of "Father" in
l. 278 of the present text. No corresponding uncanceled text for the rest
of the scene is known. What has been preserved is the original C2, ap-
parently an additional scene that began on C1v. The text follows (for
"Malchus" in the first line see John, XVIII, 10).

Mood. But one blow at him, I will so Malchus his Ears.
       What do you mean by that Sir?
Mood. To have him by the Ears, and you too if you be prating.
Sir John. I beg of you to have a little patience.
Mood. So I may have a little patience, and yet knock him soundly: oh
how my Fingers itch at him!
Sir John. Quiet your self I beseech you, and but hear me and believe
me, for I will speak nothing but truth.
Mood. Well, speak, for I will both hear thee and believe thee, for I
know thou art an honest man, speak!
Sir John. Sir, of my Soul I never meant you any injury, or the least affront, but all Civility and Service to you; for this expression of *Pardon*
me, is the new fashion of speaking, *a la mode,* as much as to say *Excuse*
me.
Mood. By Cox-nouns I hate Excuses; for they are but lyes, and I am
all for truth.
       Sir, Pardon me is as much as Excuse me, or, By your Favour I
am of another opinion.
Mood. By your Favour, is it no more? I understand that perfectly, 'tis
civil, By your favour, though a man be never so ill-favour'd.
       Pray be friends Sir.
Mood. Let the Gentleman express it so, and I am content. Speak Sir for
your self.
Sir John. Truly Sir, Pardon me, in King *Charles* the Seconds time, has
no more offence or hurt in it, than, By your Favour, in *primo* of Queen
Elizabeth.
Though your favour has been terrible to me.
Mood. Well! if it be so, then give me thy hand.
Sir John. I will lend it you Sir.
Mood. Well, and I'le pay thee agen presently, and there's an end of the
business.
So, let's go then, and *Beati pacifici.*   [*Exeunt.*

II, i

Note: The original C2v of Q1 was reprinted on the cancel C1v without
change.   ACT II. SCENE I.] D; ACT II. Q1–5, F (ACT. Q2–3).   *s.d.*
Lady] Q4–5, F, D; Lady Q1–3.   1–2   *as in D; set as verse in Q1–5, F*
(. . . / But).   4   took] Q1–5, F; take D.   8–10   *as in D; set as*
verse in Q1–5, F (. . . / Yonder . . . / Your).   11+   *s.d. Enter Lord*]
F, D; [*Enter* Lord Q1–5 (*Lord* Q4–5).   12–13   *as in D; set as verse in*

Q*1–5*, F (. . . / How).　15 'fraid] Q1, Q4–5, F; fraid Q2–3; afraid
D.　21 *Lord.*] Q2–5, F, D; ~∧ Q1.　21–23 *as in D; set as verse
in Q1–5, F* (. . . / To suspect . . . / I am . . . / So soon . . . / I hope).
25–27 *as in D; set as verse in Q1–5, F* (. . . / But . . . / Kindness
. . . / Crime).　28 mine Aunt] Q2–3, D; mine Aunt an Q1; my Aunt
Q4–5, F.　29 for . . . good] *set as a line of verse in F.*　29 good.]
Q1; ~ ; Q2–5, F, D.　29–30 But . . . agen.] *as in D; set as a line of
verse in Q1–5, F.*　31–34 *as in D; set as verse in Q1–5, F* (. . . /
You do . . . / I vow . . . pure———— / My . . . / Were . . . / With a).
32 bear you:] Q1; ~ . Q2–5, F, D.　33 Sister or a Daughter] Q1–3,
D (Sister,); Daughter or a Sister Q4–5, F (Daughter, F).　41–42 *as in
D; set as verse in Q1–5, F* (. . . / And in).　44+ *s.d.* [*Touching*] Q2–5,
F, D; ∧~ Q1.　47 to] Q1–5, D; too F.　49 *glove.*] Q3–5, F, D; ~∧
Q1–2.　51–52 *as in D; set as verse in Q1–5, F* (you, / And,).　52
Laws] Q1–3, D; Law Q4–5, F.　56 *Hugging*] Q4–5, F, D; hugging
Q1–3.　61–62 *as in D; set as verse in Q1–5, F* (. . . / All).　70+
s.d. Lady] Q4–5, F, D; Lady Q1–3.　75 *Lord*] D; Lord Q1–5, F.
76–77 *as in D; set as verse in Q1–5, F* (. . . / I).　78 Lad.] Q1–5;
La. *Dupe.* F, D.　78–80 *as in D; set as verse in Q1–5, F* (. . . / Never
. . . / The).　82–85 *as in D; set as verse in Q1–5, F* (. . . / Whether
. . . / Then . . . / So).　88–90 *as in D; set as verse in Q1–5, F*
(. . . / As . . . / Hence-forward).　94 that is] Q1–3, D; that's Q4–5, F.
100 you, and] you. And Q1–5, F, D.　100 than] Q1–2, Q5, F, D;
then Q3–4.　100 Page Post] Q1, D; Page-Post Q2–5, F.　105–107 *as
in D; set as verse in Q1–5, F* (. . . / What? . . . / Defame . . . / To).
108–109 *as in D; set as verse in Q1–5, F* (. . . / Urge).　110 Arguments.] Q1; ~ ; Q2–5, F, D.　110–111 *as in D; set as verse in Q1–5, F*
(. . . / But).　112–114 *as in D; set as verse in Q1–5, F* (. . . / Hee'l
. . . / Take).

II, ii

SCENE II. *Enter*] Enter Q1–5, F, D.　1–2 *as in D; set partly as
verse in Q1–5, F* (. . . / Your Father).　4–5 *as in D; set as verse in
Q1–5, F* (. . . / This).　6–7 *as in D; set as verse in Q1–5, F* (. . . /
You might).　9 him] Q1, F; it Q2–5, D.　18–24 *as in D; set more
or less as verse in Q1–5, F* (. . . / His wit . . . / Madam, . . . / your
scorn . . . [. . . / Scorn Q4–5, F] / By . . . / to keep this . . . [. . . /
This Q5, F] / The Lawyers . . . / And I . . . / But).　22 him;] Q1–3,
D; ~ . Q4–5, F.　25 Servant?] ~ ! Q1–5, F, D.　26 ere] Q1, Q4–5;
e're Q2–3, F, D.　26 him;] Q1–2, D; ~ . Q3–5, F.　26–27 *as in D;
set as verse in Q1–5, F* (. . . / Consider).　28–29 *as in D; set as verse
in Q1–5, F* (. . . / Methought).　33 is!] [*Aside.*] is! Q1–5, F, D.　34–
35 *as in D; set as verse in Q1–5, F* (. . . / I . . . / If).　35 me?] ~ .
Q1–3, D; ~ ! Q4–5, F.　36–37 *as in D; set as verse in Q1–5, F* (. . . /
If).　37 you————] ~ . Q1–5, F; ~ ? D.　45–46 *as in D; set as verse
in Q1–5, F* (. . . / Knowing).　55 him?] Q1–4, D; ~ ! Q5, F.　57
did———— [*Aside.*] did———— Q1–5, F, D.　59–60 *as in D; set as verse
in Q1–5, F* (. . . / Unless).　62–63 *as in D; set as verse in Q1–5, F*
(. . . / But).　65 innocent.] Q1–3; ~ ? Q4–5, F, D.　66–67 *as in*

D; set as verse in Q1–5, F (. . . / Pray . . . / Ungrateful, or [. . . / Or Q4–5, F]).   69–72 *as in D; set as verse in Q1–5, F* (. . . / But . . . / As . . . / I wish).   73–74 *as in D; set as verse in Q1–5, F* (. . . / If). 75–76 *as in D; set as verse in Q1–5, F* (. . . / I'le).   78 *within.*∧] Q2–5, F, D; ~ .] Q1.   79 do?] ~ ! Q1–5, F, D.   79–80 *as in D; set as verse in Q1–5, F* (. . . / 'Tis).   82 [*He goes out.*] F, D (*Warner goes* D); *on line below in Q1–5.*   86 laid?] Q1–4, D; ~ ! Q5, F.   88 *Door.*∧] Q2–5, F, D; ~ .] Q1.   92–93 *as in D; set as verse in Q1–5, F* (. . . / 'Tis).   94 leave.——] Q1–3; ~∧—— Q4–5, F, D.   97–98 *as in D; set as verse in Q1–5, F* (. . . / To).   101–102 *as in D; set as verse in Q1–5, F* (. . . / That).   103–104 *as in D; set as verse in Q1–5, F* (. . . / To).   105 *Warn.*] Q1–3, D; *Warn. at the door.* Q4–5, F.   105–106 *as in D; set as verse in Q1–5, F* (. . . / An).   107 you] Q1 (*corrected state*), Q2–5, F, D; you I Q1 (*uncorrected state*).   108–110 *as in D; set as verse in Q1–5, F* (. . . / Of an . . . / Where . . . / The).   110–111 him, and . . . me.] him. / *Sir John.* And . . . me, Q1–5, F, D.   112 *Sir John.* Indeed] Indeed Q1–5, F, D.   112–113 *as in D; set as verse in Q1–5, F* (. . . / But).   115 *Warn.*] Q1–3, D; *Warn. at the door.* Q4–5, F.   115 *Warn.* . . . him!] *as in D; set as a line of verse in Q1–5, F.*   116 Woman-kind, how] Q1–3, D; Woman-kind! / How Q4–5; Woman-kind! How F.   117–118 *as in D; set as verse in Q1–5, F* (. . . / He shall).   121 *Warn.*] Q1; *Warn. entring.* Q2–5, F, D ([*Entring.*] D).   121 Madam?] Q1 (*corrected state*), Q2–5, F, D; Madam? / *Enter* Millisent. Q1 (*uncorrected state*).   122–123 *as in D; set as verse in Q1–5, F* (. . . / To).   124 *Warn.* . . . laid] *as in D; set as a line of verse in Q1–5, F.*   124 a] D; A Q1–5, F.   127 *Warn.* . . . it.] *as in D; set as a line of verse in Q1–5, F.*   129–130 You'l . . . presently.] *as in D; set as a line of verse in Q1–5, F.*   139 off. [*Aside.*] off. Q1–5, F, D.   140 order.——] Q1–3; ~∧—— Q4–5, F; ~ , —— D.   142 *Warn.* . . . Sir;] *as in D; set as a line of verse in Q1–5, F.*   149–150 *as in D; set as verse in Q1–5, F* (. . . / And).   154–155 In . . . me.] *as in D; set as verse in Q1–5, F* (. . . / Both).   156–157 over-reach'd. [*Aside.*] over-reach'd. Q1–5, F, D.   157+ *s.d. Landlord*] D; Landlord Q1–5, F.   160 Countenance.——] Q1–3, D; ~∧—— Q4–5, F.   161 *Swallow;*] Q1–4, D; ~ ? Q5, F.   164 faith] Q1, D; 'Faith Q2–5, F.   164–166 *as in D; set as verse in Q1–5, F* (. . . / But . . . / There's).   170 far.——] Q1–3, D; ~∧—— Q4–5, F.   173 who.] Q1–3, D; who? Q4–5; hoo? F.   175 pluck] Q1, Q3–5, F, D; puck Q2.   176 Grimbard] Q1–3, D; *Grimbald* Q4–5, F.   186–187 *as in D; set as verse in Q1–5, F* (. . . / And).   187 morning——] Q4–5, F, D; ~ .—— Q1–3.   196+ *s.d. Sir*] Q2–5, F, D; Sir Q1.   197–198 *as in D; set as verse in Q1–5, F* (. . . / Let).   199 salute!] Q1–3, D; ~ ? Q4–5, F.   200 *Aside*] Q2–5, F, D; *aside* Q1.   205–206 *as in D; set as verse in Q1–5, F* (. . . / Were).   206 we would] Q1; would we Q2–5, F, D.   206 together!] ~ ? Q1–5, F, D.   206 *Aside*] Q2–5, F, D; *aside* Q1.   207–208 *as in D; set as verse in Q1–5, F* (. . . / To . . . / But).   208 from me.] Q1; ~ ; Q2–5, F, D.   213–214 *as in D; set as verse in Q1–5, F* (. . . / I am).   219 Fists.——] ~ : ∧ Q1; ~ ; ∧ Q2–5, F, D.   221

Company. [*Aside.*] Company. Q1–5, F, D. 222 *Aside*] Q2–5, F, D; *aside* Q1. 223 *John to him.*] Q3–5, F; *John. to him.* Q1–2; *John.* [*To him.*] D. 226 *Aside*] Q2–5, F, D; *aside* Q1. 227–228 *as in D; set as verse in Q1–5, F* (. . . / A . . . / I'le). 228 I'me] Q1–3, D; I am Q4–5, F. 229–231 *as in D; set as verse in Q1–5, F* (. . . / He should . . . / When). 232–233 *as in D; set as verse in Q1–5, F* (. . . / I). 233 [*Exeunt*] Q3–5, F, D; ∧∼ Q1–2. 233 Mill.] Q1–5, F; Mill. *and* D. 234–235 *as in D; set as verse in Q1–5, F* (. . . / For). 237–238 Mistress] Q1–2, D; Mrs. Q3–5, F. 241–242 *as in D; set as verse in Q1–5, F* (. . . / It was . . . / To). 244 all.——Say] all: say Q1–5, F, D (Say D). 244 Sir] Q2, Q4–5, F, D; *Sir* Q1, Q3. 245 *Aside*] Q2–5, F, D; *aside* Q1. 247 counsel. [*Aside.*] Q4–5, F; counsel. Q1–3, D. 252 another. [*Aside.*] Q4–5, F; another. Q1–3, D. 253 make] Q1–3; makes Q4–5, F, D. 264 trouble] Q1; to trouble Q2–5, F, D. 274–275 you think] Q1 (*corrected state*), Q2–5, F, D; you you think Q1 (*uncorrected state*). 276 How] Q1–5, D; ∼ ! F. 287–288 *as in D; set as verse in Q1–5, F* (. . . / And). 290+ *s.d.* Enter Rose. / *Rose.* Sir] D; *Enter Rose.* Sir Q1–5, F. 292–293 Repast?] Q1 (*corrected state*), Q2–5, F, D; ∼ . Q1 (*uncorrected state*). 296 out. [*Aside.*] Q4–5, F; out. Q1–3, D. 298 Sir.] Q1 (*corrected state*), Q2–5, F, D; ∼ ; Q1 (*uncorrected state*). 301–302 *as in D; set as verse in Q1–5, F* (. . . / He). 301 Rogue] Q1 (*corrected state*), Q2–5, F, D; ∼ , Q1 (*uncorrected state*). 303–304 *as in D; set as verse in Q1–5, F* (. . . / In). 306 Sirrah?] Q1, D; ∼ . Q2–5, F. 307–310 *as in D; set as verse in Q1–5, F* (. . . / Your quarrelling . . . / Landlord, and [. . . Land- / lord Q2; . . . / And Q3–5, F] . . . / All). 309 Mistress.] Q1, D; ∼ : Q2–5, F. 316 Why] Q1, Q3–5, F; ∼ , Q2, D. 322–323 *as in D; set as verse in Q1–3* (. . . / What), Q4–5, F (. . . / But). 326–327 Well; . . . pate.] *as in D; set as a line of verse in Q1–5, F.* 329–330 *as in D; set as verse in Q1–5, F* (. . . / You . . . / Fathers). 333 possible] Q1–5, F; possibly D.

III, i

ACT III. SCENE I.] D; ACT III. Q1–5, F (ACT. Q2–3). 12, 14 Mistress] Q1–5, D; Mrs. F. 20 her. [*Exit.*] Q1–4, F, D; her. Q5. 20+ *s.d. Mistress*] Q1–3, D; *Mrs.* Q4–5, F. 20+ *s.d.* Millisent] Q4–5, D; Millesent Q1–3, F. 26–28 *as in D; set as verse in Q1–5, F* (. . . / For . . . Town, [Town. F] One . . . / They've). 28 English] Q3–5, F, D; English Q1–2. 30 Perriwig] Q1–5, F; Peruke D. 37 me?] ∼ ! Q1–5, F, D. 38 first—— [*Aside.*] first—— Q1–5, F, D. 61 *O so*] Q1–4, D; *oso* Q5, F. 68 *Aside*] Q4–5, F, D; *aside* Q1–3. 70–71 you—— [*Aside. / I*] you——I Q1–5, F, D. 71–74 I am not . . . that, in fine, Sir——] *as in D; set as verse in Q1–5, F* (. . . for in fine, / Sir . . . / Only . . . / In fine, Sir——). 75 *Aside*] Q4–5, F, D; *aside* Q1–3. 77 *Madge*] Madge Q1–5, F, D. 82 *English, in fine*] Q3, D; English, in fine Q1; English, *in fine* Q2, Q4–5, F. 85 *English . . . English*] Q3–5, F, D; English . . . English Q1–2. 87 In fine] Q1; *in fine* Q2–5, F, D. 88 *Aside*] Q2, Q4–5, F, D; *aside* Q1, Q3.

92   It is] Q1-2, D; 'Tis Q3-5, F.   95   *Aside*] Q4-5, F, D; *aside* Q1-3.
108   done?] ~ ! Q1-5, F, D.   109   out before] before Q1-5, F, D.
114   over-act] Q1, Q3-5, F, D; over act Q2.   114   *Aside*] Q4-5, F, D;
aside Q1-3.   116+   *s.d.* [*Exeunt*] Q3-5, F, D; ∧~ Q1-2.   116+
s.d. Lady] Lady Q1-5; La. Dupe F; *Lady* Dupe, *and* D.   118   me;] Q1-
3; ~ ? Q4-5, F, D.   120   you, a] Q1-2, D; y'ar Q3-5, F.   122   Child
that's to] Q3-5, F; Child's that Q1-2, D.   124   word———] Q3-5, F;
~ .——— Q1-2, D.

III, ii

SCENE II. / *Enter Lady* Dupe. / *La.* Truly] *Enter old La.* Truly Q1-3;
Enter La. Dupe. Truly Q4-5, F; *Enter Lady* Dupe. / *L. Dupe.* Truly D.
6+   *s.d. To her* Christian. / *Chr.* O] D (*Enter to*); *To her Chr.* O Q1-5,
F.   7   am a] Q1; am Q2-5, F, D.   10   foundations] Q1-4, D; Founda-
tion Q5, F.   26+   *s.d.* Lord] D; Lord Q1-5, F.   27   impart,] Q1; ~ .
Q2-4, D; ~ ; Q5, F.   27-28   *as in D; set as verse in Q1-5, F (. . . / A
sad).*   37   there is] Q1-3, D; there's Q4-5, F.   41-43   *as in D; set as
verse in Q1-5, F (. . . / Or . . . / I should).*   44   La. . . . in,] *as in
D; set as a line of verse in Q1-5, F.*   51   Christian] Q1, Q4-5, F, D;
Christian's Q2-3.   52-57   *as in D; set mostly as verse in Q1-4 (. . . /
Some . . . / Youth . . . / One is . . . [prose to end]), entirely as verse in
Q5, F (. . . / One is . . . / They'll . . . / But).*   53   Beggar;] Q1-4,
D; ~ ! Q5, F.   64   believe it] Q1-3, F, D; believe Q4-5.   68   help!]
~ . Q1-5, F, D.   68+   *s.d.* Millisent.] Penelope. Q1-5, F; *and* Penel-
ope. D.   86   forefend] Q2, D; foresend Q1; forefend, Q3-5; forefend!
F.   88   but be] Q1-4, F, D; be but Q5.   95   me.] Q1-3, F, D; ~
——— Q4-5.   96   help!] ~ . Q1-5, F, D.   104-105   Salvation!] Q1-
3, F, D; ~ ? Q4-5.

III, iii

SCENE III. / Warner, Rose.] *Warner, Rose.* Q1-3; *Enter* Warner, *and*
Rose. Q4-5, F, D.   1   you] Q1-4, F, D; ye Q5.   4   Mistress: my] Q1-
5, D; ~ . My F.   30   I will] Q1-4, F, D; will I Q5.   33+   *s.d.* Martin,]
Q1-5, F; Martin, *and* D.   35   beforehand] Q1; before-hand Q2-4, F, D;
before hand Q5.   36   to me.———] ~∧——— Q1-5, F, D.   38   'um]
Q1-3, F, D; them Q4-5.   42   'um?] Q1-3, F, D; ~ ! Q4-5.   43
Ladys] Q1, F; Lady's Q4-5, D; Ladies Q2-3.   45-48   *as in D; set as
verse in Q1-5, F (. . . / Madam, . . . / And . . . / I leave . . . / My).*
51-52   *as in D; set as verse in Q1-5, F (. . . / Here).*   52   Paper]
Q1-4, D; Papers Q5, F.   54   Warn. aside.] Warn. Q1-3, D; *Warn.
Aside.*] Q4-5; *Warn.* [*Aside.*] F.   55   what,] Q2-5, D; ~∧ Q1, F.   61
do?] Q2-5, F, D; ~ , Q1.   62   Sir.] Q4-5, F, D; ~ ? Q1; ~ ; Q2-3.
65   love] Q1 (*corrected state*), Q2-5, F, D; are Q1 (*uncorrected state*).
83   now.———] ~∧——— Q1-5, F, D.   102   point's] Q3-5, F, D;
points Q1-2.   121-122   *as in D; set as verse in Q1-5, F (. . . / Once).*

IV, i

ACT IV.] Q4-5, F; ACT. IV. Q1-3; ACT IV. SCENE I. D.   *s.d.*
Martin] Q1-5, F; Martin Mar-all D.   10   now;] Q1-2, F, D; ~ ? Q3-5.

17 lay it] Q1-4, F, D; lay Q5.   21 *John &*] Q1-5, D; *John* F.   30
A'] Q1-3, D; He Q4-5, F.   33 Cox nowns] Q1-2; Cox-nowns Q3-5, D;
Coxnowns F.   33 ill-natur'd] Q1-5, D; ill natur'd F.   35 In] D; in
Q1-5, F.   39 *Bartlemew————*] Q4-5, F; ~ .———— Q1-3, D.   41
time;] ~ , Q1-5, F, D.   45 Fate.————] Q1-3; ~∧———— Q4-5, F, D.
46-47 *Scander-bag* Rogue] Scander-bag-Rogue   Q1-2; Scander-bag
Rogue Q3-5, F, D.   51 Father————] ~ .———— Q1-2, D; ~ .∧ Q3-5,
F.   75 Mistress *Millisent*] Q1-5, D; Mrs. *Millisent* F.   80 *Serving-
men*] Q1-5, D; *Serving men* F.   80+   *s.d. Messenger*] D; Messenger Q1-
5, F.   85 him. / *Re-enter* Moody.] him. Q1-3; him. / [*Re-enter* Moody.
Q4-5, F *(one line in F)*; him. / *Enter* Moody. D.   89 *Ex. Mess.*] D; *Ex.
Mess.* Q1-5, F.   90 *Mood. reads.*] Mood. reads. Q1-5, F, D.   93
them] Q1-3, D; '*em* Q4-5, F.   99 *Englishmen*] D; Englishmen Q1-5,
F.   100 *French Outalian* Rogues] French Outalion-Rogues Q1-2;
French Outalian Rogues Q3-5, F; *French* Outalian-Rogues D.   105-
106 *Outalians*] Outalians Q1-5, F, D.   113+   *s.d. Enter Sir* Martin
laughing.] *as in D; in preceding speech, at right margin in two lines in QI-
2* ([~]), *run in after "thinks" in Q3* ([~]), *at right margin in Q4-5,
F* ([~).   115-116 *as in D; set as verse in QI-5, F* (. . . / Where).
120 shalt] Q2-5, F, D; shall Q1.   143 a' Gods] Q4-5, F; a'gods Q1-3,
D.   144 without giving] Q5, F; without Q1-4, D.   147 own] Q1-
3, Q5, F, D; one Q4.   148 couldest] Q1-2; could'st Q3-5, F, D.   150
us'd] Q4-5, F; use Q1-3; uses D.   151 so!] Q1-4, D; ~ ? Q5, F.   157
busie-brain] Q3-5, F; busie brain Q1-2, D.   166-167 *as in D; set as
verse in QI-5, F* (. . . / Will).   174+   *s.d. Lord*] D; Lord Q1-5, F.
177 she has] Q1; she passes Q2-5, F, D.   186 Mistress] Q1-3, D; Mrs.
Q4-5, F.   190 at] Q1; at the Q2-5, F, D.   191 *l.*!] *l.*∧ Q1-5, F;
Pounds! D.   195 yet?] ~———— Q1-5, F, D.   197 difficult] Q2-5,
F, D; difficultly Q1.   208 Jill] Q1-3; Jilt Q4-5, F, D.   213 find]
Q1-5, D; found F.   221 clearer] Q1-5, F, D; dearer S-S.   224 Grav-
ies;] Q1-3, D; ~ ! Q4-5, F.   235 tell!] Q1, Q4-5, F; ~ ? Q2-3; ~ ; D.
240 Littleplot] Q1-2, D; *Littleplot* Q3-5, F.   242 *Mercury*] Q3-5, F,
D; Mercury Q1-2.   244 Serving-man-like] Q2, Q4-5, F; Serving-man
like Q1, D; Serving man-like Q3.   251+   *s.d. Enter* Moody.] *as in D;
at right on line above in QI-4* ([~); *after next line in Q5, F*.   274
Ignoramus] Q1-5; *Ignoramus* F, D.   275 *Martin.*] Q1-4, F, D; *Mart.*
Q5.   285 you;] Q4-5, F; ~ , Q1-3, D.   285 Grandam] Q2-5, F,
D; Grandham Q1.   286 enough] Q1, D; enough how Q2-5, F.   286
English] D; English Q1-5, F.   290 Mistress] Q1-3, D; Mrs. Q4-5, F.
293 this?] Q3-5, F; ~ : Q1-2, D.   309 on't?] Q1-4, D; ~ ! Q5, F.
315 Sir, I] Q1-4, D; I Q5, F.   326 'sur'd] Q1-4, F; 'sure Q5; sure D.
328 no.] Q1, D; ~ ? Q2-5, F.   338-339 before-hand] Q1-2, Q4-5, D;
beforehand Q3; before hand F.   339-340 you; . . . one] Q2-5, F, D;
~∧ . . . ~ ; Q1.   342 miserable] Q1-3, F, D; ~ , Q4-5.   355 that]
Q1, F, D; there Q2-5.   359 thing] Q1 *(corrected state)*, Q2-5, F, D;
~ , Q1 *(uncorrected state)*.   361 such] Q1-2, D; such a Q3-5, F.
367 before-hand] Q1-2, D; beforehand Q3; before hand Q4-5, F.   369
l.] Q4-5, F; l. Q1-3; Pounds D.   381 so sweet] Q1-2, D; sweet Q3-5,
F.   381 'um] Q1-5, F; 'em D.   387 Suitor.] Q2-5, F, D; ~ : Q1.

393 beards] D; beards it Q1–5, F.   395 never yet was] Q1–4, D; was
never yet Q5, F.   397 laugh] Q1–3, D; ∼ ; Q4–5, F.   397–398
[*Aside. / Sweet Lady———*] Sweet Lady.——— [*Aside.* Q1–5, F, D (Lady∧
——— Q2–5, F, D).   405 Sweet-heart] Q1–3, D; sweet Heart Q4–5, F.
409 a Lady] Q1, F; Lady Q2–5, D.   412 thing] Q1–5, D; think F.
415 absolv'd. [*Aside.*] absolv'd. Q1–5, F, D.   418 should] Q1–3, D;
shall Q4–5, F.   424 *La.*] Q2–5, F, D; ∼∧ Q1.   431+ *s.d.* Martin;
Sir John] Martin, and *Sir* John, Q1–5, F (Martin∧ Q1–2); Martin, *to Sir*
John D.   446 *Hebrew-Greek*] D; Hebrew-Greek Q1–5, F.   449 it,]
Q1 (*corrected state*), Q3–5, F, D; ∼ ; Q1 (*uncorrected state*), Q2.   453
I'le make] F, D; make Q1–5.   454 privy-house] Q2–5, F, D; privy
house Q1.   480 so?] ∼ ! Q1–5, F, D.   481–482 devising. [*Aside to
Sir* Martin.] devising. Q1–5, F, D.   484–485 *English*] Q3–5, D; English
Q1–2, F.   484 understand] *some copies of Q2 read* udderstand.   486
Pox,] ∼∧ Q1–5, F, D.   490 what,] D; ∼∧ Q1–5, F.   490 scape]
Q1–2, 'scape Q3–5, F, D.   505 Servant.] Q1–2, D; ∼ ? Q3–5, F.
506 a going] Q1; going Q2–5, F, D.   507 too. [*Aside.*] too. Q1–5, F,
D.   511 Hey-day] Q1–2, Q4–5, F, D; Hey day Q3.   516 [*Aside.*] *on
last line of preceding speech in Q1–5, F, D.*   525 ho!] Q1; ∼ , Q2–3,
D; oh, Q4–5, F.   527 Lye———] D; ∼ .——— Q1–5, F.   533 had
I] Q1; I had Q2–5, F, D.   533 bosom!] ∼ ? Q1–5, F, D.   534–535
you, I advise you.] Q1–5, D; you. F.   541–542 Liberality?] Q1, Q4, D;
∼ ; Q2–3; ∼ . Q5, F.   542 your] Q1; my Q2–5, F, D.   545 and]
Q1; or Q2–5, F, D.   546 an'] Q4–5, F, D; ou' Q1; on' Q2–3.   556
you———] D; ∼ .——— Q1–5, F.   557 advising!———] ∼ .——— Q1–
2; ∼∧——— Q3–5, F, D.   559 Counsel] Q1; Council Q2–5, F, D.
564 were] Q1–4, F; *we're* Q5; are D.

V, i

ACT V. SCENE I.] D; ACT. V. Q1–3; ACT V. Q4–5, F.   *s.d.* Lord]
D; Lord Q1–5, F.   7 Mistress's] Q1–2, D; Mistresses Q3–5, F.   27
Hey-day] Q1–5, D; Hey day F.   37 Mistress] Q1; Mrs. Q2–5, F, D.
41–42 thinking time. In] Q1–3, D; thinking-time. In Q4; thinking-time
in Q5, F.   43 Mistress] Q1; Mrs. Q2–5, F, D.   48 *Lord, La.* D.]
Lord, La. D. Mill. Q1; Lord. La. *Du.* Mill. Q2; Lord, *Lady* Dupe, Mill.
Q3–5; Lord, *Lady* Dupe, F; *Lord, L.* Dupe. Mill. *and* D.   48 Chr. /
Enter Millisent *above.*] Chr. Q1–5, F, D.   50 *Mill.*] Q1–5, F; *Mill.*
[*above*]. D.   56 Master.] Q1–5, F; ∼ ? D.   62 them;] ∼ , Q1–5, F,
D.   65 one another] Q2–5, F, D; another Q1.   77 *French*] Q3–5,
F, D; French Q1–2.   83 Madam.———But] Madam: but Q1–3;
Madam: But Q4–5, F, D.   85 Lute. [*Aside.*] Q4–5, F; Lute. Q1–3, D.
100 head] Q1–2, D; ∼ , Q3–5, F.   102 your] Q4–5, F; her Q1–3, D.
107 for] D; with Q1–5, F.   111 *Exit* Rose.] Q3–5, F; *Exit.* Rose. Q1–
2; *Exit.* D.   113 *premunire*] Q3–5, F; premunire Q1–2, D.   116+
s.d. Martin] Q1–5, F; Martin Mar-all D.   123 is!] Q4–5, F; ∼ ? Q1–3,
D.   131 do not] Q1–3, D; don't Q4–5, F.   134 see;] Q1–3, D; ∼ !
Q4–5, F.   138 who] Q2–5, F, D; who who Q1.   148+ *s.d.* Millisent,]
Q2–3; Millesent, Q1; Millisent *and* Q4–5, F, D.   160 me] Q1 (*cor-*

rected state), Q2-5, F, D; ~ , Q1 (*uncorrected state*).   166 is] Q1-2,
Q4-5, F, D; ~ , Q3.   197 Heaven] Q1-5, F; *Heav'n* D.   198 *ev'ry*]
Q1-3, F, D; *e'ry* Q4-5.   202+ *s.d.* [The] Q4-5, F; ∧~ Q1-3, D.
213 Why,] Q4-5, F, D; ~∧ Q1-3.   223 in?] ~ ! Q1-5, F, D.   224
matter.] Q1-3, D; ~ ? Q4-5, F.   229 Rose] Q1-5, F; *and* Rose D.
234 *Cokes*] F, D; Cokes Q1-5.   235+ *s.d.* [*Exit*] Q3-5, F, D; ∧~ Q1-
2.   235+ *s.d.* Enter] Q1-3, D; *Re-enter* Q4-5, F.   248-249 next
—— / *Enter* Warner. / Monsieur *Warner*] next———Monsieur——
[*Enter* Warner. / *Warner* Q1-5, F, D (/ ∧ *Enter* D).   255 Sir;] Q1-3,
F, D; ~ ? Q4-5.   267 ingenious] Q1, Q3-5, F; ingenuous Q2, D.
268+ *s.d.* Enter] Q5, F, D; [~ Q1-4.   271 Wit and] Q1-2, Q4-5, F,
D; Wit Q3.   271 further] Q1-5, D; farther F.   279 *Jacobus . . .*
Carolus] Q3-5, F, D; Jacobus . . . Carolus Q1-2.   281+ *s.d.* dis-
guises.] Q3-5, F, D; ~∧] Q1; ~ .] Q2.   284 time,] Q1-5, F; ~ . D.   284-
285 help, help,] Help! Help! Q1; Help! help! Q2, D; help! help! Q3-5, F.
286 his Servant,] his Q1; his, Q2-5, F, D.   287 Hey-tarockit] Q1-2,
D; Hey-tarock-it Q3-5, F.   309 name?] Q1-3, D; ~ . Q4-5, F.   322
what a] Q1; what the Q2-5, F, D.   334 now] Q1-2, Q4-5, F, D; how
Q3.   336+ *s.d.* Rose] Q1-5, F; *and* Rose D.   352 her. [*Aside.*]
her. Q1-5, F, D.   366 Sister!] Q1, Q5, F, D; ~ : Q2; ~ ? Q3-4.   370
you] Q1-5, D; you may F.   370 Sister!] Q1-2, D; ~ ; F; ~ ? Q3-5.
377 *Turk*] D; Turk Q1-5, F.   384 *Warn. aside.*] *Warn.* Q1-5, F, D.
394 *Warn.*] Q2-5, F, D; ~∧ Q1.   394 *aside.*∧] Q1-3; aside.] Q4-5, F,
D.   405 Warner? [*Aside to him.*] Warner? Q1-5, F, D.   407 her!]
~ ? Q1-5, F, D.   415 *Scanderbag*] scanderbag Q1; Scanderbag Q2-5,
F, D.   421 withall] Q1; with Q2-5, F, D.   422 *Warner! [Aside to*
him.] Warner! Q1-5, F, D.   427 further] Q1-5, D; farther F.   429
need] Q1-4, F, D; needs Q5.   436-437 Horseback.] Q1-4, D; ~ ? Q5,
F.   440 I'm] Q1-3, D; I am Q4-5, F.   441 *Aside*] Q3-5, F, D;
aside Q1-2.   444 off!] Q3-5, F; ~ ? Q1-2, D.   444+ *s.d. Enter*]
Q3-5, F, D; [~ Q1-2.   448 him. [*Aside.*] Q4-5, F; him. Q1-3, D.
451 *East-Indian*] Q1; *East-India* Q2-5, F, D.   452 Why,] Q1, Q4-5,
F; ~∧ Q2-3, D.   456 Counterfeit?] Q4-5, F; ~ ; Q1-3, D.   458
i'faith,] Q1-3, D; ~ ! Q4-5, F.   463 off. [*Aside.*] Q4-5, F; off. Q1-3, D.
467 Imposter!] Q1-5, F; ~ : D.   474+ *s.d. Mart. and* Warn.] Mart.
Q1-5, F, D.   475+ *s.d. Enter again*] Q1-3, D; *Re-enter* Q4-5, F.
500 me—— [*Aside.*] me—— Q1-5, F, D.   500+ *s.d. Enter*] D
(*but after next speech*); [~ Q1-5, F (*at end of next line*).   501 So,
so,] Q1-2, D; So∧ so, Q3; So, so; Q4-5, F.   523 Landlord] Q3-5, F, D;
Lordland Q1-2.   531 Sir?] ~ ! Q1-5, F, D.   538 Plot] Q1-2, D;
Plot, Q3-4; Plot, Sir? Q5, F.   544 *Whispers*] Q3-5, F, D; *whispers* Q1-
2.   553 'em. [*Exeunt.*] Q1-5, D; 'em F.

V, ii

SCENE II. / *Enter*] Enter Q1-5, F, D.   *s.d.* Lord] Q3, D; Lord Q1-
2, Q4-5, F.   3 has] Q1-4, F, D; was Q5.   8+ *s.d. Enter*] Q5, D;
[~ Q1-4, F.   12 Fool's Handsel] Q1, Q3-5, F, D; Fools's Handsel Q2.
21 here!] Q1-3, D; ~ ? Q4-5, F.   22+ *s.d.* John,] Q1-5, F; John, *and*

D.   23 *French*] D; French Q1-5, F.   32 *Indian* gowns] Q2-5, F,
D; Indian-gowns Q1.   33   Vizard-masks] Q1-2, D; Vizard Masks Q3-5,
F.   35+   *s.d.* Martin,] Q1-5, F; Martin Mar-all, D.   35+   *s.d. Landlord*] D; Landlord Q1-5, F.   37   *stage direction at right margin in Q1-
5, F, D.*   37   *signs*] Q1-2, Q4-5, F, D; *sings* Q3.   38   welcome,] Q1-
5, F; ~ . D.   41   had the] Q1-5, F; had your D.   49   I'le] Q1-4,
D; I Q5, F.   50+   *s.d. and* Warn.∧] Q3-5, F, D; *and* Warn.] Q1-2.
52-53   Allons,] A Lou's∧ Q1-2, D; A Lon's∧ Q3-5, F.   53+   *s.d.*
[*While . . . down.*] *as in D; at right margin of next three speeches and
continuous with next stage direction, which is similarly arranged, in
Q1-3 (*∧ ~ *); after following speech in Q4-5, F.*   57+   *s.d.* [*When
. . . Jig.*] F, D; ∧~ Q1-3; { ~ Q4-5.   63   enough:] Q1, F; ~ ! Q2-5,
D.   63   undone! my] Q1-3, D; undone! / My Q4-5, F.   67+   *s.d.
stools.*∧] Q4-5, F, D; ~ .] Q1-3.   71   *Scanderbag*] Scanderbag Q1-5, F,
D.   75   Coxcomb] Q4-5, F, D; Coxcombs Q1-3.   80+   *s.d. Lord*]
Q3, D; Lord Q1-2, Q4-5, F.   80+   *s.d.* Dupe,] Q2-5, F, D; ~ . Q1.
80+   *s.d.* vail'd,] Q1-5, F; *vail'd, and* D.   80+   *s.d. Landl.*] Q3, D;
Landl. Q1-2, Q4-5, F.   81   what,] Q3-5, D; ~∧ Q1-2, F.   81   your
selves?] ~ ! Q1-5, F, D.   82   play,] Q1-3, D; ~ ; Q4-5, F.   93+
s.d. [*Pulls*] Q3-5, F, D; ∧~ Q1-2.   93+   *s.d. off*] Q1-3, Q5, F, D; *of*
Q4.   107   *Warner!*] Q1-5, D; ~ . F.   114   till] Q1-5, F; 'till D.
121   have] Q5, F, D; hath Q1-4.   122   Serving-man] Q1-5, D; Serving
Man F.   153   near.] Q1 (*corrected state*), Q2-5, F, D; ~∧ Q1 (*uncorrected state*).

INDEX TO THE COMMENTARY